WRITING AFRICAN HISTORY

ROCHESTER STUDIES in AFRICAN HISTORY and the DIASPORA

Toyin Falola, Senior Editor
The Frances Higginbotham Nalle Centennial Professor in History
University of Texas at Austin

(ISSN: 1092-5228)

Power Relations in Nigeria: Ilorin Slaves and their Successors
Ann O'Hear

Dilemmas of Democracy in Nigeria
Edited by Paul Beckett and Crawford Young

Science and Power in Colonial Mauritius
William Kelleher Storey

Namibia's Post-Apartheid Regional Institutions: The Founding Year
Joshua B. Forrest

A Saro Community in the Niger Delta, 1912–1984: The Potts-Johnsons of Port Harcourt and Their Heirs
Mac Dixon-Fyle

Contested Power in Angola: 1840s to the Present
Linda Heywood

Nigerian Chiefs: Traditional Power in Modern Politics, 1890s–1990s
Olufemi Vaughan

West Indians in West Africa, 1808–1880: The African Diaspora in Reverse
Nemata Blyden

The United States and Decolonization in West Africa, 1950–1960
Ebere Nwaubani

Health, State, and Society in Kenya
George Oduor Ndege

Black Business and Economic Power
Edited by Alusine Jalloh and Toyin Falola

Voices of the Poor in Africa
Elizabeth Isichei

Colonial Rule and Crisis in Equatorial Africa: Southern Gabon ca. 1850–1940
Christopher J. Gray

The Politics of Frenchness in Colonial Algeria, 1930–1954
Jonathan K. Gosnell

Sources and Methods in African History: Spoken, Written, Unearthed
Edited by Toyin Falola and Christian Jennings

Sudan's Blood Memory: The Legacy of War, Ethnicity, and Slavery in Early South Sudan
Stephanie Beswick

Writing Ghana, Imagining Africa: Nation and African Modernity
Kwaku Larbi Korang

Labour, Land, and Capital in Ghana: From Slavery to Free Labour in Asante, 1807–1956
Gareth Austin

Not So Plain as Black and White: Afro-German Culture and History, 1890–2000
Edited by Patricia Mazón and Reinhild Steingröver

Writing African History
Edited by John Edward Philips

WRITING AFRICAN HISTORY

Edited by

John Edward Philips

Ⓡ UNIVERSITY OF ROCHESTER PRESS

First published 2005
Softcover edition published 2006
Transferred to digital printing 2013

University of Rochester Press
668 Mt. Hope Avenue, Rochester, NY 14620, USA
www.urpress.com
and Boydell & Brewer Limited
PO Box 9, Woodbridge, Suffolk IP12 3DF, UK
www.boydellandbrewer.com

ISSN: 1092-5228
Cloth ISBN-13: 978-1-58046-164-1
Cloth ISBN-10: 1-58046-164-6
Paperback ISBN-13: 978-1-58046-256-3
Paperback ISBN-10: 1-58046-256-1

Library of Congress Cataloging-in-Publication Data
Writing African history / edited by John Edward Philips.
    p. cm. – (Rochester studies in African history and the diaspora,
ISSN 1092-5228 v. 20)
    Includes bibliographical references and index.
    ISBN 1-58046-164-6 (hardcover : alk. paper)
    1. Africa–Historiography. 2. Africa–History. I. Philips, John Edward,
1952- II. Series.
    DT19.W75 2005
    960'.072–dc22
                                                                  2005000377

A catalogue record for this title is available from the British Library.

This publication is printed on acid-free paper.
Printed in the United States of America

IN MEMORIAM

John Lavers
Boniface Obichere
Gloria Waite

And in special rememberance of Bala Achi

CONTENTS

Acknowledgments   xi

Introduction   1
Daniel McCall

Part I. Background

1   What is African History?   25
        John Edward Philips

Part II. Sources of Data

2   Archaeology and the Reconstruction of the African Past   51
        Susan Keech McIntosh

3   Writing African History from Linguistic Evidence   86
        Christopher Ehret

4   Physical Anthropology and African History   112
        S.O.Y. Keita

5   The Importance of Botanical Data to Historical Research
        on Africa   152
        Dorothea Bedigian

6   Oral Tradition as a Means of Reconstructing the Past   169
        David Henige

7   Oral Sources and the Challenge of African History   191
        Barbara M. Cooper

8   Arabic Sources for African History   216
         John Hunwick

9   European Documents and African History   254
         John Thornton

10   Mission and Colonial Documents   266
         Toyin Falola

Part III. Perspectives on History

11   Data Collection and Interpretation in the Social History
         of Africa   287
         Isaac Olawale Albert

12   African Economic History: Approaches to Research   308
         Masao Yoshida

13   Signs of Time, Shapes of Thought: The Contributions
         of Art History and Visual Culture to Historical Methods
         in Africa   329
         Henry John Drewal

14   Methodologies in Yorùbá Oral Historiography
         and Aesthetics   348
         Diedre L. Bádéjo

15   Local History in Post-Independent Africa   374
         Bala Achi

16   Africa and World-Systems Analysis:
         A Post-Nationalist Project?   381
         William G. Martin

17   "What Africa Has Given America": African Continuities
         in the North American Diaspora   403
         Joseph E. Holloway

18   History and Memory   439
         Donatien Dibwe dia Mwembu

19   Writing About Women: Approaches to a Gendered
         Perspective in African History   465
         Kathleen Sheldon

Part IV. Conclusion

20 Writing African History 493
John Edward Philips

Contributors 511

Index 517

ACKNOWLEDGMENTS

This book has been a few years in the writing, and all who have contributed to its production deserve thanks. It would be impossible to mention everyone who contributed in some way, but as editor I would like to thank some of those who helped the most.

First I would like to thank my wife, not for typing or any of the other duties that scholars of a previous generation thanked their wives for, when so few scholars had husbands to thank. Instead, I thank Professor Ritsuko Miyamoto for putting up with my working on my own book when I had originally promised to work on one with her. We had hoped to write a short introduction to African history in Japanese. When I began the preliminary research for such a book, I found that no basic introduction to the topic in English had been done since Daniel McCall's *Africa in Time Perspective* was written a generation ago. After some thought, I realized that African history had now evolved into an undertaking too diverse and complex to be introduced by one person. I contacted several scholars, who agreed that a book like this was necessary and that I should prepare it. The result, after much effort by many people, is now in your hands. I can only hope that my wife will be willing to start another project with me, or perhaps complete the one that this project replaced.

The first chapter was drafted while I was on a research grant to the National Museum of Ethnology in Osaka, Japan. Although this book was not among the purposes of the grant, the museum's library and other research facilities made possible rapid completion of the other research I had come to do. The research for this volume, and additional research as well, was therefore carried out during the time of the grant. The facilities and support staff at the museum are truly astounding and make possible a scholarly productivity that I feel honored to have taken part in. I thank not only the museum for hosting me but my university for giving me leave and my colleagues who took over classes in my absence.

The readers for Rochester University Press also deserve thanks for their excellent contributions. They recommended many revisions that made this book better. For example, although a final chapter had been in the original outline, I thought after reading the draft without it that the book could work without such a chapter. One of the readers suggested, however, that something more was needed to finish the book—and therefore a valuable final chapter was added. I am grateful for this and other constructive criticism from the readers.

My mother, a professional copy editor, took time from her own business to look at every chapter. This resulted in some revisions to almost all chapters, although she should not be held responsible for the final versions. My advice, in the final chapter, to have one's manuscript gone over by an educated person in a different field, is based on experience, as my articles and books have often benefited from my mother's frank criticism and other comments.

Finally, without the contributors themselves this book would not exist. Not only is the book more theirs than mine, but several of the contributors also read my own chapters and offered suggestions for revising them as well. They deserve special thanks for that. Each of the authors has endured a lot, sometimes including repeated demands for complicated, multiple revisions. They suffered during the production of this book. One was going through a divorce. Another had a stroke. Bala Achi died. Without their strong faith in me as editor, the project would not have been possible, much less successfully completed. I only hope I have been worthy of their trust.

INTRODUCTION

Daniel McCall

When the first edition of *Africa in Time Perspective: A Discussion of Historical Reconstruction from Unwritten Sources* was published in 1964, I had been exploring in what was then a largely uncharted field: specifying how to identify and utilize unwritten sources for discovering African history. It is in that context that the editor, John Philips, asked me to provide an introduction to this collection of writings on historical methodology as applicable to the conditions of the African continent. The works represented in this volume demonstrate the progress made in four decades.

This is not a volume on the history of Africa; it is a compilation of discussions and advice by specialists in diverse approaches to research in particular kinds of evidence that have been found useful in elucidating African history and identifying problems encountered in their use.

One traditional conception of history was that it was based on documentation in the form of written texts. If there were no written documents there could be no history. It was logical to designate as prehistory any period before writing. This rubric is still not entirely obsolete. The more common conception today is that history is based on evidence. Prehistory, then, should be a non-entity. If there is evidence, there can be history; if there is no evidence, there is nothing to write about. Using this formula, which was proposed in the teens of the twentieth century,[1] but for a long time not often utilized, historians can go beyond written sources. Archaeology, historical linguistics, oral traditions, ethnobotany, and some other fields were early flagged as significant for history, and gradually studies pertinent to Africa, using such sources, began to appear. Some of these works we can call "pre-documentary history," a designation used by one of the contributors to this volume.[2]

It is now recognized as essential to co-opt the results of other disciplines into history in the manner that concepts and data of sociology, economics, and psychology (which have been essentially synchronic) have

1

long since been incorporated into historiography. For most of sub-Saharan Africa until a few centuries ago, as for pre-Columbian America, Oceania, Australia, and some areas of Asia, history must be largely derived from unwritten sources of evidence. Indeed, African history is developing as world history is coalescing to provide a global context of similarities and distinctions among and between geographical branches of human populations.

Archaeologists, linguists, demographers, population geneticists, as well as historians, are observers of human societies through time, but their specialities are organized in separate disciplines. Increasingly an overlap occurs and multidisciplinary strategies are being pursued. *Consilience: The Unity of Knowledge* by E. O. Wilson[3] is a defense of breaking the boundaries of specializations. The amazing success of the Pulitzer Prize-winning bestseller *Guns, Germs, and Steel* by Jarred Diamond[4] is an example of what can be accomplished by bringing many disciplines into cooperation to produce a historical narrative. Not every historian need choose such a wide format, but each may produce elements that will be available for an eventual synthesis.

African history is not by any means all "pre-literate history," to use a phrase of Harry Elmer Barnes.[5] A continuity exists from nonliterate times to literate periods, but the moment when that juncture occurs varies greatly according to the regions of Africa. The number of languages, African and otherwise, in which writings of historical import exist is extensive and the number of scripts is larger than one might have supposed.

All the traditional genres of history plus some new varieties are required to achieve a narrative encompassing the story through the various eras of human activities on this continent. The very earliest human history begins in Africa. This volume represents this generation's efforts to define the means required to supply the ingredients for a continental history.

In 1995 the National Endowment for the Humanities sponsored a summer seminar on "Imagining the Past." This must have sounded antihistorical to some: history is based on facts, not imagination. After evidence has been collected and sorted, however, imagination has a role in perceiving how a bit here and a piece there fit together. Disciplined imagination is required to bring together the results of linguistic analysis, archaeological excavations, genetic distances, oral evidence of various genres, art, and written documents. This is not a defense of license to build willful constructs; data must always be the foundation for interpretation. Disputes are less often about facts than about whether the pertinent facts are sufficient to sustain an interpretation. And differences in interpretation do not always "result in intellectual incompatibilities or error." Mark Gilderhus in *History and Historians*[6] points out that "divergent renditions may result in larger, complementary forms of understanding in which one enriches and animates the other from separate vantage points." The historians selected here to present the possibilities and problems inherent in various methods of investigation have the right kind of imagination as well as a command of particular methodologies that must be carefully applied.

The old charge by Hugh Trevor-Roper that Africans have no history has been nullified by the number of studies published in the last several decades. In the future there is certain to be an increase in efforts to achieve coordination of African history with historical linguistics, archaeology, art history, human population genetics, botany and zoology of domesticated species, oral traditions, periodization of climatic change, and other fields of research. This will be true especially, but not exclusively, of periods prior to 1500 C.E.

Kinship between history and two other disciplines, archaeology and historical linguistics, has long been recognized. The eminent archeologist, Sir Leonard Woolley, titled a book *History Unearthed.*[7] His own excavations in Mesopotamia yielded cuneiform tablets. These texts, read, edited, translated, and published by Assyriologists, created an entry for historians. In excavated sites without writing, where writing did not exist at the period, or where the material on which writing once existed has decomposed, history is less readily recognized. In North Africa, outside the Nile Valley, inscriptions are usually brief, formalistic, and limited to stone monuments or metal objects. Even Carthage has yielded only a modicum of its literary production; its literature on parchment or papyrus has not survived except as translated by Romans, and they were uninterested in most of it, choosing as the longest work to render into Latin a work on agriculture. A history of Libya (i.e., Africa) by King Juba II of Roman Mauritania, based on Punic records, has not, unfortunately, survived.

The interaction between historians and archaeologists, we may note, has been closer in the exploration of the African past than is true of some other continents insofar as "mute sites" (those without excavated inscriptions) are concerned. In the mid-1950s the School of Oriental and African Studies initiated conferences on History and Archaeology of Africa.

Linguistics, with the recognition of the genetic relationship between the various languages of the Indo-European language-family in the eighteenth century, has an even longer existence as a scientific discipline than archaeology which became organized in mid-nineteenth century. African history, which became academically recognized only in the 1950s, has from the beginning recognized the significance of linguistic data. Other historically oriented disciplines are now gaining acceptance by historians as will be exemplified by the chapters of this book.

At the outset one should remember that the adjective African, without additional qualification, can refer only to the continent itself. Peoples, cultures, ecology, and everything else vary enormously from one part of the continent to another. Every scholar, in whatever discipline, who deems her/himself an Africanist is a specialist on some segment of African reality and is at most only a generalist in regard to other aspects and regions. Thus the discussions that follow all focus on Africa, but on one or another of a variety of geographical constructs rather then on the whole continent, though usually the principles employed will be useful elsewhere.

All the techniques used to investigate the history of Africa can be used to investigate the actions of men or women in Africa—or elsewhere. Historians of the island peoples of the Pacific, seeking to learn what went on prior to the eighteenth century, are groping with the same problems and are finding comparable solutions.

John Philips, in chapter 1, notes that "observation of change" is the foundation of history. "Time is a measure of change," is a physicist's axiom. Physicists may be thinking in terms of the eons of astronomy or geology, but historians look at the more finite eras and generations of human experience. Our perspectives on history also change: History, Philips says, "as an interpretation of the past changes because it is a human-created artifact." Every generation will interpret the past in ways that agree with its fund of knowledge and with current social theory. "History is a conversation the present holds with the past." History therefore will always be a work-in-progress because the "present" is continually becoming occupied by new generations. New evidence becomes available and new ways of thinking about evidence are developed. We need to have a sense of our past in order to define ourselves in the world of the present.

Philips neatly dispels some old aspersions on history: that it is "bunk," or lies agreed to; that it is written (exclusively) by the winners; or is twenty-twenty hindsight. He insists on honesty and fairness as indispensable to the writing of history, and gives a quick survey of methodologies of history. A distinction is made between "history" as a present-day narrative of past events and "history" as the actual events. The narratives of historians are subject to revision; the actual events are not. The necessity of reinterpretation is that "history must make sense," and history is both a social science and one of the humanities, therefore subject to critique from both sides.

Susan McIntosh, in chapter 2, has tried to identify some of the perceptions and misperceptions that Africanist historians have of archaeological practice and to clarify the nature of archeological findings for historians who use those findings in reconstructing the past. She focuses especially on the issue of chronology, since that is critical to both archaeology and history, and she has tried to help historians understand how they could use archaeological data more critically in their work.

The classification of archaeology with anthropology in the United States has unfortunately led to a lack of understanding of the discipline among many historians, and of history among archaeologists, whatever good effects it may have had on anthropologists. Since historians of Africa commonly use archaeological data, they must understand that data, what it means and doesn't mean, what its uses and shortcomings are. To do this they must learn to think like archaeologists.

Historians have always recognized archaeology as a kindred discipline in researching the past, but the points of departure for each are so different that coordination of the two has some difficulties. One produces its own sources—excavated artifacts found in specific horizontal and vertical spatial relationships. The other has been accustomed to requiring recorded words from an identifiable time and place. McIntosh emphasizes that archaeological data are not so much "given" (the literal Latin meaning of "data") as "taken" (or, in Latin, "capta"). Archaeological texts must be interrogated by historians for reliability as any other texts would be. She echos my own call of forty years ago, for historians to try to follow the reasoning that archaeologists use in coming to their conclusions, and to use actual archaeological excavation reports, not just the interpretations archaeologists have made of their findings, as raw data, and explains to historians how they can understand those reports.

Perhaps the most important difference between historians and archaeologists is the two-dimensional, linear nature of the textually oriented historian who works mainly with words, and the three-dimensional, mute world of the archaeological excavation. Understanding that world involves reconstructing the process of deposition that resulted in the site that the archaeologist excavates. That process is usually complex and difficult to understand. It also often involves removal and/or relocation of material before the archaeologist even comes on the scene. However, in general, things on the bottom were placed there first, and the site was constructed from the bottom up, an understanding that makes stratigraphy important in constructing chronology, for materials from lower layers, in undisturbed conditions, will be older than materials from upper layers. Materials from the same layer can be assumed to be of roughly contemporaneous date, a conclusion known as "association." Of course, "contemporaneous" in archaeology is a much fuzzier concept than historians are used to, but understanding the hazards and imprecisions of radio-carbon and other methods of dating is something historians must do to make intelligent use of archaeological data.

Language as a source for African history has been acknowledged at least since the classification of African languages by J. H. Greenberg. Christopher Ehret has been one of the practitioners of this kind of historical research, saying, for example, that linguistics yields a "very democratic resource," as language history "does not allow one to identify individual characters in history" but lends itself to "the whole array of cultural elements" of the communities using the language(s) surveyed (chapter 3). Family trees of languages, such as Nilo-Saharan, or Niger-Congo, invite reconstruction of as much as possible of the vocabulary of the proto-language. When that, or a part thereof, has been accomplished, a "long term societal continuity" in a "sequence of periods" (the periods defined by the branches within the language family) is displayed. Vocabulary reflects society; deriving a proto-form of a noun from cognates in related languages testifies to the earlier existence of the object signified as definitely as does an artifact excavated by archaeologists.

In addition to the "vertical" transmission of a language from parents to offspring, there may occur a "lateral" transmission, as in the cited case of Dahalo in Kenya, whose ancestors spoke a Khoisan language, but who now speak a Cushitic language. The evidence of the change in speech is in a number of retained words from their previous Khoisan-speaking period. This instance of prehistoric change of language by a society is one that could be supplemented by obtaining genetic samples from Dahalo and their Cushitic neighbors. The "genetic distance" between the two would show to what extent intermarriage (or mating, at any rate) took place along with the adoption of the alien language. Kenya is an area of Khoisan, Cushitic, and Bantu convergence, and the order of their appearance in the region seems to be that of this listing.

Words can be borrowed without accepting the entire language and may be an indication of cultural influence. "Inherited words" on the other hand inform us of long traditions: a Niger-Congo protoword for "goat" tells us that Niger-Congo peoples possessed goats since the earliest time of that language family. World histories also shows that goats and sheep were obtained by Nilo-Saharan speakers from Afroasiatic speakers, but that cattle, on this evidence anyway, were not obtained from that (or any other perceived) source. Ehret sketches the methods of linguistic analysis to yield historical evidence, and how to locate societies of protolanguages in space and in time.

In many localities of Africa, as David Henige observes in chapter 6, due to the absence of written documents, historians concerned with the continent before about the mid-nineteenth century had two choices: archaeology and/or oral traditions. From the late 1950's a "new enterprise" of great magnitude to collect oral traditions got underway. Jan Vansina, the première scholar in this field, inspired many followers. There were three kinds of reactions to their works: one group refused to grant any validity to oral traditions; a second judged critically the results, accepting some after examination, and rejecting some as inadequate; and a third uncompromisingly defended the new territory against both of the other groups. Obviously, the second prevails.

Henige faults collectors of traditions for not making the actual texts available to other scholars in a depository or library within a reasonable time after the completion of field work, or at least after publishing the collector's interpretation. Failure to make accessible the recorded oral texts prevents other historians from judging the interpretation made by the collector; this is an intolerable situation. There is also the situation now that some older tapes on which traditions were recorded have deteriorated and these are no longer accessible to compare with some published works.

Vasina paid particular attention to interpretation, but Henige stresses that the problem for those who used oral traditions was not necessarily in interpretation, but generally in the collecting of the traditions. Many of the doctoral candidates seeking data for dissertations arrived in the field with tape recorders, but little or no knowledge of the language. The choice of interpreter, who must be bilingual (as most local people are not), can be a problem; each individual in the community has a place in the local social structure and the interpreter's relation, or lack of one, to an interviewee can obstruct straightforward responses. Was a collector of oral data aware of how, and to what extent, the interpreter may have skewed information?

Africans, affiliated with research facilities in Africa, where there are depositories financed locally or by UNESCO, are now collecting traditions in their mother tongue. In addition to mastery of the language and knowledge of the society, they often have the advantage of not being under the stringent limits of time that a graduate student has because of the conditions of the grant and a schedule for earning a degree. Even mature scholars on leave may have concerns with inadequate time. Thus, awareness of problems has been achieved; future results may be expected to be better. Under the best of circumstances, there are pitfalls in interviewing, as Henige forewarns anyone who wishes to deal with orally transmitted data of potentially historical value.

In chapter 7, Barbara M. Cooper reminds us that archaeologists pay attention to oral traditions in the area of an excavation. The site, in fact, may have been suggested by a reference in a tradition. The way oral tradition complements other sources, historical linguistics, as well as archaeology, is its strong defense against its deniers. She also recommends "a closely related but distinguishable" kind of oral evidence: interviews with "some of the central but sometimes neglected participants" in events that may have occurred decades earlier. This "oral history" has been developed in countries with plenty of written accounts. The questioning of participants or observers of significant events, it is recognized, adds supplementary information of value. This approach also captures "the unrecognized voices and experiences of the disadvantaged." This can be an antidote to exclusively elite history.

Do oral traditions, as functionalists among anthropologists assert, function to justify existing social conditions? Do they tell us more about the present than about the past? Or are these traditions, as structuralists following Claude Levi-Strauss contend, merely symbolic representations of universal human paradoxes, and thus timeless, devoid of historical content? Contributors to *The African Past Speaks*,[8] provide discussion and some answers. Debates on oral tradition, unfortunately, were carried out "oblivious to, or deliberately distanced from developments in oral history or gender research." There is common ground, as some chapters demonstrate in R. Perks and A. Thompson (eds.), *The Oral History Reader.*[9]

Concepts of postmodernism, deconstruction, and multiculturalism have brought a "disquiet" to the whole historical profession; this in turn undercuts new, still developing, and controversial historical methods.

Life histories, which American anthropologists began collecting before World War II (e.g., P. Radin, *Crashing Thunder*) avoid some of the problems of oral data. M. F. Smith's *Baba of Karo: A Woman of the Muslim Hausa*[10] (1981) is an early example from Africa.

Cooper, drawing on folklore, sociology, anthropology and ethnomusicology, argues "all oral evidence is essentially poetic and performative." This distinguishes it from "written sources, which are not bound to the sensory experience of the hearer or audience in the same way." Stories told are shaped by the public-speaking conventions of the community, but that does not make them "inauthentic." Scholars should be aware of "the performance context," or text and context, as folklorists have put it. Her own research, viewed with the caveats she outlined, rounds out the discussion.

Shomarka Keita, a physical anthropologist, discusses human biology in relation to African history in chapter 4. He first laments the confusion caused by use and misuse of the concept of "race." Ethnic group (defined culturally) and race (defined physically) may (as with the Inuit) or may not (as in most cases) coincide, but in any case should be distinguished. Physical anthropologists study living peoples and skeletal remains of past societies. The plastic quality of bone in a living person allows postures and repetitive activities of an occupation to affect the final form of particular bones; fossil bones tell of the kinds of stresses that affected the living person and from this can be inferred something about the lifestyle of persons whose bones were studied. From a number of skeletons from the same community, if periodization is established, socioeconomic conditions of the society often may be elucidated.

The presence of some diseases among a specific population in the past can be detected in bone. DNA is sometimes still present in some fossil bones; when this is so it "enlarges possibilities" of historical deduction. The few studies of genetic data from different regions of Africa so far completed show variations within local populations commonly considered one race. Geneticists find the diversity within a "race" to be greater than that between races.

"Art is a visual document of a creative process shaped by historical and cultural circumstances," Henry Drewal states as his point of departure in chapter 13. Forms and/or images are documents just as certainly as written texts are. Ernst Casirer's multivolume *Philosophy of Symbolic Forms*[11] asserted that art is a language, as did Goethe before him, but neither gave us a manual for "reading" art. Historians are more comfortable with texts, written or oral, whereas art historians are more at home with images. But the two fields can reinforce each other.

Drewal finds the center of gravity of art history in the realm of culture, and therefore "priorities of historians and art historians differ." He is correct that the influence of (British and American) anthropologists on African art history resulted in mostly synchronic studies—the history aspect ignored—but German, Swedish, and French anthropology have been more historically oriented than British social anthropology. American cultural anthropology was more historical, under A. L. Kroeber for example, before social anthropology began to dominate U.S. academia. Fortunately, African art history, as Drewal demonstrates, has been overcoming, with the aid of archaeologists, the exclusive attention to synchronic studies.

Dorothea Bedigian contributes a broad perspective on botanical evidence (chapter 5), derived from agronomy, ethnography, genetics, and other sources, as it is reflected in art, pharmacy, myth, economy, and other facets of society. Anthropologist G. P. Murdock's *Africa; Its Peoples and their Culture History*[12] pioneered the survey of the botany of many peoples in an historical perspective. J. R. Harlan, a specialist in crop domestication, refined geneticist N. I. Vavilov's proposed centers of domestication, some of which are in Africa. Harlan argued that agriculture originated by a coevolution of plants and peoples. Bedigian does not confine her view to Africa, preferring to let general principles be applied where they may, but in the over twenty cited publications of Harlan there are several that focus on Africa—the domestication of sorghum, for instance, and African rice. One gets an appreciation from Bedigian's discussion of the resources available for botanical research, one of which is linguistic analysis of plant names, a technique also used by Ehret. Folktales and proverbs often reveal the importance of, and attitudes toward, particular foods.

I was personally pleased to find Bedigian's reference to G. Rossel's 1998 publication, "Taxonomic-Linguistic study of plantain in Africa." Plantains and bananas are in the same genus, which originated in Southeast Asia, and I gave a paper, "Where did the Bantu meet the Banana?" at the 1957 History and Archaeology Conference in London. A word for "banana" appears in proto-Bantu, indicating that the plant reached Africa from Southeast Asia millennia ago.

African history does not depend entirely on unwritten sources. John Thornton looks at records in European languages in chapter 9. Coastal areas of Africa appear in documents in various European languages since the late fifteenth century. These accounts make the history of Asante, Benin, Dahomey, Kilwa, Mombasa, Ngola, Senegal, and Sierra Leone recoverable, in contrast to Adamawa, Azande, Luba, Lunda, and other interior states that are unmentioned "even in the early nineteenth century." Historians, who have utilized the accounts, have compiled guides to the various European sources that do exist. Many of the writers suffered from the disadvantages Henige pointed out in the collection of oral traditions: they may have been short-time visitors, lacking knowledge of local languages. The longer-time residents generally had an additional characteristic: they were interested only in commerce or in converting Africans to Christianity—in either case often harboring prejudices against "natives." Collectors of oral traditions typically were free of these biases but were not on the spot early enough to give the eyewitness accounts that can be found in missionary or trader records. Biases in the records are a problem, but one that can be handled by the historian.

An eighteenth century Danish trader on the Gold Coast identified his informants, but was unusual in this respect. Vansina, of course, advised collectors of oral traditions to name the persons making statements and place them in the structure of the society. It is seldom possible to tell from European documents whether a statement is based on information from a "noble" or a slave in an African state or from another European observer, and thus we do not know "what interests these people may have served." Despite these handicaps, there is a quantity of information from an earlier period, the value of which "cannot be exaggerated."

Areas attractive to merchants are well represented in the surviving documents; areas not commercially profitable have scant records. The Gold Coast, named for a commodity much sought after, has Dutch, Danish, English, French, German, Portuguese, Spanish, and Swedish accounts, but some in greater numbers than others.

Missionaries, having a different purpose from the merchants, looked at Africans in a more investigative way since it was necessary to know something about the way of life if they hoped to effectively proselytize these "pagans." "They were hostile to African religions . . . but their hostility did not prevent them from making detailed descriptions." Missionaries were more likely to learn local languages, making them more reliable observers, and when they compiled dictionaries or analyzed grammars they provided material for historians as well as linguists. In sixteenth-century Ethiopia (which has its own literate records), where Jesuits were active, their records "complement the local histories." At that time this Catholic order was making vast conversions in French Canada, Paraguay, India and Japan; there was also an effort to wean Ethiopia from its Coptic Christian affiliation to alignment with the Vatican; this set up a tension between the two sources.

A number of Africans learned to write in European languages. Letters from the king of Kongo, Afonso I, to the king of Portugal and others, are extant. And personal accounts by certain slaves taken overseas are not to be overlooked. These African and European writings are mostly stored outside the African localities to which they refer. Guides now exist for many collections, but the archives being scattered in many countries results in excessive travel costs for research. And of course language skills are necessary to use these disparate materials. "Many scholars never learn all the languages that would be relevant to their particular area"; thus far it has typically been scholars who are "not native speakers of the languages they mostly deal with." Modern editions of archival collections, with commentaries, are needed and some have appeared. Translations of important writings are also appearing.

With the beginning of the colonial period there was a great increase in the production of written sources that could be used in the reconstruction of African history. These sources were created not only by the colonial governments but by missionaries, whose presence began before the colonial period but which greatly increased during it. Such sources were also created by Africans, who were interested in documenting their past during the colonial period of extreme change, and who were competing with other African communities for resources. The history thus produced not only fed anticolonial nationalist movements by focusing on precolonial greatness, it served competition by African groups in the colonial and postcolonial state. Thus it paved the way both for the postcolonial production of national history textbooks for the schools, and for the boom in local history, which Bala Achi discusses in chapter 15.

Missionaries, both black and white, produced not only written histories, but newspapers and archives of documents that can today be used as raw materials in the production of written history. Thus mission archives can sometimes be as important as colonial archives in the production of colonial history. They can also be complementary since the concerns, and sometimes even the biases, of missionaries and colonial officials can sometimes be strikingly different, as we are reminded by Toyin Falola in chapter 10.

John Hunwick surveys "Arabic sources" in chapter 8, in which he includes not only works written in Arabic but also those in Hausa, Swahili, and other African languages using Arabic script. He gives the full bibliographical data on sources published in Arabic, and translations if available, since the eighteenth century, with assessments on the accuracy of the editions. He details the content of the works of historians, such as Tadeusz Lewicki, who use Arabic sources. When an Arabic work is mainly a translation of a Greek publication, e.g., Claudius Ptolemy, this fact is stated. Several Arabic accounts use the Ptolemaic system of "clima" and many "were conceived of as handbooks for travelers and incorporated the most up-to-date information, which . . . may only have been a repetition of what an earlier writer had to say . . ." But "Ibn al-Hakam (d. 871 C.E.), al-Ya'qubi (wrote 891), or Ibn Khaldun (d. 1406) were essentially historians," while others (e.g., al-Umari) were "arm-chair encyclopedists," though he, as well as Ibn Khaldun, collected some oral information.

The Maghreb, the Sahara, and West Africa feature in many Arabic sources; otherwise the area covered is the Indian Ocean coast. The interior of sub-Saharan Africa and the Atlantic coast are largely without reliable information, and on maps, with north at the bottom, sub-Saharan Africa is "a large blob." Hunwick discusses the Arabic confusion of the Nile and the Niger. He also notes some modern studies of Muslim trade with the "Land of the Blacks." Postmedieval writings exist in Arabic and in Turkish (in Arabic script)—for instance, on the Moroccan invasion of the West Sudan in 1591—but some are "so far untranslated into any European language." Turkish texts are "the least known and least exploited" for African history. Also largely unexploited are the resources of "the archives of North African states." The contents of writings by black Africans in Arabic, or in their natal languages in Arabic script, are only gradually becoming known to scholars. Plans and programs to publish Arabic sources are identified.

Another neglected source (not mentioned by Hunwick since it does not fall within his rubric) is that of the Chinese for the East African coast prior to European arrival in that region; the only translations, save one in English, are in Italian and in Russian. No listing of pertinent works is available.[13]

The opportunities for research floodlighted by Hunwick should stimulate neophyte historians looking for an orientation in a specialization that urgently needs development.

The various sources noted above, selected individually or however combined, provide the data that will be the basis of whatever historical narrative is eventually extracted from the sources by analysis and interpretation. The resultant history will fall into one or another recognized field of history: social history, economic history, art history, cultural history, and local history. The variety of these fields and the perspectives, or points of view, from which history can be written, is potentially limitless. This book can only sample a few of the most common ones in use today.

Social history is focused on the entire society, not only the kings and their courts. Some African societies were acephalous, lacking kings, or even headmen; social history should encompass these societies as well as kingdoms. Robin Horton made this appeal years ago.[14]

Isaac Albert (in chapter 11) welcomes getting beyond hegemonic orientation in African history. That orientation was stimulated by the

ambience of independence, but European history has been just as hegemonic, and there is nothing wrong in detailing the history of Sonni Ali,
Mansa Musa, Osai Tutu, Chaka, and other African rulers or lesser authorities, such as colonial district officers, so long as the life of the people
under these figures is also made as visible as possible.

Contemporary history should not be left entirely to political scientists; historians have the perspective to access and assess the sources of
evidence of today's events, crises, and movements. Albert points to medical
history and migrations as some of the challenges social historians need to
deal with. Perhaps we should add to the works mentioned in his endnotes
History and Geography of Human Genes.[15] Population genetics has a method
for elucidating old migrations. Population genetics is a resource for both of
these foci. Whatever the source of evidence, there will still be the necessity,
as Albert stresses, "to be grounded in social context." Ethnography provides
a present, or recent present, from which to interrogate the deeper past. Oral
traditions plumb beyond ethnographies. Ultimately, interpretation of the
assembled data in a rigorous way depends on theory, or worldview, whether
consciously employed or not. All techniques discussed in this volume yield
social history.

Economic history, as Albert recognized, can be teamed with social
history. Masao Yoshida keeps his attention on strictly economic aspects as
he looks at precolonial and colonial trade, rural and agricultural development, emergence of indigenous capitalism, markets, and states, and where
to find evidence for these topics. He adds Japanese Consular Reports to
those of other national archives as useful sources.

In the 1960s, country by country, Africans achieved independence,
or at the least colonialism evolved into neocolonialism. Four decades of
international aid for economic development from the former colonial
metropoles, the United States, the Soviet Union, China, Japan, and even
newly founded Israel, invite the attention of economic historians. There is
a literature of moderate size under the rubric of "economic anthropology"
in which the socioeconomic relationships within particular traditional
societies are described. Trade has its beginnings in the Paleolithic with
usable stones for tools. The later trade of the itinerant blacksmith in
West Africa selling or bartering his metal hoes and knives on a regular
route through a number of ethnic territories goes back probably to the fifth
century B.C.E. The trade of salt to the south and dried dates to the north
is an ancient pattern of Saharan economy. Copper had circles of trade in
West and in Central Africa in precolonial epochs. Evidence for early periods is scant, and is perhaps principally in the province of archaeology.

Bala Achi (chapter 15) focuses on how a local history of a people essentially neglected in colonial times can be rescued. The Atyap occupy part of the area of the Nok complex that once produced the famous terra cotta figurines. During the colonial period writers on the Kaduna region of Nigeria, where the Atyap live, referred to them as "pagans," or "head hunters." "British writers relied on Hausa as interpreters and in some cases as direct sources for their information," resulting in prejudiced accounts. Under Indirect Rule, this group was placed in the administration of Emirate of Zaria, and so was obscured in the Muslim Native Authority. "The growth of local history in post-independent Africa, particularly among minorities long exploited and oppressed . . . is phenomenal."

In 1981 a conference "involving Academia, local historians, traditional leaders and clan heads of the community" resulted in a bound volume of "proceedings [that] could not be presented as an authentic and acceptable history of the people" but it was a beginning. An Aytap History Committee was formed. "It was mandated to document and publish all available aspects" of local history. Funds were raised; the community was sensitized to the cause. Eventually writers were assigned to write twelve chapters by 1992. A 320-page manuscript was sent to press, but to date has not been published, though it now seems it may be soon. This is a work largely based on oral traditions, and could not be obtained and used without "making the area a hotbed of crisis" because traditions have to do with claims as to who were "aboriginal" and/or who were the first settlers. These issues are disputed because, among other reasons, they are the basis of legal ownership of land. "Obtaining consensus on viewpoints has not been easy."

The question of the relationship of the present population to that of the terra cotta artists millennia ago is not mentioned, and probably cannot be investigated by the method employed.

Diedre Badejo (in chapter 14) considers Yoruba aesthetics and how it fits in with other kinds of studies of the Yoruba people, whose aesthetics and history go back at least to the period when the bronze heads were made in Ife. This essay spans the study of art and of oral literature, both of which, as Drewal and Cooper have shown, are relevant to historians. And aesthetics subsumes all aspects of the culture, a condition social historians require. Historians must place Yoruba oral traditions in the context of the genres of Yoruba orature and cosmology, aesthetics, political and social structure, and all other aspects of Yoruba life and culture to comprehend them fully. This seems an almost superhuman requirement, but can be collectively accomplished in a field where, as in Yoruba studies, there are large numbers of scholars with a wide variety of skills and orientations. Badejo focuses entirely on the Yoruba people, but her approach can be applied to other peoples if there are enough studies on as many aspects of the culture.

She shows how many previous researchers have erred in using translations of Yoruba oral traditions taken out of their social context. For example, the Yoruba language has no gender, and thus whether the great Yoruba founding ancestor Oduduwa was male or female is ambiguous in the texts. Translated into English in the nineteenth century as "he," Oduduwa has been misunderstood, but understanding of African languages and ideologies "supports the possibility of a more fruitful re-analysis of the notion of patriarchy, matriarchy, and gender ideology" not only among the Yoruba, her case study here, but among all African peoples. Africanizing history must begin with a holistic attempt to understand the total world view and cosmology of African peoples, for without looking at their oral history in the total context of their thought we cannot understand the meaning that that history has for them, and why they have preserved it.

African continuities in the New World, a topic Melville Herskovits inaugurated in mid-twentieth century with *The Myth of the Negro Past*,[16] has been, and is being, pursued by another generation of scholars. Joseph Holloway concentrates on the United States (chapter 17). The Carribbean, and Brazil, in particular, but Hispanic America and Canada as well also figure in the Atlantic diaspora of Africans, as Asia figures in the Indian Ocean diaspora, and Europe received trans-Mediterranean migrants from sub-Saharan regions, in all cases almost entirely as part of the slave-trade. In some areas of the diaspora African culture traits survived and flourished, in other areas not conspicuously. African crops, such as sorghum, coffee, melons, yams, etc. helped feed peoples on other continents, and African labor helped build New World economies. African folktales, notably Br'er Rabbit, amuse Euro-Americans as well as African Americans. Music and dance in the Americas have been conspicuously influenced by African cultures. Herbal treatments and other medical practices were sometimes adopted in the new homes of Africans. "O.K.," the origin of which has had many suggestions, may be Wolof *waw kay.* African speech had some influence on American English.

In keeping with the spirit of this book, Holloway demonstrates how many sources of evidence, combined with insights he gained from study under the anthropologist Jacques Maquet, can be used to illuminate cultural continuities between Africa and America, even in the United States, where such continuities are not as readily apparent as they are in Brazil and the Caribbean. African cultural influences are far from confined to African Americans, of course, and Holloway is able to show how different African cultures influenced different aspects of American life, in different levels of society and in different geographical areas at different times. Recent research by Holloway and others on the impact of African culture among whites in the United States is already forcing a reevaluation of the nature of American society, suggesting that even such hallowed icons of popular culture as Bugs Bunny are of partly African origin. America's favorite cartoon trickster rabbit is now recognized as a descendant of that famous African immigrant, Br'er Rabbit.

In chapter 18, Donatien Dibwe dia Mwembu sees history as partial, relative, and fragile when exposed to political pressures. Memoirs can make for a counterweight to official histories, permitting the rewriting of history by taking account of first-hand reports of witnesses and actors on the political scene. The Democratic Republic of Congo is the example he discusses.

Colonial history is a history of whites in Africa defending their conquests. The lives of the local people was left to ethnographers. It was, however, in the Belgian colonial domain that Jan Vansina developed his method of historical research using oral traditions, going into the precolonial period. And *evolues*, i.e., western-educated Africans, recorded their opinions in a periodical *La Voix du Congolais*. Congo independence was achieved in 1960, but until about 1970, Congolese history remained in the hands of non-Africans from Eastern and Western Europe and America. Historians from these areas began training Congo students in the newly formed Department of History in 1965 at Louvanium University. Economic, social, political, and cultural and ethnic history was promoted. Congolese historians began to "decolonize" their recent history. The faculty was "Africanized" in 1976, and a new stage of history writing began in which precolonial history was seen as necessary to restore African history, but postcolonial history was largely neglected. The *Annales* school, and Anglo-American, and Marxist methods continued to influence history writing after Africanization of the University. Feminist history was not cultivated.

After 1970 life histories were recorded. They reached back to the colonial period. These accounts, at least those of the *bourgeoisie nationale*, filled in lacunae in official colonial records. Biographies began to be published in 1980. These publications touched on many domains: religious testimonies, political debates about the exclusion of Kasai people for

Katanga province, the life of workers in the Union Miniere du Haut-Katanga, the liberation of Congo by soldiers of AFDL, and so on.

It is the task of the historian to decipher and interpret from many memoirs the range of realities in the country in a given time. Popular art (and cartoons) may be added as a source for understanding the mood of the historical moment. Although Dibwe dia Mwembu's discussion pertains to Congo, the approach, in principle, may be applied elsewhere.

African history and gender history were recognized in academia in the same time-frame, that is, after World War II. Kathleen Sheldon takes this conjuncture of research on African history and on women in history to assess a gendered perspective in African history. "Where are the missing women?" as Gerda Lerner for decades has persistently asked. Half, or more, of the population are female; why are not half the persons in history female? Where is the evidence of women as actors in African history? Sheldon focuses on sub-Saharan Africa and on methodological issues. Studies by male authors often use the term "people" as if it included women as well as men but in practice the reference generally applies exclusively to men and their activities.

Before 1970, publications that referred to African women were mainly in ethnographies, but women were featured in some "development studies." Unabashed women's history began to be appear in a "new wave" in the 1970s, with women activists arising in both political and economic spheres. Prior to the wave, there was the essentially isolated report by Silvia Lieth-Ross on the "women's riot" among the Igbo in eastern Nigeria.

Two studies are cited for use of linguistic analysis to yield "gendered history." And archaeological evidence can reveal the division of labor in early societies. Interpretation of data from excavations relies cautiously on ethnographic descriptions of which tasks were performed by women and which by men, but patterns of who does what can change. Men's oral histories tended to omit details about women who ruled in the past in Bunyoro-Kitara. Female rulers in Oyo are not specifically identified as women because Yoruba language does not designate gender. Women who held the office of *ahemma* in Asante, incorrectly called in English "queen-mothers," were the counterpart of the *ahene*, or kings, but received little attention by British colonial authorities. However, art comes to the aid of the historian: Carvings of royal women in several African kingdoms suggest an exalted position by details of adornment in contrast to commoner women. There are some archival sources for the activities of elite women. Queen Nzinga, sixteenth-century ruler of Matamba, and the *Signares* of Senegal, have been revealed in some detail by recent studies. Edna Bay's study of women of the royal court of Dahomey analyzes "changes in social configurations that are illuminated by understanding women's situation." Several studies show a decline in various societies of the elite position of royal women. Newer studies elicit significant data on women that is understated in older publications. European and American women have written their observations of, and interactions with, African women. There are also some private papers of African women.

Oral testimony has been used with great success in collecting information about women's lives today and in the recent past." Women's songs, stories, and proverbs also tell interesting social facts. Marriage patterns change as economic changes occur. Plow agriculture, replacing hoe agriculture, favored men's interests over women's, and colonial agents preferred to promote men's authority and not women's, inducing a shift in some societies from matrilineal brideservice to eventually a system of paternal control over polygynous families. Changing house form from round to square, under missionary influence, involved a shift from women to men in building the homes, creating a psychological downgrading of women's importance in the built home.

Masculinity is recognized as the counterpoise to femininity, but not all societies define genders using the same precise distinctions. Do we impose Western concepts on African realities? Who is writing histories and for what audiences? These questions arise as African women join European and American women in investigating women's issues in African societies.

There are barriers not anticipated at the outset of research—for example, a woman historian interviewing women would want also to get men's attitudes and opinions. But women told one such interviewer, Barbara Cooper, that talking to men would be seen as a violation of the trust they have given her. A male collaborator would seem necessary to complete the picture.

Everyone has a point of view. Historians now realize that one's upbringing involves acquiring certain ways of viewing human activities, and that these mind-sets affect one's reaction to social events. In addition, one may, as an adult, adopt an ideological approach to life in the present, which colors understanding events in the past. Interpretation is an activity guided in part by theory. In chapter 16, William Martin gives us a perspective that situates Africa in the global system. It is one of a number of perspectives currently taken by historians, while some others can be seen in Martin's reactions to them, and several are listed in Philips's notes.

John Philips ties the whole project together in the final chapter. Here he tries to make sense out of the sometimes chaotic process of writing history by dividing it into stages: choosing a topic, gathering data, evaluating the data, organizing the data, and writing up the conclusions. Of course in actual practice the stages can become quite mixed and out of this logical order, but in explaining them they can be artificially separated.

Philips also makes clear the differences between "data" (a Latin plural meaning "given") and information and knowledge. The differences are often lost sight of, but can be crucial. More importantly, he shows how data from one source can be crosschecked by data from another source, showing how, for instance, linguistic data from the Hausa language can be used to decide which source, the Kano Chronicle or Leo Africanus's description of Africa, is more accurate in its portrayal of political relations between the city-state of Kano and the Songhay Empire. Historians, especially in Africa, must use data from a wide variety of sources in writing history, even if they specialize in gathering new information from only one source. This book has been compiled to help them understand those sources.

These several essays, each focused on a particular orientation, also tend to use more than one type of source. One source may be the primary one, but others are used in a supplementary way. Essentially the common stance is one of approving the employment of multiple strategies. There is no doubt that all standard branches of history—art, cultural, economic, intellectual, literary, medical, military, political, psychological, religious, and social—will be pursued in Africa, but also there will be an efflorescence of new crossdisciplinary studies with archaeology, ethnobotany, genetics, linguistics, oral evidence of various kinds, and other fields thus far only scratched by historians.

Neophyte historians about to embark on research into the history of Africa will find useful advice in these commentaries. Other readers curious as to how one strives to know how knowledge is established may also find value here.

Notes

1. James Harvey Robinson, *The New History* (New York, 1915).
2. Christopher Ehret, *Southern Nilotic History* (Evanston, Il. 1971).
3. E. O. Wilson, *Consilience: The Unity of Knowledge* (New York, 1998).
4. Jarred Diamond, *Guns, Germs, and Steel* (New York, 1997).
5. Harry Elmer Barnes, *The New History and the Social Studies* (New York, 1925).
6. Mark Gilderhus, *History and Historians*, 4th ed. (Garden City, NJ, 2000), 84.
7. Leonard Woolley, *History Unearthed* (London, 1958).

8. Joseph C. Miller, ed., *The African Past Speaks: Essays on Oral Tradition and History* (Folkestone, Eng., 1980).

9. R. Perks and A. Thompson, eds., *The Oral History Reader* (London and New York, 1998).

10. P. Radin, *Crashing Thunder* (Ann Arbor, Mich., 1999); M. F. Smith, *Baba of Karo: A Woman of the Muslim Hausa* (New Haven, Conn., 1981).

11. Ernst Casirer, *Philosophy of Symbolic Forms* (New Haven, 1953–64).

12. G. P. Murdock, *Africa; Its Peoples and Their Culture History* (New York, 1959).

13. A paperback edition of Nehemiah Levtzion and Humphrey J. Fisher's *Corpus of Early Arabic Sources for West Africa* (Princeton, 2000) has become available since this chapter was written.

14. "Stateless Societies in the History of West Africa," in Jacob Ajaye and Michael Crowder, eds., *History of West Africa* (New York, 1976).

15. L. L. Cavalli-Sforza, et al., *History and Geography of Human Genes* (Princeton, 1994).

16. Melville Herskovits, *The Myth of the Negro Past* (Boston, 1941).

PART I

Background

1

WHAT IS AFRICAN HISTORY?

John Edward Philips

> Whether Buddhas arise, O priests, or whether Buddhas do not arise,
> it remains a fact and the fixed and necessary constitution of being,
> that all its constituents are transitory.
> —Siddhartha Gautama, Shakyamuni Buddha
> (*Anguttara-Nikaya iii.1134*)

All history begins with the necessary and inescapable observation of
change around us. Writing the history of anything, including Africa,
involves finding out the nature, extent and pace of that change and trying
to explain it.[1]

The craft of writing history is best learned by reading history itself,
rather than by reading theories or philosophies of history.[2] Reading history is the best way to learn to write history in part because history is a
form of literature, and the best way to learn to write any kind of literature
is to read it. If you want to write for the theater you should read a lot of
plays. If you want to write mysteries you should read a lot of detective stories. If you want to write African history you should read a lot of African
history, especially history written by the historians you most admire for
their research, their interpretations, and their writing abilities. There are
almost as many kinds and styles of history to choose from as there are historians, probably more, since many historians write more than one kind
of history, and many works combine different types of history.

Because writing history, including African history, is a practical
affair, this book is about the practice of African history. It will describe
how historians of Africa investigate Africa's past, what sources they use and
some of the ways they interpret those sources. It will also talk about several

of the major issues and themes of African history, because no historian can ignore such issues. But this is not a book about the theory or philosophy of history; rather, it is a practical guide to understanding and writing about Africa's past. Those who want to learn more than a minimum about historical theory will have to look at other books.[3] This chapter, and the concluding one, will try to give as much theory as is necessary to understand and write African history.

A minimum of theory is necessary for a historian. Not all writing, not even all writing about the past, is history. Nor is all history good history. The assumptions of historical methods and perspectives are necessarily part of history. These assumptions are not really different for historians working on African topics and historians working on other areas of history. The historian who is aware of these assumptions will be able to write better history. But there are so many different historical perspectives concerning even such important and basic concepts as objectivity that the fledgling historian could be excused for thinking that even such a minimum consensus does not exist. Indeed, it is probably easier to define what history is not, than to define what exactly it is.

What History Is Not

History is not (necessarily) written by the winners. It is true that history is written by survivors, but as the late John Keynes pointed out, in the long run we are all dead. Much, perhaps most, of the history of certain periods and events seems to have been written by the losers, who returned home to lick their wounds and write self-justifications. One such case in Africa is the Kano Civil War of 1893–94. The first comprehensive account, and an abridged version of that account, were both written from the point of view of the losing side.[4] No one writing a history of the Kano Civil War can afford to ignore these eyewitness accounts.

History today is full of "winners" with bad press. In Africa this includes slave trade kingdoms, colonial imperialists, and assorted individual tyrants, but in this respect Africa is no different from other parts of the globe, where the historical evaluation of different individuals, institutions, and movements rises and falls with each generation's reevaluation and rewriting of history. This revisionism, as it is called, is a regular part of the process of producing historical literature. Today's winners are tomorrow's losers, and tomorrow's historians (assuming there are any) will see things differently than today's do. No condition is permanent.

History is not lies agreed upon. Because history is supposed to be nonfiction, fiction is by definition *not* history, although novels and film (like any other remains from the past) can be useful sources for a historian trying to make sense of the past in which they were produced, though not the past in which they were set. Just because official lies are taught in a "history" class does not make them history. Without getting into the debate about whether "objectivity" is possible for historians,[5] we can insist on the need for professional ethics. At the top of the list of such ethical values for historians must come honesty and fairness. Without honesty there can be no true history and without fairness, giving even the devils of history their due, our histories can be as unreliable as if they were simply not true. Ignoring important facts that don't fit our theories or prejudices can cause others to ignore our conclusions. Writing about events or persons which clearly never happened or existed is a quick way to have one's writings dismissed as fiction. In African history, as in other fields of history, this means taking the bad along with the good, and making an honest assessment of African shortcomings and failures, as well as the causes of those failures. History should be more than mere nationalist propaganda if it is to be taken seriously by intelligent adults.

History is not bunk. History may be unique among learned disciplines in that it has no specialized vocabulary of its own, but rather uses the specialized vocabulary of whatever field's history it is. Thus economic history uses the specialized vocabulary of economics, military history uses a military vocabulary, and so on. In addition, since one purpose of historical writing is to explain the past to nonspecialists, the good historian will avoid the use of specialized jargon that merely obfuscates its subject matter.

One result of this lack of specialized jargon and of bringing the subject matter down to a popular level is that many people think they know as much about history as a historian who has researched the primary sources.[6] Of course they may know particular facts that even a historian of the period and topic might not know. No one can know everything. It is also a cliche that some of the best history is written by those who are not professional historians, but most such history is written by specialists of the subject matter—for instance, economic history written by economists and medical history written by medical doctors. But history that has been researched and written by a trained, professional historian (or by anyone else who understands the history he or she has researched) cannot be dismissed as bunk. It is an interpretation of the past that needs to be considered seriously as a statement about that past, and thus about how the present came to be.[7]

History is not just twenty-twenty hindsight. In trying to explain the past we should remember that events unfold in real time. We might spend years or even decades pondering someone else's mistake, but that mistake probably resulted from a decision that had to be made on the spur of the moment, with imperfect information and with several other problems impinging on the consciousness of the decision maker. It is easy to ransack archives to find evidence which can prove that such a quick decision was wrong. It is quite another matter to know what information was actually available to the decision-maker, much less why they made the decision they did. We should also remember that just as past people made mistakes, so do present historians. No one can know everything, and thus all history is provisional and incomplete. The need for modesty in our interpretations can be understood better by contemplating two films which present very plausible critiques of historians' methods and perspectives: Akira Kurosawa's *Rashomon* (1950) and John Ford's *The Man who Shot Liberty Valance* (1962).

The Man who Shot Liberty Valance could easily be interpreted as John Ford's response to the many historians who have criticized his films for the role they played in mythologizing the history of the American west, creating the images that historians now must struggle against in our attempt to make students understand that era in American history. During the film the hero, played by James Stewart, apparently kills a gunfighter, played by Lee Marvin, who has been terrorizing the settlers of a small community of farmers on behalf of powerful interests in the area. In a seemingly fair fight, with little but his own courage to support him, but with nearly the entire town as eyewitnesses, Stewart's character emerges as the hero of the common man, the defender of decency and law-abiding citizens. He goes on to a career as Senator and ambassador.

The truth, however, is not what it appears to be. Stewart's character doesn't really have the skill to have won a gunfight with a professional gunslinger. The man who really shoots Liberty Valance is John Wayne's character, who waits in the shadows off a side street while the rest of the town watches the conspicuous, noisy drama on the main street. When it looks like Stewart's character will lose the fight, Wayne's character fires at Marvin's. The sound of his gun is masked by the sound of the other guns in the fight, and with so many reliable witnesses, no one thinks to question the incident. Wayne's character can't admit to shooting a man who wasn't looking, of course, although he does tell Stewart's character later so that Stewart's character will not have problems with his conscience. Years later, in the film's framing device, Stewart's character tells the story to the editor of the newspaper in the town where it all happened, while a reporter takes notes. At the end of the interview the editor seizes the reporter's notes and suppresses the story. "When the legend becomes fact," he says, "print the legend."

Ford has made a plausible case, if a necessarily fictional one, for an incident that probably no historian could find out the truth about. With eyewitnesses, newspaper accounts and other information available aplenty, few of us would even bother to investigate. Yet surely there could be many such instances in history, no matter how well documented. As a call to humility in our conclusions by historians it is worth listening to. If intended as a criticism of historians by a filmmaker it leaves something to be desired. Historians may not always get things right, but we do try to be accurate. Film directors, other than documentary makers, don't even try, and really shouldn't. They are producing fiction. Producing fiction is as legitimate an activity as writing nonfiction, but those who get their history from filmed (or any other) fiction should beware.[8]

Another, more famous movie, by a director much influenced by John Ford, poses an even more serious challenge to historians. Akira Kurosawa's *Rashomon* (1950) anticipated much of postmodernist discourse in dealing with questions of bias and the limits of human knowledge.[9] Like *Liberty Valance*, this film is also narrated as a flashback, but instead of a single narrator delivering a truth that has been and will continue to be hidden, there are multiple narrators giving equally convincing (or equally unconvincing) accounts. This tale is also told even more indirectly than *Liberty Valance*. A monk and a woodcutter who witnessed the police investigation of a death narrate the testimony of others to a third man.

There is a corpse to be explained, and the violent death of a samurai. A bandit has confessed to the murder, but a woman he raped seems to implicate herself as the murderer. The ghost of the dead samurai also testifies through a medium, explaining that he has killed himself. All of the stories seem equally implausible, but instead of blaming others for the death, each witness implicates him or herself. Finally the woodcutter, who claims to have found the corpse in the woods, reveals that he knows more than he has told the police. He admits that he witnessed the killing, although he has hidden this knowledge from the police, but his account is no more convincing than the others. It even turns out that he has robbed the crime scene of a valuable dagger, and hidden his knowledge of the affair for his own profit. As the man listening to the narrated stories points out, humans can't tell the truth, even to themselves. We all want to forget something, so we make up stories.

History, too, whether based on written documents, oral tradition, physical evidence, or other sources, is as much a product of forgetfulness and deceit, deliberate and/or unconscious, as it is of remembering and recording, not only on the part of those who lived in the past, but on the part of historians in the present as well. Since no historian has enough time or space to reveal everything in the sources, history is inexorably as much about forgetting and concealing as it is about remembering, discovering, and revealing the truth. How can anyone really know the truth of what happened in the past, even the recent past?

> *And ye shall know the truth, and the truth shall make you free.*
> —*Jesus of Nazareth (John 8:32)*

What Is History, Really?

The very mundane fact is that history is a job, which may or may not pay very well, or at all, but which requires work and a certain set of skills, like any other job. According to the United States Department of Labor, Bureau of Labor Statistics, a historian is a kind of social scientist. Specifically,

> Historians research, analyze, and interpret the past. They use many sources of information in their research, including government and institutional records, newspapers and other periodicals, photographs, interviews, films, and unpublished manuscripts such as personal diaries and letters. Historians usually specialize in a specific country or region; in a particular time period; or in a particular field, such as social, intellectual, political, or diplomatic history. Biographers collect detailed information on individuals. Genealogists trace family histories. Other historians help study and preserve archival materials, artifacts, and historic buildings and sites.[10]

To put that briefly, a historian is someone who creates history, a coherent interpretation of the past based on remains of the past that survive into the present. This created "history" is, of course, different from "history" in the sense of actual past events, with which it should never be confused. Even that raw reality is different from the way that persons in the past experienced it, for human experience is always mediated, first by our senses and then by the interpretations our mind gives to the raw data of our senses. Few of us remember this fact in daily life, much less in our academic interpretations of past reality.[11] History as we know it in the present is a form of created literature about the past. It is, or should be in so far as is possible, nonfiction literature, but it is still a form of created literature, an interpretation of the past in the present.

Thus history changes, but not because the past events it describes have changed. They no longer exist and thus can no longer change, except insofar as they have changed to become the present. History as an interpretation of the past changes because it is a human created artifact. We humans have limited brains and imperfect sense organs, and our understanding of the world around us, including its past, is necessarily limited by those brains and sense organs. We hope to collectively accumulate more information about our world, including its past, but there are inherent limits to human knowledge.

History changes not only because what human beings can know about our past changes but also because what humans want to know about our past changes. The problems of the present always inspire history in some way and to some extent, because history is written in the present, for an audience in the present, although (like everything else) it quickly becomes the past. The relative importance given to certain persons and events will change not only because new information about those persons and events is discovered, but because the perceived importance of their effects on the present has changed. Thus history will always be interpreted differently by each generation.

An important example of constantly changing interpretations of African history is the question of the nature, rate, and starting date of the Bantu expansion.[12] Bantu languages, including Swahili, Zulu, Kikuyu, Lingala, Kikongo and many, many others, are spread over a vast area, covering most of central, southern, and eastern Africa. They are spoken by so many of the inhabitants of Africa that they constitute a common stereotype of Africa in the minds of many non-Africans, and in many contexts, most notoriously in apartheid South Africa, the term "Bantu" has been more racial than linguistic. The close resemblance and relationship between Bantu languages was recognized by outsiders very readily. These languages must have diverged from a common ancestor and spread relatively recently, but in the absence of documentation, or even systematic archaeological investigation of such a vast area, the nature and direction of that spread, not just the details but even the point of origin (in both time and space) and general pattern of the expansion, have been controversial ever since historians and others first began to investigate the matter.

Joseph Greenberg's historically based reconstruction of the relations between African languages, including the internal relationships of the Bantu languages,[13] was not widely accepted at first, especially by anthropologists and linguists who had not been trained to think historically. Malcolm Guthrie, a linguist who knew little of the principles of historical linguistics, made a geographical classification of Bantu languages, and looked at their vocabulary to find the area which was the most "Bantu" of all.[14] Not surprisingly, he found this area in the middle of the Bantu language distribution area, where other language families and their loanwords had had the least influence. Roland Oliver, a historian who also knew little of linguistics and who was thus unable to evaluate the relative merits of the arguments of Greenberg and Guthrie, tried to combine Greenberg's apples with Guthrie's oranges, and came up with a fruit salad of an article about the Bantu expansion, that demonstrated, if little else, the necessity for historians to learn to understand the nature of source materials before using them.[15] Discussion of Guthrie's Bantu data and conclusions at the School of Oriental and African Studies (SOAS) revolved around methods and sources that the historians of Africa at that time were largely unqualified to evaluate, and which they therefore made little comment on. "One surprising feature of this discussion is the lack of participation by historians."[16] Oliver's influential conclusions were dictated more by academic politics than by ordinary rules of evidence, either linguistic or historical.[17] His paradigm was gradually abandoned as more and more specialists looked at the data it was built on, especially Guthrie's classification of Bantu languages.[18] This book is intended, in large part, to educate historians of Africa about the nature of the diverse sources that they use, so that they can better use those sources in reconstructing the African past.

Methods and sources other than linguistic are of course relevant to the historical construction of the spread of Bantu languages. The archaeologist D. W. Phillipson well summarized the then available archaeological evidence relating to the Bantu expansion for historians in an article he wrote some years back in *Scientific American*,[19] later elaborated in his book *The Later Prehistory of Eastern and Southern Africa*.[20] More recently Jan Vansina used detailed linguistic and other evidence to address the issue in his study of the history of central Africa, *Paths in the Rain Forest*,[21] and has explained the methodology behind his new reconstructions in an article in the *Journal of African History*.[22]

All of these interpretations, different as they are, share the belief that there was a recognizable group of people speaking a language that is now called "Western Bantu." Most recently of all this linguistic category of "Western Bantu" as a distinct group has been challenged by Christopher Ehret, one of the authors of this volume, in an unpublished paper, "Is there a Western Bantu?" Ehret, following the work of several other historical linguists, argues that the "Western Bantu" languages are actually not a distinct group of Bantu languages descended from a single protolanguage, but rather are the residue of several distinct groups, which have not spread as widely as the languages in the Eastern Bantu group. So-called Western Bantu is, in this reconstruction, not a distinct genetic group itself, but a number of groups, each roughly coordinate with Eastern Bantu, incorrectly classified together.

Although each succeeding work should be (but isn't always) better informed, and its author may have more data than his or her predecessors did, none of them is the final word on the issue of the Bantu expansion. There never will be a final word on the Bantu expansion, and never can be, as long as there are historians around to study the issue. Historians in new times and various places will not only have new information and new perspectives on the issue, they will have their own ways of looking at the issue and writing about it, and they will be addressing new audiences who have new concerns they want answered by historians.

History is a conversation the present holds with the past. Each new generation in every society, from the time its members are old enough to ask "Why?" wants to know how the present came to be, what persons and forces created this world they were born into, and why it is the way it is. The exact questions and answers have always changed as each new generation has different interests and different problems, and as each older generation provides different answers. Each new generation in its turn becomes an older generation before passing away, and writes new answers for itself and for its heirs.

Because history is a conversation with the past, historians must keep in mind that the past used words differently. While history as a form of literature has no specialized vocabulary, history as research must have a specialized passive vocabulary, even if one is studying one's own society. All languages change, and the semantics of their vocabularies change also. Thus historians must be aware that the words of the past, whether transmitted in written documents or in oral traditions, may have had different meanings in the past than they do in the present. The meaning of oral and written testimonies from the past may not be readily apparent. Explaining those different meanings to readers in the present is an important aspect of writing history.

History is the sense we humans make of our past. The human experience may or may not really make sense in some absolute, transcendent sense. Human life may really be, as Macbeth comes to think, "a tale told by an idiot, full of sound and fury, signifying nothing."[23] But we do not like to think such things about the human experience, because it is our experience, and we, as humans, have a need to make sense of it. Thus history is a "humanity" and is often part of a college or department of humanities in universities.

By creating a written (or oral or filmed or multimedia) history in the present we impose "history" as a created narrative on the past. I do not mean, of course, that we can travel to the past to change it, but it is our interpretation of the past that turns the former reality of the past into a coherent narrative, a kind of story called "history." Historians must mediate the questions of the present and the reality of the past, thus keeping one foot in each time, and communicating between them. The stories we build for our contemporaries (and for those who will read our histories in the future) must take account of the concerns of the present as well as those of the past. Those of the future we can only dimly guess.

The need for coherent narration is a human universal. Every people tells folktales, from the smallest, most isolated, and technologically primitive stateless societies with their myths and legends, to the largest, most urban, and technologically advanced empires and federations. Folklorists have turned increasingly to the study of rumor and urban legends, and the Internet has proved a fertile spawning ground for new folklore.[24] Among all societies, at least some of this narration includes presumed nonfiction about the past. Such narration is history, whether it is oral history, written history, documentary historical film, or multimedia digital history.

History grew out of myth and legend. Such famous works of history as the Bible and the Japanese *Kojiki* (record of ancient events) begin with what many today would consider myth, regardless of how many people in former times, or even today, would consider them literal facts. Such ancient Greek historians as Herodotus believed literally in the physical existence of the Greek gods, as well as in the prescience of the pronouncements of the oracle of Delphi, things that few (if any) in the contemporary world would subscribe to. In Africa the "Kano Chronicle" similarly began with incredible events, such as a hunter, Dala, who slew elephants with a stick and carried them for nine miles on his head. The Kano Chronicle slowly extended its narrative to more recent periods and more plausible events.

Between oral societies and earlier ages of human existence on the one hand, and the contemporary world of computers and the Internet on the other, written narratives appeared almost as soon as writing itself. Among those written narratives, nonfiction (or at least presumed nonfiction) about the past, or written history, has usually been a prominent genre. In Greek mythology history had its own muse, Clio, a spirit who inspired historians to create their stories. Thus historians, although we are supposed to be writing nonfiction, should also be inspired both in the interpretations we give the past and in the words we use to express those interpretations.

The fact that history is a form of literature implies the possibility that the logic and coherence of the historical narrative historians create is not inherent in the past but is imposed by historians. Certainly the fact that historians have created many changing interpretations suggests that the logic of our narratives is something that we impose on the past, not something inherent in past events themselves. The very universality of narrative should remind us that such narrative logic is a human universal, and perhaps only a trick that our minds play on us. Part of our duty as historians is to uncover the logic of the humans of the past, and to understand the meaning they gave to their lives, why they did the things they did. To understand the sense they made of their lives and to explain it to our contemporaries is part of the task of historians in interpreting the past to the present. Thus we must remind ourselves that our predecessors, being human, saw stories in their own lives and times just as we do in our own. To write African history we must strive to understand the mindset and worldview of the Africans of the past that we write about.

History must make sense. Without narrative coherence the mere listing of facts might make a chronology, but it is not a history. Yet the interpretations that have been given to history are strikingly diverse, from the great-man and divine-plan theories of history, to racial interpretations, class struggle, and postmodernist paradigms. The search for interpretive logic has propelled history beyond itself, and thus history has given birth to other disciplines.

> Therefore, today, the scholar in this field [history] needs to know the principles of politics, the (true) nature of existent things, and the differences among nations, places and periods with regards to ways of life, character qualities, customs, sects, schools and everything else. He further needs a comprehensive knowledge of present conditions in all these respects.
> —Ibn Khaldun, *Muqaddimah* (Rosenthal translation I:55–56)

History and Social Science[25]

History is the mother of all social science. Not only is it the oldest and greatest of the social sciences, but it gave birth to the others. Social sciences were created to explain the facts of history, and their interrelationships. The first social scientist, Ibn Khaldun, was a historian who invented his *'ilm al 'umran* (science of society) in an attempt to explain the instability of dynasties in his native north Africa.[26] Good history today, even history that is not specifically sociological in orientation, often uses social scientific theories of causation and social structure. Good social science also retains its roots in history, and looks at how societies change over time, as all societies must. The ahistorical nature of so much colonial anthropology, always written in an "ethnographic present" that actually described the recent past, not only severely limited its ability to investigate change over time, but it also resulted in conclusions so mistaken that it gave itself a bad name. Those anthropologists whose work proved most enduring were those most interested in history.[27] Modern history and social science must stay in touch, for each is poorer without the other.

Because history is human history, the human-created story of humanity, it makes social science, systematic knowledge about human beings, possible. It was only as a result of the accumulation of historical data that serious comparison and analysis of societies became possible. A certain detachment, which might be called objectivity, was also necessary, as historians came to study enough different societies and enough different times to think about them, even about their own society, as just another human society to be analyzed. This intellectual *sang froid* became indispensable to the social sciences in such forms as cultural relativism, the ability to look at another society on its own terms in order to understand it better.

While Godlike objectivity is clearly impossible for a mere human, and almost any historian must select from more primary source material than he or she can use, not to mention interpret and arrange for intellectual consumption by others, honesty and fairness are necessary for writing good history. At the very least, the lack of obvious partisanship shown by historians who bend over backwards to accommodate the perspectives of others will make their conclusions more believable. In the debates that develop history, as in any debates, the ability to listen honestly and open-mindedly to one's opponents' arguments, and therefore to counter or incorporate them as necessary, is important for historians.

Objectivity to a historian—like cultural relativism to a good cultural anthropologist—is an important tool for understanding a different society (in this case the past) and a working assumption basic to the method of the discipline. It is not an end in itself, and it is also an ideal which can only be approached, impossible to fully attain.

Unconscious assumptions are generally the most powerful, and the hardest to check. Those who most loudly proclaim their objectivity are often those farthest from their own ideal, precisely because they have never examined their own assumptions. Therefore a certain humility is necessary for a historian. This should perhaps be easiest for those working in a society other than the one we have grown up in, since there is so much we don't know about the society we study, and which the members of that society have to show and tell us, but the arrogance of so many colonial officers rings out from so many colonial archives, as an embarrassment to those who research those archives and a warning against complacency and self-satisfaction.

History is more than just a social scientific analysis of change over time, of course. It is a detective story. Readers of history want to know what really happened, and so historians investigate the past to find answers. Of course we can never know the whole truth of what happened, so historians are limited by our data, which exist in the present, in our quest to find out as much as we can about the past. Our conclusions are not restrained, however, by the Anglo-American criminal trial standard of proof beyond a reasonable doubt. They are rather similar to the standard of proof in a civil trial: the preponderance of the evidence, or (in other words) the most likely case.

The courtroom metaphor is apt because of the adversarial nature of so much historical writing. Historiographical controversies are often referred to as debates. Historians must present a case, not just facts but an argument about these facts and their significance, to a jury of our academic peers, as well as to the wider public. Because historians often think and work in this argumentative manner, building a case for their interpretation of events and trying to logically prove that case, history is good training for lawyers and politicians, who must also make arguments for their interpretations and their policies respectively.

The historian's obsession with facts is also similar to that of detectives trying to build a case about what actually happened in the past. This has led to a form of attempted objectivity which some wits have dubbed the "Dragnet" school of history, after the famously repeated line of Sergeant Joe Friday in that popular American television drama of the

1950s: "Just the facts, Ma'am." Of course historians write more than just facts. Simply by selecting the facts we use we build an argument about what happened in the past and its significance. Thus even the most factually objective history, devoid of any editorializing, is inherently making an argument. Joe Friday may have asked for "just the facts" when he was interrogating a potential witness, but he certainly selected from those facts and arranged them so that the District Attorney could build a case in court. Historians likewise use facts to make an argument, in our case to our colleagues and to public opinion.

Historians' primary sources are also similar to sources of evidence used by detectives. Linguistic evidence alone, among the major sources of evidence used by historians, is not used by detectives, because the time depth involved exceeds not only legal statutes of limitations but the lifespan of any known individual.

Both historians and detectives use physical evidence. The physical evidence used by historians is generally older, usually archaeological, but this is because historians usually work at greater time depth, not because there is an inherent difference in the argumentation about causation that the two professions make. The use of physical evidence makes advances in scientific analysis of data important for both detectives and historians, since we must both understand how to make the best use of the available physical evidence.

Historians and detectives also both use oral evidence. Detectives and historians working in more recent periods generally confine themselves to direct interviews, contemporary historians because most of their sources are alive, and detectives because indirect (hearsay) evidence is generally disallowed by courts, although it may provide detectives with useful leads to further evidence. The rules for evaluating oral evidence are different than those for evaluating other kinds of evidence, or course. But oral evidence is particularly important to African history, as it was to ancient western history. Herodotus, known as the "Father of History" for his writings about the ancient world, used oral sources, including much oral tradition, though he also used them far less carefully than would almost any historian today.

The modern Eurocentric assumption that historians can only work with written documents is a strange idea. Where it originated is hard to discover. Peter Novick[28] credited the idea to Langlois and Seignobos, specialists in the use of written historical documents who wrote around the end of the nineteenth century. He quoted their maxim "Pas de documents, pas d'histoire," making a mistranslation or misunderstanding of what these two historians were saying. In fact they defined "documents" not as written materials but as any survivals of the past in the present.[29] Not only that, they explicitly included oral traditions, not just oral testimony taken down in written form, among historical sources: "...when the events to be related were ancient, so that no man then living could have witnessed them, and no account of them had been preserved by oral tradition, what then? Nothing was left but to collect documents of every kind, principally written ones, relating to the distant past which was to be studied."[30] This seems to suggest that oral traditions are to be preferred to purely documentary history.

The idea that historians work (or should work) only with written documents has had unfortunate effects on history in general (imagine if detectives were only allowed to introduce written evidence in court!), although the lack of written evidence for much of African history has mitigated those effects on the history of Africa. The idea, borrowed from literary criticism, that nothing exists outside the text,[31] is useless for history. In fiction, of course, there *is* nothing outside the text. Shakespeare's *Othello* has a double time scheme, one in which the action takes place within a few days, the other in which it stretches over years.[32] Such a dual time line is possible only in fiction, never in history. Was Hamlet really insane? That's up to the director. When did regular trade across the Sahara begin? That is to be investigated by historians to the best of their abilities by various means. It is not up to the historian's whim. Historians must never forget that we are writing a detective story about real human beings who lived and died. We can never read their true intentions, any more than we can read the minds of our contemporaries. If we doubt that their minds were just as real in their times as our own are in ours we ought not to write history.

The claim that Africa has no history because so much of its past was not documented in writing is an artifact of colonialism and a misrepresentation of both history and Africa. The emergence of African history as a field within history coincided with the rise of African nationalist and independence movements.[33] As African governments have come to play an independent role in world affairs, there has been more and more need to know and understand the history of Africa. As African educational and publishing industries have developed, Africans have researched and published more and more of their own history. Today African history is so well established that few, if any, scholars would doubt its place as a serious intellectual endeavor.[34]

Despite the fact that the production of history does not depend on the existence of written documents, historians of course are always interested in finding written documents. This is not because history cannot exist without written documents, but because written documents combine the attributes of two other kinds of documents in one. They are physical, and like the physical remains of the past that archaeologists are so expert in bringing to light and analyzing, they are survivals of the past whose existence does not depend on continuous retransmission in the minds of human beings. However, like oral tradition, they are verbal, they are human-created testimonies of the nature of the past which are therefore more easily understood by humans in the present, even though, like oral traditions, they reflect the biases of their creators. Written documents thus combine the advantages of archaeological evidence with the advantages of oral tradition, and are important sources of historical information, whenever they can be found, though of course they should always be supplemented with as many other kinds of sources as possible. They are simply another way in which the past speaks to the present, explaining, in their own way, how the present came to be.

> What's past is prologue.
> —William Shakespeare, *The Tempest* 2.1.247

What Makes History Different from Other Disciplines?

Hard lines should not and cannot be drawn between history and other disciplines. This is true not only because there are various approaches to history, but because there are histories of various subjects, each with its own disciplinary imperatives. In addition, all disciplinary boundaries are ultimately arbitrary human creations, thus subjective and subject to change, as has been shown by the recent explosion of interdisciplinary scholarship. In Japan archaeologists are considered historians. In the U.S. they are classified as anthropologists. Where lines are drawn between disciplines is arbitrary. The important thing is not to leave anything out in dividing up scholarship. Nevertheless, history has been recognized as a separate subject for so long that it is certainly legitimate to ask "What makes history history?"

History involves development over time. The interest in change in the past almost defines history. But the backward-looking nature of the historian, like the Sankofa bird of the Akan people, is peculiarly strong. Most of us have a self-image of facing forward into the future. This is true not only for westerners, but for many Africans, as shown by the example of the Sankofa bird, which turns backward to face the past. If we are realistic however, we must admit that we cannot see the future clearly at all. We are all facing backwards from the caboose of the train of history, watching as the future races to become the past at the startling speed of sixty minutes an hour, twenty-four hours a day, nonstop for our whole lives. As events hurtle past us, and we try to influence them in our favor, they become the past almost before we know it, and move ever farther from our view. To understand and explain those past events, even (or perhaps especially) the ones from before we were born, is the task of historians.

Understanding the story of the past is the key to the most important aspect of historical narration: the problem of causation. This is what makes some facts more important than others, the fact that they helped to cause more other, later facts than did other facts in their own day. Many Muslim preachers denounced sinful practices. Why did Usuman Danfodiyo's denunciations lead to revolts, and become so influential even far from where he lived? What factors led to the collapse of the Oyo Empire? That the second question sounds as if it came from an undergraduate midterm is no coincidence. It shows how historians think, and the kind of thinking we want to give our students. Of course every cause that can be enumerated has its own causes in turn, extending back to the Big Bang, God, or perhaps *ad infinitum*. Thus history is a complex, even chaotic, web in which every event is an effect (usually of several causes, known and unknown) and many of those effects are themselves causes of other events. Trying to understand and explain this web of cause and effect is the job of the historian.

This same obsession with causation is the key to the notorious obsession historians have with dates. The more exact a date the better it is, but relative dates have an important place, especially if those are the only dates we can get. Dates are necessary to prove causation. *Post hoc ergo propter hoc* (after this, therefore because of this) may be a common fallacy, but *Ante hoc ergo propter hoc* (*before* this, therefore because of this) is so absurd as to be unimaginable. Things that happen earlier in time may (but don't necessarily) cause things which happen later. Things that happen later can never cause things that happen earlier, at least in our universe.

History is not an experimental science. "What would have happened if?" questions are inherently counterfactual, and therefore fictional, beyond the realm of history, however much we historians may like to indulge ourselves at times in imagining them. Historians are not God. We cannot construct an alternate universe in which the Berlin West Africa Conference failed to reach agreement, or in which Kwame Nkrumah died young, just to see what would have happened. Such inability to scientifically replicate conditions makes proving any causation difficult, as in many social sciences, and even in some physical sciences. But causation is of the essence in history and therefore chronology is equally essential. If it can be shown that Africans living south of the Sahara practiced iron smelting before north Africans, Indonesians, or any other people who might have been in contact with them did, then there must have been an independent invention of iron-smelting in Africa south of the Sahara. The future cannot cause the past.

Why belabor this seemingly obvious point? Because it is so obvious that it can be lost sight of. Consider the case of the French anthropologist Claude Lévi-Strauss. In his book *The Savage Mind*[35] he attempted an understanding of history that frustrated or infuriated many historians. He contrasted history with anthropology by claiming that anthropology, in his conception, was ahistorical, concerned only with things synchronically, as they are at a single point in time. History, to Lévi-Strauss, was simply a discontinuous but chronological catalogue of discrete facts, to illustrate which he drew a "rectangular matrix" (actually just a pattern of dots.) He actually argued that "It is thus not only fallacious but contradictory to conceive of the historical process as a continuous development."[36]

Too many other historians have taken on the poor professor's misunderstandings of history for me to waste time repeating all their arguments.[37] Instead I would like to show some sympathy for him. His version of history can easily be recognized by anyone who has sat through a boring secondary school history class, in which the lesson consisted of a series of disconnected and apparently irrelevant names and dates that were to be memorized for an examination. Lévi-Strauss must have sworn never to take another history class again, and to study only societies that had no history and knew nothing of the subject. Was it his fault that the ungrateful primitives with their savage minds now wanted to insist that they had their own history? He would never have anything to do with it. And so his kind of structural anthropology would become more irrelevant with each passing day, until he himself became just a historical curiosity.

Other social science becomes more relevant with every new day. New theories of causation draw particular attention. Historians must soon move from our dominant, nineteenth-century, logical-positivist assumptions about straightforward, clearly intelligible causation and begin to embrace such insights as chaos theory and self-organized criticality into the way we conceive of change. We have already come far from the time of Herodotus, whose sense of causation sometimes involved little more than "Thus the oracle was fulfilled." We can never really fully understand reality, of course, but we can strive to do better than previous generations have done by incorporating new insights from other disciplines not only into our sources of data but also into our understanding of causation.[38] Historical paradigms, like any other paradigms, change and will continue to change over time, but they will continue to try to make sense of the past to the present.

> In their history verily there is a lesson for men of understanding.
> —*Qur'an (12:111)*

What Makes History Good?

While we historians look at history as an end in itself, most of our students and readers see it as a means to an end, and look for lessons in history, lessons that historians may be reluctant to draw. Historians should, as the most important lesson of history, try to give our readers an insight into another time and perhaps even another place. We should not just provide new information, raw facts, but should also make people think in new ways by explaining to them how things were in an era they can never enter into. This will truly make history a kind of education, a word whose Latin origin means "leading out," suggesting the analogy of Plato's cave, the inhabitants of which mistook the flickering shadows thrown by a fire behind them on the walls of the cave for reality, until they were led out of the darkness and shown the world outside. Teaching must be a leading out from the darkness of ignorance, a sharing of the results of our investigations with others.

We do research to be surprised. After all, if we already knew what we would find, why would we need to do the research? We should also expect to surprise others with our research findings. One thing I have learned doing research is that all that stuff "everybody knows" to be true isn't necessarily so. This is not to advocate mere revisionism for revisionism's sake, a problem in a competitive academic environment where one may have to justify yet another study of an already overstudied question. It is rather to point out that we must challenge ourselves to learn and to change our ideas even as we seek to change the ideas of our readers and students.

The most important way we can help our readers and students to understand the time and place of our subject matter is by Africanizing history. This is an essential and obvious fact about African history, but one that cannot be stressed too much. It is also easier to say than to do, even for Africans, since Africa is such a wide and complex continent and since its history is so old. This can make other times and places of Africa's past almost as strange to Africans from other times and places as to anyone else. But all of us, African or not, must strive, first to understand the time and place we research and write about, then to help our students and readers understand it, so that it is no longer simply an exotic and mysterious "other."

Whether we call it Afrocentrism or Afrocentricity, Africanizing history must mean more than just the insistence that the ancient Egyptians were Black (however "Black" is defined). If Alan Moorehead's books *The Blue Nile* and *The White Nile*[39] had begun with paragraphs asserting the Black African identity of the Egyptians, they would have been no less Eurocentric for having said so, since those books were not really about Africans at all. They were concerned with the story of Europeans in Africa, and Africans, of whatever color, were no more part of the story than were the wild animals and exotic tropical scenery that also filled those books.

Africa is not just a continent, but a people or related and interacting peoples. Because history is about human beings, the history of Africa is not the history of the African continent as much as it is the history of African people. To write African history is to write the history of African people and the changes Africans have gone through. Thus the history of Africa must connect to the history of the African diaspora more than it connects to any other part of the world, not just because the slave trade both affected Africa and created its diaspora, but because the stories of Africa and of the African diaspora have been intertwined since the time of the slave trade.

Africanization of history cannot stop at simply pointing out the connections between the inhabitants of the continent and the African diaspora, either. We must, as much as possible, use African sources, both primary and secondary, in reconstructing the African past. We must strive to understand the ideas of the African time and place we study, to realize how Africans of the past conceptualized the world around them, including their societies, and to try to figure out how they would have thought about the changes that were happening around them and to them. Thus even archaeologists must consult living Africans, especially those with knowledge of how Africans of the past made and used the artifacts found in archaeological sites, in order to properly understand the remains of the past that Africa's land contains. This may involve learning African languages, not just as a means to communicate with ordinary Africans (for which interpreters may suffice) but in order to open the doors of our perception to the conceptual universe of the Africans we study. This is especially true, of course, for historians from outside the continent, but it can also be true for historians from Africa, if they want to understand other parts of Africa, or the interactions of different peoples.

Thus not only our sources but also our conclusions should be expressible in the African language of the people we study, if we are to write a true story about African people. We are trying to understand how some people experienced the past and then to explain that experience of the past to others in our own and future times. The multiplicity of African experiences, peoples, languages and sources make this a problem for Africans almost as much as for anyone else, of course, especially if they wish to try to be fair and honest about peoples they may not have been brought up to see as friendly. But that very multiplicity of African perspectives is one of the points we have to explain, at least outside of Africa, where the continent is often mistakenly seen as somehow homogenous.

Writing history perfectly is an impossible task, like any kind of perfection. But without striving for perfection we would never be able to do the best we can. Africa deserves to be understood better than it is. Africa's past is part of it that needs to be understood most, since that is how its present came to be. Let all of us who work to write Africa's past strive to write it as best we can.

Notes

1. A previous version of this chapter was read on August 23, 2000, to the Department of History, University of Jos, Nigeria, as "The Case for African History."

2. One of the few exceptions, a philosophical book about history that is extremely practical, is David Hackett Fischer, *Historians' Fallacies: Toward a Logic of Historical Thought* (New York, 1970). This systematic catalogue of historians' muddled thinking should be studied by every historian and reader of history as a guide to clear thinking.

3. There are several good general introductions to contemporary historical studies, although none of them deal with Africa specifically and few of them do more than mention African history. A highly theoretical treatment of history is found in Robert J. Berkhofer's *Beyond the Great Story* (Cambridge, Mass. and London, 1995). It is especially useful for its thorough review of the relevant literature in the various debates about the meaning and importance of history. More accessible introductions to current literature and debates include Joyce Appleby, Lynn Hunt, and Margaret Jacob's *Telling the Truth about History* (New York and London, 1994) and Richard Evans's In *Defense of History* (London, 1997). This latter is likely to replace both Marc Bloch's *The Historian's Craft* (New York, 1953) and E. H. Carr's *What is History* (New York, 1961) as standard textbooks.

4. Muhammad Aminu, *Fayd al-Qadir li-awsaf al-malik al-khatir* manuscript 51 in Jos Museum Arabic collection; Muhammad Aminu, *Wajiz Mulakhkhas min al-awal al-tawil* manuscript 52 in Jos Museum Arabic collection (abridged summary of *Fayd al-Qadir*).

5. The debate was surveyed in Peter Novick's *That Noble Dream* (Cambridge and New York, 1988).

6. Primary sources are sources that are not based on other sources, or whose sources are lost. Thus we cannot find the sources they are based on in our search for information, and they are "primary." Secondary sources are based on other sources which are still available. Historians use primary sources to write secondary sources.

7. In the field of African history Basil Davidson comes to mind as one of the great historians who was not professionally trained as a historian. His work depends on the extensive use of secondary works by professionally trained historians, and represents a popularization of their work. His contributions to African history show not only the importance of connection to a wider public for the discipline of history, but also the necessity of skilled writing for making that connection. History is as much literature as it is a social science, and it must keep one foot firmly in the humanities, even as it keeps the other foot firmly in the social sciences.

8. A collection of responses by historians to specific Hollywood films can be found in *Past Imperfect: History According to the Movies* (New York, 1996) edited by Mark C. Carnes, Ted Mico, and John Miller-Monzon.

9. Rashomon has arguably become an English word. Daqing Yang described the controversy in Japan over the 'Rape of Nanjing' as "a twentieth century Rashomon" ("The Nanjing Atrocity: The Making of a Twentieth Century Rashomon," Masters thesis [University of Hawaii at Manoa, 1989], cited in Daqing Yang, "Convergence or Divergence? Recent Historical Writings on the Rape of Nanjing," *The American Historical Review* 104 (3 June 1999): 859).

10. http://www.bls.gov/oco/ocos054.htm.

11. Jan Vansina, *Paths in the Rain Forests* (Madison, 1990), 71–73.

12. For a good analysis of the historiography of the problem of the Bantu expansion see Jan Vansina's "Bantu in the Crystal Ball," *History in Africa*, vol. 6 (Atlanta, Ga., 1979), 287–333, and vol. 7 (1980), 293–325.

13. Joseph Greenberg, *The Languages of Africa* (Indianapolis, 1960).

14. Malcolm Guthrie, *Comparative Bantu: An Introduction to the Comparative Linguistics and Prehistory of the Bantu Languages* (London, 1960).

15. Roland Oliver, "The Problem of the Bantu Expansion," *Journal of African History* 7 (1966) p. et seq.

16. Colin Flight, "The Bantu Expansion and the SOAS Network," *History in Africa* 15 (1988): 261–301.

17. Unfortunately, as Vansina has pointed out ("Bantu in the Crystal Ball," 1:294) this has been typical in academic and other investigations of the Bantu expansion.

18. For details see Vansina, "Bantu in the Crystal Ball," vol. 2, esp. 300–311.

19. D. W. Phillipson, "The Spread of the Bantu Language," *Scientific American* (April 1977): 106.

20. D. W. Phillipson, *The Later Prehistory of Eastern and Southern Africa* (New York, 1979). See also his *African Archaeology* (Cambridge, 1985, 1993).

21. Op. cit.

22. "New Linguistic Evidence and 'the Bantu Expansion,'" *Journal of African History* 36, 2 (1995): 173–95.

23. William Shakespeare, *Macbeth* 5.5. 27–28.

24. There are many Internet sites devoted to urban legends and Internet folklore. Among search engine sites devoted to these phenomena are http://urbanlegends.miningco.com/culture/urbanlegends/ and http://dir.yahoo.com/Society_and_Culture/Mythology_and_Folklore/Urban_Legends/.

25. Observant readers will already have noted that I straddle the divide between those who hold that history belongs in the humanities and those who feel that history should be counted among the social sciences. In fact I once unsubscribed to an Internet mailing list when the other participants began arguing this very topic. Ultimately it may matter little how the various subsets of human knowledge are divided into classes, as long as nothing is left out of the division. Very good arguments can be made on either side of this dichotomy, and in fact the categories of "humanities" and "social sciences" are rather artificial and not necessarily mutually exclusive.

In practice, most historians take a pragmatic approach to the question of whether history belongs in the humanities or the social sciences. If the National Endowment for the Humanities is handing out money, historians are all humanists. If the Social Science Research Council is in charge of the funding, they are just as firmly social scientists.

26. For a study of Ibn Khaldun's place in the history of modern thought, which places his new social science in the context of its contributions to Western thought, see Fuad Baali, *Society, State and Urbanism: Ibn Khaldun's Sociological Thought* (Albany, 1988).

27. E.g., M. G. Smith, *Government in Kano, 1350–1950* (Boulder, 1997), edited by Shula Marks and Paul E. Lovejoy.

28. Novick, *That Noble Dream*, 39.

29. "Les documents sont les traces qu'ont laissées les pensées et les actes des hommes d'autrefois," Langlois and Ch. Seignobos, *Introduction aux études historiques*, chap. 5 (Paris 1898, 1992). The English translation reads: "Documents are the traces which have been left by the thoughts and actions of men of former times" (G. G. Berry, trans., *Introduction to the Study of History* (New York 1898).

30. Berry, *Introduction to the Study of History*, 20. The original reads "Mais s'agissait-il d'événements ancien, qu'aucun homme vivant n'avait pu voir et dont la tradition orale n'avait gardé aucun souvenir? Il n'y a avait pas d'autre moyen que de réunir des documents de toute sorte, principalement des écrits relatifs au passé lointain dont on s'occupait" (Langlois and Seignobos, *Introduction aux études historiques*, 31).

31. Jacques Derrida's famous "Il n'y a pas d'hors texte," often translated as "There is nothing outside the text," quoted in Berkhofer, *Beyond the Great Story*, 10.

32. E. A. J. Honigmann, *The Arden Shakespeare: Othello* (Surrey, 1997), 68–72.

33. A recent symposium on the beginnings of African history as an academic subject in Britain was published as *The Emergence of African History at British Universities*, ed. Anthony Kirk-Greene (Oxford, 1995).

34. "Nobody in his right mind would argue any more that African history does not exist." Henk Wesseling, "Overseas History," in Peter Burke, ed., *New Perspectives on Historical Writing* (University Park, Pa., 1992), 75.

35. Claude Lévi-Strauss, *The Savage Mind* (Chicago, 1966), translation from the French original, *La Pensée sauvage* (Paris, 1962).

36. Lévi-Strauss, *Savage Mind*, 260.

37. A good example is M. I. Finley *The Use and Abuse of History* (New York, 1975). An example from an Africanist is Jan Vansina, *Oral Tradition as History* (Madison; 1985), 162–65.

38. A good first step towards incorporating chaos theory into history was Nikki Keddie's study of the historical process of the Iranian revolution in *Debating Revolutions* (New York, 1995).

39. Alan Moorehead, *The Blue Nile* (New York, 1962) and *The White Nile* (New York, 1971).

PART II

Sources of Data

2

ARCHAEOLOGY AND THE RECONSTRUCTION OF THE AFRICAN PAST

Susan Keech McIntosh

In his Preface to *Africa in Time Perspective*, the classic work that was the inspiration for the present volume, Daniel McCall notes that he had visualized the volume "as a handbook which would provide the neophyte with an adequate guide to the use of all the techniques of research in the varied and confusing fields of historical research. Certainly, we need such a book."[1] Almost forty years after the publication of McCall's book, which so admirably served this purpose, an update is just as certainly needed. But the archaeologist contributing to this project is faced with the same dilemma noted by McCall, namely, that archaeology already has "adequate handbooks which are in greater amplitude than could be squeezed into a book that has to cover so many other topics."[2] McCall resolved this dilemma by writing with brevity on the subject of archaeology, restricting himself to a number of essential points, several of which have lost none of their relevance.

Following McCall's example, I attempt here to present a number of issues that I believe to be central for anyone, but especially historians, hoping to better understand the enterprise of archaeology in Africa today. McCall's admirable brevity will not, alas, be repeated, partly because archaeology is today a much more contentious and diverse discipline than it was in the 1950s and early 1960s. At that time, African archaeology was the enterprise of a remarkably small and relatively homogenous group of active fieldworkers. Virtually all were European, a fact which united them, in terms of archaeological practice and interpretation, more than their different nationalities

51

divided them. They shared a common understanding of history and "prehistory" as distinctly different domains, and agreed broadly that a major objective of archaeological research was the description of artifact assemblages and the construction of artifact typologies, which corresponded in some meaningful way to past cultural identity. By mapping assemblages through time, they sought to produce a sequence, or history, of cultures through time.

Although culture histories are still constructed as the main goal of archaeology in parts of Africa today, the practice of archaeology is characterized by considerable diversity, comprising a variety of sometimes contradictory theoretical stances about the kind of histories archaeologists should try to write. No wonder historians get confused about how archaeologists reconstruct the past! I interviewed several Africanist historians in preparation for this chapter, asking them what they understood to be the goal of archaeological research. Some thought it was to reconstruct particular sequences for individual sites or areas and lamented that archaeology seemed to eschew generalizing narratives. Others considered that archaeological practice was too devoted to generalization and differed from historical reconstruction mainly in its refusal to engage with the particular and the contingent. Because archaeological practice in Africa is diverse, both observations may well be correct. I begin this chapter, then, with an overview of the main "archaeologies" in Africa. I will then consider the epistemological challenge shared by both archaeology and history: how do we link the present, in which artifacts/documents are perceived and experienced, and the past, in which they were made and used? Neither texts with their messages nor mute artifacts (for all their fulsome materiality) provide direct, unmediated access to the past. Both rely on interpretive linking principles to establish the evidentiary relevance of their data as a record of the past. Historians use a particular set of rules to interrogate documentary sources. Archaeologists use a very different set to translate artifacts and their spatial configurations into meaningful accounts of the past. I will argue here that a general appreciation how archaeologists apply those rules to three-dimensional configurations of artifacts and structures to produce historical narratives is one fundamental key to a better understanding of archaeological practice.

Archaeologies in Africa

Although archaeological theory and practice in Africa are not as fragmented and factionalized as they are in Europe and North America, diverse research styles, different propositions about how the past worked, and different theories about how it should be recovered and interpreted characterize the discipline.[3] In some areas of Africa, traditional culture history, with a primary goal of describing and classifying archaeological material, and mapping the spatial and chronological distributions of various artifact sets, continues, in much the same manner as it did in other, better-studied parts of the world earlier in the twentieth century.[4]

While contributing indispensable information on chronological sequences, this approach was critiqued in the 1960s by "New Archaeologists" in the U.S. and Britain for three reasons, among others: its descriptive approach did not provide very satisfactory explanations of *why* cultural and technological change occurred; its methodology was overly inductive and predicated on the assumption that the data were nonproblematic and could speak for themselves; its conceptions of culture and culture change were insufficiently anthropological. The Processual approach advocated by the New Archaeology envisioned culture as a complex system of functionally interrelated subsystems—economic, religious, subsistence, technological— that were adapted to the environment and ecosystem (figure 2.1).

The goal was to understand general, long-term processes of change,[5] rather than particular historical events, and the emphasis was on local perturbations that produced adaptive change within the system. This processual approach proved to be a valuable perspective for African archaeology, where innovation had previously been assumed to be the product of external factors, such as diffusion from more "dynamic" societies to the north. The classic work of Munson on the shift to food production as the lakes dried up at Tichitt was inspired by this new paradigm, as was the research that led to the recognition of indigenous urbanism at Jenne-jeno.[6]

Another important aspect of the New Archaeology was an emphasis on making biases explicit, stating clear research questions and indicating how they are linked to data recovery and analysis, and attempting to eliminate intuition and implicit assumptions. Generally, the goal was to make archaeology more scientific and rigorous in its procedures. David Clarke, in particular, stressed the need to define one's terms explicitly to replace "the murky exhalation that passes for 'interpretive thinking' in archaeology."[7] Problem orientation and modeling were techniques used to enhance clarity and explicitness in data recovery and analysis.[8] Many, if not most, practicing Africanist archaeologists still find modeling extremely useful, for it obliges the researcher to identity and justify a focus on specific variables, thereby highlighting the information that needs to be collected to properly evaluate the model. Modeling brings clarity to the argument linking data to human action in the past.

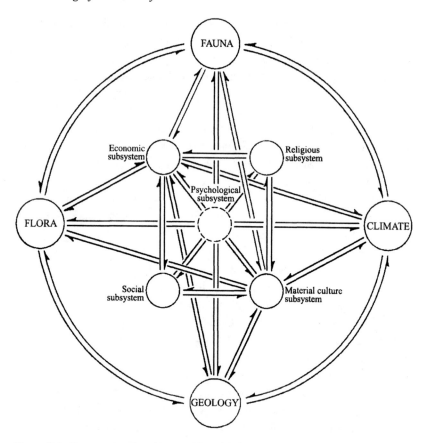

Figure 2.1. Processual archaeology envisioned culture as a system composed of various subsystems in dynamic equilibrium with the total Environment System. (Redrawn and modified from D. L. Clark, *Analytical Archaeology*, 1968, p. 125.)

The generalizing scientism of processual archaeology soon came under attack. Was the behavior of humans really predictable and subject to generalization in the same manner as atoms? Processualism's functional models of cultural systems and definition of culture as "man's extrasomatic means of adaptation" ignored the fact that the locus of culture was first and foremost in the human mind. Critiques of processualism emerged in the 1980s, stressing that human actions can be explained only by reference to human ideas and intentions. Interpretation of archaeology therefore had to be *hermeneutic* (about ideas, meanings, and symbols) in nature rather than scientific.[9]

Structuralist approaches represent a very different way of interpreting the patterning of archaeological remains in terms of human behavior. Where processualists viewed culture like a functionally integrated organism, with different parts performing different functions and the whole adapted to its environment, structuralists view culture as like a language—an expressive system of hidden, cognitive meanings.[10] Using theory derived ultimately from linguistics, structuralism seeks to identify culturally mediated and recurrent patterns of thought organized as pairs of polar opposites (male-female, raw-cooked) that are manifested in the cultural organization and use of space and production of material culture. The anthropologist Adam Kuper provided considerable fodder for structuralist archaeologists when he used a wide range of southern African ethnographies to argue that structural oppositions determined the layout of all villages built by Bantu-speaking people. Based on structuralism's assertion that these cognitive systems persist through space and time, Tom Huffman has identified the characteristic elements of this "Southern Bantu Cattle Pattern" in fragmentary remains of villages up to fifteen hundred years old.[11] Huffman has also used a structuralist approach to interpret Great Zimbabwe.[12] Peter Schmidt used a structuralist approach in his important study of iron working and associated shrines as a feature of the cultural landscape over time in the Buhaya region of Tanzania.[13] Critics of structural interpretation have pointed out that "the application of structuralist theory—which sacrifices time for the sake of explanation—perpetuates the notion that Africa is in a permanent ethnographic present,"[14] that is, timeless and unchanging.

Particularly in eastern and southern Africa, Marxist narratives have enjoyed considerable prominence. Marxist approaches see human societies as shaped by historical circumstances involving the "forces of production" (raw materials, labor power, artifacts, and other resources available to a given community) and the "relations of production" (the ways in which people organize themselves in order to use the forces of production). "Together, these constitute specific 'modes of production.' To varying degrees, forces of production are seen as controlled by minorities within a specific social formation, resulting in inherently conflictual situations—class struggle."[15] Martin Hall's widely read *Farmers, Kings and Traders in Southern Africa, 200–1860* invokes a Marxist framework at various points in the narrative to explain various transformations that have taken place in African society.

More broadly, however, it is Marx's notion of ideology, as elaborated by neo-Marxists, that has had the most pervasive influence in archaeological thought. Ideology functions to legitimize social inequalities, which it accomplishes in one or more ways: by naturalizing the existing social order and making it seem inevitable; by making sectional interests appear universal, or by masking the true nature of the existing inequalities. Although Marxism began as a materialist model, through the influence of the Frankfurt School of critical theory, it has been used to unmask the role of ideology not only in the past, but in Western knowledge claims in the present.[16] Many critical accounts of colonial archaeology in Africa draw on Marxist perspectives on ideology in the construction of narratives of the past.[17]

The notion that archaeological discourse serves political ends in the present because of its ideological dimension was a prominent theme of a group of new theoretical strands in the 1980s that came to be known as postprocessual archaeology. It initially emerged in Britain as a critique of processual archaeology and came to cover a wide range of ideas. Postprocessual archaeology can be described as interpretive and self-reflexive, favoring conflict-driven models of society, emphasizing the individual, agency, and historical context, and encouraging a diversity of views in the interpretation of the past.[18] Although Africanist archaeology has experienced nothing like the development, elaboration, and academic hegemony of postprocessual views that has occurred in Britain, many archaeologists in Africa have added a critical dimension to their own work, striving to identify the ideological elements, culturally imposed biases, and hidden assumptions that shape the practice of archaeology in Africa.[19]

The final "ism" we must mention—postmodernism—has contributed to archaeological thought a skepticism towards the Enlightenment meta-narrative of progress and stadial models of human social evolution, or any other kind of totalizing discourse that claims to apply at all times and in all places. The legacy of progressivist and neo-evolutionary models is undeniably present in African archaeology. As Ann Stahl has pointed out, one manifestation of this is the tendency to focus on case studies of increasing social complexity at the expense of studies of contemporaneous smaller scale or interstitial societies.[20] The resistance of American-based archaeologists to discarding generalizing concepts such as cultural evolution or processualism is in part due to the dominance of science-based funding (principally from the National Science Foundation) for archaeology in the U.S. The extent to which the humanistic and idiographic agendas of postprocessualists would find equivalent levels of research support is open to question. The funding structure for archaeology reflects the historical development of nonclassical archaeology as a comparative and generalizing discipline located within the social sciences in the U.S. rather than within history departments, as in Europe. Many American archaeologists therefore find it hard to ignore or deny the pattern of linearity and directionality (involving the appearance of larger-scale, more internally differentiated societies) that has been a pronounced feature of the past ten thousand years, despite postmodernist efforts to deny this pattern as a legitimate field of study.[21]

Many Africanist archaeologists continue to conduct research from a perspective that is conducive to cross-cultural comparisons, whether they adopt a generalizing stance *a priori*, or structure their research with a view to evaluating/testing the validity of various generalizing propositions. The use of models to isolate the main variables of interest and specify their interactions makes it possible to test patterns in one region against claims for cross-cultural regularities.[22] There is growing appreciation among archaeologists of the role of contingency in long-term processes of change.[23] This appreciation has been fed by the success of Jared Diamond's *Guns, Germs, and Steel*, for example, in creating a single narrative for the history of the whole world, based on the operation of precisely such large-scale processes with regional differences shaped by the opportunities and constraints offered by contingencies of geography and climate.[24]

From this brief overview, we see that African archaeological practice, while hardly uniform or monolithic, has nevertheless been somewhat insulated from the energetic theoretical debates between materialists (processualists, Marxists) and idealists (structuralists, postprocessualists) that have fragmented archaeology in Britain and the U.S. To a certain extent, this is a reflection of the relatively small number of Africanist archaeologists and the lack of a significant reward structure (positions, advancement, salary) within the discipline for theory development. For North American archaeologists generally, Africa remains relatively marginal to their theoretical agendas, with the obvious exception of "early man" research. For African archaeologists, theory development is a low priority for the many well-credentialed archaeologists who are employed in government administration of heritage. Many conduct fieldwork only occasionally, and when they do, rely on the methods learned in graduate school. The result is a chronic underdevelopment of indigenous archaeologies in Africa. When faced with the shifting winds of theory blowing from the North, it is little wonder that African archaeologists in some cases disengage from the debate: "Do I need to engage in unraveling archaeological problems through application of theories that are of no immediate relevance to solving [my country's] pressing cultural, social, and scientific difficulties?"[25] The dire underdevelopment of field archaeology in Africa prompts many of us to take a pragmatic stance focused on the urgent recovery of *some* subset of information about the African archaeological past before it all disappears in the face of development, agriculture, or looting. Once that is gone, our ability to represent the deep-time, predocumentary history of Africa will have largely disappeared as well. This is an alarming prospect, for archaeology alone can provide the data necessary to examine and challenge historical assumptions about

Africa's predocumentary past. How archaeologists go about creating meaningful accounts of that past is the topic we turn to next.

From Source Material to Narrative: Linking Arguments and Archaeology

We have seen in the preceding section that archaeologists produce various
kinds of accounts of the African past. Some create descriptive sequences
of artifacts; some try to explain the hidden cultural logic that accounts
for particular spatial configurations of material culture; others attempt to
explain changes that unfold through time, involving many different, interrelated aspects of a past culture. All of these accounts rely on interpretations
of the patterning in time and space of material residues of human activities.
These are the source materials, the actual building blocks of archaeology.
Much ink has been expended on how different these data are from the
source materials of history. And it is true—it makes a huge difference when
sources are primarily based in language. Historical sources are intentional in
a way that archaeological evidence is not. Peter Kosso draws the analogy to
testimony and evidence in a courtroom.[26] In spoken testimony, witnesses
might distort their accounts through conscious agendas or unconscious
biases, or they might be plain wrong. Expert interrogation of the witness is
required to bring to these problems to light. Material traces, such as finger-
prints, tire tracks, DNA, or the murder weapon, have no agenda. But these
data, too, require expert interrogation of a different sort to establish their relevance and robustness as evidence in the reconstruction of the crime.

History has developed a stringent set of rules and procedures for interrogating the sources and conducting source side criticism. Archaeology, likewise, has its own procedures for establishing and evaluating the evidential
significance of material identified as a record of the past. Producing an
account of the past from artifacts, features (nonmoveable traces such as
houses, burials, and hearths) and their spatial configurations, requires several
levels of linking arguments. If historians want to evaluate archaeological
accounts, some understanding of these linking principles is essential.

Chronology

The first bedrock principle is that chronology matters. Archaeological
reconstructions are built on claims that certain sets of archaeological entities were produced contemporaneously as part of a cultural system. These

contemporaneity claims exist at all levels of archaeological analysis, from a single activity locus (e.g., a cooking hearth, where it is claimed that the broken pottery, the fish bone and charred grain, the ash, and a small circle of rocks are contemporaneous and were produced in conjunction with one another) to its immediate context (a domestic structure), to the larger context (a village, a group of related villages). We build up a picture of the past by constructing webs of chronological arguments about materials and patterns that could have been produced by contemporaneous human action and interaction. We are seriously misled if we interpret the residues from very different time periods as part of a single, contemporaneous pattern, in much the same way that the historian is led astray by unrecognized document forgeries. Rigorous excavation methods designed to identify materials and features deposited at broadly the same time lie at the heart of the archaeological enterprise. We will return shortly to a discussion of some of these methods.

When archaeologists produce narratives that describe and explain change through time, these are based on recognizing changes in the patterning of a sequentially ordered series of contemporaneous sets of material. Temporal sequences are obviously of great important to archaeological narratives about the past because the order in which events occurred shapes the account we present. The demonstration that urban settlements in sub-Saharan Africa predated the trans-Saharan trade, rather than vice versa, for example, completely changed historical expectations for Africa's past.

Analogy

A second linking argument that is unavoidable in archaeology is the use of analogy to interpret the past. This ranges from the most mundane interpretation of function—"this is a house foundation made of *daga* (mud)," which we assign because it resembles such features in the present. We then build our case by adding other arguments from analogy—the presence of "domestic" residues of hearths, and meals, and pottery, for example. The problem, as Lewis Binford pointed out, is that the patterning we discern in the archaeological record is static, while the past cultural systems we seek to understand were dynamic. How can analogy mediate between these two? His answer is Middle Range Theory,[27] which uses ethnoarchaeological studies to develop theories of artifact use and deposition that permit more explicit linkages between particular observations of the archaeological record and general theories about the past. As an example, Binford cites observations of animal butchering by a variety of hunter-gatherers, noting that discarded bones accumulate in a ring as they are tossed back over the shoulders of the circle of butchers. The "toss zone" is therefore a meaningful pattern and where it is noted archaeologically, there is warrant to infer that butchering took place.[28] The strength of the argument identifying a pattern of archaeological bones as a toss zone will depend on coherence with other data (do the bones have butchery marks?) and other criteria.

An analogy can be strengthened if some form of cultural continuity can be demonstrated between present and past groups. Thurstan Shaw interpreted the stunning ninth/tenth-century burial at Igbo Ukwu as that of a high-status titleholder in a nonhierarchically organized society, based on similarities in burial ritual of a titleholder (the Eze Nri) in Igbo culture historically.[29] This is an African example of the direct historical method originally developed by North American archaeologists, in which the cultural antecedents of existing Native American groups were traced back through time. Cultural relationship and continuity are considered to produce the strongest arguments by analogy.

Pre- and Post-Depositional Processes

A third important linking principle considers the potential effect on archaeological patterning and its interpretation of pre- and post-depositional processes that may have altered or biased the record available for observation.

Almost thirty years ago, David Clarke discussed the incompleteness of the archaeological record as a chronicle of past human activity and acknowledged that selection and subjectivity in data recovery and analysis further reduce the available record.[30] He conceptualized the relationship between past human behavior and archaeological data as a nested series of samples. Of the total range of human behavior that took place at a particular site or area (*pre-depositional behavioral sample*), only a sample of those behaviors were expressed in material remains and then deposited (*depositional sample*). Of those that received material expression and were deposited, only a portion survived intact and undisturbed (*post-depositional sample*). Of those, only a sample was recovered and recorded by the archaeologist (*retrieved sample*); and then, only a portion of the recovered material was selected for analysis and interpretation (*analyzed and interpreted sample*—what usually gets published). Clarke then specified that it is the job of theory to relate these different levels and samples by specifying appropriate reasoning and methods. In Clarke's view, archaeology is "the discipline with the theory and practice for the recovery of unobservable human behavior from indirect traces in bad samples."[31]

Following up on these points with particular reference to depositional processes, Michael Schiffer proposed that human behavior could not be "read off" directly from archaeological remains, because the deposits had experienced various distorting transformations through the operation of natural and cultural processes.[32] Moving water, wind erosion, burrowing or gnawing animals are all elements that could add, subtract or shift material at a site. Similarly, cultural practices such as sweeping, digging, and reuse of dropped artifacts alter the initial context of material deposited in an archaeological site. The basic tenet of post-depositional theory is that the potential information contained in the archaeological record is always decreasing. Schiffer's focus on interpreting the various processes involved in site formation shares many similarities with the taphonomic studies that have so altered our understanding of many early hominid sites in Africa. The realization that a variety of natural agents, from running water to various animals, contributed to the addition and subtraction of material at early stone-tool sites in East Africa completely altered our interpretation of the hominid behaviors that may have occurred at them.[33]

The significant point emerging from this brief discussion is the fact that the archaeological record starts out as an unavoidably incomplete and/or disturbed record of past human behavior due to factors that have nothing to do with the actions of archaeologists. We cannot know the full extent of human behavior that never received material or artifactual expression, we cannot recover material that was never deposited, and we cannot know the full extent of destruction or distortion that has occurred to deposited material prior to its discovery by archaeologists. We can, however, determine the likelihood that such processes occurred. This interrogation of the archaeological record is analogous to historical source side criticism that seeks to understand bias (what was recorded and why?), degree of preservation (how much is missing?), and reliability. As with historical documents, there are inherent limitations in the archaeological record. Clearly, a certain amount of ambiguity and imprecision is already built in. The archaeologist hopes that through the development of appropriate theories and application of rigorous methods derived from them, she can minimize the gratuitous introduction of new biases and distortions in the course of data retrieval. However, since the archaeological record offers an infinite amount of potential information at every level, from that of the individual artifact up to the site and the regional population of sites, the archaeologist is always making selections, taking samples, and limiting what she can reconstruct of the past to some small subset of the potentially available information. Ideally (but too infrequently, in practice) the selective process is justified by explicitly linking certain data to the propositions about the past that are of interest.

The Nature of Data

Calling this recovered information "data" may lead to a misplaced sense of concreteness and objectivity. While it is true that much of what archaeologists recover has a concrete, material existence, or consists of spatial coordinates recording position in three-dimensional space, the "data" manipulated and interpreted to produce archaeological reconstructions and narratives consist predominantly of categories of information that have no necessary objective existence. As already alluded to, artifacts and features do not announce themselves as iron gongs, copper ingots, Urewe ware, or daga house foundations. Archaeologists draw inferences about function and create particular analytical groupings because some aspect of their approach to the past has convinced them that it is useful and meaningful to do so. What is considered useful and meaningful can shift, depending on the focus of the inquiry. Categorizations, both unconscious and conscious, are a feature of archaeological information retrieval and interpretation at all levels.

Precisely because the established archaeological record is composed of information recorded in descriptive or analytical or interpretive units devised by archaeologists, Chris Chippendale suggests that this information is better described as *capta* than as *data*. The etymology of *data* (sing. *datum*) is the Latin term meaning "given," and since data are almost never given to us by the archaeological record, Chippendale asserts, *capta* better reflects the fact that these are "things that we have ventured forth in search of and captured."[34] The choice of elements that we capture at the expense of others is based on an archaeological understanding at any particular point in time of which variables visible in material culture can usefully serve as proxies for variables of human behavior and organization that are not directly visible to us. As already discussed, a whole process of inference, linking principles, and assumption ties this choice of proxy variables and the way we have captured them (by defining, measuring, and analyzing them) to the archaeological event or phenomenon we seek to understand.

Assessing Evidentiary Significance

McCall's advice to historians forty years ago to try to follow how archaeologists reason and draw inferences about the past remains on target.[35] It's a tougher job now that the number of techniques available to probe the past has increased so dramatically, and archaeological data are produced by interdisciplinary teams of specialists. All of which increases the complexity of the inferential process and arguments deployed to link together so many different threads. However, critical assessment of evidentiary significance really boils down to a mere handful of general questions:[36]

- Is the argument linking the proxy phenomenon (archaeological evidence) to the human behavior for which reconstruction is attempted fully and convincingly developed?[37]
- If the proxy phenomena selected seem reasonable, have the relevant data about them been collected, counted, measured, and analyzed rigorously and appropriately, with due attention to sampling? Again, a key element is whether the archaeologist has set forth and explicitly discussed retrieval, sampling, and quantification issues.[38] The approaches used by the archaeologist will vary with the particular archaeological sites and survey areas being investigated and the particular questions being asked.[39]
- Have recovery methods been designed to detect and evaluate the distortions of pre- and post-depositional processes?
- Has due attention been paid to questions of chronology and contemporaneity?
- Where analytical groupings are created, have they been defined and inclusion criteria specified so that we may assess whether the entities created are indeed groups of individual things that can be fairly discussed together?[40]

Thus far, I have described the practice of archaeology in Africa as diverse, but generally oriented towards the creation of narratives in which chronological sequences of archaeologically detectable occurrences and events are linked and organized into an explanatory account of change through time. The chronological sequence of archaeologically detectable occurrences and events constrains the causal relationships we can hypothesize and incorporate in our narratives. Many of the narratives that historians count on archaeology to provide involve transitions from one state (of economy, social or political organization, technology, etc.) to another in prehistory. Even when these events take place over long time scales (millennia, in the case of the transition to food production, for example), the narratives still require reliable chronological information at all levels to identify earliest occurrences, environmental and social context of those occurrences, development and spread, consequences, etc. Because chronology is often the one thing that is "given" to historians (if they deal with dated or datable documents), the archaeological apprehension of time is likely to be alien terrain for many of them. Yet it is at the heart of the archaeological enterprise, and I would rank it as one of the most important aspects of archaeology for historians to understand.

For the historian, making the conceptual shift from the two-dimensional world of texts to the three-dimensional space of the archaeological site is possibly the most challenging aspect of understanding archaeology's approach to the past. Unless this shift is accomplished, historians are likely to remain tied to their preferred two-dimensional short-cuts to archaeological time—radiocarbon dates.[41] And these, as we shall see, using a case study of dates for early iron-smelting in West Africa, cannot be considered as data *tout court*, but must always be scrutinized as *capta* whose relationship to the archaeological phenomenon of interest—iron smelting, in this case—must be carefully argued and not assumed.

Thinking Like an Archaeologist: The Material Domain of Time

Within the archaeological site, time occupies a material domain: the layering of deposited material through vertical and horizontal space as the result of a sequence of events.[42] Accurately reconstructing this sequence of events, and making sure that material from different events doesn't get mixed together during the excavation process, are the foundation stones on which the rest of the edifice of site interpretation and chronology is constructed. Because the sequence of events may be complex, with later events penetrating and disturbing earlier layers (post-depositional disturbance), keeping deposits created at different times separate during excavation is often tricky. Their differences may be signaled by only small changes in the color or texture of the soil.[43] Pit fill, for example, may be slightly darker and softer than the surrounding deposits. The final reconstruction of the order of depositional events often cannot be determined until after the excavation is completed because, in the course of excavation, the archaeologist can see only a portion of any set of related deposits at any one time. And she must destroy what she can see in order to get a view of what lies beneath.

Working out the chronological relationships of various deposits thus takes place after at least some of the deposits are removed and is almost entirely dependent on the quality of the records (photos, drawings, measurements, notes, and observations) the archaeologist has made of the three-dimensional excavation unit that was dismantled in the process. There can be no going back to the site to check on exactly where a particular structure, or artifact, or ash lens was found. Information excluded from consideration and recording is gone forever. Consider the significance that your recording procedures, as a historian, would assume if you were given the opportunity to study an important, previously unknown text, part of which is in an unknown language, but you were told that photocopying it or taking it with you was not possible, and that the act of examining it would destroy the examined sections.

Perhaps the best way to grasp what is required in this act of archaeological observation and reconstruction is to imagine that you are faced with a box one meter in every dimension (one cubic meter) into which one hundred artifacts have been deposited with different types of soil. In some cases, artifacts and a particular type of soil have been poured in together. In others, small pits have been dug in already-deposited soils and a different kind of soil plus artifacts added to fill the pit. Your job is to excavate the cubic meter of deposits in the box and take notes such that another person, by consulting them, could reconstruct the box in its original configuration, with the artifacts in their original positions, or at least associated with their original soil types. What kind of information must be recorded to do this? Obviously, there must be a great deal of measurement data on the extent of particular kinds of soils in vertical and horizontal space as well as on the artifacts found associated with them. One sometimes sees photos of excavations in caves where a measurement grid has been erected by suspending strings from the roof of the cave. This gives an immediate appreciation of the three-dimensional world of excavation. To understand the magnitude of what the archaeologist routinely accomplishes, one must realize that the size of the units most commonly excavated are a normally tens or hundreds of time larger than our one-cubic-meter box. And in addition to artifacts, they commonly include a variety of features, such as pits, hearths, burials, and structural remains, which must also be plotted in three dimensions.

Depositional events are the raw material of chronology within an archaeological site. Often, a depositional event may represent a decades-long period, such as a layer created as the walls of a mud brick house slowly crumbled and eroded. We may not, even through application of chronometric dating methods such as radiocarbon, be able to place that decay episode within a range of time much smaller than three hundred years.[44] Historians accustomed to sources that announce the year and sometimes the month and day of their creation may feel some impatience at the broader scale of time the archaeologist must generally employ.

In prehistoric archaeology, the finest chronological distinctions we are able to detect come at the level of single depositional events that occupy a very short period of time: a burial, for example, may represent the brief amount of time it took to deposit the body and the accompanying grave goods. Even with radiocarbon dating, we will still not be able to indicate the year in which the burial took place more precisely than within a range of one hundred to two hundred years (if the calibration curve cooperates; greater precision is possible only with tree-ring dating, which has not yet been shown to be feasible in most of Africa), but we can make an argument, based on stratigraphic reasoning, that all the items and the body were deposited together within the same brief time span. This notion of material remains "associated" within a particular depositional event is extremely important in archaeology. It is the means by which we extend outwards our webs of chronological reasoning. Say, for example, that I have an object of known chronology in a layer (for example, a dinar struck in 519 A.H. (1125–26 C.E.)—so I know the layer is that date *or* younger). Then, by demonstrating through stratigraphic argument that other artifacts and features are in the same depositional layer—or temporally "associated"—with the coin, I can propose that the dating information obtained from the coin is valid for all other associated objects and features. Note, however, that the question of whether the date the coin was struck is approximately contemporaneous with the date of the associated deposits requires supporting evidence from other artifacts or datable materials. Because people keep heirlooms and otherwise retain old objects for one reason or another, deposits cannot be dated by a single object, any more than a church can be dated by its relics.[45] Alternatively, stratigraphic observations may indicate that the coin is an intrusion into the layer from above and its chronology has nothing to do with the other artifacts in the layer, other than to post-date them by some unknown amount of time.

Stratigraphy is the theory that permits archaeologists to create arguments about the relative temporal placement (contemporary with, earlier than, later than) of the artifacts and features recovered from excavated deposits, and it is the foundation of all other, higher-level interpretations of an archaeological site that depend on chronology (and most do). Using the concept of association, the webs of chronology move from the stratigraphic layers at a site to the various elements found at the site to different sites that interacted or were otherwise related (figure 2.2).

Historians concerned with understanding archaeological practice must, above all, appreciate how vital the concepts of stratigraphy and association are to archaeological interpretation. Together, these constitute the "context" of any given find, and it is the context, rather than the artifact

Figure 2.4. Photographic record of the excavation at the point recorded in the plan presented in figure 2.5. Walls, courtyards, pits have all been excavated separately to ensure that material deposited during different events is not mixed together. (Photography by Mark Horton. Source: Horton 1996, Pl. 42, p. 95, © BIEA, reproduced with permission.)

basis of soil color, texture, and inclusions, is assigned a different number pegged to a master list. The horizontal plans of excavated areas (see figures 2.4, and 2.5, which depict the same excavated level in a photo and a drawn plan, respectively) use the same master list and show that walls, pits, and other features have been delineated, and excavated and recorded separately. Depth measurements on the drawn plan tell us that the excavated floor surfaces ranged in depth from 2.48 meters to 2.84 meters below an established point (called a datum) at the top of the unit. These figures illustrate the care and attention to detail that archaeology requires.

The absence or paucity of profile drawings, plans or discussion of stratigraphy in a site report should arouse suspicion: was adequate attention paid during excavation? Can you have confidence in the author's claims about chronology and the sequence of events at the site? If not, how credible is the narrative offered about what happened through time at the site and how it interacted with other sites?

One difficulty involved in interrogating the primary sources for archaeology—i.e., the record of observations and data drawn from excavation

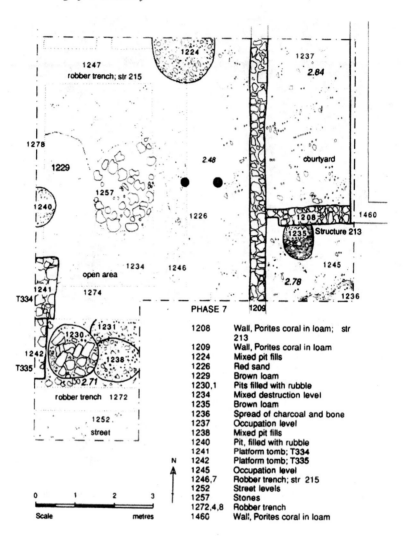

Figure 2.5. Horizontal plan drawing of features—walls, robber trenches, and pits—encountered during excavations in one unit at Shanga. Vertical depths are in italics; soil units have 4-digit numbers. (Source: Horton 1996, Fig. 49, p. 93, © BIEA, reproduced with permission.)

and survey—is that so few excavations are thoroughly published. While monographic treatment of field research was the norm forty years ago, publishers today shun monographs with high production costs (all those illustrations!) and limited sales. John Alexander's B.A.R. Monograph Series in African Archaeology, published in Oxford, is a welcome exception.

Beyond that, it is primarily government-funded research labs in Europe, with in-house publication series, that continue to produce site reports. For American and African-based archaeologists, providing timely access to the primary source materials of archaeology is a critical problem. How else shall we be able to assess claims about the past and evaluate evidence? That very issue plays a major role in the case study that follows.

Early Iron in Niger: A Case Study in Chronology and Context

We turn now to a case study illustrating the vital role that stratigraphy, association, and archaeological practice plays in the interpretation of radio-carbon dates. Historians, and some archaeologists too, I suspect, have supposed that radiocarbon dating produces reliable chronologies through the magic of physics—the very scientific measurement of radioactive decay. The problem is that the event that radiocarbon testing dates is usually not an archaeological event at all. A radiocarbon date tells us, in calendar years when properly calibrated,[47] when the carbon in the atmospheric reservoir became fixed in the organic material being dated. The ratio of the radioactive isotope C^{14} to the stable isotope C^{12} begins to diminish at fixation due to radioactive decay. Fixation occurs when cellular processes and cycling of carbon cease, either due to the organism's death or the shifting of active cellular metabolism to other parts of the organism. Trees, for example, have living cells only in their outer layers (phloem). For a long-lived tree, the carbon in the heartwood at the center of the trunk may have been fixed centuries before that adjacent to the phloem. Furthermore, in regions that have become too arid to support agents of decay, dead trees may persist for centuries before being collected for fuel during a later period of climatic amelioration.[48] Today, many archaeologists try to date short-lived samples, such as seeds, to eliminate the uncertainties created by the "old wood" problem.

Calibration is essential because C^{14} dates (reported in radiocarbon years Before Present, with Present standardized to 1950) do not correspond in a consistent manner to calendar years. The amount of C^{14} remaining for measurement in a sample is not simply a function of how much time has elapsed since the death (half of the C^{14} decays in 5730 years) but also of how much C^{14} was in the atmosphere during the life of the organism.

Over the past two decades, new technologies have permitted high precision radiocarbon dating of tree rings of known calendar date. The resulting calibration curve plots calendar years against radiocarbon years and shows their complex relationship, reflecting fluctuations in atmospheric C^{14} through time. Figure 2.6 shows how to translate a radiocarbon date into a calibrated date range. The range can be large for periods when the curve is flat. One of these is the 800–400 B.C.E. time period that is so important for understanding the chronology of early iron smelting in Africa. Overly precise claims—for example that an iron-smelting furnace dates to 800 B.C.E.—must be interrogated. How has such a specific date been determined if calibration was used and if, as we have seen, calibration always produces a range of dates? A second set of questions should address issues of context and association. Has the researcher demonstrated sufficient rigor in excavation to inspire confidence in the claim of association of the organic sample dated and the iron smelting furnace for which the age is sought?

The question that must always be considered in assessing radiocarbon dates is what the relationship is between the fixing of carbon in the material being dated (the *radiocarbon event*) and the *archaeological event* for which a date is desired.[49] Once issues of long-lived vs. short-lived samples have been taken into consideration, it is essential to thoroughly assess the association of the dated sample with the iron smelting event, in this example, that it is claimed to date. Such an assessment depends on detailed observation at the time of excavation or sample retrieval. The archaeologist bears the burden of presenting a convincing argument supporting the claim of association, providing detailed scale drawings and descriptions of the dated furnace, accompanied by minute details on how and from where the dated charcoal sample was taken, plus any observations at the time the sample was taken of possible contamination, including insect and animal burrows. Critters move material through deposits much more frequently than we usually suspect. In Chippendale's view, when an archaeologist cannot present an argument about the relationship between the sample and the archaeological event for which dating is sought, "the prudent laboratory will not waste its effort on making a determination."[50]

The assumption that physical proximity equals association is a frequently encountered error. A consideration of site formation processes is important at smelting sites, because smelting furnaces may be dug into an earlier occupation surface, or people may settle on surfaces with centuries-old eroded furnaces. In either case, it would be wrong to assume that cultural material and charcoal at the same level as the furnace is contemporaneous with it. In the Middle Senegal Valley, for example, we encountered a large concentration of smelting furnaces, many of which were dug into deposits with Early Iron Age ceramics dating to the period

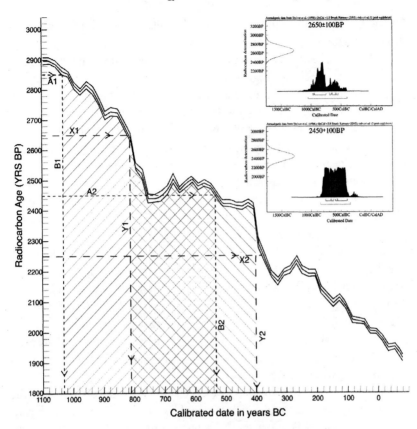

Figure 2.6. Because the radiocarbon calibration curve is flat between 800 and 400 B.C.E., radiocarbon ages that appear to be quite different may overlap considerably when calibrated. Here, the radiocarbon date 2650 ± 100 B.P. can be roughly calibrated at the 95% probability level by (a) running horizontal line A1 from 2850 [2650 + (2 × 100)] and A2 from 2450 [2650 − (2 × 100)] to intercept the calibration curve and (b) dropping vertical lines B1 and B2 from these intercept points to the calendar axis. The resulting date range is 1030–530 B.C.E. When the same procedure is followed for 2450 ± 100 B.P. (lines X1, Y1 and X2, Y2), the calibrated date range is approximately 800–400 B.C.E. The cross-hatched intersection of these ranges shows how extensive the overlap is. Without additional, independent chronological evidence, it is impossible to know which of the dated samples is actually earlier. The insets show the highly irregular probability distributions within the date ranges. For the 2450 date, all calendar dates within the range are approximately equally probable, while the probabilities vary more for the calibrated range of the 2650 date. It should be clear why calibrated dates must be reported as possible date ranges. (Insets graphed using OxCal v.3.8—Bronk Ramsey, 2002: http://www.rlaha.ox.ac.uk/orau/06_01.htm) (Curve intercept method illustrated using high-precision curve published by Stuiver and Pearson, *Radiocarbon* 28 (2B) 1986: 805–62).

200–400 C.E. Radiocarbon dates on charcoal extracted from the slag produced dates of 1200–1400 C.E., however.[51]

A series of early dates claimed to be associated with iron smelting has come out of the Termit region of Niger. The French research team has argued emphatically that these dates unambiguously establish that the first iron appears in the area, as a result of local invention, at a date close to 1500 cal B.C.E. in what was still a Neolithic cultural context.[52] The discipline is divided concerning these conclusions. A number of French and African archaeologists accept them and suggest that anyone contesting the conclusions must be motivated by racist ideology or bad faith.[53] Others find it hard to assess the claims of association of dates and iron because the detailed documentation necessary to fully support them has never been produced. The case largely rests on six radiocarbon dates on vegetable matter in the fabric of Neolithic potsherds collected from the surface of five different sites in the Termit region that also had iron artifacts. At one of these sites, a charcoal sample was also dated. All seven dates fall between 3265 ± 100 B.P. and 2880 ± 120 B.P. Calibrated to 2 standard deviations (95% certainty) according to the recommended practice and using the popular CALIB program, these dates range between 1895 and 803 cal B.C.E. So all predate the evidence so far available for the appearance of iron elsewhere in West and North Africa.

Obviously, the question is a crucial one for reconstructing the history of iron technology. It is commonly understood by archaeometallurgists and materials scientists that iron smelting was late in the history of metals because it requires higher temperatures (1100–1400°C) than can be achieved in a cooking or campfire (900°C), plus careful balancing of variables including air flow rates, fuel to ore ratio, ore type, and charcoal density. The chemical bonds that lock metallic iron in ores are much tougher to break through heating than those of copper or tin, for example. It therefore does not seem surprising to them that the earliest metals used were those that occur naturally in a metallic state (gold, silver, copper, meteoric iron), and those that can be reduced from ores at a relatively low temperature (copper, tin).[54] Because reduction of iron ores is so complex, involving so many variables, it is assumed by most archaeometallurgists and materials scientists to have been preceded by considerable experience with pyrotechnology—involving production of controlled, high temperatures using forced draft (bellows)—and with smelting other metals.[55] Other commentators, however, take a postmodernist stance, suggesting that only modern science advances progressively. Early technology in sub-Saharan Africa, where no pyrotechnology or metals prior to the use of iron are yet known, might have advanced by "qualitative leaps" via accidental discovery, producing iron smelting furnaces in Niger "whose configuration and mode of functioning do not seem to obey any logic."[56] Ultimately, archaeology will permit us to understand the actual trajectory of iron technology cross-culturally in antiquity, but this will require that issues of chronology be thoroughly resolved. This brings us back to the issues posed by the chronological claims at Termit.

The Termit data are challenging from the outset because they are all from deflation surfaces, meaning that the sandy matrix of earlier deposits has blown away over the centuries, leaving behind the much heavier artifacts and features such as furnace bottoms. As the researchers at Termit are well aware, it is never possible to conclude that materials in proximity are contemporaneous in the absence of other evidence supporting this conclusion (see figure 2.7 for a scenario in which furnace bottoms and or iron objects could come to be on the surface in apparent association with much earlier potsherds.) Ideally, the arguments that link radiometric dates and the archaeological phenomenon of interest will take the form of strong *cables* of multiple, independent strands of mutually constraining evidence, rather than a chain of individual links. A *chain* of argument is only as strong as its weakest link, while a cable of independent strands of evidence may be much stronger than its weakest constituent, indeed, stronger than the sum of its parts.[57] Our chronological arguments are strongest, I have already argued, when independent assessments are undertaken using stratigraphy, temporal changes in material culture, and radiometric or historical dating. These can then be evaluated against other categories of evidence, such as pollen analysis, to see if chronologies for smelting coincide with time periods when trees were present for fuel, for example. One of the great advantages of archaeology is precisely that it offers the possibility of such a wide range of multidisciplinary, mutually constraining sources.

What is the nature of the inferential argument at Termit? The facts of the argument are (1) the observed presence of iron artifacts on the surface of some sites that also have Neolithic potsherds; (2) six radiocarbon dates on short-lived organic material in potsherds, plus one charcoal sample from these sites produced calibrated dates in the range ca. 1800–800 B.C.E. The conclusion drawn from these data is that iron was in use and being produced in the Termit region by ca. 1500 B.C.E. The all-important linking argument between the data and the conclusion is what interests us. One strand of the potential cable is the dates themselves. The old wood issue does not arise here, as the researchers have been careful to date

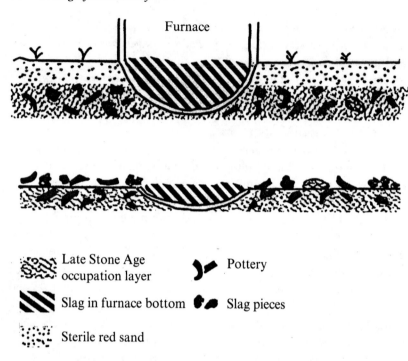

Figure 2.7. Deflation can produce surface assemblages of materials from different time periods. In this example, an iron-smelting furnace is dug through a layer of wind-blown sand into an earlier occupation layer with Late Stone Age pottery and stone tools. After the furnace is used and the site abandoned, erosion breaks down the furnace walls and scours away the red sand layer, exposing the Late Stone Age deposits. The pottery and stone tools end up on the surface mixed with slag from the eroding furnace, of which only the bottom remains intact.

short-lived chaff used as temper in the pottery. These are likely to be very reliable dates for the pottery itself, but is the pottery really associated with the iron artifacts? Here is a difficulty. Ideally, association is assessed using evidence from stratigraphy, which isn't present on a deflation surface. Instead, the claim is made that the patterning of activity areas, artifacts, and features is so clear that the surface sites can be considered to have the same integrity as a stratigraphically closed context in excavation.[58] Even if detailed drawings of the surface material were supplied in support of this claim (they are not), this would still be difficult to assess on its own. Evidence from another, independent avenue of chronological inquiry would be required. Have detailed, well-dated sequences of pottery been established for the area? If iron artifacts from a later occupation became mixed with Neolithic material through deflation, there might be more recent potsherds present as well. Ideally, again, sequences of change in pottery are most reliably established by using material from careful, stratigraphic excavation. However, sites with sub-surface deposits may be very rare in a heavily deflated region such as Termit. In that case, it is necessary to use methods that systematically describe, count, and compare the styles and types of pottery present on the surface of many sites to make an argument for chronology based on changing popularity of various categories of pottery.[59] Often, only after a great deal of systematic study of this kind is it possible to identify surface materials that represent more than one time period. The Termit researchers claim that all the surface assemblages with iron have the exact same pottery, so that both must be contemporary. Again, the problem is that the claim of identical assemblages and association is merely asserted rather than supported with documentation.

The Termit researchers have made a valiant effort to construct a strong cable of linking arguments, but, in the end, insufficient documentation is provided to permit us to evaluate the claims for association of iron and dated potsherds. It then becomes a matter of individual preference, to a certain extent, concerning how high the bar should be set for standards of evidence in arguments for unusual antiquity. Wrangling about this issue is very common in archaeology. The issue of *Antiquity* for March 2003 has articles about resolving conflicting radiocarbon dates for the earliest settlement of New Zealand and the dating of the stunning Paleolithic rock art at Chauvet Cave in France. Or, consider the decades-long debates about pre-Clovis occupation in the New World. Numerous sites, some meticulously excavated and documented and some not, have produced radiocarbon dates considerably earlier than the approximately 11,000 B.C.E. Clovis horizon. Ultimately, the argument turned on the most meticulously excavated sites (Monte Verde in Chile, Meadowcroft Rock Shelter in Pennsylvania) and a growing body of evidence suggesting a previously unrecognized pattern of earlier occupation. Some archaeologists, however, set the bar for standards of evidence so high that several years after the mainstream has reached a consensus to accept the evidence, they continue to contest it.[60]

The suggestion that the debates about early dates for iron in Africa are, at base, ideological and that standards of evidence are invoked merely to mask this bias[61] is simply at odds with the way archaeology proceeds everywhere else in the world to resolve dating ambiguities. Disputes about the dating of early metallurgy are not unique to Africa; claims for early copper metallurgy in Thailand and China have been questioned or revised.[62] While not denying the influence of ideology and bias in archaeology, a far more likely explanation for resistance to the Termit dates is that archaeology has usually demanded extraordinary proof of extraordinary claims. If iron was in fact being produced in Niger in 1500 B.C.E. as a result of independent invention, then we shall need to rethink substantially the existing account of the history of metallurgy. While there is no *a priori* reason why we shouldn't do just that if the evidence warrants, the question raised here is, does the current evidence warrant such a tectonic shift? The chemical rules that make iron production such a complex, difficult, and unpredictable process are not suspended for Africa. We will need to embark on a whole new set of inquiries to help us understand the context for iron's discovery in Africa, its subsequent development, and why it seems to have remained an isolated invention that did not affect a persistent stone-tool based technology or penetrate into neighboring regions for at least half a millennium.[63] What, in this scenario, can account for the rapid, if perhaps uneven, spread of iron smelting only after 2500 B.P. (800–400 cal B.C.E.)? It is an interesting fact that the three radiocarbon dates available for actual iron smelting furnaces in the Termit region overlap with or are later than this critical 2500 B.P. radiocarbon threshold when calibrated.[64] Given the increased feasibility of dating iron artifacts directly,[65] it is entirely possible that undertaking C^{14} dating of some of the Termit iron objects will help resolve the current chronological conundrum.

The purpose of this discussion has not been to criticize the research carried out at Termit in an extremely inhospitable environment for archaeology. Rather, it has been to illustrate how far radiocarbon dates are from being self-evident. The prudent historian looks carefully at the arguments and documentation that link radiocarbon events and archaeological events.

Conclusions

Many Africanist historians continue to expect that archaeology will furnish the chronological sequences and narratives that summarize and explain the large-scale patterns of change in human behavior over the course of the continent's prehistory. While there is a diversity of approaches to producing archaeological narratives in Africa, the postmodern "crisis of representation" that has led to open hostilities in the disciplines of history and British archaeology has had rather limited effect on the methods and practice of Africanist archaeology thus far. Still, archaeology has become much more multivoiced, and the presentation in this chapter does not pretend to be anything but a rather personal, at times parochial view of the essentials of archaeological interpretation. I have defined archaeological narratives in such as way as to privilege chronology and sequence. There will be archaeologists who find chronology a chimera or an irrelevancy. I believe they are a very small minority among Africanists. For most of us, and for many historians, I believe, it is the documentation of sequences of occurrences and events, linking environmental change, subsistence, technology, trade and interaction, and social and political organization together into explanatory narratives that we look to archaeology to provide. The archaeological record, with all its flaws, is a somewhat blunt instrument; temporal resolution on the scale of decades or more remains elusive at many sites. The historian's dream of identifying "daily routines" and *l'histoire evenementielle*[66] is currently beyond our reach, due only in part to the shortcomings of our methods. Historians interested in evaluating archaeological claims can find a useful starting point in comparing the temporal resolution necessary for the narrative provided and the chronological resolution that is possible, given the nature of the deposits, the radiocarbon samples, and other ancillary dating information.

The endless promise of archaeology is the possibility it holds for bringing evidence from the deep past to bear on our assorted pre-understandings and assumptions about human behavior and achievement in prehistory. New discoveries, with new dates that change the accepted sequence of events or interject new elements into existing narratives, can overturn existing paradigms and send us scrambling to rethink and revise our narratives. In the rapidly developing field of historical archaeology, the conjoint use of texts and archaeology provides a powerful way to challenge assumptions drawn from text-based evidence alone and to interrogate its silences.[67]

Too much of an emphasis on the chronology and not the context of change is unhealthy, as we saw with reference to radiocarbon dates for early iron metallurgy. Why was Jenne-jeno, as an early indigenous urban center in sub-Saharan Africa, so readily accepted, despite its explosive implications for traditional historical narratives on complexity in Africa,[68] while Termit as a putative early center of indigenous innovation in metallurgy remains contested decades after the first radiocarbon dates were produced? Part of the answer surely is that the narrative of change at Jenne-jeno unfolded continuously over a long time period (1600 years) and it described the process and the context of the changes accompanying growth. Iron technology at Termit, by contrast, does not unfold through time. The period of time from the earliest site with iron artifacts and the site with dated furnaces is potentially a millennium or more, but there is no sense from evidence presented of any changes in the technology. Furthermore, we have no information from other early iron smelting sites that would help us understand the process of experimentation that must have preceded successful smelting. Everywhere else in the world, human societies discovered the use of particular metals in the order of the ease with which they could be liberated from ores. In the Andes, smiths developed a variety of very sophisticated copper and silver alloys over a two-thousand-year period and never discovered iron technology. How were Africans, apparently alone among the peoples of the world, able to leapfrog over multiple technological thresholds? Chronology alone cannot provide a persuasive narrative of how and why. Archaeological narratives link chronology and context into an explanation of change.

Having identified in the last part of this chapter how archaeologists assess stratigraphy and context, it is my hope that readers will feel confident enough to follow Daniel McCall's advice to check out archaeological reports. While following all the threads of an archaeological argument may be a challenge, if you have begun to understand the material domain of time, you have the basic knowledge to evaluate the strength of an archaeological argument for stratigraphy and association. All higher level inferences that depend on assessment of chronology build upon this foundation, so it is an excellent place to focus your efforts.

Acknowledgements

I am grateful for the feedback provided by members of the Houston Area African Studies Group in response to a lecture on April 30, 2000 that covered several of the issues developed in this chapter. The historians in that group helped me further refine my thoughts on appropriate coverage. I am also grateful to Peter Robertshaw, David Killick, Roderick McIntosh, and Stanley Alpern who read earlier drafts of this text and provided valuable comments which led to revisions and improvements. All remaining weaknesses are mine alone. Adrienne Reinsvold redrafted figures 2.1 and 2.2. Thanks to Mark Horton for providing the Shanga figures.

Notes

1. Daniel McCall, *Africa in Time Perspective* (Oxford, 1964).
2. For example, Brian Fagan, *Archaeology: A Brief Introduction*, 7th ed. (Prentice Hall, 1999) or Fagan's *Ancient Lives: An Introduction to Archaeology* (Prentice Hall, 2000),

or the far more detailed text by Colin Renfrew and Paul Bahn, *Archaeology: Theories, Methods, and Practice*, 3rd ed. (Thames and Hudson, 2000), to mention only three excellent introductions to archaeology from among the dozens available. For African archaeology in particular, Martin Hall's *Archaeology Africa* (James Currey, 1996) is superb.

3. This chapter can only touch on these in summary form, and the reader is directed to other sources, notably Martin Hall's excellent *Archaeology Africa* (London, 1996) and *A History of African Archaeology* (ed. Peter Robertshaw, London, 1990) for a much fuller, more satisfying treatment.

4. Recent examples include the work of some French prehistorians dealing with stone-using cultures in the Sahara, where the job of categorizing numerous surface manifestations particularly lends itself to this approach. Culture history identified movements of people (detected through the spread of particular types of artifacts) and diffusion as the causal mechanisms of change through time.

5. Matthew Johnson suggests that the New Archaeology "shared many of the concerns with the rhythms of long-term histories as discussed by *Annales* historians such as F. Braudel, though at the time these parallels in thinking were little noted" (*Archaeological Theory: An Introduction* [Oxford, 1999], 25). Interestingly, French medieval archaeologists working in Africa who were, of all archaeologists, perhaps the most aware of the Annales approach, did little to develop field methods that were attentive to geology, climate, and other environmental elements operative at the level of the *longue durée*.

6. Patrick Munson, "Archaeological data on the origins of cultivation in the southwestern Sahara and their implications for West Africa," in J. R. Harlan, J. M. J. de Wet and A. B. L. Stemler (eds.), *Origins of African Plant Domestication* (The Hague, 1976), 187–210; R. J. and S. K. McIntosh, "The Inland Niger Delta before the Empire of Mali: evidence from Jenné-jeno," *Journal of African History* 22, vol. 1 (1981): 1–22.

7. David Clarke, *Analytical Archaeology* (London, 1968).

8. David Clarke (ed.), *Models in Archaeology* (London, 1972).

9. Johnson, *Archaeological Theory*, 43.

10. Ibid., 91.

11. This summary on structuralism was drawn from Hall, *Archaeology Africa*, 64–5. Works cited in this passage are A. Kuper, "Symbolic dimensions of the Southern Bantu homestead," *Africa* 50, vol. 1 (1980): 8–23; T. Huffman, "Archaeology and the ethnohistory of the African Iron Age," *Annual Review of Anthropology* 11 (1982): 133–50.

12. T. Huffman, "Snakes and Birds: expressive space at Great Zimbabwe," *African Studies* 40, vol. 2 (1981): 131–50.

13. P. Schmidt, *Historical Archaeology: A Structural Approach in an African Culture* (Westport, Conn., 1978).

14. Martin Hall, "Snakes and crocodiles: power and symbolism in ancient Zimbabwe," *South African Archaeological Bulletin* 52 (1998): 129–32.

15. Hall, *Archaeology Africa*, 67.

16. Johnson, *Archaeological Theory*, 94–5.

17. See chapters on Africa by A. Holl, B. Andah, and P. Schmidt in Peter Schmidt and Thomas Patterson (eds.), *Making Alternative Histories: The Practice of Archaeology and History in Non-Western Settings* (School of American Research, 1995). Also, Michael Rowlands "The archaeology of colonialism and constituting the African peasantry," in D. Miller, M. Rowlands, and C. Tilley (eds.), *Domination and Resistance* (Unwin-Hyman, 1989), 261–83.

18. Ian Hodder, *The Archaeological Process* (Blackwell, 1999), 5.

19. See, e.g., Ann Stahl "Perceiving variability in time and space: the evolutionary mapping of African societies," in S. K. McIntosh (ed.), *Beyond Chiefdoms: Pathways to Complexity in Africa* (Cambridge, 2000), 39–55; Ann Stahl, "Concepts of time and approaches to analogical reasoning in historical perspective," *American Antiquity* 58 (1993): 235–60; Michael Rowlands, "A question of complexity," 29–40, in D. Miller, M. Rowlands, and C. Tilley (eds.), *Domination and Resistance* (Unwin-Hyman, 1989); R. J. McIntosh, "Western representations of urbanism and invisible African towns," in McIntosh (ed.), *Beyond Chiefdoms*, 56–65.

20. Stahl, "Perceiving variability."

21. Bruce Trigger, *Sociocultural Evolution* (London, 1998), 1–14.

22. In this manner, it has been possible to show that settlement patterns at Jenne-jeno, for example, do not conform to predictions for a site of its size. This then leads to an attempt to understand the local circumstances that may be in play—see S. K. McIntosh, "Modeling political organization in large-scale settlement clusters: a case study from the Inland Niger delta," in McIntosh (ed.), *Beyond Chiefdoms*, 66–79.

23. The classic example of historical contingency operating within a universal process was provided by Charles Darwin in *The Origin of Species*. This point is also noted by Peter Robertshaw, "Sibling Rivalry? The Intersection of Archaeology and History," *History in Africa* 27 (2000): 261–86.

24. Jared Diamond, *Guns, Germs, and Steel: The Fates of Human Societies* (Norton, 1997). Diamond's narrative is, in fact, a resounding triumph for its successful and eye-opening incorporation of archaeology, geography, plant ecology, animal behavior, and climate change in the several chapters on domestication. Even critical reviewers such as William H. McNeill (*The New York Review of Books*, May 15, 1997, 48–50), who disliked Diamond's dismissive attitude towards cultural factors and human agency, found his discussion of food production compelling. Clearly, historians respond positively to the big narratives at long time scales that archaeology provides. For Africanists, however Diamond's last-place treatment of Africa disappoints. The fact that only Bantu Africa is discussed, to the exclusion of the entire Sahelian zone where cereal agriculture originated and where Diamond's theory about the spread of agriculture through a single ecological zone can most appropriately be tested, makes Africa the weakest of the chapters in the book, in my opinion.

25. Francis Musonda, "African Archaeology: looking forward," *African Archaeological Review* 8 (1990): 3–22.

26. P. Kosso, *Knowing the Past* (Humanity Books, 2001), 30–31.

27. A term originally coined by Lewis Binford in *Bones: Ancient Men and Modern Myths* (Academic, 1981), 21–30.

28. Cited in Kosso, *Knowing the Past*, 99.

29. Thurstan Shaw, *Igbo Ukwu* (London, 1970).

30. David Clarke, "Archaeology: the loss of innocence," *Antiquity* 57 (1973): 6–18.

31. Ibid.

32. M. B. Schiffer, *Behavioral Archaeology* (Academic, 1974); *Formation Processes of the Archaeological Record* (University of New Mexico Press, 1987).

33. For a summary, see Glynn Isaac, "The archaeology of human origins," *Advances in World Archaeology* 3 (1984): 21–41.

34. Chris Chippendale, "Capta and Data: On the true nature of archaeological information," *American Antiquity* 65 (2000): 605–12. B. Hayden and H. Sansonnet-Hayden,

"Congnata, capta, and data: Hunting for meaning," *The SAA Archaeological Record* (May 2001): 34–6 suggest that *cognata* would be a more suitable replacement for data, reflecting "the many psychological factors that enter into the 'cognizing' of interpretations from the archaeological record."

35. McCall, *Africa in Time Perspective*, 35.

36. Chippendale, "Capta," 612.

37. One would be skeptical, for example, of an argument in which pottery styles were used as proxies for groups of people. As several authors have pointed out, the advancing geographical distributions of certain types of pottery in eastern and southern Africa cannot be used nonproblematically to identify the Bantu expansion. As convincing proxy evidence of an actual spread of peoples, rather than ideas, we would want biological evidence comparing skeletal series before and after the appearance of pottery, and possibly DNA studies as well.

38. Chippendale, "Capta," 606–7, provides several examples, including the seemingly straightforward but in reality complicated issues of how to meaningfully quantify the numbers of potsherds and animal bones recovered from excavation.

39. With regard to sampling, for example, the important criteria are relevance and reliability. First, the sample must be relevant to the research questions being asked; and second, it must seek to represent the range of relevant material present in the larger population with some degree of reliability, which is achieved by using selection methods (of areas to dig or sites to survey, for example) that reduce the possibility of introducing bias. Neither relevance nor reliability is necessarily increased by simply making the sample bigger, a point that is easy to miss because it seems counterintuitive.

40. Chippendale, "Capta," 612. Clay beads and spindle whorls, for example, may overlap in shape and size. Before constructing higher-level arguments about the patterning of spindle whorls within a site and gendered perspectives on spinning activity, has the fuzziness of the boundary between whorls and bead been satisfactorily dealt with?

41. Peter Robertshaw ("Sibling Rivalry," 277) recalls Roland Oliver's famous musing on what archaeologists could contribute to the reconstruction of the Bantu expansion—"dates" (Roland Oliver "The problem of the Bantu expansion, *Journal of Africa History* 7 [1966]: 165–82).

42. Just to make things interesting, time-sequential events can also play out over horizontal space, as when people establish a new residence a short distance from their old, abandoned one.

43. Hodder, *Archaeological process*, 52–6, points out that the identification of similarities and differences among deposits while excavating is a subjective enterprise, just like all other archaeological description. While we know that the deposits were formed by a series of events that added, subtracted, moved, or otherwise distorted material, our proxy variables of soil texture, compactness, and color are not always reliable guides to these events, nor are variations within these categories of information perceived the same by different observers. Nevertheless, it is only through concerted effort and rigorous attention to the issue, despite its subjectivities, that one can avoid creating a far greater magnitude of temporal fuzziness than is already present.

44. For a detailed explanation, see S. K. and R. J. McIntosh, "Archaeological research and dates from West Africa," *Journal of African History* 27 (1986): 413–16.

45. This is one of the reasons why the study and delineation of sequences of entire artifact assemblages is crucial to the construction of chronological sequences. The presence

of one or two distinctive types of artifact of known date in a deposit or on the surface of a site may give us some chronological information, but it is only when the entire assemblage of material is assessed for contemporaneity that we can interpret that information properly. Although historians often find these descriptive sequences of pottery and stone tools tedious and irrelevant, it is these studies that permit the assessments of contemporaneity that are fundamental to almost any question of historical interest, from changing political organization within site systems, to changing patterns of trade.

46. M. Horton, *Shanga: The Archaeology of a Muslim Trading Community on the Coast of East Africa* (British Institute in East Africa, 1996).

47. The most commonly used calibration program is CALIB, developed by Minze Stuiver and P. J. Reimer at the University of Washington, based on hundreds of high-precision (i.e., having a very small standard error) radiocarbon dates on wood samples of known calendar age, as determined by tree-ring dating.

48. David Killick, "On the dating of African metallurgical sites," *Nyame Akuma* 28 (1987): 29–39.

49. Chippendale, "Capta," 607.

50. Ibid.

51. This work was directed by R. J. McIntosh, S. K. McIntosh, and H. Bocoum, with the collaboration of D. Killick, who excavated several of the furnaces, extracted the samples for dating, and is analyzing the slag. A monograph is in preparation. Extraction of charcoal from the slag itself, such that the fuel used in the smelt is being dated, is one of the most reliable associations between the sample to be dated and the smelting event.

52. G. Quechon, "Les datations anciennes du fer et de la métallurgie à Termit (Niger): leur fiabilité, leur signification," in *Aux Origines de la Metallurgie du Fer en Afrique*, ed. H. Bocoum (UNESCO, 2002).

53. Ibid., 114; A. Person and G. Quechon, "Données chronométriques et chronologiques de la métallurgie à Termit," in Bocoum (ed.), *Aux Origines de la Metallurgie du Fer en Afrique*, 115–22.

54. D. Killick, "Science, Speculation and the Origins of Extractive Metallurgy," in D. R. Brothwell and A. Pollard (eds.), *Handbook of Archaeological Sciences* (John Wiley, 2001), 479–87.

55. J. E. Rehder, *The Mastery and Uses of Fire in Antiquity* (Montreal, 2000); T. Wertime and J. D. Muhly, *The Coming of the Age of Iron* (New Haven, 1980).

56. H. Bocoum, "La métallurgie du fer en Afrique: un patrimoine et une ressource au service du développement," in Bocoum (ed.), *Aux Origines de la Metallurgie du Fer en Afrique*, 93–103, quote from p. 100.

57. A. Wylie, "Why should historical archaeologists study capitalism?" in M. Leone and P. Potter (eds.), *Historical Archaeologies of Capitalism* (New York, 1999), 23–50, quote on p. 41.

58. Quechon, "Les datations," 107.

59. This technique is called seriation. A description of the method can be found in most introductory texts on archaeological method.

60. For example, A. C. Roosevelt, "Who's on first?" *Natural History* (July/August 2000): 76–9, who objects that "the tools at Monte Verde cannot be firmly connected with the dates."

61. J. Vansina, "Historians, are archaeologists your siblings?" *History in Africa* 22 (1995): 369–408.

62. Killick, "Science, Speculation," 485.

63. Here, Quechon's warning that "absence of evidence is not evidence of absence" must be kept in mind.

64. Quechon, "Les datations," 110.

65. R. Cresswell, "Radiocarbon Dating of Iron Artifacts," *Radiocarbon* 34, no. 3 (1992): 898–905. The idea was first advanced by N. van der Merwe, *The Carbon-14 Dating of Iron* (University of Chicago Press, 1969).

66. Vansina, "Siblings?" 375, 399.

67. A. Stahl, *Making History in Banda: Anthropological Visions of Africa's Past* (Cambridge, 2001); but see Peter Robertshaw, "African Historical Archaeology(ies): Past, Present, and a Possible Future," in A. M. Reid and P. J. Lane (eds.), *African Historical Archaeologies* (New York, 2004), 375–91, on defining historical archaeology in Africa.

68. Vansina, "Siblings," p. 365.

3

WRITING AFRICAN HISTORY FROM LINGUISTIC EVIDENCE

Christopher Ehret

Language History and Human History

Historians of Africa, more than those of any other part of the world, have used linguistic evidence to enrich the contributions of their craft. They have made use of a basic linguistic characteristic, namely, that every language contains a wealth of potential information on the history of the people who have spoken it in the past. It remains only for historians to take even more advantage of that store of evidence.[1]

What is meant by this claim of "wealth"? What data can a language provide for the writing of human history?

Every language is an archive of many thousands of individual artifacts of the past. These artifacts are the words of the language, hard evidence that can be rigorously placed into a linguistic stratigraphy. Each language contains the full range of vocabulary necessary to express all knowledge, experience, and cultural practice as pursued by the various members of the society using that language. As ideas, behaviors, and practices changed in the earlier history of that society, the vocabulary that described these features of culture also underwent changes: in the meanings applied to existing words, in the adoption or deriving of new words, in the loss or obsolescence of older words. The history of past change and development across the full range of culture and economy leaves its imprint on the histories of the thousands of individual words with which members of a society express all the various aspects of their lives.

The evidence of language history is a very democratic resource. Although it does not normally identify individual characters in history, it provides a powerful set of tools for probing the widest range of past developments within communities and societies as a whole, and it lends itself well to studies of history over the long term. For while linguistically based history may not allow precise dating, the data gained will relate directly to a whole array of cultural elements that comprise the longer-term trends and sustained courses of human development.

Establishing a Linguistic Stratigraphy

How are individual word histories uncovered in a language or group of languages? The essential first step is to establish what is often called a linguistic stratigraphy.

The most basic form of such a stratigraphy can be represented by a family tree of the relationships among the languages being studied. The technical linguistic aspects of establishing a family tree, and the complications that often arise in carrying out the task, are too extensive for the limitations of a chapter such as this. But the historical meaning of such "genetic" relationships among languages does need explaining here if we are to understand how human history can be recovered from linguistic documentation.

At its most fundamental level, the genetic metaphor implies a linguistic relationship not unlike that found in many single-cell organisms. Two or more languages are related because they descend from a common mother language, called a "protolanguage." This protolanguage evolved at an earlier time in history into two or more daughter languages; it diverged into its daughters, much as the mother cell divides into daughter cells. The daughter languages can subsequently become protolanguages themselves, diverging at later periods into daughter languages of their own, and this process can, of course, repeat again and again in language history.

If this schema is applied to the early branchings of the important Nilo-Saharan family of African languages, the following tree diagram results.

This diagram identifies a series of historical periods. First, the original "mother" language, which we call proto-Nilo-Saharan, diverged into two daughter languages, proto-Koman and proto-Sudanic. Subsequently, proto-Koman evolved into Gumuz and proto-Western Koman, while proto-Sudanic, the other original daughter language of

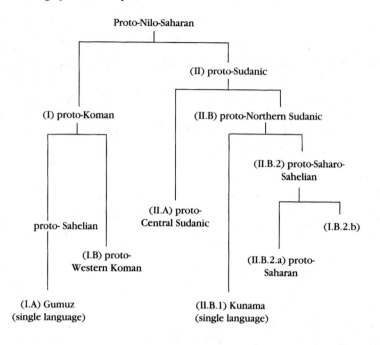

proto-Nilo-Saharan, evolved into two daughters of its own, proto-Central Sudanic and proto-Northern Sudanic. Proto-Northern Sudanic then gave rise to Kunama and proto-Saharo-Sahelian. Still later proto-Saharo-Sahelian diverged into proto-Saharan and proto-Sahelian. A complex and varied array of later divergences took place in the history of this family of languages, but for the sake of clarity only the earliest developments are presented here.[2]

This sequence of periods constitutes the basic linguistic stratigraphy of the early ages of Nilo-Saharan history. The first stratum, affecting all of the language family, is the period of history represented by proto-Nilo-Saharan. Thereafter each branching line of descent forms its own separate stratigraphic sequence. For the Koman language group, the second stratum covers the long period of the evolution of proto-Koman out of proto-Nilo-Saharan. In the third stratum Gumuz and proto-Western Koman become distinct. If, instead, we follow the chain of eras that leads down to the Saharan subgroup, the second stratum is formed by the period in which proto-Sudanic came to be spoken; the third covers the evolution of the separate languages, proto-Central and proto-Northern Sudanic, out of proto-Sudanic; and the fourth is marked by proto-Northern Sudanic's divergence into its proto-Saharo-Sahelian and Kunama branches. Finally, the fifth stratum in this historical sequence comprises the period of the emergence of proto-Saharan, as well as proto-Sahelian, out of proto-Saharo-Sahelian.

When describing language history, it is important to use terms like "diverged" and "evolved," which imply extended processes of development. The straight lines of a family tree diagram sometimes mislead people into thinking that sharp language splits are involved. But in fact the breakup of a mother language into daughters is gradual. Language change is an ongoing process in any living, spoken language: a slow, progressive accumulation of many small changes—in vocabulary, grammatical usage, and pronunciation—as time goes on. In the special case of linguistic divergence, a language initially begins to undergo different changes in different parts of its speech territory. These diverging courses of change lead at first to the emergence of different dialects of the language in different locations and then, over a period of centuries, to the evolving of these dialects into distinct languages, no longer intelligible to each other's speakers.

The mitotic metaphor for linguistic relationship and divergence, drawn from biology, is an apt one in most respects. The most important insight is that the mother language diverges into its daughters, just as the microscopic mother single cell in biology splits into its own daughters. The protolanguage does not "give birth" to its daughters and remain distinct from them; it evolves directly into each of its daughters as part of a continuing historical process: It becomes its daughters. One significant difference between the metaphor and its concrete biological referent is that the mother language can sometimes give rise to several daughters during the same period of time, whereas mitotic division normally produces just two daughter cells out of one mother cell.

Languages and Societies

One more step is required before we begin to situate linguistic historical evidence in the linguistic stratigraphy: we must comprehend the social and historical dimensions of language relationship. To do this is to understand how language and society connect to each other. Throughout most of human history, a language could exist only because there was a society to which that language belonged and whose members used it as their vehicle of social and cultural communication. When, for whatever historical reason, people lose the sense that they belong to a commonality distinct from those of other peoples, the language they speak soon ceases to be passed down to younger generations and so begins to die out. Conversely, the continuing existence of a language over a long span of time reveals a corresponding long-term societal continuity of one kind or another among the speakers of the language, extending across the different periods of its history.

The longer the period of time since the divergence of a daughter language out of the protolanguage, the more varied and diverse the ways in which the accompanying history of social continuities is likely to be played out. Most often a language is transmitted through direct historical lines of societal descent, even though as the centuries pass the society itself may change out of all recognition, and even though at times the disruptions of war or internal societal strife, or the challenges of nature, may greatly attenuate the connection.

Less often, lateral transmission of a language can take place. Dahalo, a language of the Southern Cushitic subgroup of the Afrasian (Afroasiatic) language family spoken in Kenya, provides an good example. Originally, sometime before two thousand years ago, the Dahalo people were gatherer-hunters who spoke a language belonging to the Khoisan family. After a probably long period of close relations with a neighboring, dominant Southern Cushitic-speaking herding society, the Dahalo gave up using their original Khoisan language. They began instead to speak the Southern Cushitic language of their neighbors, although they continued to follow their older food-collecting ways of life. They also carried many words of their old language into their new one, and this is how we know today that they used to speak a Khoisan tongue. Then, during the first millennium C.E., the Southern Cushitic farmers were all assimilated into another Cushitic herding society, the Garree. Only the Dahalo continued to speak the Southern Cushitic language. Because they still maintained their economically distinct way of life, they were able to retain the adopted language, despite having a new society move in all around them.[3]

So the history of related languages is at one and the same time a history of societies. To reconstruct the relationships among a group of languages is to simultaneously establish the historical existence of the societies that spoke the languages. We also establish that some sort of societal continuity connects the histories of the speakers of each language right back in time to the people who spoke the ancestral language, the "proto-language," of the family as a whole. Our tree of relationships among the Nilo-Saharan daughter languages is a history of a succession of Nilo-Saharan-speaking societies. It forms a social and historical as well as a linguistic stratigraphy.

Words as Historical Artifacts

Once we have used the evidence of language relationship to lay out the historical links among the related societies and to formulate the linguistic stratigraphy of this history, we are ready to tackle the most challenging and most rewarding part of the enterprise of recovering history from language evidence. We are ready to position the individual artifacts of history, the words that make up the vocabularies of the languages of the topic of study, in the stratigraphy. Two criteria guide our placement of the artifacts.

Situating Words in a Linguistic Stratigraphy

One criterion is the actual distribution of the words in particular modern-day languages. To derive an extant word from a root word used in an earlier protolanguage, the modern-day forms of the root (its *reflexes*) must appear in at least one language in each of two primary branches of the family. To be considered, for example, a proto-Nilo-Saharan root word, the word must still have reflexes today in at least one language of each of the two primary branches of Nilo-Saharan, Koman and Sudanic.

The process of determining whether a modern-day word can be traced back to an intermediate daughter language, such as proto-Northern Sudanic, has an additional wrinkle. The most obvious basis for reconstruction would be for the root word, as before, to have reflexes in at least one language in each of the two primary divisions of Northern Sudanic, namely, in Kunama and Saharo-Sahelian. But the criterion could be satisfied just as well in another fashion. If the same root word occurred in a language of the Central Sudanic group, it would need only to be found either in Kunama or in any one of the Saharo-Sahelian tongues to be considered a proto-Northern Sudanic item. The reason is made clear by reference back to the tree diagram of the Nilo-Saharan family. To trace a modern-day word back to an earlier protolanguage is to say that the word was transmitted from that protolanguage via the direct line of social and linguistic descent of the language in which it is found in later times. By following the outlines of the Nilo-Saharan family tree, we see that the lines of descent that link Kunama and proto-Saharo-Sahelian to Central Sudanic connect back through two successive intermediate daughter languages, proto-Northern Sudanic and proto-Sudanic. The only way a word could be part of the common inheritance of both a Central Sudanic language and Kunama, or of both a Central Sudanic language and a Saharo-Sahelian one, would be if it also had been present in the proto-Northern Sudanic language.

Regular Sound Change in Language History

A second criterion must be met, however, if we are to consider such root forms to be fully valid reconstructions, and this is the criterion of regular sound correspondence. Regular sound correspondence allows a determination as to whether two closely similar words are cognates or borrowings (or just chance resemblances).

What is meant by regular sound correspondence? As part of the normal course of history in any language, changes arise from time to time in how particular sounds are pronounced. When such a sound change, as it is called, takes hold, it tends to affect all cases of the sound in question. For example, if a *b* becomes a *p* at the end of one word in a language, it normally does so because of the operation of a sound change rule that changes all cases of former word-final *b* into *p*. In other words, sound change in any language proceeds, on the whole, according to regularly formulatable rules.

Because of this characteristic, history always creates a regular correspondence of sounds between related languages. Let us chose an example from the Bantu branch of the Niger-Congo language family. A proto-Bantu consonant represented by linguists as *b regularly became a *w* in the daughter language Swahili and dropped out of pronunciation entirely in another daughter language, Gikuyu, spoken in highland Kenya. By two other sound shifts, the proto-Bantu consonant sequence *nt changed into simple *t* in Swahili, while becoming *nd* in Gikuyu. And by two further sound change histories, original Bantu *a remained *a* in both languages, and original *u stayed *u* in Swahili while producing a sound spelled ū (but pronounced like *o*) in Gikuyu. Thus we say that Swahili *w* regularly corresponds to Gikuyu Ø (zero), that the examples of Swahili *t* that derive from proto-Bantu *nt correspond regularly to Gikuyu *nd*, and that Swahili *a* and Gikuyu *a* and also Swahili *u* and Gikuyu ū show regular sound correspondences. Reflecting these regularities, the proto-Bantu root word *bantu "persons, people" evolved into the modern-day words *watu* in Swahili and *andū* in Gikuyu.

Regular sound change is the criterion that identifies those words in the related languages that have been preserved in a direct line of descent from the vocabulary of the common mother language, or protolanguage.

We can then distinguish from such inherited items the words that a particular language has instead adopted—or as linguists say, "borrowed"—from other languages over the course of its history. If the sound correspondences are regular *throughout* in the words being compared, as they are in the instance of Swahili *watu* and Gikuyu *andū* just cited, then the probabilities are usually exceedingly high that the words are cognates, directly inherited in each language from their distant, ancestral protolanguage. Each word is, in linguistic terminology, a "regular" reflex of the same root word. If sound correspondences fail in even one of the sounds in the two words being compared, then some other kind of history, usually involving the borrowing of the word into one or both languages, has to be invoked instead.[4]

Varieties of Word Histories

The essential intermediate step, then, in tracing the history of any word is to test its sound correspondences. From that exercise we discover whether the word is likely to be part of the long-term inheritance of a language or an item originally adopted ("borrowed") into the language from another language.

But that only begins the process of unveiling its history. If the word is old in the language, we must then determine whether the word has undergone meaning changes or changes in its grammatical form. If the word was borrowed, we must consider it in relation to other loanwords in the language. Is it one of a wider set of loanwords borrowed during a particular era from a particular language, and if so what kinds of words make up that set? Have they a wide variety of meanings, or do they tend mostly to refer to a particular category of human activity, such as farming or religious ideas or the like? Each kind of word history reveals something different about the history of the people who used the word.

Inherited Words

Some words occurring today in the daughter languages will prove to have been in use, with the same meanings, ever since the time the mother language was spoken. They will thus attest to long-term cultural continuities—to areas and elements of conservatism and retention in culture and life. The widespread use in Bantu languages of the Niger-Congo family, for example, of an old, inherited word for "bow," *-ta—which can be reconstructed back to the proto-Bantu period and, in fact, right back to proto-Niger-Congo—tells us that the proto-Bantu people used bows and arrows and that their descendants maintained the knowledge of this weaponry from that period down to the present.

In contrast, the semantic derivations of words often reveal older, now lost, ways of thinking or former ways of doing things. For example, in the proto-Mashariki language, a daughter language of proto-Bantu spoken near the great Western Rift valleys of Africa at around 1000 B.C.E., a new word *-pand- for "to plant (crops)" came into use. Because previously in Bantu history this verb meant "to split," its new meaning tells us that the proto-Mashariki people continued to emphasize a particular, earlier, rainforest-based agricultural technique. This technique, protective of fragile soils, involved cutting a narrow slit in the ground and planting a new cutting from a yam or other similar food plant in the slit. Over the next several centuries after 1000 B.C.E., the settlement of Mashariki people in lands with richer soils, along with changes in their crops, led to the complete loss of this practice among their descendants. Without this piece of linguistic testimony, an insight about earlier agricultural technology would have been lost.

Other words of ancient use in a language family will have undergone meaning shifts in one or another daughter tongue. In the Horn of Africa, for example, several words in proto-Soomaali, a language of the Afrasan (or Afroasiatic) language family, originally referred to the different life-stages of cattle. In the daughter language of proto-Soomaali that we call Maxay (or "Northern Soomaali"), these words came instead to refer to the equivalent life-stages of camels. These meaning shifts reveal the replacement of cattle by camels among the early Maxay, who about 1200 years ago spread their settlement into very dry parts of the Horn, where camels but not cattle could thrive.[5]

In still other cases derivational affixes may be added to an old root word to create a new term. For example, among the early Mashariki Bantu of about 3000–2500 years ago in the African Great Lakes region, a new word for salt, *-ínò, came into use. Its derivation from an ancient Bantu verb, *-ín- "to dip," indicates that the early Mashariki had begun by then to extract salt from certain briny lake deposits, somewhat earlier than the archaeology can yet confirm.[6]

Other kinds of meaning change can reveal the appearance of new ideas or the development of new economic or social practices. Examples of this kind of historical inference include an ancient Nilo-Saharan verb *khày "to break off, tear off," which, after the inception of cultivation, took on a more specific application to the clearing-off of vegetation. Another example is the early Nilo-Saharan verb *ndɔ. After the adoption of cattle raising this verb changed meaning from "to squeeze, press out" in general to the technical meaning "to milk."

Borrowed Words

Still other words turn out to have been "borrowed," that is, adopted into a particular language from another language rather than inherited from the protolanguage. Borrowed words, or loanwords as they are also called, reveal cross-cultural influences. Many different kinds of word borrowing have taken place in history. There is space here to mention just a few.

The patterns of word borrowing between languages fall into a variety of categories and subcategories, and each of these reflects something different about the historical interactions among the peoples involved in this adoption of new words. For example, the borrowing of a single word normally indicates the adoption of the item named by the word. The generic term *ng'ikaal* for camel in Turkana of northern Kenya, for example, is a loanword from Rendille *gaal,* showing that the Turkana first learned of these animals from speakers of that language.

At the other extreme, a very large number of words may have been borrowed, all in a relatively short period of time, from one language into another. Very often this kind of word borrowing tells us that large numbers of the people who formerly spoke the donor language of the loanwords were assimilated into the society of the people who adopted the words.

Between these extremes lies a variety of other patterns of word borrowing among languages, all of which require a delicate interpretive hand. The differing kinds, quantity, and rapidity of borrowing in such instances can reflect a great variety of different kinds and intensities of intersocietal contact, and it is in fact essential to an adequate historical interpretation of word borrowing that such wider historically linked sets of loanwords in a language be identified.

It is useful to divide up the types of borrowing that take place between languages into four broad categories: (1) single-word borrowings; (2) restricted sets of borrowings; (3) general sets of borrowings; and (4) pidginization. Categories (2) and (3) each can be further divided into several subcategories:[7]

Category of word borrowing	How word borrowing takes place	Parts of vocabulary in which the borrowing occurs	Minimum duration of word borrowing
1—Single-word borrowings	Through contacts among individuals or groups belonging to two or more speech communities	An individual word for a new item of culture is adopted	A few hours or days may sometimes be enough
2A—Semantically restricted sets of word borrowings	Through contacts of the members of one speech community with those of another	A set of words all having to do with a particular field of technical or cultural knowledge is borrowed	Uncertain; possibly as little as one or two generations in some instances
2B—Grammatically restricted sets of word borrowings	From a suppressed collection of minority populations to a dominant majority or plurality speech community	Interjections and some adverbs are borrowed	Uncertain; but probably as little as a century
2C—Status-restricted sets of word borrowings	From a lower-status minority to a dominant majority speech community	Jocular, deprecatory, or tabooed vocabulary is borrowed	Uncertain; but probably 2 to 3 generations
3A—Intensive general sets of word borrowings	From a (usually dominant) majority to a co-existing economically distinctive minority speech community or in some cases the adoption by a majority community of the language of a prestigious minority community	Borrowings take place all through vocabulary (basic words are adopted at a rate of about 1 to 3 percent per century; other vocabulary is borrowed more rapidly)	Usually about 2 to 3 centuries
3B—Heavy general sets of word borrowings	Pattern described in 3A preceding, but of shorter duration than 2 to 3 centuries; or pattern described in 3C following, but of longer duration than 1 to 2 centuries	Borrowings take place in all parts of vocabulary, *except* for basic vocabulary	1 to 2 centuries if short period of category 3A borrowing is involved; longer than 1 to 2 centuries if category 3C borrowing is involved

(*continued on next page*)

Category of word borrowing	How word borrowing takes place	Parts of vocabulary in which the borrowing occurs	Minimum duration of word borrowing
3C—Extensive general sets of word borrowing	From one speech community to another, as part of the merging of the one community into the other (and the loss of its former language in the process)	Borrowings take place in all parts of the vocabulary, *except* for basic vocabulary and terms for large animals	Uncertain; but probably about 1 to 2 centuries
3D—Light general sets of word borrowings	From one neighboring speech community to another	A sparse, semantically diverse scatter of culture vocabulary is borrowed	2 to 3 generations
4—Pidginization	By a collection of distinct speech communities thrown together by historical circumstance in the same region; as part of their adoption of a new common language	Rapid and extensive word borrowing takes place in all parts of the vocabulary, accompanied by severe grammatical simplification of the adopted new common language	Less than one generation

Folk Organizations of Knowledge as Revealed in Word Histories

A different, but equally productive, approach to the grouping together of word histories takes account of the findings of a now out-of-vogue field of anthropological investigation called "ethnoscience." Scholars have shown that societies, each in their own various culture-specific ways, systematize their knowledge and their understanding of the cultural and natural worlds in which they operate. Their folk understandings are expressed in the semantic patterning of words that deal with the different subsets of human knowledge. This makes it possible to elicit the modern folk epistemological systems of peoples who speak related languages and then to seek to reconstruct from these data the earlier systems of their common ancestors. From the individual word-histories within a semantic subset, we can make further inferences about how ideas and beliefs have changed between earlier and more recent periods. Both inherited and borrowed vocabulary may figure in this type of investigation. The borrowed words in particular reveal whether the cultural shift has a debt, wholly or in part, to influences from neighboring societies.[8]

The religious history of the Southern Nilotic peoples in the first millennium B.C.E. offers a fairly straightforward example of this kind of historical inference. The proto-Southern Nilotes of about 800–500 B.C.E. took over a new set of ideas about the realm of spirit from their Southern Cushitic neighbors in central Kenya.

Before 1000 B.C.E. the beliefs of the Southern Nilotes were those of the Sudanic religion. Most other related Nilotic peoples, such as the Maasai and the Dinka, still follow this belief system today. In Sudanic religion there is a single category of Spirit or spiritual Power in the universe, called by names that scholars usually translate into English with the word "Divinity." Divinity is the source of good and evil; the bad happenings of life are the result of Divine retribution, visited upon people for the wrongs they or their parents before them have committed. In religious metaphor, Divinity is identified with the sky and with rain and lightning.

The proto-Southern Nilotes, however, changed their belief system sometime between 800 and 500 B.C.E. They adopted a new identification of Divinity with the sun, and they also began to recognize the existence of lesser, dangerous spirits, able to bring about bad happenings to people. The Southern Cushitic societies of East Africa followed virtually the same division of the realm of spirit into two categories, in which Divinity or God was identified with the power of the sun, and lesser spirits were believed able to cause harm. So it seems clear that one of the two peoples must have borrowed their ideas from the other.

But how do we know that it was in fact the Southern Nilotes who adopted the new views from the Southern Cushites? The answer is, from the testimony of word histories. The proto-Southern Nilotes acquired at least one key word in their new religious terminology from the Southern Cushites, their word for Divinity or God, *asis. This word was a borrowing of the old Southern Cushitic term for "sun" and in fact meant both "sun" and "Divinity/God" in the proto-Southern Nilotic language.[9]

Applying the Principles of Linguistic Reconstruction of Human History

It is now time to see in a more practical manner how these principles can be applied in African historical studies. For a case study, we will explore certain aspects of very early Nilo-Saharan history, showing how to use a linguistic stratigraphy of key changes in vocabulary to plot the course of social and economic change.

Building a Stratigraphy: The Nilo-Saharan Example

The Nilo-Saharan family has undergone a complex history of repeated divergence into subgroupings and languages, a history that took well over eleven thousand years to unfold. Over those thousands of years, great shifts in human economies and in customary life and political and social institutions have taken place in Africa, as well as all across the world, and Nilo-Saharan-speaking peoples have been at the center of many of the most important reshapings of life and livelihood in the African continent. Their languages, as would be expected, have time and again mirrored those changes. A particularly striking and telling range of examples of how linguistic historical methods and techniques work out in practice can be adduced if we restrict ourselves to the period 11,000–7,000 years ago, when most Nilo-Saharan peoples shifted from gatherer-hunter to herding and cultivating economies.

Nilo-Saharan societies took on key roles in the earliest creation and spread of agricultural ways of life in the African continent, and the evidence of this history provides a striking illustration of the power of linguistic evidence in unveiling the ancient past. But we can go further in the case of early Nilo-Saharan agricultural history, correlating the history inferred from the linguistic evidence with the findings of archaeology. In this example, virtually the same sequence of changes appears in the archaeological record of the eastern Sahara as in the linguistic record of the Nilo-Saharan family. The correlation of the linguistic and archaeological stratigraphies then allows us to pinpoint in time and place the common set of developments apparent in both records.

The linguistic evidence and arguments for Nilo-Saharan history are extensive and complex, and the history itself was long and immensely varied; thus, only a simplified sampling of the relevant data can be presented here. In the data cited, however, the regularity of sound correspondences can be assumed to have been established,[10] unless irregularities are specifically noted. The reader should refer to the Nilo-Saharan family tree (see the first section, above) for the linguistic stratigraphy with which to trace the lines of descent of the particular reflexes of each root word. To assist the reader in identifying the descent lines, each citation of a reflex and its language has its branch of Nilo-Saharan also listed. The examples illustrating this story are drawn from the history of the Sudanic branch of the family.

A Stratigraphy of Nilo-Saharan Word Evidence for Food Production

In the first two stages of Nilo-Saharan history, represented by the proto-Nilo-Saharan and proto-Sudanic strata, the societies that spoke the Nilo-Saharan languages were still all probably gatherer-hunters in economy. No vocabulary diagnostic of any type of food production can be tracked back to those two eras. To the proto-Northern Sudanic period can be traced the first words that indicate the deliberate raising of domestic animals, while the earliest stratum in which words diagnostic of cultivation appear is the immediately following proto-Saharo-Sahelian era.[11] Finally, only after the proto-Saharo-Sahelian society itself had diverged into two daughter societies, proto-Saharan and proto-Sahelian, were sheep and goats added to this economy.

The histories of the individual root words that make up this body of evidence are of several types. Sometimes we simply cannot as yet track the words back before the beginnings of food production. The earliest term for a cultivated field, traceable to the proto-Saharo-Sahelian language, is such a case:

---

*oḍomp "cultivated field"

II.B.2.a. Saharan: KANURI dǝ′mbà "bed for sweet potatoes, small irrigation dike"
II.B.2.b. Sahelian: TEMEIN ɔjɔm, PL. kɔjɔm "(cultivated) field"
  Nilotic: JYANG dom, PL. dum "(cultivated) field"

In many other examples, however, the words turn out to be older roots shifted in meaning to express activities or things connected to livestock raising or to the cultivation of crops. Examples of this kind of history are provided by three proto-Nilo-Saharan (PNS) verb roots that originally referred to activities not specifically involving cultivation. The first of these formerly denoted breaking or tearing off of any kind, but at the Saharo-Sahelian stage took on the narrower technical meaning of cutting and clearing away plant material, particularly in relation to cultivation. The second meant simply "to dig," without implying cultivation, while the third meant "to stick something into the ground." Each of these two also shifted in application at the proto-Saharo-Sahelian period specifically to activities of cultivation.

*kʰày "to break off, tear off (tr.)"

I. Koman: OPO kai "to break"
II.A. Central Sudanic: proto-Central Sudanic *kɛ OR *kʼɛ "to tear off"
II.B.2.a. Saharan: KANURI cè, kè "to plow, remove earth"
II.B.2.b. Sahelian: FOR kauy- "to weed; to skin"
SONGAY kèyè "to weed field a second time"
NYIMANG kai "to chop" (i.e., vegetation with an ax)
Nilotic: proto-Western Nilotic *kay "to harvest"
Rub: IK kaw- "to cut (e.g., with ax), to clear land"

*tɔɔk "to stick in the ground"

II.B.1. KUNAMA tokai- "to dig the ground with a spear" (*tok-ay-, stem plus extended action suffix in *y)
II.B.2.a. Saharan: KANURI dòwóp "to sow, plant" (*dogop-, stem plus *p extended action suffix
II.B.2.b. Sahelian: SONGAY dóogó "to weed"
Rub: proto-Rub *tɔkɔb "to cultivate" (stem with same suffix as in Kanuri)

*ɖììp OR *ɖììpʼ "to dig"

II.A. Central Sudanic: proto-Central Sudanic * ɖʼi OR *dʼi "to dig" (the second consonant is missing because the proto-Central Sudanic language dropped final consonants in its words)
II.B.2.a. Saharan: KANURI jìwá "to weed, harrow"
II.B.2.b. Sahelian: GAAM ɖəw- "to sow seeds"

The fact that each of these verbs derives from a root word that earlier in Nilo-Saharan language history had a nonagricultural meaning suggests that the cultivation of crops may well have begun as a set of independent inventions among the proto-Saharo-Sahelians.

If we turn our attention to word histories relating to livestock raising, an equally varied picture emerges. Again some root words cannot yet be traced back to earlier pre-food-producing periods, as, for example, a verb for "to drive herd" used as early as the Saharo-Sahelian period:

*yókw "to drive herd"

II.B.2.a. Saharan: KANURI yók "to drive, herd"
II.B.2.b. Sahelian: SONGAY yógó "to bustle, stir, move about to gather the herd and send it to pasture"
Nilotic: proto-Eastern Nilotic *-yok "to herd"
proto-Southern Nilotic *yakw "to herd"

But again also, other old root words specifically do reveal in their histories the transition to animal domestication. For example, the earliest verb indicative of driving livestock to pasture, present in proto-Northern Sudanic in our linguistic stratigraphy, was formed by attaching the Nilo-Saharan causative suffix *k to the older proto-Nilo-Saharan (PNS) verb *ṣù "to lead off, to start off":

---

*ṣùùk "to drive (animals)" [PNS *ṣu "to lead off, start off" plus old *k causative]

II.B.1. KUNAMA sugune- "to cultivate, to raise animals" (back-formation from an earlier noun, consisting of stem plus *n noun suffix)
II.B.2.a. Saharan: KANURI sùk "to drive (many things), to speed horse"
II.B.2.b. Sahelian: Nubian: DONGOLAWI šu:g "to drive along, off"

The particular animals driven by the people of the proto-Northern Sudanic stage appear to have been cattle, as the following old cognate set indicates:

---

*yááyr "cow, head of cattle" [PNS *yaay "meat" plus *-(V)r noun suffix]

II.B.1. KUNAMA aira, aila "cow"
[ara "wild cow, antelope, small buffalo": loan apparently from early form of the Nara language (see II.B.2.b)]
II.B.2.a. Saharan: BERTI eir "cow"
II.B.2.b. Sahelian: SONGAY yàarù "bull; brave; to be brave"
   NARA ar, PL. are "cow"
   Nilotic: proto-Southern Nilotic *(y)e:R "male cattle"

Most interesting, this root word can be derived, by addition of a Nilo-Saharan noun suffix *-(V)r, from a still earlier proto-Nilo-Saharan term *yaay "meat." This particular semantic history suggests that the Northern Sudanic people used cattle as their main source of meat. The indigenous derivation of the word would fit a history in which the Northern Sudanic people themselves domesticated cattle, rather than adopting them from somewhere else, although it does not require such a history.

Incidentally, the borrowed term for "wild cow," etc., in Kunama is one of a large set of Nara loanwords in that language, of the kind that fits the category 3B, "heavy general" (see the table above of the types of word borrowing). Apparently a long history of close interactions and assimilation of people has taken place between the speakers of the earlier forms of the Kunama and Nara languages.

Still other root words dealing with livestock raising have histories that include their having been borrowed from one language to another. Histories of this kind, of course, indicate the diffusion of the things or ideas from one early society or group of societies to another. An instructive example is provided by the earliest verb for "to milk." The history of this word involves both its derivation by meaning shift from an earlier Nilo-Saharan pre-food-production root word that did not mean "to milk," and its later spread by borrowing, with its new meaning, from one Nilo-Saharan branch to another. Originally meaning "to squeeze," the root word added a verb suffix at the Northern Sudanic stage in our linguistic stratigraphy and, along with that suffixation, a new meaning, "to milk."

---

*ndɔ "to squeeze"

II.A. Central Sudanic: proto-Central Sudanic *nzɔ "to squeeze out, press out"
  proto-Central Sudanic [*jo "to milk": loan from Sahelian language]
II.B.1. KUNAMA šu- "to milk" [from earlier *šow stem plus *w focused-action
  extension]
II.B.2.b. Sahelian: TAMA juw- "to milk" [stem plus *w focused-action extension]
  Rub: proto-Rub *'jut "to milk" [earlier *'jow-t stem plus *w focused-action extension
  plus continued action extension *tʰ]

In the Central Sudanic branch, this verb appears in two forms: with regular sound correspondence and the meaning "to press out," and in a borrowed form with the meaning "to milk." The borrowed shape, of course, fits the category of a single-word borrowing (category 1 in our chart of word-borrowing types) in that it reflects the diffusion of a new cultural practice to the Central Sudanic peoples. It is one of a number of similar word histories in Central Sudanic languages indicating that the early Central Sudanic people, who diverged along a separate line of historical development before the Northern Sudanic period, did not participate in the original establishment of livestock raising among Nilo-Saharan peoples. The ideas and practices of herding diffused to them from other Nilo-Saharan societies only much later in time.

Even more arresting is the evidence dealing with the raising of sheep and goats. Here the histories of a number of key early root words show that the raising of these two animals did not originate among the Nilo-Saharans at all, but spread to them after the proto-Saharo-Sahelian period in our stratigraphy. The sources in each case were languages of the Afrasan (Afroasiatic) family. For example, the generic term *tam for "sheep" in the

Saharan group of languages was an ancient loanword from the Chadic branch of the Afrasan language family. Similarly, the proto-Sahelian root word for "goat," *ay, came originally from the northern, Beja, sub-branch of the Cushitic branch of the Afrasan family.[12] Again, these examples belong to the category of single-word borrowings, indicative of the diffusion to the early Sahelian and Saharan peoples of the new cultural items named by those words:

---

*áy "goat"

II.B.2.b. Sahelian: FOR déí, PL. keita "he-goat"
   TEMEIN kai "goats (suppletive plural)" [*kʰ plural prefix plus stem]
   Daju: proto-Daju *aiše "goat" [stem plus *s noun suffix]
   Surmic: Didinga-Murle *εεθ "goat" [stem plus *s noun suffix]

The conclusion drawn from this evidence exactly fits the zoological and archaeological evidence, which shows that goats and sheep did indeed spread into Nilo-Saharan-speaking areas from the Afrasan-speaking societies to the north, and that they spread after cattle-raising had already developed among peoples of the Northern Sudanic branch of the family.[13]

To recapitulate, these sets of evidence are part of a much larger body of data demonstrating that, in the earliest periods of the linguistically recoverable history, the Nilo-Saharan peoples were gatherer-hunters in economy. Food production took hold among the peoples of one sub-branch of the early Nilo-Saharans in a three-stage process. First, a tending in some fashion of cattle began among the proto-Northern Sudanic communities. Then, in the subsequent historical period, the Saharo-Sahelian descendants of the proto-Northern Sudanians took up the cultivation of crops. Finally, still later in time, the proto-Sahelian and proto-Saharan societies separately added goats and sheep to their economies.

Locating Past Societies: An Example from Nilo-Saharan History

To turn the linguistic findings into even more satisfactory history we must correlate them with other datable evidence of the past, such as archaeology or written documents. To accomplish this correlation, two other lines of linguistic historical argumentation must be applied. One is to use the more recent locations of the languages of a family to argue for the most probable areas in which their earlier protolanguages would have been found. The other is to apply a tool called glottochronology to estimate the broad time frame within which particular protolanguages would have been spoken.

Locating Societies in Place

In arguing for earlier language locations, the most probable historical scheme is the one that requires the least population displacement and the fewest population movements to account for the modern locations of the languages of the family. The sequence of argumentation begins with the most recent branchings among the languages and moves backward in time. We sometimes call this approach by its own name, the principle of fewest moves, but it is simply a version of the usual scientific principle of Occam's razor, as adapted to historical argumentation from linguistic evidence.

What does this method say about the geographical history of the Nilo-Saharan development of food production? The latest of the three stages identified for this history took place among the proto-Sahelians (see the Nilo-Saharan family tree above). With the exception of a single subgroup, Eastern Sahelian—which extends from the Nubian languages of the Nile in the northern Sudan to the Maasai language of north-central Tanzania—all the Sahelian groups today are located in the sahel geographical belt, along the southern edges of the Sahara Desert, extending from Songay, spoken in Mali near the interior delta of the Niger River, to the For language of the Marra Mountains in Sudan. The simplest history of population movements is therefore one that places the lands of proto-Sahelian broadly somewhere along the southern edge of the Sahara region.

At the next previous stage in this history, proto-Sahelian diverged as a sister language of proto-Saharan out of their common ancestor, proto-Saharo-Sahelian. The modern-day distribution of the daughter languages of proto-Saharan reaches from the Sahara Desert fringes north of the Marra Mountains, where Zaghawa and Berti are spoken, to the Tibesti region of the east-central Sahara Desert, occupied by the Tibu people, and to the Lake Chad Basin at the south edge of the central Sahara, in which the Kanuri language is spoken. The proto-Saharan speech territory therefore most probably lay in the southern or eastern parts of what is today the central Sahara Desert. If we combine the arguments for locating the proto-Saharan and proto-Sahelian territories, the simplest history we can construct would attribute the wide spread of the Sahelian languages to a single early east-west expansion, with that expansion beginning in a region adjacent to the proposed proto-Saharan lands in the east-central or southeast-central Sahara.

Finally, we consider the first of the three stages. In that period the proto-Northern Sudanic language diverged into two branchings—proto-Saharo-Sahelian and ancestral Kunama. The lands of the proto-Saharo-Sahelian society, as we have just shown, would best be placed in the east-central or southeast-central Sahara. Kunama is today a single language spoken just beyond the far southeast edge of the Sahara Desert, in the far northwestern part of the Ethiopian Highlands. The simplest account of this historical stage would involve a single expansion, either (1) of the speakers of the proto-Saharo-Sahelian daughter language of proto-Northern Sudanic westward from the southeastern Sahara, (2) of the speakers of the earliest form of the Kunama language eastward from the southeast-central Sahara, or (3) of both groups outward from a common center somewhere in the eastern half of the southern Sahara regions.

Locating Societies in Time

One way to give a dating framework to this history is to apply a technique known by the unprepossessing name of glottochronology. The approach is based on empirical observations, taken in a variety of language families from different parts of the world, that reveal a recurrent patterning of lexical change in what has been called "basic" or "core" vocabulary. Using a standard list of one hundred or two hundred meanings, sometimes called the "Swadesh" lists, that are basic and nearly universal in the world's languages, scholars have found that similar percentages of the words for those meanings tend to be replaced by new words over similar periods of time in all languages.

The method has been widely criticized, but the criticisms have all too often been expressed as simple disbelief, an unscholarly substitute for argumentation from evidence.[14] A possible reason for this disbelief is that both the detractors of glottochronology and many of its early supporters misunderstood it as a phenomenon involving a *regular and predictable* rate of vocabulary change. On the contrary, glottochronology counts up accumulation over time of individual word replacements, each of which is *random and unpredictable*. This sort of accumulated change in the different languages can then be analyzed and described by statistics and distribution curves. This kind of analysis is familiar to sociologists studying human behavior, of course, but has not been part of the usual training of linguists.[15]

Glottochronology has been shown to fit well with known language histories in the Americas, Europe, Asia, and Africa. It works well for languages of the very distantly related Semitic and Cushitic branches of the Afrasan family, for the Turkic language group, for Carib, and for Japanese, among others, as well as for a variety of Indo-European cases.[16] Nor does the size or social complexity of the speech community appear to modify the long-term outcome of this kind of vocabulary change. The applicability of glottochronological estimation to societies of widely varying demography and culture is amply evident in the variety of strong correlations of archaeology with language that have been developed in the past three decades for several parts of Africa.[17]

In the case of two languages that began to diverge out of their common mother a thousand years ago, the proportion of words in the 100-meaning list that both will retain with the same meaning tends to range around a median of 74 percent. After two thousand years of divergence, the count of shared basic words distributes around a median of 55 percent; after three thousand years, around 40 percent; and so on down the scale. It must be emphasized that these figures are empirically observed median values, based on actual counts undertaken for a great many languages. As with any statistical distribution, a majority of the observed figures fall close to these medians, but the figure for any particular language pair over a particular time period might well be considerably lower or higher than the median.

Rough median dating (B.P.)	Median common retention figures between related languages (%)
1000	74
2000	55
3000	40
4000	30
5000	22
6000	16
7000	12
8000	9
9000	7
10000	5

In the case of the Northern Sudanic branch of Nilo-Saharan, the languages of its Kunama and Saharo-Sahelian subbranches are separated by cognation figures centering around three percent, indicative of a time period for the divergence of proto-Northern Sudanic of around eleven thousand years ago, or perhaps a bit more—in other words, somewhere very, very approximately in the range of the ninth millennium B.C.E.

For just that period in the history of the Sahara, which was then a land of mostly steppe, grassland, and dry savanna environments, a strikingly close set of parallels can be identified between the archaeology and the linguistic history of early Nilo-Saharan food production. In areas that included far southwestern Egypt, a three-stage development of food production took place between about 9000 and 5000 B.C.E. It began with the tending of cattle before 8000, followed by the appearance of prima facie evidence for a second development, of cultivation, by the second half of the eighth millennium, and at a still later point in time, possibly about 6000 B.C.E., by the first evidence of sheep and goats.[19]

The archaeological dates of the three stages fit within the general range of time proposed from linguistics for the proto-Northern Sudanic society and for the next two strata of its descendant societies, first the proto-Saharo-Sahelians and then the proto-Saharans and proto-Sahelians. Moreover, the locations of the finds lie in a part of the same overall region, the southern half of the eastern Sahara, in which the linguistic arguments would place these peoples. The same succession of economic changes appear, from the beginnings of cattle-tending among the proto-Northern Sudanians, to the adding of crop cultivation by their proto-Saharo-Sahelian descendants, to the adoption of sheep and goats by the still later proto-Sahelian and proto-Saharan daughter societies of the proto-Saharo-Sahelian people.

Writing History for Historians from Language Evidence

These examples from Nilo-Saharan history apply some of the long-established methods and formats that historians follow in the recovery of history from the evidence of language. They give us a first hint of just how far-reaching and valuable this work can be. Imagine, then, how much more complex a story we can tell when applying these methods in detailed ways—when studying word histories from all parts of the vocabulary and bringing forth evidence from all the languages of a region.

The most sophisticated and original applications of linguistic methods so far in the writing of African history deal with the past three to four thousand years. The key recent works of this type are Jan Vansina's *Paths in the Rainforests*,[20] David Schoenbrun's *A Green Place, A Good Place*,[21] and my own *An African Classical Age*. Each author intertwines the evidence of many hundreds or, in the case of my book, many thousands of word histories. Each marshals a great body of comparative ethnographic evidence to evoke and articulate the social and cultural changes those word histories encompass. Each engages as well the long-term social and political developments, the multiple trajectories of agricultural and technological history, and the consequences of trade and the diffusion of things and ideas over longer and shorter distances.

The importance of these books reaches far beyond just the uncovering of the African past. They are models for the writing of full and satisfying social and economic histories of large regions, applicable to *any* part of the world where written documentation is absent and also to many locations where it exists but is sparse and uneven. They demonstrate the great power of language evidence in displaying the history of the inner as well as the outer lives of those societies. Vansina's work constructs the political history of the Bantu peoples of the equatorial rainforest regions of Africa, a story of ancient genesis and great complexity and longevity. Schoenbrun evocatively plots out the changing cultural and social milieus of the African Great Lakes region, from the small-scale societies of 500 B.C.E. up to the threshold of the emergence of large states in the first half of the second millennium C.E. My own book depicts the complex unfolding of cross-cultural interactions in interior East Africa in the last millennium B.C.E., involving peoples of all four of the major African language families. Out of those interactions emerged a new historical tradition, which then spread in the early first millennium C.E. all across the eastern and southern sides of the continent. My study sets that history, as well, within the wide African and world historical contexts of its times.

Other scholars are now pursuing the same kinds of directions in their work, and we can confidently expect further exciting advances in the coming years. What is presented here only scratches the surface of what linguistic techniques can bring to the study of history in Africa and to the building of rich and deep understandings of all the neglected histories of preliterate or otherwise under-documented societies around the world.

Notes

1. This chapter is a revised version for historians of "Language and History," in B. Heine and D. Nurse (eds.), *African Languages: An Introduction* (Cambridge: Cambridge University Press, 2000).

2. C. Ehret, *A Historical-Comparative Reconstruction of Nilo-Saharan* (Cologne: Rüdiger Köppe Verlag, 2002). An alternative Nilo-Saharan subclassification different in several key aspects is followed by M. L. Bender in *NiloSaharan Language* (Lansing: Michigan State University Press, 1984) and elsewhere. The differences derive primarily from the fact that his works use a less wide range of classificatory evidence and a more incomplete phonological reconstruction of proto-Nilo-Saharan than is found in Ehret.

3. C. Ehret, *Ethiopians and East Africans: The Problem of Contacts* (Nairobi: East African Publishing House, 1974).

4. The preceding two paragraphs reproduce materials in C. Ehret, *An African Classical Age: Eastern and Southern Africa in World History, 1000 BCE to CE 400* (Charlottesville: University Press of Virginia; Oxford: James Currey, 1998).

5. Mohamed Nuuh Ali, "History in the Horn of Africa," Ph.D. diss., University of California at Los Angeles, 1985.

6. C. Ehret, "Linguistics, Historical," in J. Middleton (ed.), *Encyclopedia of Africa South of the Sahara* (New York: Charles Scribner's Sons, 1997), 2:579–80.

7. C. Ehret, "The Demographic Implications of Linguistic Change and Language Shift," in Christopher Fyfe and David McMaster (eds.), *African Historical Demography*, vol. 2 (Edinburgh; Centre of African Studies, 1981).

8. C. Ehret, "Historical Inference from Transformations in Culture Vocabularies," *Sprache und Geschichte in Afrika* 2 (1980): 189–218, shows how this kind of analysis can be applied in the context of early East African History.

9. C. Ehret, *An African Classical Age*, 164.

10. C. Ehret, *A Historical-Comparative Reconstruction of Nilo-Saharan* presents the evidence for these in great detail.

11. C. Ehret, "Nilo-Saharans and the Saharo-Sudanese Neolithic," in T. Shaw, P. Sinclair, B. Andah, and A. Okpoko (ed.), *The Archaeology of Africa: Foods, Metals and Towns* (London and New York: Routledge, 1993), 104–25.

12. Ibid.; C. Ehret, "Wer Waren die Felsbildkünstler der Sahara" *Almogaren* 20 (1999): 77–94.

13. Ehret, "Wer Waren die Felsbildkünstler der Sahara" and "Nilo-Saharans and the Saharo-Sudanese Neolithic"; F. Wendorf and R. Schild, "Nabta Playa and Its Role in Northeastern African History," *Anthropological Archaeology* 20 (1998): 97–123.

14. Sheila Embleton, *Statistics in Historical Linguistics* (Quantitative Linguistics, vol. 30; Bochum: Studienverlag Dr. N. Brockmeyer, 1986), 61, makes a similar point.

15. Very few studies have sought to apply actual evidence to disprove glottochronology. One kind of substantive work dealt with languages in which the apparent rate of change in basic vocabulary was significantly less than that expected by the method (in particular Knut Bergslund and Hans Vogt, "On the Validity of Glottochronology," *Current Anthropology* New York, 1962). But these languages each had a long history of being associated with the special social preservation and recital of the older literary forms, a situation that provided a strong and recurrent potential for feedback from those ancient literary sources to the spoken language, thus reinforcing the use of older vocabulary and slowing the replacement of old words by new. The results of these studies in fact fit in with the expectations of the method and do nothing that brings into question the utility of glottochronology in the study of unwritten languages.

Other scholars have been bothered by the fact that lesser apparent rates of change apply to neighboring languages in a chain of contiguous, closely related dialects. But these examples derive from histories in which the society that spoke the mother language underwent an incomplete divergence into daughter communities and in which the intersocietal boundaries never became well defined. They regularly produce a recognizable patterning of percentages that allows them to be easily identified and understood. Normally the dialects located farthest apart, at opposite ends of the chain, have cognate percentages with each other that fit well with the glottochronological expectations. The dialects located in between them have percentages that are skewed higher in direct proportion to how close they are to each other, with adjacent dialects sharing the highest percentages of all.

16. Some of the relevant sources can be found in C. Ehret, "Language Change and the Material Correlates of Language and Ethnic Shift," *Antiquity* (1988) 62: 564–74.

17. Stanley Ambrose, "Archaeology and Linguistic Reconstruction of History in East Africa," in C. Ehret and M. Posnansky (eds.), *The Archaeological and Linguistic Reconstruction of African History* (Berkeley, Los Angeles: University of California Press, 1982), 104–57; Ehret, *An African Classical Age*; Christine Choi Ahmed, "Before Eve Was Eve: 2200 Years of Gendered History in East Central Africa," Ph.D. diss., University of California at Los Angeles, 1996; Ehret, "Testing the Expectations of Glottochronology Against the Correlations of Language and Archaeology in Africa," in C. Renfrew, A. McMahon, and L. Trask (eds.), *Time Depth in Historical Linguistics*, vol. 2 (Cambridge: The McDonald Institute of Archaeological Research, 2000).

18. It has been argued that, because the words for some meanings on the list tend to be retained longer than others, very ancient periods of language divergence will be reflected mainly by retention of the words most resistant to replacement, with the consequence that over very long spans of time the rate of change in the one hundred-word list will seem to slow down (the literature on this point is reviewed by S. M. Embleton, *Statistics in Historical Linguistics* [Bochum, 1986]). The point is a reasonable one, but the experience of correlating linguistic findings and archaeology in eastern Africa suggests this element may be a relatively minor distorting factor in interpreting what is, after all, a very, very wide range of measurement indeed. For that reason, the simple list of approximated datings has been relied on here.

19. F. Wendorf, R. Schild, and A. E. Close *Cattle Keepers of the Eastern Sahara: The Neolithic of Bir Kiseiba* (Dallas: Southern Methodist University Press, 1984). This work has been brought up to date by F. Wendorf and R. Schild, "Nabta Playa and its role in northeastern African history," *Anthropological Archaeology* 20 (1998): 97–123.

20. Jan Vansina, *Paths in the Rainforests* (Madison: University of Wisconsin Press, 1990).

21. David Schoenbrun, *A Green Place, A Good Place* (London: Heinemann, 1998).

4

PHYSICAL ANTHROPOLOGY AND AFRICAN HISTORY

Shomarka Omar Y. Keita

Prologue

Physical anthropology, sometimes called biological anthropology or human biology, looks at synchronic and diachronic biological aspects of the human species. It includes palaeoanthropology, which examines aspects of Homo sapiens' macroevolution. Its topics are as diverse as the energetics of agricultural labor in the tropics, and disease patterns in the skeletons of Late Stone Age populations.

Comparison, whether explicit or implicit, is usually the goal. Whether looking at physiological adaptations of high altitude peoples or the genetics of diseases in migrant groups, researchers try to contrast study populations with others, either real or theoretical.

In its earlier period, physical anthropology was primarily concerned with describing and classifying humankind, and with its evolution. This interest in classification, usually by "race," has left its mark on the historical studies of all of the continents. Africa is no exception.

All Africanist scholars are aware of the Hamitic "hypothesis," a biocultural construct that purported to explain various aspects of African biological, linguistic and cultural reality.[1] Scholars are also aware that the African continent's peoples have been divided into "races," units regarded as fundamental or even foundational, and that previous discussions of African historiography have frequently used "race" as part of an explanatory model, or as a necessary part of any description of historical actors.

112

The issue of race cannot be avoided in any exploration of biological anthropology and African history, sad as this may be. The subject of "race" will be treated at greater length, as it is very important.

What can human biology offer to the "reconstruction" of African history? The question is complicated because it includes the word "history," and serving all of "history's" many areas of study is difficult.[2] To look at African history and biological anthropology as a unit brings to mind a variety of activities. For example, the human biologist may study the skeletons of southern Africans from before and after contact with Europeans, assessing changes in health, disease and ways of life in frontier communities; these new data can clarify how a particular contact affects the local population. Studies of skeletons from successive time periods in Nubia, Egypt, or Mali could add to knowledge about health and population diversity over time.[3] In these examples, archaeology or historical texts have identified the subjects. The biological anthropologist then provides data to shed more light on, or add dimensions to, what is known about the peoples or societies of interest. The unique methods of physical anthropology provide a biological viewpoint on "historically" known (at some level) communities.[4]

In addition to research such as this, which could be called "social biology,"[5] one type of "history," which could be called biohistory or biological history, places biology first. This history most often refers to the microevolution of populations, and the processes involved, as having generated current patterns of genetic and morphological diversity. A few studies have examined available biological data from the various regions of Africa and attempted to explain current continental patterns of serogenetic and morphological variation.[6] Also, numerous studies use DNA, although samples are usually small. These studies make an effort to infer process from pattern, and "process" here, unlike in other situations, becomes nearly synonymous with "history," a term that can be problematic.[7]

This assessment may be too positive, however, for at the root of much discussion on genetics and African history lies the concept of race, which is greatly influenced by ideal typological thinking. The concept presupposes primordial units of analysis ("races") that permit a deductive approach to explaining the biology of peoples in some total sense. This approach explains much by migration/colonization and admixture.

The issues are many. Should the units of analysis be geographical spaces, with research focusing on the biological histories of populations in regions and their interconnections? Would the "history" be better served if the subjects were "ethnic groups" and the work attempted to unravel genealogical relationships? Could "African history" be served by understanding the "history" of certain biological traits, in the sense that the concepts of adaptive selection or genetic drift from evolutionary theory would "explain" the presence of particular characteristics in certain environments? What is the "history" that bio-anthropology can help elucidate? Can it produce, or help produce, a "narrative" outside of "evolutionary" time in the macro sense, say of the time depth that Africanist historical linguists would give the major language families of Africa (i.e., between ten and fifteen thousand years ago), truly a *longue duree*, as Braudel might say?[8] Again, is it to "trace" or attempt to infer the biology of historically known groups or the "history" of biological traits, or disease patterns over time in particular regions, or their cause? Indeed, might biological history encompass all of these?

What about the term "reconstruction"? Is it proper to say that the purpose is to "reconstruct" African history? Properly speaking, reconstruction of something can only take place if the original is known. A goal of recovering African history would involve examination of various kinds of sources and data, to construct a historical narrative consistent with available information. The writing of history requires a critical interrogation of sources.[9] A coherent structure, as sources permit, is sought.[10]

No doubt for some scholars these questions are not important because the historical inquiry can benefit from any information that allows an explanation of particular events or outcomes in terms of unique factors. But "biological history" may often not be workable outside of general principles or theory. For example, the issue of the "peopling" of the African continent must be addressed in both evolutionary and historical terms. Certain situations can illustrate biological change in a socially defined group. For example, the Gnawa, a social group in Morocco whose primary occupation is music and who have a quasi-religious social function, are said to have originated in the Sahel belt region.[11] They are generally believed to have been slaves in social-status origin and are said to have had a Sahel belt West African physiognomy in the mid-twentieth century. However, by the end of the century the group contained many individuals who were closer to a typical Moroccan appearance (personal observation). Assuming that adaptive microevolution had hardly any role, was this change in appearance due to intermarriage by Gnawa with local people, with descendants of such unions being identified as Gnawa (emically or etically)? Or, was it due to recruitment or assimilation by the Gnawa of others, who thus became Gnawa by choice? Has sexual selection from within the Gnawa (perhaps highly variable from the start) produced the change internally? Or are all of these processes at work? As the Gnawa are still very much with us, it would be easy enough to ask their elders what has happened in the last several generations. Genetic studies on the oldest living members of the group and their descendants could generate a transgenerational "genetic history" of the group, and because we could collect genealogical information on spouses or recruits defined as non-Gnawa *in origin*, we could test various hypotheses depending on the group's demographic structure. We could compare different Gnawa sub-groups. Depending on general trends and mores in Moroccan society (and the wealth of the Gnawa?), we might be tempted to hypothesize or predict what will happen to the Gnawa physiognomy over time. This, of course, would not be "history" at this point, but is worth considering. It is quite possible that in the future the Gnawa, whose genesis lay across the desert in a biological and cultural (style of music) sense, will be transformed such that, although still known as Gnawa, their faces will not distinguish them from the Moroccan average. (A range of physical traits has been evident in Morocco and supra-Saharan Africa from ancient times, hence we can only speak of an average, knowing it to be different from that of, for example, contemporary Senegal.) An ethnic (socio-cultural) group may "diversify" biologically and genealogically by the assimilation of outsiders, or even change completely in the visible traits of which so much has been made (skin color, lip form, nose form, etc.), unless the group's cultural rules will not allow people with such a range of appearances to be members. (It is hard to imagine an Afrikaner who looks like Nelson Mandela, but apparently a few Afrikaners are genealogically in part the descendants of indigenous Africans.[12] Therefore, the distinction between a "remote" connection and the possession of traits to which there can be a *social reaction* must be made. Nonetheless, only in recent times have physical traits been used as the foundational basis for social identities or defining social groups.)

Likewise a group having particular physical traits could change culture (and language) in particular sociopolitical environments over time, without intermarriage, thus changing ethnicity but retaining the biological traits of its ancestors (e.g., the "arabization" of some Nubian groups, and even earlier, some Egyptian communities). Of course there is a problem here since many from the Arabian peninsula were East African in origin in early Islamic armies;[13] also the range of variation of ancient indigenous "Arabs" is yet unknown. There could be many permutations of these biocultural scenarios. Furthermore, the scenarios presented, though heuristic and having real examples, have problems in terms of categories like ethnicity and race (although this latter term was not used). Ethnic boundaries and the acceptability of physical variation are socially mediated and negotiated, and values could shift over time. Perceptions by outsiders may differ about the meanings of various terms in different epochs. For example, Shakespeare's Othello is called a Moor and described as having black skin and full lips, yet the "Moors" of Mauritania today do not generally fit this description and may consider it outside of their somatic norm; they may even seldom refer to themselves as Moors. We might speculate that, of the Muslims encountered by early Europeans, those most unlike them physically were best remembered.

Many issues and themes have been raised, and will recur, in this chapter. The "problem" of the proper use of the term "biological history" can be set aside as we address roles for physical anthropology in African history, or perhaps better still, historiography. "Biological history" as a concept will be continuously questioned, however.

Physical anthropology has as its potential material for study both living and skeletal samples.

The living offer the opportunity to understand aspects of recent events (in Braudel's sense), for example, the results on growth patterns of a historically known famine, lowered crop yields, forced migration, use of vitamin supplements, etc., for one population versus another in the same country. As already noted, the genetic sampling of living groups in order to infer process from pattern (as historical linguists do), and to attempt a microevolutionary history, might help tell a story of the generation of biological populations now known by certain ethnic labels. Ethnicities, of course, are known to be quite fluid.

Skeletal samples of groups long dead offer the opportunity under the right conditions (and with constraints) to study demography, health and disease states, body build and posture, microevolution, and possible genetic relationships and connections, as demonstrated by the late Lawrence Angel in *The People of Lerna* (1971).[14] Such studies can be modestly attempted with even small samples, by a knowledgeable researcher. The ideal "right conditions," however, would be very large samples with males, females, and subadults, from different but temporally narrow levels of the same site, covering a thousand years or more and with sufficient contextual data. These conditions do not exist for any one site, as far as can be ascertained; even predynastic Egypt, for which a skeletal record has been preserved, leaves much to be desired. Clearly the issue of population replacement (by another group) would be of interest, and biological anthropologists have also addressed the issue.[15] A combination of standard morphometric methods, plus ancient DNA techniques (that permit the evaluation of DNA from skeletal remains), enlarges possibilities.

Biological anthropology can help add to the context of past social actors, facilitating a more "inside" view of their circumstances as advocated in principle by Collingwood.[16] A detailed skeletal analysis of remains from a site could contribute to understanding the factors impinging on a past community's life.[17] This would clearly be a "historical" use of human biology, in that it is particularistic.[18] Explanations in history versus those in science can generally be said to be differentiated by the degree of reliance on general theoretical constructs.[19] "Scientific" explanations explain change and phenomena in terms of general theoretical principles, deemed to be "laws." Historians emphasize the unique and contingent circumstances in which events occur.

This chapter will not fully explore the philosophical and theoretical issues raised about human biology and history in the African sphere, but some of these will be recurrent themes. Skeletal biology is the subarea most likely to contribute to African history. Its possibilities, plus some discussion of genetics, will be presented below, with three major areas to be covered: lifeways, health and disease states, and population affinity and relationships. Some discussion on the legacy and persistence of the race concept/construct in African history, unfortunately physical anthropology's best-known impact on the field, will also be presented. Population genetics has taken up where the "old" biological anthropology left off. These studies, while holding out much promise, have also sometimes been carried out under the racial paradigm, with predictable results.

Archaeological Populations: Sampling Issues

The recovery of biological information from a skeletal (archaeological) population, although providing useful information, does have limitations. Skeletons from a single site are not necessarily from one generation, and indeed may span thousands of years. Hence some method of periodization is advisable, and without it only the most general statements are possible. Skeletal series are samples of samples. Several nonbiological factors indicate how much the skeletal sample is a subset of those who have lived at a given time, which influences the number of remains available. These factors include the proportion of those dying who are buried at the site studied, the proportion of those buried who survive to discovery, the proportion discovered, and the total recovered.[20] To these can be added the number shipped to a museum or university, especially after the excavations of the nineteenth and twentieth centuries, as well as the proportion of these in good enough condition to study the specific problem at hand, and the reasons for saving the remains in the first place.[21]

Lifeways

Bone has plastic qualities. The forces exerted by muscles, differential weight bearing, and habitual postures can all affect the shape of various bones.[22] Based on accumulated observations and analogic reasoning, one can interpret bony changes and construct an account that may be a fair representation of the lifeways of past peoples, as well as how lifeways may have changed.[23] "Lifeways" here broadly refers to the totality of activity patterns, cultural practices, and range of activities in a community. The recovery of aspects of lifeways may provide insight into the daily lives of individuals and groups. The nonskeletal archaeological data and their interpretation provide a larger context for the interpretation of the biological remains.

Activity patterns can be surmised from tooth wear, variations in joints, and the differences in shape and robustness between left and right sides in paired long bones.

Tooth wear refers to alteration in shape of the enamel and dentin of the tooth by abrasion or erosion. Some wear results from the use of the dentition as a tool,[24] a practice that continues in some human communities. Grooves in the anterior teeth occlusal surfaces have been noted to occur when materials are used to prepare materials for other uses. Greater wear on the anterior teeth is more generally found among hunters and gatherers than agriculturalists,[25] the latter having instead a cupped ("scooped out") wear pattern on the molars.[26] Occlusal patterns of wear have been observed to differ among agriculturalists and hunter-gatherers from different environments,[27] the former showing highly angled wear planes and the latter a pattern of even and flat erosion. The differences have been attributed to variation in the masticability of diet, with agriculturalists having a "softer" diet. However, such differences have not been consistently noted between agriculturalists and nonagriculturalists.[28] Dental wear patterns can nonetheless be useful at the conceptual level, beyond assessing economy (in circumstances where other data are scarce); the existence of different wear patterns implies variability in activities and foods. The level of heterogeneity in a site or setting would interest historians, as would the specific meanings. Possible differences in the wear pattern between sexes may allow inferences about variability of diets and activities. Between-group variability in wear between those from elite and lower status cemeteries or burials may suggest social class differences.

If serial chronological samples are available, changes in wear patterns can be used to infer changes in diet or the use of teeth as tools, thus revealing an aspect of life not necessarily in the archaeological or written record.

The issue of data sources and research design in terms of categories must be noted here, although it is beyond the scope of this presentation. Data collected from groups termed "hunters-gatherers" and "agriculturalists" present problems because the categories suggest absolute bounded sets of ways of living, and have their roots in problematic social evolutionary models.[29]

Dental mutilation also involves the deformation of calcified tooth tissues. It is easily imaginable that the shaping of teeth, or selective removal of them, can be markers of "ethnicity" under the assumption that these represent ritualized behavior. In Africa dental evulsion is known from the epipalaeolithic Maghreb[30] and from the recent Sudan.[31] Hence the alteration of teeth as functions of diet or use as tools or as cultural markers may inform the historian about various facets of life "on the ground." These kinds of data may sometimes be used as evidence in postulating historical continuity in a region.

Craniofacial form may also vary as a function of cultural practice or diet. Deliberate cranial deformation was practiced in various populations.[32] This would also have value in social interpretations when comparing skeletal populations synchronically or diachronically. Palate dimensions and masticatory muscle attachments vary with types, or levels of preparation, of foodstuffs.[33] Changes in diet could have long-term effects on craniofacial form; for example, Nubian craniofacial form may have changed (evolved) in situ from epipaleolithic through neolithic periods as a response to the alteration in diet.[34] It is hypothesized that the softer diet of the agriculturalists made the more massive craniofacial skeleton less necessary. Perhaps those with smaller facial skeletons and teeth, theoretically requiring less energy for growth and development and less protein, would experience a differential survival. Another explanation for this aspect of Nubian "biohistory" is that the later Nubians were not primarily or at all the descendants of the epipalaeolithic people. (Population replacement would be the hypothesis.) This is one instance where a general principle (either adaptive or "relaxed" selection) is used to explain a diachronic change, thus again raising the issue of "biohistory." However, this concern, although a return to it is unavoidable, may be overdone. It is important to recall that Nubia (and Egypt) are African regions where the mechanism of culture and historical change was frequently postulated in the past to be due to migrations. At one level conceptually this view is a "historical" explanation due to the specificity and contingency implied in migrations. At another level, however, migration was defined as an inflexible principle: culture change always meant new people who had migrated from a different locale and had different, usually advanced, culture.

Another aspect of activity can be inferred from joint variation, which can be categorized as pathological or nonpathological.[35] Biologists have noted skeletal modifications believed to be primarily caused by squatting. Anatomical features on the bones of the ankle, knee and foot joints have been noted. While anthropologists have generally viewed the changes, usually bony extensions or facets, as being due to squatting, other activities causing flexion and extension might be responsible.[36] Generically such changes can, however, be viewed as due to repetitive activities, which may be inferred with the use of other information. In the upper extremity, changes around the glenohumeral (shoulder) joint may indicate something about daily activities such as hammering. The humerus may hypertrophy in response to activity,[37] and the site of muscle attachment may be more pronounced.

Pathological joint variation would include changes associated with osteoarthritis, which is also called degenerative joint disease and hypertrophic arthritis.[38] This is usually seen in individuals who have been involved in activities that cause long-term repetitive stress to joints. However, one form, traumatic osteoarthritis, may be seen in a young person whose injury has crushed the articular surface. Arthritis is a disease of synovium and cartilage of a joint but with progression may extend to include changes at the joint margins and surfaces in the bone. This severity of disease is recognizable in a skeleton. Osteoarthritis in elbow joints has shown sex differences in agricultural communities and has also been related to corn grinding, other plant processing, or use of the atlatl.[39]

The distribution of arthritis or joint changes in a skeleton likely reflects the major activities. Skeletal biologists have been able to validate the use of these patterns by ethnographic accounts of behaviors. For example, some Inuit males have shown a pattern of arthritis that correlates with hunting activities, specifically kayak paddling and harpoon throwing, whereas females showed a high incidence of temporomandibular joint disease, which likely reflects the jaw action associated with hide softening.[40]

Osteoarthritis, in some archaeological populations, shows association with social rank. An analysis of early native American samples from the Middle Woodland period indicates that higher-status individuals had different patterns and lower degrees of pathology, thus suggesting a different group of behaviors. However osteoarthritis may also have a genetic component.[41]

Studies for activity patterns of early skeletons in earlier African societies, even those of the Nile Valley, are few. As to osteoarthritis, Judd has shown a different pattern for spinal osteoarthritis for women and men at Kerma.[42] Women have a higher proportion of cervical disease, which may suggest they were more engaged in potterage.

Patterns of longbone fractures may give some indication about behavior, at least for the snapshot of skeletal sample. Random fractures of upper and lower extremities may merely reflect the dangers of agricultural life;[43] high numbers of ulnar fractures, caused when an attempt is made to block a blow, may suggest a situation where interpersonal violence is common.

The cited skeletal changes, while largely validated, still require interpretation with other data. The same changes may be caused by different activities. Osteoarthritis also is a function of aging and general health, hence caution is required in the construction of what can be called the osteobiography of a site, or biohistory of time-successive samples.

Health and Disease

Palaeopathology has the potential to serve historians by providing information about disease in specific ecological, social and "historical" situations. The term *palaeopathology*, like "ancient DNA" refers not only to work on very old remains, but to that on skeletal populations that may be less than a century old.

Skeletal analyses can provide reasonable data for understanding the growth and development, infectious risk, and physiological challenges of youth in earlier populations.[44] Space considerations do not permit a detailed survey of all topics of interest to palaeopathologists. Some are covered elsewhere,[45] and those chosen here are more likely to be of interest to historians.

One "voice" frequently omitted from history is that of the child. The study of adolescent and preadolescent remains to ascertain health may illuminate social and physical environmental quality.[46] Unfortunately, the remains of large numbers of children are not usually available in museum collections, for reasons that include poor preservation and perhaps lack of interest on the part of early twentieth-century excavators. (Current workers attempt to save all remains.) However, adult remains can also provide data, as the skeleton may preserve evidence of physiological challenges that occurred in childhood. Pathological markers of stress can be divided into those reflective of episodic and chronic disease, broadly defined.[47] Both groups can be found in teeth and bone. Episodic markers include linear enamel hypoplasias and Harris lines. Chronic markers include porotic hyperostosis, stature, and skull base height.

Linear enamel hypoplasias are defects of tooth crowns that can be observed by the naked eye, or at another level by microscopic techniques. They are caused by the arrest or decreased secretion of enamel by ameloblasts during the development of the crown.[48] Enamel completion occurs for the teeth of interest by the age of eight or nine. (The third molar, or wisdom tooth, is unstable in its development and is generally not used as a primary health data source.) Ameloblast activity may be compromised by general physiological challenges such as poor nutrition or episodes of infectious disease. Hypoplasias were noted to frequently correspond to recalled disease episodes of childhood.[49] However, not all individuals with moderate or severe illness will sustain defects on even the most sensitive teeth (i.e., the upper central incisors and lower canines, favored by palaeopathologists, which develop roughly between birth and five to six years of age).[50] The premolars and molars are less sensitive to growth-disturbing insults. Hence this lesion is not perfect. Nevertheless it quantifies aspects of the health experiences or history of individuals and "populations" (to the degree that an archaeological series can represent the latter).

Harris lines are also indicators of growth arrest, but found on the metaphyses of long bones. They are likewise found in growing individuals, but can only be identified by X-ray. Also, not all individuals having a general physiological challenge will manifest a lesion. Harris lines pose a problem: they may become undetectable because bone, unlike enamel, does remodel, thus obscuring the number of episodes of growth disruption experienced.

Porotic hyperostosis, or more generally skull vault and orbital porosities, are believed to generally be indicative of iron-deficiency anemia,[51] especially if associated with bone thickening. Other anemias, including those of genetic aetiologies (sickle cell, thalassemia), may be responsible, along with Vitamin D and C deficiencies, but the latter cases show less or no skull-vault thickening. The pathophysiology of the lesions is not well understood. In classic porotic hyperostosis, it is hypothesized that compensatory marrow hypertrophy causes pressure necrosis on the outer skull

the ultimate origin of new genetic variation. The three basic microevolutionary processes are adaptation, genetic drift, and gene flow.[57] Adaptation refers to what is called natural selection, transgenerational differential survival due to the advantage conferred by some particular gene. Genetic drift can be described as random diachronic genetic change due to nonrepresentative reproduction of the gene pool from one generation to the next, that is, from sampling error. A special case of this is founder effect, in which a genetically nonrepresentative subset of a population migrates elsewhere, and starts (founds) a new population with different gene frequencies; all things being equal, over time this new population will continue a different genetic pattern from its "parent." Gene flow refers to the genes received by mating with individuals of another "distinct" population. To measure this, obviously, the genetic variants that "distinguish" the groups would have to be measured.

In a hypothetical example, if significant incorporation of outsiders who were on average biologically "different" occurred, in a process of total biocultural assimilation, then this group with ethno-cultural continuity would have also "gained" a biological relationship with another group, that is, a new biological heritage, an additional genealogy. The group, across time, would be categorically the same ethnically (socioculturally) and yet also have "foreign" ancestry—enough to make it different from its ancestral group. In fact, it could be nearly as different from the ancestral group as a biologically foreign group that entered the region and then adopted in toto the culture of the resident population. Other scenarios can be envisioned in which biology is "unchanged" but cultural continuity is broken. And how can we know if the cultural replacement was by a group that biologically was not significantly different, or vice versa? Many of our techniques, but more important our worldviews, search for discontinuities and emphasize these. It may not be possible to firmly answer questions about the meaning of diachronic differences in biology and culture in even a single locale. Much depends on the time scale and the gap between samples. It is important to keep this in mind for the ensuing discussion of (biological) population histories. Issues of identity, continuity, geography, migration, gene flow, linguistic shift, population extinction, and micro demography will clearly confound our efforts.

The Problem of Race

African peoples are among the subjects in various works on "race." Several earlier books have had an enduring impact on the description and interpretation of aspects of the biology of African peoples. These will be used as the references for ideas that need criticism because of their ongoing influence, which is sometimes not recognized by current writers from various fields.

Seligman's *The Races of Africa*, Coon's *The Origin of Races*, and *The Living Races of Mankind*—the "classic" works with concepts that still permeate discussions about African peoples[58]—are fundamentally organized around the concept/construct of race. This tradition was largely (but not completely) broken by Hiernaux in *The People of Africa* in 1975.[59]

Although deemed passé officially by most anthropologists, the race concept and racial thinking underlie much of the interpretation of molecular or morphological diversity. Racial thinking and interpretation as discussed here connotes a form of typological (Platonist) discourse. Plato postulated that reality was actually composed of pure essences or *eidos* (types), and that variation from these represented imperfection.[60] In the extreme racial world view, human biological variation is conceptualized as being explicable in terms of racial types. These "types" are treated as primordial fundamental or even foundational units. Individuals or populations who do not conform to the types are interpreted as being the products of admixture between them. In concrete terms, the races in earlier works were *defined* entities, and definitions were based on constellations of anatomical traits, especially those of the face and head, and their bony substructure. These definitions were largely abstractions although based on some observation and can be called ideal types. In some earlier works, the hypothesized basic units were called "primary races," and others usually conceptualized as the products of admixture between them, designated "secondary races."[61] It is easy to see that since a *type* must conform to a definition, that variation from it ("imperfection") must be explained. (The word "type" implies that all individuals bearing its name must be nearly uniform, in strict usage.) "Human diversity" in this approach would be understood as the variation represented by the fundamental types (races) and the interactions between them that produced admixed groups.

Racial thinking has other components. These include accepting the actual racial schema or taxonomies that were developed, the implicit or explicit idea that races "emerged" in distinct widely separated geographical cradles, and—most important for Africanists—"stereotyped notions about which set of traits most authentically represents each continent."[62] This last is especially critical since the concept of what is understood to be biologically African has frequently been a restricted range of physiognomical "types" even from sub-Saharan Africa. This is not a minor issue because the notion of race is "historicized" in such a way that the names of the well-known racial ("Mongoloid," "Caucasian," "Negroid") taxa *imply* a geographical origin. For example, the narrow noses of some Fulani, Somali, Nubians, and Masaai are frequently called "Caucasian"; because of the equation of names with definitions, and terms being theory-laden, this would suggest to many that these narrow noses are the result of gene flow (admixture) between "Caucasians" and "Negroes," even without knowledge of the Hamitic hypothesis. Notions of causation are built into the terms, and they should not be used in adjectival form, or at all for that matter.

This may be problematic for some who might reason by analogy and extrapolation from personal experience that individuals or groups with "nonstereotyped" or "intermediate" traits are the products of matings between "different races." Although the word "race" here is inappropriate, for reasons discussed later, their observations are not to be denied. However, their experience derives from circumstances in which people from regions and populations with usually notably different anatomical traits did exchange genes. This historically known situation is very different from one in which there is no evidence for the massive migration and contact required for admixture as the primary explanation for a particular combination of traits. This way of interpreting human variation across vast regions in Africa or any other continent fails to take other evolutionary mechanisms into account. It also presumes that the biology of the ancestors was little different from their descendants, and from any time depth. Races, being defined as "types," are constrained to being static entities, since any difference from the type would constitute a violation of its definition. While few workers adhere to a strict racio-typological perspective in theory, this mode of thinking is still influential. An example for Africa is Coon's postulating[63] that *in origin* supra-Saharan and Saharan African populations are an admixture of indigenous (specifically "Bushman") groups and invading Europeans or European-derived peoples. This way of thinking can still be found in the literature.

In the racial paradigm, as noted, human variation is conceptualized as being fundamentally organized into several distinct units comprised of nearly uniform individuals ("types"). "Individuals by definition are more similar to each other in all measurable parameters, and any individual can serve as a representative of the group."[64] The "measurable parameters" include traits beyond those used to define the type (race), and it is assumed that boundaries marked out by the defining traits would hold up when other traits are used. In other words, concordance is expected.

Furthermore, the type concept implies that any individual can represent the group.

It is important to understand that zoologists not interested in humans have long questioned the validity of the subspecies rank to which race corresponds in the Linnean taxonomic hierarchy.[65] Subspecies were largely defined as types. Zoologists largely critiqued the subspecies for its typological qualities, which implied absolute boundaries. Subspecies were delimited by external anatomical traits coupled with geographical information (a flaw if criteria are to be strictly biological). The subspecies rank is officially recognized by zoologists and covered by the Law of Priority, which acknowledges the first name registered for a newly discovered subspecies.

The problems with subspecies as taxa (actual living organisms) have been noted to be numerous.[66] These include (1) the nonconcordance of traits, (2) the existence of clines, (3) the presence of demes, (4) polytopicity, and (5) the arbitrariness of the criteria used to delimit subspecies. It is important to note that the issue emerged as to whether or not subspecies were units of evolution or simply collections of populations that were named for convenience.

Nonconcordance refers to the observation that individuals may form one set of groups based on a particular battery of traits, and other very different units if other traits are used. Different groupings of the same individuals could occur. The term *cline* refers to the finding that traits may vary gradually across geography, and sharp discontinuities do not exist. Human examples include skin color and nasal width. Clines are normally thought of as reflecting varying selective forces, but kin-structured founder effects could create them.[67] Demes are sharply demarcated populations that have good concordance of traits and are true breeding units; these have been found within subspecies that were defined by a few external anatomical traits. In polytopicity, the "same" constellation of traits used to define a unit is also found in another place, quite some distance away. An example from living *Homo sapiens* would be the "taxa" "Oceanic Negroes" and "African Negroes," as found in older texts. The question for taxonomists in the abstract or concrete example was, should these people be lumped together because of their similarity in certain traits? Simple similarity has frequently been taken (incorrectly) to mean a recent common origin or direct derivation. Zoologists observed polytopicity frequently. It caused a problem for the taxonomists, who raised the issue, previously mentioned, of the purpose of taxonomy below the species level: was it to depict microevolutionary relationships, or provide a pigeonholing device for classification? In the case of the Melanesians and New Guineans ("Oceanic Negroes"), nuclear DNA and serogenetic (blood group and proteins) clearly place them much nearer to far East Asians than to stereotypically defined Africans.[68] Finally, it is to be noted that zoologists used varying criteria for deciding when a group or population under study should be raised to the level of subspecies and official recognition. Thus, consistency was a problem.

The criticisms of the classical subspecies indicate that each is a special case, strictly speaking, in that all subsequent variation is interpreted within a classification scheme based on variations of particular characters (e.g., coat color), irrespective of their biological meaning. Subspecies were typologically defined in terms of trait complexes. Using strictly genetic criteria derived from documented breeding populations, geneticists have developed criteria that indicate significant divergence of populations within a species deserving of the designation "subspecies."[69] The emphasis is on breeding population, which connotes the concept of a mating system. The range of variation of individuals within a breeding population may be immense.

Further criticisms can be made of the biological race (subspecies) concept as applied to humans. It must be reiterated that the objects of the critique are groups based on morphological traits, and that the racial paradigm implies a distinctiveness for these groups, a coherence in numerous biological systems, which would reproduce similar groupings out of the same set of individuals. Nonconcordance has been described at the level of group classification and exists because the traits used to define human "racial types" are not genetically linked. A narrow nose and thin lips can be found associated with black skin and frizzy hair, as well as light skin and wavy or straight hair. It has been found, using serogenetic data, that the within-group variation is greater than that between the groups (races) of the standard racial scheme.[70] This means that numerous individuals are more similar to individuals outside their own "race" for traits other than the morphological ones used to establish the groups. Direct lineage data are provided by mitochondrial DNA and Y-chromosome variants that are transmitted through the female and male lines respectively. Studies of individuals from around the world having different morphologies (i.e., from different "races") show individuals frequently clustering with those from different groups.[71] Exclusively "racial" clustering is rare, indicating that there are no coherent lines of descent. The findings probably reflect the manner in which individuals left Africa in the process of global colonization and before the demonstrable emergence of the current morphologies found in various regions. Evidence exists that the greatest longstanding diversity is in Africa.[72]

Studies of various genetic systems that use the received races as units of analysis indicate so-called divergence times of more than 120,000 B.P. for the initial split within the species. However, no modern humans were known to be outside of Africa at this time. These "divergence" times likely represent population expansions and differentiation within Africa.[73] The various studies that claim to show racial divergence times actually reveal the times of differentiation of the particular genes used. These genes are not linked to the multiple genes responsible for skin color, hair form, nasal width, facial profile, and so forth (i.e., the trait complexes used to define "racial types.") Only a study that could show the divergence times of these polygenic traits as complexes would evince "racial divergence" if the validity of the race category for humans is accepted. This is a tall order, given that these traits are not linked, that is, no race gene or chromosome is known. At what point in time the current molecular profiles now observed with certain morphologies became associated is not known. To reiterate, they are *casually* and not *causally* associated. There is no deterministic relationship. "The phrase *racial divergence*, in a strict sense, must first imply the appearance of the morphologies used to define races."[74] Modern human biological evolutionary history or variation is not described by the phrase "racial divergence." Infraspecific human variation does not conform to a simple bifurcational splitting model whose distinctiveness reaches a value indicative of the existence of subspecies.[75]

Classification systems should logically be exhaustive and mutually exclusive. Exhaustive means they account for all objects subject to classification. Mutual exclusivity means the object being classified should belong to only one group. The tripartite racial system (the broadest) fails on both points in obvious, and not so obvious, ways. The lack of true boundaries has already been discussed but can be amplified. In terms of morphology, not all living "nonadmixed" individuals will fit into any of the received racial taxa. It is also observed that the application of different traits may lead to an individual being placed in different groups. Some molecular studies have shown groups switching between "races" on repeated analyses. These genetic studies use probabilistic models in the generation of dendrograms, tree-like representations postulated as depicting infraspecific biogeographical structure (either a phylogenetic "history" or just degrees of relationship). A sample of Berber speakers in one study shifts between clustering with Europeans and a select (stereotypical) group of tropical Africans, and statistical significance for "treeness" was not attained.[76] This further reveals one of the problems with the race concept. Incidentally, that the forensic uses of DNA frequently successfully place people in groups called "races" does not negate the critique, because the forensic applications use probabilistic models based on synchronic biological snapshots of the living reference populations, and current (accidental) associations between some DNA variations and certain physiognomies (races). This is identification, not taxonomic classification.[77] If the same DNA markers now associated with "northern Europeans" were found from samples in New Guinea (or Central Asia, or the Maghreb) dating to 60,000 years ago, they could not be called "northern European" since there were no northern European *Homo sapiens sapiens* at this time. All of these observations indicate that the biological boundaries implied by the morphological definitions of the received racial taxa are nonexistent, and that the taxa are not foundational units, consisting of uniform individuals having coherent lines of descent from unique origins.

Furthermore, it is worth noting that the received racial taxa are not themselves breeding units (mating systems). They are based on traits not demography. Therefore the assembly of random individuals from these groups does not constitute a real population unit. However, this does not mean that a breeding group of individuals with similar morphologies is not possible, or does not exist. It does mean that it is possible to have a mating system, that is, a breeding population, that has individuals having diverse morphologies.

A "Prospectus" for African Biological Population History

The discussion about race and other ways of thinking about biological variation is relevant to any discussion of "African biological history," which must be understood as a problematic and something perhaps to be yet defined or better still described. What is covered by this phrase? Is it the microevolutionary "history" of biological populations (mating systems), traits, or trait complexes (such as the elongated physiognomy elucidated by Hiernaux,[78] which exists in speakers of all of the larger African language families)? Or is its subject matter the regional biological populations of Africa viewed through objective time in the search for origins, changes, or the lack of them? Or is African biological history, the "history" of the biology of the speakers of particular languages, language families or "ethnicities," or, more accurately, "communities"?

Perhaps the answer is all of these. The exploration of this requires revisiting some of the previously mentioned genetic work. African population biological history can be schematicized as having geographical and temporal dimensions. There are several considerations that relate to periodization. First there is the issue of when to speak of *African* versus general *human* biological history. Both of these cover long time spans. The "middle range" of time might include the early communities suggested by some historical linguists[79] that appear in the reconstructions of families as their "genealogies" are constructed. Next would be the later communities recovered by archaeology (and also linguistics), along with even later periods in which "ethnicities" become visible up through the present time. African biological history can be conceived as the study of the pathways—and the processes driving them—that account for current observable patterns of variation at the gene, character, and population levels.[80] However, the issue of the possible adaptive value of different nasal shapes, varying skin colors, permutations of body forms, et cetera, as addressed by Hiernaux,[81] is clearly an evolutionary question whose temporal dimensions cannot be addressed with confidence. The skeletal record is incomplete. Although a "unique" African biohistory can be said to begin after there are modern people outside of Africa, the long view is difficult to narrate. It would be dependent on relatively unbroken archaeological sequences containing human remains from all locales. These would still be difficult to "historicize" in terms of the present since sociocultural "identities" are the basis of communities. Perhaps the aforementioned "middle range" is the place to start the recovery and construction of African history. Even at this time period determining the concrete units of analysis is difficult.

It is possible to develop various frameworks for studying African biological population history, with the clear understanding that the goal is to describe African realities. The concept of "biological African" logically refers to those whose population "histories" have occurred in Africa. The *locale* of biological history is the objective basis on which to structure any enquiry of biological Africanity. The focus is on indigenous peoples and regions known to have indigenous populations in a biological sense, even if this is now somewhat obscured by socially constructed conceptualizations. Of interest is developing a critical approach to reading the human genetics literature, treating it as a source and not the final word as a narrative.

A synthesis of data from genetics, paleontology, and geography with a due consideration of the time of occurrence of datable events leads to the understanding that we can think in terms of *African biohistorical variants*. This is an advance over the raciotypological paradigm that dictates a particular mode of thinking and interpretation. It is worthwhile reviewing some of the findings that allow a basic framework for examining African biological population history. This is useful in order to construct a method of approach to the biological population history of geographical regions and ethnic groups, as well as helping to explore the possible explanations for specific cellular, molecular, or morphological traits. The fundamental theoretical bias here is that anatomically modern people (modern *Homo sapiens sapiens*) emerged in Africa first and subsequently dispersed,[82] although this is not a prerequisite for the framework to be presented. There will be some repetition of previously mentioned findings. This is necessary for clarity and emphasis.

There is an unbroken record of hominid habitation of Africa.[83] Humanity's ancestors emerged there as members of the australopithicines. The australopithicines were "succeeded" by the genus *Homo*, which over the course of time gave rise to our species, and strictly speaking subspecies, since the proper designated for "modern" humans is *Homo sapiens sapiens* if taxonomic tradition is followed. However, this tradition and designation is not unmuddled by issues of interpretation and taxonomic procedure. These are beyond the scope of this presentation. What is of interest is the appearance of anatomically modern folk in Africa and their subsequent biogeography.

Fossil evidence is generally interpreted as indicating the presence of modern humans in Africa at early dates.[84] These date to 130,000–120,000 years in eastern Africa based on remains from Ethiopia, 80,000–100,000 years B.P. in southern Africa, and at least 60,000 B.P. in northwest supra-Saharan Africa.[85] The Taramsa child, from southern Egypt, is estimated to be 50,000 years old.[86] Another modern hominid from southern Egypt (Nazlet Khater) dates to approximately 33,000 years B.P.[87] While there are no complete remains of these ages from central Africa (Democratic Republic of the Congo) there is evidence for modern human behavior in this region some 80,000 to 90,000 years B.P.[88] Thus most of the regions of Africa have evidence of modern human habitation of at least 50,000 years.

Genetic data from various kinds of groups of individuals and sometimes just individuals from the various continents have been analyzed. The results of these studies have been interpreted to suggest the emergence or expansion of modern people at between 100,000 to 200,000 years ago, based in part on coalescence theory.[89] This theory predicts that the date of an ancestral gene can be estimated using mutation rates and other information. Assuming no natural selection, or disturbing extinction events, geneticists can work back from current variation to the date of an ancestral state. Genetic studies that attempt to recover the biological history of the species have generally found that there is a split between their restricted African samples and the "rest of the world."[90] These approaches conceptualize human population history as a series of bifurcations with each node being relatively uniform. The "Africans" usually used are either the short statured Aka or Mbuti, Khoisan speakers, or West African stereotypes, in keeping with a socially, not scientifically constructed concept of African.[91] The results have been interpreted as indicating a "racial divergence." Studies using individuals as the unit of analysis evince a different pattern. A select subset of Africans called the "group of 49" forms a unit versus the rest of humankind.[92] However the latter individuals ("rest of humankind") also include non-East African sub-Saharans. Hence there is no "racial" split. As has been stated, the idea that human variation can be described as being structured by subspecies (races) that are treated as lineages is fundamentally false. In actuality, also, although averages are used, the gene studies usually give us gene histories that are not necessarily the same as population histories.[93]

Synthesizing the fossil data (dates, location) with times of genetic differentiation leads to the conclusion that indigenous African variability should be tremendous. The studies interpreted as indicating an African-"non-African" divergence are actually recovering differentiation in Africa, events in early modern human history, in the view taken here. A high level of biological diversity for morphological and molecular "traits" is predicted for Africa by the various findings, the geographical structuring of early populations, and current understanding of microevolutionary processes. To this can be added time and demographic factors, including those caused by ecological changes. The length of time of human residence in Africa means a greater accumulation of mutations. This has been one of the arguments for the African single origins hypothesis—this greater diversity, specifically at the molecular level. However it has been shown that a larger population (effective population size) would be more diverse. It matters little which of these is true for this discussion, and they are not mutually exclusive propositions. What is important to understand is that this diversity is indigenous to Africa. This indigenous African diversity must be operationalized as an analytic tool.

African continental biological history can be said to begin after the appearance of people with modern morphologies outside of Africa, which occurred approximately 90,000 years B.P. in the Near East. The data taken together would seem to suggest that no regional African population could be labeled as "more" African or *the* authentic African. The so-called "Negro" morphology has no privileged place in the panorama of biological Africanity from a scientific perspective. Modern studies do indicate that some samples of supra-Saharan populations evince genetic profiles for various systems that are usually more similar to groups outside of Africa than to others within the continent. It also has been observed that supra-Saharan and Horn populations have a subset of the variation found in non-Horn tropical Africa; non-Africans have a subset of the African variation.[94] The data when interpreted in a historical causal model based on all of the evidence explains this. Biohistorically, populations from the rest of the world are derived from early supra-Saharan and eastern African groups, not vice versa. This occurred long before modern ethnicities. This is not to say that the historically (including archaeologically) known migrations had no impact, rather that the majority of the variation is more likely much older than these. In order to accurately assess how much variation in Africa (any region) is due to non-African admixture it is required that we have population unique variants ("private" alleles) in the donor groups that can be dated accurately, and to times after the colonization of the regions from which gene flow or colonization are postulated. (Otherwise it would not be possible to know that a different source was involved.) Similarity between populations in two regions must be explained in an objective time framework, not mythologized by the race construct. Supra-Saharan Africans in core origin are not European ("Caucasian") offshoots, because there were modern people in northern Africa first, and there is no indication of population extinction. The baseline variation of Africa could be deduced, theoretically, by factoring out the known migrations and settlements into the continent, after the peopling of the other continents. Of course mutation and evolution are ongoing. Recent circum-Mediterranean gene flow, and natural selection may have "homogenized" the region more in the last seven thousand years. There have yet to be done detailed studies with large samples of interior supra-Saharan, Saharan, and Nile Valley peoples from a model that integrates the fossil record, ancient DNA (Saharan, Nile Valley, and Maghreban) and the historical (including archaeological) record. Africanists can use existing studies and those of skeletal remains in the recovery of "population history" by critically integrating all of the evidence. Some scholars still work largely from the racial model that does not incorporate an understanding of the evolutionary history of modern humans in Africa.[95] These scholars still explain narrow noses and faces in large regions of Africa as being due to "Caucasian" admixture or colonization (i.e., a racial approach). Popular writers (and some scholars) will simply sometimes label a trait as "Caucasian." The cognitive map and racial paradigm supply the causation, thus "historicizing" it in terms of "racial" interaction or migration. (This is a different situation from the Gnawa.) Hiernaux[96] has developed explanations for tropical African variability based on micro-evolutionary principles. These can be extended to supra-Saharan Africa. It cannot be said enough that there is no set of traits that has a scientifically privileged place in biological Africanity.

Even in the best of circumstances, and using the most integrative approach there will be problems. Notable among these is the meaning of "population." Sometimes random samples of individuals from "races" are treated as populations; some scholars use samples from true breeding populations (mating systems). Sometimes linguistic groups have been sampled and treated as breeding groups. Africanists are fully aware that ethnicities have been created in remembered time, that breeding units split and fuse, that men and women have been biologically incorporated into societies other than their own, and that identities can be fluid. Archaeologists are aware of difficulties in equating artifacts with ethnicity, languages, and biology. What happened to language, biology, and ethnicity of the Greek colonists at Cyrenaica, or the Roman soldiers (which includes families) who settled Tunisia after the defeat of Hannibal? Who painted the Saharan rock art, and whose biological ancestors (if any) are they in terms of living groups? Do modern maraboutic families in the Sahara reflect the kind of "admixture" suggested by the mixing of genealogies described as occurring in scholarly families in Timbuktu?[97] How do we conceptualize Berber speakers who became thoroughly "Mandesized" in time and space?[98] Can we always distinguish between the possible causes of the particular patterns of biological traits within a locale? How much of the current variation in the Egyptian delta region and Algerian oases reflects the indigenous long-time biological history of Africans, versus the biocultural assimilation of non-African outsiders? How much do the external traits reflect drift, adaptation, admixture, or social and sexual selection by which humans actually "shape" features like skin color, facial form and hair type, in order to approach some idealized aesthetic norm? Did proto-Afro-Asiatic speakers all "look" the same in the beginning and then later diversify by gene flow after their migration from the Horn, and in the course of the family's historical development? Or were they highly variable from the beginning and various random events sorted them out? How did the very first Semitic speakers "look"? They seemed to have arrived in the Near East after Sumerian speakers according to one view.[99] However, perhaps this is an artifact and the Semitic languages that survived emerged late. When does the use of various kinds of data lead to circularity?

These questions provide critical examples of what we should be aware of in attempts to recover the "history" of populations.

Recovering (Biological) Population History

The issue of baseline biological variation in Africa must be considered in any efforts to recover biopopulation history. The molecular findings and palaeontological evidence when viewed in relationship to the *dates* of coalescence (and likely differentiation) and fossils clearly suggest an immense molecular genetic diversity in Africa of great antiquity. Morphological variability is also tremendous, even in tropical Africa alone, which would also suggest a long residence influenced by the various microevolutionary mechanisms. Skeletal remains are rare when the size and length of habitation of the continent are considered. In part this is an artifact of the lack of research. Only in the Nile Valley, and perhaps the Maghreb, are there remains that form a reasonable chronological series, for a restricted area, and even in these cases there are gaps and generally small sample sizes.

This background genetic variation is important to keep in mind as a backdrop to discussing shorter-term biopopulation, biocultural and ethnic, or better still community histories. Stated in another fashion, this diversity is the background against which subsequent pathways and processes of biological variation are to be modeled and understood. It can be likened to an ocean in which there are streams and currents with distinctive characteristics but are nevertheless of the ocean. The African biological world is generally not conceptualized in this fashion. Rather racial thinking, which seems to be operationalized as a theory, still has great influence. No more need be said about this other than that African (from Algerian to Zimbabwe) genetic diversity at root cannot be interpreted as the product of racial types from different homelands invading and mixing in the continent. The indigenous Berbers cannot be conceived at root as lost Europeans, nor the earliest Egyptians. While the home regions of these groups have bioculturally assimilated outsiders, and perhaps in great quantity, the evidence indicates a longstanding habitation of the areas. No studies have attempted the formidable task of factoring out the changes wrought by the non-African admixture in order to recover the probable initial genetic profiles. Of interest is how discrete any "European" genetic influence would be since some work using nuclear (recombining) DNA suggests that at least some Europeans can be conceptualized themselves as groups whose genesis is due to intermixture between those having proto-African and proto-East-Asian genetic profiles.[100]

The methods used to examine "population" history generally employ the concept of biological distance. Genetic or morphometric data from predefined groups are analyzed with various mathematical techniques in order to determine their relative similarity, which is conceived in geometrical models.[101] In most approaches the larger the biological distance the more dissimilar are the groups being compared. The degree of similarity (resemblance) is taken to indicate the degree of relationship. If only overall resemblance is considered, the type of affinity is said to be phenetic. If the data are chosen or analyzed in such a way as to recover lines of descent, the resulting taxonomy is called phyletic or cladistic. These different concepts of affinity were generally developed for taxonomic considerations at and above the species level, but are applied to studies of living humans.

After biological distances are determined the resultant matrix is usually analyzed for structure. Tree-like depictions called dendrograms can be generated by cluster analysis.[102] These group the populations by various rules. Different clustering routines can give vastly different results.[103] This is a problem given that dendrograms are frequently read as phylogenies in models of microevolution that postulate differentiation solely by isolation and drift. Geneticists have developed various methods to test for the validity of a tree-like structure in various analyses. Human diversity does not fit neatly into a fissioning model where variation is conceived as being coterminous with successive population splits productive of uniform groups. Gene exchange is ongoing; no groups are composed of uniform individuals. Also, high levels of genetic differentiation could exist within an ancestor population and a subsequent history of buddings from this group would result in "fuzzy" descendant populations that are not sharply demarcated. This is different from a situation where population division is nearly coterminous with mutation events or the "segregation" of distinct variants into different daughter populations. Gene histories and population histories are not the same. This must be kept in mind whenever reviewing biopopulation studies. It may not be possible to be certain when population divergences (for particular groups of traits) follow a linear "deterministic" versus random "stochastic" path.

The "method" used by bioanthropologists to assess population history involves inferring process from pattern, when no earlier remains are available. Current gene or morphological distributions are viewed as "structures" that can be historically explained or that can reveal aspects of history. For example Euro-South Africans have an unexpectedly high hemoglobin C frequency, which would suggest that West Africans were incorporated into that community.[104] The interpretation is largely dependent on the models brought to bear on the question. These are dependent in part on one's understanding of the biology of the traits, social processes, and histories of regions, but also on one's range of acceptable possibilities. When genes under study are known to be adaptive (e.g., sickle cell) frequencies may reflect the intensity of natural selection. If variants are neutral care still must be taken in interpretation; the age of alleles, geographical origin and distribution, and the possibility of presence in a common ancestral population as well as gene flow must be considered in attempting a historical use of these data. It will not always be possible to use the distribution of biological variants or variation to infer movements, or gene exchange. Differential distribution of rare alleles may reflect numerous processes. The place of origin and place of greatest frequency may not be the same.

Dendrograms are not the only means to depict group similarity. Ordination methods make possible a two- and three-dimensional presentation of data. These include principal components, canonical variates, principal coordinates, and related approaches.[105] These techniques place the studied groups in relation to each other in the multivariate space described by the raw data, which has been transformed to generate axes that emphasize polarities within the variation. Inspection of the groups' positions relative to each other gives an idea about relative similarity. The ordination methods also permit an understanding of differences as a part of a continuum. Again no interpretation is "automatic." Sound biological principles and theory are needed. Dendrograms are reflections of algorithms of grouping, irrespective this approach's validity in given situations. Information is lost by either method.

In summary, the view taken here is that in order to recover "population" history it is necessary to define the parameters of "population," and integrate geographical, archaeological, and skeletal data into the enquiry. It is also important to define the time frame of the investigation. Finally, it is necessary to distinguish between examining the history of particular biological traits or genetic variants and populations. At this time it has to be admitted that African data are scarce, paradigms need reworking, and the past burdens the field with problematic constructs.

Afro-Asiatic Speakers: An Exploration

It is always important to be wary of the traps of circular reasoning and affirming the consequent. Establishing many lines of independent evidence is crucial in exploring any historical question. Nevertheless if the field of inquiry is narrowed the kinds of permissible evidence are necessarily limited.

Populations may undergo various changes. These include dispersal (migration), subdivision, expansion in size, extinction, exchange of individuals or merger with other populations, and reduction in size. All of these may leave genetic signatures, but it is not clear that these can be read except when great changes have occurred. When it comes to genetic variation, for example, before admixture is invoked it has to be ascertained that the population in question could not have had high indigenous variation. This of course may not be easy, and at what point does the definition of original or indigenous have meaning, since humans can and do move between groups? Obviously, known recent contacts between peoples of very diverse origin is one situation where probabilities indicate the cause of a particular profile. This model can only with great care be extrapolated to peoples like those in the Horn or Sahara where there is great antiquity of residence.

For the historian, knowing that any particular population event occurred, such as an expansion, as inferred from mathematical analyses of genetic data, can only have meaning when given some kind of absolute or relative chronology. The possibility of associating purely biopopulation "events" with other sorts of information is the only way in which these former can become useful to historical study.

A consideration of the distribution of the Afro-Asiatic language family invites an exploration of the utility of biological, geographical and linguistic data. Afro-Asiatic languages are spoken in a modified crescent-shaped range, which stretches from northern Kenya through Ethiopia, the Nile Valley, supra-Saharan Africa, the southern Sahara-Shael, and the Near East. The genetics and anatomical variation in the African portion of these regions are on average in some sense intermediate to those of other Africans and Europeans. The word "intermediate" is chosen to convey only a position in a relational scheme. *Why* they are intermediate remains to be explored. It is also important to note that in varying degrees this is true not only for the biology of Afro-Asiatic speakers, but for that of peoples from other linguistic families, such as Nubian or Teda Nilo-Saharan speakers. This "intermediate" characterization is best gleaned by an examination of the raw data and "reading between the lines" of reports that state conclusions in terms of race, or clines. Of note is the lack of knowledge about the early inhabitants of the Arabian peninsula.

There is skeletal material from Kenya (Gamble's Cave) associated with an early Holocene culture called the Eburran.[106] The craniofacial characteristics of this material have the narrow face and nose and profile seen amongst various non-supra-Saharan Africans today, traits mistakenly called "Caucasian." The presence of these traits clearly antedates the coming of merchants or even "colonists" from Arabia in the first millennium, as evidenced by language. Some of the Gamble's Cave material will group with late dynastic northern Egyptians.[107] Under the racial paradigm the anatomy of these folk would have de-Africanized them. Today some scholars still interpret the narrower noses and faces in Ethiopia and various genetic variants as being primarily due to Arabian colonists.[108] Given the early evidence of this morphology in East Africa, the origin of Afro-Asiatic languages in the Horn region, the long presence people in East Africa, the coalescence times, and findings that illustrate gradients or clines for various alleles,[109] it is reasonable to question whether or not some of the genetic variation in the Horn attributed to Arabian migrants was not there originally. This question bears asking and repeating: What was the range of biological variation of early Afro-Asiatic speakers, and amongst the indigenous peoples of the Horn?

At the skeletal level similarities exist between the remains of material from the late Pleistocene and Holocene in a broad crescent-shaped belt from parts of East Africa through the Maghreb.[110] Unfortunately, the data are not complete, even in the sense of having remains from each country. The proper assessment of ancient populations in the regions requires the evaluation of remains from between 20,000 and 8,000 B.P. "along and beyond the Nile drainages, from the mountainous and forested terrain of Zaire to the savannah lake country, northward toward the Delta…, and finally with the chain of North African populations."[111] These regions can be conceived as containing a chain of populations represented by remains from Ishango, Elmenteita, Gamble's Cave, Wadi Halfa, Jebel Sahaba, Badari (early predynastic Egypt), Mechta, Afalou, and Taforalt. Angel noted

> Along this long line of lakes, rivers, hills and seacoast, the very linear and quite low skull vault with sloping broad forehead extends north to Egypt, but becomes broader and higher, with more vertical but pinched or relatively narrow forehead, when we reach the northwest African sites.[112]

After describing other trends, Angel postulates that there is probably "a smooth transition from the Ishango-Lothagam-Elmenteita proto-Nilotics to the Mechta-Afalou proto-Moors and proto-Berbers"; this "chain of populations" is the direct ancestors of modern Nilotics, Nubians, Egyptians, probably Libyans and Berbers. This is the far-sighted, comparative view."[113] This conclusion is reasonable and is to be seen in the context of indigenous African variability and evolution. It applies to the biology of these peoples, not to them as culturo-linguistic entities. Of interest is that the variability in this broad region, while largely clinal, is not strictly so. For example the nasal apertures of some of the Gamble's Cave (Kenya) skeletons are narrower (and higher) than that of epipalaeolithic remains from further north in the Sudan and Egypt.

The Afro-Asiatic language family seems to have originated in or near the Horn, or the Sahara.[114] Linguists, while disagreeing on details, have constructed family phylogenies that may be interpreted as suggestive of successive speech communities. The development of the current members of Afro-Asiatic passed through several stages of language diversification. One suggested construction postulates that common Afro-Asiatic diverged initially into Omotic and another group leading to the remainder of the family.[115] This latter, in turn, split into Cushitic and a speech community that develops into Chadic and a group called "Boreafrasian." Eventually ancient Egyptian (and probably some extinct related languages), Berber, and Semitic emerge from Boreafrasian. This process of subfamily development was associated with geographic spread over a vast distance. Some of this spread was due to language shift, colonization, and probably imposition. How much physical migration occurred is unknown and unknowable. Common Afro-Asiatic has no terms for food production, indicating that the initial speakers were "hunters and gatherers." The family is likely between 15,000 and 10,000 years old, with the upper limit perhaps being more likely. Given the low population density in the range of Afro-Asiatic speakers even today, it is likely that physical migration played a primary role in its spread.

This background and the consideration of the time of origin and spatial distribution of any genetic marker are the necessary tools to explore the biology of communities of Afro-Asiatic speakers. For example in order to investigate the question of migration or a traceable common biological ancestry, it would be best to have a genetic marker that arose between ten and twenty thousand years ago in the Horn. Its presence in all populations of Afro-Asiatic speakers would be circumstantial evidence for sharing of some biological ancestors. If a gene is being labeled "Semitic," then it should date to or after the time of the emergence of the ancestral proto-Semitic language, since this is the most objective use of the term "Semitic." If a genetic variant predates the emergence of a language or ethnic group then it is wrong to label it with that group's name, even if it seems confined to a specific group now.

These concepts help address the Afro-Asiatic question. There were already people in the Maghreb, Nile Valley, and Chad basin, as well as the Near East, before Afro-Asiatic's spread. Who were these people—in any sense? Is it to be assumed that they were totally replaced as in the Hamitic hypothesis? To what degree did climatic events, like the increase in Saharan water resources in the early Holocene and subsequent aridification, influence the mobility of people. The famous Saharan rock paintings suggest communities possessing a range of economies.[116] Their linguistic affiliation is unknown, but it is likely that both Nilo-Saharan and Afro-Asiatic speakers were involved.[117] The Saharan climatic cycles may have functioned as a microevolutionary "processor" and "pump"; during the wet phases more habitation (and increased population) was possible, and with increasing aridity emigration was more likely. The Egyptian predynastic is believed to owe much to Saharans.[118] These emigres and Nile Valley inhabitants likely spoke a language or languages from which ancient Egyptian emerged. Climatically linked droughts in the Sinai also likely encouraged some immigration into supra-Saharan regions and northern Egypt.

When did proto-Semitic speakers first appear in the Near East, or more accurately their ancestors speaking a still undifferentiated version of the language that was also ancestral to Berber and Egyptian? Archaeological data possibly indicate migration from Africa into the Near East at between 11,000 and 14,000 years ago, and sufficient enough to perhaps cause population pressure.[119] This is less certain, however, linguistic data have been interpreted as suggesting that the early Semitic speakers did not participate in the transition to agriculture.[120] The wheat and barley cultivated in the supra-Saharan and Nile Valley Africa, as well as the domesticated goat and sheep seem to be of Near Eastern origin.[121] Interestingly, the terms for these domesticates in Berber and Egyptian are not Sumerian or Semitic. There is no archaeological evidence, however, of a mass population movement from the Near East. Perhaps Berber emerged in situ from the common ancestor previously noted. Linguistic separation (nor genetic differentiation) times need not be coterminous with notable geographical subdivision. Proto-Chadic speakers were perhaps involved in the early Saharan way of life.

The biological variability seen among Afro-Asiatic speakers is immense and can be understood with evolutionary and "historical" approaches. It is worth noting that general clines in skin color, hair form, and other traits are to be observed from the Horn through Morocco. Interestingly, at the end of this range Berbers vary immensely in physiognomy.[122] The implications of synthesizing the fossil and genetic data have been discussed: African genetic diversity is high and has a geographical structuring, which likely reflects many processes, but primarily in situ differentiation. Accepting this diversity and assuming that the Afro-Asiatic family was spread by both migration and language shift, it is easy to envision that a subset of highly variable people from the Horn migrated northward and westward, with successive splits and subdivisions of the primary speakers and subsequent spread of the family. It is conceivable that early Afro-Asiatic speakers migrated in sufficient numbers to transmit their speech. Successive founder effects would have led to molecular and morphological differences over space and time, such that the major variability of Afro-Asiatic speakers is to be explained in evolutionary, not raciotypological terms. Their way of life, as gleaned from linguistics, indicates that intensive plant collecting was a major part of the subsistence strategy. This would have enabled the spread of the speakers and transmission of the language family in its early stage of development. By a combination of physical migration and language shift, the family at different stages was transmitted over its current geographical range, which also contained populations that may or may not have been numerically larger. It is reasonable to view Afro-Asiatic speakers as having high variability among its original speakers who also undergo differentiation in their travels. At a later period immigration into the territories of Afro-Asiatic speakers occurs from various regions.

Summary

Physical anthropology has methods of value in recovering data that can be used in the construction of the historical narratives of various African communities. Skeletal analyses can provide information useful to understanding patterns of health, lifeways, population affinity, and microevolution. The explanation of the spatial patterning of DNA and serogenetic variant in living populations requires the use of evolutionary models and other considerations to infer the causal reasons for their distributions. The racial paradigm is of no use. Genetic studies when considered with fossil data and geography suggest immense genetic variability on the continent at a date that precedes external invasion and admixture. All biological variation in Africa has to be considered against this backdrop, and in relationship to the various known climatic events and likely internal migrations.

Notes

1. C. G. Seligman, *The Races of Africa* (Oxford: Oxford University Press, 1930; reprinted 1966).

2. F. Braudel, *On History*, trans. Sarah Matthews (Chicago: University of Chicago Press, 1980); J. R. Hall, "The time of history and the history of times," *History and Theory* (1980) 19:113–31; I. Hodder, "The contribution of the long term," in I. Hodder (ed.), *Archaeology as Long-Term History* (Cambridge: Cambridge University Press, 1987), 1–8; V. Y. Mudimbe and B. Jewsiewicki, "Africans, memories and contemporary history of Africa," in *History Making in Africa: History and Theory* (1993) Beiheft 32:1–12.

3. J. Rudney, "Dental indicators of growth disturbance in a series of ancient Lower Nubian populations: changes over time," *American Journal of Physical Anthropology* (1983) 60:463–70; D. Van Gerven, D. Carlson, and A. Rohr, "Continuity and change in cranial morphology of three Nubian archaeological populations," *Man* (1977)12:270–77; S. O. Y. Keita, "Aspects of the Human Biology of Sociohistorical Change in Ancient Upper Egypt," Ph.D. diss., University of Oxford, 1997.

4. P. Rosa, "Physical anthropology and the reconstruction of recent precolonial history in Africa," *History in Africa* (1985) 12:281–305; F. P. Saul and J. M. Saul, "Osteobiography: a Maya example," in M. Y. Iscan and K. A. R. Kennedy (eds.), *Reconstruction of Life from the Skeleton* (New York: Wiley Liss, 1989), 287–302.

5. J. L. Angel, "Social biology of Greek culture growth," *American Anthropologist* (1946) 48:493–525.

6. C. Gabel, *Prehistoric Populations of Africa*, in J. Butler (ed.), *Boston University Papers on Africa*, vol. 2 (Boston: Boston University Press, 1966), 3–37; J. Hiernaux, *The People of Africa* (New York: Charles Scribner's Sons, 1975); A. J. Hausman, "Holocene human evolution in southern Africa," in J. D. Clark and S. Brandt (eds.), *From Hunters to Farmers: The Causes and Consequences of Food Production in Africa* (Berkeley: University of California Press, 1984), 261–71; L. Excoffier, B. Pellegrini, A. Sanchez-Mazas, C. Simon, and A. Langaney, "Genetics and history of sub-Saharan Africa," *Yearbook of Physical Anthropology* (1987) 30:151–94; L. L. Cavalli-Sforza, A. Piazza, and P. Menozzi, "Africa," chap. 3 in *The History and Geography of Human Genes* (Princeton: Princeton University Press, 1994).

7. R. G. Collingwood, *The Idea of History* (Oxford: Clarendon Press, 1946).

8. Braudel, *On History*.

9. Collingwood, *The Idea of History*.

10. J. Topolski, "Historical narrative: towards a coherent structure," in *The Representation of Historical Events: History and Theory* (1987), Beiheft 26:75–86.

11. Hsain Ilahiane, personal communication.

12. G. T. Nurse, H. Harpending, and T. Jenkins, "Biology and history of southern African populations," in R. J. Meier, C. Otten, and F. Abdel-Hameed (eds.), *Evolutionary Models and Studies in Human Diversity* (The Hague: Mouton, 1972), 245–54.

13. 'Abd-al-'Aziz' Abd-al-Qadir Kamil, *Islam and the Race Question* (Paris: UNESCO, 1970); M. F. Gaballah, "An Anthropological Study of Egyptians in Ancient and Recent Periods," M.D. thesis, Department of Anatomy, Cairo University (1970).

14. J. L. Angel, *The People of Lerna* (Washington, DC: The Smithsonian Institution Press 1971).

15. K. Weiss, "In search of times past: gene flow and invasion in the generation of human diversity," in N. Mascie-Taylor and G. W. Lasker (eds.), *Biological Aspects of Human Migration* (Cambridge: Cambridge University Press, 1988), 130–66.

16. Collingwood, *The Idea of History.*

17. D. W. Owsley, "Human bones from archaeological context: an important source of information," *Tennessee Anthropologist* (1983) 8:20–27.

18. I. Hodder, "The contribution of the long term," in I. Hodder (ed.), *Archaeology as Long-Term History* (Cambridge: Cambridge University Press, 1987), 1–8.

19. R. Martin, "The essential difference between history and science," *History and Theory* (1997) 36(1):1–14.

20. T. Waldron, *Counting the Dead* (Chichester: John Wiley and Sons, 1994).

21. M. Hoffman, *Egypt Before the Pharaohs* (London: Routledge and Kegan Paul, 1979).

22. H. H. Jones, J. D. Priest, W. C. Hayes, C. C. Tichenor, and D. A. Nagel, "Humeral hypertrophy in response to exercise," *Journal of Bone and Joint Surgery* (1977) 59-A:204–8.

23. C. S. Larsen, *Bioarchaeology, Interpreting Behavior from the Human Skeleton,* Cambridge Studies in Biological Anthropology 21 (Cambridge: Cambridge University Press, 1997); D. Ortner and W. G. J. Putschar, *Identification of Pathological Conditions in Human Skeletal Remains* (Washington: Smithsonian Institution Press, 1981).

24. S. Molnar, "Human tooth wear, tooth function and cultural variability," *American Journal of Physical Anthropology* (1971) 34:175–89 and S. Molnar, "Tooth wear and a culture: a survey of tooth functions among some prehistoric populations," *Current Anthropology* (1972) 13:511–26.

25. R. J. Hinton, "Form and patterning of anterior tooth wear among aboriginal human groups," *American Journal of Physical Anthropology* (1981) 54:555–64.

26. C. S. Larsen, "Bioarchaeological interpretations of subsistence economy and behavior from human skeletal remains," in *Advances in Archaeological Theory and Method* (New York: Academic Press, 1987), 339–445.

27. B. H. Smith, "Patterns of molar wear in hunter-gatherers and agriculturalists," *American Journal of Physical Anthropology* (1984) 63:39–56.

28. B. J. Schmucker, "Dental attrition: a correlative study of dietary and subsistence patterns," in C. F. Merbs and R. J. Miller (eds.), *Health and Disease in the Prehistoric Southwest,* Arizona State University Anthropological Research Papers (1985) 34:275–323.

29. J- L. Amselle, "Anthropology and historicity," in *History Making in Africa: History and Theory* (1993), Beiheft 32:12–31; J. Vansina, "Historians, are archaeologists your siblings?" *History in Africa* (1995) 22:369–408.

30. L. C. Briggs, *The Stone Age Races of Northwest Africa* (Cambridge: Peabody Museum, 1955).

31. Seligman, *The Races of Africa.*

32. E. J. Dingwall, *Artificial Cranial Deformation: A Contribution to the Study of Ethnic Mutilations* (London: University College, 1936).

33. M. McCann, D. Torney, and T. Grant, "Occlusal attrition, transpalatal dimensions and the early New Zealand Maori," *American Journal of Physical Anthropology* (1966) 25:87–90.

34. D. Carlson and D. Van Gerven, "Masticatory function and post-Pleistocene evolution in Nubia," *American Journal of Physical Anthropology* (1977) 46(3):495–506.

35. Larsen, "Bioarchaeological interpretations."

36. E. Trinkhaus, "Squatting among Neanderthals: a problem in the behavioral interpretation of skeletal morphology," *Journal of Archaeological Science* (1975) 2:327–51.

37. Jones et al., "Humeral hypertrophy in response to exercise."

38. Ortner and Putschar, *Identification of Pathological Conditions.*

39. J. L. Angel, "Porotic hyperostosis, anemias, malarias, and marshes in the prehistoric eastern Mediterranean," *Science* (1966) 153:760–63; [Miller 1982 and Haney 1974?]

40. C. F. Merbs, "Patterns of Activity-Induced Pathology in a Canadian Inuit Population," *Archaeology Survey of Canada*, Mercury Series Paper (1983), 119.

41. Larsen, *Bioarchaeology, Interpreting Behavior from the Human Skeleton.*

42. M. Judd, "Paleotrauma: A profile of personal injury during the Kerma period," *Sudan and Nubia* (2001) 5: 21–28.

43. Ibid.

44. Larsen, "Bioarchaeological interpretations"; J. E. Buikstra, "Differential diagnosis: an epidemiological model," *Yearbook of Physical Anthropology* (1977) 20:316–28; S. Kent, "The influence of sedentism and aggregation on porotic hyperostosis and anaemia: a case study," *Man* (1986) 21:605–36.

45. T. Steinbock, *Palaeopathological Diagnosis and Interpretation* (Springfield: CC Thomas, 1976); Larsen, *Bioarchaeology, Interpreting Behavior from the Human Skeleton*; Ortner and Putschar, *Identification of Pathological Conditions.*

46. M. L. Blakey and G. J. Armelagos, "Deciduous enamel defects in prehistoric Americans from Dickson Mounds: prenatal and postnatal stress," *American Journal of Physical Anthropology* (1985) 66:371–80.

47. For broader categories see A. Goodman, D. L. Martin, G. Armelagos, and G. Clark, "Indications of stress from bone and teeth," in R. Cohen and G. Armelagos (eds.), *Palaeopathology at the Origins of Agriculture* (New York: Academic Press, 1984), 13–50.

48. Alt. Goodman and J. C. Rose, "Assessment of systemic physiological perturbations from dental enamel hypoplasias and associated histological structures," *Yearbook of Physical Anthropology* (1990) 33:59–110.

49. B. G. Sarnat and I. Schour, "Enamel hypoplasia (chronologic enamel aplasia) in relation to systemic disease: a chronologic, morphologic and etiologic classification," *Journal of the American Dental Association* (1942) 29:67–75.

50. R. Huss-Ashmore, A. H. Goodman, and G. J. Armelagos, "Nutritional inference from palaeopathology," *Advances in Archaeological Method and Theory* (1982) 5:395–474; Goodman and Rose, "Assessment of systemic physiological perturbations."

51. M. K. Sandford, D. P. Van Gerven, and R. R. Meglen, "Elemental hair analysis: new evidence on the etiology of cribra orbitalia in Sudanese Nubia," *Human Biology* (1983) 55(4):831–44; P. L. Stuart-MacAdam, "Nutritional deficiency diseases: a survey of

scurvy, rickets, and iron deficiency anemia," in M. Y. Iscan and K. A. R. Kennedy (eds.), *Reconstruction of Life from the Skeleton* (New York: Wiley Liss, 1989), 201–22.

52. P. Stuart-MacAdam, "Porotic hyperostosis: representative of a childhood condition," *American Journal of Physical Anthropology* (1985) 66:391–98.

53. Angel, *The People of Lerna.*

54. D. R. Martin, G. T. Armelagos, and D. P. Van Gerven, "The effects of socioeconomic change in prehistoric Africa: Sudanese Nubia as a case study," in M. Cohen and G. J. Armelagos (eds.), *Palaeopathology at the Origins of Agriculture* (New York: Academic Press, 1984), 193–214.

55. A. C. Aufderhide, "Chemical analysis of skeletal remains," in M. Y. Iscan, and K. A. R. Kennedy (eds.), *Reconstruction of Life from the Skeleton* (New York: Wiley Liss, 1989), 237–60; S. H. Ambrose and M. J. DeNiro, "Reconstruction of African human diet using bone collagen and carbon and nitrogen isotope ratios," *Nature* (1986) 319:321–24; Larsen, *Bioarchaeology, Interpreting Behavior from the Human Skeleton.*

56. Larsen, "Bioarchaeological interpretations."

57. Hiernaux, *The People of Africa.*

58. Seligman, *The Races of Africa*; C. Coon, *The Origin of Races* (New York: Alfred Knopf, 1962); C. Coon, *The Living Races of Man* (New York: Alfred Knopf, 1965); for more recent discussions influenced by these classics see, e.g., C. R. Guglielmino, P. Menozzi, A. Piazza, and L. L. Cavalli-Sforza, "Measures of genetic admixture for north African populations," *Atti Associazione Genetica Italiana* (1987) 33:177–78, E. Bosch, F. Calafell, A. Perez-Lezaun, D. Comas, E. Mateu, and J. Betranpetit, "Population history of north Africa: evidence from classical genetic markers," *Human Biology* (1997) 69(3):295–311, and J. L. Newman, *The Peopling of Africa, A Geographic Interpretation* (New Haven: Yale University Press, 1995).

59. Hiernaux, *The People of Africa.*

60. E. Mayr and P. D. Ashlock, *Principles of Systematic Zoology* (New York: McGraw Hill, 1991).

61. See comment in A. Brues, *Peoples and Races* (New York: MacMillan, 1977).

62. S. O. Y. Keita and R. A. Kittles, "The persistence of racial thinking and the myth of racial divergence," *American Anthropologist* (1997) 99(3):534–44.

63. Coon, *The Living Races of Man.*

64. Keita and Kittles, "The persistence of racial thinking."

65. Mayr and Ashlock, *Principles of Systematic Zoology*, 1953–59.

66. Ibid.

67. A. G. Fix, "Gene frequency clines produced by kin-structured founder effects," *Human Biology* (1997) 69(5):663–73.

68. A. Bowcock, J. Kidd, J. Mountain, J. Herbert, and L. L. Cavalli-Sforza, "Drift, admixture and selection in human evolution: A study with DNA polymorphisms," *Proceedings of the National Academy of Sciences (USA)* (1991) 88:839–43.

69. A. Templeton, "Human races: a genetic and evolutionary perspective," *American Anthropologist* (1999) 100(3):632–50.

70. B. D. Latter, "Genetic differences within and between populations of the major human subgroups," *American Naturalist* (1980) 116(2):220–37.

71. D. Penny, M. Steel, P. J. Waddell, and M. D. Hendy, "Improved analyses of human mtDNA support a recent African origin for *Homo sapiens*," *Molecular Biology and Evolution* (1995) 12:863–82; L. Vigilant, R. Pennington, H. Harpending, T. Kocher,

A. Wilson, "Mitochondrial DNA sequences in single hairs from a southern African population," *Proceedings of the National Academy of Sciences (USA)* (1989) 86:9350–54; L. Vigilant, M. Stoneking, H. Harpending, K. Hawkes, and A. Wilson, "African populations and the evolution of human mitochondrial DNA," *Science* (1991) 253:1503–7; R. D'Andrade and P. A. Morin, "Chimpanzee and human mitochondrial DNA," *American Anthropologist* (1996) 98(2):352–70; A. Ruiz Linares et al., "Geographic clustering of human Y-chromosome haplotypes," *Annual of Human Genetics* (1996) 60:401–8.

72. Keita and Kittles, "The persistence of racial thinking"; A. G. Thorne, M. H. Wolpoff, and R. B. Eckhardt, "Genetic variation in Africa" (letter), *Science* (1993) 261:1507–8; L. L. Cavalli-Sforza, Paolo Menozzi, and A. Piazza, "Genetic variation in Africa" (response to Thorne et al.), *Science* (1993) 261:1508.

73. Kittles and Keita, "The persistence of racial thinking."

74. Ibid.

75. Templeton, "Human races."

76. L. L. Cavalli-Sforza, A. Piazza, P. Menozzi, and J. Mountain, "Reconstruction of human evolution: Bringing together genetic, archaeological and linguistic data," *Proceedings of the National Academy of Sciences (USA)* (1988) 85:6002–6.

77. Mayr and Ashlock, *Principles of Systematic Zoology.*

78. Hiernaux, *The People of Africa.*

79. C. Ehret, "Historical linguistic evidence for early African food production," in J. D. Clark and S. Brandt (eds.), *From Hunters to Farmers* (Berkeley: University of California Press, 1984), 26–36.

80. For a discussion of this in the Pacific, see J. Terrell, "Causal pathways and causal processes: studying the evolutionary prehistory of human diversity in language, customs and biology," *Journal of Anthropological Archaeology* (1986) 5:187–98.

81. Hiernaux, *The People of Africa.*

82. C. Stringer and R. McKie, *African Exodus* (New York: Henry Holt and Company, 1993); R. Foley and M. Lahr, "Mode 3 technologies and the evolution of modern humans," *Cambridge Archaeological Journal* (1997) 7:3–36.

83. D. W. Phillipson, *African Archaeology* (Cambridge: Cambridge University Press, 1985); Stringer and McKie, *African Exodus.*

84. Stringer and McKie, *African Exodus*; Foley and Lahr, "Mode 3 technologies."

85. J. D. Clark, "The origin and spread of modern humans: A broad perspective on the African evidence," in P. Mellars and C. Stringer (eds.), *The Human Revolution: Behavioral and Biological Perspectives on the Origins of Modern Humans* (Princeton: Princeton University Press, 1989).

86. P. M. Vermeersch, E. Paulissen, S. Stokes, C. Charlier, P. Van Peer, C. Stringer, and W. Lindsay, "A Middle Palaeolithic burial of a modern human at Taramsa Hill, Egypt," *Antiquity* (1998) 72:475–84.

87. P. M. Vermeersch, E. Paulissen, G. Gijselings, M. Otte, A. Thoma, P. Van Peer, and R. Lauwers, "33,000-yr-old chert mining site and related *Homo* in the Egyptian Nile Valley," *Nature* (1984) 309:342–44.

88. A. S. Brooks, D. M. Helgren, J. S. Cramer, et al., "Dating and the context of three Middle Stone Age sites with bone points in the Upper Semliki Valley, Zaire," *Science* (1995) 268:548–53; J. E. Yellen, A. S. Brooks, E. Cornelissen, M. J. Melhman, K. Stewart, "A Middle Stone Age worked bone industry from Katanda, Upper Semliki Valley, Zaire," *Science* (1995) 268:553–56.

89. G. Hudson, "Gene genealogies and the coalescent process," in D. Futuyma and J. Antonovics (eds.), *Oxford Surveys in Evolutionary Biology* 7:1–44 (Oxford: Oxford University Press, 1991); M. Slatkin and B. Rannala, "Estimating the age of alleles by use of intrallelic variability," *American Journal of Human Genetics* (1997) 60:447–58.

90. Kittles and Keita, "The persistence of racial thinking."

91. Ibid.

92. Penny, et al., "Improved analyses of human mtDNA."

93. For technical discussions see A. R. Templeton, E. Routman, and C. A. Phillips, "Separating population structure from population history: a cladistic analysis of the geographical distribution of mitochondrial DNA haplotypes in the tiger salamander, *Ambystoma tigrinum,*" *Genetics* (1995) 140:767–82, and M. Ruvolo, "Molecular evolutionary processes and conflicting gene trees," *American Journal of Physical Anthropology* (1994) 94:89–113.

94. S. A. Tishkoff, E. Dietzsch, W. Speed, et al., "Global patterns of linkage disequilibrium at the CD4 locus and modern human origins," *Science* (1996) 271:1380–87.

95. See, e.g., Newman, *The Peopling of Africa,* and to a lesser degree Excoffier, et al., "Genetics and history of sub-Saharan Africa."

96. Hiernaux, *The People of Africa.*

97. E. N. Saad, *The Social History of Timbuktu: The Role of Muslim Scholars and Notables 1400–1900* (Cambridge: Cambridge University Press, 1983).

98. P. D. Lange, "Les Rois de Gao-Sané et les Almoravides," *Journal of African History* (1991) 32:251–75.

99. I. M. Diakonov (Diakonoff), "Earliest Semites in Asia," *Altorientalische Forschungen* (1981) 8:23–74.

100. Bowcock, et al., "Drift, admixture and selection in human evolution."

101. J. S. Weiner and J. Huizinga, *The Assessment of Population Affinities in Man* (Oxford: Clarendon Press, 1972); T. S. Constandse-Westermann, *Coefficients of Biological Distance* (Oosterhout [The Netherlands]: Anthropological Publications, 1972).

102. L. A. Abbott, F. A. Bisby, and D. J. Rogers, *Taxonomic Analysis in Biology* (New York: Columbia University Press, 1985); A. J. Boyce, "Mapping diversity: a comparative study of some numerical methods," in A. J. Cole (ed.), *Numerical Taxonomy* (New York: Academic Press, 1969), 1–31.

103. E.g., W. Howells, "Cranial Variation in Man," *Papers of the Peabody Museum* (Cambridge, Mass.: Harvard University Press, 1973).

104. Nurse, et al., "Biology and history of southern African populations."

105. Abbott, et al., *Taxonomic Analysis in Biology.*

106. Phillipson, *African Archaeology.*

107. G. P. Rightmire, "Problems of the study of later Pleistocene man in Africa," *American Anthropologist* (1975) 77:28–52.

108. E.g., Excoffier, et al., "Genetics and history of sub-Saharan Africa."

109. Tishkoff, et al., "Global patterns of linkage disequilibrium."

110. This discussion relies in part on observations by the late J. L. Angel (as well as my own).

111. L. Angel and J. O. Kelley, "Description and comparison of the skeleton," in F. Wendorf and R. Schild (eds.), *The Wadi Kubbaniya Skeleton: A Late Palaeolithic Burial from Southern Egypt* (Dallas, 1986), 66.

112. Ibid.

113. Ibid., 68.

114. I. M. Diakonov (Diakonoff) *Semito-Hamitic Languages: An Essay in Classification* (Moscow: Nauka Publishing House, 1965); L. Bender *Omotic: A New Afro-Asiatic Language Family* (Carbondale: Southern Illinois University, 1975); Ehret, "Historical linguistic evidence for early African food production"; C. Ehret, *Reconstructing Proto-Afroasiatic (Proto-Afrasian): Vowels, Tone, Consonants and Vocabulary* (Berkeley: University of California Press, 1995); R. Blench, "Recent developments in African language classification and their implications for prehistory," in T. Shaw, P. Sinclair, B. Andah and A. Okpoko (eds.), *The Archaeology of Africa* (London: Routledge, 1993), 126–38.

115. Ehret, *Reconstructing Proto-Afroasiatic.*

116. H. Lhote, *The Search for the Tassili Frescoes* (London: Hutichinson, 1959).

117. J. E. G. Sutton, "The aquatic civilisation of middle Africa," *Journal of African History* (1974) 15:527–46; C. Ehret, "The Afrasan (Afro-Asiatic) language family originated in Africa, and other true tales for archaeologists and biological anthropologists," paper presented at annual meeting of the American Anthropological Association, November 19, 1999.

118. F. Hassan, "The predynastic of Egypt," *Journal of World Prehistory* (1988) 2:135–85; M. Kobusiewicz, "Neolithic and predynastic development in the Egyptian Nile Valley," in F. Klees and R. Kuper (eds.), *New Light on the Northeast African Past* (Cologne: Heinrich Barth Institut, 1992), 208–17.

119. O. Bar-Yosef, "Pleistocene connexions between Africa and Southwest Asia," *African Archaeological Review* (1987) 5:29–38.

120. Diakonov, *Semito-Hamitic Languages.*

121. Hassan, "The predynastic of Egypt."

122. See photographs in Coon, *The Living Races of Man.*

5

THE IMPORTANCE OF BOTANICAL DATA TO HISTORICAL RESEARCH ON AFRICA

Dorothea Bedigian

Introduction

This chapter will apply a broad definition of botanical evidence, as it incorporates information from the disciplines of agronomy, genetics, anthropology, archaeology, and ethnographic records. The subject matter is vast, touching on many additional fields, including art, religion, economics, geography, the pharmaceutical, mystical, ceremonial, and ritual uses of plants, and the symbolic meanings of plants in art and decoration, myths, legends, and folklore. When illustrations are required, the examples will refer to sesame, my own specialty.

Plants have altered the course of human history. Prehistoric hunter-gatherers depended on their knowledge of native food plants. From earliest time, plants provided people with food, shelter, clothing, fuel, medicine, and other necessities. The rise of agriculture provided a food source reliable enough to sustain advanced village society. People who once collected plants from the wild came to rely on crops grown for food, thus making stable societies possible and eventually leading to the advances of great civilizations.

Prehistorical Sources

Direct Evidence from Antiquity

Plant remains, such as flowers in the form of funerary bouquets, garlands, or wreaths, fruits, and above all, seeds, can reveal what people ate and used in trade in early historic times. One example of plant remains that can serve as valuable historical resources is the complete inventory of plants found in the tomb of King Tutankhamon. The inventory was finally completed by a student, Christian de Vartevan,[1] after the plants sat untouched in storage at the Royal Botanic Gardens, Kew, for sixty years after the death of Leonard Boodle, who had been studying them.

Seeds can reveal whether a plant was wild or domesticated. One well-defined morphological feature in cereals is the rachis, which attaches the seed to the receptacle. Cultivated seeds often remain attached to the plant at maturity, while wild seeds possess a brittle rachis that breaks off upon maturity, causing the seed to shatter. Seed shattering is an important trait that can be used to distinguish wild species from their cultivated relatives, thus identifying a morphological change that occurs during plant domestication. Wheat species possess tremendous polymorphisms in reproductive parts, and the plants can frequently be categorized on the basis of these as diploid, tetraploid, or hexaploid, and often as cultivated or wild. Polyploid chromosome numbers frequently increase seed or fruit size, and this character also suggests that a plant has undergone domestication. These traits are a good indication of whether the seed was domesticated or wild, as Jack R. Harlan showed in his innovative publication in *Scientific American.*[2]

Carbonized wood can sometimes be used to identify species, using microscopic examination of the anatomy of growth rings, arrangement of vascular bundles, ray cells, pith cell size, and so on. Pollen grains can be viewed and photographed with a scanning electron microscope, and later compared with reference specimens published in atlases. Although these photographs can be useful for making identifications, the difference between the pollen of related species is not always sufficient to distinguish species.

Grasses contain silica bodies called phytoliths that are embedded in the leaves and stems. When a plant dies, the phytoliths are not subject to disintegration, and consequently they remain in the earth long after the organic matter of the plants has deteriorated. Phytoliths, too, have unique crystalline structures and assist some archaeobotanists to identify the species that were once present, by examining soil samples or the remains in tombs.

Agriculture and Cultivated Plants

Harlan was a pioneer in the study of the origins of agriculture and crop domestication. Since agricultural origins in Africa have a unique explanation, his theoretical contributions are fundamental to understanding the history of Africa from an agricultural and historical perspective. Harlan was a keen student of the work of Russian agronomist and geneticist N. I. Vavilov in the early twentieth century. Vavilov had proposed eight centers of origin, representing most of the cultivated plants of the world. Harlan refined Vavilov's concept to include space, time, and variation. As he observed crops and wild species throughout the world, he could see, as a few others had also recognized, that the centers of crop origins described by Vavilov were centers of diversity and centers of long-standing agricultural activity, which may or may not represent centers of crop evolution or domestication. He synthesized his observations in a classic paper, "Agricultural Origins: Centers and Non-centers,"[3] and introduced the concept of "non-centers" as a complement and refinement of Vavilovian theories of crop origins and diversity:

> I propose the theory that agriculture originated independently in three different areas and that, in each case, there was a system composed of a center of origin and a non-center, in which activities of domestication were dispersed over a span of 5,000 to 10,000 kilometers. One system includes a definable Near East center and a non-center in Africa; another system includes a North Chinese center and a non-center in Southeast Asia and the South Pacific; the third system includes a Meso-American center and a South American non-center. There are suggestions that, in each case, the center and non-center interact with each other. Crops did not necessarily originate in centers (in any conventional concept of the term), nor did agriculture necessarily develop in a geographical center.[4]

He revisited this matter almost twenty-five years later in *The Living Fields* (1995):

> How did the Vavilovian theory fare? We can credit him with three bull's eyes: Peru, Oaxaca (Mexico), and Palestine are dead center in three of his eight centers. Furthermore, agriculture also evolved independently in China, southeast Asia and Ethiopia, centers in his scheme. Ethiopia is the only

country in sub-Saharan Africa visited by Vavilov, and the Russian scientists did not know Africa well until his final two decades. This left some gaps in the theory. There were other independent origins, but by and large his essay of 1926 was a landmark and still influential. As of that date it was a remarkable perception, but based more on intuition than data.[5]

Harlan readily recognized the great value of wild relatives of crop plants as gene resources for plant breeding. While this concept was not new, he and his colleague, J. M. J. deWet, in "Towards a Rational Classification of Cultivated Plants,"[6] formalized the concept of gene pools for use in plant breeding into primary (i.e., hybridization of cultigens [cultivated plants] within the same species), secondary (i.e., hybridization of cultigens with closely related compatible species), and tertiary (i.e., hybridization of cultigens with more distantly related species, often requiring unusual steps, such as embryo rescue with artificial media). This classification has been useful in setting priorities for collecting plant genetic resources and as a reference point for use in designing breeding strategies.

He returned to the need for conservation of wild species in a post-Green Revolution paper, "Genetics of Disaster,"[7] in which he formulated many of his concerns about "genetic vulnerability" and "genetic wipeout." This paper also hints at the need for *in situ* conservation, a topic that he held in secondary importance to *ex situ* conservation for practical reasons, as revealed in "Evolution of cultivated plants":

> For the sake of future generations, we MUST collect and study wild and weedy relatives of our cultivated plants as well as the domesticated races. These sources of germplasm (genetic material) have been dangerously neglected in the past, but the future may not be so tolerant. In the plant breeding programs of tomorrow we cannot afford to ignore *any* source of useable genes.[8]

Still, Harlan's words in "Our Vanishing Genetic Resources" ring true today:

> The co-evolution of crops and man in subsistence agricultural economies is one of the most fascinating of all subjects for the student of evolution whether he be interested in plant or human cultural evolution. But, as with so many things in this world, the past is being destroyed by the present. Centers of diversity have been wiped out in recent decades. Indigenous tribal cultures and social customs have collapsed as well.

Authentic indigenous cultivars [abridgement of cultivated varieties] and landraces [those varieties that are the product of selection by local farmers in traditional settings, and not manipulated by researchers at experiment stations] are becoming collector's items as much as Luristan bronzes, African masks and figurines, or pre-Columbian Indian art. The world of N. I. Vavilov is vanishing and the sources of genetic variability he knew are drying up. The patterns of variation . . . may no longer be discernible in a few decades and living traces of the long co-evolution of cultivated plants may well disappear forever.[9]

Harlan's philosophy of the origins of agriculture echoes throughout the decades. While many details about the origins of agriculture remain to be discovered, Harlan offered this guiding principal in some of his final writings:

First, we will not and cannot find a time or place where agriculture originated. We will not and cannot because it did not happen that way. Agriculture is not the result of a happening, an idea, an invention, discovery or instruction by a god or goddess. It emerged as a result of long periods of intimate co-evolution between plants and man. Animals are not essential; plants supply over 90% of the food consumed by humans. The co-evolution took place over millennia and over vast regions measured in terms of thousands of kilometers. There were many independent attempts in many locations that fused over time to produce effective food production systems. Origins are diffuse in both time and space.[10]

We see that his long-standing view of spatial diffuseness, particularly in the case of Africa, and multiple origins of agriculture, first expressed in his 1951 paper "Anatomy of Gene Centers,"[11] and elaborated in "Agricultural Origins: Centers and Non-centers,"[12] has stood over several decades. This is one of the legacies of Harlan that clarify the framework of knowledge about the origins and maintenance of crop genetic diversity.

Harlan was completely committed to the concept that *ex situ* conservation of crops was necessary to capture the products of millennia of crop evolution. These genetic resources may not be used for a long time to come in plant breeding or other studies, but the use of even one of the thousands of accessions he collected justified the whole effort. Harlan enjoyed telling of a nondescript wheat he collected in eastern Turkey:

The potential value of a collection cannot be assessed in the field. Perhaps this statement could best be illustrated by PI 178383, a wheat I collected in a remote part of Eastern Turkey in 1948. It is a miserable looking wheat, tall, thin-stemmed, lodges badly, is susceptible to leaf rust, lacks winter hardiness yet is difficult to vernalize, and has poor baking qualities. Understandably, no one paid any attention to it for some 15 years. Suddenly, stripe rust became serious in the north-western states and PI 178383 turned out to be resistant to four races of stripe rust, 35 races of common bunt, ten races of dwarf bunt and to have good tolerance to flag smut and snow mould. The improved cultivars based on PI 178383 are reducing losses by a matter of some millions of dollars per year.[13]

Indirect Evidence

Recorded history provides other sources of information beside published accounts and seed remains. Egyptian tomb reliefs and paintings provide a wealth of information about plant use. Harlan's enthusiastic study of these ancient colorful drawings led to a publication that was presented as one of his last public lectures at the University of Illinois. Its title, "Lettuce and the Sycamore: Sex and Romance in Ancient Egypt," was intriguing and the presentation attracted a huge audience from many disciplines.[14]

Loret's *La flore pharaonique*[15] and Lucas's *Ancient Egyptian Materials and Industries*[16] are examples of review of this combination of botanical and historical detail by respected authorities. Economic botanists frequently mention the monumental relief at Queen Hatshepsut's temple at Thebes that immortalizes her inauguration of the first plant-collecting expedition, to the land of Punt in search of seedling trees of the highly prized frankincense and myrrh.

Ancient historians provide a wealth of information based on their own firsthand observations as well as anecdotal accounts. Herodotus, Theophrastus, Pliny, Columella, and the Periplus of the Erythracean Sea are useful sources about plants cultivated and traded in the ancient world.

Modern Sources

Herbarium Specimens

Herbaria are institutions where botanical specimens are kept. Herbarium specimens contain a wealth of ethnographic detail that has never been published anywhere else, but this information has been largely neglected because it is tedious to extract, and it requires a specialist to obtain access to the collections. A herbarium is a storehouse of dried plant specimens collected by amateurs as well as scientists for well over a century, or more in some cases.

Karl Linnaeus published the landmark *Genera Plantarum*, which launched herbarium collections in the mid-1730s by introducing the concept of binomial nomenclature, i.e., identification of each plant by its general and specific name. The plant kingdom is hierarchically subdivided into phyla, classes, orders, families, genera, and species. The fundamental unit of classification in herbaria is the family. Botanists initially view the plant they study in terms of its family. The size of plant families can differ greatly, based on evolution, antiquity, and specialized floral and vegetative structures. A number of genera are included within a single family, and each genus contains a number of species.

For humans, the single most important plant family is the grass family, Poaceae, which includes the cereal staples eaten by nearly all peoples of the world, wheat, rice, maize, and sorghum—that is, the genera *Triticum*, *Oryza*, *Zea*, and *Sorghum*, respectively. Some species of *Triticum* include *T. aestivum*, *T. urartu*, and *T. timophevii*; rice can be either *Oryza sativa* or, from Mali's inland delta of the River Niger, *O. glabberima*; maize is *Zea mays*; and *Sorghum bicolor* feeds much of Africa's sub-Saharan population. (Note that Latin binomials are always underlined or italicized.)

During their exploration of Africa, the colonial powers attempted to assemble an inventory of the plant resources as well as the botanical curiosities of their colonies. This was the beginning of the venerable collections of today, including the herbarium of the Royal Botanical Garden, Kew, of the Jardin des Plantes in Paris, the Jardin Botanique in Meise, near Brussels, the Universities at Coimbra and Lisbon, and in Florence. Major collections were also made, and continue to grow in Vienna, in Munich, at the Agricultural University in Wageningen, the Netherlands, in Copenhagen, and at Uppsala. A significant portion of the valuable collection at Berlin was destroyed during World War II, illustrating the point that duplicate collections are essential. The Missouri Botanical Garden in St. Louis holds the largest and most balanced collection of African material in the United States, obtained by direct collecting expeditions as well as by exchange with other institutions. Each herbarium has unique strengths in terms of the geographic regions represented, and the species in the collection are frequently accumulated because a researcher has an interest in a particular group.

Herbaria differ in the way they arrange their collections. Some, such as those in Missouri and at Kew, are arranged using evolutionary relationships among the families, although these arcane criteria are controversial and debated among systematists. Usually the scheme of a leading taxonomist such as Cronquist or Takhtadzhian is adopted or modified and followed. A different approach to the arrangement of families is taken at Brussels, where they are placed alphabetically, avoiding the question of relationships, and simply following a convenient order that can be universally understood. Within a family, the genera are arranged alphabetically; likewise, within a genus, the species are organized alphabetically. The general location where each plant was collected is shown by the color of the folder into which it is placed. Since the herbaria in Belgium are strong in collections from Congo, Burundi, and Rwanda, brown folders are used for these nations. Green folders identify the other African countries.

Variation below the species level is especially important to botanists in the case of economically useful plants. The progenitor of a crop is sometimes identified by the number of cultivars that resemble the wild ancestor in morphological features, including branching pattern, leaf shape and color, hairiness, flower color and markings, fruit characteristics, and seed color. Also, discovery of a large number of different genotypes of a single species that are established in an isolated region might reflect the antiquity of the crop at that location. It suggests intense human activity using selection to improve qualities such as seed color and size, oil content, days to maturity, disease resistance and resistance to insect predators, plant height, and sturdiness of stem. Statistical resemblance of the traits of a large number of distinct landraces from a region, with the wild relative's traits, might point to a geographic center of origin.

The procedures for preparing, curating, and studying plant collections in herbaria are a specialty in themselves. Some distinguished manuals for herbarium practices include Leenhouts's *Guide to Practice of Herbarium Taxonomy*,[17] de Vogel's *Manual of Herbarium Taxonomy*,[18] Stace's *Plant Taxonomy and Biosystematics*,[19] Stuessy's *Plant Taxonomy: The Systematic Evaluation of Comparative Data*,[20] and *The Biological Monograph*, by Hopkins et al.[21]

Ideally, every specimen is pressed immediately in newspapers, before the color of the leaves and flowers can fade. Details about location are essential, as are a description of the habitat, the plant itself, date, altitude, associated species, soil conditions, vernacular names, and culinary, medicinal, and other uses.

Reproductive portions, that is, flowers, fruits, and seeds, are the most diagnostic of plant parts, and ideally these should accompany each specimen. Leaf characteristics are more variable, depending on the placement on the plant: seedling leaves often look very different from mature ones, but they too provide information that can be used to distinguish many species from one another. If possible, roots should also be collected, as they too contribute unique data.

The specimens may suffer from decay, fading flower color, insect damage, and the like, unless conservation measures are persistently carried out. Additionally, those working with specimens sometimes encounter handwriting that is difficult to read, or that was written on paper that is disintegrating, or with glue that is bleeding through with age, obscuring the writing.

Specimens are now mounted on heavy-grade acid-free cardboard, with professional labels that include precise location information that was gathered with professional geographic positioning devices. But these modern tools were not available a century ago when some of the most important historical collections were being made. Many countries are no longer or not easily accessible to researchers because of wars and insecurity, political conflicts, xenophobia, and strict restrictions on collecting biological materials. This means the old, historically important, collections are invaluable, regardless of condition.

Herbarium specimens can offer interesting information, assuming that the collector took the trouble to enter these details. Sometimes the sheets contain information that is not available anywhere else, not published in any book. The many hands that painstakingly collected and pressed specimens decades ago, as a hobby or out of scientific curiosity, have provided us with a wealth of data that is ripe for collection. Some early examples of these riches were compiled by Siri von Reis Altshul and von Reis and Lipp, who gathered vast quantities of information about medical uses of plants from herbarium labels.[22]

Linguistic Analysis

Linguistic analysis can be used to reconstruct trade routes and traded goods, with a thorough compilation of all known names and geographic locations. For example, Gerda Rossel, in her doctoral dissertation at the Agricultural University, Wageningen, gathered all available information on the distribution of *Musa* germplasm in Africa and used linguistic evidence to suggest its first introduction to an area, plus the donor location. This study was finally published after twenty years of work, in 1998, as *Taxonomic-Linguistic Study of Plantain in Africa*.[23] Here is a fairly unusual and effective interdisciplinary approach to the study of crop origins. Conventional wisdom about crop evolution dictates that seed evidence is the ultimate authority to document crop history. That is fine when one is dealing with seed crops, if and when those archaeological seeds survive through the ages. However, seed crops that do not stand up over time or to charring, such as sesame, or crops having other edible parts, create some challenges for evolutionary botanists. *Musa* plants do not leave archaeological traces behind and historical sources are scarce. One alternative approach to studying a crop's history is an exhaustive analysis of its names.

We learn from Rossel's preface that there are 120 plantain cultivars in Africa, more than ten times the number that occur in Asia, the continent of origin. She was dealing with an interspecific, triploid hybrid of *Musa balbisiana* and one or more sub-species of *M. acuminata*, with the genome AAB. The plant is sterile and can only be multiplied by clones, which is why breeding is difficult.

The two main components of the study concern various aspects about the distribution of plantain diversity and the scientific and ethnobotanical classification and nomenclature of the crop. The analysis combines the linguistic and geographic study with historical, cultural, ecological, agronomic, and economic data, and integrates all constituents into a theory about the introduction, spread, and diversification of plantain in the African continent. The study takes into account the ecological conditions in the parts of Africa where plantain is grown, as well as the economies and cultural histories of the people cultivating plantain. One technical problem Rossel encountered was the classification and nomenclature of plantain cultivars, and her suggestions are presented in this study.

The work is well documented, with an extensive bibliography and four appendices that record all the locations and variants of the names of each cultivar. It epitomizes the interdisciplinary approach to a crop's history.

Medicinal Plants

The ethnopharmacological literature that contributes to our knowledge of African history by means of folk medicine and healing plants is increasing each year. Some outstanding compilations are Watt and Breyer-Brandwijk's masterful (1962) *Medicinal and Poisonous Plants of Southern and Eastern Africa*,[24] Haerdi's *Afrikanische Heilpflanzen*,[25] Venzlaff's *Marokkanische Drogenhändler und seine Ware*,[26] Sofowora's *Medicinal Plants and Traditional Medicine in Africa*,[27] Morris's *Chewa Medical Botany: A Study of Herbalism in Southern Malawi*,[28] Neuwinger's *African Ethnobotany*,[29] and from an older era, Deines and Grapow's *Wörterbuch der Aegyptischen Drogennamen.*[30]

Experts in allied fields, particularly chemistry, should be consulted when investigating the active constituents in plants mentioned in anecdotal accounts. Plants produce natural metabolites that are responsible for the characteristic smells, colors, flavors and medicinal properties. These are remarkably diverse and are distributed throughout the plant kingdom in characteristic patterns. Although some may simply be the waste products of physiological processes, most of these compounds aid plants in adapting to environmental conditions, competing with other plants, and either warding off attacks by predatory insects and animals or attracting ones that play a role in pollination, fruit dispersal, or protection. Essential oils, for example, help reduce water loss in plants growing in arid zones, repel insects, and deter grazing animals. Some alkaloids, bitter-tasting compounds that are often poisonous, discourage predators. For plants that grow in poor soils and cannot recycle nitrogen or derive it from bacteria, alkaloids serve as a storehouse of nitrogen.[31]

Anthropology

Ethnographic accounts such as Westermarck's distinguished two-volume *Ritual and Belief in Morocco,*[32] Nadel's epic work *The Nuba,*[33] and Busson's classic ethnobotanical source, *Plantes Alimentaires de l'Ouest Africain,*[34] contain rich agricultural, botanical, and cultural details, as well as direct observations about the period, that can be used to help reconstruct African history.

The Society of Economic Botany is devoted to scholarship about human plant use, both ancient and modern; its journal is *Economic Botany.* Anthropologists and archaeologists, agricultural historians, agronomists, and botanists all find it a desirable venue.[35] The report by Chhabra and Mahunnah contains data relevant to a study in progress about the wild relatives of sesame, although their findings contradict information that I myself have obtained in interviews.[36] However, agronomists and botanists must be cautious about communicating unambiguously with the people they visit, as illustrated by Pierre de Schlippe's foreword to his enduring *Shifting Cultivation in Africa,* below:

> The first impulse to study African traditional agriculture by anthropological methods came to me in the form of an ever-recurring "social situation" between agricultural extension officers and native cultivators. One scene of this sort, imaginary but typical, may therefore be the best introduction to this book.

The extension officer: You will measure squares of fifty by fifty yards along this line. Each man will cultivate one square and sow it with sesame. Right?

One of the African cultivators:—Yes, sir.

—Is this land good for sesame?

—Yes, sir.

—How do you know?

—You are the Government. You tell us to sow sesame on this land. The land is good.

—You don't understand me. You will cultivate sesame for your own profit, not for me. I shall come and buy it from you. You are the people who know how to choose good land for sesame. The better your land, the more sesame you will sell, the more money you will get. All I want is that your plots should be arranged in fifty-yard squares along a line, so that I can come and see that there are no lazy people amongst you.

—There are no lazy people, sir.

—Well now, is this land good or do you want to choose another place?

—All the land is God's land, sir.

—So you are satisfied with my choice?

—You are our father, we are your children. How can we not be satisfied?

And so on and so forth. Exasperated, my friend decides that firmness is the best guarantee of success.

—You are going to cultivate this land and woe to him, who will not produce good sesame.

—Yes, sir.

The sesame is a failure. In front of the few meagre stalks choked by grass I may have had later the following conversation with my friend, the African cultivator.

—Why has the sesame failed?

—Is it not God's will?

—Have you grown sesame for yourself elsewhere?

—Yes, sir.

—Did it fail?

—No, sir.

—Now, what was the difference between your sesame and this one which you call the Government's sesame?

—There was no difference, sir, but there is one thing. We do not grow sesame on first-year land.

—Why did you not tell that to the extension officer?

—He is the Government. He knows.

—But he asked you to choose your land yourself.

—We had no second-year land in fifty-yard squares along a line.

—Was the sowing date at least correct?

—No. It was much too late.

—How did you know?

—The pods of the *maza* tree were already brown.

—But surely the extension officer laid out your plots long before you sowed your last sesame?

—Yes, sir, he gave us the seeds long ago.

—So it was, after all, your own fault that the sowing was done too late.

—How could we sow before the grass was that high? and he puts his hand some eight inches from the ground, which would correspond to some three weeks of growth.

—Why was such a delay necessary?

—If you sow sesame into land just burnt, will it grow?"[37]

Travelers' Accounts

J. D. Hooker (1878) was the second director of the Royal Botanical Garden, Kew, and his account of his travels with Ball in "Marocco" and the Great Atlas makes suspenseful reading and includes breathtaking descriptions of the plants encountered in the high mountain valleys.[38] A great deal of historical detail is also included in the report. Barth's travels along the Niger in the mid-nineteenth century[39] supply detail about the plants and people encountered. Maire and Monod covered an inaccessible route to the Tibesti mountains that can fill certain gaps.[40]

Colonial Records

A rich repository of historical detail, records in the Kenya National Archives, indicates that the British actively discouraged the cultivation of sesame by offering more favorable rail shipping rates for maize.[41] In fact, the British influenced a change in the pattern of preference and use of vegetables, cereals, oilseeds, and all food categories, as well as sugar consumption. Farmers in most other regions of Kenya (aside from the Luo lands) have almost completely replaced their traditional leafy vegetables with collards (*sukuma wiki*) and cabbages.

Further evidence of these policies is provided by M. Little.[42]

> Colonialism strained the indigenous subsistence production system of the Sukuma people in northwestern Tanganyika. For example, the colonial authorities shifted labor from food production and attempted to create a surplus of a labor-intensive nonfood cash crop, cotton. The government also diverted two minor, high-protein food crops, peanuts and sesame, into the export market and eliminated or reduced indigenous production of high-protein dietary staples such as millet and sorghum.(375)

Literary Sources

Proverbs and poetry can illustrate the significance of a plant in society. The importance of sesame in the cultural life of Kenya is illustrated by its mention in a Swahili proverb: *Mwenyezi mungu atakushinda kama shinda la ufuta* (Almighty God will reduce you as the left-overs of simsim)—a curse.[43]

Among the Luo, the *simsim* mortar is one of the objects for oath-taking: to cross by the mortar is considered a very serious thing. The consequence is that the whole family lineage may perish if one crossed the mortar (Ocholla-Ayago 1980).[44]

The literary references of Okol p'Bitek show the cultural significance of sesame among the Acholi in Uganda. Simsim appears in the title poem, number 6 from *Song of Lawino*, "The Mother Stone has a Hollow Stomach," which p'Bitek recites:

> the earthen dish
> Contains simsim paste
>
> Clean and beautifully oiled
> Like a girl
> Ready for the *jok* dance
> Is the simsim grinding stone.
>
> And when my sister
> Is grinding simsim
> Mixed with groundnuts
> And I am grinding
> Millet mixed with sorghum
> You hear the song of the stones
> You hear the song of the grains
> And the seeds
> And above all these
> The beautiful duets
> By Lawino and her sister[45]

Notes

1. C. de Vartavan, "Contaminated plant-foods from the tomb of Tutankhamun: a new interpretive system," *Journal of Archaeological Science* (1990) 17: 473–94.

2. J. R. Harlan, "The plants and animals that nourish man," *Scientific American* (1976) 235: 88–97.

3. J. R. Harlan, "Agricultural origins: Centers and non-centers," *Science* (1971) 174: 468–74.

4. Ibid.

5. J. R. Harlan, *The Living Fields: Our Agricultural Heritage.* Cambridge University Press, Cambridge, UK. (1995) 237.

6. J. R. Harlan and J. M. J. de Wet, "Toward a rational classification of cultivated plants," *Taxon* (1971) 20: 509–17.

7. J. R. Harlan, "Genetics of disaster," *Journal of Environmental Quality* (1972) 1: 212–15.

8. J. R. Harlan, "Evolution of cultivated plants," in *Genetic Resources in Plants: Their Exploration and Conservation,* O. H. Frankel and E. Bennett, eds. Aldine, Chicago. (1970) 19–32.

9. J. R. Harlan, "Our vanishing genetic resources," *Science* (1975) 188: 618–21.

10. Harlan, *The Living Fields,* 239–40.

11. J. R. Harlan, "Anatomy of gene centers," *American Naturalist* (1951) 85: 97–103.

12. Harlan, "Agricultural origins."

13. J. R. Harlan, "Practical problems in exploration: Seed crops," in *Crop Genetic Resources for Today and Tomorrow,* O. H. Frankel and J. G. Hawkes, eds. Cambridge University Press, Cambridge, UK. (1975) 111–15.

14. J. R. Harlan, "Lettuce and the sycamore: sex and romance in ancient Egypt," *Economic Botany* (1986) 40: 4–15.

15. V. Loret, *La flore pharaonique,* rev. 2nd ed. Paris. (1892).

16. A. Lucas, *Ancient Egyptian Materials and Industries.* London. (1962).

17. P. W. Leenhouts, *A Guide to the Practice of Herbarium Taxonomy.* Utrecht, International Bureau for Plant Taxonomy and Nomenclature of the International Association for Plant Taxonomy. (1968).

18. E. F. De Vogel, *Manual of Herbarium Taxonomy: Theory and Practice.* Indonesia, UNESCO, Regional office for science and technology. (1987).

19. C. A. Stace, *Plant Taxonomy and Biosystematics,* 2nd ed. Edward Arnold, a division of Hodder & Stoughton, London; NY. (1989). (See particularly chap. 10, "Taxonomy in the service of man," where taxonomic priorities, floras, and monographs are described.)

20. T. F. Stuessy, *Plant taxonomy: the systematic evaluation of comparative data.* Columbia University Press, NY. (1990).

21. H. C. F. Hopkins, C. R. Huxley, C. M. Pannell, G. T. Prance, and F. White. *The Biological Monograph:The Importance of Field Studies and Functional Syndromes for Taxonomy and Evolution of Tropical Plants.* A Festschrift for Frank White Royal Botanical Gardens, Kew, UK. (1998).

22. S. von Reis Altschul, *Drugs and Foods from Little-Known Plants.* Harvard University Press, Cambridge, MA. (1973); S. Von Reis and F. J. Lipp, *New Plant Sources for Drugs and Foods from the New York Botanical Garden Herbarium.* Harvard University Press, Cambridge, MA. (1982).

23. G. Rossel, *Taxonomic-Linguistic Study of Plantain in Africa.* CNWS Publications, c/o Research School CNWS, Leiden University, Leiden, The Netherlands. (1998).

24. J. M. Watt and M. G. Breyer-Brandwijk, *Medicinal and Poisonous Plants of Southern and Eastern Africa,* 2nd ed. E. & S. Livingstone, Edinburgh and London. (1962).

25. F. Haerdi, "Afrikanische Heilpflanzen. Die eingeborenen-Heilpflanzen des Ulanga-Districtes Tanganjikas (Ostafrika)" *Acta Tropica* Suppl. (1964) 8: 1–278.

26. H. Venzlaff, *Der Marokkanische drogenhändler und seine ware* Franz Steiner Verlag GMBH, Wiesbaden. (1977).

27. A. Sofowora, *Medicinal Plants and Traditional Medicine in Africa.* Chichester, West Sussex; John Wiley, NY. (1982).

28. B. Morris, *Chewa Medical Botany: A Study of Herbalism in Southern Malawi.* International African Institute, LIT Verlag, Hamburg. (1996).

29. H. -D. Neuwinger, *African Ethnobotany.* Chapman and Hall, London. (1996).

30. H. Deines and H. Grapow, *Wörterbuch der Aegyptischen drogennamen.* Grundriss der medizin de alten Aegypter. Vol. 6. Berlin, Germany. (1959).

31. G. J. Martin, *Ethnobotany: A Methods Manual.* Chapman and Hall, London. (1996).

32. E. Westermarck, *Ritual and Belief in Morocco*, vols. 1 and 2. Macmillan & Co., London. (1926).

33. S. F. Nadel, *The Nuba.* Oxford University Press, London. (1947).

34. F. Busson, *Plantes alimentaires de l'ouest. Africain.* Leconte, Marseille. (1965).

35. For instance, the following have all appeared in *Economic Botany*: J. R. Harlan, "Ethiopia: A center of diversity," *Economic Botany* (1969) 23: 309–14; Harlan, "Lettuce and the sycamore"; J. R. Harlan and J. Pasquerleau, "D'ecrue agriculture in Mali," *Economic Botany* (1969) 23: 70–74; G. E. Wickens, "What is Economic Botany?" *Economic Botany* (1990) 44: 12–28; D. Bedigian and J. R. Harlan, "Nuba agriculture and ethnobotany, with particular reference to sesame and sorghum," *Economic Botany* (1983) 37: 384–95; D. Bedigian and J. R. Harlan, "Evidence for cultivation of sesame in the ancient world," *Economic Botany* (1986) 40: 137–54; D. Bedigian, C. A. Smyth, and J. R. Harlan, "Patterns of morphological variation in sesame," *Economic Botany* (1986) 40: 353–65.

36. S. C. Chhabra and R. L. A. Mahunnah, "Plants used in traditional medicine by Hayas of Kagera Region, Tanzania," *Economic Botany* (1994) 48: 121–29.

37. Pierre De Schlippe, *Shifting Cultivation in Africa: The Zande System of Agriculture.* Routledge & Paul, London. (1956) ix–x. Reprinted with permission of the publisher.

38. J. D. Hooker and J. Ball, *A Tour in Marocco and the Great Atlas.* Macmillan, London. (1878).

39. H. Barth, *Travels and discoveries in north and central Africa, being a journal of an expedition undertaken under the auspices of HRM's government in the years 1849–1855.* Reprinted 1965, Frank Cass & Co. Ltd., London.

40. R. Maire, "Contrib a l'etude de la flore du Tibesti," in Marius Dalloni, *Mission au Tibesti* II: 1–39. (1935); D. R. Maire and T. Monod, "Etudes sur la flore et la végétation du Tibesti," *Mémoires de l'Institut Français d'Afrique Noire.* Librairie Larose, Paris. (1950).

41. D. Bedigian, unpublished data, Kenya National Archives, Nairobi, and field research, Nyanza Province. (1994).

42. M. Little, "Colonial policy and subsistence in Tanganyika 1925–1945." *Geographical Review* (1991) 81: 375–88.

43. A. Scheven, *Swahili Proverbs: nia zikiwa moja, kilicho mbaliuja.* Washington, DC (1981) p. 9, no. 34; *Shinda*, the dregs of the simsim seeds after oil has been extracted from them.

44. Ocholla-Ayago, *The Luo Culture.* Studien zur kulturkunde 54. Franz Steiner Verlag, Wiesbaden. (1980).

45. O. p'Bitek, *Song of Lawino & Song of Ocol.* Heinemann, International, Oxford. (1984) 59–60.

6

ORAL TRADITION AS A MEANS OF RECONSTRUCTING THE PAST

David Henige

One

When, in the wake of World War II, serious historians began to try to write serious histories of Africa before the arrival of the Europeans, they faced what seemed to be an insuperable hurdle.[1] For most of the continent there were no written records before the mid-nineteenth century—in several places even later. What to do? After all, this was a dilemma that was all but unprecedented. True enough, anthropologists had been studying African societies for fifty years or more, and in the process had occasion to probe the past as well as the present. But for most anthropologists of the time, the past *was* the present—that is, they saw dynamic change as virtually nonexistent, meaning that what the saw in the field was essentially what any outsider would have seen 300, 400, 500 years ago, or even longer. For historians, on the other hand, the past is interesting precisely *because* of change. Historians then, must seek out new ways of reconstructing the African past, or give the project up as hopeless.

There were only two choices, really. They could depend on the work of archaeology, but this was in its infancy and in any case archaeological evidence requires specialized handling and interpretation. The alternative was oral tradition, that is, memories of the past handed down from one generation to the next, until, the idea went, it would be collected, written down, and published. From the late 1950s then, Africanist historians set out to recover the more distant African past.

Two

In its magnitude the new enterprise had no model. Still, it is true that history based on oral evidence was everywhere one cared to look. Take the Bible. Most biblical scholars today emphasize the role that oral tradition must have played in the writing of the pre-monarchical books, those that traced the Israelites from Adam through Abraham, on to Joseph and into Egypt, out of Egypt again, to begin a campaign of conquest that lasted several centuries until David united the twelve tribes into a state. Others would insist that even the history of the Divided Monarchy after Solomon was largely based on oral evidence.

Herodotus, widely recognized as the father of history in the western world, palpably relied on data he had collected in the field; in fact, if all he wrote were true, he would be the father of fieldwork as well as the father of history. Herodotus ushered in a period of more than two millennia that was marked by historians and others seeking oral data and then writing it down.[2] After all, until the twentieth century, most of the people in the world were not literate enough to read a book, let alone to write one. In this respect, the notion of discovering a past by questioning people rather than opening a book was not new, but the scope of it was. Collecting oral tradition was not to be a complement to accessing written history, but almost the entire process.

Three

It was a daunting prospect, although a decade or two elapsed before the enthusiasm abated enough to realize just how daunting. Perhaps the greatest challenges were for historians to turn themselves into anthropologist-like fieldworkers instead of library and archive rats, and then to convince the historical establishment that this worked—that respectable history could actually be gleaned from mouths rather than pages, and that those who did it were respectable historians.

The discipline of precolonial African history actually began in the persons of several European historians, mostly of imperial history, who themselves did little collecting in the field, although many of them spent much time in Africa. Their job was to establish some line-drawing historical maps and then to train others to fill in the voids.

One of the pioneers was Jan Vansina. A medievalist by training, Vansina did not go to Africa specifically to write precolonial African history, but it did not take him long to conclude that the task bore a hopeful resemblance to the ways in which medieval historians collected their data, that is, how they sought out and used oral materials. Vansina sensed a need for a work that would justify oral traditions as historical sources, while at the same time providing a methodological point of departure. In 1961 he published *De la tradition orale*, which, when translated into English four years later as *Oral Tradition*, became the clarion call of those who by then had come to believe in the efficacy of oral data.[3]

Oral Tradition was, in effect, a trial balloon. Trained in a traditional historiographical milieu, Vansina was instinctively cautious as to the claims he made. As he saw it, oral tradition was one of many possible paths to the past, but an important enough one to be tread on often. Although he did not espouse the *sufficiency* of oral tradition for this purpose, his work was enthusiastically taken up as a justification for the enterprise and became one of the most influential works ever written on African history. Its timing was impeccable, its arguments hopeful, its conclusions congenial.

The decade or so after the appearance of *Oral Tradition* can be seen in retrospect as the high tide of the notion that oral tradition was an unimpeded path to centuries of history throughout Africa, and that there was little more to it than going into the field and asking questions. Like most initial enthusiasms, this was to prove illusory. In his book Vansina devoted most attention to interpretation, but as experience mounted, it could be seen that problems peculiar to the *collection* of oral tradition needed to be addressed. Some of these are discussed below.

In any event, the second law of thermodynamics began to set in. There were those who felt that no history of Africa before the nineteenth century was possible, those who felt that at least some of the ground seemingly gained had to be surrendered, and those who fought against both positions by reaffirming the sufficiency of oral data to answer most questions that could be asked.[4]

Members of the first group was so firmly wed to written sources that that they clearly would brook no defense of the value of oral data in historical reconstruction. If there were a confrontation of oral and written evidence, the former was always to be dismissed in favor of the latter. When only oral data existed, they were to treated, not only as uncorroborated, but also uncorroborable. The third group illustrated another setting for Newton's second law of thermodynamics. The more that oral data were criticized, the more they sprang up to defend them. They wrote as if it were still the

1950s, even in light of much well-founded criticism. They became overly defensive and dealt with their critics largely by ignoring them. However, they were no longer the leading standard-bearers of precolonial African history. That honor fell to the second group mentioned above. This was composed largely of those trained after the 1960s and early 1970s and could be seen merely as manifesting the commonplace young-Turk syndrome, in which the next generation always finds reasons to minimize their forebears' contributions. Even so, this group brought to the table a series of advantages not enjoyed by the enthusiasts. A new, more critical, instinct underlay the changes. Oral data were to be collected, but also analyzed, and dispensed with if necessary.

The criticisms were not the kneejerk attitudes of the first group, but generally were more reasoned and more soundly based. Often they were based on wider comparative research, a task the earlier generation had eschewed in favor of gathering data. More attention was paid to the interactive aspects of fieldwork and the problems attending thereto. Archaeology, historical linguistics, and other allied disciplines were brought more frontally into the interpretative mix. The result of all this was a retreat from facile certainty to a show-me attitude. In the process, the results of the first generation's work were subjected to some fairly serious assaults, but that work remains publicly accessible. Unfortunately, members of this pioneer generation largely declined to engage in the kind of extended colloquy that could have benefited later generations.

Among the most important of the new issues were the baneful effects of failing to share primary sources, the equally problematical results of interactive research, the role that acculturation plays in this kind of activity, the role of feedback into and then out of oral testimonies, and the dubious chronology imposed by, and on, oral traditions. Each of these is dealt with in turn below.

Four

In terms of sources, the collection and interpretation of oral data were unlike anything preceding. Traditionally, historians consulted printed or archival sources, drew conclusions from them, published these conclusions, and waited for others to respond. If such responses were not always forthcoming, it was not because it was particularly difficult to do so. Doubters had merely to consult the same sources used by those they doubted. In the spirit of the discipline, these were laid out in notes and bibliographies; all it required then for the critics was a sense of purpose and travel expenses. In this system no published interpretation was immune to the direst of attacks.

Unfortunately for the progress of the discipline, the historiography of precolonial Africa has not developed this way at all. From the very beginning, Africanist historians took to the field with notebooks and tape recorders, used them furiously—or so we are to gather—and wrote articles and books based on them. These contained a panoply of citations to interviews—names and identifications, dates, places, sometimes even references to complex alphanumeric classification systems. And then nothing. Perhaps in no more than 10 percent of the cases were the notebooks and/or field tapes deposited anywhere else than the historian's basement, attic, or office, despite the establishment of several depositories for just this purpose.

The potential effects of this course of action for the credibility of the discipline are enormous—and all bad. We may assume that by now these tapes have deteriorated to the point of complete uselessness. We are left then with the interpretation of these tapes and a referential system that, however elaborate, is of no value whatever other than for showcasing. As a result, those who summarily dismiss oral evidence as well as those who would like to test it can use the impossibility of disconfirming interpretations to denigrate such evidence, not only on its own terms, but on the basis that it is utterly unverifiable.[5]

Is this an extreme response? Not at all. No arguments or interpretations are of lasting value unless and until they can be tested. If someone were put into a windowless inner room and told that it was sprinkling or raining hard or even raining cats and dogs and then asked which of these seems most probable, they would have every right to say: "Why should I try to answer a question when I have been unfairly deprived of the chance to know enough to do so?" Sadly, this practice has not perceptibly diminished. Even though the interest in precolonial Africa has waned, at least temporarily, those working on colonial and contemporary issues still engage in oral interviews, have perhaps graduated to videotapes, but not advanced yet to the stage of offering their materials for scrutiny.

This inevitably brings up the matter of ownership of such materials, and to this there are moral, intellectual, and legal dimensions. By definition, an interview is at least two-sided. Which side owns the results? To date it has been taken for granted that the physical products of such interviews belong exclusively to the interviewer. If he or she cares to share them with informants—or with other scholars—this is his/her privilege, but it is not his/her obligation.

To my knowledge, those who talk about "hegemonic" behavior and attitudes have not discussed this very central and very palpable example. If nothing else, fieldwork is exploitation. The historian gains experience, raw materials, and a start on a life of scholarship. The interviewees, if nothing else, gain a new perspective on ingratitude, a place in bibliographies and, if lucky, in prefaces. This is to put it harshly, but it is not to put it too harshly. Still, the situation has no easy or consistent answer. The fact remains that information can be gained only in these ways, and it would be difficult to imagine an equitable scenario.

But it does seem that one palliation would be to return copies of tapes to informants, and to allow them their full input by depositing the same tapes in more accessible locations. To claim sole ownership of such tapes and to use that in turn to withhold them from fair use by others is not only disingenuous, but just plain wrong.

The reason often advanced for doing this is that dumping tapes and transcripts into the public domain would allow unscrupulous persons to use them even before that collectors themselves could. This is a reasonable excuse—for *delaying* the deposit for a reasonable time; however, the period should be shorter than forever. "Reasonable" is a treacherous word, but a period of no less than five years nor more than ten years seems to fit the word fairly well.

In the present circumstances, anthropologists and historians often publish one piece after another on the groups that they studied in the field. The pieces appear, are duly noted, possibly believed, but never scrutinized, because the evidence is never presented to permit this. This could be described as a house of cards, susceptible to unpredictable but total demolition. Suppose, for instance, that historian X was followed in the field twenty years later by historian Y, who happens to find that informants tell him that they lied to historian X, or simply produce evidence that contradicts the published conclusions of historian X.

As it happens, this recently occurred when Derek Freeman roundly criticized Margaret Mead's fieldwork in Samoa, and was in turn roundly criticized himself. Freeman claimed that Mead had been gulled in a crucial way by a couple of informants playing a practical joke. Mead was dead and could not respond directly, and the issue might well have lain there without resolution at all. However, in the 1920s Mead was forced to use pencil and paper rather than perishable tapes, and these she had conscientiously, if only eventually, deposited in the Library of Congress.

Consulting them could not answer the question—practical joke or not?—but did throw light on her interviewing and reasoning processes, and shows that both were careless.[6]

Whether they were more careless than those of other fieldworkers in the 1920s is less certain, but irrelevant. What matters is that access to Mead's fieldnotes has allowed scholars sounder grounds for assessing her conclusions—conclusions that have had an extraordinary influence both in anthropology and in the wider world. If Mead had deposited her fieldnotes within ten years after she took them, who knows how different this impact would have been?

Five

Whatever certain schools of thought maintain, reading a printed or manuscript text is not an interpersonal experience, however divergent the results might be. The text remains the same and does not change simply by being studied. Of all the differences between gathering written data and oral data, this must be the most significant.

Armed with whatever information they have gleaned from written sources, and with perhaps a few practice interviews under their belt, the researchers head for the field.[7] No matter how much they think they have learned about the *mores* of the group they are studying, it will never be anything like enough, but it will have to do—their time is limited, their goals high. In the first few interviews, historians are likely to be informants themselves, as they wend their way through bureaucratic channels to get the necessary authorizations to be on their way to wherever they are going. If they are paying attention, they learn a bit in these interviews about saying what the interviewer wants to hear. If the local authority asks them what they propose to study, they know, we hope, what not to say. Perhaps they have even been coached in this. At any rate, they respond to various questions in ways that they hope will be pleasing and get them their credentials.

If this works, they head to the field and immediately begin to think that interviewing is a straightforward process. Why? Because it makes life simpler? In any case, they must now organize themselves by deciding whom to interview, whether to indulge in group interviews, whether to hire interpreters and under what terms, and so forth. All these are part of learning—and learning fairly briskly—local intersocial protocols, no easy task. Even Africanist historians who work in their own societies, and who may therefore be presumed to understand its protocols better, fit into the social structure in ways that expatriates do not. Just as they understand their interviewers better than an expatriate might, their interviewees understand them better than they would an expatriate. This can make the process of dissembling not only easier for informants but imperative.

It is the rare expatriate Africanist historian who first goes to the field in fluent command of the local language/s. In many cases even African scholars are now working in areas beyond the reach of their mother tongue, so the question is less whether to engage an interpreter, but how and whom. Typically, interpreters are locals who have attained a secondary education and are sufficiently bilingual to perform an interpreter's usual duties. But what are these? In some respects, the interpreter is like the translator in the case of written sources—crucial yet problematic. Without him neither interviewer nor informants know what the other is saying. But do they know, even with an interpreter? Who is to say?

Of the many ways to transmit a message only one can be correct. An interpreter can repeat the historian's questions but only by interpreting them as well, since *verbatim* translations are most unlikely from radically different languages. Many times, in fact, a word, a concept, or an abstraction simply cannot be translated from one idiom to another. This means, among other things, that interpreters interpret far more than just words, far more even than just thoughts and ideas, and that along the way the process is inevitably distorted, however unwillingly or unwittingly.

Chances are that the historian is not, or is insufficiently, aware that this is happening, although only a moment's thought should tell him or her that it cannot be otherwise. Moreover, when the interpreter is present at the interview itself—which would be most of the time—that very presence can have a further distorting effect. Most societies, even the smallest, have social fissures and, if the historian is researching these widely, these will be cut across. This might be acceptable for a rank outsider, but where does the locally grounded interpreter fit in? He can never really be neutral, or at least will never be perceived as neutral. This might mean that he cannot transmit some questions as asked, or answers as answered, or that he will not receive frank answers to pass along because this would transgress some aspect of local etiquette.

In time perspicacious historians will improve their own language or social skills to the point where they will come to realize their predicament. Knowing this will seldom spur them to reinterviewing; in view of logistical constraints, this will seem wasteful. The pragmatic solution is to assume that it didn't happen often enough to matter and, better yet, that when it happened, it didn't matter because the occasions were peripheral.

Six

The exploitative nature of field research is often masked by payments of one kind of another to informants. Deciding what these should be and how they should be managed is one of the thorniest problems of fieldwork. If the payments are in the form of some negotiable currency, there is a real danger that informants will be encouraged to maximize their return, either by providing "more" or more "congenial" information. This commonsense, bottom-line approach to what has been turned into a business transaction is thoroughly understandable, and indeed, above reproach. But if historians fail to pick up on the changed terms, they are lost. And if they do, they might also be lost since they will have no other choice but to appear niggardly by withdrawing their largesse.

A slightly better alternative would be to express gratitude on an occasional, even spontaneous, basis by means of local sumptuary goods. This has the advantage of being less obviously *pro rata*, but hardly the advantage of having no effect on the question-and-answer process.

Yet a third alternative is to offer no payment at all, or at least any payment that can be construed solely as remuneration. Payment might be preempted by promises of sending back photographs, any books or articles that result from the experience, or whatever. The trouble with this is that it sounds, even from a distance, to be specious and patronizing, especially if the promises are not followed up—and what virtue is in shorter supply than gratitude? There are no foolproof ways of turning the effects of this inherently exploiter-exploited relationship into anything that can ensure objectivity, because there is no way to pretend successfully that field interviews are an equalized process.

Seven

Most fieldwork is a period of time squeezed between other periods of time that often make greater demands on the historian. The single most common impetus for fieldwork is to fulfill certain requirements for some kind of higher degree, which allows the successful historian to launch his career. Time and money constraints are ubiquitous in these circumstances. To keep overall momentum going, fieldwork is usually sandwiched tightly between course work and dissertation-writing. Funding is usually granted on the assumption that a year or less in the field—including archives—is sufficient for the task. If the money can be stretched, so much the better, but it often cannot, especially if the historian has a family. All this tempts him into finding ways to do more in less time—an understandable but perilous objective.

A common way to do this is to make do with group interviews. Why not get a dozen people's opinion at no more cost than interviewing only one of them? It is no surprise that, in the heady early days of African history, the group interview proved to be popular. The price though is either a completely fragmented notion of the past or one so homogenized that it constitutes no more than common opinion.

The problem with group interviews is actually fairly obvious. Group interviews are public interviews. The same social fissures mentioned above serve to pall the expressions of opinion so publicly that all can hear. Even in modernized societies this constraint applies: who has not heard the common phrase on the news: "*X* declined to be interviewed on camera." Worse, those who dissent from the reigning local orthodoxies are the least likely to speak out. The careless or lazy historian is quite likely to gain the impression that there are no disagreements about the past and go merrily on his way, blissful in his ignorance.

The same eventuality is likely when one or more individuals dominate the proceedings. Group dynamicists soon learn that all people are not equal after all. In any group, one or a few people will dominate the discussion, whether by ascription or force of personality. Again, if historians are careless, they will miss this, or they might assume that the dominators have been deputed to speak on behalf of the majority. This might even prove to be true, but the conclusion should be drawn only after further investigation.

All this is not to say that there is no value in group interviewing. But it *is* to say that the value is diagnostic and not informational. The shrewd fieldworker tries to conduct group interviews at an early stage precisely in order to gauge the *complexity* of opinions about the past. When the dominator/s speak, the careful historian is busy looking around for scowls, shakings of the head, abrupt departures, and the like. It is these people that the historian should make sure to interview. Of course the historian should interview the dominant voices as well, but should be sure to plumb the reasons why they appear to monopolize discussion. Is it a general deference to their presumed knowledge, or merely a desire to avoid crossing them because of their wealth, position, or temperament?

At some point interviews reach the individualized stage. Here the ambiance is critical. Is it at a place or time preferred by the informant, or by the historian? Is anyone present who should not be? Is the tape recorder discreetly positioned to avoid allowing the informant to speak to it rather than to the historian? Is there a local etiquette (not using the left hand, for instance) that needs to be followed scrupulously?

All protocols having been observed, the historian at last begins to ask questions. Asking the right questions in the best way is no easy task at all. First, the historian should probably try to take the informant into his or her confidence by explaining why he or she is there, what he or she hopes to accomplish, and how it will benefit the informant and his community. Doing this not only is a courtesy to the informant, but it helps to break the ice and even to crystallize in the historian's own mind what he or she is up to.

Everyone knows, if they stop to think about it, that the form of the question goes a long way to shaping the form of the answer. In courtrooms, lawyers often object to "leading questions," designed to elicit from the witness the very testimony the interlocutor wants on the record. Judges usually agree with the objectors. Leading questions can be defined as any questions that contains a hint of the desired response. Suppose the historian prefers to believe that X led a migration to Y at time Z. He could be particularly heavy-handed by asking: "Isn't it true that X came here from Y about Z?" Or he might tone it down just a little by rephrasing it: "Did X come here from Y at Z?" Still less persistent but hardly less obvious, he might put it this way: "Did someone from Y come here at Z?" Even if the informant doesn't know who X was, if he fails to question the rest of the premise, the eager historian might well feel legitimated. Even an apparently innocuous question such as "How did you get here?" implies some kind of population movement rather than an autochthonous development.

Judging rigorously, all these questions, and others like them, would have to be rejected as inappropriate and leading. What is left? A great deal, actually. It is to be assumed that the historian comes to interviewing with at least a fuzzy hypothesis in mind. That is fair enough, but it becomes unfair as soon as he transmits this hypothesis directly to any informants, for this fatally compromises the exercise. Much the best way to start would be to move seamlessly from the introduction discussed above into more, but not directed, specifics. Having explained himself, the historian can then ask his informant if he has any information that seems to fit into the historian's perspective. If the informant responds with someone along the lines of "like what?" the historians stays vague but persistent, asking him perhaps to tell him what his parents or grandparents had told him about their lives and the lives of those who preceded them.

There are many paths to take, but the only ones that matter are those that begin with open-ended, non-revealing questions. The historian who goes to the field determined to have his view of things confirmed, no matter what, is a danger to himself and his discipline. Not doing so, though, requires more than a modicum of self-discipline. Seeing an informant floundering, the historian will find it hard to contain his anxiety to help the informant at the cost of helping himself.

Eight

Written sources do not perform; human beings are always performing. Although a truism, it is often forgotten in the chase. In all societies high-level performing is well-regarded and in smaller-scale, largely oral, societies it seems to be valued all the more, or at least all the more obviously. Many accounts of such societies' pasts are consciously shaped into texts that reward performance by subordinating the story-line to the performing opportunities. In these cases it becomes all but impossible to relay the information *without* couching it in theatrical terms.

This is true even in one-on-one occasions, but substantially truer when there is an audience—not a group of listeners, mind, but an audience. On these occasions, narrating the past is a community affair, with the narrator and the choir sharing and shaping the story as they go along. On these occasions improvisation may be more highly regarded than mere accuracy of content or transmission, which might well mean as little to the performers as it does much to the historian. In these cases, it is the "story" in "history" that is being told, and while it might contain historical information that borders on knowledge, these parts are indistinguishable from their laden contexts.

Nine

The historian using written documents is likely to find it easy to recheck her sources should a problem arise. She merely goes to a copy of the manuscript or book or offprint, finds the crux, and then proceeds. At worst the historian will have to write off for a copy. What does the oral historian do? At one level the task is much the same. She can pull out a tape (presuming it hasn't disintegrated) or notebook and check the data there and then proceed just as a colleague rechecking written sources would.

But that is checking *in* a source; how about checking *on* a source? The documentary historian does not have this problem, for in such case the two operations are the same. When the historian looks a second time she will *see* exactly what she saw the first time. If she *apprehends* it differently, it is the historian who has changed, not the source. But the historian who concedes that people change, and that her sources were people, has a major headache if she wants to conduct a pilot project to test for change. If such a historian is provident, she will have thought of this before leaving the field, or even before entering it, and will have a conscious strategy of asking the same informants the same questions at widely separated times or in differing circumstances. Some informants will take umbrage at the implications, others will have forgotten that she had already asked them these very questions, or maybe any questions at all. Either way, the historian must persist. The less provident but still scrupulous historian, who only realizes after leaving the field that there are serious discrepancies in the collected evidence that can only be resolved by asking questions again, must return, however inconvenient this would be.

Whatever the circumstances, when the idea has been converted into the deed, the historian might find disaster in the form of different answers from the same informants. How different can they be? This is a hard question to answer since context matters; suffice to say that there is little room for generosity here; slight variations in names or dates are probably acceptable, any more should raise the reddest of warning flags.

Assuming the worst, how should the historian proceed? The options are few here, conscientious ones even fewer. A historian could damn the torpedos and proceed as if unimpeded by their shock waves until finally hitting one or blundering through, knowing one should never have cast off in the first place—knowing as well that one will be forever susceptible to another torpedo attack. A historian might take special care to explain in footnotes or in a methodological appendix what kinds of changes were encountered and why they do—or do not—matter.

Or, he might do as Paul Irwin did for Liptako in Burkina Faso.[8] Having completed his fieldwork there and his dissertation on it, Irwin realized that the oral interviews he conducted presented far more discrepancies than he felt comfortable with. He could have proceeded pell-mell; probably no one would have known otherwise, but his scholarly conscience forbade this expedient. Instead, he returned to Liptako, reinterviewed numerous informants, got numerous differing answers, and came home to work out the implications. In the event the book he wrote was not only different from his dissertation—most are expected to be—but actually constituted the first—and last—assault on his earlier work.

Irwin's book is frequently cited today, but less for his interpretation of the historical experience of Liptako, than for his own experiences there. To some it will actually seem postmodern in that regard, but for Africanist historians, it is a cautionary tale that tells us that penetrating the oral past is no easy task. It is a pity that it is one of the few *mea culpa* books of this kind, for its heuristic value quite surpasses what would otherwise have been a straightline narrative interpretation of Liptako's nineteenth- and twentieth-century past.

Anthropologists practice what they call restudies on a formal, if not routine, basis. That is, an aspiring anthropologist or perhaps one already ensconced in the field attempts to revisit a society already "classically" treated by a predecessor anthropologist from twenty to fifty years earlier. The process includes reading all the literature on the group in question, whether by the original anthropologist or by others, as well as whatever fieldnotes survive. The purpose is twofold. The first is to try to discern, and if possible measure, any changes in the society in the interim. To do this effectively, certainly to measure it, would require that the original anthropologist—unchanged himself in the interim—carried out the experiment, much in the way of Paul Irwin and Liptako.

A second result, perhaps at first unintended, is to pass judgment on the work of the pioneer anthropologist. In some cases, change is illusory because the earliest anthropologist got too many things wrong, invalidating any attempt to plot change from point A to point B, simply because point A is found not to exist. The Mead-Freeman controversy mentioned above emanated from just such a situation. Freeman did not go to Samoa twenty years or so after Mead in order to check her work, but when he came to conclude that she was wrong, he engaged in a fuller-scale and more systematic inquiry. The next step, of course, is to follow in Freeman's own footsteps in order to restudy and reevaluate *his* work.

There is little of this in African oral history. The reasons for this deficiency are not hard to find. Some argue that African historiography is still too inchoate. Rather than bothering to recheck someone's earlier work, it is more important to carry out different work before it is "too late." This is specious reasoning, since such restudies are imperative for evaluating the methodology of the entire field.[9] If many early studies are found wanting, it certainly brings into question the overall theory and method behind fieldwork in oral history. If they are not, then there can be renewed confidence, and renewed energy, devoted to this part of Africa's history.

Then too, the field is so young that restudies almost necessarily tread on the toes of the living, perhaps even the active. There is little reward in this, especially for the historian who is only aspiring to eminence. There is more merit in this, if unfortunately so. Academic politics takes second place to no known cutthroat activity of thinking man, and, sad to say, many, probably most, senior academics frown spectrally on efforts to show their work at fault.

A third reason is more significant, not least in that it can cover for the first two reasons. Fieldwork is time-consuming, expensive, and even unhealthy. Why engage in it only to check the work of others? Where are the restudiers to come from? The senior Africanist historians are too old for active fieldwork and in any case would not often be satisfied to criticize themselves.

Finally, the best—and the worst—reason of all. From all appearances, the restudier, the rethinker, is his or her own worst enemy. Like textual editing, relooking at the works of others, no matter how significant methodologically, does not put the historian on the fast track. Too often it is regarded as hackwork—and hatchet work. The restudier is deprecated by those whom he or she has challenged and their epigones, and lightly regarded by those who have no vested interests. It might not be without significance that Paul Irwin did not receive tenure a few years after *Liptako Speaks* appeared. Whether he was regarded as dangerously uncollegial for criticizing himself, I cannot say, but those who know the case feel they have cause to wonder about just this.

Ten

Those who conduct fieldwork in oral societies have a tendency to take the word "oral" too seriously, and thus to ignore too readily signs that written works have affected traditions that they would prefer to think of as pristine. The process, which folklorists call "feedback," is sometimes risibly obvious, but more often not. And obviously it applies with different degrees of *gravitas* from one area to another.

My experience in southern Ghana, where we might expect a very high incidence of feedback, confirmed that suspicion.[10] It must be said that I did not enter the archives with such a suspicion in mind. Instead, I gradually grew suspicious of the evidence that kept appearing before me. It probably began when I was reading some testimony regarding succession to one of the numberless tiny polities there called "stools." The stool authorities proved a litigious lot and the files were bursting with one inquiry after another. As I read these I began to be struck by references to "Bosman" or "Claridge" or "Reindorf." I knew these as earlier historians of southern Ghana and knew what their testimony was. I had presumed (I think) that they had gathered this testimony from oral inquiries of their own and I was in the archives hoping to find more examples where oral tradition confirmed it, and thus, *ex hypothesi*, themselves.

It began to appear, though, that the exact opposite was happening. More and more references to earlier published works on the history of the Gold Coast (the previous name of the area) forced me to consider what I regarded, in my naïveté, as unwelcome news. After a while I began to notice that the traditions proffered at the inquiries (largely from the 1920s to the 1950s) always mentioned the names of alleged previous rulers that appeared in these published sources. I also began to notice that if X was mentioned in the sixteenth or seventeenth centuries, then some twentieth-century stoolholder named X II would turn up. Unrealistically, there appeared to be no rulers named X in the in the intervening centuries, but only shortly after the original X's name had appeared in one of these publications. I also found correspondence that showed that disputants made a habit of asking the colonial government for copies of one or another of these works.

Since the real history of most of these stools is virtually unknown before the early twentieth century, it is impossible to be sure that masses of feedbacking explained the situation. But the pattern was widespread enough and consistent enough to make it a virtual certainty and, at the very least, the most reasonable default hypothesis.

This epiphany convinced me to look elsewhere in the world of oral tradition, particularly in Polynesia, where the history of historical sources is much the same as for Africa. There I found stories of a primordial couple, a universal flood, a redeemer god, and other things that made sense only if there was once universal knowledge of the Christian Bible or if the teachings of nineteenth-century missionaries had quickly and silently infiltrated into what appeared to be indigenous traditions.[11] To me the choice was easy: hypothesis number two.

The harsh among us would call this plagiarism, for sources were very seldom acknowledged. However, others might think of it as fighting fire wth fire. The colonial masters palpably placed greater value on written sources than on oral traditions and those invoking the past did the same thing, but, cleverly, did it *sub rosa*. To them plagiarism was not even a notion, and certainly not a sin. Copyright meant nothing and intellectual property was freely shared. Most of us would probably do the same to maintain or advance our interests. The problem is that Africanist historians were a long time in noticing that their subjects were not empty test tubes, but of a mind to learn about their own past without being prodded by the researcher. In doing so, they freely added to their store of knowledge in this respect. If the colonialists' book recorded that *X* ruled in 1670, who were they to diasgree?

To counter this refreshing, but still debilitating, fact, the historian must do at least three things. The first is to determine the visibility of earlier published materials in the community they work in, and then to compare carefully the results of their own inquest to these published materials. The second is to learn more about the education of their informants and others in the community and, with that, the degree of acculturation. The third, and often the most important, is to study closely the missionary experience and influence in the community, tracing it as far back as possible and investing whatever effort is necessary to consult the relevant mission records.

This seems like a lot of work, and it is. But without it, the important task of validating oral tradition by showing its independence is impossible, and leads only to a loss of credibility outside the immediate family. It was once thought—and still is by some—that oral tradition comprised a unified, coherent, consistent body of information that passed down from generation to generation essentially unchanged until the modern historian had at it. The absurdity of this notion should be self-evident, but for those who wish to believe anyway, any evidence of feedback is crippling. And this is the very reason to search vigorously for it.

Eleven

There is a centuries-old saying to the effect that without chronology there can be no history. The reasons are obvious enough. If history, as most agree, is the study of, and explanation for, change, then the progression and duration of events must be established as accurately as possible so that the pace, direction, and essence of such change can be identified properly.

The new generation of African historians recognized this well, and from the very beginning they attempted to apply chronology to the available oral data. Several options were open to them, all of them indirect and approximate. In rare lucky cases, a name appeared in oral tradition which seemed very much like a name that appeared in a published text and that could be roughly or exactly dated. Of course, it was always assumed that close was close enough in these instances, and such identifications were routinely made and followed. Often they proved to be correct.

Lacking such benchmarks, which was the vast majority of the time, intending chronologers had to rely on such things as generational dating, purported eclipses, and archaeological dating.[12] To date, generational averaging has been the most common means to ascribe dates to the names in the traditions. The first, and still the most popular, figure for a generation's length, was twenty-seven years. On the face of it, the number is entirely plausible, but we are immediately faced with a classic GIGO (garbage in, garbage out) situation.[13] The number might be plausible, but are the data accurate? That is, were both the number of names *and* the genealogical filiations correct? At first the temptation was to think that they were, but it did not take much scrutiny to prove otherwise. The lists were suspicious on several grounds. They were late bloomers, and when they did bloom, it was under the usual exigencies of Indirect Rule ("my lineage can beat your lineage"). There was an unlikely number of father-to-son successions, which tended to add to the prescribed length of the kinglists but detracted from their credibility.

These things became known, however, only when the weight of comparative evidence was applied, for one of the great weaknesses of the first several generations of African historians was their lack of exposure to the historical experience of other parts of the world. Failing this, they were forced—or allowed themselves—to draw conclusions in isolation that proved unlikely (in most cases; sometimes they were *prima facie* ridiculous) as soon as they were contrasted with a much larger database.

The attempt to date precolonial African history by lunar or solar eclipses was doomed from the start.[14] Again, it suffered from a missing comparative perspective, which shows how readily astronomical phenomena become agglutinated with historic, but terrestrial, events. In most cases, the descriptions handed down in oral tradition (or borrowed through feedback) were entirely too vague to be treated as eclipses in any case. Generally, astronomical dating has fallen by the wayside more emphatically than generational dating, for whatever reasons. Presumably, for some, it seems just too dangerous. For the moment, then, the dating of precolonial Africa is pretty much undecided. Those who believe in the testimony of traditions find ways to push royal lines, and thus official history, back to, and even before, the beginning of the second millennium. Others doubt that many of the rulers named in the tradition ever existed. It is not an issue likely to be resolved.

Twelve

While oral data are practically the only source for early African history, they serve as well to supplement inquiry into more recent periods, especially in works that follow the "bottom-up" or "subaltern" approach. These seek to provide a better balance by subordinating the official ("elite") record to the recollections of those whose voices seldom appear in this record, and then only in an adversarial way. In effect these are contributions to the life-history genre, in which individuals great and small testify to their lives, the lives of others as they saw them, and events from a perspective far different than the canonical one.

The life history developed in the U.S. during the 1930s, when ex-slaves were interviewed in large numbers. These then were preserved and have been used many times since to offer counter-images to the more readily available historical record. Those who collected these narratives were trained in interviewing techniques, but did not intend to write history. The results are variable, but served as an exemplar for those who were to follow.

Ironically, these concentrated on the powerful and influential at first, only later (from the 1970s) shifting to the underclasses. Several journals have been established to represent workers in this field, some of whom are academics while others are hobbyists and sometimes eager genealogists.[15] One result of the oral history movement is the development of sets of guidelines that collectors are asked to follow in order to improve the quality and consistency of their work.

One of the issues in the oral history movement is particularly relevant to African historians working in the field. At issue is whether it is preferable to spend time collecting audiodata or to devote the time to transcribing. It seems that the weight of choice runs toward the second of these, under the assumption that most users prefer transcriptions to tapes. Maybe so, but it is not a preference to be catered to. Each transcription takes many hours per hour of tape, time that could be spent collecting further materials for later processing.

More important, only the tape can provide telling indications of the informant's attitudes while testifying. Laughter, hesitations, vocal disagreement from the audience, corrections, and several other diagnostics come through on tape but are lost forever in the transcription. Whatever precautions and care are taken to carry them forward, there can be no substitute for the real thing, and any historian who is willing to settle for the transcriptions when the tapes are available is unforgivably remiss in the same sense that historians who use documents settle for a translation or an abridgement.

Thirteen

If this litany of precautions seems excessive, it is because the collection, interpretation, and presentation of oral data can only remain a central feature of African historiography—admittedly, not as central as it was thirty or more years ago, but important enough that its use be assured by as many safeguards as possible. Moreover, the opportunities to reprocess oral data collected in the field are severely restricted—usually there is only one bite of this apple. In fact, looking back, it is tragic how much of the oral tradition that was collected in the early years has proved unusable. More tragic is that, from this perspective, we cannot know whether the futility was intrinsic, the result of deficient collecting methods, or a combination of both. For better or worse, a great deal of that work has to be written off as history, even if still useful as condign examples of the effects of growing pains in a new discipline.

In several cases archaeological evidence has reinforced the oral testimony, a situation that seems necessary if the testimony is to be believed. In fact, the best hope is that oral data and other evidence combine in ways that produce complementarity and symbiosis. Data that have been collected under ideal circumstances could be reliable; at the least they deserve a suspension of disbelief.

To become fully operational, the use of oral data must encompass *at least* the deposit of raw materials with limited or no restrictions on their use; accompanying details of interviewing and collecting techniques; and a full list of informants and formal questions. Until these happen, at a minimum, oral data cannot be regarded as full-fledged historical sources and can be disregarded without further ado. This is a high price to pay, but a cardinal rule of historical interpretations is that their audience have the right to test these to the fullest possible extent. Depriving them of this opportunity is scholarly malfeasance. Universities and funding institutions are in the best position to encourage these developments, merely by insisting on them as a condition of funding or degree-granting. We can depend on innate altruism as an alternative, but experience shows little reason to expect success.

Fourteen

It cannot be emphasized too strongly here that, although this discussion has centered on the *collection* of oral tradition, whether encountered in the raw or in printed form, the points made are valid for the *collection* of all forms of historical inquiry, even though most of them do not have some of the handicaps (e.g., the interpersonal aspects, the untold number of transmissions) that so characterize the creation of oral data. In particular, the attitude of mind when approaching historical evidence is very much the same. Succinctly put, it amounts to this: search widely, suspend judgment, be self-critical at every stage of the process, never assume that your interpretations cannot be challenged, and be willing to challenge them yourself if it seems necessary. These are admittedly abstract goals, but not unrealizable for that. When they are successfully carried out, the work submitted for the approval of the present and the future will be able better to resist assaults. It will also be intrinsically more reliable, even, in some ways, more authentic. Given the critical importance of oral data to the study of the past—and not only the African past—this is not inconsequential.

Notes

1. Although this essay happens to concentrate on Africa, the principles argued here are applicable to oral research under any circumstances, and many of them to research with written sources as well. I covered some of these points in my *Oral Historiography* (London, 1982).

2. Susan Niditch, *Oral World and Written World: Ancient Israelite Literature* (Louisville, 1996); Rosalind Thomas, *Oral Tradition and Written Records in Classical Athens* (Cambridge, 1989) and *Literacy and Orality in Ancient Greece* (Cambridge, 1992).

3. Jan Vansina, *Oral Tradition* (Chicago, 1965). Later Vansina cast his argument in a more explicitly historical framework; see his *Oral Tradition as History* (Madison, Wis., 1985).

4. For examples of the two extremes see David Henige, *The Chronology of Oral Tradition: Quest for a Chimera* (Oxford, 1974), and J. B. Webster, ed., *Chronology, Migration, and Drought in Interlacustrine Africa* (New York, 1978).

5. David Henige, "'In the Possession of the Author': the Problem of Source Monopoly in Oral Historiography," *International Journal of Oral History* 1 (1980): 181–94.

6. Derek Freeman, *Margaret Mead and Samoa: the Making and Unmaking of an Anthropological Myth* (Cambridge, Mass., 1983) and *The Fateful Hoaxing of Margaret Mead: a Historical Analysis of her Samoan Research* (Boulder, Colo., 1999); Martin Orans, *Not Even Wrong: Margaret Mead, Derek Freeman, and the Samoans* (Novato, Cal., 1996).

7. Carolyn Keyes Adenaike and Jan Vansina, eds., *In Pursuit of History: Fieldwork in Africa* (Portsmouth, UK, 1996).

8. Paul Irwin, *Liptako Speaks: History from Oral Tradition in Africa* (Princeton, 1981).

9. A chastening example of the salutary effects of retracing earlier fieldwork is Walter E. A. van Beek, "Dogon Restudied: A Field Evaluation of the Work of Marcel

Griaule," *Current Anthropology* 32 (1991): 139–67 (including comments and response), which appears to throw into considerable doubt many of the conclusions Griaule drew about Dogon life and cosmology.

10. David Henige, "The Problem of Feedback in Oral Tradition: Four Examples from the Fante Coastlands," *Journal of African History* 14 (1973): 223–35.

11. David Henige, "'Truths Yet Unborn'? Oral Tradition as a Casualty of Culture Contact," *Journal of African History* 23 (1982): 395–412, and sources cited there.

12. The matter is treated at great length in Henige, *Chronology of Oral Tradition*.

13. GIGO, for "garbage in, garbage out," is an old computer saying.

14. Richard Gray, "Eclipse Maps," *Journal of African History* 6 (1965): 251–62 and "Annular Eclipse Maps," *Journal of African History* 9 (1968): 147–57; David Henige, "'Day Was of Sudden Turned into Night': On the Use of Eclipses for Dating Oral History," *Comparative Studies in Society and History* 18 (1976): 476–501.

15. E.g., *Oral History, Oral History Review*, and *International Journal of Oral History*.

7

ORAL SOURCES AND THE CHALLENGE OF AFRICAN HISTORY

Barbara M. Cooper

African history, perhaps more than other domains of history, has had to be inventive in its use of sources and eclectic in its approach to evidence: Africanists draw upon linguistic, archaeological, ethnographic, genealogical, oral-performative, and oral-interview evidence in addition to the documentary sources more conventionally understood as primary sources within the discipline. This broad view of sources is due in large part to the relative paucity of written documentary materials for the continent. It would be a mistake, however, to overstate the absence of documentary sources for the construction of African history (see chapter 9, by John Thornton, in this volume): depending on the region and period in question, documentary evidence can be quite rich. It would be an even bigger mistake to imagine that African historians by and large rely on any one kind of evidence to the exclusion of others—the long history of debate over the nature and suitability of oral tradition for the reconstruction of the African past, which I shall discuss below, has obscured the reality that few historians rely exclusively on oral evidence in their work. Historical linguists supplement their thinking with archaeological evidence, archaeological historians draw inspiration from oral tradition, champions of oral evidence complement their work with documentary sources, and so on. Our confidence in our reconstructions of the past derives in part from the ways in which these various sources and methods, when used together, can refine, challenge, inspire, reinforce, or confirm one another. One of the most dramatic ways in which sources complement one another has been when oral traditions have been used to successfully locate important archaeological sites.[1]

In what follows I shall focus on oral historical data that is solicited by the researcher, in order to contextualize work on Africa that I regard as being in dialogue with the broader post-war development of oral history within the discipline of history. David Henige's contribution to this volume (chapter 6) has addressed one important kind of oral evidence that has been central to the development of African history as a discipline, namely oral tradition. Oral traditions are generally stories about the past that local populations produce and reproduce through oral performative transmission, as a means of preserving their own history and consolidating or contesting a sense of belonging and identity. Oral traditions can be cosmologically grounded; they often begin with myths of creation and go on to provide tales of origin for particular communities; they frequently celebrate the exploits of more or less legendary culture heroes; and they are dramatic and episodic. The performers of oral tradition are, perhaps above all else, as Joseph Miller remarks, good storytellers.[2]

In this chapter I will discuss a closely related but distinguishable kind of evidence that is undoubtedly more familiar as historical evidence to historians of other regions, namely oral history. Since the development of reasonably portable recording technology after 1945, historians have attempted to supplement the biases and gaps in documentary data by eliciting interviews with some of the central but sometimes neglected participants in late nineteenth and twentieth century history: workers, women, minorities, ex-slaves, peasants, and community leaders. Such evidence has not been limited to the histories of those who are generally marginalized, however; oral evidence has enlivened biographies of well-known personages by providing perspectives, details, and color that are not available in primary documents.[3] Oral history, then, is personal reminiscence solicited by the researcher in an interview format, and it may focus on the life history of the person being interviewed, on specific events of interest to the historian, or on the subject's perhaps idiosyncratic memories of a family, neighborhood, community, or movement. Generally the temporal depth the historian attempts to recover through such evidence is limited to the actual memories of events in which the interlocutor took part and perhaps the interlocutor's reminiscences about hearing stories relevant to the topic of research. Here the stories are treated as idiosyncratic memories rather than as "oral traditions." The researcher tends not to lose sight of the individuality of the person being interviewed, however shaped his or her narrative might be by communal concerns.

The long commitment of Africanists to oral sources, whether they be traditions or personal narratives, derives from a healthy skepticism about permitting written sources, often produced by outsiders to the continent, to stand as the only recognized evidence about Africa's past. However complex or problematic the use of oral sources might be, the now-established tradition of commitment to their use is of a piece with a broader post-World War II commitment within history as a discipline to recuperate the unrecognized voices and experiences of the disadvantaged. That the use of oral sources is bound up with this broader democratic impulse has not always been recognized by Africanists, largely because debates about the use of oral sources have tended to focus upon how to systematically deploy "oral tradition" to gain chunks of usable evidence about the past rather than upon how to think about oral evidence, memory, and subjectivity more broadly. These debates have occluded somewhat the ways in which our work is in fact typical of much work done in social and cultural history since the 1960s. In our defensiveness about the recoverability of the history of the "barbarous tribes" derided by Hugh Trevor-Roper, we have neglected to engage in debate with the many historians of other parts of the world whose work has been very much in sympathy with our own. We have also, on the whole, missed an opportunity to share our own methodological insights with historians who might find them striking and useful. In this chapter I urge developing historians to draw on the shared methodological ground of oral history to begin to make African history more exciting and more accessible to our colleagues outside of African studies. Because African Studies is inevitably interdisciplinary, and because the use of oral history requires an interdisciplinary sensibility, we can for once turn our perceived weakness into a strength if we think more carefully about how our work intersects with work in history more broadly, and if we learn to pitch our writing in such a way that its relevance is more visible to outsiders.

Debates Concerning Oral Tradition

There have been four major moments of debate about the use and interpretation of oral tradition as history since the rise of African history as a formal academic discipline in the late 1950s. The first debate was implicitly between the champions of Africa as a place with a significant and recoverable history and those historians who, with Hugh Trevor-Roper, would dismiss the African past out of hand. Jan Vansina and his students in particular worked tirelessly to develop a rigorous approach to the use of oral traditional evidence to recover the history of nonliterate peoples.[4] Unfortunately this work did not engage particularly directly with two other important movements within history and popular memory in the same era, namely the growth of "democratic and popular" oral history projects in Britain under the aegis of such historians as Paul Thompson and the increased interest among African Americans seeking access to their own past inspired by Alex Haley's *Roots*.[5] If anything Africanist historians, in the rush to gain credibility relative to more established historical fields, minimized the common ground between oral tradition and oral history and between African history and popular history. This has meant that Africanists have not tended to cite or engage with oral historians of other regions. It has also meant that, beyond the obligatory footnote, few oral historians of other regions have delved deeply into the work of central figures in African history such as Jan Vansina.[6]

More tragically, behind the scenes Africanist historians tended to belittle both the methods and the emotional impulse undergirding the African-American enthusiasm for oral history, with consequences that have been extremely damaging to African Studies as a whole. Rather than engage in constructive debate in a cooperative and supportive spirit, mainstream African history retreated to an academic high ground disengaged from the interests and resources of African-American popular authors and scholars. One result of this was that very little of the work produced by mainstream Africanist historians was taken up by a popular American audience. I regret that my own work, as much as anyone's, bears the marks of this legacy of omissions. This chapter is an opening venture towards ways in which Africanists might make their way into broader conversations.

Within a decade or so a new stage in the debates had developed, for while Vansina and his students might have silenced (if not convinced) the skeptical historians, their argument that oral traditions consisted at least in part of orally transmitted memories of actual past events were vigorously challenged by anthropologists. Functionalists such as Laura Bohannon, following Malinowski, pointed out that much oral traditional evidence served as a charter to support contemporary political and social orders. Oral traditions, by this understanding, function to reproduce, adjudicate, and justify existing practices—they tell us a great deal about the present and relatively little about the past. To treat them as records of the past is to render into fixity something which, in order to function properly as a homeostatic mechanism of social order, must in reality remain fluid and changeable. This is what one might call the presentist critique of oral tradition as history.[7] Structuralists such as Luc de Heusch, following Claude Lévi-Strauss, emphasized instead the symbolic and universal dimensions of oral traditions that would seem to render them timeless rather than historical. Pointing out that historians tended to underplay the mythical elements in traditions, structuralists explored the central human dilemmas played out through myth, offering what one might call the cosmological critique of oral traditions as history. This critique made comparatively literal readings of mythical elements of traditions seem like wishful thinking. Instead structuralist anthropologists presented elegant interpretations of the mythic elements as symbols through which the human mind explores painful human paradoxes.[8]

Historians of Africa responded vigorously to the structuralist (cosmological) critique in 1980 in a major collection edited by Joseph Miller, *The African Past Speaks*, in which historians reflected more explicitly than usual upon the means by which evidence and hypotheses about the past can be derived from oral tradition. The volume clarifies how a close attention to the ways in which cultural understanding, political struggle, and memory shape or "structure" oral traditions will provide important methodological insights. In many ways the contributions revealed that it was more useful to focus on inconsistencies, disagreements, "seams," and other anomalies within and between different oral traditions than to rely on the claims of the narratives themselves taken at face value. Historians had already begun to develop arguments for traditions as "complex ethnographic documents in which the narrative aspects may be among the least important elements for inferring history."[9] The very structuring processes to be found shaping oral traditional evidence inevitably give rise to contradictions and inconsistencies that signal to the literate historian central problems, shifts, struggles, and noisy silences.

Interestingly, in the same period historians such as Luisa Passerini and Alessandro Portelli were urging oral historians to shift away from seeing oral history as simply providing chunks of evidence about the past. They criticized the naive populism that uncritically accepts and celebrates oral interview evidence as the authentic vantage point of the subordinated population. Rather, they pointed to the role of subjectivity in history, drawing on silences, discrepancies, and idiosyncrasies to think about the social production of history and its contradictions. This vantage point not only led to a more critical use of oral sources but also opened the way to make fuller use of what is distinctive about oral sources: their foregrounding of the partiality and subjectivity of historical memory. As Portelli remarks: "Oral history changes the writing of history much as the modern novel transformed the writing of literary fiction: the most important change is that the narrator is now pulled into the narrative and becomes a party of the story . . . the *telling* of the story is part of the story being told."[10] It is, to my mind, a terrible shame that the communities of historians working on tradition in Africa and on oral historical evidence elsewhere did not begin to find significant grounds for convergence, comparison, and regrouping around the very issues of partiality, structuring, and subjectivity that both were attempting to come to terms with.

One significant area in which such common ground of inquiry might have been forged was consideration of the role of feminist approaches to history and their implications for oral historical work. It is striking how much of the important work on oral history in Africa has in fact arisen in the literature on women and gender (for a fuller treatment of the literature on gender in Africa, see chapter 19, by Kathleen Sheldon, in this volume). Scholars seem to have been particularly inclined to turn to oral approaches to redress the triple erasure of African women from conventional documentary sources due to race, gender, and class positions. As a dual result, one rich literature uses women's life histories to anchor the work on oral history in Africa and another draws on oral sources to inform the work on gender in Africa.[11] One reason why the work on women's personal narratives has not fully articulated with oral historical work more often has been that much of it has been done by female scholars in disciplines other than history. Central examples would include Mary Smith's *Baba of Karo* and Marjorie Shostak's *Nisa!*[12] Many historians of Africa who have attempted to seek out models for life history approaches have accordingly relied heavily on work in anthropology and sociology that has been less concerned to engage in explicit debates about oral history and has focused, rather, on debates in feminism, including discussions of the ethics of the research situation and the plausibility of imagining that oral history is in some way transformative or liberating in itself.[13]

Debates on oral tradition were, on the whole, oblivious to or deliberately distanced from developments in the realms of oral history and gender research. Even if, by the late 1980s, African historians committed to oral traditional sources had quieted the critiques of the structuralist anthropologists (having in the process become a good deal more sophisticated in terms of symbolic analysis as a result), the problems raised by the functionalists were harder to dismiss, partly because history as a discipline was itself struggling to come to terms with the problem of the invention of tradition more broadly. This discovery often occurred precisely among those Africanist scholars who had focused on the rare documentary space in which women were indeed likely to appear, if only in idealized form, namely the law. Works by such authors as Martin Chanock and Marcia Wright were making clear that as oral "tradition" was translated into the literate legal domain under colonial rule, the "customary law" that emerged was in fact a vehicle for struggles between men and women, elders and juniors, under the shifting circumstances of colonialism.[14] An awareness that tradition is not inert but is rather the product of human agency and can serve the agendas of various parties is, of course, one of the tools the historian can use to decode the structure of oral traditional accounts. The insights of Africanists such as Terence Ranger were central to the growing attention to the issue of the uses of "tradition" throughout the discipline.[15] The functionalist observation—that "tradition" can be modified to accommodate and legitimize political positions in the present—opened the door to more troubling reflections about the construction of the past and the nature of interpretive authority. In the context of recent interest in deconstruction (through which the logic of any text can be dismantled from within to reveal the subjectiveness of its claims to knowledge), this insight has been profoundly unsettling to historians. It calls into question the objectivity of all historical accounts, implicates history in the very politics it strains to describe objectively, and undermines historians' confidence in the possibility of arriving at any final interpretation of the past.

Most recently the debates about the uses of "tradition" in contemporary struggles have centered around Cohen and Odhiambo's *Burying SM.*[16] The book describes, yet refuses ultimately to come to a conclusive interpretation of, a legal battle in Kenya between the widow of a prominent lawyer and the members of his clan over how he should be buried. In this legal battle in a modern courtroom, the central problem of how "authentic" understandings of traditional practices are to be determined came to a head as different modes of interpretive authority clashed. In the context of a legal battle, the phrases "traditional history" and "oral evidence" take on heightened meaning, for here the evidence is not simply to be used to construct a written text arguing for one interpretation or another of the past. The broader understanding of property, women's rights in Kenya, the role of the State in private lives, the ability of individuals to choose particular lifestyles, the nature of ethnicity—all were at stake in this case. The authors wryly note that "if one would bring methods of deconstruction to the close reading of the text of the case, one should also recognize that practices of deconstruction were extensively deployed within the case by the cast of litigants, witnesses, counsel, and jurists themselves."[17] Anthropological, historical, and "traditional" evidence were all brought to bear in order to stake claims of different kinds over the body and to undermine other claims; these struggles, the authors argue, are constitutive of, rather than simply reflections of, Kenyan history and culture. History becomes, then, not the past itself, but struggles over the meaning of the past.

A Manifesto

The disquiet within the historical profession concerning postmodernism, deconstruction, and, more diffusely, multiculturalism is likely to continue for some time to come. As Steven Feierman points out, the central paradox of our moment as historians is that "our faith in objective historical knowledge has been shaken precisely because of the advance of 'knowledge' in its objective sense. The authoritative version of historical knowledge has been undermined because historians, in recent decades, have built bodies of knowledge about which their predecessors could only have dreamed. By carrying assumptions about historical knowledge through to their conclusions, historians have discovered some of the limits of those assumptions."[18] In true Socratic fashion, the lack of certainty is a measure of how much better historians are today than in the past. Rather than spin our wheels debating the question of just what kind of "qualified objectivity" is suited to contemporary historical work,[19] historians need to take their increasingly sophisticated understandings of the past into debates beyond the confines of history as a discipline.

From the point of view of someone who has often been situated institutionally outside of a history department, the most urgent debates raging concerning the nature of oral "texts" today appear to be dominated by scholars in literary studies and media studies who appear to have little interest in actually testing their propositions against what historians have painstakingly discovered about orality and the settings in which oral performances are deeply valued. There has been a resurgence of interest in Marshall McLuhan's work in the wake of reflections about continuing illiteracy in the context of a literate culture. It is hard to find a popular scholar who has done more to misrepresent Africa and Africans than McLuhan, for whom Africa represents the mindless constrained darkness of illiteracy in contrast with the freedom and light that comes with print culture. Scholars such as Eric Havelock, Walter Ong, and anthropologist Jack Goody have also contributed to a complex of assumptions about the nature of "oral man" that include formulaic oral production in the service of memory, profound "homeostatic" conservatism, concrete rather than abstract thought, collective rather than individual identity, an emphasis on the sense of sound over the sense of sight, and so on.[20] With the exception of Goody, none of these authors has any real experience with cultures in which orality serves as a significant mode of intellectual and cultural production. Goody is the most subtle (not to say slippery) of these authors, but he is not a historian and his work does not provide the kind of evidentiary grounding a historian would find compelling. It is worth pointing out that the average historian who does not work on Africa is far more likely to have read Goody than, say, Vansina.

The "invention of oral man," to borrow Vail and White's phrase, seems to me to have very troubling racist overtones.[21] For any Africanist, this is familiar ground and would not be particularly startling if it did not also seem to be compounded with other binary oppositions at play in contemporary discourse about global processes. The binaries of the cold war seem to be sliding into other binaries in which Africa and Islamic "civilizations" are cast in fundamental opposition to a counter-complex characterized by dynamism, technology, literacy, "democratic" political and social forms, and individual freedom. Yet the discoveries from thirty years of work with oral evidence in Africa fly in the face of these assumptions. Parenthetically, thirty years of work on literacy across cultures also throws the implicit binary of literate versus oral culture into disarray.[22]

Life Histories as Oral Performance

All of this would seem rather far from the question of how to use oral interviews in the construction of African history. Let me now tie together the scattered strands of the argument. Even if some recent work in literary studies has been unproductive in its reification of the difference between oral and literate worlds, nevertheless the most exciting historical work drawing on oral sources has in fact been greatly enhanced by a more literary and textual approach to oral works. For example, a number of recent texts draw not on conventional oral interviews but rather on oral performative evidence often treated in the vein of "oral tradition." Vail and White, in their magisterial study of praise poems in southern African history, propose that oral texts be understood through an aesthetic they call "poetic licence." Their approach places at the center of attention once again the creativity and active agency of the oral poet that Milman Parry so admired, without becoming hampered by Perry's more problematic assertion that oral poetry is formulaic. To put to the fore the creativity of the speaker and the privileged nature of poetic speech is to reorient ourselves towards oral evidence as fundamentally creative rather than as a repository for inert chunks of the past. This emphasis is far more in keeping with the self-commentary of the oral poets themselves than the more analytical approaches that Vansina, Miller, and others developed—in the context, admittedly, of less clearly poetic forms. "To relegate aesthetic considerations to felicities of expression and then raid the content of these songs and poems for 'history' would be to abuse them profoundly," remark Vail and White.[23] For oral poets, the meaning of their oral performances rests in the performance itself, not in the interpretations of the words: as one of Scheub's storytellers observed in implicit criticism of Scheub's symbolic analysis of her story, "If I am to tell you what my story means...I must tell it again."[24] The sentiment is echoed at a more musical register in a rebuke David Coplan received from a singer-poet whose song he was seeking to understand, "If you want to understand my song, mister, just listen to the music."[25]

The force of these texts then emerges not from the fixed arrangements of words, but from the dynamic, relational, aspect of the encounter between the performer and audience. In a similar vein Karin Barber has argued that Yoruba oriki or epithetic speech are a particularly rich source for understanding how a people constitute their own society because in such texts "we find the possibility of entering into people's own discourse about their social world."[26] Seeing them as bursting with intended and unintended meanings, she notes that such texts invite an exploration of indigenous interpretive techniques as well. In these dense, unbounded, and cryptic concatenations of meaning and history are embedded intense struggles for power, a dimension of oral forms sometimes neglected on the one hand by historians in their search for usable chunks of data and on the other hand by literary folklorists in their gentle appreciation of the finer aesthetic dimensions of oral poetry. By combining historical and literary approaches in an anthropological optic in which struggles for power are central, Barber brings the potency of these texts to the fore as means through which struggles are enacted. These texts don't *represent* powerful individuals in speech—they *call that power into being* through speech.

Barber argues persuasively that the deconstructionist criticism that has so troubled historians is in many ways inadequate to interpret oral texts, despite its seeming resonance with some surface attributes of oral works. In a much-quoted passage she remarks,

> at a deeper level post-structuralist criticism is inimical to oral texts. It immobilises the human agent at the same time that it empowers the text itself: texts interact, fructify, produce meaning; the human beings participate merely as loci or functions within a vast network of codes. Oral texts do not permit this evasion of the question of agency (ultimately a question of power)—of who is saying these things, to whom, in whose interests—for the speaker and the hearers are always visibly and concretely present, and text clearly has no existence apart from them.[27]

Barber's work shows how productive an approach can be that brings together close ethnographic knowledge of a locale, careful contextualization in a range of literary genres, and an eye for the ways in which the silences, disjunctions, and contradictions within these texts can reveal something about how the past is always still active in the present. Elizabeth Tonkin's *Narrating Our Pasts* is another work from an anthropologist that usefully brings together literary, historical, and anthropological approaches. Tonkin systematically explores how oral texts are authorized and how they in turn bring authority to those who produce them, how genre shapes accounts, and how our sense of self and time is constructed in past-directed accounts. By focusing on how, in creating past-directed speech, oral artists at the same time construct themselves, Tonkin once again highlights the agency of the artist and the potential of oral texts to have social effectiveness.[28] Kwesi Yankah's work on surrogate speech in Akan royal oratory reminds us that artful speech is not simply the province of the weak or powerless but is central to the very construction of legitimate authority.[29]

Inspired by the works of Tonkin, Barber, and Vail and White, Isabel Hofmeyr has written an interesting study of oral historical narrative in the Northern Transvaal. Hofmeyr studies oral storytelling, oral historical narrative, and literacy in their complex interrelations to offer a rich history of change in the region.[30] As in other such studies linking history, anthropology, and literary analysis, Hofmeyr's approach places the sociology of historical understanding at the heart of her work. Like Barber and Tonkin, her work gives us not only a vision of the history of the region, but also and fundamentally a glimpse of how that history has been variously constructed and experienced by those to whom it belongs. Her attention to the relationships among gender, space, and historical memory is particularly thought-provoking.

As Belinda Bozzoli notes in her ambitious study of consciousness among women in Phokeng, oral historical sources need not simply provide us with "more history" to fill in gaps in other kinds of sources. Oral texts, because of their highly discursive character, can be "unsurpassed sources for revealing otherwise hidden forms of consciousness."[31] Bozzoli draws on the insights of oral historians such as Ronald Grele, Michael Frisch, Alessandro Portelli, and Luisa Passerini in developing a portrait of the shifting consciousness of the women of Phokeng. Interestingly, in the context of the broader historiography of oral work on Africa, it is Bozzoli, a sociologist, who undertakes a sustained exploration of oral interview materials from South Africa in the spirit of the kinds of work generated by historians of the Popular Memory Group at Birmingham. By foregrounding rather than hiding the interactions between Mmantho Nkotsoe and the women she interviewed, Bozzoli uses the interviews to bring out not simply "what happened" but also the complex and contradictory subjectivities of the women who experienced the events, as well as their active involvement in constructing a self, a life, and a world. While the book is not entirely successful as an exploration of "consciousness," the fullness of the interviews and the inventiveness with which Bozzoli approaches them makes it an extremely thought-provoking model for both performing and using oral interviews.

My argument, then, drawing in part on work by oral historians outside the African history canon and on historically grounded work by scholars of disciplines such as folklore, sociology, anthropology, and ethnomusicology, is that all oral evidence is essentially poetic and performative. In this it differs profoundly from written sources, which are not bound to the sensory experience of the hearer or audience in the same way. It follows from this that any historian who wants to use oral interviews, regardless of how prosaic they may at first appear, must include the performance context—in which the historians are central players as the intended audience—in the analysis and interpretation of the material collected. Another corollary would be that oral evidence, even when it appears most private and intimate, is in its very nature public. Finally, oral materials (whether traditions, songs, poems, or apparently straightforward narrative life histories) are always shaped by the poetic and performative conventions by which the speaker is informed. This is not to say that they are nonauthentic because they are "artificial." It is to suggest that all our interchanges are given structure and meaning by cultural themes, categories, values, symbols, and common practices without which we would not have the resources to actively shape ourselves or our worlds. While individual informants cannot be taken as "representative" of any whole social group in which they might be imbedded, nevertheless individual memory and broader collective representations of the past are in complex relationship with one another. Any careful work with oral texts must begin with a thoroughgoing exploration of the constellation of performance genres in which the given text is embedded. Tradition then becomes not fixed formulas or forms but rather a longstanding processual practice of invention, drawing on existing images and forms of expression to create a present and future self that is imbued with meaning precisely because the past is immanent within it. The past thus both constrains and enables the present. Cohen refers to this in the context of Basotho aesthetic inventions as "cultural self-preservation through transformation."[32]

Coming into oral interviews with this orientation is quite different from coming into them with the assumptions that many feminist researchers held in the early 1970s. Because oral historical methods are particularly appealing to historians who want to reclaim the lost or neglected voices of the disadvantaged, feminist possibilities of the field-work encounter have often been romanticized. Certainly I myself entered the field with a rather naive notion that I was going to reclaim the authentic experiences of Hausa women through their life histories. My image of fieldwork was of a pristine dyadic relationship between me, a woman, and my informant, a woman, in which in the privacy of an individual interview her "real" experience would be made visible in part because of our shared gender.

My first discovery was that there is no such thing as privacy. Why this should have come as a surprise to me, given that my interviews were indeed intended to become part of a published, and therefore public, work is itself in retrospect the greater mystery. My second lesson came from watching the very humane and experienced researcher, a man named Habou Magaji, *perform* an interview. He literally acted as a *naamusayer* for a woman we had invited into the research center in Maradi. Griots typically employ an auxiliary assistant, a *naamu naamu*, whose job is to utter such affirmative expressions as "yes, indeed, truly, it is so" regularly throughout their performance. Malam Habou gently but enthusiastically said *naamu!* ("yes!" in Arabic) after every breath and clause of this woman's story, exactly as if she were a bard and he her assistant. She produced a life story at a breathtaking clip that bore no resemblance to ordinary speech, and I understood not one word of what she said. But the lesson struck home: if I wanted women to speak to me, I would have to be resolutely affirmative, I would need to let them shift into discursive modes no interviewer would recognize in the United States, I would have to forestall my own understanding at least temporarily, and ultimately I would have to recognize the creative dimensions of these performances.

In practical terms, I came to discover how important it was not to interrupt women too frequently. I had to let them find their own ways into describing their lives, even at the cost of relatively little control over their performances. To ask perfect questions was less important than to listen patiently and politely, no matter how long the silence, how arcane the story, or how seemingly irrelevant the response. I had to literally play it by ear. The direction and content of the book that emerged from this research, *Marriage in Maradi*,[33] was profoundly shaped by the women interviewed, even if the argument is not one they would have been inclined to make themselves.

I came to write a book about marriage largely because that is a subject on which the women I interviewed were comfortable and fluent. Marriage and wedding ritual were simultaneously the repository of "traditional" practices and relations, and the locus of tremendous adaptability and uncertainty. Marriage was thus eminently suitable as a topic of history, for it fell safely under the rubric of "tradition" (after all, that is what *tarihi*, the Hausa word also used for "history," generally means in Maradi), while providing the occasion for women to relate how they themselves had experienced and negotiated rapid change. Although I sometimes chafed under this restricted definition of which subjects were suitable for discussion and which ones were not, in the end I followed my informants' lead in attending closely to how marriage had shaped and been shaped by the rapidly changing political economy of twentieth-century Maradi.

Thus the seeming apolitical nature of the subject of marriage and domestic life rendered it available as a topic of conversation to me as a researcher, while its accepted status as the locus of custom and conservatism rendered it suitable as the material for "history" understood as "tradition." Ironically the assumption among scholars that the domestic sphere is the site of conservatism has occluded the ways in which the very taken-for-grantedness of that realm renders it the ideal medium through which women, in particular, can effect change. In stubbornly insisting on marriage as a safe topic of conversation, women I worked with were seizing on the domestic realm as the stage for their own inventiveness, agency, and subjective experience. Paradoxically, they were using the signifier of tradition to point up the centrality of their experience of and contribution to change. The importance of my informants' sense of history to the direction of my own research and interviews suggests to me that, however salutary the postmodernist critical reevaluation of fieldwork, scholars who employ oral historical methods must nevertheless attend to the ways in which the "objects" of "representation" are themselves active in shaping those representations, if only imperfectly. As Henrietta Moore and Megan Vaughan remark, "The current criticisms by anthropologists and others of the invention of societies and cultures through the process of textualization have an important role to play both inside and outside the discipline, but to claim that these processes float free of all the significant others involved in their production is a strange kind of inverted arrogance."[34]

It is worth noting that although the content of my interviews was in many ways channeled by the women themselves, my most important initial lessons about how to interview Hausa women came from a Hausa man. Feminist standpoint theory had predicted that somehow the shared positioning of a female fieldworker and female informant would lead to greater access to the feminine experience than a man could have. Ultimately my own interviewing style was quite different from Malam Magaji's, but any success I might have had probably has little to do with my gender alone. My point is not that it makes no difference who does the interviewing, but that humans are all variously equipped to perform humane and productive interviews, and one's gender alone is a poor predictor of how successful one will be in any given interview. Clearly some individuals are particularly skilled as oral researchers, and it is not obvious which of the many qualities they have as humans render them so gifted. Mmantho Nkotsoe's extraordinary interviews in Belinda Bozzoli's *Women of Phokeng* are telling in this regard: Which of her many attributes make her the unparalleled field researcher she seems to be? Her education? Her origins? Her respectful but direct style? Her genuine interest in her "subjects"?

I used interviews in a variety of ways and to a variety of ends, and they always went best if I took my cues from my interlocutors rather than attempting to "conduct" or direct the conversation too forcefully myself. In working to construct extended life histories of women I found that structuring the chronology of a woman's life, in a sense, through the woman's *spatial* movements (from natal home through various virilocal marriages and often finally to a home of her own) was more successful than my initial efforts to get women to produce a temporal sequence. Sometimes props such as wedding gifts, cloth, or photographs could be useful in triggering the discussion. I then often extended the next stages of the interviews to branch out into the woman's family tree to discover what she could tell me about her own mother (or mothers) and her own grandmother (or grandmothers), sometimes using the same kinds of prompts. Some women were central to a specific problem I wanted to think about, and so I devoted considerable discussion time to their under-standing of the history of, for example, spirit possession or women's asso-ciations; such interviews were greatly enhanced by my actual participation in events related to the subjects. Occasionally it was necessary to engage in a group interview, and the contrast between what different women said in such a setting and what they might say in a more personal context was interesting and useful. Getting into the spirit of the group in such contexts was important, and might require me to take part in some collective activ-ity (such as gardening) relevant to the group before any real conversation could occur. In other words, oral history interviewing required a great deal of flexibility and imagination and called for considerable investments of time in activities other than interviewing. I had to earn women's confi-dence first if I was to work with them.

The information in such interviews can be put to very different kinds of uses. Far more than most oral historians of other regions, who have long since turned their attention to the problems of memory and subjectivity, Africanists do indeed still rely on oral interviews for access to "facts" of a variety of kinds. Oral interviews are important ways of val-orizing and making more widely accessible the rich local knowledge of Africans about their own worlds and environments. Often this kind of detailed knowledge has to do with things like population movements, dis-ease control, agricultural practices, shifts in environmental conditions, and so on. Being grounded in political economy, I value this kind of infor-mation and would be reluctant to ever give up entirely the sense that oral interviews can produce practical objective knowledge. It is noteworthy that in the methods section of Perks and Thomson's *Oral History Reader* the only contributions that seem to retain that sense of the utility of oral research are the ones most directly related to research outside the overde-veloped world.[35] By working in settings such as fields and marketplaces, and by drawing on material cultural props such as agricultural imple-ments, it is indeed possible to gain access to a great deal of detailed infor-mation that is not necessarily embedded either in oral tradition or in personal narratives. Getting people to talk about such issues does require a great deal of prompting precisely because they themselves regard the information as so obvious as to be uninteresting. It can take time to show them that the visitor does not regard this knowledge as trivial, and values it because it is known to them and not to other kinds of "experts."

Still within the realm of a relatively positivist understanding of knowledge, I do emphatically use my interview materials to gain a general sense for the shape of women's lives over time, for example to learn how women have earned and invested money. Much of *Marriage in Maradi* develops this strand of my interviews, exploring them for patterns linking shifts in the political economy with practical strategies in women's lives. The interviews made it more evident to me than would probably have been the case from documentary sources alone the ways in which women have had a hand in shaping the agricultural economy, the urban environment, children's attendance at school, the circulation of commodities, and so on.

However, oral sources do more than simply offer alternative sources of information or slightly different vantage points from with to describe processes. They offer us the possibility of exploring the social production of memory, self, and subjectivity. In my own research it took me a long time to understand that the women I was interviewing had a vision of history as continuity and reiteration that was very different from my own sense of history, and that that understanding of history as "tradition" was shaping the narratives I was collecting. Thinking about the sense of worth and personhood that accompanied such an understanding of history made it a great deal easier, in turn, to make sense of the investment strategies these women were likely to make. It also made me more alert to the silences in my interviews with women: the numbers of children they had lost, the "fact" of their first marriages, their unexplored feelings about their lives. These silences were not merely absences of evidence but issues to reflect on in thinking about women's constructions of self, their struggles and traumas, and the relationship between private self and public self.

One element of my own research style, perhaps as much a weakness as a strength, is that if I sense hesitancy on the part of a woman, I don't push hard to get her to work with me or discuss a topic about which she seems reticent. I value my own privacy too highly to relish the prospect of consciously intruding into someone else's. This does not mean women I worked with did not experience me as intrusive, but it does mean that my willingness to intrude, to be combative, to cross-examine, or to probe sensitive or painful topics has very real limits that have as much to do with my own personality as with any articulated ethical stance. I have tended to trust my readers to weigh such silences as heavily as I do myself, both for what they reveal about me as a researcher and for what they reveal about the women themselves. Not all interviewers have the same approach; I am conscious of the contrast between my style and that of, for example, Peter Friedlander, whose work I admire.[36] One rather intimidating dimension of doing oral history research is the rather constant fear that one is doing it wrong. When working with documents, the fear that one might be doing violence of a sort is attenuated because the violence one might inflict has the appearance of at least being indirect and impersonal. Similarly, any meditations surrounding absences in the documentary evidence appear somehow as hypotheses rather than as projections.

When I returned from the field I was immensely comforted to discover the work of the Personal Narratives Group, for here I found scholars discussing directly the complex dynamics at play in interactions between researchers and the women whose lives they hope to document. I was particularly influenced by a piece by Marjorie Mbilinyi in which she discusses honestly her intense working relationship with Rebecca Kalindile and how she gradually learned to listen more carefully to Kalindile, bearing in mind that her informant's words were chosen out of a concern for her own and other women's safety.[37] What I have taken from these and other such works is a sense of humility and a commitment to openness. No matter how pure our intentions, our research will never be flawless. In fact, some of the most important learning in research happens when one makes a particularly egregious mistake. Research is, by definition, the process of coming into knowledge about something that is as yet unknown. It is not possible to do useful research without making mistakes. One reason for abandoning certain Marxist and feminist models of the merits of oral research is that they presuppose a kind of superior consciousness on the part of the researcher that will be somehow bestowed upon the "subjects" through the oral history process. But in reality there is no moral high ground on which the researcher (feminist or otherwise) can stand and remain untouched by the murky ambiguities of the research encounter. The best we can do is to be endlessly self-conscious, to be as full and honest as possible about the circumstances that shape the evidence presented, and to do no harm consciously. But on the other hand it would be naive and condescending to imagine that the people we interview are passive or lacking in creative agency. By remaining alert to that agency, we both honor them as creative human beings and learn from them as individuals who have something to say about themselves, their own worlds, and the human condition we share.

My experiences in the field led me to James Scott's reflections on the performative dimensions of human interaction in contexts of unequal power relations.[38] Vail and White's notion of "poetic licence" is again useful here, for what I have found is that the discursive modes into which my informants shifted were frequently ones that guaranteed some degree of safety while at the same time authorizing the performance itself. Where Scott helps us to understand the power relations, the dramatic dimensions, and the agency in these moments, his work is less helpful in bringing out the individual creativity and potency of oral interviews, partly because for Scott the collective sociological experience is always more centrally in evidence than the individual experience.

However, in these safe discursive modes some particularly gifted women produced extraordinarily powerful performances, ones I have been unable to leave behind. Since writing *Marriage in Maradi* I have devoted a great deal of thought to the performative dimensions of a particular subset of my own interviews involving an array of unusually articulate women. These interviews at the same time (and not incidentally) shed light on the emergence of what I see as a new oral genre, the oral (re)performance of the hajj to Mecca.[39] My work on women's performance of the hajj is very much in keeping with other recent work on genre development and how it encodes social transformation. I suppose in some ways I have in part found myself compelled to think through these issues due to the depth of feeling some of these interviews evoke in me. That is to say, some of the women I interviewed were so skilled in their oratory, so capable as artists, that they succeeded in planting in an outsider and non-Muslim a deep-felt sense of the moving, changing world they as artists simultaneously occupy and create. Their performances succeeded as evocations of the "structure of feeling" that brings us into an acute consciousness of our shared humanity even where circumstance and experience may differ.

Conclusion

Earlier I said it would be a mistake to imagine that African historians rely on any single kind of source. Instead most historians seek to test and confirm propositions developed from one source through evidence from another. However, these sources do not simply reiterate one another, and that is why African history is an exciting field. I see our highly interdisciplinary work as full of vitality in at least two ways. First, our sense of how our work as historians is distinctive is sharpened by an awareness of how we might differ from our colleagues in other disciplines in our use of and attitude towards particular modes of argumentation and kinds of evidence. Not surprisingly, therefore, we have tended to direct our arguments as much to anthropologists and other Africanists as to historians of other regions. While there have been long periods of friction as a result of these debates, there has also been, as I have suggested above, much fruitful borrowing and rapprochement. African social and cultural history, for example, is today very close to historical anthropology in its concerns, approaches, and sources of evidence. This makes for very lively intellectual communities and sustained explorations of related issues from more than one vantage point.

Second, our thinking has inevitably been shaped or shaken by modes of historical understanding on the ground in Africa. In making up for the absence of documentary evidence, we have had to ask Africans themselves about their own pasts, with interesting and complicated consequences. Where a historian of rural France might turn to mute cadastral records to understand shifts in land tenure, the historian of Africa is likely to seek out oral evidence of one kind or another. Cadastral records teach us much about the use of land in the past but relatively little about the cosmological and historical sensibility of the French peasant. Oral evidence inevitably comes, in the apt phrase of Leroy Vail and Landeg White, "with the metaphysics included."[40] While the academic discipline of history is clearly western in origin, much of our work in African history has, in the end, challenged the complacency of western historical assumptions. Because we have had to rely on African modes of historical thought, frequently oral, we have come up against the ways in which those modes record understandings of history, personhood, power, memory, time, human excellence, and so on, and these may or may not accord with the assumptions and questions taken for granted by history as a discipline founded in the west. This is not because "oral man" has, in some Lévi-Bruhlian sense, a fundamentally different mental outlook from "civilized" man, but rather because Africans have made sense of the world and their own histories in ways that are simultaneously consistent with and formative of the realities on the ground around them.

Those realities frequently fly in the face of the most taken-for-granted of western concepts. Feierman has pointed out that we now know that the complex of elements once understood to be at the heart of civilization ("political and economic hierarchy, towns, commerce and intercommunication, writing, the plough, high densities of population, and historical dynamism"), which in the past drove the questions western-trained historians asked, often don't hold in Africa. In an economically dynamic region such as southeastern Nigeria, productive agriculture eschewed the plough, high population densities throve without political hierarchy, and commercial transactions flourished in the absence of writing:

> [T]he historical experience of southeastern Nigeria followed a pattern for which the historians' category of "civilization" was largely irrelevant. In this part of Nigeria, clearly, a different set of interrelations was at work. It is no wonder that historians, faced with the obligation to take seriously the history of Igboland, complain of "fragmentation" and "chaos" in historical knowledge. Some of the long-accepted categories of historical understanding are irrelevant.[41]

In this case both the modes of historical memory and the history they encode challenge central assumptions of history as a discipline.

Such challenges are healthy and exciting. Unfortunately the reality is that the methodological and conceptual challenges produced by African history have rendered it largely unintelligible to academic historians in general. It is becoming urgent that scholars of African history frame questions and enter into conversations in such a way that our colleagues outside African Studies can learn from us and we from them. African history is far too important to remain a lively but largely ignored subdiscipline of history. Furthermore, the issue of the legibility of our field has important implications for hiring and promotion, which in turn has repercussions on the visibility of African history within the discipline and within higher education as a whole.

In some ways, African history is caught in a whirlpool partly of its own making, having not succeeded, on the whole, in conveying the import of its discoveries to those outside African Studies and having missed a number of important opportunities to contribute lively participants to important debates. Until we find ways of bringing our work into the light, it will continue to be marginal and poorly understood. The way out, I suggest, is to recast somewhat our sense of audience and become more self-conscious about the multitude of discourses about Africa that shape how our work is received. For better or for worse, if we can't demonstrate how what we have learned is relevant in broader historical debates, then openings in African history will continue to go empty year after year. The challenge is to do this without giving up the interdisciplinarity that is the source of the field's vigor and without letting go of a longstanding commitment to placing Africans' experiences, beliefs, and modes of knowing at the heart of our work. Foregrounding our reflections on the use of

oral sources is one way we can find common ground with other historians, on the one hand, and popular audiences, on the other.

Notes

1. Peter Schmidt, "Oral Traditions, Archaeology, and History," in Peter Robershaw,
ed., *A History of African Archaeology* (London: James Currey, 1990), 252–70.

2. Joseph Miller, ed., *The African Past Speaks* (Folkestone: Wm Dawson and Sons,
1980), 51.

3. One of the most useful texts a budding oral historian might turn to in order to
develop a good sense for how to conduct interviews would be Charles Morrissey's "On
Oral History Interviewing," in Robert Perks and Alistair Thomson's *The Oral History
Reader* (London: Routledge, 1998), 107–13. Morrissey is known for his work with major
political figures in the United States. The Perks and Thomson reader is an invaluable
resource for the student of oral history, and the reader is urged to take advantage of the
many rich and accessible articles cited below. Those articles in turn provide rich bibliographies for further exploration.

4. No student of oral history should pass up the insights of Jan Vasina's *Oral
Tradition as History* (Madison: University of Wisconsin Press, 1985), despite its emphasis
upon "traditional" oral texts as opposed to the more personal narratives dealt with here.

5. See Paul Thompson, "The Voice of the Past," in Perks and Thomson, *The Oral
History Reader*, 21–28 and Alex Haley, "Black History, Oral History and Genealogy," in
Perks and Thomson, *The Oral History Reader*, 9–20.

6. Tellingly, Perks and Thomson's *The Oral History Reader*'s broad-ranging collection of foundational works in the realm of oral history includes Vansina in the index but
does not see any need to reproduce an article from his corpus.

7. For a particularly elegant exposition of this problem, see Laura Bohannan,
"A Genealogical Charter," *Africa* 22 (1952): 301–15.

8. To get a feeling for the critiques at the heart of this controversy, see Luc de
Heusch, "What Shall We Do with the Drunken King," *Africa* 45, (4) (1975): 363–72;
T. O. Beidelman, "Myth, Legend, and Oral History," *Anthropos* 65, (5–6) (1965): 74–97;
Wyatt MacGaffey, "African History, Anthropology, and the Rationality of Natives," *History
in Africa* 5 (1978): 101–20.

9. Miller, ed., *The African Past Speaks*, 45.

10. Alessandro Portelli, "What Makes Oral History Different," in Perks and
Thomson, *The Oral History Reader*, 72. See also Luisa Passerini, "Work Ideology and
Consensus under Italian Fascism," in Perks and Thomson, *The Oral History Reader*, 53–62.

11. One thinks of such classics as Margaret Strobel's *Muslim Women in Mombasa,
1890–1975* (New Haven: Yale University Press, 1979) and Claire Robertson's *Sharing the
Same Bowl: A Socioeconomic History of Women and Class in Accra, Ghana* (Ann Arbor:
University of Michigan Press, 1984). Luis White's *The Comforts of Home: Prostitution in
Colonial Nairobi* (Chicago: Chicago University Press 1990) is particularly important in this
regard, since it signaled the importance of reading African history through the language
and categories that African women themselves employ in order to make sense of broader
patterns of urban life and struggles for social control. Nina Mba's marvelous book,

Nigerian Women Mobilized: Women's Political Activity in Southern Nigeria, 1900–1965 (Berkeley: Institute of International Studies, 1982), shows that oral sources can be central to the construction of political history as well as social and economic history. Obviously this is a partial and idiosyncratic list.

12. Mary F. Smith, *Baba of Karo: a Woman of the Muslim Hausa* (New Haven: Yale University Press, 1981 [1954]); Marjorie Shostak, *Nisa: the Life and Words of a !Kung Woman* (New York: Random House, 1983). See also Jean Davison with the women of Mutira, *Voices from Mutira: Change in the Lives or Rural Gikuyu Women, 1910–1995* (Boulder: Lynne Rienner Publishers, 1996). Not all such texts draw primarily from life histories; see Lila Abu-Lughod's *Veiled Sentiments: Honor and Poetry in a Bedouin Society* (Berkeley: University of California Press, 1986).

13. For a direct reflection on some of the assumptions undergirding this literature see Susan Geiger, "What's So Feminist About Women's Oral History?" *Journal of Women's History* (2) 1 (1990): 169–70. My own work has been shaped, for better or for worse, far more by such texts as S. B. Gluck and D. Patai, eds., *Women's Words: The Feminist Practice of Oral History* (London: Routledge, 1991), Diane Wolf, ed., *Feminist Dilemmas in Fieldwork* (Boulder: Westview, 1996), and Micheline R. Malson et al., *Feminist Theory in Practice and Process* (Chicago: University of Chicago Press, 1989) than by foundational texts in the canon of oral history that do not directly touch on gender. This reflects my entry into the subject via work on gender rather than through the methodological door of oral history proper. This chapter would perhaps have taken a rather different hue had it been written by an Africanist whose interest in oral history came via peasant studies or labor history. It is striking that much of the strong work in oral history does indeed cluster in the Southern African region, where the literature on industrial labor is central, and in Kenya, whose historiography reveals a long linkage with peasant studies.

14. See Margaret Jean Hay and Marcia Wright, eds., *African Women and the Law: Historical Perspectives* (Boston: Boston University, 1984).

15. The now classic text is, of course, Eric Hobsbawm and Terence Ranger, eds., *The Invention of Tradition* (Cambridge: The University of Cambridge Press, 1983).

16. David Cohen and E. S. Atieno Odhiambo, *Burying SM: The Politics of Knowledge and the Sociology of Power in Africa* (Portsmouth: Heinemann, 1992).

17. Ibid., 92.

18. Steven Feierman, "African Histories and the Dissolution of World History," in Robert Bates, V. Y. Mudimbe, and Jean O'Barr, *Africa and the Disciplines: the Contributions of Research in Africa to the Social Sciences and Humanities* (Chicago: University of Chicago Press, 1993), 168.

19. Joyce Appleby, Lynn Hunt, and Margaret Jacob, *Telling the Truth About History* (New York: W. W. Norton & Co., 1994), 259.

20. See Marshall McLuhan, *Understanding Media: The Extensions of Man* (Cambridge: MIT Press, 1964); Eric Havelock, "The Coming of Literate Communication to Western Culture," *Journal of Communication* (winter, 1980): 90–98; Walter Ong, "Writing Is a Technology that Restructures Thought," in Gerd Baumann, ed., *The Written Word: Literacy in Transition* (Oxford: Clarendon Press, 1986); Jack Goody, *The Logic of Writing and the Organization of Society* (Cambridge: Cambridge University Press, 1986).

21. For a fuller exposition of this troubling literature see Leroy Vail and Landeg White, *Power and the Praise Poem: Southern African Voices in History* (Charlottesville: University of Virginia Press, 1991), 1–39.

22. For two texts that in very different ways illustrate my point see Jonathan Boyarin, ed., *The Ethnography of Reading* (Berkeley: The University of California Press, 1993) and Robert Darnton, "An Early Information Society: News and the Media in Eighteenth-Century Paris," *American Historical Review* 105, (1) (2000): 1–35.

23. Vail and White, *Power and the Praise Poem*, 72.

24. Harold Scheub, *The Tongue is Fire: South African Storytellers and Apartheid* (Madison: University of Wisconsin Press: 1996), xviii.

25. David B. Coplan, *In the Time of Cannibals: The Word Music of South Africa's Basotho Migrants* (Chicago: University of Chicago Press, 1994), 9.

26. Karin Barber, *I Could Speak Until Tomorrow* (Edinborough: Edinborough University Press, 1991), 2.

27. Ibid., 24.

28. Elizabeth Tonkin, *Narrating Our Pasts: The Social Construction of Oral History* (Cambridge: Cambridge University Press, 1992).

29. Kwesi Yankah, *Speaking for the Chief: Okyeame and the Politics of Akan Royal Oratory* (Bloomington: Indiana University Press, 1995).

30. Isabel Hofmeyr, *"We Spend our Years as a Tale that is Told": Oral Historical Narrative in a South African Chiefdom* (Portsmouth: Heinemann, 1993).

31. Belinda Bozzoli with Mmantho Nkotsoe, *Women of Phokeng: Consciousness, Life Strategy and Migrancy in South Africa, 1900–1983* (Portsmouth: Heinemann, 1991), 7.

32. David B. Coplan, *In the Time of Cannibals: The Word Music of South Africa's Basotho Migrants* (Chicago: University of Chicago Press, 1994), 15.

33. Barbara M. Cooper, *Marriage in Maradi: Gender and Culture in a Hausa Society in Niger, 1900–1989* (Portsmouth: Heinemann, 1997).

34. Henrietta Moore and Megan Vaughan, *Cutting Down Trees: Gender, Nutrition, and Agricultural Change in the Northern Province of Zambia, 1890–1990* (Portsmouth: Heinemann, 1994), xx. The sense that Africans have had a hand in shaping historical discourses and that in turn the legacy of past moments of shaping can itself become a constraint is powerfully captured in Carolyn Hamilton's intriguing book, *Terrific Majesty: The Powers of Shaka Zulu and the Limits of Historical Invention* (Cambridge: Harvard University Press, 1998).

35. I am thinking of Hugo Slim and Paul Thompson, with Olivia Bennett and Nigel Cross, "Ways of Listening," in Perks and Thomson, *The Oral History Reader*, 114–25, and Nigel Cross and Rhiannon Barker, "The Sahel Oral History Project," in Perks and Thomson, *The Oral History Reader*, 246–57.

36. Peter Friedlander, "Theory, Method and Oral History," in Perks and Thomson, *The Oral History Reader*, 311–19.

37. Marjorie Mbilinyi's " 'I'd have been a Man': Politics and the Labor Process in Producing Personal Narratives," in Personal Narratives Group, *Interpreting Women's Lives* (Bloomington: Indiana University Press, 1989): 204–27. Other useful contributions to this volume by scholars of Africa include Shula Marks, "The Context of Personal Narrative: Reflections on *'Not Either an Experimental Doll'—The Separate Worlds of Three South African Women,* 39–58; Marcia Wright, "Personal Narratives, Dynasties, and Women's Campaigns: Two Examples from Africa," 155–72; and Marjorie Shostak, " 'What the Wind Won't Take Away': The Genesis of *Nisa—The Life and Words of a !Kung Woman,*" 228–40.

38. James C. Scott, *Domination and the Arts of Resistance: Hidden Transcripts* (New Haven: Yale University Press, 1990).

39. Barbara M. Cooper, "The Strength in the Song: Muslim Personhood, Audible Capital, and Hausa Women's Performance of the Hajj," *Social Text* 60, (17) (1999): 87–109.

40. Vail and White, *Power and the Praise Poem*, 73.

41. Feierman, "African Histories and the Dissolution of World History," 77, 178.

8

ARABIC SOURCES FOR AFRICAN HISTORY

John Hunwick

This contribution aims to review the known Arabic sources for African history, both published and unpublished, and at the same time to review some of the problems in interpreting them. Although the title of this paper uses the phrase "Arabic sources," I will also be referring to sources in African languages written in the Arabic script, notably Hausa and Swahili. While using the term "African history," I shall effectively confine my attention to Saharan and sub-Saharan Africa, with occasional references to North, or Mediterranean, Africa, in so far as the Arabic sources for this segment of the continent illuminate the history of other parts of it.

The External Sources

Arab knowledge of Africa dates from the earliest days of Islam; indeed, the Arabs of the Ḥijāz and the Yemen evidently had some knowledge, at least of "Ethiopia" (al-Ḥabasha, however that may be defined), before the rise of Islam. The first *hijra* of persecuted Muslims of Mecca was to Ethiopia in 615 C.E., and the Ethiopians retained a respected status in the eyes of Arabic writers, who exalted their "virtues" (*faḍā'il, maḥāsin*).[1] Ethiopia's proximity to Arabia, and its relative proximity to Egypt (and Coptic Christian links to Ethiopian Christianity), helped to sustain Arab interest in the area, and several Arab writers produced works on that land.[2] Nubia was also one of the earliest lands of Black Africa to become known to the Arabs, who concluded a bilateral agreement (*baqṭ*) with the Nubian king at Old Dongola in 645. The Arabic texts referring to Nubia, and in some cases to other areas of what is now the Sudan, written between the ninth and the early sixteenth century, have been conveniently gathered together in a single volume edited by Muṣṭafā Muḥammad Saʿd.[3]

There are several works that assemble Arabic texts dealing with Africa, or parts of it. The largest, both physically and in regard to coverage, is the magnificent *Monumenta Cartographica Africae et Aegypti,* edited by Prince Youssouf Kamal of Egypt, and originally privately published by him.[4] As its name indicates, its primary purpose is to present a collection of maps of Africa, but it also includes all known descriptions of Egypt and Africa in their original languages with translations into French or English.[5] It begins with pre-Ptolomæan times and ends with Portuguese maps and descriptions of Africa, with an addendum containing maps only from more recent centuries. This is a rich source of Arabic external sources for African history as it takes a continent-wide approach (excluding the Maghreb). The only other work to take such a broad approach is the four-volume *Arabskie Istochniki,* compiled by V. Matveeva and L. Koubbel (and the fourth volume with Marina Tolmacheva), published in Leningrad, 1960–95,[6] a very thorough coverage which includes sources found in no other collection, and includes Egypt as well as Black Africa. Arabic texts are given, followed by Russian translations.

The two other collections of sources both concern West Africa only and consist entirely of translations without any Arabic texts, though indications are always given of the sources from which the translations were made. The first to appear was that of Fr. Joseph Cuoq in 1975,[7] followed six years later by the volume translated and annotated by J. F. P. Hopkins and N. Levtzion.[8] Obviously the two collections of sources overlap to a great extent, but is should be pointed out that Cuoq's collection contains twenty-three extracts not to be found in the Hopkins and Levtzion volume, while the latter contains seventeen pieces not found in Cuoq's volume. One major difference between the two is that Cuoq includes the epitaphs of Gao translated by J. Sauvaget,[9] and a translation of the replies of al-Maghīlī to the questions of Askiya *al-Ḥājj* Muḥammad of Songhay, more strictly to be regarded as an "internal" source.[10]

Four external texts have received particular attention: al-Bakrī's account (1087) of the region between the R. Senegal and the R. Niger, Ibn Saʿīd's account of the Lake Chad region (written between 1269 and 1286), the "Travels" of Ibn Baṭṭūṭa (d. 1369) who visited both East and West Africa, and al-Maqrīzī's text on the peoples of sub-Saharan Africa. Al-Bakrī's account was first published in Arabic and translated into

French. as part of his account of North Africa by Bn. MacGuckin De Slane,[11] and in 1968 Vincent Monteil published his own annotated translation of the West African portion only;[12] later, in 1982 three scholars published together their individual reconstructions of al-Bakrī's West Africa.[13] The texts of Ibn Saʿīd and al-Maqrīzī were both worked on by the German scholar Dierk Lange, who painstakingly edited both texts from original manuscripts and translated them into French.[14] Ibn Baṭṭūṭa's "Travels" have been known and studied since the mid-nineteenth century. A complete text with parallel French translation was published in 1853–59, and it remains to this day the definitive edition.[15] In 1927 H. A. R. Gibb published an abridged one-volume English translation that included most of the material on West Africa;[16] he also embarked on a full translation in four volumes, which was completed after his death by Charles F. Beckingham.[17] In the mean time Raymond Mauny with others published a French translation of the West African sections,[18] while Said Hamdun and Noel Q. King translated both the East and West African portions into English in 1971.[19] In 1986 Ross Dunn published an account of Ibn Baṭṭūṭa and his travels, following his global peregrinations, including his visit to Mali.[20]

There has been relatively little critical appraisal or detailed analysis of these external sources over the past century and a half. The most brilliant exception to this is the work of Joseph Marquart, which has attracted little attention, partly, perhaps, because it is in German, and partly because its nature is concealed by its being an "introduction" (in fact a "Prolegomena" running to some 367 pages!) to an analysis of the Benin bronzes of the Royal Museum of Folk Culture in Leiden (Holland). It is, in fact, a masterpiece of philological investigation covering the whole of Sahelian Africa from Senegal to Ethiopia, and utilizing material in Aramaic, Amharic, and Greek as well as Arabic.[21] The Polish scholar Tadeusz Lewicki has also been active in combing through these external Arabic sources to gather material on various specific topics, his best known work in this domain being his mini-encyclopedia *West African Food in the Middle Ages According to Arabic Sources*, translated from the Polish by Marianne Abrahamowicz, and edited by Marion Johnson.[22] He is also the author of a general introduction to the external Arabic sources for African history.[23]

The first Arab writer whose work had anything to say about sub-Saharan Africa was al-Khᵂārazmī. He wrote at a time when ancient Greek works had begun to be translated into Arabic at the behest of the ʿAbbāsid caliphs and his *Ṣūrat al-arḍ* ["Depiction of the Earth"] is essentially a work of geographical coordinates that seems to have been instructions for making a map. The title declares that it was abstracted from the "Book of Geography" of Baṭalmayūs al-Qulūdhī, i.e., Ptolemy the Claudian, otherwise Claudius Ptolemaeus of Alexandria, who was active in the middle of the first century C.E. Most of its information is thus merely an Arabic rendering of the Greek work, with the toponyms transliterated the best way he knew how, though he added several names of towns, regions, and peoples that had recently become known to the Arabs, and made certain other corrections.[24] Many of these Ptolemaic names continue to feature in Arabic geographical works over the next five hundred years, thus creating numerous red herrings for readers of Arabic interested in the African interior. Al-Kh^Wārazmī also adopted the Greek *climata* (Ar. *iqlīm*) scheme under which the known world is divided up for reference purposes into seven roughly equal latitudinal bands from the equator to the Arctic regions. This system was to be used by several subsequent Arab writers and for some it goes beyond a mere reference function and becomes a framework for theories about skin color and mental and moral qualities.[25]

Veneration of earlier authorities is a common feature of Arabic writing of the pre-modern period, most especially in the religious sciences—the "transmitted sciences" (*al-ʿulūm al-naqliyya*) as they are known—but also, as is noteworthy in geographical writings, in the "cognitive sciences" (*al-ʿulūm al-ʿaqliyya*). Scholars were loathe to excise information derived from earlier authorities, but sought rather to fit new empirical data into older frameworks, and the fit was often uncomfortable and apt to create confusion. Celebrated scholars of the ancient Greek world, such as Plato, Aristotle, Euclid, Galen, and Ptolemy, were granted a status in their own fields similar to that of the great Muslim scholars in the sciences of Qurʾān, *Ḥadīth* and *Fiqh*.

Geography in the Medieval Sources

Accounts of Saharan and sub-Saharan Africa appear in a number of different types of Arabic works, not all of which have as their aim to impart geographical or ethnographic knowledge. Of those that have geographical pretensions, several use the Ptolemaic foundation—the "Geography" *par excellence*—and add in whatever new material they may have acquired. Others divide up the known (i.e., Muslim) world on the basis of regions, such as the Arabian peninsula, Iraq, the Maghreb, Egypt, the "Land of the Blacks," and so on. Some, like the works of Ibn Khurradādhbih (c. 885), Ibn Ḥawqal (c. 977), and al-Bakrī (1087), were conceived of as handbooks for travelers and incorporated the most up-to-date information, which in some cases may only have been a repetition of what an earlier writer had to say, or may, by contrast, have been based on actual new observation; others such as Ibn ʿAbd al-Ḥakam (d. 871), al-Yaʿqūbī (wrote 891), or Ibn Khaldūn (d. 1406) were essentially historians whose information is thus oriented; yet others, especially later writers such as Abū 'l-Fidāʾ (wrote 1321), al-Dimashqī (d. 1321), al-ʿUmarī (wrote 1337), and al-Qalqashandi (d. 1418), were arm-chair encyclopedists, though both al-ʿUmarī and Ibn Khaldūn gathered valuable oral information too. We have only a small handful of truly first-hand accounts of sub-Saharan Africa: the tenth-century historian-encyclopedist al-Masʿūdī visited East Africa and has left us a descriptive page or two; the thirteenth-century writer Ibn Saʿīd quotes passages from an otherwise unknown travel account by one Ibn Fāṭima relating to the Lake Chad area, while in the mid-fourteenth century the intrepid Ibn Baṭṭūṭa first visited East Africa, and then visited Mali, the Niger Bend and Tagidda (in present day Niger), and wrote up an account of the trip at in the last section of his travel memoirs.

How, then, did medieval Arab writers construct their image of the African interior, and how can historians make use of their data? Cartography makes its appearance from the very inception of Arab geographical writing, presumably because Ptolemy's work contained a map. In fact most medieval Arab world maps bear a fairly close resemblance to the Ptolemaiac model. On Arab maps such as those of Ibn Ḥawqal (10th century), or al-Idrīsī (12th century), Africa occupies almost half of the circular space, while Europe and Asia occupy the other half (conventionally the south is at the top of maps and the north at the bottom). The three continents are surrounded by water, usually called the "Encompassing Sea" (*al-baḥr al-muṣāṭ*). Not surprisingly writers who lived in Baghdad, or Cairo, or Cordoba, were best acquainted with the region in which they lived. Their maps of the Mediterranean at least bear some resemblance to physical realities, even though medieval maps are essentially diagrammatic, and features that their authors considered important are shown as disproportionately large. Correspondingly, the farther away from the Mediterranean they got, the vaguer was their knowledge of topography. Africa south of the Sahara, following Ptolemy, simply becomes a large blob, filling out the semi-circle of the map and extending eastwards until southern Africa is shown "facing" China. In Ptolemy's map it even appears joined to Asia, creating an inland sea out of the Indian Ocean. The failure of Arab cartographers to correct Ptolemy (except for detaching Africa physically from east Asia) is not merely an artifact of the follow-the-master syndrome. It also reflects what Arabs "knew" from the accounts of merchant seaman who plied sea routes between Mombasa, Kilwa, and Sofala in East Africa and ports in Gujerat, Malabar, the Maldives, and beyond. To them it must have seemed that such places really were "opposite" the East African coast.

Since the whole of the southern half of Africa was unknown to Arab merchants and travelers, except for the East African coast which, for them ran due east from Cape Gardafui (in Somalia), it was represented as being essentially uninhabited. This posited lack of population was explained by the fact that the farther south one went, beyond the equator, the hotter the climate became. Even in the "land of the Blacks" just north of the equator people's brains almost boiled from the heat, as one author put it.[26] People could not live in heat more intense than that; *ergo* there could be no people living south of the equator! As we shall see later, the intense African heat, even in the inhabited first clime just above the equator, and to some extent the second clime to the north of it, was thought to affect both body color and intelligence. Extreme cold in the seventh clime in northern Europe was thought to have similar effects, bleaching skins and numbing brains.

The dominant physical feature of Arab maps of Africa is the continent's hydrographical system as constructed from Ptolemy and complemented by further theorizing, informed (or, as its turns out, misinformed) by new "empirical" knowledge. Ptolemy, living in Alexandria at the head of the Nile delta in Egypt, was clearly able to obtain knowledge of the course of the Nile which, though it becomes stylized on his map and much more so on later Arab maps, bears a general resemblance to the physical facts. Later, Arab geographers came to know of what they thought was another great river in West Africa, though in fact it seems to have been a conflation of three separate rivers (Senegal, Niger, and Komadugu Yobe), and they assumed that it/they must be another branch or arm of the great Nile River system. Some also knew of a third large river—evidently the Wabi Shebelle—and they also related this to the Nile system, sometimes calling it the "Nile of Mogadishu."

The "Nile of the Blacks" (*Nīl al-sūdān*), as the composite West African river came to be known, first makes its appearance in the literature with the "Book of Routes and Kingdoms" (*Kitāb al-masālik wa'l-mamālik*) of the Andalusian scholar Abū ʿUbayd al-Bakrī, who was not apparently indebted to Ptolemy. Writing in 1067, he made use of the work of al-Warrāq, a North African geographer of the previous century, but drew extensively on oral accounts of merchants who had visited

West Africa. He refers to "the Nile" in several places: first as the river on which Takrūr and a number of other small states stood. This is clearly the river Senegal, which al-Bakrī indicates, but does not directly state, flows into the Encompassing Sea (i.e., the Atlantic). Later, when describing a route from ancient Ghana eastwards to Tādmakkat, he remarks that at a certain point the traveler "meets the Nile coming out of the land of the Blacks." One travels along it to Tiraqqā when it turns south into, once again, the "land of the Blacks." Here he is clearly referring to the great bend of the river Niger which flows through the Inland Delta, along the Saharan fringes and then turns south near modern Bourem to continue on to its delta in modern Nigeria. Al-Bakrī, then, does not distinguish in his nomenclature between the river Senegal and the river Niger. Even though a close reading of his text would show that his first "Nile" flows east-west and his second Nile west-east, the implications of this were not grasped by later geographers. So strong was the theory that the "Nile" was the mother of all African hydrography that when Ibn Baṭṭūṭa reached the Niger near Segu in 1352 he assumed it was the Nile (and did not apparently ask its name). Learning that it flowed on *eastwards* past Timbuktu and Gao he tells his readers that it flowed on eventually passing Dongola in Nubia, from which one would suppose that he thought it was either the "great" (Egyptian) Nile or a tributary of it.[27]

Perhaps the most influential of all Arab geographers, both on Arab writers and later European geographers, was al-Sharīf al-Idrīsī, who wrote his universal geography *Nuzhat al-mushtāq fī ikhtirāq al-āfāq* (A pleasure trip for him who longs to penetrate distant lands), a sort of armchair tourism, for the Norman king Roger II of Sicily in 1150—hence its nickname, "*Kitāb Rujār.*" The basis of al-Idrīsī's physical geography of Africa is Ptolemy, but he has clearly been influenced by Arab writers on the hydrography of western Africa, even though he does not, for example, mention al-Bakrī among his sources. In al-Idrīsī's work we find the full theoretical development of the two Niles river system and this reappears in several later writers down to Ibn Khaldūn who repeats it without question. The key passage reads as follows:

> In this [fourth] section [of the 1st Clime] occurs the splitting of the two Niles. I mean the Nile of Egypt which cuts through the land and flows from south to north. Most of the towns of Egypt are on both banks of it and on its islands also. The second part of the Nile flows from the east to the far west and on this part of the Nile are all the towns of the Blacks, or most of them. These two Niles have a common source in the Mountain of Q-m-r

[read "Qamar" (?)—"moon," *cf.* Ptolemy's "Mons Lunae"], the first part of which is sixteen degrees beyond the equator. The source of the Nile is in this mountain from ten springs. Five of these pour forth and gather in a large swamp; the other five also flow into another swamp. From each of these swamps three rivers flow, all of which empty into a single very large swamp.[28]

This swamp (which we may identify with the actual Sudd region of southern Sudan) is soon called a "lake" by al-Idrīsī and he says that at its lower end there is a mountain which splits the lake in two. One part of the mountain goes to the northwest taking along with it the Nile of the Blacks, while the other part follows the eastern half of the mountain and goes in a northerly direction to become the Nile of Egypt. The "Nile of the Blacks" empties into the "Sea of Darkness" (i.e., the Atlantic Ocean). His hydrographic scheme is clearly illustrated in the map of Africa he drew up, which is also reproduced by Ibn Khaldūn in his *Muqaddima*.[29]

Medieval Arab scholars recognized four great rivers in the world, reflecting the biblical tradition, though their identity varies among authors. Common to all lists are the Euphrates and the Nile.[30] It was natural, then, to suppose that a river such as the Niger, of similar grand proportions to the Nile, was just a branch of it. From this position it was perhaps but a small step to see the two other major rivers that Arabs came across in West Africa, the Senegal and the Komadugu Yobe, as being part of this branch. No one, it would seem, ever saw all three, and the fact that two of them—the Niger and the Komadugu Yobe—flowed west-east was conveniently overlooked. The key factors seem to have been that one *did* flow east-west and empty into the Encompassing Sea, just as the Egyptian Nile emptied into the Mediterranean and the Mogadishu "Nile" emptied into the Indian Ocean (the eastern reaches of the Encompassing Sea)— a fine example of the symmetry of nature. Another factor may have been the association of one of the rivers, the Komadugu Yobe, with a large, swamp-like lake—Lake Chad—even though the river flowed into it and not out of it.

This West African "Nile" was more important as a symbol than it was as a physical fact, or series of reconstructed "facts"—just like the European geographers' later construction of the "mountains of Kong," stretching from the Senegal River to Lake Chad at about 12° N, which served to discourage consideration of the possibility that the Niger turned south and emptied into the Atlantic.[31] Using the comparative reality of the Egyptian situation and the partial evidence of some Arab geographers in relation to West Africa, al-Idrīsī plants almost all known towns of the region along this "Nile." The river is shown as a virtually straight line, and it is designed to represent not merely a physical but a psychological barrier.

To the north of it, on the frontiers of the "lands of Islam," were the towns visited by Muslim merchants, the populations of which were by the twelfth century, at least in part, Muslim: Takrūr, Silla, Tiraqqa, Kawkaw, and others. On the banks of both the Senegal and the Niger, they met with West African merchants who bought their goods and sold them gold, slaves, and other items. They did not, so far as we can tell, venture across this "Nile," the other banks of which were said to be inhabited by naked pagans (often reputed to be cannibals) known under the cant name of Lamlam, Damdam, or Namnam, who seem to turn up wherever there is any "Nile." On the one hand the Muslims had no real need to cross this Nile, unless they sought to discover the sources of gold; on the other hand, crossing the river would have taken them beyond the lands of Islam and beyond a point where they could mount their camels and simply head back home. It was dangerous country for both body and soul.[32] In reality, most of the towns that the North African informants of al-Idrīsī and his predecessors did business in were, in fact, on one of the great rivers. It is not very surprising, then, that Idrīsī should also place the "town" of Ghana on the "Nile" (indeed, on both banks) in conformity with his theory.[33] In fact, Kumbi Ṣāliḥ, the likely site of the merchant town of Ghana, was several hundred kilometers from either the Senegal or the Niger.

This leads us to another geographical red herring for which Idrīsī seems to be responsible, but which proved to be of such longevity that British geographers were solemnly discussing it and trying to locate it on their maps in the early nineteenth century: that is the "island of Wangara." The term "Wangara" is first used (though with a confused spelling) by al-Bakrī, who applies it to a group of non-Arab long-distance traders who dealt in gold in ancient Ghana—essentially correct, for it is a term used until recently in the Middle Niger and Hausaland for long-distance merchants of Manding origin otherwise known as Dyula.[34] Idrīsī, however, makes of "Wangara" a piece of land, an island surrounded by the "Nile" to the east of Ghana. In his text he tells us that it is inundated by the "Nile" waters annually and that after the flood people swarm over it to search for gold. Susan McIntosh has suggested that what Idrīsī was really describing was the Inland Delta of the Niger (in modern Mali) which stretches from about the vicinity of San in the south to the Goundam area in the north.[35] Certainly Idrīsī's dimensions for the "island"—300 miles long and 150 miles wide—are close enough, and his statement that the flood begins in August also matches the reality of the river Niger's inundation regime. But the identification is not so simple as that, for theory and reality are inextricably intertwined in Idrīsī and he combines two separate types of information to produce a hybrid and mythical third. The original area of "Wangara" was undoubtedly the auriferous Bambuhu (or Bambuk) region situated between the Bafing and Bakhoy tributaries of the river Senegal, and still known as Gangaran,[36] which probably gave its name to the merchants who visited it regularly in pursuit of gold to sell to North African merchants. Though it does not become inundated annually, it is, nevertheless, surrounded almost completely by rivers. On the other hand, it is likely that "Wangara" merchants were establishing themselves in towns of the interior delta such as Dia (Ar. Zāgha) and perhaps Kābara as early as the first half of the twelfth century.[37] "Modern" Jenne, too, may have originally been settled by Wangara merchants who made it their base while doing business with the non-Muslims of "Old" Jenne (Jenne-jeno) until the ruler of that town converted to Islam *ca.* 1200 and moved his court to the new site. Accounts of the area from such merchants of the area would have filtered back up the Saharan trails and into North Africa. Thus what we most probably have is a conflated description of the Bafing-Bakhoy Wangara, where people really did find gold, and the interior delta of the Niger where Wangara merchants were operating (and trading in gold), and which really did become inundated annually.[38] It is even possible that Idrīsī's "Ghāna," which he describes as consisting of two towns on opposite banks of the river ["Nile"] near the land of "Wangara," may be a conflation of accounts relating to an earlier "capital" of ancient Ghana and more recent accounts of old and new Jenne.

Deconstructing the Sources

The above examples illustrate some of the problems of interpretation inherent in these external medieval Arabic sources. It is clear that in order to extract usable historical material from them we must first deconstruct these sources by examining the sources which a given author may have drawn on, and the assumptions he may have had in regard to geography, ethnography, and the workings of history.[39] In order to do this it may be necessary to read more than the meager passages concerning the area we are concerned with, and perhaps to read widely in the entire work in which such material appears, or even in other works of the same author. Thus, while translated anthologies of closely focused material extracted from medieval Arab writers may seem an apparent convenience, in that they spare us from consulting a large array of original Arabic texts (including some as yet unpublished), we should be aware of the pitfalls of such an approach. For the serious scholar such collections serve best as a key to what to examine in the broader literature from which they are drawn, and remind us that there is no substitute for a contextualized study of the texts themselves.

While attention has been focused so far on medieval external sources, we should not forget that the postmedieval period also offers a range of external sources for certain areas and periods, both in Arabic and in Turkish. Because Morocco became involved in the history of the Middle Niger region, following the conquest of the area by a Sa‘dian expeditionary force in 1591, there is a continuing interest in West Africa on the part of Moroccan historians. A highly partial account of the Sa‘dian conquest appears in the history of the Sa‘dian dynasty of the court historian ‘Abd al-‘Azīz al-Fishtālī (d. 1621), so far untranslated into any European language.[40] The Moroccan historian of the eleventh century of the Hijra (seventeenth century C.E.), Muḥammad al-Ṣaghīr b. *al-ḥājj* Muḥammad b. ‘Abd Allāh al-Ifrānī (d. 1743 or 1745), also includes an account of the Sa‘dian conquest in his *Nuzhat al-ḥādī bi-akhbār al-qarn al-ḥādī*, written shortly before 1724.[41] While this is apologetic in tone, it does contain two passages of interest: a brief account of the Askiya dynasty taken from a book entitled *Naṣīḥat ahl al-Sūdān*, by a man simply identified as al-Imām al-Takrūrī, and thus presumably a West African, and some material on the experiences of the Timbuktu scholar Aḥmad Bābā in exile in Marrakesh.[42] Finally, in the late nineteenth century Aḥmad b. Khālid al-Nāṣirī wrote his celebrated history of Morocco during the Islamic era, *Kitāb al-istiqṣā' li-akhbār duwal al-Maghrib al-aqṣā*, first published in 1894–95.[43] This contains a lengthy account of the Sa‘dian conquest of the Middle Niger drawn from a variety of sources, some identified and some not, and concludes with a sharp attack on the practice of taking Black Africans into slavery and the assumption that blackness of skin is alone a justification for enslavement.[44]

Turkish texts are one of the least known and least exploited sources for African history. The full extent of them is not yet known, as no one has undertaken a systematic exploration of the Istanbul archives. One literary work that has been partially examined is the *Seyāḥatname* of Ewliyā Celebi (d. 1684), a ten-volume account of his travels, written to entertain rather than to give scientific information, but nevertheless a valuable source if used carefully. The tenth volume, written towards the end of his life during an extended stay in Egypt, concerns Egypt, the Sudan, and Ethiopia.[45] No translation into any other language exists, but some work has been done by Polish scholars on his passing remarks on West Africa.[46] The Turkish scholar Cengiz Orhonlu had an abiding interest in the Ottomans in Africa. He wrote on Ottoman-Bornu relations in the sixteenth century utilizing Ottoman archival documents,[47] and edited a volume of documents concerning the Ottoman attempts to establish a province in Eritrea.[48]

Another scarcely explored source of historical data concerning West Africa lies in the archives of North African states: Morocco, Algeria, Tunisia, and Libya. To date the only material published from such archives is parts of some correspondence from Tripoli and Fezzan relating to Bornu and to trans-Saharan trade in the early nineteenth century.[49] There is as yet only one study that exploits Arabic archival material for the study of trans-Saharan trade: the study by the late Ulrich Harmann of documents of Ghadāmsī traders,[50] though much more material must exist. There are certainly similar documents in Timbuktu,[51] and no doubt in Kano, the other main trading link of these merchants in the nineteenth century.

North African archives need to be explored also for another aspect of African history: the trade in Black slaves, and the social history of Black slave and ex-slave communities in North Africa. This is a topic that is beginning to attract increasing attention, both from North African and American scholars. Abdel Jelil Temimi has been something of a pioneer, publishing in 1981 an account by a Timbuktu pilgrim of Hausa *bori* practice in Tunis in 1814,[52] and exploring other local sources.[53] Two earlier texts on slavery have been published by Fatima Harrak and myself: the *Miʿrāj al-ṣuʿūd* of Aḥmad Bābā of Timbuktu (written 1615) and replies he gave when in Morocco to his student Aḥmad al-Īsī.[54]

Internal Sources

Whatever may now be said about internal Arabic sources for African history represents only the tip of the iceberg. While considerable progress has been made in the past half century in bringing to light, cataloguing, editing, and translating Arabic materials, it is still true to say that the more one probes the more one finds. The number of scholars whose competency in Arabic is sufficient to exploit these resources is still so minimal that it will take many more decades before we have a reasonably accurate picture of what exists.[55] It will take even longer before enough of this material is translated into international languages such as English or French to allow it to be integrated into the broader literature of African history. The unfortunate thing is that scholars can gain very little credit from the editing and translation of sources, and journals are generally reluctant to publish translations of sources (even with critical analyses), let alone original texts.

There have, however, been some attempts to establish scholarly loci for the publication of Arabic sources for African history (including African language materials in the Arabic script), with most of which I am happy to have had an association. In 1964, while teaching at the University of Ibadan, I was able to establish a Centre of Arabic Documentation within the Institute of African Studies. Arabic manuscripts from Northern (and later Western) Nigeria were loaned for microfilming and the originals returned to their owners. A journal, simply entitled *Research Bulletin*, was established in the same year, in which were published analyses of the manuscripts microfilmed and articles concerning Arabic sources, or containing texts and translations. Unfortunately, over the years the microfilms deteriorated to the point of being unusable, due to inadequately climate-controlled conservation; the *Research Bulletin* survived better, and sporadic issues were still appearing in the late 1980s.

Slightly before this, in 1962, the Czech scholar Ivan Hrbek proposed an international project to publish sources of African history under the title *Fontes Historiae Africanae*. The project was adopted by the International Academic Union (situated in Brussels) as Commission XXII, but political turmoil in Czechoslovakia in 1967 prevented Hrbek and the Czech academy from getting the project off the ground. In 1972 I was invited by the IAU to assume direction of the project, and I continued in this role until 1985. Four series were established: Series Arabica, Series Aethiopica, Series Varia, and Subsidia Bibliographica. Over the period 1978 to 1988 ten Arabic texts and translations were published,[56] and an inventory of the Arabic manuscripts from the royal palace of Segu preserved in the Bibliothèque Nationale, Paris.[57] Publication subsidies were initially provided by UNESCO. From 1985 onward the project was directed by the late Charles F. Beckingham through the British Academy, but the emphasis was placed on sources in European languages; in 2001 the overall direction of the project returned to the Czech Republic, directed by Viera Pawliková-Vilhanová, but the committee of the British Academy continues to be a very active participant in the project.

During my time as director of the project I was asked to produce a newsletter. The first issue of the *Bulletin d'Information* was published when I was teaching at the University of Ghana, in 1975. Originally simply a source of news about the project, it rapidly developed into a locus for publishing documents, especially Arabic documents (many of these arabic documents were republished in *Sudanic Africa*, 13 (2002).), and each issue also contained a bibliography of new publications of, or about, sources for African history. The last issue of the *Bulletin* appeared in 1986–87 (nos. 11/12), published through the Program of African Studies, Northwestern University.

As the *Fontes* project seemed to move away from Arabic sources and its *Bulletin* fade away, two other initiatives emerged to take their place: one in the United States, and one in Norway. In the United States an Association for the Publication of African Historical Sources was founded through the efforts of David Robinson and Jay Spaulding; funding to support publication was provided by the National Endowment for the Humanities. The first volume to appear (in 1989), *Public Documents from Sinnār*, edited by Jay Spaulding and Muḥammad Ibrāhīm Abū Salīm, was also volume 11 of the Series Arabica of the Fontes Historiae Africanae. This was a revised version of what had been originally planned as volume 2 of that series, but never published. This new series, simply entitled "African Historical Sources," has continued to be published by Michigan State University Press, and has included several Arabic sources among its volumes.[58]

The Fontes *Bulletin* was "replaced" by *Sudanic Africa: a Journal of Historical Sources*. Sean O'Fahey and I had long talked about the need for establishing a solid ongoing journal to deal with Arabic and Arabic script sources for African History. In 1990, with the help of Knut Vikør and the Centre for Middle Eastern and Islamic Studies at the University of Bergen, we were able to publish the first issue of this new journal, which has continued its annual publication ever since and has both broadened the scope of its content and further internationalized its editorial committee. As regards journals that publish (or have published) Arabic sources, honorable mention should be made of the *Bulletin of the School of Oriental and African Studies*, which published Arabic and Hausa sources for northern Nigeria edited by A. D. H. Bivar and Mervyn Hiskett in the 1950s and 1960s, and for Mauritania by Harry Norris in the 1960s and 1970s; the *Africana Bulletin* of the University of Warsaw has also published Hausa material from Ghana in text and English translation, while the *Bulletin de l'IFAN* has published French translations of a number of Arabic writings by West Africa authors, many of which are broadly historical in content.

The internal sources for African history can conveniently be divided into two types: literary and archival, with some writings sharing in the two categories. By "literary" I mean those that were written by (generally) named scholars, who had a point of view to express and an audience in mind, the principle subcategories being chronicles, annals, and biographies. Archival sources are writings of a documentary nature, generally in the public domain; they include court records, legal documents, proclamations, and political correspondence. In the crossover category are political poetry (both praise and satire), religiopolitical polemics, and juristic responsa (*ajwiba, fatāwī, nawāzil*) covering a wide variety of topics, social, economic, and political.

Possibly the oldest chronicle of any sub-Saharan African locality is the so-called "Kilwa Chronicle," of which a Portuguese translation was published in 1552, through it was perhaps written ca. 1520.[59] Indeed, the Swahili coast and islands has been well chronicled over time, both in Arabic and Swahili, and a number of such chronicles have been published, though most were written in the nineteenth century.[60] Chronologically, the next major African Arabic chronicle is the two-part history of Bornu written by the imam Aḥmad b. Furṭuwā: the history of the first twelve years of Mai Idrīs Aloma's rule, written soon after 1576,[61] and his account of that mai's wars against Kanem, written in 1578. This latter work is said to have been inspired by a now lost work of Masfarma ʿUmar b. ʿUthmān about the campaign of Mai Idrīs Katakamarbe (*reg.* ca. 1497–1519), therefore perhaps contemporary with the writing of the first Kilwa chronicle.

The next generation of chronicles comes from Timbuktu in the sixteenth and seventeenth centuries, and this is also the period that sees the appearance of the first biographical dictionary. The two major chronicles of the Middle Niger region are the *Taʾrīkh al-fattāsh* and the *Taʾrīkh al-sūdān*. The history of the writing of the former is complex, but appears to have been begun by a certain Maḥmūd Kaʿti, perhaps a descendant of an Andalusian immigrant to the region,[62] and continued by some of his descendants down to around 1655. Later in the early nineteenth century the text of some copies of it was manipulated to reflect certain political and territorial claims of Shaykh Aḥmad Lobbo of Masina, and it is this version that was published and translated by O. Houdas and M. Delafosse in 1911.[63] With the coming to light of the library of Maḥmūd Kaʿti (now stored in Timbuktu), a new edition may now be possible, based on the author's notes, and possible earlier versions of the text of the chronicle.[64] The *Taʾrīkh al-sūdān* of ʿAbd al-Raḥmān al-Saʿdī has no such complicated history. Its main focus is the history of Songhay from the reign of Sunni ʿAlī to the Saʿdian conquest of 1591, and the first sixty or so years of Arma rule of the region, the last date mentioned in it being 1065 A.H./ 1655–56 C.E. A text and translation were published by O. Houdas in 1898–1900, and an English translation by myself of the first thirty chapters (covering the period down to 1613) was published in 1999.[65]

One of the features of al-Saʿdī's work is its periodic chapters containing obituaries (*wafayāt*) of scholars and other notable persons of the years covered, and a brief mention of other important events (such as the flood waters of the River Niger reaching Timbuktu), beginning from the year of the Saʿdian conquest. This annalistic style later became a genre in its own right, both in Timbuktu and in Mauritania,[66] the chronicles of Walāta and Néma being prime examples, and on a more elaborate scale the *Minaḥ al-Rabb al-Ghafūr* (see below). A late eighteenth-century history of Timbuktu from 1160/1747 down to 1215/1815 follows the same pattern.[67] It was in this period, too, that the biographical genre, so widely practiced in the greater Islamic world for many centuries, manifested itself in sub-Saharan Africa. In fact, the earliest work, the *Nayl al-ibtihāj* of Aḥmad Bābā al-Tinbuktī, was completed while this scholar was in exile in Marrakesh in 1596, and was modeled on, and formed a supplement to, the biographical compendium of Mālikī scholars of Ibn Farḥūn (d. 1397), *al-Dībāj al-mudhahhab*. Only a small portion of the entries deal with West African scholars (mainly Aḥmad Bābā's relatives), but this proved a valuable source for al-Saʿdī, who devoted two entire chapters of his history to biographies of Timbuktu scholars, lifted verbatim from Aḥmad Bābā's *Kifāyat al-muḥtāj*, an abbreviated and revised version of his *Nayl al-ibtihāj*. The text of the *Nayl al-ibtihāj* itself has been published several times, and in the mid-nineteenth century Cherbonneau translated the biographies of West African scholars.[68] In the eighteenth century an anonymous history of the pashas of Timbuktu, entitled *Dīwān al-mulūk fī salāṭīn al-sūdān*, was produced, and was rearranged as a biographical dictionary, the *Tadhkirat al-nisyān fī akhbār mulūk al-sūdān*, which Houdas also published.[69]

In the twentieth century two works of brief biographical notices concerning Timbuktu were written, though neither has yet been published: the *Izālat al-rayb waʾl-shakk waʾl-tafrīṭ fī dhikr al-ʿulamāʾ al-muʾallifīn min ahl al-Takrūr waʾl-Ṣaḥrāʾ wa-ahl Shinqīt* of Aḥmad b. Abī'l-Aʿrāf al-Takanī (d. 1955),[70] and *al-Saʿāda al-abadiyya fī ʾl-taʿrīf bi-ʿulamāʾ Tinbuktu al-bahiyya* of Aḥmad Bāber (d. 1997),[71] which also includes historical narratives, mainly derivative from earlier chronicles. I should also mention a biographical dictionary written by a Walāta scholar, which includes some Middle Niger material, the *Fatḥ al-Shakūr fī maʿrifat aʿyān ʿulamāʾ al-Takrūr* of Muḥammad ʿAbd Allāh b. Abī Bakr al-Ṣiddīq al-Barritaylī (or al-Bartilī), compiled in 1214/1799–1800.[72] It was complemented by the as yet unpublished *Minaḥ al-Rabb al-Ghafūr fī mā aḥmalahu ṣāḥib Fatḥ al-Shakūr* of Abū Bakr b. Aḥmad al-Walātī (d. 1917).[73] This, in fact, goes beyond the simple compass of a biographical dictionary and merges this genre with the annalistic genre, and in so doing provides much valuable information on the history of southern Mauritania and northern Mali in the nineteenth century.[74]

In addition to numerous small annals of Timbuktu, Māsina, Jenne, Arawān, and so on, there are some unpublished chronicles of the region written in the twentieth century that deserve attention. Notable among these is the *Kitāb al-turjumān fī taʾrīkh al-Ṣaḥrāʾ waʾl-Sūdān wa-balad Tinbuktu wa-Shinqīṭ wa-Arawān* of Muḥammad Maḥmūd b. al-Shaykh al-Arawānī, one time *qāḍī* of Timbuktu (d. 1973),[75] and two works by Aḥmad Bāber: his *Taʾrīkh Azawād*, an edited version with footnotes of a history of the Barābīsh of Azawād by Maḥmūd b. Daḥmān, written in 1368/1948–49;[76] and his *Jawāhir al-ḥisān fī akhbār al-sūdān*, a work intended in some sense to replace the apparently lost sixteenth-century work of the same name by Bābā Gūr(ū) b. *al-ḥājj* Muḥammad al-Amīn.[77] For the period down to the early nineteenth century the work follows the standard histories in the main, but the material for the nineteenth and twentieth centuries is more original, especially in synthesizing tribal histories.

Turning now to northern Nigeria, the nineteenth and twentieth centuries witnessed a proliferation of historical writing associated with the *jihād* of Shaykh ʿUthmān b. Muḥammad Fodiye (d. 1817), and the Islamic state which arose out of it (sometimes called the "Sokoto Caliphate"). The earliest of these is the *Infāq al-maysūr fī taʾrīkh bilād al-Takrūr* of Shaykh ʿUthmān's son and military commander Muḥammad Bello (d. 1837), an account of the *jihād* campaigns, with valuable material on the history of Islam in the central *bilād al-sūdān* (including some biographical sketches),[78] written in 1227/1812. The Arabic text has twice been very incompetently edited, but recently a viable edition was published in Morocco,[79] though as yet no translation is in sight.[80] Shaykh ʿUthmān's brother ʿAbd Allāh, who had written much poetry celebrating the victories of the *jihād*, collected his poems together and wove an historical account around them, completing in 1228/1813 his *Tazyīn al-waraqāt*, a work in the tradition of Ibn Hishām's *Sīra*.[81] Another early account is that of ʿAbd al-Qādir b. al-Muṣṭafā (d. 1280/1864), the so-called *Rawḍāt al-afkār*, which also contains a unique account of Gobir history in the eighteenth century.[82] No Arabic text has yet been published, only a mediocre, unannotated, translation by H. R. Palmer.[83] The annals of the state founded by Shaykh ʿUthmān have largely been written by the viziers of the succeeding sultans,[84] the most comprehensive being the *Ḍabṭ al-multaqaṭāt* of the late vizier Junayd b. Muḥammad al-Bukhārī (d. 1997).[85] Less well known are the *Taqāyīd mimmā waṣala ilaynā min aḥwāl umarāʾ al-muslimīn salāṭīn Ḥawsa* of a man simply known as *al-ḥājj* Saʿīd, an ousider to the institution, covering the period down to 1854;[86] and the unpublished *Kanz al-awlād wa 'l-dharārī* of Muḥammad Sambo b. Aḥmad al-Kulawī, written in 1234/1818–19, a long and rambling work of general Islamic history, pious biography, and Fulani genealogy and history, not well regarded by Sokoto scholars and hence neglected.[87] Of local accounts of the *jihād* and its aftermath two deserve mention, one published, and the other not: the *Taqyīd al-akhbār* of Muḥammad Zangi concerning the establishment of Fulani rule in Kano (written in 1284/1868, see *ALA* II, 342),[88] and the *Taʾlīf akhbār al-qurūn* of Aḥmad b. Abī Bakr called Ọmọ Ikokoro, concerning Ilorin (written 1330/1912, see *ALA* II, 447).[89] There are numerous short chronicles of particular states and emirates in northern Nigeria, generally anonymous, and often in Hausa, and these are listed in *ALA* II, chapter 14. The best known is the so-called Kano Chronicle, written, so I have argued, in the 1890s (it ends ca. 1893, though relates Kano history back to the eleventh century) by someone who thought in Hausa but wrote in Arabic.[90] This is evident from his Arabic style, which includes a number of very clear calques of Hausa phrases, as well as numerous terms in Hausa despite the existence of suitable Arabic terms. Similar traits are to be found in many African Arabic chronicles, which were often written by persons who, while literate in Arabic, were not members of the high scholarly class, and therefore did not think in Arabic, but in their native tongue, and then translated their thoughts into Arabic. This is even evident in an historian such as al-Saʿdī, who includes phrases that are literal translations of Songhay expressions. In order to make fully accurate translations of such works it is necessary to know the mother tongue of the author, or to collaborate with an African scholar who does.

Ghana was influenced by both the Hausa tradition of learning and the Manding Dyula tradition, the latter being the earlier of the two to make its presence felt there. It is to the Dyula tradition that the local chronicles of the Volta Basin largely belong, a tradition that has its origins in the Inland Delta region of Mali, and which spread wherever Dyula and Jakhanke merchants and scholars roamed from the river Gambia to the river Volta. Dyula traditions of Islamic scholarship have been ably chronicled by Ivor Wilks, who is also the only scholar so far to have published texts and translations of chronicles grounded in this tradition from Ghana,[91] though other scholars such as Lamin Sanneh, Thomas Hunter, and Michael Gomez have used similar materials to illuminate the history of communities farther west.[92] The entire tradition of Islamic learning in Ghana is documented in chapter 12 of volume 4 of *Arabic Literature of Africa*, in which Wilks's detailed knowledge of the chronicling tradition is set forth.[93] Perhaps the best known Ghanaian Muslim writer of the pre-twentieth century was *al-ḥājj* ʿUmar b. Abī Bakr al-Ṣalghawī, who wrote much that is of historical interest, both in Arabic and Hausa. His poems on the Salaga civil war of 1892 and on the beginnings of European colonialism are particularly important.[94] He also collaborated with the German administrator Mischlich to produce a Hausa prose account of Hausa society, based on his own memories,[95] and he wrote Hausa histories of both Kebbi (his place of origin) and Ilorin.[96] Another writer of the early colonial period, simply known as Mallam Abu wrote Hausa chronicles of the invasions of Babatu and Samori into northern Ghana.[97]

The Fulfulde-speaking peoples of the Senegambia region also have a tradition of chronicle writing that probably goes back to the eighteenth century. The Islamic states of Futa Toro and Futa Jalon had their chroniclers, both identified and anonymous, some writing in Arabic and some in Fulfulde.[98] The single most outstanding historian of the region is the twentieth-century scholar Mūsā Kamara (1864–1943). Trained in traditional fashion in his homeland of Futa Toro, and in Futa Jalon and southern Mauritania, he established good relations with such French scholars of Senegal as Paul Marty, Maurice Delafosse, and Henri Gaden. He wrote over thirty works on a wide range of subjects, but some of his weightiest were works of history. Among these are *al-Majmūʿ al-nafīs*, a history of some Moorish and Fulbe chiefs, which still remains in manuscript,[99] and his best-known work, the encyclopedic *Zuhūr al-basātīn fī taʾrīkh al-sawādīn*, a history of Futa Toro and adjacent lands and peoples, several sections of which have been translated into French.[100] Mūsā Kamara also wrote a biography of *al-ḥājj* ʿUmar,[101] a history of the Torodɓe,[102] and a history of the Yalalɓe, Denyankoɓe, Wawamɓe, and the Tukulor.[103]

The *jihād* and state-building movements of *al-ḥājj* ʿUmar, Shaykh Aḥmad Lobbo, and their successors lack major chroniclers. There are, however, numerous short and partial accounts of aspects of at least the first of these two and some material that may be regarded as hagiographical rather than historical.[104] *Al-ḥājj* ʿUmar, though a prolific writer did not write of his own deeds, though he did, in the manner of Shaykh ʿUthmān b. Fodiye, write a justification of his attack on a fellow Muslim—in *al-ḥājj* ʿUmar's case Shaykh Aḥmad Lobbo of Māsina, whom he denounced as an infidel. This is the only work of his to have been translated in full,[105] though parts of his major doctrinal work, the *Kitāb al-rimāḥ*, have been translated, and the whole work analyzed.[106]

In the present state of our knowledge the chronicle tradition appears to be strongest in West Africa, though this may merely reflect the relative state of our knowledge. A great deal of work has been done in West Africa to bring to light personal libraries and archives and to establish public collections, and while much still remains to be done, it far exceeds what has been done in the Sudan, Eritrea, Ethiopia, or the Horn of Africa. Hence, our knowledge of the manuscript heritage of those areas remains defective, and their traditions of historical writing underexplored. Whereas in Nigeria there are ten public collections of Arabic manuscripts, in the Sudan there is only one—the Public Records Office in Khartoum. While this is extremely rich in archival materials, few scholars are aware that its "Miscellaneous" (*mutanwwiʿāt*) collection contains some five thousand items that fall into the "literary" category, since there is no available handlist of them. Ethiopia and Eritrea are as yet almost completely unexplored territories, though it is certain that in these countries, as in the Sudan, there are scholarly private libraries, and libraries attached to Sufi *zāwiya*s and teaching institutions. Due to internal strife and the breakdown of central government in Somalia, no collection of manuscripts has been possible and this remains another area of relative ignorance. Apart from histories written in Arabic and Somali in the second half of the twentieth century, the only earlier work is the anonymous *Kitāb al-zunūj*, which summarizes the history of the lands of the Indian Ocean coast of Africa from Mogadishu southwards, from earliest times to the beginning of the twentieth century;[107] one other work, *al-Kawākib al-durriyya li-akhbār Ifrīqiyya*, written in 1928 by one ʿUthmān b. Muḥammad ʿAbdī covers similar ground, but the relationship between the two works is not yet ascertained. As far as Ethiopia is concerned, apart from the chronicles of Harar that Ewald Wagner has so conscientiously edited and translated,[108] the only other major work of history is the chronicle of the campaigns of Aḥmad Grañ down to 1535, entitled *Bahjat al-zamān*, or more commonly, *Futū ̣ al-Ḥabasha*, by Shihāb al-Dīn Aḥmad b. ʿAbd al-Qādir, known as ʿArab Faqīh.[109]

Returning now to the Nilotic Sudan, there is only one major dynastic chronicle, and that is, in fact, a composite work, often known as "The Funj Chronicle," although it covers not only the Funj period (1504–1821), but most of the period of Turco-Egyptian rule down to 1871. Its textual history is complex, and is admirably laid out in the introduction to

P. M. Holt's recent complete translation of all the recensions and fragments.[110] The other work dealing with the Funj era is the bio/hagio/graph-
ical work, the *Tabaqāt* of Muḥammad al-Nūr b. Ḍayf Allāh, known as Wad
Ḍayf Allāh (d. 1224/1809–10), which, as its full title indicates, contains
material on the "saints," the righteous, the scholars, and the poets.[111]

The Mahdist period in the Sudan (1881–98) inspired several works
of an historical nature, though in fact they were describing contemporary
events. The only published biography of the Mahdī Muḥammad Aḥmad
(d. 1885) is that of Ismāʿīl b. ʿAbd al-Qādir (d. 1897), of which a con-
densed English translation was produced by Haim Shaked.[112] This is a
detailed account of his life and campaigns by an insider, who also wrote an
account of the war between the Mahdī's successor, the *Khalīfa* ʿAbdullahi
and King Yohannis of Ethiopia in 1889.[113] There are also two important
accounts by contemporary non-Sudanese: a two-volume memoir by
Ibrāhīm Fawzī, who was an Egyptian officer commanding troops when the
Mahdī took Khartoum in 1885, and who was then confined to Omdurman
until the Anglo-Egyptian expedition occupied the area in 1898;[114] and a
three part "history and geography" of the Sudan by Naʿūm Shukayr, an
Egyptian Intelligence officer in Cairo, who had access to much confidential
information and who was the first person to be able to exploit Mahdist
archives.[115] One further contemporary outsider account deserves mention.
The last pages of Aḥmad b. Zaynī Dahlān's *al-Futūḥāt al-Islāmiyya*, first
published in Mecca (of which city Aḥmad b. Zaynī was the *muftī*) in
1884–85, discusses the claims of the Mahdī. Although he is able to chronicle the Mahdī's life only by hearsay, the importance of his work lies in what
it reveals about the way "neutral" Muslims of the age thought about him.[116]

Archival Sources

Archival sources in Arabic are even less known than literary sources, yet
Arabic was the official chancery language of many Muslim polities in
Saharan and sub-Saharan Africa; it was the language of legal documents, of
business records, family affairs and personal correspondence. It was also the
language of religious polemic, and politico-religious disputation between
learned leaders of communities, especially in the nineteenth century.
Although some of these archival materials are now preserved in public
collections, a great deal more remains in the hands of those who generated
the material or were recipients of it.

A few examples will suffice. In the archives of Zanzibar there is a complete set of the *qāḍī*'s court records in Arabic from 1880 to 1960. These

would offer unique insights into social life in Zanzibar and shed light on the way in which law was practiced there, but so far they remained unstudied. As regards Ethiopia, two volumes of nineteenth-century documents (mainly from collections outside Ethiopia) have been published under the editorship of Sven Rubenson; most are in Amharic, but there are also many in Arabic.[117] In the Sudan, the National Records Office holds over a million documents relating to the Mahdiyya period of Sudanese history (1882–98)—probably the largest state archive of any precolonial African state. Many of these documents have been used by historians writing the history of this period, such as P. M. Holt, Makkī Shibayka, Muḥammad Ibrāhīm Abū Salīm, and Muḥammad Saʿīd Qaddāl. Abū Salīm has also published the texts of all the known writings of the Mahdī in seven volumes,[118] and is currently preparing a parallel set of volumes of the writings of the Khalīfa ʿAbdullāhi. However, Muḥammad Ibrāhīm Abū Salīm died before that volume was published. The archival records of the previous period of Sudan's history, the Turkiyya (1821–82), are not held in the Sudan, but in Egypt, and most of these are in Turkish. An inventory of these materials was published in French in 1930,[119] but to study the period in depth the archives of several European powers that had consuls in Egypt or the Sudan at the time need to be studied.[120]

The seventeenth and eighteenth centuries have also been surprisingly well served. The pioneer here was Muḥammad Ibrāhīm Abū Salīm, for many years the director of the Sudanese Public Records Office. He published a volume of Funj land charters in 1967, and a similar volume relating to Dār Fūr in 1975.[121] A volume of texts and translations of documents relating to the Funj state was published by Abū Salīm and Jay Spaulding, while Abū Salīm collaborated with Sean O'Fahey to produce a volume of translated land documents from Dār Fūr.[122] These volumes are illustrative of a custom that seems to have existed right across the *bilād al-sūdan* in the period roughly 1500 to 1800, that is, the granting by rulers of parcels of land, sometimes with rights over attached free or slave populations, as well as certain other privileges (e.g., freedom from certain forms of taxation) to holymen whose services were needed, and to significant political figures. These documents were known in the Sudan as *jāh* (privilege) or *ḥākūra* (estate), while in Bornu they were called *maḥram* (locus of inviolability), and in Songhay *ḥurma*.[123] The *maḥram*s of Bornu have not yet been published in full, though some were published in translation by H. R. Palmer, and an extensive analysis of their historical function was made by Hamidu Bobboyi.[124] Dār Fūr, and its relations with Wadai on the one hand, and the Sanūsiyya of Libya/Chad on the other, has had the good fortune to attract the attention of Jay Spaulding and Lidwien Kapteijns, who have published two volumes including both texts and translations of correspondence preserved in the National Record Office, Khartoum.[125]

Nigeria has been less fortunate as regards archival documents in Arabic. Although large numbers of Arabic manuscripts have been amassed in university libraries in particular, and in the National Museum, Jos, little attention was paid to archival documents except by H. F. C. (Abdullahi) Smith when he directed the Northern History Research Scheme in the 1970s and early 1980s. Clearly there was a great deal of correspondence between Sokoto and the various emirates of the Sokoto Caliphate, as well as inter-emirate correspondence, and some of this has been preserved in the collection of the Northern History Research Scheme at Ahmadu Bello University, Zaria, and at Arewa House, Kaduna.[126] But this is probably only the tip of the iceberg, and certainly only a very small portion of this is published in either text or translation.[127] The Kano State History Bureau also collected some Kano archival material under the direction of Garba Said, but no listing of this has been published. However, a fascinating little volume of summaries of cases held before the emir's court in 1913–14 was published by Allen Christelow, with facsimile texts and translations and commentaries.[128] From the other end of Nigeria some chancery documents have been published from the papers of the Olubadan ʿAbbās Oleshinloye in the 1930s. These show how Arabic began to be used as a language of recording an official view of history, employing what may best be described as a semiliterate style, with curious turns of phrase, often attempted calques of Qurʾānic style, mixed with Yoruba terminology, skillfully interpreted by the editors of the published version.[129] These attempts to use Arabic in the service of recording valued information, despite lack of literary skills, bring to mind the use of Arabic in Asante in the nineteenth century.[130]

So far, I have discussed only published sources, but, as noted above, there are large numbers of unpublished Arabic documents in public and private libraries in Africa, and in a few public collections elsewhere. The most important of these collections are detailed in the Appendix below.

To conclude, let me draw attention to the Institute for the Study of Islamic Thought in Africa, directed by Sean O'Fahey and myself, and based jointly in Northwestern University and the University of Bergen. Its mission is to discover and preserve collections of Arabic manuscripts in sub-Saharan Africa; to analyze their content, and to sponsor the publication and translation of their most important items, especially works of historical significance. In twenty years we expect an account of Arabic sources for African history to be considerably more full than this present one.

APPENDIX

AFRICAN ARCHIVAL COLLECTIONS

I. *The Zanzibar archives*, which contain, among other things, a complete set of court records (in Arabic), covering the years 1880–1960.

II. *The Public Records Office of the Sudan (Khartoum)*. Preserved there are over a million documents relating to the Mahdist era (1881–98),[131] and a considerable number of writings by Sudanese authors in the "Miscellaneous" (*mutanawwiʿāt*) section.

III. *The Centre de Documentation et de Recherches Historiques Ahmad Baba (CEDRAB), Timbuktu*. Established in 1973, this collection now contains some 20,000 items, ranging from local chronicles and large collections of *fatwas* to single page legal documents on slavery, land transactions, and commercial matters.[132]

The great majority of the items preserved at the Centre Ahmad Baba are of local authorship, though some nonlocal items have been acquired if they have some historical or aesthetic interest. Among the latter we may note a beautiful illuminated copy of the *Shifāʾ* of Qāḍī ʿIyāḍ penned in Morocco (no. 3178) and one volume (in 80ff.) of the *Wafayāt al-aʿyān* of Ibn Khallikān in the hand of Aḥmad Bābā, copied by him in Marrakesh in Jumādā I 1008/19 Nov.–18 Dec. 1599 (no. 3866). Almost all the items are in the Arabic language, though the index does record the existence of a letter in Tamacheq and several poems and letters in the Songhay language—the only examples of this language written in the Arabic script so far preserved to the best of my knowledge. Other noteworthy items include:

1. *Religious Treatises.* Prominent among these are works by Kunta scholars, Sīdī al-Mukhtār b. Aḥmad al-Kuntī (d. 1811), his son Sīdī Muḥammad (d. 1826) and his grandson Sīdī Aḥmad al-Bakkāʾī (d. 1865), who was also the effective civil power in Timbuktu in the mid-nineteenth century and the host and protector of Heinrich

Barth. Earlier Timbuktu scholarship is represented by a number
of works by Aḥmad Bābā (though less than one would have
expected), by the *al-Minaḥ al-ḥamīda* of Muḥmammad Bābā b.
al-Amīn (d 1606) on grammar (no. 1563), the *al-Futūḥ al-*
Qayyūmiyya of Aḥmad b. Anda-Ag Muḥammad (d. 1635) (nos.
1927, 1928, 2008), and the commentary by Aḥmad Bābā's grandfather Aḥmad b. ʿUmar b. Muḥammad Aqīt (d. 1583) on al-
Maghīlī's poem on logic—the *Amnāḥ al-aḥbāb min minaḥ*
al-Wahhāb (no. 1945). There are also numerous works by
Mauritanian authors, especially those of Walāta, such as the celebrated *qāḍī* Muḥammad Yaḥyā b. Muḥammad al-Mukhtār
(d. 1912). Finally in this category we may note the existence of
copies of a number of works by the early nineteenth-century
Sokoto family of scholars and state builders, the Shaykh ʿUthmān
b. Fūdī (d. 1817), his brother ʿAbd Allāh (d. 1829) and his son
Muḥammad Bello (d. 1837). In particular, there are several copies
of each of the two volumes of ʿAbd Allāh's *tafsīr* the *Ḍiyāʾ al-taʾwīl*.
Earlier generations of "Nigerian" writers are represented by the
seventeenth-century Muḥammad al-Wālī b. Sulaymān al-Fullānī
of Katsina and his contemporary Muḥammad Masanih, also of
Katsina, and the eighteenth-century Muḥammad al-?āhir b. Ibrāhīm
al-Fallātī of Bornu.

2. *Chronicles.* There are two copies of al-Saʿdī's *Taʾrīkh al-Sūdān*,[133]
   Neither is dated, but both appear to be nineteenth-century copies
   and both are in neat hands with fairly generous vocalization of
   most place and personal names. One of them (no. 660 in 163 ff.)
   was obtained from the papers of Maurice Delafosse which were
   sold to the Centre by his surviving daughter, and lacks a small portion at the end. The other (no. 681) is complete in 199 ff. There
   are also two copies of the *Taʾrīkh al-fattāsh*. The one which I briefly
   examined (no. 3927) follows the text of MS A/B of the published
   edition but lacks the opening sections down to the account of
   Mansa Mūsā and has one or more folios missing at the end.
   The following is a summary list of the other principal chronicles and biographical dictionaries to be found at the Centre:

279. History of Azawād and the Barabīsh (21 ff.).

280. History of the people of al-Sūq (ancient Tādmakkat) by ʿAbd
Allāh b. al-Shaykh b. *al-ḥājj* Muḥammad Adda (6 ff.).

492. *Izālat al-rayb wa'l-shakk wa'l-tafrīṭ fī dhikr al-mu°allifīn min ahl al-Takrūr wa'l-Ṣaḥrā° wa-ahl Shinqīṭ*—the incomplete biographical dictionary of the Timbuktu scholar of Moroccan origin Aḥmad Bū 'l-Aʿrāf compiled in 1941–42 (no. 492, a draft in 80 ff. of which no. 4987 in 110 ff. is a fair copy).[134]

621. History of Azawād and Taoudeni by Abū 'l-Khayr b. ʿAbd Allāh b. Marzūq al-Arawānī (6 ff.).

684. *Fatḥ al-Shakūr fī maʿrifat aʿyān ʿulamāʾ al-Takrūr*, a biographical dictionary of the scholars of Timbuktu and the western Sahara down to the end of the eighteenth century by the Walāta scholar Abū Bakr Muḥammad b. al-Ṭālib al-Bartīlī (62 ff.), of which an inferior edition was published in Beirut a few years ago.[135] The collection also contains a much larger (and presumably fuller) copy at no. 5344 (182 ff.).

669. An expansion and annalistic continuation of the preceding item entitled *Minan al-rabb al-ghafūr fī dhikr mā ahmalahu ṣāḥib Fatḥ al-Shakūr* by Abū Bakr b. Aḥmad al-Walātī (d. 1917) in 173 ff., another item from the Delafosse collection and at present the only known copy of this important work.

769. *Kitāb al-turjumān fī taʾrīkh al-Ṣaḥrāʾ wa'l-Sūdān wa-balad Tinbuktu wa-Shinqīṭ wa-Arawān* by Muḥammad Maḥmūd b. al Shaykh al-Arawānī (56 ff.).

1051. A copy of the well-known *Infāq al-maysūr* of Muḥammad Bello.

1210. An account of the wars of the Tuareg against the French (9 ff.).

1293. A listing of important events in the region beginning from 1100/1688–89 (16 ff.).

2078. Listing of major events in the region from the ninth to the thirteenth centuries of the *hijra*.

2318. Listing of events in Timbuktu, 1200/1785–86 to 1215/1800–01 (11 ff.).

2775. A short history of the lands of Takrūr and the towns of the region by Muḥammad b. Muḥammad al-Aytī/Ītī (31 ff.).

3315. Events and obituaries of Jenne and Timbuktu, *c.* 1748–1800 (30 ff.).

4284–85. Dates of birth and death of some notable people of Timbuktu (7 ff.).

5343. *Diwān al-mulūk fī salāṭīn al-Sūdān* (56 ff.), an anonymous history of Timbuktu from the Saʿdian conquest of 1591 down to the middle of the eighteenth century. This is the chronicle version of a work that was published in the form of a biographical dictionary of the Bāshās of Timbuktu with the title *Tadhkirat al-nisyān* by Octave Houdas (with French translation, Paris, 1899–1901). There is also an incomplete copy at no. 2221 (12 ff.).[136]

Items of a documentary character

i) *Documents relating to property ownership.*

3848. Documents concerning the renting of houses (15ff.).

4468–4563. Inheritance schedules (98 ff.).

4672–4678. Land ownership documents (17 ff.).

5335. Three documents of ownership of land, wells, and houses in Walāta.

5407. Documents on sales of houses in Timbuktu.

ii) *Documents of regional and trans-Saharan trade.*

3850. Documents concerned with the transactions of Ghadamsi merchants in Timbuktu (24 ff.).

4283. Documents on the gum arabic trade (6 ff.).

4998–5002. Six letters to and from al-Bashīr al-Talmūdī, a Maghribi merchant resident in Timbuktu.

5305. Letters concerning trade between Timbuktu and Jenne (11 ff.).

5455–5515. Sixty letters to and from Ghadamsi merchants, mainly dating from the 1290s (1873–1883).

5516–5546. Thirty documents relating to prices and rates of exchange as between gold dust, cowries and salt dating from the 1280s and 1290s/*c.* 1863–1883.

iii) *Documents relating to slavery*

1532. A quarter share of a slave obtained through inheritance by a woman is given away as a charitable donation by her in expiation of her sins.

1534. Sale of a slave woman.

1555. Document of manumission.

1615. Delegation of a *qāḍī* to divide up slaves forming part of an inheritance.

1640. Letter about an offence committed by a *maʾdhūn* slave.

1716. *Fatwā* about a slave woman who apostatized.

2044. Letter from the Bāshā Ba-Ḥaddu b. Bū Bakr (reg. 1761–62) concerning the free status of a family of Bamba.

2089. A legal problem concerning the sale of free persons.

2283. *Fatwā* about a man who acted agressively (*taʿaddā*) against some one else's slave woman.

2602. *Fatwā* about whether a master should pay his slave's taxes during the colonial period.

2947. The case of a man of unknown ancestry who was enslaved (4 ff.).

3329–3342. Documents on the prices of slaves and other goods at Timbuktu and Jenne.

3555. Document on a claim to free status.

3558. Document dated 1276/1859–60 granting freedom to a slave woman upon her master's death.

5666. A judgment issued concerning a man who beat his slave women to death.

iv) *Collections of fatwās.*

There are a dozen or so major collections of *fatwās* at the Centre Ahmad Baba, totaling over 1,800 ff. Some of these are collections of the legal opinions of a particular scholar while others are more diverse collections of opinions of the scholars of the region as a whole. Most of the collections by single individuals are, in fact, by scholars of Mauritanian origin, though the major one is by the late nineteenth-early twentieth-century Kunta scholar Bāy b. Sīdī ʿUmar (b. 1865),[137] which runs to some 488 ff. in nine volumes (nos. 118–126). There are three copies of the major collection of the *fatwās* of the scholars of 'Takrūr'—*al-ʿAmal al-mashkūr fī jamʿ nawāzil ʿulamāʾ al-Takrūr* by al-Muṣṭafā b. Aḥmad al-Ghallāwī (nos. 521, 1031, and 5346).[138] There is also a collection of the opinions Aḥmad Bū l-Aʿrāf (no. 711 in 49 ff.).

IV. *Public collections in Nigeria*: the National Archives, Kaduna; Arewa House, Kaduna (a research and documentation center of Ahmadu

Bello University); Bayero University, Kano, Library; Sokoto State History Bureau; Kano State History Bureau; the Nigerian National Museum, Jos; the Waziri Junaid Library, Sokoto (private, but accessible to *bona fide* scholars); the collection of the Northern History Research Scheme, Ahmadu Bello University, Zaria. All of these collections contain both literary and archival items of local authorship, but few have detailed published listings.[139]

Notes

1. See Akbar Muhammad, "The image of Africans in Arabic literature: some unpublished manuscripts," in John Ralph Willis (ed.), *Slaves and Slavery in Muslim Africa*, Vol. I: *Islam and the Ideology of Slavery*, London, 1985, 47–74; Elizabeth Hodgkin, "A Discussion of Ibn al-Jawzī's *Tanwīr al-ghabash fī faḍl al-Sūdān wa'l-Ḥabash*," M.A. thesis, University of Birmingham, 1978; Imran Hamza Alawiye, "Ibn al-Jawzī's Apologia on behalf of the Black People and their Status in Islam: a Critical Edition and Translation of *Kitāb Tanwīr al-Ghabash fī Faḍl al-Sūdān wa'l-Ḥabash*," Ph.D. diss., University of London, 1985; Saud H. al-Khathlan, "A critical edition of *Rafʿshaʾn al-ḥubshān* by Jalāl al-Dīn al-Suyūṭī', Ph.D. diss., St Andrews University, 1983.

2. Notably, Ibn Faḍl Allāh al-ʿUmarī (d. 1349), *Masālik al-abṣīr fī mamālik al-amṣīr*, ch. 8, trans. M. Gaudefroy Demombynes, *Masālik El Abṣīr fī Mamālik El Amṣīr*, I: *L'Afrique moins l'Égypte*, Paris, 1927; Arabic text in Youssouf Kamal, *Monumenta Cartographica Africae et Aegypti*, Cairo-Leiden, 1926–51, repr. Frankfurt: Institut für Arabisch-Islamischen Wissenschaften an der Johann Wolfgang Goethe-Universität, 1987, IV, fasc. 2, 297–9; and al-Maqrīzī (d. 1442), *Kitāb al-ilmām bi-akhbār man bi-arḍ al-Ḥabasha min mulūk al-Islām*, Arabic text and Latin trans. F. T. Rinck, *Historia regum Islamiticorum in Abyssinia*, Leiden, 1790; Arabic text only, Cairo, 1895; see also Enrico Cerulli, *Documenti arabi per la storia dell'Etiopia*, Rome, 1931 [Memorie della Reale Accademia dei Lincei]. For a brief general overview, see C. F. Beckingham, "The Ḥabash in Muslim geographical works," in *Encyclopaedia of Islam* (new edn., hereafter *EI²*), Leiden, 1960–2002, iii, 6–7.

3. Muṣṭafā Muhammad Saʿd, *al-Maktaba al-Sūdāniyya al-ʿArabiyya: majmūʿat al-nuṣūṣ wa'l-wathāʾiq al-ʿarabiyya al-khaṣṣa bi-taʾrīkh al-Sūdān fī 'l-ʿuṣūr al-wusṭā*, Cairo, 1972; see also G. Vantini, *Oriental Sources concerning Nubia*, Heidelberg and Warsaw, 1975, a volume to be used with caution as it contains numerous inaccuracies.

4. See n. 2 above.

5. If there is an existing translation of a text into French or English, he uses it; if not, in the case of Arabic texts, he translates the text into French.

6. Series: Drevnie i srednevekovye istochniki po etnografii i istorii Afriki iuzhnee Sakhary.

7. Joseph Cuoq, *Receuil des Sources Arabes concernant l'Afrique Occidentale du VIIᵉ au XVIᵉ siècle*, Paris, 1975.

8. *Corpus of Early Arabic Sources for West African History*, trans. J. F. P. Hopkins, ed. and annotated by N. Levtzion and J. F. P. Hopkins, Cambridge, 1981 [Fontes Historiae

Africanae: Series Arabica IV], reprint (paperback edition) Princeton: Markus Wiener, 2000.

9. A complete corpus of the epitaphs of Gao, as well as inscriptions from Bentia (Kūkiya) and Es-Souk (Tādmakkat), assembled, translated and commented upon by Paulo F. de Moraes Farias, published by the British Academy, 2001.

10. An earlier French translation was published by El-Hadji Ravane M'baye, "Un aperçu de l'Islam songhay," *Bull. de l'IFAN*, 34 (1972), 237–67; an unsatisfactory Arabic text was published by ʿAbd al-Qādir Zabādiya, Algiers, 1974; a critical Arabic text with English translation is to be found in John Hunwick, *Sharīʿa in Songhay: the Replies of al-Maghīlī to the Questions of Askia al-ḥājj Muḥammad*, Oxford University Press for the British Academy, 1985.

11. *Description de l'Afrique du Nord*, Alger, 1857–58.

12. Vincent Monteil, "Al-Bakrî (Cordoue 1068), routier de l'Afrique blanche et noire du Nord-Ouest," *Bull. de l'IFAN*, 30 (1968), 39–116.

13. Cl. Meillassoux J. -L. Triaud and John Hunwick, "La géographie du Soudan d'après al-Bakrī: trois lectures," in J. P. Chrétien et al., *2000 Ans d'histoire africaine: le sol, la parole et l'écrit. Mélanges en hommage à Raymond Mauny*, Paris: Société Français d'Outre-mer, 416–25.

14. Dierk Lange, "La région du Lac Tchad d'après la Géographie d'Ibn Saʿīd: textes s et cartes," *Annales Islamologiques*, 16 (1980), 149–81; *idem*, "Un texte de Maqrīzī sur ⟨Les Races du Soudan⟩," *Annales Islamologiques*, 15 (1979), 187–209.

15. Ibn Baṭṭūṭa, *Tuḥfat al-nuzzar fī gharāʾib al-amṣār wa-ʿajāʾib al-asfār. Voyages d'Ibn Baṭṭūṭa*, texte arabe accompagné d'une traduction par C. Defrémery et B. Sanguinetti, Paris, 4 vols., 1853–9; *ibid*, réimpr. augmentée d'une préface et de notes de Vincent Monteil, Paris, n.d. [*c.* 1970].

16. *The Travels of Ibn Battuta*, London: Routledge [Broadway Travellers], 1929, repr. [Darf], 1983.

17. *The Travels of Ibn Baṭṭūṭa A.D. 1325–1354*, 4 vols., Cambridge-London, 1958–94 [Hakluyt Society, Second Series, Vols. 110, 117, 141, 178].

18. R. Mauny, V. Monteil, A. Djenidi, S. Robert, J. Devisse, *Textes et Documents Relatifs à l'Histoire de l'Afrique: Extraits tirés de Voyages d'Ibn Baṭṭūṭa*, Dakar, 1966 [Université de Dakar: Publ. de la Faculté des Lettres et Sci. Humaines, Section d'Histoire, no. 9].

19. *Ibn Battuta in Black Africa*, London: Rex Collings, 1975, repr. several times, most recently by Markus Wiener, Princeton.

20. Ross E. Dunn, *The Adventures of Ibn Battuta, a Muslim Traveler of the 14th Century*, Berkeley, 1986. For discussions of Ibn Baṭṭūṭa's itinerary in West Africa, see Claude Meillassoux, "L'itinéraire d'Ibn Battuta de Walata à Mali," *J. African Hist.*, 13 (1972), 389–95; J. O. Hunwick, "The mid-fourteenth century capital of Mali," *J. African Hist.*, 14 (1973), 195–208.

21. Jos. Marquart, *Die Benin-Sammlung des Reichsmuseums fur Völkerkunde in Leiden: Beschrieben und mit ausfurlichen Prolegomena zur Geschichte der Handelswege und Völkerbewegungen in Nordafrika*, Leiden, 1913.

22. *West African Food in the Middle Ages According to Arabic Sources*, Cambridge, 1974.

23. Tadeusz Lewicki, *Arabic External Sources for the History of Africa to the South of the Sahara*, translated by Marianne Abrahamowicz, Wroclaw, 1969. For a bibliography of

Lewicki's writings, see Elizabeth Savage, *A Gateway to Hell, a Gateway to Paradise: the North African Response to the Arab Conquest*, Princeton, 1997, 184–9.

24. See J. Vernet, art "al-Khʷārazmī, Abū Jaᶜfar Muḥammad b. Mūsā," in *EI²*, iv, 1070–71. His name indicates he came from Khuwārizm on the Lower Oxus River south of the Aral Sea, though he lived and worked in Mesopotamia.

25. See John O. Hunwick, *West Africa and the Arab World: Historical and Contemporary Perspectives*, Accra, 1991, 4–9.

26. Al-Dimashqī, see Hopkins & Levtzion, *Corpus*, 205.

27. Sultan Muḥammad Bello of Sokoto seems also to have subscribed to this theory, see the sketch map he gave to Capt. Clapperton in 1824 in *Missions to the Niger*, ed. E. W. Bovill, Vol. 4, Cambridge, 1966, facing p. 698. The river Niger bears the legend (in Arabic): "This is the river Kwāra. It is the one that reaches Egypt and is called the Nile."

28. al-Idrīsī, *Opus Geographicum, sive "Liber ad eorum delectationem qui terras peragrare studeant,"* ed. A.Bombaci, U. Rizzitano, R. Rubinacci, L. Veccia Vaglieri; Naples-Rome, 1970–84, i, 32–3. (Translation by J. O. H.)

29. See Ibn Khaldūn, *The Muqaddima: an Introduction to History*, trans. Franz Rosenthal, Princeton, 1967, i, map facing p. 110.

30. Favorites for the other two are the Tigris, the Amu-Darya and the Sir-Darya, these last two flowing into the Aral Sea in Central Asia. See André Miquel, *La géographie humaine du monde musulman*, The Hague-Paris, 1967–80, iii, 118.

31. See Thomas J. Bassett and Philip W. Porter, "'From the best authorities':the mountains of Kong in the cartography of West Africa," *J. African Hist.*, 32 (1991), 367–413.

32. Hence the North African jurist Ibn Abī Zayd al-Qayrawānī declared that "Trade to the Land of the Blacks and the land of the enemy [i.e. Europe] is disapproved of"; see *La Risâla ou Épître sur les éléments du dogme et de la loi de l'Islâm selon le rite mâlikite*, texte arabe et traduction française . . . par Léon Bercher, 3rd ed., Alger, 1949, 319. The commentators of this text explain that the reason for this is the threat such travel poses to a Muslim's spiritual integrity. See also M. Brett, "Islam and trade in the Bilād al-Sūdān from tenth-eleventh century A.D.," *J. African History*, 24 (1983), 431–40.

33. I have suggested elsewhere that al-Bakrī may have at one point confused Ghana with Ghiyaru, which was on the "Nile" (R. Senegal), and it is possible that al-Idrīsī was heir to this confusion. See Meillassoux, Triaud and Hunwick, "La Géographie du Soudan d'aprés al-Bakrī: trois lectures," Troisième Lecture, 420.

34. See B. Marie Perinbam, "The Julas in Western Sudanese history: long-distance traders and developers of resources," in B. Swartz & R. E. Dumett (eds.), *West African Culture Dynamics: Archaeological and Historical Perspectives*, The Hague: Mouton & Co., 1980, 455–75.

35. See Susan Keech McIntosh, "A reconsideration of Wangara/Palolus, island of gold," *J. African Hist.*, 22 (1981), 145–58.

36. M. Delafosse, *Haut-Sénégal-Niger*, Paris, 1912, i, 55. See also his *La langue mandingue et ses dialectes*, vol. 2, *Dictionnaire mandingue-français*, Paris, 1955, 260, where he lists: "gbā-gara ou gā-gara (litt. 'trou du terrain'), puits à or, région aurifère."

37. When Ibn Baṭṭūṭa was on the Niger near, I believe, Sansanding in 1352 he obtained information about these two towns and was told that the inhabitants of Zāgha (read: Diakha) were Muslims of long standing. See Hopkins and Levtzion, *Corpus*, 287. In the fifteenth-century Timbuktu there seems to have been a tradition of learned Kābara

scholars migrating there, again indicative of an ancient tradition of Islam. See Hunwick, *Timbuktu and the Songhay Empire*, 47–48.

38. I have made these arguments before in my article "Gao and the Almoravids: ethnicity, political change, and the limits of interpretation," *J. African Hist.*, 35 (1994), 251–73.

39. The key work in the analysis of early medieval Arab geographical writings is André Miquel, *La géographie du monde musulman jusqu'au milieu du 11ᵉ siècle*, 4 vols., Paris-La Haye: Mouton, 1967–88. For a specific discussion of Africa, see vol. 2, 127–202. Regrettably, there is no parallel study for the period after the mid-eleventh century.

40. See his *Manāhil al-ṣafā fī maʿāthir mawālīnā al-shurafā*, ed. ʿAbd al-Karīm Kurayyim, n.p. [Rabat: Maṭbūʿāt wizārat al-awqāf wa'l-shuʿūn al-Islāmiyya wa'l-thaqāfiyya], n.d. Some of the state correspondence included in this text is translated in my *Timbuktu and the Songhay Empire*, 292–308, where sources of other letters on the conquest are also listed.

41. Text and translation by Octave Houdas, Paris, 1888–89; new edition of the Arabic text ed. By ʿAbd al-Laṭīf al-Shādilī, n.p. [Casablanca], 1998.

42. For a selective translation of the passages concerning West Africa, see my *Timbuktu and the Songhay Empire*, 309–17.

43. The standard edition in nine vols. was published in Casablanca, 1954–55, edited by the author's two sons Jaʿfar and Muḥammad. This has been translated into French by various scholars and published in *Archives Marocaines*.

44. See vol. 5, 99–134.

45. Published in Istanbul, 1938.

46. See T. Habraszewski, "Kanuri—language and people—in the 'Travelbook' (*Siyahetname*) of Evliya Çelebi," *Africana Bulletin* [Warsaw], vi (1967), XXX; T. Ciercierska-Chlapowa, "Extraits de fragments du Siyāḥatnāme d'Evliya Celebī concernant l'Afrique noire," *Folia Orientalia*, 6 (1964), 239–43.

47. "Osmanli-Bornu mµnâsebetine ait belgeler," *Tarih Dergisi*, 23 (1969), 111–30. See also B. G. Martin, "Mai Idrīs of Bornu and the Ottoman Turks, 1571–1578," *Int. J. of Middle East Studies*, 3 (1972), XXX; *idem*, "Turkish archival sources for West African history," *African Studies Bulletin*, 10/iii (Dec. 1967), XXX. Martin also draws attention to a Turkish work on Ottoman North Africa, which appears to have something to say about West Africa: A. S. Ilter, *Simali Afrikada Tµrkler*, Istanbul, 1937.

48. *Habash Eyeleti.*

49. See B. G. Martin, "Five letters from the Tripoli archives," *J. Hist. Soc. of Nigeria,*, 2/iii (1962), XXX; H. I. Gwarzo, "Seven letters from the Tripoli archives," *Kano Studies* (o.s.), 1/iv (1968), 50–60.

50. Ulruch Harmann, "The dead ostrich: lofe and trade in Ghadames (Libya) in the nineteenth century," *Die Welt des Islams*, 38 (1998), 9–94.

51. Some is preserved in the Centre de Documentation et de Recherches Historiques Ahmad Baba (CEDRAB); see below. I have published translations of two merchant documents from this archive; see John Hunwick, "Islamic ffinancial institutions: theoretical structures and some of their practical applications in sub-Saharan Africa," in *Currencies, Credit and Culture: African Financial Insitutions in Historical Perspective*, ed. Endre Stiansen and Jane Guyer, Uppsala: Nordiska Afrikainstututet, 2000, 1–32.

52. See Abdeljelil Temimi, *Les Affinités culturelles entre la Tunisie, la Libye, le Centre et l'Ouest de l'Afrique à l'époque moderne/al-Rawābiṭ al-thaqāfiyya al-mutabādila bayn Tūnus*

wa-Lībiyā wa-wasṭ wa-gharb Ifrīqiyā khilāl al-ʿaṣr al-ḥadīth, Tunis, 1981 [Publications de la Revue d'Histoire Maghrébine, Vol. 7]. A new edition of this text with an English translation, together with another text of the same Timbuktu author written in Morocco, has been published by Mohamed El Mansur and Fatima Harrak, under the title *Muṣliḥ Fūlānī fī bilād al-Maghrib/A Fulāni Jihādist in the Maghrib*, Rabat: Institute of African Studies, Mohamed V University [Texts and Documents, 6].

53. *Idem*, "L'affranchissement des esclaves et leur rescensements au milieu du XIXe siècle dans la Régence de Tunis," *Revue d'Histoire Maghrébine*, 39–40 (1985). See also a more recent study based on archival sources, Muḥammad al-Hādī al-Juwaylī, *Mujtamaʿāt li 'l-dhākira—mujtamaʿāt li 'l-nisyān: dirāsat mūnūghrāfiyya li-aqalliyya sawd_ bi 'l-janūb al-Tūnisī*, n.p. [Tunis]: Editions Cérès, 1994.

54. John Hunwick and Fatima Harrak, *Miʿrāj al-Ṣuʿūd: Aḥmad Bābā's Replies on Slavery*, edited and translated with annotations and an introduction, Rabat: Université Mohammed V, 2000 [Publications de l'Institut des Études Africaines. Textes et Documents, 7].

55. A preliminary "census" of all Arabic materials is being made by myself and R. S. O'Fahey in our ongoing multi-volume work *Arabic Literature of Africa*, volumes 1 and 2 of which were published by E. J. Brill, Leiden, 1994, 1995. We have found that, quite literally, "one thing leads to another." As soon as we start to push inquiries, material we had no idea existed comes to light.

56. All volumes contained introductions and annotation, and some had lengthy commentaries. (1) F. H. El Masri, *Bayān wujūb al-hijra* of ʿUthmān b. Fūdī, Oxford University Press-Khartoum University Press, 1978; (2) Not published; (3) R. S. O'Fahey & M. I. Abū Salīm, *Land in Dār Fūr: Charter and related Documents from the Dār Fūr Sultanate*, Cambridge University Press, 1983; (4) J. F. P. Hopkins & N. Levtzion, *Corpus of Early Arabic Sources for West African History*, 1980 (5) J. O. Hunwick, *Sharīʿa in Songhay: the Replies of al-Maghīlī to the Questions of Askia al-ḥājj Muḥammad*, Oxford University Press for the British Academy, 1985; (6) N. Cigar, *Muḥammad al-Qādirī's Mashr al-Mathānī*, Oxford University Press for the British Academy, 1980; (7) M. Abitbol, *Tombouctou au milieu du XVIIIᵉ siècle*, Paris: Maisonneuve et Larose, 1982; (8) Sidi Mohamed Mahibou & Jean-Louis Triaud, *Voilà ce qui est arrivé: Bayân māa waqaʿa d'al-Ḥāǧǧ Umar*, Paris: Edns. du CNRS, 1983; (9) Ivor Wilks, *Chronicles of Gonja: a Tradition of West African Historiography*, Cambridge University Press, 1986; (10) *After the Millenium: Diplomatic Correspondence from Wadai and Dār Fūr on the Eve of Colonial Conquest, 1885–1916*, East Lansing: Michigan State University African Studies Center, 1988.

57. Noureddine Ghali, Sidi Mohamed Mahibou, Louis Brenner, *Inventaire de la Bibliothèque_Umarienne de Ségou conservée à la Bibliothèque Nationale, Paris*, Paris: Edns. du CNRS, 1985.

58. Notably, John Hanson, and David Robinson, *After the Jihad: the Reign of Aḥmad al-Kabīr in the Western Sudan*; A. Christelow, *Thus Spake Emir ʿAbbās*; Jean Boyd & Beverly Mack, *Collected Works of Nana Asnaʾu, Daughter of Usman 'dan Fodiyo (1793–1964)*; M. Tolmacheva, *The Pate Chronicle*.

59. The only Arabic version of the Kilwa chronicle, entitled *al-Sulwa fī akhbār Kilwa*, apparently an abbreviated version with the last three chapters missing, was copied in the nineteenth century, and published in translation by S. A. Strong, "A history of Kilwa," *Journal of the Royal Asiatic Society*, 54 (1895), 385–430; an Arabic text was published in Muscat [Oman], 1985.

60. For details see R. S. O'Fahey, *Arabic Literature of Africa*, Vol. 3B, *The Writings of Muslim East Africa*, Leiden: Brill, forthcoming.

61. Text, trans., and gazetteer in D. Lange, *A Sudanic Chronicle: the Borno Expeditions of Idrīs Alauma*, Stuttgart: Franz Steiner Verlag, 1988. It was earliest translated into English by J. W. Redhouse in *J. Royal Asiatic Society* (ser. 1), 19 (1862), 43–123, who also translated the chronicle of the wars against Kanem in the same issue of that journal, 199–259; see also H. R. Palmer, *The History of the First Twelve Years of the Reign of Mai Idris Alooma of Bornu (1571–1583)*, Lagos: Government Printer, 1926, repr. London: Frank Cass, 1970.

62. This is what is implied in some genealogical information in the margins of books belonging to the descendants of Maḥmūd Kati, which I examined in Timbuktu in 1999. The full picture is as yet unclear.

63. *Tarikh el-Fettach ou Chronique du Chercheur pour servir à l'histoire des villes, des armées et des principaux personnages du Tekrour* par Mahmoûd Kâti ben El-Hâdj El-Motaouakkel Kâti et l'un de ses petits-fils, traduction française . . . par O. Houdas [et] M. Delafosse, Paris: Publications de l'École des Langues Orientales Vivantes, Ve série, Vol. 10, 1913–14, repr., Paris: Adrien-Maisonneuve, 1964.

64. Ismael Diadié Haidara was able in 1999–2000 to assemble the Kaʿti family library from various members of the clan of his descendants in Kirchamba, near Goundam, and bring it to Timbuktu for conservation. Some manuscripts in the collection date back to the fifteenth and sixteenth centuries.

65. *Tarikh Es-Soudân*, ed. and trans. O. Houdas, Paris: Publications de l'École des Langues Orientales Vivantes, IVe série, Vol. 13, 1898–1900, repr., Paris: Adrien-Maisonneuve, 1964; J. O. Hunwick, *Timbuktu and the Songhay Empire: Al-Saʿdī's Taʾrīkh al-Sūdān down to 1613, and other Contemporary Documents*, Leiden: E. J. Brill, 1999.

66. Translated by Paul Marty, *Les chroniques de Oualata et de Nema (Soudan français)*, Paris, P. Geuthner, 1927.

67. See Michel Abitbol, *Tombouctou au milieu du XVIII*ᵉ *siècle d'après la Chronique de Mawlāy al-Qāsim b. Mawlāy Sulaymān*, Paris, 1982: Maisonneuve et Larose.

68. M. A. Cherbonneau, "Essai sur la littérature arabe au Soudan d'après le Tekmilet ed-Dibadje d'Ahmed Baba le Tombouctien," *Annales de la société. archéolologique de Constantine*, ii, 1–42. Also published separately, Constantine-Paris, 1856.

69. *Tedzkiret en-Nisian fi akhbar molouk es-Soudan*, ed. and trans. O. Houdas, Paris: Publications de l'École des Langues Orientales Vivantes, IVe série, Vol. 20, 1899–1901, repr. Paris: Adrien-Maisonneuve, 1966.

70. MSS: CEDRAB, 492, 991 (inc.). An edited ms with a biography of the author has been prepared by Maḥmūd Muḥammad Dedeb (known as Hamu), a present-day scholar of Timbuktu and a pupil of Aḥmad b. Abī 'l-Aʿrāf's son. It awaits publication.

71. MS: CEDRAB, 2752.

72. Ed. Muḥammad Ibrāhīm al-Kattānī & Muḥammad Ḥajjī. Beirut: Dār al-Gharb al-Islāmī, 1401/1981. Trans Chouki Hamal; see review by Jean-Louis Triaud in *Islam et Sociétés au sud du Sahara*, 7 (1993), 233–4.

73. MS: CEDRAB, 669.

74. Note also Ismaël Hamet (trans.), *Chroniques de la Mauritanie sénégalaise*, Paris, 1911, a collection of short chronicles including one that deals with the *jihād* of the eleventh/seventeenth century Nāṣir al-Dīn al-Yadālī.

75. MS: CEDRAB, 769.

76. MS: Niamey (Institut de Recherches en Sciences Humaines), 1475.

77. MS: Niamey, 106.

78. See further John O. Hunwick, "A supplement to *Infāq al-maysūr*: the biographical notes of ʿAbd al-Qādir b. al-Muṣṭafā," *Sudanic Africa*, 7 (1996), 35–52.

79. The two older and incompetent editions are the one edited by C. E. J. Whitting, London, 1951, and one privately published in Cairo, 1964; the recently published edition is edited by Bahīja al-Shādhilī, Rabat, 1996.

80. A "paraphrase and in some parts a translation" was made by E. J. Arnett, under the title *The Rise of the Sokoto Fulani*, Kano, 1922; it is quite unreliable. An abridged Hausa translation by Sidi Sayuṭi Muhammad and Jean Boyd was published by the Sokoto State History Bureau, 1974.

81. Ed. and trans. M. Hiskett, Ibadan, 1963.

82. In fact, the work has no formal title. The author never produced a finial version, and the text we now have is merely a draft.

83. Published in *J. African Soc.*, 15 (1915/16), 261–73.

84. See D. M. Last, *The Sokoto Caliphate*, London, 1967; *idem*, "Arabic source material and historiography in Sokoto," *Research Bull.* [Centre of Arabic Documentation, University of Ibadan], i/2 (1965), 3–19, i/3 (1965), 1–7); see also *ALA* II, 185 ff.

85. Arabic text publ. Sokoto, n.d.; Hausa trans, *Tarihin Fulani*, Zaria, 1957.

86. Only part 2 has been published, ed. and trans. O. Houdas, *Histoire du Sokoto*, at end of his trans. of *Tadhkirat al-nisyān*.

87. See *ALA* II, 230–1.

88. English trans. *The Jihad in Kano*, by Ibrahim Ado Kurawa, Kano: Kurawa Holdings, 1989, with a preface asserting the need for continued *jihād*.

89. The *Taʾlīf*'s contents are paraphrased in B. G. Martin, "A new Arabic history of Ilorin," *Research Bull.* [Centre of Arabic Documentation], 1, ii (1965), 20–27.

90. See J. O. Hunwick, "A historical whodunit: the so-called "Kano Chronicle" and its place in the historiography of Kano," in *History in Africa*, 21 (1994), 127–46. The "Kano Chronicle" has never been published in Arabic; an unannotated translation was published by H. R. Palmer, *Sudanese Memoirs*, Lagos, 1938, iii, 92–132) and a Hausa translation was made under the direction of Rupert East, *Labarun Hausa da Makwabtansu*, Zaria 1933, ii, 3–58, with additional material covering the period down to 1926.

91. See Ivor Wilks, Nehemia Levtzion and Bruce Haight, *Chronicles from Gonja: a Tradition of West African Historiography*, Cambridge University Press, 1986. He also published brief chronicles of Wa in both Arabic and Hausa in his *Wa and the Wala: Islam and Polity in Northwestern Ghana*, Cambridge University Press, 1989.

92. See Lamin O. Sanneh, *The Jahamke: the History of an Islamic Clerical People of the Senegambia*, London: International African Institute, 1979; Michael Gomez, *Pragmatism in the Age of Jihad: the Precolonial State of Bundu*, Cambridge University Press, 1992; Thomas Hunter, "The Development of an Islamic Tradition of Learning among the Jahanke of West Africa," Ph.D. diss., University of Chicago, 1977.

93. Published by E. J. Brill, Leiden, in 2003.

94. See B. G. Martin, "Two poems by al-ḥājj ʿUmar of Keti-Krachi," in J. A. Braimah & J. R. Goody, *Salaga: the Struggle for Power*, London: Longmans, 189–209; S. Pilaszewicz, "The arrival of the Christians: a Hausa poem on the colonial conquest of West Africa by al-ḥāji ʿUmaru," *Africana Bulletin* [Warsaw], xxii, 55–129.

95. Adam Mischlich, "über Sitten und Gebrauche in Hausa," *MSOS*, x (1907), 155–81, xi (1908), 1–81, xii (1909), 215–74, and in his *¯ber die Kulturen im Mittel-Sudan*, Berlin: Reimer, 1942.

96. H. Sölken, "Die Geschichte von Kabi nach Imam Umaru," *Mitteilungen des Instituts für Orientforschung*, vii (1959–60), 123–62.

97. S. Pilaszewicz, *The Zabarma Conquest of North-West Ghana and Upper Volta. A Hausa Narrative "Histories of Samory and Babatu and others" by Mallam Abu*. Warsaw: Polish Academic Publishers.

98. For Fulfulde chronicles, see Alfâ Ibrâhîm Sow, *La femme, la vache, la foi: écrivains et poètes du Fouta Djalon*, Paris: Juillard, 1966; idem, *Chroniques et récits du Fouta Djalon*, Paris, 1968.

99. MS: IFAN, Fonds Musa Kamara, 5–6 (photocopy in Niamey, Institut de Recherches en Sciences Humaines, 1139, in 350 pp.).

100. "Histoire du Boundou," trans. M. Ndiaye, *BIFAN*, 37 (1975) 784–816; "Histoire de Ségou," trans. M. Ndiaye, *BIFAN*, 40 (1978), 458–88; "L'histoire de l'Almaami Abdul (1727/8–1806) par Shaykh Muusa Kamara," traduit par S. Bousbina et édité par J. Schmitz, *Islam et Sociétés au Sud du Sahara*, 7 (1993), 59–95. The entire work is now in the process of being translated into French, and one volume has already been published by a team of scholars under the direction of Jean Schmitz: *Florilège au jardin de l'histoire des Noirs. Zuhûr al-basâtîn*. Tome I, vol. 1, sous la direction et avec une introduction de Jean Schmitz, traduction de Saïd Bousbine, Paris: CNRS Éditions, 1998.

101. Trans. A. Samb, *BIFAN*, 32 (1970), 56–135, 770–818.

102. See Constance Hilliard, "Zuhur al-basatin and Taᵓrikh al-Turubbe: some legal and ethical aspects of slavery in the Sudan as seen in the works of Shaykh Musa Kamara." In J. R. Willis, *Slaves and Slavery in Muslim Africa*, London: Frank Cass, 1985, ii, 160–81.

103. *Tanqiyat al-afhām min shubuhāt al-awhām*, MS: IFAN, Fonds Musa Kamara, 7.

104. E.g. the anonymous account in Hanson and Robinson, *After the Jihad*, 27–37. These shorter accounts are listed in *ALA* IV, chapter 13.

105. *Voilà ce qui est arrivé: Bayân mâ waqaʿa d'al-Ḥâgg ʿUmar al-Fûtî. Plaidoyer pour une guerre sainte en Afrique de l'ouest au XIXe siècle*, trans. M. Mahibou & Jean-Louis Triaud, Paris: Éditions du C.N.R.S., 1983.

106. See Mauriace, Puech, "Les Rimāḥ. Les Lances du parti du Misericordieux à l'attaque du parti du diable. Un traité de sciences religieuses musulmanes écrit en arabe par le Chaikh El Hadj ʿOmar, en 1845," *Diplôme d'études supérieures*, Université de Dakar, 1967; Saïd Bousbina, "Analyse et commentaire du livre *Rimāḥ ḥizb al-Raḥi m ʿalā nuḥūr ḥizb al-rajīm* d'al-ḥājj ʿUmar al-Fūtī," *Diplôme d'études approfondies*, Universités ParisI/Paris VII, 1988; J. O. Hunwick [with the assistance of Robert Kramer, Richard McGrail and Daniel Shaw] "An introduction to the Tijānī path: being an annotated translation of the chapter headings of the *Kitāb al-rimāḥ* of al-ḥājj ʿUmar," *Islam et Sociétés au Sud du Sahara*, 6 (1992), 17–32; Bernd Radtke, "Studies on the sources of the *Kitāb Rimāḥ ḥizb al-Raḥim* of al-ḥājj ʿUmar," *Sudanic Africa*, 6 (1995), 73–114.

107. Text and Italian trans. by E. Cerulli in his *Somalia: scritti vari editi ed inediti*, n.p. [Rome], 1957, i. 231–357.

108. These and other minor items on Ethiopian history are listed in the forthcoming vol. 3A of *ALA*, edited by R. S. O'Fahey.

109. See *Histoire de la conquête de l'Abyssinie*, ed. and trans. R. Basset, 2 vols., Paris 1897–1901.

110. *The Sudan of the Three Niles: the Funj Chronicle 910–1288/1504–1871*, Leiden: E. J. Brill, 1999. See also *ALA* I, 42–5. O'Fahey also lists a number of family histories and works of genealogy. Partial Arabic texts of the Funj Chronicle were published by Makkī Shibayka, *Taʾrīkh mulūk al-sūdān*, Khartoum, 1947; Shāṭir Buṣaylī, *Makhṭūṭat Kātib al-shūna*, n.p. [Cairo], n.d. [1963].

111. *Kitāb al-ṭabaqāt fī khuṣūṣ al-awliyāʾ waʾl-ṣāliḥīn waʾl-ʿulamāʾ waʾl-shuʿarāʾ*. The work is analyzed in Neil McHugh, *Holymen of the Blue Nile: the Making of an Arab-Islamic Community in the Nilotic Sudan, 1500–1850*, Evanston: Northwestern University Press, 1994, 203–12. A partial English trans. was published by Harold Macmichael, *A History of the Arabs of the Sudan*, Cambridge University Press, 1922, ii, 217–323. Several texts have been published, the most scholarly being that edited by Yūsuf Faḍl Ḥasan, Kartoum University Press, 3rd ed., 1985.

112. *The Life of the Sudanese Mahdi: a Historical Study of Kitāb Saʿādat al-mustahdī fī sīrat al-imām al-Mahdī*, New York: Transaction Books, 1978.

113. *al-Ṭirāz al-manqūsh bi-bushrā qatl Yuḥannā malik al-Ḥubūsh*, ed. M.I. Abū Salīm and S. Qaddāl, Khartoum, 1972.

114. Published as *al-Sūdān bayn yadāt Ghurdūn wa-Kitshinar*, Cairo, 1319/1901–2.

115. Published as *Taʾrīkh al-Sūdān al-qadīm waʾl-ḥadīth wa-jughrāfiyyatuhu*, Cairo, 1903. Although strictly a secondary work, its unique insights and its proximity to the events it chronicles qualify it as a primary source.

116. See Heather Sharkey, "Aḥmad Zaynī Dahlān's *al-Futūḥāt al-Islāmiyya*: a contemporary view of the Sudanese Mahdī," *Sudanic Africa*, 5 (1994), 67–75. See also Muḥammad Ibrāhīm Abū Salīm & Knut Vikør, "The man who believed in the Mahdī," *Sudanic Africa*, 2 (1991), 29–52.

117. *Acta Aethiopica*, vol. 1, Evanston: Northwestern University Press, 1987; Vol. 2, Addis Ababa: Addis Ababa University Press and Lund: Lund University Press, 1994.

118. *al-Āthār al-kāmila liʾl-Mahdī*, Khartoum: Khartoum University Press, 1990–1995. These volumes include, correspondence, proclamations, sermons, and accounts of his "assemblies" (*majālis*).

119. J. Deny, *Sommaire des archives turques du Cairo*, Cairo, 1930.

120. See Richard Hill, *Egypt and the Sudan, 1820–1881*, Oxford University Press, 1959, 172–3.

121. *al-Fūnj waʾl-arḍ: wathāʾiq tamlīk*, Khartoum, 1967.

122. Jay Spaulding and Muḥammad Ibrāhīm Abū Salīm, *Public Documents from Sinnār*, East Lansing: Michigan State University Press, 1989. R. S. O'Fahey and Muḥammad Ibrāhīm Abū Salīm, *Land in Dār Fūr: Charters and Related Documents from the Dār Fūr Sultanate*, Cambridge University Press, 1985.

123. For a survey of the institution in its pan-Sudanic perspective, see R. S. O'Fahey, "Endowment, privilege and estate in the central and eastern Sudan," *Islamic Law and Society*, 4/iii (1997), 33–51.

124. See H. R. Palmer, *Sudanese Memoirs*, Lagos, 1928; *idem*, *The Bornu Sahara and Sudan*, London, 1936; Hamidu Bobboyi, "Relations of the Bornu *ʿulamāʾ* with the Sayfawa rulers: the role of the *maḥrams*," *Sudanic Africa*, 4 (1993), 175–204.

125. See *After the Millennium: Diplomatic correspondence from Wadai and Dâr Fûr on the Eve of Colonial Conquest, 1885–1916*, n.p. [East Lansing]: African Studies Center, Michigan State University, 1988; *An Islamic Alliance: ʿAlī Dīnār and the Sanūsiyya, 1906–1916*, Evanston: Northwestern University Press, 1994. A number of Arabic

documents relating to Sanūsī activity in Niger were published in facsimile, with French translation in Jean-Louis Triaud, *La légende noire de la Sanûsiyya: une confrérie musulmane saharienne sous le regard français (1840–1930)*, Paris: Éditions de la Maisons des Sciences de l'Homme, 1995, ii, 970–1057.

126. It is listed in the various "interim reports" of the Northern History Research Scheme, published in 1967, 1975, 1977, and 1981.

127. For a list of these, see the appendix to John Hunwick, "Falkeiana II: A letter from the amīr of Mafara to the amīr of Zamfara," *Sudanic Africa*, 3 (1992), 95–108.

128. Allen Christelow, *This Spake Emir Abbas: Selected Cases from the Records of the Emir of Kano's Judicial Council*, East Lansing: Michigan State University Press, 1994. The value of the volume is somewhat diminished by the poor reproduction of the facsimiles, some of which are unreadable.

129. Isaac A. Ogunbiyi and Stefan Reichmuth, "Arabic papers from the *Olubadan* chancery I: a rebellion of the Ibadan chieftans, or At the Origins of Yoruba Islamic prose," *Sudanic Africa*, 8 (1997), 109–36; *idem*, "Arabic papers from the *Olubadan* chancery II: Toying with the Caliphate," *Sudanic Africa*, 9 (1998), 135–62.

130. See the routes described in Arabic in the appendix to Joseph Dupuis, *Journal of a Residence in Ashantee*, London, 1824; and the nineteenth-century letters published in N. Levtzion, "Early nineteenth century Arabic manuscripts from Kumase," *Transactions Hist. Soc. of Ghana*, 7 (1965), 99–119.

131. The writings of the Mahdī Muḥammad Aḥmad have been published by Muḥammad Ibrāhīm Abū Salīm, *al-Āthār al-kāmila li'l-imām al-Mahdī*, 7 vols., Khartoum: Dār Jāmiʿat al-Kharṭūm. 1990 An edition of the writings of the Khalīfa ʿAbdullāhi is in progress.

132. See *Fihris makhṭūṭāt Markaz Aḥmad Bābā li'l-tawthīq wa'l-buḥūth al-taʾrīkhiyya*, 5 vols., London: al-Furqān Islamic Heritage Foundation, 1995–98, containing only 9,000 items.

133. I have published an annotated English translation of this work, based on the published text of Houdas compared with all other known manuscripts; see n. 65 above.

134. See the note on this work by W. A. Brown, "A new bibliographical aid: the IZA-LAT AL-RAIB of Aḥmad Abū 'l-Aʿrāf al-Tinbuktī," *Research Bull.* (Centre of Arabic Docn.), 3, ii, July 1967, 135–36.

135. Ed. Muḥammad Ibrāhīm al-Kattānī & Muḥammad Ḥajjī, Beirut: Dār al-gharb al-Islāmī, 1401/1981.

136. There is another MS in the Bibliothèque Nationale, Paris, mss. arabes, 5259, ff. 88r.–152v.

137. For a brief account of him from the French colonial perspective, see Lt. Cortier, *D'une rive à l'autre du Sahara*, Paris 1908, 286–9.

138. On this work see the note by W. A. Brown, "A monument of legal scholarship: the NAWAZIL ʿULAMAʾ AL-TAKRŪR of al-Muṣtafā b. Aḥmad al-Ghallāwī," *Research Bull.* (Centre of Arabic Docn.), 3, ii, July 1967, 137–8.

139. An exception to this is the catalogue of part of the National Archives, Kaduna, 2 vols., prepared by Baba Yunus Muhammad, edited and annotated by John Hunwick, London: Al-Furqan Islamic Heritage Foundation, 1995–97.

9

EUROPEAN DOCUMENTS AND AFRICAN HISTORY

John Thornton

In the heady 1960s, oral tradition was billed as the means by which African history would be recovered. Scholars of those days believed that the fact many African societies did not keep any form of written records was not an insuperable problem. Historians would simply have to tap oral sources to find African history. The years since then have dimmed this vision. Oral tradition has not proven to be a substitute for the on-the-spot, eyewitness documentation that can come from written sources. Moreover, the study of oral tradition raises difficult problems of interpretation and ambiguity. Even in the 1960s, historians who wrote the histories of coastal African societies, such as Asante, Benin, Dahomey, the states of the Senegal valley, Angola, and Sierra Leone made extensive use of written documents of European origin. They made scant use of oral tradition although, like others, they championed its collection and use.

The value of written documents is revealed even more clearly when regions located far from the coast, and outside the range of European literate observers, are considered. Thus, for example, the states of the Benue valley, the Adamawa region, the Azande and Mangbetu region, the Luba, Lunda, Lozi, and other great interior central African states are poorly known, even in the early nineteenth century, despite their obvious sophistication and culture.

Thus, no historian can begin writing the history of most of coastal Africa south of the Sahara without recourse to these European sources. They do, of course, present some problems, most of which are well known. A major conference, held in Bad Homburg, West Germany, in 1986, examined and produced an overview of the critical problems of using such sources.[1] First, they are the work of outsiders with often limited interest in the societies they describe. Many of the authors lived on the coast for only a few years, did not speak local languages, and were often interested only in commercial affairs. Many also had strong prejudices about Africans, which made them biased observers.

For example, Capuchin missionaries made numerous and sometimes detailed assessments of local religious life during their evangelical work in Kongo. Much of this work takes the form of denunciations of local customs, thus revealing a strong Christian bias. This bias is reflected, for example, in their tendency to identify all supernatural beings worshipped in Kongo as manifestations of the Devil. Their accounts are never quite clear as to whether the Kongolese truly were worshipping a figure they regarded as wicked and evil in the same way Christians regard the Devil, or even whether Kongolese cosmology included a figure who served as an opponent for God, or whether the missionaries were simply assigning all supernatural beliefs to the Devil.[2] Most historians address this difficulty by studying modern anthropological accounts or the testimony of modern Kongolese and hoping that they can see the local cosmology more fully. Nonetheless, the missionaries were contemporary eyewitnesses and thus can never be discounted as a source of information, whatever problems their bias creates.

Another issue relates to the informants of European writers. Clearly, some Europeans who wrote long and detailed accounts of Africa did not themselves directly observe everything they wrote about. Although some probably drew knowledge from better-informed long-term European residents, it is obvious that many were informed by Africans. These African informants are rarely named. Ludevig Rømer, a Danish factor resident on the Gold Coast in the first half of the eighteenth century, was unusual in naming his informants and attributing to them most statements for which he himself was not an observer. The same sort of people, including nobles in local states, merchants, and the slaves of the commercial company, probably served the less scrupulous European writers as well, but without specific identification the source of the information cannot be known. Historians must proceed cautiously, not knowing what interests these informants might have served.

In addition, geographical scope was limited, for large areas fell outside the European visitors' observations and even outside their indirect knowledge from local informants. Adam Jones produced a set of revealing maps at the Bad Homburg conference in which he outlined the areas illuminated by European observers and showed that 80 percent of sub-Saharan Africa was not covered.[3] Even allowing that Jones's definition of observation was a strict one—only those writers who could actually witness events were counted and only the areas they could actually see were included—it is still obvious that much of African was left out.

These problems aside, the value of these sources cannot be exaggerated. Their special problems, scope, and study are critical to beginning the study of precolonial African history.

Scope of European Sources

Europeans visited Africa primarily because of commercial interests, and therefore their sources cluster in the areas of greatest commercial activity. Some regions, such as the Gabon coast and parts of the Ivory Coast, were not commercially attractive and thus were described. Also, visiting an area was generally not enough. Hundreds of ships visited the Niger Delta in the eighteenth century, for example, but they left a scant and generally uninformative record behind them. Most of what is known of the region comes from a handful of observers, and some sailing records. The reason for this is that Europeans did not normally live there, but only visited to receive slaves. Their contact with Africans was limited to a few rulers and brokers, who often did not allow them to go far from a single port or place of entry.

In contrast, the Gold Coast is well documented. The Dutch "Elmina Diary," a daily record of events around the Dutch factory-fort at Elmina, as well as occasional letters from factories in other parts of the coast, provide a substantial record. The total record of this collection of material probably covers close to sixty thousand pages of testimony.[4] Whereas much of it deals with commercial matters, and the life of the small Dutch community, it also has detailed records of events in the surrounding African communities. Because the Dutch maintained a fort there, they had an interest not only in their commercial transactions, but also in all the political developments of the societies of the interior that might affect or impinge on their business. Therefore, detailed Dutch records provide information about not only what was going on in the interior, but also their own efforts at diplomacy. Records of the Danish West India Company support the Dutch records. Although the Danish were not major players in the international slave trade, compared to other powers, their maintenance of a post required a similar documentary body.[5] Also, extensive English records (unfortunately not as well preserved as the Dutch) stem from the same concerns.[6]

Commercial records of this sort, primarily interested in trade but by necessity also reporting political developments, are found in several areas. From 1450 to about 1650, the Portuguese were the only European power to have extensive commercial dealings with Africa. Portuguese records of activities in Africa were certainly once very plentiful, and probably could have provided the basis for detailed reconstruction of events in many areas. Unfortunately, most of these records were destroyed in the great earthquake of 1755, although the surviving ones, mostly in the 1500–1540 period, show something of the wealth that was once available, especially for the Gold Coast.[7]

The other European powers began to contest Portuguese dominance of trade in the mid-seventeenth century, and as they became successful, their posts generated commercial records of great interest and value. There were commercial centers on the Senegal coast from the mid-seventeenth century, although detailed records only survive from the late seventeenth century onward, especially in the French archives. These records also include a valuable series dealing with the length of the Senegal River during the roughly half a century when France maintained a string of posts along the river.[8] England also had posts in the region, especially in the Gambia area and Sierra Leone, although unfortunately the generally poor survival of full early records from the English company has made their sources much more limited.

The Gold Coast records, the richest of the commercial ones, form another block, joined by those of the various factories maintained by European concerns on the "Slave Coast" (the region centered on Dahomey).[9] Portuguese records from the island of São Tomé, as well as from commercial concerns and Portuguese possessions in Brazil, provide information on the area, although they are scattered and incomplete. Portugal's records are also important for Angola, where they are supplemented by an extensive collection of local records from the largest European colony in Africa. Here there are administrative records for a large domain as well as commercial records.[10]

A similar situation prevails in southern and eastern Africa. Dutch commercial records for their colony in South Africa (founded 1652) are fairly abundant, and augmented by administrative records as well.[11] Portuguese records of their colony in Mozambique (and other posts along the east African coast) are also both commercial and administrative.[12]

Commercial records have shortcomings despite their volume (far greater than any other type of European records), primarily because of their limited interests. They have virtually nothing to say about cultural matters or religion, and often the political references are terse or lack larger context. Thus, the longer narrative records left by travelers are often the most important source for these aspects of African life. People left travel records for a variety of reasons. For some they were official reports, describing the situation in an area in depth. The earliest accounts of West Africa, especially those of early Portuguese compilers and visitors, such as the sources of Valentim Fernandes' work, Alvise da Mosto (or, Cadamosto), and Duarte Pacheco Pereira, were typically commercial in orientation, like their authors.[13] Two of the earliest and best accounts of the Senegambian and Sierra Leone region in the late sixteenth century were by André Donelha and André Alvares de Almada, Cape Verde-based traders who clearly learned about a great deal more than trade in their numerous visits to the coast.[14] Willem Bosman's description of Guinea published in 1704, for another example, was presented in the form of letters from a factor on the coast to his superiors, but in response to a questionnaire that demanded more than simply commercial reports.[15] On the other hand, Ludevig Rømer, who worked as a factor for the Danish West India Company at the post at Fredriksburg (located in such a way that he has information on both the Gold and Slave Coasts), seems to have written his memoirs of the coast to satisfy a general readership in Denmark.[16] The soldier chronicler António de Oliveira Cadornega wrote his lengthy history of the Angolan wars to publicize them in Portugal,[17] while justification of and attacks on the slave trade underlie the long histories of Dahomey written by several English authors. Here, the critical historian must proceed with great care through the quantity of information such writers produced.[18] Commercial interests underlie the earliest Portuguese accounts of east and southeast Africa, and probably also informed the great historian João de Barros' account of southeast Africa.[19]

Whereas trader-authors did produce valuable work, perhaps missionaries wrote the most informative.[20] Their interests diverged substantially from the traders, and naturally their desire to convert Africans made them interested in African culture. They were hostile to African religions, of course, and often to other customs as well, but their hostility did not prevent them from making detailed descriptions of these traditions. Missionaries were also likely to be knowledgeable of local languages, and some left important linguistic work. Wilhelm Johann Müller, a Lutheran missionary on the Gold Coast in the mid-seventeenth century, left detailed accounts of the religion of the Akan people as well as a lengthy and carefully constructed word list. Likewise, Portuguese Jesuits such as Baltasar Barreira and Manuel Álvares[21] left detailed accounts of life, culture, and religion in Sierra Leone in the opening years of the seventeenth century.

The greatest of the missionary documents probably come from west central Africa, Jesuit and Capuchin accounts of work in Kongo and Angola. Without the missionaries, with only the commercial records, historians would know little about Kongo, but the missionary work makes it instead the best-documented Atlantic African country.[22] Although missionary documents are less helpful for Angola after the initial Jesuit accounts of the late sixteenth and early seventeenth century, Giovanni Antonio Cavazzi da Montecuccolo's massive mid-seventeenth-century history of the region is one of the best accounts of Mbundu religion and society.[23]

Missionary records are also crucial for understanding the history of the east African coast, especially the southeast zone. João dos Santos' compendium of the early seventeenth century is one of the best of these. Although Ethiopia is one of the relatively few African countries to have a fully literate elite and to have left extensive historical chronicles of its own, the missionary sources, especially Jesuit ones, complement the local histories in interesting and important ways. European commercial sources are of little help for that region,[24] and the Ethiopian chronicles focus almost exclusively on the politics of the court and country, or military activities, taking much of the daily life of the country for granted. However, the Jesuit material, especially Francisco Alvares's account of the early sixteenth century, includes many details of daily life that considerably expand our knowledge of Ethiopian social history.[25]

European contact with Africa also produced a small but significant body of documentary material written by Africans in European languages. Probably the most famous of these is the series of letters written by Afonso I (1509–1542) of Kongo to various addressees, and Afonso was followed by other Kongo kings who also wrote letters, some equally interesting and lengthy. There are other documents from Kongo as well, including judicial inquests that can be good sources for law and politics. Angola's Queen Njinga, another famous and interesting central African, wrote a sizable collection of documents. In recent years, historians have uncovered local archives of documents written by or for a variety of local African rulers in Angola, and these archives also promise to yield interesting fruit.[26] While most of these documents are in collections in Europe, quite a few are in Angola, whose National Archives contain some seventeenth-century and many eighteenth-century documents. Other documents have been located in several provincial archives, some dating as far back as the late eighteenth and nineteenth centuries. In the 1980s, Eva Sebastiyén, a Hungarian researcher, located eighteenth-century documents in private collections and clan treasuries of the Dembos region of northern Angola. There is every indication that these are only a few of what may be a much richer store of documents, but the intense fighting of the civil war has made research anywhere outside of Luanda very difficult. A number of Angolan scholars are planning to systematically seek out these rural documents when peace returns to Angola.

Outside of Angola, correspondence by African rulers is scarce, and much of it is potentially unreliable. For example, a letter written to England's George I in 1726 is often regarded as a fabrication, as is a similar letter written by the Oba of Benin to Capuchin priests. On the other hand, a spectacular trove of correspondence from Dahomey kings in the early nineteenth century, recently discovered in Rio de Janeiro, seems to be directed by the king, though not written by him. Most of these rulers, unlike the central Africans, were not personally literate, but their secretaries wrote on their behalf. Certainly such correspondence needs to be examined with care, but it is likely to reveal elements of African history that may be lost in documentation written by European visitors or travelers.

Problems of European Sources

A major problem in the use of European sources is their vast scatter. It is ironic that hardly any of the sources in European languages are located in the country they concern. Even the records of the European African colonies of Angola, Mozambique, São Tomé, Guinea, or Cape Verde have survived poorly and probably never possessed the richness of the metropolitan records. In other areas, with no European colony until the nineteenth or early twentieth century, records about the area might be housed in a European country other than the colonial one, and even in a different language. For example, Ghana, a former British colony, has no Danish records even though a Danish fort was on Ghanaian territory, and observers in Danish service provided a number of important accounts of the country's past. Because Ghana was not a Danish colony, there has also been little interest in Denmark in preserving or studying Danish records relating to Ghana. In another example, many documents about the Kingdom of Kongo, finally colonized by Belgium and Portugal, are found in Italy and Spain, and others are in the Netherlands. Also, whereas many documents relevant to early periods are found in Portugal, almost none are found in Belgium.[27]

This means that historians have had to travel widely to consult the documents relevant for the study of their areas of specialty. Only in relatively recent times have guides been published to aid in this research.[28] Microfilming of archival collections has helped as well. Northwestern University and the University of Wisconsin, for example, have compiled substantial collections of microfilm. Of these, Northwestern's collection of materials from Dutch, Danish, and English archives pertaining to the Gold Coast is the most impressive, with hundreds of reels.[29]

The linguistic spread of material for African history is another problem, related to that of its geographical spread. Much is written in languages, such as Dutch, Swedish, or Danish, that are rarely offered at universities, and even Italian and Portuguese do not appear in the curricula of any but the largest research institutions. Scholars need to know these languages to do thorough research. The Gold Coast, possibly the worst example, has in addition to English- and German-language documents substantial and important documents in Dutch, Danish, and Swedish (not to mention material written in Arabic, or after 1850 two Ghanaian languages, Twi and Gā). To make matters worse, these countries have not had a colonial presence in West Africa, therefore native speakers of these languages rarely have an interest in the subject, nor are the languages spoken in modern Ghana. The result is that virtually all scholars who work on Gold Coast subjects are not native speakers of most of the languages they work with. Many scholars never learn all the languages relevant to their particular areas; even those who do tend to avoid comparative work from primary sources precisely because of the linguistic burden such work poses.

In some measure the geographic scatter of sources, and the fact that so many important collections are in countries that no longer have historic ties with the African regions described in the sources, may explain the lack of many basic research aids. For example, the records of the various trading companies in Africa have not been thoroughly surveyed or calendared. They are not easy sources to consult. Africanists who study the English commercial records are generally confronted with files organized chronologically: items of little relevance are mixed with important material. In the absence of a calendar or guide, the researcher has no choice but to leaf through the entire volume, gleaning perhaps a few pages of notes for a thousand pages of reading. Dutch-language material about the Gold Coast is at least one hundred thousand manuscript pages, much of it in difficult handwriting, so it is to be expected that this collection has not been thoroughly searched. Information of considerable significance is likely to still be awaiting discovery in this collection.

For many years, however, some scholars have labored to produce modern editions and versions of the most important of the vast quantities of European language materials.[30] Portuguese scholars have led the way, and their work has generally started with the older materials, both because the Portuguese are more important in the earlier periods and because it is natural to publish a collection starting with the earliest date. Probably the most extensive collection of this sort has been António Brásio's spectacular *Monumenta Missionaria Africana*. Composed of twenty thick volumes of documentation on western Africa, Brásio's collection covers the period up to 1700 for Angola and 1650 for Guinea. Recently, a new series of Portuguese documents has begun publication under the Centro de Cartografia Antiga in Lisbon, and it promises to exceed even Brásio's effort if it reaches completion. Another important effort, primarily by French and Senegalese scholars, has published dozens of French translations and original documents in French in the *Bulletin* of the Institute Foundamentale de l'Afrique Noire. Paul Hair has also produced many translation of documents into English, first in the African Research Bulletin of Fourah Bay College in Sierra Leone, and then in small editions that circulate on request. In England and the United States, the Fontes Historiae Africanae has committed itself to publication of a wide variety of African historical materials, sometimes in original languages and often in English translation.

Early Portuguese documents on southern Africa were initially published by the great South African historian George M. Theal beginning in the last years of the nineteenth century, and his efforts were extended by a joint Portuguese-Rhodesian/Zimbabwean team in the 1960s, producing excellent texts of materials written for the most part before the seventeenth century. Similarly C. Beccari produced an important monumental collection of European writers about Ethiopia early in the century, which has been followed by a number of other editions and translations.

Publication efforts of the eighteenth-century material have been much less complete, and many of even the best texts remain unedited. Albert van Dantzig produced English translations of a selection of late seventeenth- and early eighteenth-century material from Dutch archives on the Gold and Slave Coasts, and Robin Law has regularly produced materials from English and occasionally French sources on the same area.

But so far no scholar has taken on the daunting task of producing the Danish archival materials, or the Dutch material of the later eighteenth century. Likewise, most of the French archival pieces on the Guinea region remain unpublished, although some of the best items on Senegal have been published in full by the Franco-Senegalese scholars associated with the *Bulletin* of the Institute Foundamentale de l'Afrique Noire.

Notes

1. Beatrix Heintze and Adam Jones (eds.), *European Sources for Sub-Saharan Africa before 1900: Use and Abuse* (special edition of *Paideuma* 33 (1987)).

2. Anne Hilton, "European Sources for the Study of Religious Change in Sixteenth and Seventeenth Century Kongo," *Paideuma* 33 (1987): 289–312.

3. Adam Jones, "The Dark Continent: A Preliminary Study of the Geographical Coverage in European Sources, 1400–1880," *Paideuma* 33 (1987): 19–26.

4. This collection is housed today in the Nederlands Bezittungen ter Kust Guinea section of the Algemeen Rijksarchief in The Hague. There are only a few years of entries before 1716, but from that point on, they go forward, roughly one volume per year for the rest of the century. Some of volumes are as many as eight hundred pages long.

5. Mostly found in Rigsarkivet, Vest-India Kompagnie, especially Breve og dokumenter og Uklgaede, Guineiske Journaler.

6. English sources are found in the Public Record Office, Treasury Series (T/70). Unfortunately, most of the letters are only summaries and not full text. Often the summaries amount to only a line or two when the original letter probably had several pages. As a sample of what the originals might have been like, there are the letters preserved in the Rawlinson collection in Oxford, now being published by Robin Law, *The English on the Guinea Coast* (Oxford, 1998), the first of three projected volumes.

7. The Portuguese records for this period were reorganized after the earthquake in the Corpo Cronológico section of the Arquivo Nacional de Torre do Tombo, Lisbon.

8. French records on the Senegal region are found in Archives Nationales de France, Colonies 6.

9. The Dutch records, quite full here as elsewhere, fail after about 1740, and the French records are the most important. English records are mostly summaries here as elsewhere.

10. The main depository for Portugal's records of Africa after the early seventeenth century is Arquivo Histórico Ultramarino, Lisbon. In Angola the Arquivo Histórico Nacional de Angola contains the local records, but they only effectively extend from the 1740s onwards. Earlier records were destroyed in 1641, and survival has been a problem.

11. Material on South Africa is largely found in the Algemeen Rijksarchief for the earlier periods, and then in local archives later.

12. In addition to materials on eastern Africa found in the Arquivo Histórico Ultramarino, many documents relevant to east Africa and the interior areas of southeast Africa that Portugal took an interest in are found in the Historical Archives of Gao (India), the headquarters of Portugal's Indian Ocean empire.

13. Fernandes's manuscript, compiled from other sources, was published by António Baião, *O maniuscrito Valentim Fernandes* (Lisbon, 1940), a French translation with annotation was published by Theodor Monod, Avelino Teixeira da Mota, and Raymond Mauny, *Description de l'côte occidentale d'Afrique*... (Bissau, 1951); Pacheco Pereira's work, *Esmeraldo de situ orbis* was edited and published by Augusto Epiphanio da Silva Dias in Lisbon, 1905 (reprinted 1975). An English translation by G. H. T. Kimble was published in London in 1937. Alvise da Mosto's work presents textual problems; an excellent critical edition of the various texts is Tullia Gasporini Leporace, *Le navigationi atlantiche del Veneziano Alvise da Ca' da Mosto* (Milan, 1966). An English translation from incomplete MSS sources is G. R. Crone, *The Voyages of Cadamosto and other documents* (London, 1937).

14. Alvares de Almada's work is published in António Brásio (ed.), *Monumenta Missionaria Africana* (2nd series, 5 vols., Lisbon, 1958–85), vol. 3; and an edition of Donelha appeared in vol. 5, a fuller edition and English (P. E. H. Hair) and French (Leon Bourdon) translation, *An Account of Sierra Leone and the Rivers of Guinea of Cape Verde (1625)* (Lisbon, 1977). Hair has also produced an informal edition of Alvares de Almada at the University of Liverpool.

15. Willem Bosman, *Naukeurige beschriyving van de Guinese Goud-, Tand-, en Slave-Kust* (Utrecht, 1704). An English translation, not always accurate, was published the next year as *A New and Accurate Description of the Coast of Guinea* (London, 1705, modern reprint with annotations by J. D. Fage and Ray Bradbury, London, 1967). Problems with the translation have been identified and corrected in a series of articles by Albert van Dantzig in *History in Africa* 2 (1975) to 11 (1984).

16. Ludevig Rømer, *Efterretning om negotien paa Kysten Guinea* (Copenhagen, 1756). A modern French translation is by Matte Digge-Hess, *Le golfe de Guinée 1700–1750* (Paris, 1989) does not include all the material in the original.

17. António de Oliveira Cadornega, *História geral das guerras angolanas* (mod. ed., Matias da Cunha and José Matias Delgado, 3 vols., Lisbon, 1940–42, reprinted 1972). The book was written for publication and even had an authorization, but was never published in its day.

18. For these writers and their background, see Robin Law, "Dahomey and the Slave Trade: Reflections on the Historiography of the rise of Dahomey," *Journal of African History* 27 (1986): 237–67.

19. Much of the earliest narrative histories of this region were published with English translations by George M. Theal (ed. and trans.) *Records of South-Eastern Africa* (9 volumes, Cape Town, 1898–1903); another bilingual source that includes early administrative and commercial documents is António da Silva Rego, et al. (eds.), *Documentos sobre os Portugueses em Moçambique e na Africa Central, 1497–1840* (9 vols., Lisbon, 1962–89).

20. For a large, if somewhat dated, bibliography of published and many unpublished missionary works, see Robert Streit and Johannes Dindinger, *Biblioteca Missionum* (33 vols., Aachen, 1916–present), vols. 15–17.

21. Barreira's corpus is largely published in Brásio, *Monumenta* (2nd series) vols. 2–3; Álvares's is unpublished and remains in the Biblioteca de Sociedade de Geografia de Lisboa. An informal edition and translation (into English) by Paul Hair is available from the University of Liverpool.

22. Many of the documents of missionary origin are published in Brásio, *Monumenta* (1st series), but many of the longer books, especially of the Capuchins, are not.

An excellent summary of them as well as many unpublished sources is found in Teobaldo Filesi and Isidoro Villapardiena, *La "Missio Antiqua" dei Cappuccini nel Congo (1645–1835)* (Rome, 1978).

23. The original draft of Cavazzi's work is in the private MSS of the Araldi Family. I have produced an edition and provisional translation, not yet published but available for scholars; Cavazzi's much better known published work is *Istorica Descrizione de' tre regni Congo, Matamba ed Angola* (Bologna, 1687). A modern annotated Portuguese translation by Graziano da Legguzzano is *Descrição Histórica dos três reinos Congo, Matamba e Angola* (2 vols., Lisbon, 1965).

24. Most of these sources were printed in their original languages and good editions in C. Beccari, *Rerum aethiopicarum scriptores occidentales inediti* (15 vols., Rome, 1905–17). New editions and English translations have been prominently published in various Hakluyt Society publications. Also see Charles Beckingham, "European Sources for Ethiopian History before 1634," *Paideuma* 33 (1987): 167–78.

25. A good modern edition and translation is C. F. Beckingham and G. W. B. Huntingford (eds. and trans.), *The Prester John of the Indies* (2 vols., London, 1958).

26. Many of the pre-1700 documents are printed in Brásio, *Monumenta* (1st series).

27. It must be said, however, that Belgian scholars have been very active in studying, publishing, and translating early records on Kongo. Certainly we would know much less were it not for the efforts of pioneers like Teophile Simar, Jean Cuvelier, Louis Jadin, and François Bontinck.

28. UNESCO has published a number of guides to African history in the archives and libraries of various European countries. Typically these guides were assembled by writing to the heads of archives and libraries and asking them to check catalogues for entries that seemed to pertain to Africa. The Athelone Press in London also published a series of guides to European archives for West Africa. These guides were often compiled by historians with expertise in the field as well as deploying questionaires.

29. David Henige compiled a National Union List of Microfilms in 1974. Though the text is inevitably dated, it is still a valuable guide to many collections.

30. For listings of the published books and collections whether edited in recent times or in the past, see John D. Fage, *A Guide to Original Sources for Precolonial Western African published in European Languages* (2nd ed., Madison, WI, 1994), which contains critical annotations on sources, publication history, and other vital information. For assessments of the quality of recent editions, see Adam Jones, *Raw, Medium, Well Done: A Critical Review of Editorial and Quasi-Editorial Wrok on pre-1885 European Sources for Sub-Saharan Africa* (Madison, WI, 1987).

10

MISSION AND COLONIAL DOCUMENTS

Toyin Falola

Introduction

Colonial and missionary encounters with Africa were not limited to political domination or to the pursuit of economic and religious objectives. The generation of knowledge was also part of this interaction. European missionaries and colonial officers sought information to make their work easier, to understand the "minds" of their subjects, and to be able to "engineer" appropriate strategies to civilize the so-called primitive Africans. Some were simply curious about Africans. Not only did they want to satisfy this curiosity, they then wanted to relay the information back to family, friends, sponsors, and even members of the general public who enjoyed stories of Europeans' heroic and humanitarian engagements with the "dark continent." No matter the motive or method, Africa is always the "abnormal other" in most of the documents: the continent and its people are different from Europeans, and the difference is presented by many writers in less than flattering ways.

This chapter will analyze their documents. While the general points are applicable to most of the documents, wherever generated, many examples are drawn from West Africa, because of both space limitation and the redundancy of listing all the documents in Africa. The chapter covers the full time span of events mentioned in the documents, if only to show that they address issues of space and time. The documents are abundant, range widely in their varieties, cover many important subjects in the long precolonial and colonial history of Africa, and have a number of drawbacks that should be recognized in their evaluation and use.

There is no one way of reading any particular document. Various documents illuminate various facets of the past. Disciplinary strategies of reading are multiple and reflect biases and boundaries between the various disciplines. New theories, the reality of the present, and the reality of memory all shape the ways in which a document is interpreted and reinterpreted. Documents also deal with many "pasts" rather than just one "past," and their meanings and conclusions can be contested, just as we debate the interpretations of present histories. The documents do not seek to present any coherent view of the past—as modern researchers, our task is to produce coherence from the fragments, by imposing our themes on them.

The documents can now be found in archives around the world, the majority in public archives in Europe and Africa. There are private papers as well as missionary archives (for instance, the Church Missionary Society's papers are in Birmingham, England). A substantial number have been reprinted in essays and books, while the range can be discerned from thousands of footnotes in hundreds of monographs.

The Nature of the Documents

The writings in and about Africa were generated by external and internal agencies at various periods. This chapter emphasizes materials generated by Europeans—explorers, traders, missionaries, and officials—who wrote not for Africans, but largely for an European audience. In the nineteenth and twentieth centuries, the African elite, too, joined in writing, producing vastly different accounts and representations.

With the advent and spread of Christianity in the second half of the nineteenth century, written accounts by missionaries grew by leaps and bounds. These accounts have been useful in crosschecking information from oral traditions and material evidence.

The trend continued in the first half of the twentieth century when Africa was under colonial rule. Many of these sources were generated for multiple reasons. In the first place, Europeans believed it was important to understand the history of the people they governed. Consequently, colonial officials were often instructed to document history and make this documentation available to new officers. Second, a number of European officers were eager to justify their stay in Africa by spreading stories of "primitive Africans" and their own works to liberate them. G. I. Jones has rightly observed the motives of colonial writings, which were encouraged first on historical grounds, the need to record for posterity the last vestiges of the primitive cultures which the twentieth century was about to engulf; then on the grounds of administrative convenience, the need for accurate information about the peoples whose territories were being organized into the districts, divisions, and provinces of the colonial empire.[1]

Nigeria is a good case study to illustrate the development of colonial documentation. The first very successful attempt at compiling information was in 1916 when Intelligence Records were collected in northern Nigeria. These records were collated and published in 1921 as *The Gazeteers of Northern Provinces*. Many Intelligence Reports were compiled for nearly all districts and provinces. The judicial records of both the Native and the High Courts also contain information on many Nigerian communities.

Many books were also written by officials-cum-researchers. The most distinguished among these was P. A. Talbot, who wrote a number of significant books.[2] He was a dedicated researcher who successfully provided primary data on a wide range of issues and themes, moving from what we now call anthropology to zoology with effortless ease. Another prolific writer was C. L. Temple, who gave insight into the problems of colonial administration in Nigeria in his *Native Races and the Rulers*.[3] He and his wife jointly published *Notes on the Tribes of Northern Nigeria*,[4] which described the customs of the people of that area. Other distinguished writers include R. E. Denett, who wrote *The Nigerian Studies*;[5] C. K. Meek, *A Sudanese Kingdom* (1931) and other books,[6] and A. J. N. Tremearne, another prolific author.[7]

In Nigeria and elsewhere, the colonial writers provided valuable written sources not only on aspects of colonial rule but also on local history. They collected many traditions relating to the early history of Nigerian communities. They described the mechanisms of the indigenous political system and commented elaborately on many aspects of social life such as naming, wedding and burial ceremonies, religious beliefs and modes of worship, and types of cloths and food.

The African Voice

The generating of documents was not limited to Europeans. Africans, too, added their voices, especially from the nineteenth century onwards when they began to write in European languages as well as their mother tongues.

Thus, Samuel Johnson was able to distinguish himself for his successful book, *History of the Yorubas*.[8]

The interest of Africans in writing increased during the colonial period, not necessarily because of any fascination with writing or written histories but due more to a desire to document the past for a new generation, the need to offer historical accounts in order to acquire prestige, and the belief that historical texts offer opportunities to present manifestoes for progress. The list of such writers during this period is long. One example is Jacob Egharevba among the Benin.[9] Many of these works are now referred to as local chronicles or local histories, but they are part of the development of the colonial period. Indeed, this unprecedented upsurge in the number of Africans who decided to write came about for two reasons: The first was an intense nationalistic ambition to reassert African values, institutions, and history that colonialism wanted to wipe out. A few literate Nigerians believed the best way to do this was to record for posterity the history of their fatherland. For instance, Samuel Johnson, one of Africa's greatest local historians, claimed to write from

a purely patriotic motive, that the history of our fatherland might not be lost in oblivion, especially as our old sires are fast dying out. Educated natives of Yoruba are well acquainted with the history of England and with that of Rome and Greece, but of the history of their own country they know nothing whatever.[10]

The second reason for Africans to write was that the competition of communities for political power and social amenities stimulated interest in local studies. Local historians became spokesmen of their people and tried to show and justify either the supremacy of their community over, or its equality in status with, the others. Bala Achi deals with this in a detailed study of a particular recent example in chapter 15 of this volume.

Nigeria is used here to illustrate the trend in local chronicles in colonial Africa. In northern Nigeria, the intolerable encroachment of Christianity and Western values spurred the Ulama and Amirs to vigorously pursue the writing of local history not only in Arabic, as they had hitherto done, but also in their mother tongues. One of the most outstanding works produced during this period was Mohammad B. Idris al-Sudani's *Tarik Umara Bauchi*, published in 1921, a lengthy and informative account on Bauchi. Other works of great repute include Tabyin Amr Buba Yero on Gombe, and Abubakar Imam's *Hausa Bakwai* (1958). Perhaps best known among these local historians is Al-hajj Junaidu, the

Waziri of Sokoto. Generally acknowledged to be a distinguished scholar, Junaidu had works to his credit that include *Tarihin Fulani* (Zaria, 1957) and *Mujaddadi Shehu Usman dan Fodiyo* (1953).

A major book, first written in the local language and later (1939) translated into English is Akia Sai's *Akiga's Story*. For its invaluable information and minute details on the Tiv, the book has become indispensable to researchers. Professor Daryll Forde aptly describes it as "a valuable document for its portrayal of an early phase of 'culture contact' and for its invaluable contextual accounts of traditional rituals and beliefs."[11]

In southern Nigeria, hundreds of works were written on local communities. In the east, the notable works include I. E. Iwekawune's *Akuko-ala na ohwu nke ale-Ibo Nile*; O. A. Arua's *A Short History of Oheha* (Enugu, 1951); O. O. Ekegha's *A Short History of Abriba* and M. C. N. Idigo's *The History of Aguleri*. In the southwest, among the Edo, Chief Egharevba was the leading authority. He wrote many works, the most famous being *A Short History of Benin*, first published in Edo in 1934 and later translated into English. The book discussed the Benin Empire and Edo institutions. Commenting on the work, Prof. J. D. Fage concluded that it is "one of the first and still remaining among the best of the now numerous little books in which Nigerians have written down the histories of their own peoples and states."[12]

Among the Yoruba, the work of Samuel Johnson is unrivaled. Completed in 1897 and published in 1921, *The History of the Yorubas* remains the most comprehensive record of Yoruba history, encompassing origin, customs, government, and the nineteenth century wars. The work has activated a number of other writers, notably J. D. Abiola, who wrote on the Ijesa; I. B. Akinyele, on Ibadan; J. A. Olusola, on Ijebu-Ode; Chief Ojo, the Bada of Saki, on Ilorin, Benin, and Saki; Ajisafe on Abeokuta and Oyerinde on Ogbomoso.[13]

It is almost impossible to write the history of many Nigerian communities without making use of these works. Many of the writers collected information first hand and even participated in the events they described. Samuel Johnson, for example, was an eyewitness of the Yoruba wars he described so elaborately in his book. Several of these books have now been turned into "authorized versions" of local traditions to such an extent that new field works often fail to obtain new information other than that published in local histories.

Local histories have their limitations, like all other sources. Many of them made use of oral traditions, which the original authors did not have the skill necessary to collect and evaluate. Some interpreted the traditions wrongly and distorted them to present an account in line with other purposes. For example, most of the writers were glaringly biased in favor of their own communities due to patriotic motives. They exaggerated their people's past and turned the writings into propaganda by challenging derogatory remarks others had made about their people and communities.

In contrast to the above works, it was mainly outsiders who generated the elaboration of specifically missionary and colonial documents.

Missionaries and the Production of Knowledge

The promotion of education was central to missionary activity in Africa, and missionary schools affected the production of historical documents; for example, the Africans cited above had usually attended such schools. The missionaries themselves also generated a variety of historical documents.

To facilitate the spread of Western education and the dissemination of knowledge, missionaries embarked on two other projects generally less noted than their schools: publishing houses and bookshops. Many missionary agencies did not see publishing as to be done solely for profits, and some bookshops even survived on marginal profits. The agencies were interested in proselytization, but they sponsored an extensive collection of materials on local histories and customs, even allowing some of these to be used in elementary schools. Often, however, missions were very controlling: they chose the books they wanted to publish, the bookstores to sell them, and the authors they wanted to promote. A few groups were aggressive in promoting their authors and books, as in the case of the Church Missionary Society (CMS) among the Yoruba in Nigeria. Whenever a mission saw publishing as a business, publication of other than solely religious books was further encouraged.[14] Some missions had their own publishing outfits. Some did not and relied on private publishers. Seely, a publishing house in London, published many books for the CMS.

Mission and colonial documents exist in many European languages and are found in all leading European and African archives. Many are also in private hands. The range is impressive; examples below are drawn primarily from West Africa. Missionary documents cover many subjects and use a variety of media, including reports and official correspondence. Early materials, such as those by J. F. Schön and Samuel Crowther, focused on conditions for the spread of Christianity and extensive information on African peoples and their lifestyles.[15] As the missionaries settled among Africans, they recorded their impressions in diaries, official correspondence, and little books. One famous diary, subsequently published and reissued in four editions within a space of five years, is *Seventeen Years in the Yoruba Country*, published in 1872 by Anna Hinderer, wife of David Hinderer, the first missionary in Ibadan.[16] Travelogues were many, including notable ones by Clark[17] and by Bowen.[18]

The missionaries also encouraged the publication of local histories and actually sponsored many of these. One of the earliest well-read books was on the kingdom of Abeokuta, where the progress of conversion was reported to a European audience.[19] This book was reprinted in several editions; translated into Dutch, it also sold well.

Missionary agents, whites and Africans alike, felt a need to report on mission work, namely, the progress of Africans in their march towards "civilization" and modernity. For want of a better term, we can describe these works as "progress reports" in book form or in journals and letters. Some were even sold to raise more money for missionary duties.

Religious and educational materials are numerous. These include hymn books, sermons, language and grammar text, and translated books of literature. All are documents of historical significance on various issues and subjects. Samuel Crowther, a hero among the African missionary agents, published books on Yoruba grammar and vocabulary, with remarks on history.[20] He also published on the Igbo language.[21] J. F. Schön published language books on the Hausa,[22] in addition to his works on folklore.[23] Many works are published in African languages, useful to study the problems of translation and culture change.[24] Some texts became famous in schools. One example is the Fifth Yoruba Primer (*Iwe Kika Ekarun*), used in schools in Western Nigeria. The book combines language with historical materials on Yoruba cities, wars, kings, chiefs, politics, and biographies of religious leaders.

Journals and reports were far more numerous than books. Some assumed the status of full-length books, for example some of Crowther's or of Robert Moffat in South Africa.[25] Stories of successful conversion dominate many reports. The courage of pioneer missionaries to work in a "benighted country" is always celebrated, while virtues were associated with missionary/white culture and viciousness and stupidity with "pagan Africa." The tone is consistent: missionaries are the humanitarian agents of civilization and Africans are primitive.[26]

Furthermore, the missionaries also pioneered newspaper publishing, valuable for historical materials. One prominent leader in this field was Henry Townsend, the founder of the Yoruba Mission. In the 1850s, Townsend brought a used printing press to Abeokuta to train apprentices in printing technology. In 1859, he started the *Iwe Irohin*, a fortnightly newspaper on religion and politics. The *Iwe Irohin* became bilingual in 1860. Drawing from the mission staff, a secular newspaper, the *Anglo-African*, established by a Jamaican-born Lagos entrepreneur, Robert Campbell, followed in 1862. Other religious magazines are useful as historical documents. For instance, the *Church Missionary Gleaner*, published in London by the CMS, reported political events. Local editions were started in Africa, in Lagos in 1911, so successfully that an eventual local language replacement, *Iwe Eko* (Lagos News), was able to draw contributors from eminent members of the Lagos elite. Yet another newspaper, non-denominational and published from 1880 to 1937, was the *In Leisure Hour*, a monthly bilingual on religion and current affairs. *In Leisure Hour* carried items on gender as well.

The "Colonial Library"

Another category of documents is those generated by officials, or officials-cum-scholars, associated with the various European governments. In northern Nigeria, the administrators developed a rapport with kings and the elite that led to the production of texts. High-ranking officers such as Lord Lugard wanted to sell his model of indirect rule by presenting the north as a successful case of administration. Fieldnotes appeared in printed forms as early as the first decade of the twentieth century, providing extensive documentation of many African groups, their culture and the changes that the European administration was capable of making.[27] A comprehensive book in this early period was *The Making of Northern Nigeria*, by C. Orr.[28]

As part of the consolidation of colonial power, efforts were made to collect information on various groups in northern Nigeria. The Residents, administrative heads of provinces, were instructed to collect genealogical materials of some families as well as ethnographic data on many towns and villages. C. L. Temple, the Lieutenant Governor, and his wife collated all these reports and published them in book form.[29] Temple called for more data, a challenge subsequently taken up in the following years. Officers provided "manuals" on government and histories in the *Gazetteers of the Northern Provinces of Nigeria* published in the 1920s.[30] The *Gazetteers* are one of the richest sources of information, with attention to details in those issues that mattered most to the colonial administration. Amateur ethnographers also joined in the new enterprise of writing about Africa, the

"Other." Among the famous ethnographic documents in the 1920s and 1930s were those on the Igbo by Basden[31] and on savanna dwellers by Wilson-Haffenden[32] and Oakley.[33] Comparative works were even presented, for example, Olive Temple's description of a number of chieftaincy institutions in Africa.[34]

Indeed, the 1920s inaugurated a successful era in colonial ethnography. Although not typical, Nigeria offers an example to document this development. From the 1921 census report, Amaury Talbot generated a widely cited book that provides valuable information on many ethnic groups in southern Nigeria.[35] The system of indirect rule was explained and justified in a number of important studies. C. L. Temple credited indigenous institutions with the ability to adapt to what he regarded as an innovative administrative system.[36] The most famous of all the works was by Lord Lugard, *The Dual Mandate in British Tropical Africa*, which outlined the objectives of the colonial administration and how to achieve them.[37] Colonial officers were less critical of the system, although a bold officer, H. B. Hermon-Hodge, published a critical book using a pseudonym.[38] Both the system of indirect rule and its consequences have generated a long string of scholarly literature.[39]

In a move that generated a fresh set of colonial documents, H. R. Palmer, appointed to the post of Lieutenant-Governor in 1925, instructed that the *Gazetteers* be revised. Thus, in the late 1920s, many new editions appeared. Also common all over the country in the late 1920s and 1930s was the collection and circulation of *Intelligence Reports*, which document the history, contemporary politics, and economy of many towns and villages.

Works of translation also appeared as part of the colonial documentation of Africa. Missionaries and scholars such as Charles Smith, Richard Hill, Thomas Hodgkin, and Sir Richmond Palmer translated documents from Arabic, Hausa, and some African languages into English. Palmer, a distinguished British administrator in Nigeria, succeeded in translating many Arabic writings. In the 1940s and 1950s, he collected many documents in northern Nigeria and made them available to a larger audience. Examples of translated works are numerous, and these have made a significant contribution as source-material.[40]

Contents and Scholarship

Documents do not constitute coherent reconstructed histories, but instead are raw materials that make possible the writing of history.

They can be difficult to collect and even harder to locate; many are neglected and ignored, or a researcher runs out of time to keep collecting more. Once they are available, however, they provide the opportunity—in many cases, the best opportunity—to reconstruct African history, for most of which documents are lacking, primarily because the people were nonliterate. Wherever Islam spread after the seventh century, the situation was better because of Arabic literacy. Elsewhere, written accounts grew in volume from the fifteenth century onward as Europeans began to visit Africa. In addition, the influence of Islam and Western education enabled many Africans to read and write, and many wrote about their local communities.

The documents cover many subjects.[41] Only some will be mentioned below, but the range is limitless. Many documents deal with early history, demonstrating a fascination with stories of origins. Although some dismissed these tales as African fantasies, a few did not. Africans themselves were eager to record them, if only to show the antiquity of their people. To take a few examples, H. R. Palmer, that notable translator, reported the Daura legend on the creation of the Hausa dynasties[42] and the origin of the Saifawa Dynasty in Borno.[43] E. J. Arnett also provided a translation of the origin of the Yoruba,[44] Samuel Johnson offered a much more elaborate legend about the Yoruba,[45] and Egharevba did the same for the Benin.[46] Some works attempt to trace the origins and diffusion of material objects. Thus, Adebiyi Tepowa traces the history of brass,[47] and Egharevba narrates how the technology of brass casting traveled from Ile-Ife to Benin.[48]

Missionary and colonial documents also attempted to chart the phases in African history. In Palmer's *Sudanese Memoirs* and *Bornu, Sahara and Sudan* can be found a gold mine of information on the early history of Kanem-Borno, Kano, and many other places in West Africa. Other writers of the colonial period were equally fascinated by early histories in other parts of Africa. Thus, Y. Urvoy translated Al-Bakri's works on Borno;[49] Patterson collected Kanuri folklore;[50] H. A. R. Gibb translated and edited the famous work of Ibn Battuta, the greatest Arab traveler of the fourteenth century;[51] and M. de Sleane translated the work of Ibn Khaldun, the greatest Arab historian of the fourteenth century.[52] O. Houdas translated the work of Arabic traveler, al-Sadi, on the Western Sudan.[53] The influential work of Leo Africanus on North and West Africa during the sixteenth century is available in Arabic, English and French.[54] African writers never let early history and the narratives of great kings escape their attention.

We cannot divorce the contribution of Africans from these documents. There is a category of literature that also narrates the African experience. Many deal with African interpretations of colonial changes; and others deal with issues of resistance. Out of this literature, a nationalist historiography developed, focusing on power, the need for reforms, and the demand of autonomy.[55] There are also impressive memoirs and political manifestoes that capture the mood and desire of the African intelligentsia of the nationalist era.[56]

A number of other general comments can be made. Ignoring the time when the documents were generated, and paying attention to the contents, we can say that there is a deeper dimension of time. Although a document was generated in the twentieth century, it may contain information on the tenth century C.E. There is definitely a rich body of information on historical process. Most documents capture the changes of their era, even if they exaggerate the impact of the European contact with Africa, including information both on indigenous Africa and on the impact of the West. As I have shown above, there is also the dimension of location and space, as many parts of the continent are also covered in one way or the other. The sources can be fragmentary, but they do hint at many places and issues.

As to be expected, most of the documents deal with the colonial period itself, as an attempt to record the policies and changes that were being introduced. While space does not permit a full elaboration here, these documents do provide abundant data on the process of colonial conquest, covering such issues as the process of diplomacy and military attacks, the imposition of a new set of laws, race relations (especially in South Africa), and the ultimate transfer of power to Africans.[57]

Limitations of Documents

Documents as historical sources have many limitations. For example, observers record events from their own points of view. Although historians do not necessarily take liberties with texts, even retaining names and spellings in original documents, they understand that "points of view" do require critical analysis. "Points of view" encapsulate the subjective conditions in reporting and interpretation. A common tendency in some of the reports is to attribute aspects of civilization to the outsiders. Even legends of origins, which are partly meant to create pride, have external connections, as in the example of the establishment of Hausa states narrated by Palmer.[58] Such stories are known to support a so-called Hamitic hypothesis, which suggest that the great civilization of Africa owes its creation to external origins. There were many missionaries and colonial officers who believed that they were actually generating history for the first time—that Africa had no history before their arrival. The views of many enlightened writers of the period were based on the following assumptions: North Africa was superior to the rest of the continent, and there was little or no interaction between different regions; African history was dominated by warfare and squabbles for power; the most important development in Africa occurred only recently, associated with the coming of Europeans. In the words of A. E. Afigbo, who has little respect for colonial historiography, most of the documents were "simply a display on paper of European, or in any case white, racial and cultural arrogance, an ideological legitimisation of Europe's exploitative presence in Africa, in short a chastening display of the inability of a civilization (no matter how advanced) to transcend itself."[59]

Language barriers are another issue: English speakers may not profit from texts written in Portuguese. The resources in Arabic are yet to be made known and widely used by nonnative speakers. Translated materials have problems too. They may not be accurate. In some cases, as in the works translated by Palmer, the translator can introduce concepts not necessarily in the original. For instance, Palmer used biblical language in some of his translated texts, thus making some meanings hard to understand.

The sources on which many accounts are based must also be considered. Some relied on hearsay evidence or firsthand information from other travelers. For instance, Olfert Dapper, who wrote one of the best accounts of Africa, acquired his information from Dutch travelers.[60] Where oral evidence was collected, there is no evidence that missionaries and colonial officers were able to evaluate the evidence before they provided their interpretations. When Europeans were restricted to the coast, accounts of places in the hinterland were based on secondhand sources. This is true, for instance, of much of the information on the Yoruba before the 1820s, when most of what was known came through secondhand sources. During the twentieth century, some writers relied on the works generated during the nineteenth century to make wide-ranging comments on Africa.

The sources are uneven in the areas they cover. Until late in the colonial period, the most privileged areas were along the coast, which Europeans settled or knew firsthand, followed by the adjacent hinterland. As colonial rule was established, the most privileged areas were those that produced minerals and cash crops or were administrative centers. The upshot is that many areas are mentioned in ethnographic works, but some just in passing or merely as a list of groups, villages, or language groups. Accounts of remote areas are often based on secondhand sources.

Just as quantity is not the same, so also quality is uneven with respect to subject matter. Many accounts of places and people can be sketchy because the writers did not set out to write comprehensive and detailed works. A number of the writers simply wanted to fill diaries or write those things that would interest their friends, relatives, business associates, or the media. Some do reflect narrow interests, especially commercial possibilities—what goods were available, and how willing were the people to trade.

The historical depths covered in the documents also vary. Where previous literary traditions existed, as among the Islamic population, documents may narrate histories from as far back as the eighth century. In some instances, historical depth or its lack may reflect the importance which outside interests (mainly of commerce) attached to an area. Trade with the outside world gave the Swahili coast and Borno a greater historical depth in the documents than, say, the Jukun in Nigeria's middle belt.

All creators of documents have some interests in what they write. Missionaries were interested in the expansion of Christianity and the colonial officers in the consolidation of power. The interests shape the kinds of questions they posed and the answers that they recorded. To draw from the examples of the early writers mentioned in the opening pages, they sought to learn about trade, originally in slaves and later in palm products. Their documents contain information about sources of commodities, prices, quantity and quality of products, the major markets, and issues pertaining to commerce in general. As they also either wanted to expand trade or seek the means to control the sources, the authors were interested in learning about the politics of trade. Since systems of government and the commercial interests of leaders affected trade, the documents contain information on chiefs and kings, relating systems of government with commerce. Where the African political class controlled trade, the documents describe the nature of power and its connection to trade, as in such examples as a state monopoly on trade in the Benin Empire. To take another example of secondary interests, missionary documents contain substantial information on African indigenous religions, even if their chief aims were to discredit them, present Christianity as a better alternative, and offer the vision of a new society.

Many of the writers believed that Africans were inferior to the whites. Indeed, some set out to seek facts to demonstrate a theory of racial inferiority. A. J. N. Tremearne, for example, stated that one of his aims in writing was "to show how much the uncivilized native of Northern Nigeria resemble some other aboriginal races. . . . The native is certainly not the equal of the European."[61] It is not uncommon in a number of colonial documents to find the characterization of Africans as children, lazy and without civilization.[62] Similarly, many missionaries presented African culture and customs in the unkindest manner. They saw barbarism instead of creativity, decadence instead of coherence. From both their Christian and Western backgrounds, many things African were odd, backward, and degraded. The documents may reflect the ignorance of the writers with regard to the things they describe, or simply their lack of proportion or judgment. "A clash of culture" is always at work: the foreign missionary chronicler imposed his own cultural framework on another society and reached conclusions that frightened or fascinated him.

Another aspect is also often ignored, namely, the politics of the composition of documents, as when a writer is influenced by the politics of the sponsor or the political objectives of his country. The politics can be to further the interest of commerce or of the government. A few writers can be seen to have been part of the architects of imperial policies; many represented their governments, missionary agencies, or scientific organizations. Their statements can reveal the "voice" of power or of vested interests. Thus, a number of documents generated by the Portuguese clearly reveal how the writers wanted the Portuguese government to expand its influence in Africa, its traders to benefit more, and its missionaries to gain more converts. Where the kings and chiefs controlled commerce, documents can show how to court them, or at least to influence their decisions.

Perhaps most crucial are the "points of view" that encapsulate the subjective conditions in reporting and interpretation. A common tendency in some of the reports is to attribute aspects of civilization to the outsiders. Even legends of origins that are partly meant to create pride have external connections. To cite the example from Palmer:

> The people went up out of Canaan and settled in the land of Palestine. And a certain man among them named Najib the Canaanite went up out of Palestine with all his household and journeyed westwards into Libya, which is one of the Provinces of Egypt, and there they dwelt for many years. And a certain man among them named Abdul Dar, and he was a son of Najib, went out of Libya and dwelt in the Province of Tripoli. And after a time he sought the kingship of Tripoli, but the people refused. Wheretofore he

arose with his people and journeyed to the south till he came to an oasis called Kusugu and dwelt there. And he begat children, and they were all daughters. Their names were Bukainya and Gambo and Kafai and Waizamu and Daura, and she was the youngest. All these he begat before they came to Daura.[63]

As the story continues, Abuyazidu, son of the king of Bagdad, visited Daura after a successful stay in another West African kingdom, Borno. At Daura, Abuyazidu was able to kill a snake that had prevented the people from fetching water from their only well, and had princess Daura as a reward. Their son, Bawo, had six sons that established the six "original" Hausa states in northern Nigeria.

Conclusion

The publication of mission and colonial documents should be promoted. This will make more works accessible to readers. Those who have worked on a specific theme or country can annotate the texts to clarify the meanings of many issues and provide appropriate context for researchers and students. In some cases, it may be necessary to explain technical terms and translate some archaic words. Places mentioned in many texts can be identified for students and scholars to see.

Mission and colonial documents remain one of African history's most valuable sources. Thus far, they constitute one of the largest bodies of source-materials that make possible the reconstruction of African history and one of the most respectable branches of history. The duty of the historian is to subject all written accounts to critical internal and external analysis to determine authenticity and credibility. If the accounts are thoroughly examined, and if the texts can be compared with one another and with the information contained in oral and other sources, they will continue to yield valuable information on the history of Africa.

Notes

1. G. I. Jones, "Social Anthropology in Nigeria During the Colonial Period," *Africa* 54 (3) (1974): 282.

2. P. A. Talbot, *The Budduma of Lake Chad* (London, 1911); *In the Shadow of the Bush: On the Ekoe of Oban Division* (London, 1912); *Life in Southern Nigeria: The Ibibio*

of the Eket Division (1914); *Some Nigerian Fertility Cult* (New York, 1923; reprint, 1967); *Tribes of the Niger Delta* (New York, 1914; reprint, 1967) and the four-volume *Peoples of Southern Nigeria* (London, 1926).

3. C. L. Temple, *Native Races and their Rulers: Sketches and Studies of Official Life and Administrative Problems in Nigeria* (Cape Town, 1918).

4. C. L. and O. Temple, *Notes on the Tribes, Provinces, Emirates and States of the Northern Provinces of Nigeria* (Cape Town, 1919; 2nd ed. London, 1965).

5. R. E. Dennett, *Nigerian Studies or the Religious and Political System of the Yoruba* (London, 1910).

6. C. K. Meek, *The Northern Tribes of Nigeria*, 2 vols. (London, 1925); *Law and Authority in a Nigerian Tribe* (London, 1927); *A Sudanese Kingdom* (London, 1931).

7. A. J. N. Tremearne, *The Ban of the Bori* (London, 1914); *The Tailed Headhunters of Nigeria* (London, 1912); and *Hausa Superstitions and Customs: An Introduction to the Folklore* (London, 1913).

8. Samuel Johnson, *The History of the Yorubas* (1921).

9. Jacob U. Egharevba, *A Short History of Benin* (Benin, 2nd edition, 1953).

10. Johnson, *History of the Yorubas*, vii.

11. Akia Sai, *Akiga's Story: the Tiv Tribe as Seen by One of Its Members* (London, 1939).

12. J. D. Fage, book review in *Journal of African History* 2 (2) (1961).

13. See for instance, R. C. Law, "Early Yoruba Historiography," *History in Africa: A Journal of Methods*, vol. 3 (1976), 69–89.

14. Michel R. Doortmont, "Recapturing the Past: Samuel Johnson and the construction of the history of the Yoruba," Ph.D. diss. (Erasmus University, Rotterdam, 1994), 41–47.

15. *Journal of the Rev. James Frederick Schon and Mr. Samuel Crowther, who, with the sanction of Her Majesty's Government, accompanied the expedition up the Niger and Tshadda Rivers undertaken by Macgregor Laird. Esq., in connection with the British Government in 1854* (London, 1855).

16. A. Martin Hinderer, *Seventeen Years in the Yoruba Country: Memorials of Anna Hinderer . . . gathered from her Journals and letters, with an Introduction by R. B. Hone* (London, 1872).

17. W. H. Clark, *Travels and Explorations in Yorubaland, 1854–1858* (Ibadan, 1972).

18. T. J. Bowen, *Adventures and Missionary Labour in Central Africa* (Charleston, 1857).

19. Sarah Tucker, *Abbeokuta; or, Sunrise within the Tropics: an outline of origin and progress of the Yoruba Mission* (London, 1853).

20. Samuel Ajayi Crowther, *A Vocabulary of the Yoruba Language* (London, 1843); *A Grammar of the Yoruba Language* (London, 1852).

21. Samuel Ajayi Crowther, *Isoana-Ibo Primer* (London, 1859).

22. J. F. Schon, *Grammar of the Hausa Language* (London, 1862); *Dictionary of the Hausa Language with appendices of Hausa literature* (London, 1876).

23. J. F. Schon, *Magana Hausa: Native Literature or Proverbs, Tales, Fables and Historical Fragments in the Hausa Language*, 2 vols. (London, 1881–86).

24. Among others, see, *Katekissmu ti ijo enia Olorun* (Lagos, 1901); *Iwo l'omo! Tabi, Asaro fun Iwamimo* (Lagos, 1911).

25. Robert Moffat, *Missionary Labours and Scenes in Southern Africa* (London, 1842).

26. See an analysis of some of these writings in Felix K. Ekechi, "Studies on missions in Africa," in Toyin Falola, ed., *African Historiography: Essays in Honor of Jacob Ade Ajayi* (London, 1993), 145–65.

27. Among others, see J. A. Burdon, *Northern Nigeria: historical notes on certain Emirates and Tribes* (London, 1909); F. De F. Daniel, *A History of Katsina* (Self-published, n.d., n.p.; reprinted in 1928 as *Historical Notes on Katsina Emirate* [Katsina, 1928]); J. M. Fremantle, "The Emirate of Katagum," *Journal of the Royal Society* (1911–12).

28. C. W. J. Orr, *The Making of Northern Nigeria* (London, 1911; reissued and introduced by A. H. M. Kirk-Greene, London, 1965).

29. Temple and Temple, *Notes on Tribes, Provinces, Emirates and States of the Northern Provinces of Nigeria.*

30. See for instance, A. H. M. Kirk-Greene, ed., *Gazetteers of the Northern Provinces of Nigeria* (London, 1972, 2nd imprint; reissued in 1965, with a new introduction by Kirk-Greene).

31. G. T. Basden, *Among the Ibos of Nigeria, an account of the curious and interesting habits, customs, & beliefs of a little known African people by one who has for many years lived amongst them on close and intimate terms* (London, 1921).

32. J. R. Wilson-Haffenden, *The red men of Nigeria, an account of a lengthy residence among the Fulani, or "red men," & other pagan tribes of central Nigeria, with a description of their headhunting, pastoral & other customs, habits & religion* (London, 1930).

33. R. R. Oakley, *Treks and Palavers* (London, 1938).

34. Olive Temple, *Chiefs and Cities in Africa: Across Lake Chad by way of British, French, and German Territories* (n.p., n.d.).

35. P. Amaury Talbot, *The Peoples of Southern Nigeria: A Sketch of their history, ethnology, and languages, with an abstract of the 1921 census*, 2 vols. (London, 1926).

36. C. L. Temple, *Native Races and their Rulers: Sketches and Studies of Official Life and Administrative Problems in Nigeria* (Cape Town, 1918).

37. Lord F. D. Lugard, *The Dual Mandate in British Tropical Africa* (Edinburgh, 1922).

38. Langa Langa [H. B. Hermon-Hodge], *Up Against it in Nigeria* (London, 1921).

39. Among others, see Margery Perham, *Native Administration in Nigeria* (London, 1937); J. White, *Central Administration in Nigeria, 1914–1948: the Problem of Polarity* (Dublin, 1981); and Michael Crowder and Obaro Ikime, eds., *West African Chiefs: their Changing Status under Colonial Rule and Independence* (Ile-Ife, 1970).

40. See for instance, Ibn Battuta, *Ibn Batoutah*, trans. from the Arabic by C. Defremery and B. R. Sanguinétti (Paris, 1863); *The Voyages of Cadamosto and Other Documents on Western Africa in the Second Half of the Fifteenth Century*, trans. from the Italian and ed. by G. R. Crone (New York, 1937); and Abderrahman Ben Abdallah Ben Imran Ben Amir Es-Sadi, *Tarkih es-Soudan*, trans. from the Arabic by H. O. Houdas (Paris, 1898).

41. Many have been reprinted to make them accessible to researchers. See for instance, Thomas Hodgkin, ed., *Nigerian Perspectives: An Historical Anthology* (London, 1960); Bruce Fetter, ed., *Colonial Rule in Africa: Readings from Primary Sources* (Madison, 1979).

42. H. R. Palmer, *Sudanese Memoirs*, vol. 3 (Lagos, 1928), 132–4.

43. Ibid., 15–16.

44. E. J. Arnett, *The Rise of the Sokoto Fulani* (Kano, 1929).

45. Johnson, *History of the Yorubas*, 3–5.

46. Egharevba, *Short History of Benin*, 5–9.

47. Adebiyi Tepowa, "A Short History of Brass and its People," *Journal of the African Society* (1907): 33–7.

48. Egharevba, *Short History of Benin*, 12.

49. Y. Urvoy, *Histoire de l'empire de Bronou* (Paris: Mémoires de L'IFAN, No. 7, 1949).

50. J. R. Petterson, *Kanuri Songs* (Lagos, 1926).

51. Ibn Battûta, *Travels in Asia and Africa, 1325–1354*, ed. H. A. R. Gibb (London, 1929).

52. Ibn Khaldoun, *Histoire des Berberes*, trans. M. de Slane (Paris, 1925).

53. 'Abd al-Rahmân ibn 'Abdullâh al-Sa'di, *Ta'rikh al-Sudan* [Tarikh es-Soudan, trans. O. Houdas] (Paris, 1900).

54. See for instance, Leo Africanus, *The History and Description of Africa done into English by John Pory*, ed. Robert Brown (London, 1896).

55. The nationalist documents deserve more space than is allocated here. Among others, see Abdallah ibn Maseed ibn Salim al-Mazrui, "Utendi wa al-akida," in Lyndon Harris, *Swahili Poetry* (Oxford, 1962); G. G. K. Gwassa and John Iliffe, eds., *Records of the Maji Maji Rising* (Nairobi, 1967); Haile Selassie, *Selected Speeches of His Imperial Majesty Haile Selassie 1: 1918–1967* (Addis Ababa, 1967); Ronalld H. Chilcote, ed., *Emerging Nationalism in Portuguese Africa: Documents* (Stanford, Cal., 1972); Nnamdi Azikiwe, *Zik* (Cambridge, 1961).

56. See for instance, Tom Mboya, *The Challenge of Nationhood: A Collection of Speeches and Writings* (London, 1970).

57. Among others, see Frederick William Maitland, *The Constitutional History of England*, ed. H. A. L. Fisher (Cambridge, 1908); Frederick Madden, *Imperial Constitutional Documents* (Oxford, 1953); Raymond Betts, ed., *The "Scramble" for Africa* (Boston, 1966); Sir Edward Hertslet, *The Map of Africa by Treaty*, 3 vols. (3rd ed., 1909; reprint, London, 1967); Lady Lucie Duff-Gordon, *Letters from Egypt, 1863–1865* (London, 1865); Sir Lewis Michell, *The Life of the Right Honourable Cecil John Rhodes*, 2 vols. (London, 1910); John Hargreaves, ed., *France and West Africa* (London, 1969); H. W. Wack, *The Story of the Congo Free State* (New York, 1905); Sir Arthur Conan Doyle, *The Crime of the Congo* (New York, 1909); R. L. Buell, *The Native Problem in Africa*, 2 vols. (London, 1928); Geoffrey Gorer, *Africa Dances* (London, 1935; reprint, New York, 1962).

58. Palmer, *Sudanese Memoirs*, 132.

59. A. E. Afigbo, "Colonial Historiography," in Falola, ed., *African Historiography*, 50.

60. Olfert Dapper, *Description de l'Afrique* (Amsterdam, 1686).

61. A. J. N. Tremearne, *The Tailed Headhunters of Nigeria* (London, 1921), xi.

62. See for instance the views of Lord Delamere, who believed that Kenya should be a white man's country, in Elspeth Huxley, *White Man's Country: Lord Delamere and the Making of Kenya* (London, 1935).

63. Palmer, *Sudanese Memoirs*, 132.

PART III

Perspectives on History

11

DATA COLLECTION AND INTERPRETATION IN THE SOCIAL HISTORY OF AFRICA

Isaac Olawale Albert

Introduction

Discussions at academic and policy forums all over the world are evidence of a growing interest in Africa's social history. Meanwhile, since the 1960s, when most African nations regained their independence from erstwhile colonial masters, the continent's social, political, and economic conditions have been going from bad to worse. Although attempts to explain these developments have thus far been monopolized by social scientists, African problems might be better understood from a historical standpoint, for history digs more deeply than political science, sociology, or anthropology in explaining the etiology of social problems.

Unfortunately, few historians have shown an interest in explaining the growing problems in African development. This unsatisfactory situation should be reversed; historians, especially those within Africa, should show more interest in the study of social problems on the African continent, thus enabling them to make better contributions to contemporary African development. This chapter addresses some salient methodological issues that social historians must take into consideration in their bid to understand the challenge of social development in Africa.

A historian has two main responsibilities: collecting the facts and interpreting them. These tasks are intertwined:

> To do the one without the other reduces the historian to either a chronicler or a teller of tales. From ancient times, of course, history has always been part chronicle and part tale, but in our modern age previous generations of historians, under the impact of science, have set out to collect and interpret the facts scientifically, seeking to arrive at an objective and true rendering of history.[1]

Thus, this chapter has two objectives: to discuss, first, how the data for writing the social history of Africa can be collected and, second, how to interpret these facts. The tasks before us might not, in fact, be too different from what beset those writing the social history of other parts of the world. Social history is basically interested in human actions. As Nzemeke tells us in 1989, the actions of humans everywhere have a fundamental similarity, notwithstanding the cultural variations that condition them. It is difficult to claim exclusive peculiarity for the social history of Africa, for history is simply history.

What is probably peculiar to Africa is that social history is not very popular—especially among the indigenous historians.[2] This is surprising, considering the degree of social transformation that has taken place in different parts of the continent, especially since the beginning of the twentieth century. Why is social history not popular in Africa? To answer this question, we first need to define what is meant by social history. Historians do not agree on what to include or exclude from this special field. The consensus is that it is a total history. As Eric Hobsbawn tells us:

> Social history can never be another specialisation like Economics or other hyphenated histories because its subject matter cannot be isolated. We can define certain human actions as economic, at least for analytical purposes and then study them historically. . . . In much the same way though at a lower level of theory, the old kind of intellectual history which isolated written ideas from their human context and traced their filiation from one writer to another is possible, if one wants to do that sort of thing. But the social or societal aspects of man's being cannot be separated from the other aspects of his being, except at the cost of tautology or extreme trivilisation. . . . The intellectual historian may [at a risk] pay no attention to economics, the economic historian to Shakespeare, but the social historian who neglects either will not get far. Conversely, while it is extremely improbable that a monograph on provencal poetry will be economic history or one on

inflation in the sixteenth century intellectual history, both could be treated in a way to make them social history.[3]

What Hobsbawn, like many other scholars, means is that the field of social history is very broad. Within this framework, Ade Ajayi, the doyen of African history, defined social history as a study of the change in pattern of daily life, the emphasis being on how people lived at different times in the past, what music, dance, architecture, marriage, and family life they favored, what religion insofar as this impinges on daily life, and the pattern of change in the totality of life that these imply.[4] The emphasis of this type of history is on continuity and change in how people live their lives. In other words, the basic challenge of social history can be said to be a fuller understanding of the complex processes that have led to the emergence of human society in its present form.[5]

M. H. Dawson, in a paper on the future of social history in Africa, also observed that this specialist field overlaps other aspects of history to the extent that its boundaries with political, economic, intellectual, and religious history are blurred or difficult to delineate.[6] Against the background of the opinions of these two eminent historians, social history is presented in this chapter as that aspect of history that uses a sociological approach to explain past economic, political, environmental, intellectual, and other related events. It explains changes and the factors responsible for them in historical terms.[7]

We can now go back to the question raised earlier: the underdevelopment of social history in Africa. Why is this the case? To use Ajayi's language,[8] why is the social history of Africa left to the tender mercies of political scientists and others who analyze questionnaires and so on? Attempting to answer the question, Ajayi suggested that many African historians begin by studying areas in which their own cultural and linguistic competencies confer an advantage. The historian lives in Yorubaland in Nigeria and therefore writes about one small community in Yorubaland, or belongs to the Akan in Ghana and thus focuses attention on those people. Broad-based subject matter is simply not of interest. Even more problems are faced after doctoral work is completed. Most of these historians, according to Ajayi, find it difficult to work on issues or employ methods different from those used during their doctoral research. Here lies the crux of the matter. He notes further that probably the most limiting factor determining preference is that of sources, how easily accessible and how easily digestible. Historians often pitch their tents where they can find ready-made (documentary) or oral data. I wholeheartedly agree with Ajayi that African historians find it difficult to study outside their narrow environment and field of specialization, preferring to focus their work on a narrow geographical environment. In most cases their focus is on the polity rather than on social issues. They therefore hardly need the cross-cutting research methodology that social or economic history would require.

The present situation can be further accounted for. As part of the struggle against a European ideological framework, the earliest historians in Africa were trained to write political or cultural history, to the neglect of the economic and social history of the continent.[9] The basic goal of this clearly defensive history was to counter the dangerous lies Europeans has systematized and institutionalized about the African past.[10] One major object of attack by the historians was the colonial myth that Africans lacked the capacity for governing themselves. H. R. Trevor-Roper specifically asserted that Africans had no history beyond the activities of the colonial masters and Christian missionaries from Europe.[11] Trevor-Roper, himself a historian, is reported to have wondered why historians who are supposed to be engaged in the serious business of reconstructing the past should amuse themselves with the unrewarding gyrations of barbarous tribes in picturesque but irrelevant corners of the globe. To challenge him and others like him, several early African and black American historians began to use oral traditions and other available sources to show that many Africans had a glorious past before the European incursion. The raison d'être of most of the researches conducted and courses taught in African universities was, and still is, to show that Africans could really manage their own affairs independent of the European intruders. Whereas this old system could be said to be appropriate for the time when it was developed, the present deserves a new approach if history is to play its expected role in national development. Once more we quote Ade Ajayi:

> The situation has changed from the first days of independence when the objectives of historical education were mainly those of decolonization and trying to persuade others that we have a history. We now need to examine what positive objectives historical education should have in Nigeria today and how to achieve them.[12]

The defensive history written by Africans had a class bias. The emphasis was on kings and kingdoms. The present-day African historian has therefore been trained to write more on the hegemonic class, not as much on the masses whose energy daily creates and recreates civilization.[13] We know more of the precolonial African leaders like Sonni Ali, Mansa Musa, Askia the Great, Idris Aloma, and others than of the people they governed. Those who have written the political history of colonial Africa had the same problem. They told us mostly about District Officers, Residents, Provincial Governors, and so on, as well as the leaders of resistance movements. An understanding of the social life of the colonial subjects is hardly documented by these historians. Even in the present, more is written about Mobutu, Bokkassa, Idi Amin, Abacha, etc. than the hapless and helpless people these despots governed.

Is it possible for us to have a complete picture of the past using the vocal lens of the hegemonic class? The answer is no. What we therefore know about the precolonial, colonial, and even postcolonial African past today is a small fraction of what could be known. Having a full picture of what really happened requires us to adopt the social historical approach. Social history is a remarkable departure from the traditions of history conceived in terms of the deeds of the hegemonic class; it is interested in the entire society, not just a section of it. It is within this framework that social history is interested in such crosscutting subjects as health, migrations, governance, and so on.

This kind of history becomes a necessity for Africans, given the present state of development in the continent. Several parts of Africa are today less developed than they were some thirty years ago. The role of history, in addition to proving that Africa does have a history, should be to explain why every good thing fails in modern Africa. European colonialism has been replaced by neocolonialism in all parts of the continent. War, economic crisis, poverty, corruption, political underdevelopment, and environmental degradation are everywhere. As the international community battles to give the African continent a future, in terms of humanitarian intervention in war situations, promotion of democratic principles and good governance, granting of international aid, rescheduling of unpaid loans, and sponsoring of research to stem different kinds of diseases decimating the people of the continent, the historians in the continent are still singing "We have a history."

This monologue of the deaf must stop. The production of knowledge in Africa must reflect the challenge of globalization. Historians are therefore challenged to give better attention to social history with a view to generating thoughts that could be used to solve the mounting problems of social, economic and political development in the continent. Historical works on Africa now need to be grounded in social context.

One other noticeable problem with the defensive history of the past must be mentioned. That history failed to evolve any concrete hypothesis or theory to give unity or internal coherence to the African past. To this extent, African historians have not been able to provide any detailed interpretation of the African past. The history of the Ghana, Mali, Songhai, and other empires and kingdoms are stories of different forms of imperialism—probably not too different from the European imperialism in Africa. The African imperialism was presented in most of the books as a thing of beauty and therefore a joy forever. In the light of this, should we have a second look at the works on European imperialism? The point is that most of the works on the empires and kingdoms in Africa were produced without any questions as to whether the motive force for such an empire was egocentric, dynastic, or even something baser. If, on the other hand, it was based on a noble idea, no effort has been made to find out how close each empire or kingdom, in its day-to-day performance and its political and class structure, came to that idea.[14] All these questions and problems arise simply because the African past has not been approached from the social historical perspective.

Social problems are better understood and analyzed using theories. But the African historian was trained to fight shy of theoretical issues.[15] These scholars accused African history of being theoretically impoverished, lacking in rigorous materialism, yet characterized by politically suspect radicalism and essentially limited to issues of tribes, ethnic groups, and kingdoms. The professional historian in the continent is not interested in making predictions but, instead, in just telling the stories in more detailed form than the mainstream social scientist would do. However, without theories and predictions neither social science nor a thorough social history can be written.

Another problem is that most African historians, by training and practice, were and are slaves to documentary evidence. They have little faith in the unconventional sources used by the social scientists. They still approach the written document with bowed heads and speak of it in awed tones. "If you find it in the documents, it is so."[16] The paradox is that the kinds of problems a social historian is supposed to be studying do not easily lend themselves to documentary evidence. Ethnicity, corruption, poverty, and the like are more often expressed in people's actions than what they commit into writing. Information relating to any of these issues is deliberately distorted in most cases where it is found in writing. This means that the social historian must go extra miles to sources for data, and then must also interpret them.

The conservatism of the professional historian has been an issue of discussion for a long time. In *The Fashion and Future of History*, B. E. Schmitt rightly predicted in 1960 that the death of historical scholarship in several parts of the world was just a matter of time if the professionals in the field refused to change their research themes and methods. Schmitt called for a development-relevant kind of historical scholarship and noted the need to adjust to changing times and not be bound by customary conventional approaches.[17] In a learned presentation, Ajayi has expressed concern about this same ugly development, noting that

> In our search for the philosophy to guide social evolution, for the understanding of the dynamics and consequences of economic change, for the historical perspective to provide meaning for the apparently chaotic changing going on around us, history has a vital role to play. In our training of historians and the teaching of history to nonspecialist as well as in historical education at other levels, we do need this greater awareness of society and social concerns.[18]

My interaction with historians and students of history in the developed parts of the world suggests that Schmitt's advice has been heeded in many such places. Many departments of history and historians in Africa are still where they were several decades ago. They have not changed and are not changing. This explains why these historians are not much involved in the heated social science debate on the trajectories of development in their continent. This is why social scientists are taking it upon themselves to write the historical background to their publications rather than leaving this for historians to do, although in the past historians were customarily invited to write that aspect of any work.

Sources for the Social History of Africa

Social history is a broad field that, *inter alia*, captures issues germane to governance, economics, population, labor, religion, law, medicine, family, environment, conflict, and gender studies. Like every other discipline that uses qualitative research methodology, social history probably does not have any specific theory, paradigm, or method that it can strictly claim as its own. However, it integrates information from semiotics, narrative, content discourse, archives, phonemic analysis, and even statistical data. It draws insights from the approaches, methods, and techniques of ethno-methodology, phenomenology, cliometrics, feminism, deconstructionism, ethnographies, psychoanalysis, cultural studies, survey research, and participant observation, among others.[19] The field involves the study, use, and collection of a variety of empirical materials—case studies, personal experiences, life stories, interviews, and observational, historical, interactional, and visual texts—that describe both routine and problematic moments and meanings in individuals' lives.

This kind of history enables the professional historian to actively participate in the contemporary debate on the trajectories of development in the society. To this extent, social historians around the world enjoy a prime place in the assembly of social scientists. It logically follows therefore that field methods in social history are not too different from those of the mainstream social scientists like political scientists, economists, sociologists, feminists, and so on. The major difference is that the social historian is more interested in the facts of what happened than in formulating theories—the emphasis of the mainstream social scientists. Nonetheless, to become a social historian a student of history must be ready to critically study how social scientists do their work. The social historian must have a good understanding of social science epistemology, concepts, theories, and field methods. Little wonders that the Council for the Development of Social Science in Africa (CODESRIA) noted in 1989 that African historians must begin to pay attention to criticism from the researchers in such other areas as the social sciences, the natural sciences, and the aesthetic disciplines, as well as from the common masses; historians must have the courage to step over traditional academic walls into a multidisciplinary praxis.[20] Within this framework we can consider the social historical methodology to be simply a combination of historical and mainstream social science methodologies.

The social historians of Africa have three major roles. The first is to attempt a reconstruction of the African past, with substantial consideration of social concerns. The second is to provide a social perspective of the culture and political history of Africa as written by past writers. The third is to attempt to write the contemporary history of Africa, with a view to shedding light on why Africa is underdeveloped and what could be done to give the continent a future.

There are primary and secondary data for writing any type of history. Secondary sources are materials already existing on issues germane to the subject of investigation—for example, the work of other historians, communication specialists, literary critics, and scholars in other fields of specialization, and most of all the mainstream social scientists.[21] The contemporary historian of Africa is therefore confronted with vast amounts of written material. The social scientists have taken more time than the professional historians to study and analyze social situations in Africa, but the work often lacks time depth and is sometimes impressionistic. Many social scientists have written on Africa without knowing the antecedents of what they wrote about; thus they often make misleading generalizations. A social historian reading these works can use the knowledge of history to identify what is missing and can be filled in. In some cases, the historian studying issues already addressed by social scientists just needs to dig deeper and subject the data to more rigorous explanation. Within this vital framework of explanation, the work of historians appears more acceptable than the reconstructions of the mainstream social scientists.

Social historians can also use existing references in the social science work to their advantage. For example, a social historian studying migrations in nineteenth-century Nigeria might look up the references of geographers, sociologists, and economists who have studied migrations in the contemporary period. These references in the work of social scientists might steer the social historian towards recognition of essential issues, perspectives, theories, and methodologies. This is helpful for the historian not originally trained to do social science but now compelled, as a social historian, to be half historian and half social scientist.

In reviewing relevant secondary sources and critically studying references, one must raise certain questions about what others have written. Some such questions are suggested by Tuchman:[22] Why is this author making this argument? Do other scholars dispute this argument? Why these particular materials, but not the others? Do the author's questions suggest other issues relevant to the project at hand? To answer such questions, one could check book reviews to see how the material under consideration was received.

Secondary sources do not contribute to the originality of one's work as the primary sources do. Tracking down primary historical data is very demanding, like doing detective work; it

> involves logic, intuition, persistence, and common sense—the same logic, intuition, persistence, and common sense that one would use to locate contemporary data or information pertinent to one' s daily life. For instance, if one needed a part for a refrigerator whose manufacturer had gone out of business, one would contact a specialist—an appliance service—to learn whether that firm has the part. If [it] does not, one might contact a series of appliance services. One will either find the part or learn that it is no longer available.[23]

The identification of and search for primary historical data has to follow this rigorous pattern. Thus searching for primary social historical data requires great perseverance and doggedness.

What are these primary sources that the social historian has to keep track of? The first are archival records. Many African states have National Archives that store different forms of raw data considered to be of invaluable importance to a social historian. These include official documents like annual reports, parliamentary papers, statistical surveys, population census reports, interdepartmental correspondences from which several social issues can be deciphered, intelligence reports of colonial and post-colonial state officials, reports of commissions of inquiry, petitions, etc. Most archives in Africa have past newspapers, periodicals, and journals a scholar could search for social historical data. In addition to these archives, which house general information about each country, some African communities have local archives. In Nigeria, for example, the archives of some state and local governments have information particular to their societies. Outside Africa, archives housing important documents on social developments in Africa include the Public Records Office in London, the Ministre d'outre-mer in Paris, the German Zentralarchiv in Potsdam, and others. There are also some African Studies associations and Institutes around the world that keep important information about the African continent. One needs to know these establishments and their holdings to write about some African social issues.

Information collected from archives as well as gleaned from secondary sources could suggest to the social historian what other information would be needed for writing one's paper. The sad truth, however, is that not much information can be found from written sources for writing the social history of Africans. The existing literature on Africans is about the hegemonic class, as noted above. Social history is more interested in the common folk, is about the social experience of everybody. As Ekechi has said, the ideas and emotions of the masses, the majority of the population, are not expressed in writing but in oral and artistic forms.[24] How then do we study the patterns of thought of the masses? They can more properly be studied through ethnographic and oral sources.

In using ethnographic sources, the historian is merely aping the anthropologists. Ethnography is the central method of anthropologists. Ethnographic traditions are a twentieth-century development, and their history is closely connected to the shift of fieldwork methods by which anthropologists in the late nineteenth century and early twentieth century came to base their work on firsthand information about the everyday life of the people they studied. Ethnography, as McNeil noted, simply means, "writing about a way of life." It is also referred to as "field study" or "field-work."[25] The main work of the ethnographer is to describe a people's way of life—the emphasis is on the people's culture and lifestyle, describing as faithfully as possible how the people see themselves. The work of Malinowski in the Trobriand Islands, especially, gave rise to this field method. Writing on the rigors of this method of sourcing data, Malinowski noted:

> The anthropologist must relinquish his comfortable position in the long chair on the verandah of the missionary compound, Government station, or planter's bungalow, where, armed with pencil and notebook and at times with a whisky and soda, he has been accustomed to collect statements from informants, write down stories, and fill out sheets of paper with savage texts. He must go into the villages, and see the natives at work in the gardens, on the beach, in the jungle. . . . Information must come to him full-flavoured from his own observations of native life, and not the squeezed out of reluctant informants as a trickle of talk. Field work can be done first or second hand even among the savages, in the middle of pile dwellings, not far from actual cannibalism and head-hunting. Open-air anthropology, as opposed to hearsay note-taking, is hard work, but it is also great fun. Only such anthropology can give us the all-round vision of primitive man and primitive culture.[26]

The relevance of ethnography to social historiography is evident in the fact that it enables the historian to have a feel for how the people have been living their lives. The historian is basically interested in the past. By observing how the people live today, the historian can extrapolate or ask relevant questions as to how they lived in the past. He can do this because he understands that the present is a product of the past. As Marc Bloch observed, one must first look at the present, or what was recently the present, in order to understand that past.[27]

Ethnography in the modern world is usually associated with and sometimes confused with "participant observation" by many students of African Studies. The two are not the same but are related, both being a uniquely humanistic, interpretive approach, as opposed to supposedly "scientific" and "positivist" positions. Within the ethnographic school, however, some scholars maintain "scientific" postures in their work. In practice, ethnography and participant observation methods are flexible. The work of those that embrace the "scientific" stance intertwine with those who reject such position in favor of advocacy and a critical stance.

Ethnographic methods rely in some aspects on participant observation. Ethnography as a practical social science method has the following features:[28]

1. a strong emphasis on exploring the nature of particular social phenomena, rather than setting out to test hypotheses about them;
2. a tendency to work primarily with "unstructured" data, that is, data that have not been coded at the point of data collection in terms of a closed set of analytic categories;
3. investigation of a small number of cases, perhaps just one case, in detail; and
4. analysis of data that involves explicit interpretation of the meanings and functions of human actions, the product of which mainly takes the form of verbal descriptions and explanations, with quantification and statistical analysis playing a subordinate role at most.

What the social historian adopting the ethnographic method looks at is not limited to patterns of day-to-day existence of the people but also visual objects like dressing codes, inscriptions on vehicles and walls, and so on. All these move the researcher closer to the inner world of those being researched.

Participant observation is often the primary field method of ethnographers. The former is just a method of data collection in an ethnographic research project. In their own work, Scwartz and Schwartz defined "participant observation" as "a process in which the observer's presence in a social situation is maintained for the purposes of scientific investigation."[29] What amount of time must the historian adopting this approach for sourcing data spend in the field? This question is popular with anthropologists themselves. Past attempts to answer it have led some scholars to say clearly that not all observations are "participant" observations. There may be both participant and nonparticipant observation in a fieldwork situation. As M. Stacey noted, the former involves the researcher joining, as a member, the group being studied[30] and thus functioning both as a member and as an observer of how the society or group conducts its affairs. In this case, the group is studied from inside. The latter, on the other hand, requires the researcher to operate as an outsider, not really belonging to the group in terms of seeking means of integrate with it but merely interacting with the group sometimes informally to gain access to information about its operations. Either method could be used in a research project, depending on the amount of participation sought by the researcher and what those being studied could guarantee.

Closely related to ethnography and participant observation is the oral method of sourcing data (see chapters 6 and 7 in this volume). Oral data can be divided into two types, oral traditions and oral testimonies. Oral traditions are verbally transmitted information handed down across several generations. These include myths, epics, legends, proverbs, songs, etc. Such data can only be collected from elderly people in African society because some of them are of esoteric importance. Oral testimonies, on the other hand, are orally transmitted information collected from the dramatis personae in some social events, or from people who were informed about the events. The persons providing oral testimonies talk about what they felt rather than what they were forced to believe by their culture. Such testimonies can be collected in an interview situation. More information about the interviewing methods of sourcing social historical data follows below.

Merely living among the research subjects and observing their lifestyles as the ethnographers do might not provide all the information that researchers need. They therefore have to proceed further, to ask questions on things that seem unclear to them. Indeed, researchers often go straight to the interview techniques without first engaging in any formal process of ethnography and participant observation. In a real life situation, however, it is not possible to interview without first observing. This is because the questions asked in research situations are always based on things observed but about which detailed information was not available.

As Fontana and Frey noted, asking questions and getting answers "is a much harder task than it may seem at first. . . . Yet, interviewing is one of the most common and most powerful ways we use to try to understand our fellow human beings."[31] In most cases, an interview entails face-to-face verbal interchange between the interviewer and interviewee. It could involve single individuals or a group. An interview could be a "once-for-all" exercise or could span several days, months, or even years.

In a typical interview session, the interviewer defines what the respondent(s) is going to talk about and what information will count as being relevant. The basic goal of an interview is to gain insight into people's experiences, opinions, aspirations, attitudes, and feelings. It requires a great deal of effort and skill to be able to do this. Interviews can be categorized into four major types according to how the questions are asked and answered. The four are:

1. Structured interview
2. Semi-structured interview

3. Unstructured or focused interview, and
4. Group interview.

The difference between the structured, semi-structured, and unstructured interviews could be seen in the mechanical shift from a situation in which the researcher attempts to control the interview through predetermining questions and thus teach the respondent to reply in accordance with the interview-schedule (standardization), to a situation in which the respondent is encouraged to answer a question in her or his own terms.[32] In a situation of structured interview, the researcher has absolute control over the response of the respondent whereas the unstructured interview situation empowers respondents to say what they want to say in the way they feel like saying it. Social historians often use the semi-structured and unstructured types of interviews.

The unstructured interview is also known as focused interviewing or open-ended ethnography. In this method, the interviewer does have a list of questions or topics to be investigated, but the way the questions are presented is quite discretionary. Unstructured interviewing is most suitable for topics on which depth of understanding rather than large-scale coverage is involved. Unstructured interviewing is relatively flexible; its emphasis is on discovery of meaning rather than the standardization sought by the structured interview method. It could even take the form of interviewing by comment.[33] The interviewer stimulates the interest of the respondent in a topic and encourages discussion of the topic, making it more likely that the necessary concealed facts are revealed. An unstructured interviewer gathers data gradually by posing unstructured questions as prompted by the field situation and the countenance of the interviewee. Unlike the structured interviewer, those conducting unstructured interviews allow their personal feelings to dictate the kind of questions they ask; they also answer questions the respondent might pose to them. It is a more flexible kind of interviewing, although more demanding than structured interviewing. A researcher doing unstructured interviewing must have some basic information about the subject under investigation and must therefore be able to pose all necessary questions that could give a better knowledge of the situation. As each question is posed, clues will appear that suggest other questions to ask. The interview could therefore last for several hours or days—depending on the clues the interviewer can decipher in the process of talking to the respondent. In most cases, unstructured interviewing challenges the researcher to further expand or narrow down the scope of the research. More, or possibly less, information than originally envisaged might result. This then forces an alteration of the original research focus or even the title of the project.

In collecting primary and secondary data, a social historian must be very inquisitive, critically examining every datum before taking it in. As Tuchman warned: Do not assume that anything about data is natural, inevitable, or even true.[34] To be sure, a datum has a physical presence: One may touch the page, picture, tombstone, or microfiche one has located. But that physical truth may be radically different from the interpretive truth needed to assess the application or test of a theory.

Problems of Interpretation

History is not just an assemblage of information about the past. The data have to be properly interpreted and given larger meaning than a layperson could readily apprehend from outside. After completion of fieldwork, the next major task for the social historian is therefore data interpretation. That a historian collected good data is not an absolute indication that good history will be written. Good history only flows from scientifically sound interpretation of good data. In the explanation process, the historian tries to unveil hidden meanings behind the available data. This is usually an invaluable but arduous task, given that the main goal of history is a pursuit of truth about past human situations and institutions. In interpreting data, the historian is not just shedding light but also searching for broader meanings for the research findings by linking them to other available knowledge. Such a search is geared towards two major objectives: to establish continuity in social research through linking the results of one study with those of another, and to identify new categories, explanatory concepts, and theories.[35]

Interpretation of the social events must be preceded and accompanied by some sort of abstract reasoning. To this extent, interpretation involves philosophical and theoretical issues. The general questions that the historian has to answer include "how?" "why?" and "how important?" In answering the question "how?" a narration is called for. This requires that the events be described. This kind of exercise is known as narrative history. However, answers to the question "why?" lead to analytical history,[36] with its emphasis on reasons or causes. Social history requires a combination of the narrative and analytical approaches.

Answering the question "how important?" requires the historian to situate the findings in a larger global context. Theoretical positions or generalizations could be very useful here. A social historian could therefore have recourse to Marxist, Weberian, feminist, modernist, and postmodernist interpretation of specific phenomena. Theories enable the social historian to easily apprehend patterns the mainstream or traditional historian could take for granted. This is another respect in which the social historian is forced to behave like a mainstream social scientist. The researcher's knowledge, imagination, and even wisdom is called into play here. Of course, it must be noted that social historians bring their own points of view to bear on an argument. The more interpretive social researchers are, the better able they are to interpret their data and the more development or policy-relevant their work becomes. It is within this framework that the work of social historians studying similar subject matters differs. Issues pertaining to women's development, for example, could be interpreted from either feminist or Marxist perspectives.

As is true of many western social historians or social scientists with respect to Africa, it is difficult to interpret when lacking good background knowledge, and it is difficult to produce a scientific piece about a people with whom you have had very little contact. The social life of Africans, like any other peoples, are rooted in their various cultures and traditions. Failure to understand a culture and tradition can only lead to a poor analysis of day-to-day lives. For example, issues like corruption or ethnicity in Africa are difficult to understand without a sound knowledge of the people's kinship system. A corrupt politician in Africa is more likely to be recognized as a hero in the community than as a social irritant, although the latter is probably closer to the truth. Members of the community see such a person as an ambassador who has gone to the larger world to bring home the community's fair share of the national cake. If such a politician is called to order according to the law of the country, local people allege persecution of their community. If removed from power, the people allege ethnic marginalization. Within this framework, it is necessary for the social historian to start work by acquiring the necessary background information about the people being studied.

Data interpretation does not need to start at the end of the field research. As perceptive investigators collect data, they do not turn off their intellects. Eyes and ears are opened to discern the happenings around them. Available data in the field must be critically examined in their own right. Perceptive historians should be able to identify and refuse to accept the biases of sources. Interpretations of immediate situations will enable them to ask more questions and collect more data from all possible sources, with a view to ensuring that the overall research results are scientifically sensible and plausible.

Interpretation of data in social history is more rigorous. The emphasis here is to refute or confirm claims, especially through the application of models. Interpretation facilitates an integrated understanding of human action. The historian is not satisfied just with what has been read, seen, or heard. He subjects everything to rigorous scrutiny by triangulating sources of information and subjecting information to the baptism of theoretical analysis. In the process, a social historian is able to move beyond the surface in accounting for past human actions. Imagine, for example, a social historian attempting to write on human rights in precolonial African society. Human rights is a twentieth-century concept in Africa. The historian writing about it using precolonial sources must be very perceptive, willing to test data against several human rights theories and models.

In attempting to reason beyond the surface, a social historian would not, for example, accept several conclusions reached by those who wrote on the precolonial African states, kingdoms, and empires. These polities were presented as models. Within what context? We were not told. Is a kingdom great just because of its mere existence, or because it was able to meet the needs of the people in it? There were many of these empires. In the Western Sudan, for example, were Ghana, Mali, Songhai, among others. As one empire fell, another was founded. Social historians are interested in rigorous debate of what led to the fall of the empires and kingdoms. Were they badly managed? What can the present learn from this kind of situation? Another example is the quality of leadership provided by precolonial African leaders like Sonni Ali, Mansa Musa, Askia the Great, Idris Aloma, etc. All these people were presented as great leaders. But it is difficult to understand the context within which these people could be said to be great. Were they visionary leaders, mediocre, or opportunists? A reinterpretation of what was said about them by a social historian shows clearly that they were the opposite of what past writers (most especially the political historians) considered them to be. This probably explains why nobody can uphold any of them today as exemplars of morality, accountability, and good governance. Let us take a look at some of the problems as presented by A. E. Afigbo:

> [H]istory books write approvingly of Askia Muhammad Ture, of his Jihads and pilgrimage but gloss over his failure to know when to quit the political stage on grounds of age. Blind and decrepit, he had to be

removed in coup d'etat led by his own children when he was 85 years old. In our own day we have become familiar with this kind of refusal on the part of African leaders to relinquish power with good grace. . . . Mansa Musa spent . . . wealth with such thoughtless abandon that he created an inflationary crisis in Egypt, while he himself ran out of money while still in the Holy Land and had to borrow money from an Alexandrian financier to pay his way back.

. . . If Mansa Musa's recklessness continues to be played up as having advertised the brilliance of the Western Sudan in his time, then we should stop complaining when our contemporary leaders buy up villas in Spain and elsewhere, stack up millions in Swiss banks.[37]

What past writers on the precolonial African kingdom and empires succeeded in telling us is that precolonial African societies were well organized and led by some prominent individuals. One wonders if any of the volumes written actually came out in any concrete form to dispel Trevor-Roper's characterization of African social life as "unrewarding gyrations of barbarous tribes in picturesque but irrelevant corners of the globe." The point being made is that all of African history must be reinterpreted taking into consideration social concerns. Social history has a social commitment to help ensure that past problems are not repeated. The kind of nationalist history that was written in the past hid a lot about the African past. Sick people do not get healed by pretending to be well, nor by not knowing they are sick. The genteel euphemisms that characterized the nationalist history of Africa are no longer sufficient for the present.

The above notwithstanding, African social problems must first be interpreted from the African perspective before any other perspectives. The African world is not always as the occidentals see it. Western writers often caricature the African systems. Africans are said to be corrupt, politically inept, environmentally deplorable, and so on—yet people from the same Western societies created some of the problems. But this hardly gets mentioned in the analysis of African problems. History is about truth. The pursuit of the truth, as Smith noted,[38] requires both a setting aside of all prejudice, so far as possible, and the exercise of empathy, the sensitive and imaginative effort to understand past societies and events in their own terms. Smith tried to shed better light on this in his process of discussing the question why, in history,

the historian is rarely, almost never, content to adduce only one explanatory factor. Even though he may conclude that one factor far outweighs all others in bringing about the explanandum, he will look for other factors which interacted with, delayed, stimulated, or perhaps triggered off his grand single factor. But it is much more usual to find that a multiplicity of factors must be adduced, each in itself the result of a separate chain of development. To master all this material, classification is required, and such familiar labels as political, economic, ideological and the like play their [overlapping] parts. But containing and transcending all such divisions, the historian needs, consciously or unconsciously, openly or by stylistic concealment, to categorise his material according to the different levels at which it occurs.[39]

Writing on competing approaches the historian could adopt for explaining or interpreting data, Smith noted that the following should be distinguished:

1. Long-term [or situational or dispositional or underlying] factors, which brought about a situation in which *y* became possible.
2. Medium-term or median factors which brought about a situation in which *y* became probable.
3. Occasions, precipitants or triggers, the factors [which in this case are nearly always the actions of one person or more] which made *y* all but certain—all but certain rather than certain because bullets may go wide, fuses may die out before reaching the powder barrel, and so on.[40]

The historian must also establish the order of importance of the factors he adduces.

Social historians of Africa must therefore clearly separate between the internal and external catalysts of change in Africa. Africa having experienced colonialism, and still experiencing a period of neocolonialism, it is urgent that the social historian look beyond Africa, for example, for the explanation of the problems in the continent. Those writing about corruption in Africa collect hardly any data about the Western world in which the stolen moneys are kept. They hardly interrogate the developed civilization that makes it convenient to accommodate blood money from Africa. They hardly say anything about the Western companies that serve as couriers to those taking the money outside the African continent. When some Western writers talk about the political crisis in Africa, the Western scholars hardly mention the support corrupt and inept African political leaders get from the outside world against the hapless and helpless masses as long as the affected African leaders satisfy the narrow interest of some Western powers. Several other examples can be cited. Social history is about the masses; if carefully interviewed, the African masses will openly deny some of the things the international world claimed to have contributed to African development. A single-cause explanation of African problems must stop if we are really interested in writing an objective social history of Africa. By a single-cause explanation is meant the explanation of a historical event or situation by only or primarily one single factor (cause), whether that factor is material, spiritual, or elemental.[41] The African past must not be distorted or oversimplified.

Notes

1. R. O. Collins, *Problems in African History* (Englewood Cliffs, NJ., 1968), 1.

2. E. A. Ayandele, "The task before Nigerian historians today," *Journal of the Historical Society of Nigeria* 9, no. 4 (June 1979); F. Ekechi, "The future of the history of ideas in Africa," *African Studies Review*, 30, no. 2 (June 1987): 63–82; M. H. Dawson, "The social history of Africa in the future: medical-related issues," *African Studies Review* 30, no. 2 (1987): 83–91.

3. E. J. Hobsbawn, "From social history to the history of society," *Daedalus* (Winter 1971): 24.

4. J. F. A. Ajayi, "A critique of themes preferred by Nigerian historians," *Journal of the Historical Society of Nigeria* 10, no. 3 (1980): 33–40.

5. R. Hallet, *Africa Since 1875* (London: Heinemann, 1974).

6. M. H. Dawson, "The social history of Africa in the future: medical-related issues," *African Studies Review* 30, no. 2 (1987): 83–91.

7. K. M. Phiri, "African history: An assessment and an agenda for future research," *African Studies Review* 30, no. 2 (1987): 35–48.

8. Ajayi, "A critique of themes preferred by Nigerian historians," 36–37.

9. J. F. A. Ajayi, "Introduction," *Tarikh*, vol. 9: *History and the Social Sciences* (Ikeja, Nigeria: Longman Nigeria Limited, 1990), 1; I. A. Akinjogbin, and S. O. Osoba, "Preface," in I. A. Akinjogbin, and S. O. Osoba (eds.), *Topics on Nigerian Economic and Social History* (Ile-Ife: University of Press Ltd., 1980), i; A. E. Afigbo, "The Poverty of Contemporary African Historiography," Public Lecture delivered under the auspices of the Institute of African Studies, University of Ibadan, 1976.

10. O. E. Uya, *African History: Some Problems in Methodology and Perspectives* (Cornell University Press, 1974).

11. H. R. Trevor-Roper, "The rise of Christian Europe," *Listener*, November 28, 1963, 13.

12. J. F. A. Ajayi, "Historical education in Nigeria," *Journal of the Historical Society of Nigeria* 8, no. 1 (1975): 3–8.

13. C. Ake, "History as the future of social science," *Tarikh*, vol. 9: *History and the Social Sciences* (Ikeja, Nigeria: Longman Nigeria Limited, 1990), 19–27.

14. Afigbo, "The Poverty of Contemporary African Historiography," 7.

15. Ajayi, "Introduction," 1; H. Bernstein and J. Depelchin, "The object of African history: A materialist perspective," *History in Africa* 5 (1978): 1–19, and 6 (1979): 17–42;

B. Freud, *The Making of Contemporary Africa: The Development of African Society since 1800* (Bloomington: Indiana University, 1982).

16. Edward Hallett Carr, *What is History?* (London: Penguin, 1983), 15; Carr was criticizing nineteenth-century European historians.

17. B. E. Schmitt, *The Fashion and Future of History: Historical Studies and Addresses* (Cleveland, Ohio: Press of Western Reserve University, 1960).

18. Ajayi, XXXX.

19. K. Denzin and Yvonna S. Lincoln (eds.), *Collecting and Interpreting Qualitative Materials* (Thousand Oaks, CA: Sage Publications, 1998).

20. CODESRIA Bulletin, Nos. 2 and 3, 1989, *African History: Perspectives for Tomorrow*, 6–15.

21. G. Tuchman, "Historical Social Science: Methodologies, Methods and Meanings," in K. Denzin and Yvonna S. Lincoln (eds.), *Strategies of Qualitative Inquiry* (Thousand Oaks, CA: Sage Publications, 1998).

22. Ibid., 251.

23. Ibid., 252.

24. Ekechi, "The future of the history of ideas in Africa," 66.

25. P. McNeill, *Research Methods* (Routledge: London and New York, 1989), 64.

26. B. Malinowski, *Argonauts of the Western Pacific* (London: Routledge and Kegan Paul, 1922), quoted in N. Polsky, *Hustlers, Beats and Others* (New York: Aldine, 1985).

27. M. Bloch, *French Rural History: An Essay on its Basic Characteristics*, trans. Janet Sonddheimer (Berkeley and Los Angeles: University of California, 1970), xxvi.

28. P. Atkinson, and M. Hammersley, "Ethnography and Participant Obervations," in Denzin and Lincoln (eds.), *Strategies of Qualitative Inquiry*, 10–11.

29. M. S. Scwartz and C. G. Schwartz, "Problems in participant observation," *American Journal of Sociology* (1954–55): 344.

30. M. Stacey, *Methods of Social Research* (Oxford: Pergamon Press, 1969).

31. A. Fontana, and J. H. Frey, "Interviewing: The art of science," in Denzin and Lincoln (eds.), *Collecting and Interpreting Qualitative Materials*, 47.

32. Ibid., 110.

33. D. A. Snow, L. A. Zurcher, and G. Sjoberg, "Interviewing by comment: an adjunct to the direct question," *Qualitative Sociology* 5 (1982): 285–311.

34. Tuchman, "Historical Social Science," 256.

35. C. Selltiz, et al., *Research Methods in Social Relations* (New York: Holt, Rinehart and Winston, 1959).

36. R. Smith, "Explanation in African History: How and Why," *Tarik* 21, vol. 6, no. 1: *Historical Method* (Essex: Longman Group Limited, 1978), 3.

37. A. E. Afigbo, "Reflections on the History Syllabus in Nigerian Universities," *Journal of the Historical Society of Nigeria* 8, no. 1 (1975): 9–18.

38. Smith, "Explanation in African History, 1.

39. Ibid., 3.

40. Ibid., 4.

41. A. E. Afigbo, "Monocausal explanations in African history: A prevalent distortion," *Tarik* 21, vol. 6, no. 1: *Historical Method* (Essex: Longman Group Limited, 1978).

12

AFRICAN ECONOMIC HISTORY

APPROACHES TO RESEARCH

Masao Yoshida

Discussion of Research Themes

I would like to take up four themes here that I think cover most of the recent African historiography, and which I believe would examine various African economic history subjects from different angles. Short discussions of each of these subjects will be made so that a student of African history could refer his or her subject of study to wider scholastic achievements that are available as books and journal articles. After such examination, I will take up the problems of how to search for evidence to support the expositions.

In doing this I must say that some rather important subjects had to be omitted, such as the ones dealing with predominantly early phase of economic life of hunter/gatherers or transmigrant livestock herders. These together with subsistence agriculture have been important economic activities of life sustenance. However, we should not assume the present state of agriculture in Africa to be predominantly subsistent in nature. An economic historian recently warned that "African agriculture is still described as 'shifting' and African economies characterized as 'subsistence' by many authors, despite persuasive critiques of these concepts by others."[1]

Precolonial and Colonial Trade

Under this theme, we can include various local trades such as trading done by primarily subsistence type of communities in commodities like salt and iron, which, due to the unavailability of the natural resources, the communities themselves could not produce. However, these are necessities and had to be obtained by barter or with money, or by other forms of transactions.

The major theme of precolonial trade in Africa is that of long-distance trade. This kind of trade in the first half of the second millennium (900–1500 C.E.) was so important that Catherine Coquery-Vidrovitch once called the long-distance trade the basic characteristic of "African Mode of Production."[2] The trans-Saharan caravan trade and its control by kingdoms established along the southern fringe of the Sahara Desert (the area called Sahel) is a subject of many economic as well as cultural historical studies. The examinations as to what were the material bases on which such kingdoms as ancient-Ghana, Mali, Songhai, Kanem/Bornu, and others flourished are still going on, and it is still debated whether the wealth of these kingdoms came from the direct control of gold trade, which was exchanged with salt and the Mediterranean goods, or by imposing tribute on the inhabitants of the subjected territories.

Importance of long-distant trade is not confined to the Sahelian area. It also includes the Indian Ocean coastal area. The city-state of Kilwa which controlled the gold trade coming from Zimbabwe, and later city-states of Mogadishu, Kismayu, Mombasa, and Zanzibar, etc. flourished by controlling the Indian Ocean trading with the Arabian peninsula and India. It is, however, to be noted that the long-distance trade became possible for these city-states because it was accompanied with the development of regional trade of foodstuffs and other items of subsistence nature with their hinterlands.[3] Apparently they could not flourish without eating food.

The first contact between sub-Saharan Africa and Europe came with a tragic type of long-distant trade, namely, the trans-Atlantic slave trade. The nature and the magnitude of this trade, and its effects on both African societies and Europe, have been studied by many historians as well as by politicians, and the search for truth is still going on. In recent years the importance of this subject has shifted to the black-Diaspora studies, and the economic situations of the black-Diaspora have begun to be examined.

Since the 1970s, the period immediately after the trans-Atlantic slave trade (or in actual fact in the terminal phase of that slave trade) has come to be studied under the name of the legitimate trade.[4] The importance of this period was highlighted because the notion of imperialism, explained by Hobson and Lenin as the period following the age of liberalism and characterized by monopoly capitalism, came to be seriously challenged. Many studies with new empirical data showed that the European merchant capital in the years before the 1870s was more responsible in expanding the sphere of European influence in Africa.[5] Thus the nature of European trade development with Africa during the age of legitimate trade came to the focus of attention, and the studies on competition among the trading houses and on the actors of these trading activities have become favorite subjects by economic historians.

The partition of Africa and the resultant institutionalization of colonial rules have set the scene for expanded yet controlled activities of trade, and Africa was incorporated into the world-wide trading network. In simple terms, Africa became the provider of some raw materials for European industries, and tropical food and beverages for European appetite. Africa became a market for European manufactured products although that market was never as big as India or China. The dominance of metropolitan products was threatened sometimes by newly industrialized countries. A good example is the case of East Africa in the 1930s, as the Congo Basin Treaty of 1919 prevented England from imposing differential tariffs for non-British goods, which caused the defeat of cotton products of Lancashire against the trade competition of Japanese cotton products.[6]

Many studies of international trade concerning colonial Africa focused their attentions on the operations of metropolitan commercial and trading firms. The best example of this category of research can be found in Kathleen Stahl's *The Metropolitan Organization of British Colonial Trade*, which focuses on East Africa.[7] The West African case can be found in A. G. Hopkins's, *An Economic History of West Africa*, and in a study on a single giant enterprise, the United Africa Company, written by D. K. Fieldhouse.[8] Biographies of commercial entreprenuers are good source of information. Among these, we can find a few examples of Indian and Lebanese entreprenuers—for instance in N. K. Mehta's autobiography, *Dream Half-Expressed*, and Fuad Khury's journal article "Kinship, Emigration and Trade Partnership among the Lebanese of West Africa."[9] Trading organizations within Africa, under the colonial situation touching on the African traders, are described in P. T. Bauer's *West African Trade*.[10]

Rural and Agricultural Development

The share of agriculture in the total economic activities can be described as dominant in most of the African countries south of the Sahara. Although a few countries' exports may be concentrated in minerals, and a few countries like South Africa have developed manufacturing sector with high shares in their countries' GDP (Gross Domestic Product), agriculture remains the most important economic sector in the occupational distribution of manpower, the share in GDP, and in the export incomes, even at the end of the twentieth century.

The main characteristic of sub-Saharan agriculture is that its production is borne by small-holding peasant type of farmers. Plantation type of agriculture is not as important as in Southeast Asia or in Central America, and Settlers came in with considerable numbers during the colonial period only in a few countries such as Angola, Mozambique, South Africa, Zimbabwe, and Kenya. The analysis of the development of peasant agriculture is thus crucially important in the study of African economic history.

In Africa, the land areas as well as a number of peasant farmers have usually not been measured, and are not accurately known. The production figures are notoriously inaccurate, as will be discussed later. They present serious problems in trying to analyze peasant production, as economic studies rely very much on figures. The only obtainable figures on agriculture are for agriculture for exports, as these figures can be recorded by the government at the exit points where the registering of figures is often required by law. Commercial firms also keep records of their purchases and sales of export crops. However, the most important data for analyzing the development of peasant agriculture are those relating to the amount of production for subsistence and for cash earnings, and the amount of land and labor used for such production.[11] If these figures are not available at the national, provincial, and district level, we have to rely on the case studies done at the local level, mainly as household rural surveys, and use them after compounding the figures of many households to arrive at the conclusion.

There has been debate on the character of peasant production, and whether peasant farmers are mainly self-sufficient and therefore not captured by market forces or by government coercion, or are already taken in by the market forces to such an extent that there is no exit option for them even when the market forces are adversely affecting them by, for instance, falling market prices for their products.[12] There are also debates concerning the differentiation process among the peasant farmers so that class differences are appearing. These debates are concerned with the availability of empty land or surplus labor at the peasant farmers' command. It seems that the peasants in Africa are highly mobile, and this aspect has been explored to explain why the peasant class differentiation has been slow in coming, while the export production by the indigenous farmers in Africa has progressed so rapidly.[13] This in turn raises the question as to whether these farmers who migrated to the virgin land should rather be called capitalist farmers!

Closely tied to this examination of peasant farmers is the question of land tenure and land use. It has been observed that the land holding systems in most parts of sub-Saharan Africa are communal types of land tenure where the right to occupy land is derived from a membership of a community. They have a right to occupy, cultivate, and inherit land as long as they are recognized as members of a particular community. The communal land tenure has been regulated according to the traditional authorities exercising influence in the area, but such authorities have changed their characters through the history of colonial and postcolonial administrative rules.

Also the penetration of monetary economy has changed the attitude of the peasant farmers to such an extent that the leasing of land by individuals is now very common, and even the outright sales of land have emerged. Because of this trend, and of the desire to accelerate the agricultural development, the post-independence governments are eager to introduce individual types of land tenure, and provide a legal framework for individual transactions of land. Kenya has instituted the individual freehold tenure since the end of the colonial period, but due to the complexities of overlapping customary land rights, and possible high political cost for the land tenure reform, most countries have not touched the communal land tenure systems and have been content with minor changes, such as recognizing widows' land rights through court decisions. Sometimes conversion to leasehold under government ownership has been instituted for those lands occupied mainly by foreign settlers and commercial enterprises. There are many different views on the effects of a particular land tenure system on agricultural development, and since there has been much evolution of land tenure practices even under essentially communal type, many case studies are needed at local levels to understand this institutional aspects of economic development.[14]

African land problems are increasingly taken up in relation to the natural environment issues. The rapid increase of the rural population coupled with commercialization of agriculture came to be viewed as a danger to the ecological balance, especially when such a development caused the destruction of the forest cover. The understanding of the ecological control has become an important subject of economic history study recently, and we may see a further increase in the study of this theme in the future.[15]

Emergence of Indigenous Capitalism

There has recently been renewed emphasis on the question of whether an indigenous capitalism had grown up in Africa, and as to what its characters are if it has existed in the area south of the Sahara. When the dependency theory was current among the economic historians, the idea that the periphery capitalism would always remain dependent on the center was strong, and the only rational choice for the Africans should be "socialism," as former President Nyerere of Tanzania proposed. Certainly these views were the reflection of the ideologies of the African independence movement,[16] the colonial regime's ruling everywhere was to put Africans in one category and deny them opportunities to move upwards economically and politically.[17] However, after more than a quarter century of independence for most countries, and after the economic disaster of those who chose the state-managed planned economies, and in the face of economic marginalization by the onslaught of globalization, a fresh attempt to evaluate indigenous capitalism has to be made by the economic historians who have concerns about Africa.

As J. Iliffe has stated, there have been many rich and dynamic African businessmen. But in order to say that capitalism is firmly established, it has to qualify for the condition of "the production of goods for exchange by capitalists who combine their capital and land with labour power which they buy from free and property-less workers."[18] However, Africa came into contact with capitalism in comparatively recent years, and although the essence of capitalism is the same anywhere, the actual flesh may have distinctive shapes and qualities in Africa, if I may borrow the words of Iliffe. The examination of this distinctiveness is the task for economic historians.

The first area to be examined, whether capitalist relations have emerged or not, is in the rural and agricultural sector. As I stated before, this is the dominant economic sector in Africa. However, here the existence of communal land tenure or even the feudal type of landlord/tenant system that existed in a few places prevented the full growth of capitalist relations in this sector. The migrant cocoa farmers of Southern Ghana seemed to have embarked on the road to capitalism only to move towards the "abusa" system, a kind of share-cropping system with tenant farmers retaining the option to obtain the land eventually.[19] The landlord/tenant system of the Buganda area of Uganda was altered by the British policy of favoring the tenants by fixing the rent at a very low level, and encouraging the tenants to start producing cash crops within the Mailo land system.[20] The only places with a good possibility of seeing the emergence of capitalist farmers seem to be the settler-economy areas in Kenya and Zimbabwe, where after independence Africans were allowed to buy large farms that European settlers used to own, and inherited the same type of capitalistic farming operations.[21] It must be noted that many of these

African buyers were high-ranking government officials who had advantages in accumulation of wealth and in the access to credit facilities.

The next thing to examine is the craftsmen or craft production as the possible source of indigenous capitalists. Quite well-developed crafts productions are observable in the cities of the Sahel area of West Africa. One of the craft centers here is Kano in Nigeria, and according to Iliffe, Kano's production of indigo-dyed cotton cloth was the most important craft industry in sub-Saharan Africa.[22] He tells us that a study based on oral interviews revealed that some Kano cloth merchants invested in new dye-pits and began to hire cheap migrant laborers in the late nineteenth century. However, the merchants "were never able to penetrate the cloth-beating trade, for the beaters were highly skilled men—and they worked in small, tight-knit, cooperative groups which retained control of their occupation into the twentieth century."[23] These studies of craft production seem to negate the possibility of the growth of indigenous capitalism based on craft production, but this is still inconclusive.

Another source of indigenous capitalism could well be found in the business of transport. Transport business was preceded by porterage in the precolonial period, and was one of the enterprises which was easy to enter in terms of technology. In the colonial period, porters were the earliest form of wage labor. After the automobile came to be used as the main tool of transportation, Africans quickly moved in to own lorries for transporting agricultural products and manufactured goods, using hired drivers. P. Kennedy says that "from the 1920s onwards—although much more so from the mid 1940s—indigenous owners ran small haulage firms, buses and taxis."[24] As the trunk roads have been improved in the post-independence years, transportation business became the easiest method to get rich quickly.

Other important spheres of enterprise for indigenous peoples were the various trading activities, especially of foodstuffs. Kennedy also tells of these activities as follows: "the economic expansion . . . gave a strong boost to certain kinds of trading in foodstuffs such as fish, yams and other staple crops while the long-distance trade in kola nuts and cattle, between the forest and savannah areas of West Africa also increased dramatically."[25] Women have also been able to play a leading role in many aspects of this kind of trading, especially in the forest area of West Africa, although gender issues are often taken up in relation to the patriarchy domination within the context of development of capitalism.[26]

The emergence of capitalism cannot be studied unless the creation of working class is addressed. Much of the earlier studies of industrialization in Africa pointed out the characteristics of African labor as migrant and casual. They are migrants from their rural homes, coming for a short duration to earn cash either to pay taxes or to supplement their agricultural incomes, and they eventually go back to their rural homes. Some economic studies inquired into the origin of such labor, and found that the compulsory labor recruitment by the colonial governments for construction purposes was important. However, most studies dealt with the recruitment practices by the plantation owners or mining enterprises for institutionalizing migrant labor. The enterprises opted for the short-term employment as the nature of work was unskilled, and they could get away with minimum wages for these laborers as they did not have to take care of the reproduction costs of decent and permanent living.[27]

However, as such industries as manufacturing, which need some trained and skilled laborers, have started to develop, permanently employed laborers began to increase who are paid the full reproduction costs. Under these circumstances, many rural migrants moved to the cities where such employment opportunities became available. In Kenya, since 1954, official policy was "theoretically aimed at stabilizing the urban labor force by raising urban wages to a level capable of supporting worker's families. However, at the end of the 1960s the great majority of urban workers were still essentially migrant workers."[28]

It was in the 1940s that the labor union movement started in earnest in British, French, and even Portuguese colonies. Labor movements were helped by the metropolitan labor organizations, which often had their colonial bureaus. The colonial governments feared that the labor unions might turn to political issues, and responded with both repression against strikes and positive programs fostering nonpolitical types of trade unionism.[29] After these colonies gained independence, the governments often unified the existing labor unions under their control, prohibited strikes, and instead gave them formalized wage negotiation process and arbitration tribunals, fixing rather generous minimum wages, and making allowance for a greater employed labor force. For instance, Tanzania legislated wide-ranging labor laws in 1962 and 1964 along these lines,[30] and Kenya instituted the tripartite agreement between the government, labor unions, and the Federation of Kenya Employers to control the labor dispute, with the same aims mentioned above.[31]

The main aim of this control of the labor movement was to attract foreign direct investment as well as to encourage the foreign and domestic capital to form joint ventures with parastatal enterprises, but it encouraged rather generous wage levels, and very probably increased rural exodus, swelling the urban population. As the pace of urbanization quickened, this formal-type employment could not absorb the influx of job-seekers, and most of those seeking regular jobs failed and had to survive with various menial work which constituted the so-called informal sector in cities.[32] While the organized labor, or at least its upper stratum, came to be called the "labor aristocracy" by some scholars, the rapidly increasing urban poor whose number has not even been ascertained, has become a permanent feature of the cities. After the ILO invented the term "informal sector," there were many studies that attempted to place this informal sector in the context of the development of capitalism in Africa.[33]

Market and State

From precolonial through colonial and postcolonial period government has always intervened in the market in order to obtain revenue and for other purposes. Thus the extent and the mode of government intervention constitute an important aspect of the economic history study. The economic policies of a government can be understood mostly in terms of this intervention into the market, whether that market is about the agricultural, mineral, or manufacturing products, or input goods, or about their transportation, or about their finance.

After the achievement of independence, the state's need to raise revenue was eagerly advocated. New taxes were introduced, such as pay-as-you-earn income taxes, or consumers' taxes like purchase taxes, or in recent years the value-added taxes (VAT). Power of the state bureaucrats was enormously increased, both as planners of marketing controls and as receivers of tax revenues.

As R. H. Bates explains, the state-sponsored capitalism flourished from the 1960s to the middle of the 1980s.[34] The state appropriated funds by price-fixing, and controlled agricultural marketing channels. Almost every African government after independence tried to promote industrial development, and their preferred method of promotion was to create import-substitution industries, whether they were producers of cigarettes, shoes, bottled beers, textiles, corrugated iron-sheets, or more sophisticated manufactures. For these industries, governments offered protection against foreign competition with high import tariffs and sometimes with total import restriction. Often some enterprises were given the monopoly of the domestic markets. Competition was severely curtailed under these conditions, and the productivities of these protected industries tended to decrease and not increase. Moreover, under these bureaucratic industrialization processes, corruption charges against many high-ranking bureaucrats became a big political issue.

The international economic trend was also very harmful to these African industrialization attempts. Two oil shocks of the 1970s hit African countries especially hard. Faced with the worsening of international balance of payments, and the resultant international debt accumulation, the African governments were mostly obliged to accept the "structural adjustment programs" designed by the World Bank/IMF initiatives. The relations between market and state were now fundamentally altered. The power of the state was severely curtailed, and free market economy became the overwhelming principle. The price fixing and industrial subsidies were abolished, foreign exchanges were freed, government expenditures were curtailed, and the parastatal enterprises were wound up and privatized.[35] Private business initiatives have been released by this market economy regimes, but the vulnerable sectors of the society, like the poor, handicapped, and underprivileged bore the brunt of these policy changes.[36] The external trade balance seems not to have improved since these economic liberalization policies started, and the accumulated external debts remain a heavy burden for the African countries almost without exception.[37] What all these recent development will have on the course of the emergent indigenous capitalism in Africa remains to be seen.

Where to Search for Evidence

Written Documents

The previous discussion of the various themes of the African economic history could give some guidance for deciding what topic to choose and how to approach it. These referred books and the articles can give clues about the kind of documents that would be very useful in examining the problems, and supporting one's arguments.

Usually, at the end of the books and articles, there is a list of written sources, or bibliography. This bibliography serves as a guide that might show where the written evidence can be found, and might lead to unexpected treasure mines. Sometimes footnotes give useful clues where one should search for evidence to support one's cases.

For the period when there was no indigenous writings to describe the social and economic conditions of the people, like much of the precolonial sub-Saharan African history, one has to rely on archeological evidence, or the written sources of the travelers, who were usually short-time sojourners. Oral traditions are increasingly used recently, but care must be taken to ascertain their socioeconomic accuracy, as they are sometimes very politically charged narratives that praise or discredit certain persons or groups of people. It is easier to use oral tradition for political history than for economic history.

Arabs have left many documentary sources on the long-distance trade, whether trans-Saharan or Indian Ocean trade. When the Europeans arrived in Africa, first by Portuguese and Spanish, and later by Dutch, French, English, American, and even by Danish, Swedish, and Brandenburg peoples along the African coast, documentary sources became much more available. But here also the available sources were long written by outsiders. One of the first written documents by the indigenous people about their social and economic conditions is said to be that of Olaudah Equiano, an Ibo who was taken to Europe and who wrote his autobiography in 1789, although his book may have been preceded by a few years by a book written by Ottobah Cugoano, a former slave who was sent to Grenada and England from an area presently in Ghana.[38] For the study of slave trade and so-called legitimate trade, many records of ships' cargo, and port statistics, as well as the writings of ships' captains, have been used to estimate the total amount of trade figures.[39]

When it comes to the colonial period, a huge amount of written documents becomes available. Colonial offices of the metropolitan powers documented their activities and published them as reports or kept them in files in their offices. Laws and directives were promulgated and were published in government gazettes. All these are very fruitful sources for historical research. Great Britain had a tradition of establishing a legislative council in each of its territory in the early stage of colonial rule, and the debates that took place there are recorded and published by *Hansard*. This is a very good source of documentary evidence for ascertaining the problems that occurred and the way they were treated.

Another good source of examining the troubles encountered by the colonial administration is the published report of the commission of inquiry. Typically, the British colonial administration inquired into the cause of, say, disturbances, whenever they occurred, by appointing a commission of inquiry and acting on the findings of this report. Many reports were made available to the public from Her Majesty's Stationary Office (HMSO), with the serial numbering of colonial office. Most commission reports just served to adjust and prolong the colonial rule, but occasionally some commission reports radically altered the course of events, and served to weaken the colonial rule itself.[40]

Many colonial government documents, especially Provincial and District government reports and memoranda, can be found in the national archives after the colonies became independent. Various departmental reports can be found in the respective ministerial libraries. Thus for instance, the department of agriculture annual reports can be found in the library of the ministry of agriculture. This is at least the case in the former British colonies. I have very little knowledge of the former French, Belgium, and Portuguese, and pre-World War II German colonies, but it is probably the case that the colonial documents are mostly kept in the metropolitan countries.[41] Not many colonial documents are kept in the archives of the independent countries with good catalogues, except in some countries of former British colonies. In some special cases, a university library became the deposit library of the colonial government documents. An example is the Makerere University Library in Uganda, which used to be the depository of the East African colonial government documents. When I had the privilege of using the Africana section of Makerere library in the 1960s as a Ph.D. student of the University of East Africa, the place was like a treasure mine.

In order to undertake economic analysis, statistical data are indispensable. When African countries became independent, they usually published an economic survey every year as a background for a government budget proposal. This survey is very useful for the macro-analysis of the country, because it has all the basic statistics not only for that particular year but also for the past few years. Besides, the survey usually contains the analysis of the state of affairs in each sector of the country's economy. Also the statistics bureau of a country occasionally publishes a statistical abstract. Various ministries of the government publish their own statistical reports. The statistics related to the population are published following the year when a national population census is undertaken, but the publication for the public may be delayed for several years. In some countries, notably Nigeria, population census became such a hot political issue that the census-taking exercise had to be annulled many times after 1973. This means that even such a basic figures as population must be roughly estimated, and the result is that widely different figures are being used.

For the production figures of the most important sector of the African economy, namely foodstuffs, the statistics are notoriously inaccurate. Many countries have very rough estimated figures for such staple foodstuffs as maize, rice, sorghum, millet, beans, cassava, yam, and plantain banana. Sometimes, the only available figures for these foodstuffs are the marketed volumes and prices through statutory marketing organizations (usually so-called parastatals), as they are obligated to submit the figures to the government. The wide differentials exist even among the government estimates of production figures, as are exemplified in the following maize production statistics of Tanzania (see table 12.1).

Table 12.1. Statistics of Maize Production in Tanzania

Unit: 1000 ton

Crop Year	61/62	62/63	63/64	64/65	65/66	66/67	67/68	68/69	69/70	70/71	71/72	72/73
Most likely figure	457	475	738	589	513	739	551	638	488	719	621	887
A	457	508	648	660	559	1150	800	1000	536	650	650	984
B												
C	457	475	738	589	513	739	551	638	488	719	621	887
D												
E												
F					518	920	643	700	616	758	765	914
G												980
H												
I												

Table 12.1. (*Continued*)

						Unit: 1000 ton						
Crop Year	73/74	74/75	75/76	76/77	77/78	78/79	79/80	80/81	81/82	82/83	83/84	84/85
Most likely figure	761	1367	1449	1664	1465	1720	1726	1839	1654	1651	1939	2093
A	800	550	900	1619	968	1000	900	800	750	800	2000	1131
B					1610	1888	1855	1840	1954	2324	2547	1860
C	761	1367	1449	1664	1465	1720	1726	1839	1654	1651	1939	2093
D									1402	1740	1712	2013
E												
F	893	858	1103	1150	1182	1298	1317	517				
G	750	750	825	897	968	1000	900	800				
H											1939	2093
I												2093

Table 12.1. (*Continued*)

Unit: 1000 ton

Crop Year	85/86	86/87	87/88	88/89	89/90	90/91	91/92	92/93	93/94	94/95	95/96	96/97	97/98
Most likely figure	2211	2359	2339	3128	2445	2331	2226	2282	2159	2567	2663	1832	2750
A	2093	2359	2339	3159	2445	2332	2226	2284	2159	2567	2638	2107	2750
B	2671	2245	2423	2428	2227	2332	2226	2282	1813				
C	2211	2359	2339	3128	2445	2331	2111						
D	2671												
E	2671	2245	2423	2528	2227	2332	2111	2364					
F													
G													
H	2211	2359	2339										
I	2211	2359	2339	3128	2445	2331	2226	2282	2159	2567	2663	1832	2750

Source A : FAO Production Year book, based on previous year's production.

B : Bank of Tanzania, Economic Bulletin for the Quarter ended 30 September 1994, Table 3.9.

C : Tanzania Economic Trends, Vol. 6, No. 1/2, Statistical Appendix Table 12(a), 13.

D : Planning and Marketing Division, MALD, Tanzania, Basic Data, Agriculture and Livestock Sector (198 1/82–198 5/86).

E : Planning and Marketing Division, MALD, Tanzania, Basic Data, Agriculture and Livestock Sector (198 5/86–199 0/91).

F : Ministry of Agriculture, Tanzania, Bulletin for Food Production on Statistics, 1981, Unpublished.

G : FAO/World Bank Cooperative Programme Investment Centre, Tanzania: Agricultural Sector Review Mission.

H : Bureau of Statistics, Tanzania, National Socio-Economic Profile of Tanzania, 1989, Dar es Salaam, 1989, Table EA3.

I : Marketing Development Bureau, MALD, Tanzania, 1996/97, Market Review of Maize and Rice, p. 4.

Compiled by Jun Ikeno (1999), with Masao Yoshida for Source A.

The above discussion of available documentary evidence cautions us against treating economic analyses too precisely, in a mathematical way, even for recent years in Africa.

Finding and Using Unique Documentary Sources

Here, I would like to illustrate the importance of finding and using unique documentary sources, by showing the examples of how some Japanese economic historians have worked.

The first one to examine is the doctoral dissertation of Katsuhiko Kitagawa, who wrote on the history of Japan–South Africa trade relations. For the pre-World War II period, Kitagawa extensively used the Japanese consular reports sent from the consular offices in Cape Town, Port Said, Cairo, Bombay, London, Lyon, and so on. The Japanese Ministry of Foreign Affairs started to publish its Consular Reports in 1881, mainly to promote Japanese trade with various parts of the world. The first Japanese consular office in sub-Saharan Africa was established in Cape Town in 1918. Although many scholars before him had written on the importance of consular records as important sources of information in the history of trade, it was Kitagawa who painstakingly examined the actual consular reports, and used the evidence he gathered to explain the motives of Japanese trade policies with South Africa, and the changes brought about during the course of time. He traced the origin of the South African acceptance of Japanese as "Whites" in the 1930s to the Japanese consul's vigorous efforts to increase the Japanese imports of South African wools, which persuaded the South African government to grant permission for Japanese trading companies to set up an office within their territory.[42]

Gleaning facts by painstakingly reading a voluminous amount of documents has some precedence in African economic history studies in Japan. M. Saeki has done that to obtain the amount of investment going to the mining companies of South Africa by perusing all the issues of the *Economist* published in Britain.[43] T. Yoshikuni, a social historian, has also gone through the Salisbury Town Clerk's department files, which are deposited in the National Archives of Zimbabwe. He was searching for the information of housing while writing his D. Phil. thesis for the University of Zimbabwe, entitled "Black Migrants in a White City: A Social History of African Harare: 1890–1925."[44] Sometimes, private files are deposited in a library, and this will often become a very precious primary source of evidence. When I was writing my Ph.D. thesis for the University of East Africa on "Government Intervention in Agricultural Marketing in East Africa,

1900–1965," I was very fortunate to be able to use the personal files of Sir Amar Maini, who had been a Legislative Councilor, and of the members of the boards of many important government organizations. The files had very detailed information on the allocation of cotton for ginneries in Uganda in wartime and immediately after the war period, which was almost impossible to obtain anywhere else.[45]

Oral Sources

For some type of topics, written documents are nonexistent. Such will be the economic history of rural village life in sub-Saharan Africa. In this kind of circumstances, one has to rely on collecting oral sources.

A good example of this type of research is found in I. N. Kimambo's book: *Penetration & Protest in Tanzania: the Impact of the World Economy on the Pare 1860–1960*. This is a book about the transformation of village life among the Pare people of Northern Tanzania since the time of the Arab caravan trade to the end of the colonial period.[46]

The method employed by Kimambo is as follows:

> [It] appeared to this author to require experimentation with different techniques in order to determine their suitability for the type of data needed. In 1968/69 three techniques were identified: the field interview technique (extending the oral tradition technique to eye-witness accounts); the biographical technique involving collection of life histories of individual participants at different levels of society; and finally the questionnaire method of collecting specific information.[47]

I came across with the same type of research problem when I started investigating the history of traditional, communal-type irrigation on the Pare Mountains. I could rely on the information about the general and particular Pare history written by Professor Kimambo, but beyond that I had to rely on the field interviews with the villagers, combined with visits to various remaining and abandoned irrigation facilities. There was no map to rely on, so that after visits to irrigation facilities, I had to draw maps myself, and ascertain their accuracies by consulting the inhabitants.

In order to understand the organization of irrigation management, which had started as a kinship organization but later incorporated many non-kin neighbors as members, I had to draw a kind of family-tree picture and place the names of ancestors in proper places, a difficult exercise. Only by doing this kind of work, the nature of the furrow (canal) leaders and the corporate principle of the canal group could be understood.[48]

If the land-use investigation has to be done at the same time, the researcher must visit every piece of land a household claims to occupy and use, and ascertain the area of cropping for different types of produce. The most difficult thing that one encounters in an African situation is the widely adopted practice of mixed cropping. Several crops are often planted in the same piece of land, and this makes the measurement of any planted crop area of a single variety of crop very difficult. Accurate measurement of the yield of a crop per unit of land becomes almost impossible, and one has to be contented with "about" measurements. Experiences of this kind of field work, however, would wake us up to seeing the figures of statistics in Africa cautiously, and with more insight into their real hidden meaning.

Notes

1. Tiyambe Zeleza, *A Modern Economic History of Africa*, vol. 1: *The Nineteenth Century*. Dakar: CODESRIA, 1993, 6–7.

2. C. Coquery-Vidrovitch, "Research on an African Mode of Production," originally published in French in Pensee, 144. Editions Sociales, Paris, 1969. P. C. W. Gutkind and P. Waterman (eds.), *African Social Studies: A Radical Reader*. London: Heinemann, 1977, 77–92.

3. R. Gray and D. Birmingham (eds.), *Pre-Colonial African Trade: Essays on Trade in Central and Eastern Africa before 1900*. London: Oxford University Press, 1970.

4. A. G. Hopkins, *An Economic History of West Africa*. London: Longman, 1973.

5. J. Gallagher and R. Robinson, "Imperialism of Free Trade," *Economic History Review* 6, no. 1 (1953).

6. E. Brett, *Colonialism and Underdevelopment in East Africa: the Politics of Economic Change, 1919–1939*. London: Heinemann, 1973.

7. K. M. Stahl, *Metropolitan Organization of the British Colonial Trade*. London: Faber and Faber, 1951.

8. Hopkins, *An Economic History of West Africa*, and D. K. Fieldhouse, *Merchant Capital and Economic Decolonization: The United Africa Company 1929–1985*. London: Oxford University Press, 1994.

9. N. K. Mehta, *Dream Half-Exprssed: Nanji Kalidas Mehta, an Autobiography*. Bombay: Vakils, Feffer and Simons, 1966; Fuad Khury, "Kinship, Emigration and Trade Partnership among the Lebanese of West Africa," *Africa* 36 (1965); For the Indian merchants in East Africa, see: J. S. Mangat, *A History of the Asians in East Africa c. 1886–1945*. Oxford: Clarendon Press, 1969; R. R. Ramchandani, *Uganda Asians: The End of Enterprise*. Bombay: United Asia Publications, 1976; C. Tominaga, "Merchants of the Indian Ocean and Jetha Lila—Bankers," in E. Linnebuhr (ed.), *Transition and Continuity of Identity in East Africa and Beyond*. Bayreuth: Bayreuth University, 1989.

10. P. T. Bauer, *West African Trade, A Study of Competition, Oligopoly and Monopoly in Changing Economy*. Cambridge: Cambridge University Press, 1954.

11. Inaccuracy of agricultural statistics in Africa was severely criticized by Polly Hill, *Development Economics on Trial.* Cambridge: Cambridge University Press, 1986, 30–40.

12. G. Hyden, *Beyond Ujamaa in Tanzania: Underdevelopment and an Uncaptured Peasantry.* London: Heinemann Educational, 1980; N. Kasfir, "Are African Peasants Self-sufficient?" *Development and Change* 17, no. 2 (April 1986); L. Cliffe, "The Debate on African Peasantries," *Development and Change* 18, no. 2 (April 1987); C. D. Smith, *Did Colonialism Capture the Peasantry? A Case Study of the Kagera District, Tanzania.* Uppsala: Scandinavian Institute of African Studies, 1989.

13. Polly Hill, *The Migrant Cocoa Farmers of Southern Ghana: A Study in Rural Capitalism,* Cambridge: Cambridge University Press, 1963; For Cote d'Ivoire case, see: P. Anyang' Nyong'o, "The Development of Agrarian Capitalist Classes in the Ivory Coast, 1945–1975," in P. M. Lubeck (ed.), *The African Bourgeoisie: Capitalist Development in Nigeria, Kenya, and the Ivory Coast.* Boulder: Lynne Rienner, 1987.

14. P. Shipton and M. Goheen, "Understanding African Landholding, Power, Wealth and Meaning," *Africa* 62, no. 3 (1992).

15. One of the early attempts to expose the historical processes of ecological destruction is H. Kjekshus, *Ecology Control and Economic Development in East African History: The Case of Tanzania 1850–1950.* London: Heinemann, 1977. His premises were questioned by J. Koponen, *People and Production in Late Precolonial Tanzania.* Helsinki: Finnish Society for Development Studies, 1988, 361–69.

16. J. K. Nyerere, "The Rational Choice," in J. K. Nyerere, *Freedom and Development: A Selection from Writings and Speeches 1968–1973.* Dar es Salaam, Oxford University Press, 1973.

17. M. Yoshida, *Agricultural Marketing Intervention in East Africa: A Study in the Colonial Origin of Marketing Policies, 1900–1965.* Tokyo: Institute of Developing Economies, 1984.

18. J. Iliffe, *The Emergence of African Capitalism.* London: Macmillan, 1983, 2–4.

19. Hill, *Migrant Cocoa Farmers of Southern Ghana*; Iliffe, *Emergence of African Capitalism.*

20. C. C. Wrigley, *Crops and Wealth in Uganda,* East African Studies 12. Kampala: East African Institute of Social Research, 1959. M. Mamdani points out that that the colonial policy in Uganda of implementing the law to protect the position of tenants effectively kept the landlords from becoming capitalist farmers: M. Mamdani, *Politics and Class Formation in Uganda.* Heinemann Educational, 1976, 152.

21. Colin Leys, *Underdevelopment in Kenya.* Berkeley: University of California Press, 1974, 63–66; R. Austen, *African Economic History: Internal Development and External Dependency.* London: James Currey, 1987, 254.

22. Iliffe, *Emergence of African Capitalism,* 9.

23. Ibid., 10.

24. P. Kennedy, *African Capitalism: The Struggle for Ascendancy.* Cambridge: Cambridge University Press, 1988, 44. In order to supply foods from rural areas to cities, a transport network was indispensable. See J. Guyer (ed.), *Feeding African Cities: Studies in Regional Social History.* Bloomington: Indiana University Press, 1987, 46.

25. Kennedy, *African Capitalism,* 43.

26. April A. Gordon, *Transforming Capitalism and Patriarchy: Gender and Development in Africa.* Boulder: Lynne Rienner, 1996. Various women's economic activities

are analyzed in M. J. Hay and S. Stichter (eds.), *African Women South of the Sahara*. London: Longman, 1984.

27. C. van Onselen, *Chibaro: African Mine Labour in Southern Rhodesia 1900–1933*. London: Pluto Press, 1976. On the South African case, see F. Wilson, *Labour in the South African Gold Mines*. Cambridge: Cambridge University Press, 1972. At the terminal stage of the South African apartheid regime, vigorous debate was taking place on whether or not the economic development itself would dismantle apartheid, or whether it was too much a part of its development to disappear, as was argued by M. Legassick, "Legislation, Ideology and Economy in Post–1948 South Africa," *Journal of Southern African Studies* 1, no. 1 (1974). K. Hayashi has analyzed this debate in "Industrialization and Racial Discrimination in South Africa with Special Reference to the Criticisms by Neo-Marxist Group," *Africa Kenkyu [Journal of African Studies*, in Japanese] no. 16 (March 1977).

28. Leys, *Underdevelopment in Kenya*, 178–81.

29. B. Freund, *The Making of Contemporary Africa: The Development of African Society since 1800*. Bloomington: University of Indiana Press, 1984, 203. A new edition was published in 1998 by Macmillan.

30. I. G. Shivji, *Law, State and the Working Class in Tanzania*. London: James Currey, 1988.

31. Leys, *Underdevelopment in Kenya*, 216–20.

32. G. Arrighi and J. S. Saul, *Essays on the Political Economy of Africa*. New York: Monthly Review Press, 1973. On the need for deaggregation of the concept of "informal sector," see B. Freund, *The African Worker*. Cambridge: Cambridge University Press, 1988, 75–79.

33. The concept of informal sector was elaborated in S. V. Sethuraman (ed.), *Urban Informal Sector in Developing Countries: Employment, Poverty, and Environment*. Geneva: ILO, 1981.

34. R. H. Bates, *Market and States in Tropical Africa: the Political Basis of Agricultural Policies*. Berkeley: University of California Press, 1981.

35. *Sub-Saharan Africa: From Crisis to Sustainable Growth*. Washington DC: The World Bank, 1989.

36. G. A. Cornia, et al. (eds.), *Africa's Recovery in the 1990s: From Stagnation and Adjustment to Human Development* (UNICEF study). New York: St. Martin's Press, 1992.

37. E. W. Nafziger, *The Debt Crisis in Africa*. Baltimore: Johns Hopkins University Press, 1993.

38. P. Edwards (ed.), *Equiano's Travels: His Autobiography: The Interesting Narrative of the Life of Olaudah Equiano or Gustavus Vassa the African*. London: Heinemann Educational, 1967; Ottobah Cugoano and Vincent Carretta, *Thoughts and Sentiments on the Evil of Slavery and Other Writings*. New York: Penguin, 1999.

39. P. D. Curtin, *The Atlantic Slave Trade: a Census*. Madison: University of Wisconsin Press, 1969; J. E. Inikori (ed.), *Forced Migration: The Impact of the Export Slave Trade on African Societies*. Hutchinson University Library for Africa, 1982; P. E. Lovejoy, "The Volume of the Atlantic Slave Trade: A Synthesis," *Journal of African History* 23 (1982); P. Manning, *Slavery and African Life*. Cambridge: Cambridge University Press, 1990; H. Thomas, *The Slave Trade: The History of the Atlantic Slave Trade, 1440–1870*. New York: Simon and Schuster, 1997.

40. For instance, British Government, Commission of Enquiry into Disturbances in the Gold Coast, 1948, Colonial No. 231. London: HMSO, 1948.

41. The British colonial government documents are kept in the Public Record Office in London. Also, most of the former colonies have their own National Archives, which have kept various governmental documents of their colonial period, but their catalogues are usually not well prepared. For other colonial powers, such offices as Archives Africaines, Ministere des Affaires Étrangères, Brussels, Belgium, and Bundesarchiv in Koblenz, Freiburg, and Potsdam in Germany are important. In France, official government documents on colonies are kept in Centre d'Archive d'Outre-Mer in Aix-En-Provence. Otherwise, Centre d'Étude d'Afrique Noire, Institut d'Études Politiques de Bordeaux, at Université Montesquieu-Bordeaux IV, has a good collection of historical documents. Portugal has its documents in Instituto dos Arquivos Nacionais/Torre do Tombo, and Arquivo Histórico Ultramarino, both in Lisbon.

42. K. Kitagawa, "A Study in the History of Japanese Commercial Relations with South Africa," Ph.D. thesis (in Japanese), Graduate University for Advanced Studies (Japan), 1997. A summarized version of this thesis was published as "Japan's Trade with South Africa in the Inter-war Period: A Study of Japanese Consular Report," in C. Alden and K. Hirano (eds.), *Japan and South Africa in a Globalising World: A Distant Mirror*. Hampshire: Ashgate, 2003. A book dealing with the postwar Japan-South Africa trade, utilizing heavily some unofficial documents of business organizations and NGOs, is J. Morikawa, *Japan and Africa: Big Business and Diplomacy*. London: Hurst, 1997.

43. M. Saeki, "A Study in the British Investment towards Africa," in Hideo Yamada (ed.), *Capital and Labour in Colonial Africa* [in Japanese]. Tokyo: Institute of Developing Economies, 1975.

44. T. Yoshikuni, "Black Migrants in a White City: A Social History of African Harare: 1890–1925," Ph.D. thesis, University of Zimbabwe, 1989. A part of this elaborate research was utilized in his "Notes on the Influence of Town-country Relations on African Urban History before 1957, Experiences of Salisbury and Bulawayo," in B. Raftopoulas and T. Yoshikuni (eds.), *Sites of Struggle*. Harare: Weaver Press, 1999.

45. "Memorandum by the General Manager of the Uganda Lint Marketing Board for the Board Meeting, January 23, 1950," Sir Amar Maini Files, Makerere University Library Collection.

46. I. N. Kimambo, *Penetration & Protest in Tanzania; the Impact of the World Economy on the Pare 1860–1960*. London: James Currey, 1991.

47. Ibid., xi–xii.

48. M. Yoshida, *A Socio-Economic Study of East Africa: with Special Regards to Tanzania* [in Japanese]. Tokyo: Kokon Shoin, 1997.

13

SIGNS OF TIME, SHAPES OF THOUGHT

THE CONTRIBUTIONS OF ART HISTORY AND VISUAL CULTURE TO HISTORICAL METHODS IN AFRICA

Henry John Drewal

A river that forgets its source, dries up

—Yoruba Proverb

Introduction

What is art? What is art history? How does art history relate to other kinds of art studies, to history, and to the emerging field of visual culture? These and other issues are discussed in this two-part chapter. Part I considers the following topics: 1) an African understanding of "art," 2) definitions and discussions of concepts and methods in art history, 3) a comparison of the disciplines of art history and history showing their commonalities and differences and how they may complement each other to enrich and deepen our understandings of Africa's past, and 4) an assessment of the new transdiscipline of visual culture. Part II provides an overview and assessment of art-historical and visual culture studies in Africa and the African Diaspora over the last forty years that historians of Africa may find relevant and useful.[1]

Part I

An African Understanding of "Art"

Art is a visual documentation of a creative process shaped by historical and cultural circumstances. African cultures have countless distinct, explicit, and complex terms and concepts for objects and processes that are called "art" in the "western" world. For example, Yoruba-speaking peoples in Nigeria and Benin call art *ona*—a complex term that encompasses ideas of the beautification, embellishment, decoration, skillful manipulation, and transformation of media (wood, clay, iron, bronze, pigments, etc.), and the play (*ere*) of images and ideas. *Ona* is *evocative form*—something meant to move and enlighten its audiences, helping them to experience deeply and to make sense of their world.

If we take a Yoruba understanding of "art" (and this may vary greatly in other African cultures, as it does globally), how does one analyze "evocative form" before interpreting its historical and cultural meanings or significance? We begin with form, the visible object, and analyze its visual elements—line, color, shape, texture, size/scale, composition—in order to record our perceptions and to reflect on them in order to understand the object's *style*. Style is the synthesis of its distinctive characteristics or expressive qualities and reveals how/why the work is evocative. With this analysis of form and style, we examine the work's content, meanings, or significance—the cultural and historical ideas, perceptions and attitudes it expresses. This aspect of art history has been called the study of iconography, the analysis of symbolic meanings of images, or its broader, more interpretive version, iconographical interpretations/iconology.

Recently, however, many art historians have questioned ways of interpreting meanings in art, arguing that images have no fixed inherent meaning in themselves. Rather, artists and audiences over time produce meanings from what they observe, think, and feel. Evocative form, it is argued, creates meanings. This focus on the making of meaning in art is known as reception theory.[2] However, there are limits to such inventiveness. Artists/creators of evocative images never work in a vacuum, and neither do their audiences. They are social beings who shape as well as reflect socio-cultural and historical forces. The challenge for art historians/visual culturalists is to explore and assess the meanings of evocative forms (that is, the intentions of their creators as well as the responses of their audiences) in specific socio-cultural contexts and at specific historical moments, while at the same time recognizing their own subjective positions and perspectives. If we recognize the difficulties and complexities, the limits and possibilities of art-historical research and interpretation, we may be able to illuminate, not just illustrate, the past.

What is Art History?

Art history is the study of the appearance of things. It explores how, why, where, and when images look the way they do, as well as how those images reflect and shape history and culture in both the distant and the recent past. Other kinds of art studies, such as those that focus on technique, style, iconography, patronage, quality, authenticity, aesthetics, or criticism, are generally ahistorical. Yet the analysis and interpretation of some or all of these studies *over time* can inform art-historical studies and illuminate the past in fuller, more complex, more nuanced ways.

An analysis of style changes or continuities in a series of objects arranged chronologically can reveal the dynamics and impact of historical forces in specific eras/areas. For example, the royal arts of Benin from the sixteenth to the late nineteenth century have received extensive attention from a number of scholars using a variety of disciplines—art history, history, anthropology, and archeology.[3] Using the large corpus of brass, iron, ivory, wood, leather, beads, ceramic, and cloth works taken from the palace at Benin City in 1897 by the British, together with numerous written accounts by European visitors over more than three hundred years, and extensive local oral histories, these scholars have been able to give a broad and sometimes detailed picture of the ebb and flow of Benin history and royal art history, despite continuing debates about specifics. The first broad outline, proposed by William Fagg, identified Early, Middle and Late periods (a classical Western model). This scheme was based on a set or series of one object type—cast brass heads assumed to have been used on royal ancestral altars. Since this original framework, many revisions and reformulations have been proposed as specific objects (like carved tusks or plaques) and more specific historical eras have been examined using visual, written, and oral data. The most recent, and convincing treatment can be found in Paula Girshick Ben-Amos's detailed study of the multiple sources, influences and innovations in the royal art and their changing forms and meanings in the context of interactive economic, social, cultural, ideological, institutional, and political forces in eighteenth-century Benin.[4]

Art History and History

Art history is different from *history* yet closely related to it. Art history examines, analyzes, and interprets images—their forms and meanings—as the creations of minds and hands rooted in specific historical and social contexts. Such images are signs of the times and shapes of thought. Style itself has content—form is meaning.

History usually examines "texts," oral or written, to understand the past. Art history examines forms and images instead. These visual documents, as historical evidence "shaped by imagination as well as tradition and purpose,"[5] demand a special kind of visual literacy. Although the logocentric approaches of semiotics are sometimes recommended for "reading" paintings, sculptures, photographs, and so forth, I would suggest instead that visual materials communicate by evoking ideas, attitudes, emotions, and concepts in ways distinct and apart from those of language. Artifacts derive from multiple intentions and senses. Interdisciplinary and multisensory approaches can help us understand them and the histories they document. In such ways can art history in Africa be used to illuminate and enrich our understandings of the past.

Some of the confluence, divergence, and overlap of historians' and art historians' approaches, as discussed by Rotberg and Rabb,[6] are summarized, revised, and amplified in the following paragraphs:

Historians work with materials other than objects or images, and then use visual evidence to reach conclusions. In contrast, art historians begin with objects, analyze their visual evidence (style, content, chronology), and consider various forms of contextual data beyond the object to reach conclusions about objects, artists, and audiences as well as other socio-cultural or historical matters. Thus the foci of historians and art historians may differ, yet they have significantly similar interests.

One of these is the focus on texts, whether written or oral. Historians, even some art historians, are more comfortable analyzing texts than images. The verbal often takes precedence over the visual, as is evident among art historians who have attempted to adapt logocentric theories and methods of semiotics to studies of images. Both disciplines prefer words over images, although to differing degrees. Art historians attempt to "see and say,"[7] historians most often "read and say."

Second is a shared assumption that "painters, sculptors, and architects are able to give us clues (and sometimes answers) about the universe that they inhabit that are available nowhere else. In the absence of words, artifacts can point us in directions we could not otherwise imagine."[8] For example, a corpus of images of women in chiefly or royal regalia might raise questions about gender issues (such as the positions and powers of women) that might be invisible or hidden in oral traditions or written accounts produced and controlled by men. Such a view is fundamental to the work of art historians, and to increasing numbers of historians.

A third aspect, derived from the first two, is the shared origin of both disciplines in the field of rhetoric. They share an interest in style, persuasion, and narration—telling a story convincingly using verbal and visual evidence to differing degrees and for different purposes. Both demand arguments that are plausible, coherent, and persuasive.

Fourth, a concern for both disciplines, is the role of causation, the "why" and "how" of investigations. An awareness of indeterminacy in matters of causation has increasingly infused so-called "postmodern" thinking and writing as we have confronted the limits of supposed "objectivity." In the best work, scholars have presented and argued multiple scenarios in order to reveal the complexities (and perplexities) of historical and art-historical reconstruction. This openness to alternative arguments is a recognition of the rhetorical nature of our disciplines.

A final concern, perhaps the most important, yet difficult to argue, is effectiveness, the power of images to shape as well as reflect history.[9] That power lies in part in their form and style, which possess and create meaning, content, or significance. The ways in which artists represent their worlds are as meaningful as what they choose to represent. Art historians analyze and interpret both in order to understand the past. A recent compelling argument for art's power to communicate royal legitimacy and power and thus shape political struggles is Paula Girshick Ben-Amos's study of eighteenth-century Benin. Her detailed and perceptive analyses of form, style, and content of objects and images demonstrate their strategic role in contests of legitimation.

Visual Culture

So far I have spoken of the discipline of "art history," yet in recent years some who are rethinking the scope and definition of the field call it the study of "visual culture."[10] In what ways is visual culture different from art history, and what implications does this shift have for art history's contributions to the field of African history?

The term "visual culture" refers to all forms meant to be experienced primarily, although not solely, through the sense of sight.[11] To study visual culture is to analyze and interpret the history, significance, and impact of the visual environment as it shapes and is shaped by historical processes and cultural ideas. Visual culture encompasses a number of traditionally related, yet often separated, disciplines—art history, history, studio art, art criticism, film studies, communications, cultural studies, anthropology, and aesthetics. It is therefore trans- or post-disciplinary, and as such visual culture adopts an inclusive rather than exclusive approach to human creativity in image-making and image-reception. Visual culture's inclusiveness avoids the historical and cultural "baggage" associated with the term "art" and false Eurocentric assertions that only the "West" possesses "art." It is not restricted to so-called "elite" or "fine arts" cultural productions, but rather covers a whole range of visual forms reaching mass (sometimes global) audiences. Such forms—political posters, fashions, television programs, films, billboard advertisements, carnival costumes, body arts, photographs, interior designs and furnishings, paintings, sculptures, etc.—formulate, express, and reflect socio-cultural ideas both in the past and in the present. The distinction between elite and popular culture has been elided in this era of mass communication and global interactions.

Such a broadening of horizons seems timely. Creative individuals (the distinction between "artists" and "non-artists" seems irrelevant) are presenting us with visual forms that force us to rethink the old boundaries of form, content, and intention. Those who might have been considered "non-artists"—public relations or publicity specialists, TV producers, fashion designers, computer programmers, etc.—are shaping and transforming how we see and perceive visual environments in ways that have a profound impact on cultural experiences and aesthetic sensibilities. The world is increasingly visualizing things that are not themselves visual. For example, the impacts of TV—and especially the high-energy, rapid-fire visual style of MTV—are images of sounds. In the computer revolution of the past thirty years, it is noteworthy that text-based programs such as "WordPerfect" are being replaced by vision-based graphic programs such as "Windows." Windows are something we see through, not read through. We can only speculate about the future impact of virtual imaging systems.

The field of visual culture recognizes such dramatic dynamics and attempts to identify, analyze, interpret, and understand the historical and cultural factors or forces (economic, political, religious, historical, and social) operating in three spheres: the making of images, the mechanisms by which they are seen, and finally the subjectivity of viewers, the reception and continuous creation of meanings by viewers—in other words, the study of spectatorship.

As theory, visual culture is a form of resistance. It opposes hierarchic, divisive thinking. It questions the division between so-called high and low culture and sees cultural worlds as dynamic, ever-changing holistic systems in constant process of formation, where power relationships are being continuously negotiated. Such an open, inclusive view may be particularly important for studies in Africa where questions of hierarchy vs. heterarchy, sacred vs. secular, elite vs. popular may be irrelevant, or posed in very different ways.

A visual culture approach focuses on the primacy of vision and the visual world in producing meanings, and in establishing and maintaining aesthetic values, stereotypes, or power relationships within culture. For example, visual culture might examine mechanisms of censorship—who controls what people get to see, or not see—as evidence of power relations, hegemony, and resistance over time. Visual culture also considers the dynamics of spectatorship and reveals how, based on issues such as race, gender, or class, people make sense of, make meaningful, what they see.

Yet despite these useful expansive dimensions of visual culture, this post-disciplinary approach may have potential "blind-spots" as well. Many studies tend to focus on so-called "modern" and "postmodern" eras and image technology issues. And, as its name suggests, visual culture may produce more synchronic rather than diachronic studies, and emphasize spectator/consumer issues, rather than producer/creator matters.

Visual culture is a strategy to confront cultural worlds undergoing enormous, rapid, often volatile transformations. The grand narratives of the past that sought to "explain" cultural or historical phenomena seem no longer adequate. Instead of the "good eye" of the art connoisseur, we need to develop what one scholar has called the "curious eye," which suggests an undecided state of mind. Such a "curious eye" speaks to a subject, rather than about it. This is a shift away from objectification to a space between objectivity and subjectivity—that space in which we inhabit and constantly make and remake our world, our visual culture. This perspective is what informs the arena of visual culture studies. As a new post-discipline, visual culture is engaged in an "archeology of knowledge," excavating a past and probing a present in which little is stable, acceptable, or understood with certainty.

Part II

African/African Diaspora Art-Historical/Visual Culture Studies: An Overview

During the last forty years, Africanist art historians have been eclectic in their methodologies. That is, they use the theory and practice of a method that selects perspectives from various sources depending on what appears to be most useful and effective for a particular research problem. This is both inclusive and pragmatic. A Yoruba proverb graphically illustrates such wisdom: "If you want to pick your nose, choose the finger that fits."

Eclecticism in the field is manifest in interdisciplinary approaches. The 1960s were the crucible for this development. The conjunction of many factors set the stage; among the most significant were the collapse of colonial empires, the coming of independence in Africa and elsewhere, and the civil rights and black nationalist movements in the United States, all of which raised consciousness about African peoples and cultures. The post-World War II baby boom swelled American universities and their budgets and, as a result, spawned innovative, interdisciplinary programs, many of them area studies programs. Such developments, which brought together multiple perspectives and heightened awareness of the complexity of issues and the contingency and indeterminacy of our conclusions, have contributed to discussions of so-called "postmodernist thought."

In the fields of African art history and visual culture, a scholar's preparation usually combines methods drawn primarily from anthropology, history, and art history. Anthropologists interested in art dominated the studies up to 1960. This heritage, exemplified by works of the students of Boas, Herskovits, Griaule, and Olbrechts, is clearly evident in the writing of the last forty years. It is particularly evident in the trend toward synchronic (ahistorical), contextual studies. Anthropology provided the theoretical models as well as the field methods for the majority of studies on African art, while art and architectural history contributed their perspectives on visual evidence and matters such as attribution, technique, style and sequence, iconography, and patronage. History has provided methods for the use of oral and written sources as well as detailed studies of the flow and ethos of eras that can anchor art-historical interpretations of purposes, meanings, and changes in significance over time.

Anthropologists also tended to identify art with ethnicity, but Africanist art historians now recognize that style is defined by multiple socio-cultural and historical factors in specific cases and, furthermore, that these factors may have different weights. This idea is being carried forward in studies of "borderland" art where the visual evidence of independent invention, diffusion, interaction, and exchange among peoples are important documents of peoples' histories.[12]

At the same time, along with macro/regional transcultural studies, some scholars, especially those who study Yoruba-speaking peoples, have worked at the micro-level to identify and analyze the works of specific ateliers and named artists. African artists are not anonymous to their patrons or audiences, only to outsiders who, assuming the Africans simply "reproduced" works from the past, neglected to ask for their names, their place within society, or their importance as visual historians of events, beliefs, and social worlds.[13] This research focuses on the socio-cultural context of art production in specific places and times. It has illuminated issues of patronage and the relation between master artists and apprentices, and the differences among artists' guilds, professional, semi-professional, and unprofessional artists, and the dynamics of innovative versus conservative visual traditions over time.

The record of the built environment (architectural history) has developed dramatically, from early surveys to detailed studies of specific regional or cultural traditions.[14] Architectural history, like art history, deals with the shapes of time. Style, iconography, and purpose, and changes in these over time, can reveal much about a people's socio-political forms, histories, and exchanges with others. For example, the recent work of the archeologists Roderick and Susan McIntosh on the ancient inland Niger River Delta city of Jenne-Jeno has forced scholars, especially historians and sociologists, to re-evaluate Euro-centric concepts of "urbanism" and hierarchy vs. heterarchy.[15]

Africanist art historians and visual culturalists are exploring the concepts and role of individuals in shaping culture and history. The broader discipline of anthropology, long wedded to the concept of culture, has often underestimated the impact and agency of individual persons in shaping society. In its search for the norm and for structure, anthropology tended to ignore their impact and importance in creating art and culture. Only recently has it recognized that culture is "invented" by individuals—especially creative ones like artists—who play with symbols and imbue them with new, ever-changing meanings to envision and configure society and history.[16]

Anthropology has been slow to appreciate the importance of history. Analyses framed in "the ethnographic present" suggest a sort of static timelessness that ignores or distorts the dynamics of change over time. The impact of anthropology on African art-historical studies has resulted in a preponderance of synchronic studies of the relationship between art and society. The most substantial progress has been made in detailed studies of specific cultural or sub-cultural traditions, the result of sustained field and archival research. Beginning in the 1960s, students undertook detailed fieldwork in localized areas to document all artistic activities. The 1970s and 1980s saw a proliferation of more specialized field studies of specific art traditions, and the last few years have witnessed a general decline that seems tied to the economics and politics of both this country and the independent nations of Africa. Despite some advances, a serious unevenness of knowledge remains.

What of the second element in our transdisciplinary triad, history? Although anthropologists have been essentially ahistorical in their work, they are now beginning to formulate poststructuralist models that consider change over time and take historical factors into account. Even so, as Jan Vansina correctly observed in 1984 (and it is still true today), our field lacks concerted or systematic studies of the history of art in Africa.[17] It may be that the interdisciplinary effort of the last forty years, dominated by anthropological methods, is ironically the very thing that militated against systematic historical studies. In our concern to document context and fill in the blanks in the artistic map of Africa, we have neglected historical depth, dynamics, and development. Granted, we are confronted with the challenges of works in perishable media[18] and sometimes elusive oral sources, but our aversion to historical thinking, I believe, derives more from our affinities with anthropological approaches.

Despite the problems that have in effect limited art-historical studies in Africa, a growing number of works demonstrate the possibilities.[19] Here again the efforts and results have been eclectic and mixed. Often they are concerned with "history and art" not art history as reconstructed from diverse kinds of data. Art history *per se*—the analysis and interpretation of constancy and change in the forms, styles, and meanings of objects and images *over time* and what these can tell us about cultural worlds and eras—are still rare. Integrative art-historical and visual cultural studies are only beginning.

Archeology is the third discipline important for documenting Africa's art history. Because of the impermanence of many African art forms, the limited time depth for many oral traditions (perhaps four or five generations), and the paucity of written documents, archeology is the primary recourse for reconstructing and interpreting the earliest phases of Africa's art history. Archeology's methods and data are very different from those of historians and art historians. Archeological research in Africa faces major challenges. For one, most funding agencies support research on the origins of humanity in Africa, rather than on the eras and sites that could potentially yield the kinds of material evidence art historians focus on. Second, archeologists have their own priorities and cannot be expected to analyze the visual evidence contained in artworks. But despite the general paucity of systematic archeology, some major work has been accomplished.[20]

A review of the progress made in archeological research reveals circumstances similar to those for art-historical studies generally: uneven coverage. In 1971, archeologists assessed the state of research in Ghana and found that while some significant work was carried out, partly because of the Volta River Dam Project, much of it covered the period after A.D. 1000 and the area north of the forest. Archeology in Central Africa, seriously begun only in 1970 with a joint effort between the National Museum Institute of Zaire and the African Museum, Tervuren, dealt mostly with prehistory from the Early Stone Age to the Iron Age, which did not usually include artistic materials. The same trend may be seen in work in eastern Africa as well. The major activity has been in West Africa, where archeological work is establishing the processes of urbanization that led to some of the most important art traditions within Africa. Dates now establish extensive pre-Islamic trade routes around Jenne-Jeno that help explain the setting for the terra cotta traditions of that area. In Nigeria, the dates of A.D. 1000–1100 for Old Oyo and its extension sites establish an early time frame for urban settlements. These, with the findings in the Sahel, support the ninth-century dates of Igbo Ukwu bronzes. The progress has been slow, but sustained. A record of projects has been maintained through the archeological newsletter *Nyame Akuma*. There are now several surveys of the archeological record for Africa, including North Africa, and the more recent assessment of the prospects for future archeological research was published in 1996.[21] And Peter Garlake, an archeologist known for his work on Great Zimbabwe and Ile-Ife sites, recently published a book that surveys and synthesizes the art histories of several major early traditions (mainly from archeological work) including Nubia, Aksum, the Niger River, Forest kingdoms, Great Zimbabwe and Southern African Interior, and the East African Coast.[22]

A foundation to encourage and support emergency excavations in cooperation with African colleagues and institutions (similar to the Mimbres Foundation for Native American archeology) is needed to protect and study important archeological sites that provide the only link to the early history of African art.[23] This is especially crucial in light of the recent destruction and looting of such important archeological sites as those of Nok, Ife, and Igbo Ukwu in Nigeria, and others in Niger.[24] Another perspective in reconstructing Africa's past has been interdisciplinary work combining archeology and linguistics—archeolinguistics. A volume by Ehret and Posnansky surveyed research findings for four regions of the continent.[25]

Performance studies, which often involve aspects of visual culture, can also contribute to the field of African history. Performance is a learned, embodied practice that documents and reveals a person's or group's history and culture. What a dancer, ritual specialist, or masker *does* is as important as imagery, music, or song texts in analyses of cultural/historical meanings. Theories of social process generally, and performance theory specifically, will play an important role in our understanding of African arts and history. We are moving toward an integrated approach to the histories, styles, and meanings of the various art forms that constitute performance.[26] New video/digital technologies make this practical for the first time. These need to be combined with well-thought-out theoretical models.

Breaking the Boundaries of Time and Space

Another dimension of eclecticism, of a gathering together, is beginning to appear in the reevaluation of distinctions between so-called "modern" and "non-modern" societies, between "traditional" and "contemporary," between "popular" and "elite" art. The inclusiveness of visual culture addresses such issues in its holistic approaches to material culture or artifacts and history.

Some have suggested that our highest research priority should be the documentation of artistic traditions before they disappear or are "homogenized" as a result of "global Westernization." Such an effort has been described as a salvage operation. I disagree. First, I do not believe the world is in danger of homogenization. Rather people seem to be aggressively asserting their differentness, often through their art.

Second, while some forms fade and new ones do emerge, many long-term traditions continue to be vital today. All need recording. We are not at the end of so-called "traditional" African art, whatever that means. Rather we are witnessing the changes that have always been occurring and will continue to occur as long as African people create culture and art. Those conscious of this on-goingness, the dynamics of history, study what African artists create today for their changing clientele, both domestic and foreign.[27]

Lessons from Art-Historical Methods in the African Diaspora

Research has now extended to African-inspired artistic traditions outside of Africa. Different cultural and historical circumstances in the Americas shaped African art and culture in particular ways. Slavery and oppression required Africans to devise tactics that would ensure the survival and vitality of artistic forms and concepts. Systematic documentation and analysis of these evolving traditions help to illuminate persistent, fundamental cultural concepts embodied in art, as well as divergence from these. Because the early work in these topics was carried out by Americanists, not Africanists, the sources of many traditions were unknown or poorly understood. As our field has grown, scholars with extensive field experience in Africa have begun to establish the roots of such phenomena as well as their persistence and transformation in the Americas. But basic problems persist. Both visual and textual sources are few for reconstructing African cultural practices in the era prior to major dispersal to the Americas. Early documents in the Americas are now being mined with promising results.[28] Our fullest accounts are relatively recent and record already-changed or radically transformed African diasporic traditions. Yet perhaps these very transformations may provide the keys to understanding the guiding principles and mechanisms for change that operate in the history of forms and cultural formulas.

The first step is to document as precisely as possible the African sources in African-derived forms found throughout the world today. The history of these forms, their uses and significance, can then begin. Such an encompassing approach requires cooperative efforts between Africanists and scholars of other areas of the world. Links with specialists in American, Caribbean, Iberian, Mediterranean, Egyptian, Middle Eastern, and Indian Ocean studies are all essential. The vastness of the undertaking is a major challenge. Africa is big enough; the African-influenced world is enormous. And the era under consideration is millenniums long when considering the Mediterranean, Egypt, the Middle East, and South Asia, and at least five hundred years for Afro-Atlantic diasporas. Yet such an expansive view of our field reflects realities that can bring our research to wider audiences and closer to home.[29]

These various dimensions of eclecticism that characterize African art history/visual culture since 1960 are indicative of a pervasive air of experimentation. No "paradigm" dominates; even the word itself is seldom invoked. Dissatisfied with old approaches, we are willing to try almost anything new, searching for ways to convey with words the vitality of the artistic traditions we study. The openness of the situation should allow a certain amount of playfulness—something of importance to artists. Academics sometimes find it hard to convey this sense of play. Africanist scholars have criticized anthropologists and art historians for over-emphasizing African art's ritual uses, ignoring its aesthetic and playful aspects and its secular sources. Investigations of these neglected aspects may provide a more balanced and richer view of art's place in African history and society.

Transdisciplinary Collaborations

All of which highlights the issue of collaboration. We have enormous gaps in our knowledge about the history and significance of art in Africa. Many of these require long-term team efforts that are interdisciplinary, inter-institutional, intercultural, and international. There are different kinds of collaboration. What I would call "networking" seeks only to make scholars aware of comparable work being done by colleagues, perhaps as an initial step in comparative studies. These efforts usually take the form of edited volumes on a particular theme and have appeared on various topics in *African Arts*.[30]

As our field has grown, so too has the number of scholarly "mafias" (a nickname first applied to students of the Yoruba, affectionately called "Yoruboids"). They now include those studying the Mande, Edo, Akan, Poro/Sande complex, the cultures of the DRC, the peoples of Southern Africa, the Swahili coast and Indian Ocean World. These clusters of scholars have the potential to enrich our knowledge of specific peoples or institutions, yet at present little substantial collaboration has taken place within groups, or between groups. Interdisciplinary collaboration on specific topics has also been rare.

Intercultural as well as interdisciplinary efforts are needed. Such projects present logistic problems; nevertheless, they need to be attempted and encouraged.[31] Some French scholars are working on topics jointly with their African counterparts. For example, they choose a topic and then the French scholar studies it in an Africa society and the African scholar does the same topic in France. This approach has been termed "le double-regard" (the double view). While potentially illuminating, it does not go far enough. Both scholars should work on the same topic in both places, first independently and then together—discussing, debating, and arguing commonalties and differences in theories, methods, and interpretations, to reveal the dynamics of crosscultural translations of artistic activity and cultural history.

A significant development over the last two decades is an increasing number of works by African scholars. The development of projects that extend and deepen the exchange and dialogue between African and non-African colleagues is long overdue, an issue addressed many years ago by Michael Crowder.[32] Multiple perspectives, "insider" and "outsider" views of arts, historical events, and social processes, can enrich and complex our understandings of the past.

Some projects can only be accomplished by institutions. We need massive cooperative projects uniting scholars, museums, and collectors in

America, Africa, and Europe in order to create comprehensive inventories of all visual arts in all media. Museums with vast stores of material should publish these, inviting scholars to provide data from their specific areas. Visual data banks with new computer technologies should be established.

In one aspect of collaboration, our field has made a major, although generally unrecognized, contribution. Since the 1960s, our publications have highlighted the voices of our collaborators in the field—our teachers, mentors, and friends, often inappropriately termed "informants." We have recognized their crucial participation in our efforts and represented this by citation of discussions and interviews alongside other sources. In so doing, we anticipated one of the key issues that has been discussed in the literature on writing ethnography and narrative representations in history.

African Art History/Visual Culture Studies in a "Postmodernist" Age?

We are said to live in a postmodern era. If so, what does it mean for our field? Postmodernism as a construction seems to lend a certain importance to what we are doing as somehow distinct from, and more "advanced" than, what our forebears the "modernists" did. At the same time it reveals a deep sense of insecurity and uncertainty about what we do. Such consciousness is double-edged. It can be helpful in forcing us to question and evaluate our assumptions, to continually rethink our ways of working. It can move us to newer levels of awareness, sensitivity, and understanding, not only of ourselves, but of others and their art histories. The questions we ask are at least as important as the answers we propose.

This is an era of experimentation, dialogue, and debate, of process-related approaches and new levels of collaboration. African art-historical studies anticipated this new era primarily in their eclecticism, but also by forays into process and collaborative effort. In other significant ways, however, a postmodern consciousness has not yet emerged. Such is the case with reflexivity, that is, consciousness of being conscious.

Reflexivity is a much debated issue in several disciplines. Its origins may be found in philosophical discussions of literary criticism.[33] It has been especially lively in anthropology because of what is called "a crisis of representation," that is, fundamental questions about the accuracy and validity of ethnographic descriptions or representations of the "social realities" of others, not to mention the analysis, interpretation, and theorizing about these data. And in history, it has been centered on discussions of "narrative imagination."[34]

In art history/visual culture, debates about representation appeared in critical re-evaluations of various methods, interpretations, and conclusions. The double sight provided by being reflexive can be beneficial only if it does not end in self-indulgence but instead demands that we move beyond to consider our own part in the interpretive process. Such a perspective sensitizes us to our role in the generation, selection, and manipulation of data and what they tell us, and the ways we construct and translate these data into written documents for new audiences.

Nowhere in African art-historical and visual culture studies has this "crisis of representation" surfaced, partly as a result of our priorities. We have not attained a balance between the generation of data and its analysis, synthesis, and interpretation, a point made by Arnold Rubin many years ago.[35] In our sense of urgency to simply document the vast array of art traditions across Africa (and beyond), we have concerned ourselves primarily with the content of our writing, not its form and style—its rhetoric. Thus how we describe, analyze, and make sense of what we document has largely been ignored.

One of the things that emerges from such reflexivity is a rethinking of our relationship to our subject. Rather than distancing ourselves in the interest of so-called "objectivity," we are questioning its usefulness and recognizing the importance of interaction, involvement, and shared experience as equally valid modes of operating that can lead to important insights into others' ways of living and creating. The process of dialogue, debate, and discussion requires an important precondition: a coeval relationship between the researcher and the researched, an exchange of questions and ideas. We are hopefully moving beyond the kinds of asymmetricality embodied in evolutionary, colonial, and neo-colonial thinking critiqued by Fabian.[36] If anything characterizes this postmodern era, it is a fundamental reorientation of power centers in the world that demands dialogue, not authoritarian pronouncement.

Envoi

We are pushing back the boundaries of our field on many fronts. Our transdisciplinary methods force us to consider theoretical and methodological issues broadly. The wide variety of visual cultures and histories we consider has raised questions about the nature and definition of art, artistic activity, and the power of images to both shape and reflect history, as much as—if not more than—the works of contemporary artists in our own society. As archeological, visual, written, and oral data accumulate, more historical depth in our work becomes possible. At the same time, we are considering the dynamics of the present as part of an unbroken continuum with the past. And we are beginning to systematically evaluate the impact of African artistic traditions beyond Africa's shores. In all these endeavors we might remember a Yoruba adage that helps keep things in perspective: "It is more than seven that follows six."

Notes

1. Sources cited in this essay focus on works with particular relevance for art-historical reconstructions in Africa. Most are post-1990. For extensive bibliographies on studies of African art and art history up to 1990, consult National Museum of African Art, *African Art Studies: The State of the Discipline* (Washington, DC: NMAA, 1990). Hereafter, NMAA 1990.

The first part of this chapter is new, while the second part, an overview of the field of African and African Diaspora art studies, is a revised and up-dated version of my essay on the "State of African Art Studies Today" in NMAA 1990: 29–62. I thank my colleague Thomas Spear, John Edward Philips, and the anonymous readers of this essay for their insightful and constructive editorial suggestions. Deepest gratitude goes to all my friends, colleagues, mentors, masters, artists, and audiences in Africa and beyond who have taught me so much—ADUPE. All remaining shortcomings are of course my own.

2. See James Elkins in *Critical Inquiry* 22 (1996).

3. Barbara Blackmun, "Who Commissioned the Queen Mother Tusks: A Problem in the Chronology of Benin Ivories," *African Arts* 24(2): 54–65, 90–92 (1991); Paula Girshick Ben-Amos, *The Art of Benin* (London, 1995); and *Art, Innovation, and Politics in Eighteenth-Century Benin* (Bloomington: Indiana University Press, 1999); and Irwin Tunis, "The Search for a Benin Art History: The Role of Scientific Methods," paper presented at the Symposium on Approaches to Benin Art: Past, Present, Future (Metropolitan Museum of Art, New York, 1992); and earlier sources cited in NMAA 1990.

4. Girshick Ben-Amos, *The Art of Benin.*

5. Robert I. Rotberg and Theodore K. Rabb, eds., *Art and History: Images and Their Meanings* (New York: Cambridge University Press, 1986).

6. Ibid., 1–6.

7. Sylvan Barnet, *A Short Guide to Writing about Art,* 6th ed. (New York: Longman, 2000).

8. Ibid., 2.

9. David Freedberg, *The Power of Images* (Chicago: University of Chicago Press, 1989).

10. Nicholas Mirzoeff, ed., *The Visual Cultural Reader* (London: Routledge, 1999).

11. Visual culture gives primacy to vision in understandings of our world both past and present. Closely aligned with visual culture is the field of material culture studies. Here the scope of study includes objects/things created to be perceived primarily with other senses besides sight, for example perfumes or musical instruments. See M. J. Arnoldi, C. M. Geary, and K. Hardin, eds., *African Material Culture* (Bloomington: Indiana University Press, 1996).

12. See NMAA 1990.

13. See Roslyn Walker, *Olowe of Ise: A Yoruba Sculptor to Kings* (Washington, DC: National Museum of African Art, 1998); Rowland Abiodun, Henry John Drewal, and John Pemberton III, eds., *The Yoruba Artist: New Theoretical Perspectives on African Arts* (Washington, DC: Smithsonian institution Press, 1994); Moyosore Okediji, *African Renaissance: Old Forms, New Images in Yoruba Art* (Denver: University Press of Colorado, 2002).

14. NMAA 1990.

15. Roderick and Susan McIntosh, eds., *Excavations at Jenne-Jeno, Hambarketolo, and Haniana (Inland Niger Delta), Mali, the 1981 Season* (Berkeley: University of California Press, 1995).

16. But see Thomas Spear, "Neo-Traditionalism and the Limits of Invention in British Colonial Africa," *Journal of African History* 44 (2003): 3–27, who argues that the idea of the "invention of tradition" has often been overstated.

17. Jan Vansina, *Art History in Africa* (New York: Longman, 1984).

18. The work of Ezio Bassani of African art/artifacts (many in perishable materials) in early European collections is a major accomplishment that can provide crucial data for art-historical research, especially on questions of innovative versus conservative traditions and the dynamics of change. See Ezio Bassani, *African Art and Artefacts in European Collections 1400–1800* (London: British Museum Press, 2001).

19. See NMAA 1990.

20. See NMAA 1990.

21. J. R. Ellison, et al. "The Future of African Archeology," *African Archeological Review* 13:1 (1996).

22. Peter Garlake, *Early Art and Architecture of Africa* (New York: Oxford University Press, 2002).

23. The author, with the support of many Africanist colleagues, sought funding (unsuccessfully) for the FAA, Foundation for African Archeology.

24. P. Schmidt and R. McIntosh, eds., *Plundering Africa's Past* (Bloomington: Indiana University Press, 1996).

25. Christopher Ehret and Merrick Posnansky, eds., *The Archaeological and Linguistic Reconstruction of African History* (Los Angeles: University of California Press, 1982).

26. See NMAA 1990, and Margaret T. Drewal, "The State of Research on Performance in Africa," *African Studies Review* (1991); and M. T. Drewal, *Yoruba Ritual: Performers, Play, Agency* (Bloomington: Indiana University Press, 1992).

27. See the works of Jules-Rosette, Ben-Amos, the Fabians, and Houlberg cited in NMAA 1990; Clementine Deliss, ed., *Seven Stories about Modern Art in Africa* (Paris: Flammarion, 1995); Okwui Enwezor, ed., *The Short Century: Independent and Liberation Movements in Africa, 1945–1994* (Munich: Prestel Verlag, 2001); Nicole Guez, *L'Art Africaine Contemporaine* (Paris: Association Africaine en Creation, 1996); Elizabeth Harney, *In Senghor's Shadow: Art, Politics, and Avant-Garde in Senegal* (Durham, NC: Duke University Press, 2003); Sidney Kasfir, *Contemporary African Art* (London: Thames and Hudson, 1999); Jean Kennedy, *New Currents, Ancient Rivers: Contemporary African Artists in a Generation of Change* (Washington, DC: Smithsonian Institution Press, 1992); Betty LaDuke, *Africa Through the Eyes of Women Artists* (Trenton: Africa World Press, 1992); Thomas McEvilley, *Fusion: African Artists at the Venice Biennale* (New York: Museum for African Art/Prestel, 1993); Nkiru Nzegwu, *Contemporary Textualities: Multidimensionality in Contemporary Nigerian Art* (Binghampton: International Society for the Study of Africa,

1999); Nkiru Nzegwu, ed., *Issues in Contemporary African Art* (Binghampton: International Society for the Study of Africa, 1998); Olu Oguibe and Okui Enwezor, eds., *Reading the Contemporary: African Art from Theory to the Marketplace* (Cambridge, Mass: The MIT Press, 1999); Moyosore Okediji, *African Renaissance: Old Forms, New Images in Yoruba Art* (Denver: University Press of Colorado, 2002); Simon Ottenberg, *New Traditions from Nigeria: Seven Artists of the Nsukka Group* (Washington, DC: Smithsonian Institution Press, 1997); Salah M. Hassan, ed., *Gendered Visions: The Art of Contemporary Africana Women Artists* (Trenton, NJ: Africa World Press, 1997); Andre Magnin and Jacques Soulillou, eds., *Contemporary Art of Africa* (New York: Harry N. Abrams, 1996).

28. See E. K. Agorsah, ed., *Maroon Heritage: Archeological, Ethnographic, and Historical Perspectives* (Kingston: Canoe Press, 1994); Linda Heywood, *Central Africans and Cultural Transformations in the American Diaspora* (New York: Cambridge University Press, 2002); Charles Joyner, *Down by the Riverside: A South Carolina Slave Community* (Urbana: University of Illinois Press, 1984/; Judith Carney, *Black Rice: The African Origins of Rice Cultivation in the Americas* (Cambridge, Mass.: Harvard University Press, 2001); John Vlach, *The Afro-American Tradition in Decorative Arts* (Athens: University of Georgia Press, 1990); and numerous recent works on African American religion, folklore, culture, and history.

29. Emanoel Araujo, *A Mao Afro-Brasiliera: Significado do Contribuiçao Artistica e Historica* (Sao Paolo: Tenenge, 1988); Henry J. Drewal, and John Mason, *Beads, Body, and Soul: Art and Light in the Yoruba Universe* (Los Angeles: Fowler Museum of Cultural History, 1998); Robert Farris Thompson, *Face of the Gods* (New York: Museum for African Art, 1993); Donald Cosentino, ed., *Sacred Arts of Haitian Vodou* (Los Angeles: Fowler Museum of Cultural History, 1995); Arturo Lindsay, ed., *Santeria Aesthetics* (Washington, DC: Smithsonian Institution Press, 1994); and other earlier works cited in NMAA 1990.

30. A list of all these thematic issues can be found in *African Arts* 35:3 (Autumn 2002): 10.

31. See NMAA 1990 for earlier efforts. The exhibition and publication of Haitaian Vodou sacred arts was a very successful intercultural and interdisciplinary effort. See Cosentino, ed., *Sacred Arts of Haitian Vodou.*

32. Michael Crowder, " 'Us' and 'them': The International African Institute and the Current Crisis of Identity in African Studies," *Africa* 57:1 (1987): 109–22.

33. Jacques Derrida, *Of Grammatology,* trans. Gayatri Chakravorty Spivak (Balitmore: Johns Hopkins University Press, 1974); Michel Foucault, *The Order of Things: An Archeology of the Human Sciences,* trans. Alan Sheridan (New York: Pantheon, 1970).

34. Hayden White, *The Content of the Form* (Baltimore: The Johns Hopkins University Press, 1987).

35. Marla Berns, "African Art Studies in the 1980s," *African Arts* 12:4 (1980): 15–23, 90.

36. Johaannes Fabian, *Time and the Other: How Anthropology Makes its Object* (New York: Columbia University Press, 1983).

14

METHODOLOGIES IN YORÙBÁ ORAL HISTORIOGRAPHY AND AESTHETICS

Diedre L. Bádéjo

Research is about satisfying a need to know, and a need to extend the boundaries of existing knowledge through a process of systematic inquiry.[1]

Introduction

The intent of this chapter is to further satisfy a "need to know" Africa and her ethnolinguistic cultures on her own terms by exploring "how to know" her on those terms, and premising what is "knowable given those terms." It proposes that *knowing (ìmọ̀)* requires a form of research in African studies generally, and African history specifically, that finds its *profundity (ìgbéèdè)*[2] in the knowledge core of the societies and cultures being studied. The chapter also suggests that Africa's terms for knowing are grounded in that which she deems permissible to know, and that which is knowable given the appropriate keys to a particular culture's world views. Yorùbá oral traditions and thought are the focus of this study which attempts, in the words of Linda Smith, to extend the boundaries of the existing knowledge of, and in this case, approaches to an oral historiography of an African people.

Some of the most insightful and useful African historical works have relied, to some degree, on the verbal and, occasionally, the visual record.[3] The spoken word of court historians and/or artisans whose social and political responsibility was primarily to recall and record the deeds of nobility was, and is, in some societies bound by an oath of veracity as well as artistry. The Yorùbá historian, Babatunde Agiri, makes this point in his essay, "Yorùbá Oral Tradition with Special Reference to the Early History of the Oyo Kingdom."[4] His essay illustrates how oral sources contribute to a reconstructed history of the Oyo Kingdom, and the role of linguisitics in the corroboration of that history. Agiri's epistemological approach presents a Yorùbá based distinction between "histories of the origins (which) are called *Itan Isedale*, while effective history is referred to as *Itan*."[5] As he demonstrates in his essay, this linguistic analysis of specific Yorùbá oral traditions and historiography contributed substantially to the reconstruction of the migration theme in Yorùbá history. It also disclosed the narrative inlays that reference an interconnected migration history among the Mossi, the Borgawa, and the Yorùbá as well as the spread of Islam across western Africa.[6] Such complex histories and deeds of political, religious, economic, and social rulers, courtesans, artists guilds, and military elite required a code of reliability that could be used and, sometimes, misused to articulate precedence, establish mores and social codes, and define and justify jurisdiction.[7] Although these oral traditions are relevant to, and carry significance among people such as the Yorùbá, their traditions and meanings are not unique to them. As the Malian D. T. Niane[8] described, these men and, in some cases, women are trained and dutybound to those who ruled or are destined to rule, to recount and record the developments of their people.

Obviously, the use of oral sources is neither new nor extraordinary. Herodotus made similar use of Greek verbal and visual texts in pioneering his work from oral into recorded history. Nor is the idea of an historical record limited to recorded documents as visual and music history have illustrated. Even today, the use of oral tradition as a form of evidence of an historical record finds validation in contemporary historical undertakings, as is apparent in the importance of public history and oral history today. In short, the notion of evidence includes verbal and visual sources, the solicitation of accounts by eyewitnesses as well as the recorders of memory. In any case, it is understood that oral sources, like other sources, may be or should be corroborated by other sources internal and external to any given account or subject culture. African and Africanist scholars have long since debated the relevance of oral traditions, and the ways in which such traditions are utilized in scholarly work. Kola Folayan discusses the problems and challenges of using oral sources. He notes that 'political propaganda" can influence court traditions,[9] the purpose of which is to obscure the more "unpleasant features of their history."[10] However, Folayan also proposes that the historian who uses oral sources can

> check and cross-check and supplement information derived from [court traditions] with various accounts from different lineages, wards, and families as well as individuals located over different parts of the town concerned.[11]

Like Agiri, Folayan recommends an epistemological approach to Yorùbá historiography that is grounded in the Yorùbá language itself. He notes that for the nonnative speaker or nonspecialist in the language, this approach presents special challenges and requires attention to methodological approaches. This is particularly true since, as both Agiri and Folayan note, "much of Yorùbá history is buried in oríkì, proverbs, Ifá corpus, or ceremonies . . ."[12] The challenge of accessing such histories then is both an historical and a literary one. As will be explored in this essay, within the aesthetic and linguistic verve of Yorùbá oral traditions lies the kernel of historical evidence and cultural historical relevance.

In *De La Tradition Orale: Essai de Methode Historique*,[13] Jan Vansina also attempts to distinguish central approaches to oral tradition in African studies and ethnohistories. Departing from oral traditions in European studies, he invokes major perspectives from such early Africanists' works as Van Gennep, Herskovits, Beier, Evans-Pritchard, Wilks, and Mercier. In summarizing their arguments, he notes that some dismiss the validity and usefulness of oral traditions, while others uphold such traditions as useful resources for scholars. Citing Herskovits, Beier, and Mercier, Vansina emphasizes the importance of corroborating oral sources with scholarly work in social anthropology, linguistics, archeology, and literature. Conversely, Van Gennep and Wilks minimize the usefulness of oral traditions and question the credibility of such sources. While these differing perspectives on the usefulness of oral sources remain with us today, for Vansina, the key issues confronting oral traditions as historical evidence is the historians' ability to characterize what constitutes a valid historical source, and what historical methodology can be utilized to critique such sources. Vansina states the problem thusly,

> Mais, aucune d'elles n'offre une discussion generale du caractere specifique des traditions orale comme sources pour la connaissance du passe, pas plus qu'elle n'entreprend d'appliquer la critique historique a ces sources.[14]

(But, no one has offered a general discussion of the specific characteristics of oral tradition as a source for knowing the past, nor has anyone undertaken to apply an historical critique to these sources.)

Since Vansina raised these questions in 1961, Africanist scholarship has continued to expand our understanding of the diversity of African oral traditions. With the recognition that such traditions are enfolded in mnemonic and literary forms, these scholars have reinforced the interdisciplinary nature of academic work in the Western academy.

Theoretically, this chapter also benefits from the work of Linda Tuhiwai Smith, a Maori researcher and scholar, who has developed a model for community research in Kaupapa Maori.[15] It also benefits from David Henige's classic work on field studies in oral historiography.[16] Its African-centered perspective gives testimony to more than twenty years of engagement with Nigerian and Ghanaian scholars in West Africa along with Africanist scholars globally. Methodologically, its general approach is one which works within and evolves from an engagement with Yorùbá world view, cultural history, and aesthetics. This is an attempt to reflect and validate the subject culture's articulation of and epistemological approach to a philosophical and historical knowledge of its ideal selves. It premises that those selves lie within a matrix of truths wherein Yorùbá related discourses can, and should, occur. Unlike Vansina,[17] however, it posits that internal contradiction is essential to the notion of historical discourse within such cultures, and that evidence, validation, and veracity of sources are still subject to the rigors of an historical method, albeit one that evolves from the subject culture itself. Such an historical method evolves from a careful analysis and understanding of how a specific culture articulates its historical self and validates its own truths. This approach foregrounds the epistemological base of Yorùbá thought as a subject culture revealing its greater philosophical, historical, and social world views, and represents a fundamental prerequisite to Africa's dialogue with itself and with other global cultures.

The distinct methodology asserted here requires framing questions which open the heart and character of the specific African culture being studied in partnership with the researcher. It aims at being an inside-out rather than a (superficially) outside-inside approach. The accompanying theoretical perspective (re)places African subjects as actors in their own historical and social dramas.

To know and understand the complex world of Yorùbá studies, we must ask how do those who purport to be its practitioners, scholars, and students know what constitutes evidence, historiographical or otherwise, or know what constitutes refinement, virtuosity, and elegance for the Yorùbá people themselves? Art historian, Professor Rowland Abiodun, posits a comment which, for the purpose of this essay, provides a contextual answer. He writes,

> My approach to [aesthetic and methodological issues are] best expressed by the Yorùbá proverb: "What follows six is more than seven" (Ohun ti o wa leyin Offa, o ju Oje lo). The proverb suggests that we must look beyond what is easily observed if we are to understand something. Relating it to the study of African art, we must try to understand an artwork in its *cultural depth*, as the expression of the local thought or belief systems, lest we unwittingly remove the "African" in African art.[18] [*my emphasis*]

Similarly, Yorùbá-centered research requires that *we look beyond* the liminal sensibilities of Western notions of culture and history to that which is "greater than six," or in other words, to an analysis framed by the peculiarities of Yorùbá "cultural depth." Accordingly, we can speak of an historical record that is not just found in Yorùbá oral traditions but is also found in its visual, performance, aural, and literary arts, and woven throughout a rich aesthetic tapestry of Yorùbá sensibilities. An understanding of the primary cosmological role in Yorùbá historical discourse as suggested by Agiri, the significance of the Yorùbá language texts as suggested by Wande Abimbola,[19] and an effective corroboration with linguistic and archeological sources as illustrated by Omotoso Eluyemi[20] forms the basis of our methodological approach to Yorùbá oral historiography.

Methodological Perspectives and Partnership in African-Centered Research

The *process of systematic inquiry* here consists of two components: first, the recognition of master practitioners of Yorùbá cultural knowledge as experts, and second, acknowledgment of a Yorùbá worldview and epistemology that organizes and disseminates that knowledge. The recognition of master practitioners rests upon their long years of training and discipline, a condition of becoming accomplished traditional historians, masters of the spoken word, and/or court adjudicators. The acknowledgment of a discernible Yorùbá world view and epistemology opens a way to comprehend the Yorùbá world and the organization of that world view; in other words, it illuminates the character of Yorùbá thought, and privileges it as subject and its master practitioners as experts. Such acknowledgment and comprehension in Yorùbá studies provides a vista, or a world-view bridge, for African and Africanist scholars to engage in collaborative research between diverse knowledge bases. This world-view bridge is constructed upon culturally defined knowledge and aesthetics, and supported by a Yorùbá epistemological foundation. That epistemological foundation rests firmly upon "dilogicality," or a logic based upon an embrace of the dual nature of existence, and a concomitant unity of opposites. It is the tension within our dilogical existence that sharpens character, a concept represented in the narrative of the deity Iwa and elaborated in the proverb, *Ìwa l'ewà* (character is beauty). The relationship between character and causality embellishes certain oral historical narratives. To enter into this world, the linear nature of Western historical methodology yields to a circulinear mapping of Yorùbá data and its multilayered sources of evidence. Corroboration with fields such as archeology and anthropology is inevitable and evident.

Calling into focus such indigenous ideologies suggests that the study of Yorùbá oral historiography is a vast polythetic[21] system enfolded within a multidisciplinary terrain. That terrain is defined by its dilogicality and contradictions, key points of departure for understanding how to pursue Yorùbá oral historical inquiry. Dilogicality, as a narrative strategy, defines that which is aesthetically valued in concordance with the social and political significance of a subject or event. Dilogicality and contradictions provide mechanisms for organizing and embellishing the traditional record. For engaged researchers, these devices can provide opportunities for an intrinsic and holistic "read" of diverse symbolisms and iconographies, and a revelation of a complex web of independent and interactive corroborative sources, thus giving a Yorùbá perspective on what constitutes evidence. Astute and careful researchers can uncover a treasure trove of documentation that includes written, verbal, visual, aural, and instrumental[22] texts.

Another characteristic of this methodological approach to Yorùbá oral historiography is its partnership with Yorùbá cultural caretakers including traditional sovereigns and rulers, griots, religious potentates, specialized artisans, carvers, musicians, performers, and a cornucopia of other culturally defined professionals.[23] As a whole, these professional caretakers maintain a plethora of cultural records in oral literature, art, metonym, performance, instrumentation, and major celebratory events. Their knowledge-base and skills give testimony to what they, as custodians of culturally specific wisdom, knowledge, and world views, are empowered to validate about their cultural and communal selves. Placing them at the center of our partnership research illuminates how they are trained, and how they train others to assume similar cultural responsibilities. It provides a glimpse of the high esteem and recognition that they command within their own social ethos. It is important to underscore Agiri's concrete distinction in Yorùbá tradition between general storytellers on the one hand, and professionally trained cultural caretakers on the other.[24] The latter include among others babalawo, olorisa, onijala, and iyanile orisa whose authority and practices are regulated by a master class who adhere to established criteria for membership, transmission, and training of successive practitioners.

With respect to data and evidence, researchers are challenged to include alternative texts such as Eṣẹ̀ Ifá, Ijálá, Oríkì, and Orin Ọ̀ṣun as contributing sources of an historical record. If as Wande Abimbola[25] attests, the Ifá Divination Corpus is the storehouse of Yorùbá knowledge, then the Ifa corpus itself must also be an extant source of Yorùbá history. It would follow that "knowing" (*ìmọ̀*) and "comprehending" (*ìgbéèdè*) this system, in part, provides an entre; into the essence of that which is historically substantive and aesthetically pleasing to the culture itself. As Abimbola attests and the *ẹṣẹ̀* Ifá reveal, ọdú Ifá reflects essential Yorùbá truth(s) (*òtító*) that are simultaneously literary and historical, and which underscore the effectiveness of "bicultural or partnership" methodology as articulated by Linda Smith.[26] With respect to African historical studies, this means seeking what is unique in the world view, what defines and constitutes historical significance, and how the interpretation of that world view and significance underscores historical truths as context for knowing the historical record.

The Imọ of Yorùbá Thought

Another key to approaching Yorùbá historiography is through an understanding of Yorùbá thought (*ìrònú*) which also resides in its literary orisa system and which, in part, codifies its historiography. For example, the Yorùbá sense of locality and time is located in their historical identification with Ile-Ife and its complex oral narratives. Both Ile-Ife and associative Ifá narratives continue to characterize the intricate Yorùbá political system and social hierarchy, as well as to provide legitimacy for local and interlocking governance. With Ifé as locality and Ifá traditions as mappings, the Yorùbá locate a place of origin and an extensive oral encyclopedia of events, major players, migrations, and resettlements since before and after the time of Odùduwà and their Ifẹ̀ engagements. For the researcher of Yorùbá historiography, a knowledge and understanding of the *Odú Ifá*, as a complete set of cosmogenic narratives, can, and should, lead her or him to a broader interpretation of Yorùbá sovereignty and rulership. In a nineteenth-century example, Reverend Samuel Johnson used his intimate knowledge of Yorùbá culture, interviews with the master babalawo(s) in the court of the Oní Ifẹ̀ (traditional ruler), and recitations from the *Odú Ifá* to reconstruct one of the earliest lists of rulers among the Yorùbá houses.[27] In his work as well as that of Eluyemi, we find a rich genealogical list that includes women rulers, some of whom are descendants of earlier rulers. This suggests a branch of study that focuses on an underlying gender ideology, and one that extends the idea of rulership beyond individual authority to a more Yorùbá-centered model. This could also lead a researcher to work through the Yorùbá language in partnership with its professional cultural caretakers for corroboration.

E. Bolaji Idowu in his classic cosmogenic work, *Olódumaré God in Yorùbá Belief*,[28] offers an example of an interdisciplinary lingua-cultural approach to revealing aspects of Yorùbá historiography. Although this work focuses on Yorùbá religious history, Yorùbá scholars, traditional and literate, agree that all Yorùbá-based knowledge derives from this source. To do so, Idowu notes that the only way to truly know the Yorùbá is to know their oral literature, which contains the sum total of their essences.[29] In addition to providing several etymological and mythical sources for the Supreme Deity, Olódumaré, and examines the names, attributes, and status of Olódumaré which, he concludes, represents the quintessential source of *àṣẹ*, life force or soul.[30] In his analysis of Olódumaré's will, Idowu states that other òrìṣà (deities) and beings occupied the heavens with the Supreme Deity before the creation and occupation of earth,[31] a factor relevant to the authority of divine rulership. The *Odú Ifá*, the Ifá chapters which contain *ese* or poetic narratives and verse, is instructive here. One of the major *Odú Ifá* (Ifá chapters) states that the IrúnMọlè, or primary deities included sixteen major òrìṣà plus one, or seventeen major orisa. The distinction "plus one" refers to Ọ̀ṣun, the mother principle central to Yorùbá cultural, religious, social, and political order.[32] Two major ideas are communicated in this foundational narrative: (1) that the narrative itself parallels and establishes the legitimacy of theocratic rulership which has existed in Ilé-Ifẹ̀ since its founding, and (2) that theocracy is mother-centered and gender harmonized,[33] a key to understanding both Yorùbá historical and cultural realities. The history of Odùduwà, the acknowledged Yorùbá progenitor, becomes critical here because theocratic legitimacy throughout the Yorùbá speaking kingdoms was, and is, derived from Odùduwà's descent line and from Ile-Ife. Such political and cultural legitimacy still carries influence from the Ketu areas in the present-day republic of Benin to the Bini areas along the southwestern borders of the Niger River.[34]

The ongoing debate about the gender of Odùduwà illustrates the importance of bicultural research, especially with respect to Yorùbá historiography. The odú Ifá narrates that the world began at Ilé-Ifè, and other awon itan, or effective histories, narrate that Odùduwà migrated from the East. These seemingly disparate narratives do maintain some complementarity, especially in light of the theocratic nature of Yorùbá rulership and the predominance of migration in their history. That a pre-Odùduwà people existed in Ilé-Ifè is also evident, and also that women were part of a dual-gender ruling class. J. K. Olupona's work in the Ondo region is particularly revealing. Olupona notes that the Obá of Ondo

> derives his authority partly through his mythic descent from the primogenitrix of the town, Oba Pupupu, the first woman-king and the daughter of Oduduwa, the legendary founder of the Yorùbá ethnic group. The reference to Pupupu as Ondo's primogenitor warrants further elaboration in light of the existence of three indigenous ethnic groups, Ifore, Idoko, and Ika people prior to the arrival of the Oduduwa group. In the Ondo myth of origin, it is alleged that these three original groups surrendered to the newcomers without much of a fight, and that all rights and privileges pertaining to the territory were readily ceded to the newcomers. This story is acted out during the ritual of succession of an Osemawe (the title of Ondo Oba). The Oloja of Ifore ritually reenacts the original pledge of surrender of the territory while Osemawe concedes certain medicinal powers and the control of a sizeable portion of the land, the Idoko ward, to the Oloja of Idoka.[35]

It becomes obvious here that understanding the significance of gender in Yorùbá oral traditions and cultural history is a fundamental part of reconstructing Yorùbá historiography. Indeed, one could argue that Pupupu inherited her crown from Odùduwà, her mother, if we suppose a matrilineal descent pattern, and also that she inherited it from Odùduwà, her father, if we accept Idowu's argument that Odùduwà is male, while the orisa that he brought with him from the Eastern Africa is female.[36] One could also argue that Pupupu as female and Ọrànyán as male inherited their crowns from Odùduwà, a cognomenic title, in a manner that is characteristic of bifurcated, dual-gender political, social, and cultural leadership systems among the Yorùbá. One could also suggest that the bifurcation reflects an asymmetrical gender ideology that willingly incorporated aboriginal cultures into that which became and today is known as Yorùbá. Indeed, the brilliance of Yorùbá culture and historiography is its ability to accommodate others.

Moreover, the significance of role and seniority over biological gender in its syntax and meaning is an important factor in Yorùbá ideology and rulership. Even Idowu tacitly acknowledges that "Yorùbá society was at one time based upon a matriarchical system."[37] Unfortunately, Idowu relies solely on the masculine English pronoun in his work, retaining "he" throughout his discourse. Had he move to a more culturally based discourse, his exploration and analysis of Yorùbá theology along with its concomitant theocracy would have noted the role of women in both religious and political ideology and praxis.[38] Drawing from evidence presented in Yorùbá art history, Professor Abiodun's work highlights the significance of a bicultural analysis when he states

> Even though much of Yorùbá religious activity and aesthetic concern seems to be male-dominated, we have not much authority from Yorùbá oral traditions and visual art for assuming that this picture is accurate. For example, we are not quite certain of the sex of Odùduwà, the progenitor of the Yorùbá culture, since we have as much evidence for considering Odùduwà feminine as we have for considering him masculine.[39]

Idowu's analysis of Yorùbá cosmogony and the settling of Ile-Ife highlight several historiographical themes, motifs, and points of departure for researchers. In another narrative that offers both historical and cultural significance, he posits that the fragmentation of Òrìṣà-Ńlá (the Arch-Deity), a reference to being split to pieces by a jealous servant, is a source of the òrìṣà pantheon. In brief, Ọrúnmìlà, custodian of Ifá, gathered his pieces together, and buries some of Òrìṣà-Nlá's parts in Irànje, the city of the fragmented deity. Ọrúnmìlà then scatters the rest of Òrìṣà-Nla's parts around the world,[40] analogous to the global dispersal of the òrìṣà, and reflecting the global dissemination of creative and plastic arts. Notably, the similarities between this myth and the Osiris myth of ancient Kemet are thematically striking for, in both cases, jealousy causes fragmentation (ostensibly negative) which results in the evolution of a new theocracy and political system (ostensibly positive). Metaphorically, the narrative is also striking because it references patterns of unity, enmity, migration, resettlement, and regeneration consistent with Yorùbá oral and *written* historiographies. Themes such as a) unification—fragmentation—synthesis,

b) theocracy—governance—usurpation, and 3) migration—resettlement—synthesis are major patterns in Yorùbá historiography. These patterns are played out in the narratives of major orisa such as Ṣàngó, Ọgùn, and Ọ̀sun as well as in the somewhat contradictory stories of Jákùtá, Ẹrinlẹ̀, and Ezulea. As Idowu states,

> The significance of this myth lies in its suggestion that Òrìṣà was originally a unity; that this is the Yorùbá way of giving recognition to the process of "fragmentation" which comes as a result of giving concrete shapes in the mind to certain outstanding attributes of the Deity, or of that renaming, due to circumstances, by which one and the same divinity becomes apparently several divinities.[41]

Furthermore, the Òrìṣà Ńlá narrative suggests an historical process that holds meaning for and understanding of Yorùbá society beyond its contemporary geophysical boundaries. Here the role of Ọ̀rúnmìlà, symbolic of wisdom and knowledge, is to represent and to validate Yorùbá cultural historical references and contradictions in order to know, and in fact to preserve, what lies beyond them. Indeed, one could suggest that Ọ̀rúnmìlà is also a source of unification and dissemination, as well as a consummate diplomat of the pantheon. Although Idowu is silent on the topic, the mother symbol as the source of all humanity remains a constant one in the narrative, and her relationship to the fragmented and disseminated deity structures a way of knowing the relationship among the sixteen major Yorùbá orisa as modalities of political thought and human observation.

To reiterate, our bicultural methodology for understanding (*ìgbéèdè*) the interdependence of Yorùbá orature and historiography involves knowing that orature as they themselves know, interpret, and discern value from it, that is by asserting its complex artistic, literary, and language traditions as key signifiers of that tradition. To do so, we center our approach in the middle of a Yorùbá cultural lens to gaze upon a world created by a Yorùbá dialectic engaged in its own sensibilities and meaning. It is instructive to note that the word, *ìgbéèdè* or understanding, has its etymological roots[42] in two literary indicators *gbọ́* + *èdé*, that is, to hear language—in short, comprehension of what is said.[43] In the study of Yorùbá orature and historiography, we must hear, accept, understand, and ponder the aesthetic relevance of Yorùbá orature and historiography as it is found in its tonal, subtle language and its associated cosmology in order to produce advanced and relevant historiographical research.

The Primacy and Challenges of Cultural Historical Inquiry

The question then remains, what do we know and how can what we know lead to an understanding of Yorùbá historiography? We know that the Yorùbá pantheon is laden with eclectic deities who mirror human, elemental, and chromatic phenomena. We know that these eclectic orisa signify events and concepts indicative of Yorùbá culture and history. As Sandra Barnes succinctly demonstrates,

> Attributing certain things to a deity is like placing these things under the same rubric or in the same class. Each class (or "domain" as they should be called when one is dealing with the polythetic religious system) is ordered according to logical principles. A typical one is the single common denominator principle whereby phenomenon are classified according to one feature. Using this principle, one might propose that all things related to iron belong to the Ogun domain, and therefore this is *the* diagnostic principle for deciding whether and not something is Ogun-related.[44]

While this associative diagnostic principle works to organize ideas about Ògún, a broader view of associative principles is required for other orisa and their cohorts. We know, for example, that Òṣun, the renown foundress and protectress of Oṣogbo, is also a river and an owner of brass. We know that Ṣángò, an ancient ruler of Òyó, is the deified force of thunder and lightning. We know that Óyá is Ṣangò's favorite and most loyal wife, associated in Yorùbá cosmology with strong winds and tornados. In the Ijálá oracular texts, Ògún's travels throughout Yorùbáland and beyond reveal the presence of certain plants, their medicinal properties, and animals that are slowly disappearing today.[45] Babalola, for example, illustrates how the poetic Ijálá contains the genealogy of the ruling houses and several important Ife families, warriors, and hunters.[46] With respect to the list of Ifẹ rulers, Ijálá sources provided significant information regarding the nature of Ifẹ rulership, migration patterns, and warfare. Ògún narratives also reveal internal conflicts between Yorùbá regencies and among the ruling elites. Babalola also notes that oríkì is the most important form of Ijala chanting because of its role in the preservation of the genealogical record and its role in inspiring proper conduct among the ruling elite.[47]

An analysis of the oríkì (praise poetry) and orin (songs) of Òṣun provides vital information regarding the role of women in the founding and protection of several Yorùbá towns, including Òṣogbo, Ikiti, and others.

A bicultural exploration of Ṣángò's narratives points to an historic relationship between Nupe, where Ṣángò was born, and Òyó, a town of vital importance in Yorùbá history, which he came to rule. A study of Òyá's cosmological association with the River Niger and her similarity with the Wraith in the Malian myth of Sundiata's mother, Sologon, offers a broader view of the influence of Yorùbá historiographical and migration patterns than its current physical mapping suggests.[48]

Engaging Yorùbá oracular texts in this manner requires the expertise of their cultural caretakers, whose intimate knowledge of these narratives and of their interrelationships provide the appropriate context for understanding the literary and historical value of this data. With an appropriate bicultural preparation, ancient and mythical cities, villages, and regencies reveal a web of clues for further historiographic investigation and corroboration. We learn of migration patterns, wars, and conquest that establish some cities while abandoning and sacking others. We find in the vestiges of language and dialect indications of resettlement, trade, and cultural influences swirling within and throughout the western African region. This kind of in-depth knowledge and understanding of the òrìṣà and their variations lends itself to a set of Yorùbá-specific tools of critical analysis relevant to diverse aspects of the human experience. This type of bicultural method is accomplished through cultural immersion and at least a working knowledge of the subject language with the goal of mastering its nuances and intricacies. This cultural immersion also requires that the researcher seek the proper local protocols before beginning to engage in dialogue with its cultural masters, that is, both traditional and contemporary Yorùbá scholars. With an understanding of language, structure, and protocols, a bicultural researcher can access a culture's complex codes and locate its linguistic signifiers. Indeed two decades of scholarly work and research partnership with other Yorùbá and Yorùbá-influenced artists, writers, and practitioners globally, such as Rowland Abiodun, J. Kehinde Olupona, and Wande Abimbola, Yemi Eleburuibon, and Andrea Benton Rushing have been crucial to my own work. Such partnerships have yielded continuous in-depth knowledge and understanding of Yorùbá cultural studies generally, and its historiography specifically.

Corroborative interpretation of events outside of the Yorùbá oracular, cosmological context also rests upon a partnership approach to the research question because it provides accesses to relevant internal knowledge systems. When integrity guides such discourse, the theoretical and methodological design carries with it an authoritative yet dynamic voice sufficient to address both the contradictory and corroborative sources external to the orature and relevant to the historiographical question. Such efforts must proceed with an appreciation of Yorùbá thought which begins with internal corroboration among extant visual, verbal, and aural sources. Sandra Barnes is also instructive here.

> The principle by which Ogun information is classified accepts variation in meanings. Rather than being an exclusive principle, it is inclusive. The technical term for this kind of classification is polythetic. In a polythetic system of classification, no one feature gives definition to a domain. A polythetic system identifies a domain through combinations of features. . . . A useful way of dealing with polythetic classification is to think of the chain of family resemblances, where the defining attribute changes from one link to the next.[49]

Barnes' *diagnostic principle*, which I have termed the òrìṣà principle elsewhere,[50] also functions well in designing a theoretical and methodological approach to Yorùbá orature and historiography. It applies to the multi-media and multi-sensory Yorùbá cultural delivery system which interweaves verbal and visual arts[51] with political memory[52] and religious history[53] in order to mediate sociocultural and political-religious behavior. This multimedia and multisensory delivery system is artistic, informative, and historical. Such a mode of presentation reinforces the cultural and political history of its audience and allows for dialogue with the audience as well as between them and their cultural professionals. Like a master dúndún ensemble, where each drum carries only one segment of the whole, the beauty of each drum is best appreciated in concert with the other drums. In short, Yorùbá historiography is best comprehended in concert with a knowledge of Yorùbá orature, language, cosmology, art, and political structure. Interpreting the proper oracular signs requires that the researcher understand that Yorùbá aesthetic preferences for knowledge presentation are underscored by the proverb, *iwa l'ewá*; (character is beauty). That is, as Farris Thompson succinctly states

> Character is a force infusing physical beauty with everlastingness. . . . Beauty is part of coolness but beauty does not have the force that character has. Beauty comes to an end. Character is forever.[54]

Yorùbá orature, its intrinsic self-appraisal, and its complex meanings are rooted, as Abiodun observes, in "mutual references and allusions"[55] which are only fully discernible as interlocking pieces of a complex philosophical and historical puzzle. Truly to unravel and reconstruct Yorùbá orature and historiography is to listen, interpret, engage, and surrender to a multisensory tapestry of "metaphoric allusions." It is to become a perennial learner locked in discourse with several master diviners, drummers, artists-teachers simultaneously while living at the center of things. It is to know that,

> The Yorùbá assess everything aesthetically—from the taste and color of a yam to the qualities of a dye, to the dress and deportment of a woman or a man. An entry in one of the earliest dictionaries of their language, published in 1858, was *amewa*, literally "knower-of-beauty" "connoisseur," one who looks for the manifestation of pure artistry. Beauty is seen in the mean (iwontúnwonsi)—in something not too short, not too beautiful (overhandsome people turn out to be skeletons in disguise in many folktales) or too ugly. Moreover, the Yorùbá appreciate freshness and compensation per se in the arts. These preoccupations are especially evident in the rich and vast body of art works celebrating Yorùbá religion.[56]

Yorùbá oral historiography is found within the matrix of Yorùbá aesthetics and thought. Consequently, to understand its philosophy is to ponder contradiction as normative, and linearity as banal. In language and in orature, the Yorùbá relish analogy, oxymoron, and hyperbole served in polysyllabic and polyrhythmic modalities as the true life-force of historical and literary expression. Understanding the interrelationships among literary aesthetics, creative arts, and historiography is to abide "in the mean";[57] that is, to be poised with balance in seeming disequilibrium, with truths in disparities, with beauty strewn among variegated and multidimensional sources. To relentlessly engage such profound contradictions is to reside at the vortex of Yorùbá thought on a precipice of an understanding of its complex history. This, as a part of a bicultural methodological framework, hinges on a critical engagement with Yorùbá sensibilities and its cultural constructions of analogy and metaphor. It asks the researcher to engage in the linguistic and literary interplay between orun (heaven-spiritual) and ile (earth-mundane), between diunital[58] world views that align content, meaning, and form within the complexity of its oral historiography and its other Yorùbá-defined sources.

Oral Historiography and Yorùbá Aestheticism

Cultural, literary, and historical transmissions occur in an array of Yorùbá specific venues including annual òrìṣà festivals, celebrations of numerous human events, and daily activities. In these settings, trained professionals oversee the performance and narration of the ancestors and the divinities[59] that validate Yorùbá life and history.[60] Yorùbá scholars such as Abimbola and Babalawo note that the mythical, historical and poetic knowledge of each òrìṣà as learned by its caretakers adheres to specific aesthetic and metonymic principles designed to safeguard the veracity of the cosmological and historical record while allowing the diverse creativiy and artistic verve in their public presentation. Yorùbá orature provides the texts and sources for their collective sociocultural, political, and historical memories. As demonstrated, the cosmology of each òrìṣà refers to a distinctive roll and/or attributes within the Yorùbá cosmological system. A learned priesthood of women and men, along with trained oracular poets and performing artists, preserve this collective treasure of cultural histories and mythologies. Together, these professional women and men of the religious echelon, in conjunction with a continuous stream of artists-initiates, comprise the cultural caretakers who preserve a cornucopia of diverse genres and various aspects of the Yorùbá worldview and history. In this manner, as Abiola Irele notes, Yorùbá artists "Take their own voice and speak with their own accent."[61]

Akin Euba's work, *Yorùbá Drumming*, provides an example of this relationship. He states,

> A version of the myth of origin obtained from an Ile-Ife drummer has it that dundun drums were brought to Ile Ife from heaven by the founders of Ile-Ife. According to another version, the gudugudu and iyaalu came to Ile-Ife from "Mecca," while an Ijebu-Odè drummer, who told me that his father brought dundun to Ijebu-Odè from Oyo believes that dundun originated in Oyo.[62]

This myth culled from the oral tradition and recounted by professional dundun drummers parallels the myth of origins of Odùduwà. It also interacts with the mythical history of the founding of Oṣogbo in which Timi of Ẹdẹ also plays a significant role. Further, Euba's aural itan or narrative corroborates such diverse works as Samuel Johnson's *History of the Yorùbá*, Ojo's *Yorùbá Culture: A Geograhical Anaylsis*, and Idowus's *Olodumaré: God in Yorùbá Belief*. In each work, reference to the relationships between Yorùbá migration and Mecca are reiterated.

Nevertheless, one of the richest sources for the study of Yorùbá orature and historiography remains the òrìṣà festivals. In his critical introduction to *Drama and Theater: A Critical Source Book*, Yemi Ogunbiyi summarizes the diverse genres, forms, and functions of Nigerian drama related to the orisa festivals. He states,

> The specific origins of Nigeria theater and drama are speculative. What is, however, not speculative . . . is the existence in many Nigerian societies, of the robust theatrical tradition. The primitive root of that tradition must be sought in the numerous religious rituals and festivals that exist in many Nigerian communities. For, as the expression of the relationship between a [humanity, society, and nature], drama arose out of fundamental human needs in the dawn of human civilization, and has continued to express those needs ever since, which is to say, Nigeria theater and drama originated with Nigerian himself (and herself), embodying the first preoccupations, first struggles, successes, setbacks, and all.[63]

The religious rituals and festivals, which incorporate and manifest these needs, mirror cumulative human and collective historical experiences, and are intended to fortify the collective memory of these experiences. The reinforcement of certain key historical motifs occurs in the privacy of the divination process as well as in the public display. In both the public display of festival and the private discourse of divination, literary, religious, and historical presentations are presented through aesthetically woven conduits for a community of individuals who attend such events. Or to put it another way, these presentations are conduits through which Yorùbá communities access and divine the cultural depths of metaphor and analogy, both of which reinforce and reveal cultural and historical truths. Similarly, the artistry of Yorùbá festival drama and orature presented as expressions of beauty, *amewa*, are the marrow which sustains deep historical and cultural perspective. To engage this interplay of cultural dramas is to engage in the "polythetic process" Sandra Barnes defines as the form and function of such a process.

> The thinking of Ogun as a system of classifying information—according to an inclusive, or polythetic principle—shifts the discussion of meaning from singular to plural. It therefore relieves us of finding a single common denominator with which to identify and then compare this divine figure. Taken as a domain of related ideas, diversity and unity in meeting can then be the bottom of it as well as being simultaneously present. One of the most useful implications of being able to think of meanings in the plural is that we can, by extension, visualize the processes by which some meanings remain unchanged while, at the same time, other meetings can be added, subtracted, or altered, little by little, over space and time. It allows us, further, to make order out of what seems to be contradiction, diversity, and

unevenness. Needless to say, the logic used by insiders in assigning meanings to the deities' domain is intuitive. For the outsider, it is artificial and then mainly for heuristic purposes.[64]

The Òṣun Festival, like other Yorùbá festivals, reinforces its own sociocultural norms through the recitation of classic and contemporary orature. It discerns history and contemporary issues through the dramatic staging of its polythetic performing artists, and reaffirms those ideals that foster social cohesion. The major participants and their respective responsibilities confirm this. The Atáója or traditional Oṣògbo ruler, the Ìyá Òṣun or chief priestess, and the Aworo or chief priest, are responsible for the organization of the festival since they represent the founders of Òṣogbo, including Òṣun. They officiate over the religious aspects of the festival by performing the prescribed rituals, and preparing the arugbà to carry the sacrifice, that is, an offering to Òṣun as foundress and aboriginal ruler. They also officiate and participate in numerous secular ceremonies which occur throughout the sixteen-day festival.[65] Similar to festivals described by Olupona, Abimbola, and others, the Òṣun festival reconstructs a history of Òṣogbo including its interaction with Ile-Ife, Ede, Ijumu, and other surrounding townships. It also reinforces the authority of the ruling classes, and reaffirms the interconnectedness of the religious and political elite. Herein lies another characteristic of oral historiography, that is, its reenactment in festival context, which, as Agiri and Folayan state, require the researcher to "check and cross-check" with other sources including other regencies, nonruling families and lineages, and diverse artists.

Igbéèdè: Understanding and Theorizing about Yorùbá Aesthetics and Historiography

As stated before, "What follows six is more than seven" is the logic of Yorùbá orature and historiography. To the insider, seven is a number of completion but not finality. It signifies a day of transitions and new beginnings such as naming ceremonies, rites of passage, and preparatory burial rituals. To the outsider, seven follows six but precedes eight, and can be said to reside in the middle of both, thereby forming a duality of plus or minus one. From this perspective, one can also argue that seven leads to infinity in a predictable pattern or set of patterns. But that is linear thinking. To the Yorùbá insider, there are infinite, cyclical possibilities beyond the finite number six that holds sway. In fact, this proverb itself suggests that infinity begins immediately after six, thus skipping the incremental logic in favor of a more expansive one. For the oral history researcher, such aesthetical and literary understanding helps to distinguish meaning and sift historical data from the illusory meanings and icons.

In this case, the "intuitive" logic, as Barnes points out, lies in the nuanced cultural depth of historical experiences and collective consciousness about those experiences, in other words, in the mythical edifice that validates Yorùbá thought, world view, and existence. What facilitates that intuitive logic is the collective assessment of what has preceded "six" as the foundation for what lies beyond it. In the case of traditional literary criticism and oral historiography, the collective consciousness and experiences of both indigenous and migrant populations are narrated in Ifá Divination and other diverse oracular texts. These texts form the edifice of Yorùbá world views which house the historical reconstructions in myths, legends, poetry, epics, praise poetry, and festival drama expressed in the allegorical messages and metaphors of the Yorùbá artistic imagination. To access, interpret, embellish, and disseminate these texts and their "polythetic" meanings requires, at the least, studied attention to the cultural details formed by the ambivalence of hyperbole and coded meanings found in the "*diagnostic principles*" represented by the òrìṣà. It is critical to understand the philosophical underpinnings of such oracular construction if the researcher of oral traditions is to properly engage with their meaning. It is to live in the fray of active òrìṣà principles and ideological perspectives that lie beyond the immediate tangibility of number six as the event horizon in Western parlance. Conversely, in Yorùbá parlance, infinity begins beyond our perception in such a way that divinity and infinity, like historical evidence and aesthetics, are interchangeable.

Babalola[66] and Abimbola[67] elaborate on the artistic breadth implicit within the context of very structured and identifiable literary genres. In both Ijálá, the hunters' poetry and entertainment of the òrìṣà Ògún, and Ifá, the divination poetry as the corpus of Yorùbá knowledge and purview of the òrìṣà Ọ̀rúnmìlà, Yorùbá audiences anticipate both the predictable and the unpredictable. The variations in style and performance mode are obvious inasmuch as Ijálá and Ifá are distinct oral genres. For example, the Ifá literary corpus presents a more sacred, oracular style consisting of poetic formulas and linguistic alliterations specifically relevant to the Ifá religious corpus and analogous to social discourse. Conversely, Ijálá poetry constitutes a more secular style replete with allusions to the Yorùbá physical environment, especially as viewed by hunters and metal workers. In addition, Ifá orature is more philosophical and mythical than Ijálá, which is a more environmental and functional art form. It is also noted that the literary stylistics and modes of performance constitute enough diversity in oracular arts to call attention to the need for careful analysis and methodological approaches to Yorùbá orature as well as its influence on written literature, literary criticism, and oral historiography itself. Such Yorùbá oracular aesthetics are replicated in Yorùbá dundun drummers, as indicated by Akin Euba.

> The "composer of the moment" is usually the person leading the ensemble, the iyaalu drummer, for it is he alone that is not restricted to "fixed" material. Although the other members of the ensemble are normally restricted to fixed patterns, previously composed by them or by other people, they may also now and then make spontaneous innovations, consisting of minor variations on their fixed patterns, during the course of performance. Nevertheless, their creative impulse is almost totally restricted and, in view of the fact that no member of the ensemble knows what new material will be produced until it is realized in performance, this restriction makes good sense.[68]

Obviously, these recurrent patterns are characteristic features of diverse oral genres and drumming styles that are controlled by the master drummer. However, what lies beyond such obvious characteristics rest upon a fusion of literary, visual, aural, and performing arts as transmission agents for cultural and historiographical ideologies. Each òrìṣà functions as a *diagnostic principle* that relays identity, meaning, and history through associative instruments, chronology, movements, and literary genre. These associative elements classify and catalogue an affiliation of symbols and themes that culminate in its core repertoire of knowledge and information. The master drummer leads the ensemble as the custodian of the history of a particular community, family or important individual as well as a creative artist in his own right.

Ọṣun, her worshiper, and orature, for example, are readily discernible through the gentle swaying dance movements accompanied by calabash players and water drummers, and a chorus of women singing her oríki, or praise poetry. Ṣàngó, his worshiper, and orature, on the other hand, are identified by the long majestic, powerful movements of the male dancers, the crimson red costuming, and the falsetto Ṣàngó-pipe singing. Ògún, the òrìṣà of war and iron, is the patron of warriors and military endeavors, as well as of hunters, farmers, and carvers. As Wole Soyinka demonstrates, Ògún represents both creative and destructive forces, an artistic and bellicose spirit.[69] His complexity is symbolic of human nature, thus, as a primordial deity who carved open the pathway between orun and ile as the conduit of the òrìsà , he represents ingenuity, challenge, and aggression. The oriki Osun is played on the bátá drum which also accompanies the special Ijálá poetry, a verbal artistic form of Ògún's own creation. Acknowledged as a strikingly handsome deity, Ògún wears a thigh-length overgarment known as agbada. Over this he drapes his hunter's rifle to one side and his machete to the other. His chest is covered with amulets that contain special charms or medicines of the hunter òrìṣà. Ògún thirsts for palm wine and the blood of dogs, his favorite offerings. He symbolizes challenge and the will to penetrate the "transitional gulf" between humanity and divinity as well as the conquest of the human spirit.

Ṣàngọ́, another powerful deity, who according to Reverend Samuel Johnson ruled Old Òyó around the seventeenth century.[70] Deified as the orisa of thunder and lightning, Ṣàngọ́ terrified his enemies with his ability to control fire at will. His most popular appellation, obá kò sò, refers to his mythical-historical suicide, which occurred after the Òyó people, then his favorite wife Òyá, abandoned him. Ṣàngọ́ is the consummate tragic character whose most egregious flaw is his temper and rages. His worshipers entertain him with an oral genre known as Ṣàngọ́-pipe, his dedicated praise poetry accompanied by the bata drum. Envisioned as a robust Obá, Ṣàngọ́ wears aṣọ okẹ́, a Yorùbá traditional heavy woven cotton garment. Esu is the custodian of the crossroads and of àṣẹ. He wears light garments sewn together in strips.[71] His distinctive braid and juju bag gives Esu a fitting image as the deity of chance and fate. Where Ifá knows the secrets of creation, Esu is the keeper of the ase, that is "the divine power with which Olódumarè created the universe and maintained its physical laws."[72] As guardian of the crossroads, his designated authority to judge, accept, or reject sacrifice weighs heavily upon the success or failure of each supplicant. Where Òrúnmìlà divinates, Èṣù dispenses justice, hence, the images of Esu and Òrúnmìlà are carved on the Ifá divining tray, Opon Ifá, as complementary forces in Yorùbá cosmology. Finally, Egúngún, the òrìṣà of collective ancestry, dresses in raffia, strips of cloth, and is covered completely so as to expose no part of the body. The Egúngún symbolizes the collective spirit of the deceased, and therefore embodies Yorùbá heritage. This masked spirit is always accompanied by attendants who attempt to control and protect its essence. According to Kofi Opoku Asare, the Egúngún are the protectors of Yorùbá society who guard it against evil, misfortune, and fear.

Festival Drama and Orature as Context for Yorùbá Historiography

The main purpose of traditional festivals is the reaffirmation of the society's commitment to itself. These events represent community efforts to recapitulate its mythical and historical origins, to refine its meanings and objectives for continuity. The Òṣun festival exemplifies such collective social consciousness. It engages itself simultaneously with its own internal conflicts as it attempts to resolve those conflicts and reset its own cultural course. A community gathering of individuals, the Ọ̀ṣun Òṣogbo festival finds consensus in its internal communal voice by validating its own mythical historical and objective purpose through the agency of her orature. It revisits individual and communal origins as well as addresses conflicts that threaten unity. The audience-participants "read" the meaning and identify with main characters in an effort to respond to extant festival songs and poetry as modalities of oral literary discourse. Ọ̀ṣun, as a polythetic òrìṣà subject, along with her verbal and visual metaphors symbolize the internal logic of her mythology and its social historical expression. As a corpus of knowledge Ọ̀ṣun, as subject and metaphor, expands her definitive boundaries and exploits the *diagnostic* order of Yorùbá world view. Consequently, the myth and meaning of the subject-òrìṣà principle structures the theory and practice of oral literary aesthetics and historiographical knowledge within the festival context.

Clearly, knowledge of Yorùbá historiography and understanding of Yorùbá thought presents a real opportunity for a bicultural partnership approach to the study of Yorùbá history and culture. Their identifiable voices draw together those verisimilitudes of associative meanings that are replicated in life itself. The òrìṣà do not necessarily follow us, nor do we always follow them, except by mutual agreement, *Ènìyàn kò sí, kò s'Ímàlè* without humanity there's no divinity. As the Ifá corpus reminds us, it is only Orí, our own heads and destinies, that remain with us eternally. Indeed, the narrative of Òrìṣà-Ńlá reminds us that unity is not necessarily conformity, and that fragmentation can seed regenerative energies, which, in turn, can address a spectrum of human needs. In fact, the characteristic ability of the Yorùbá òrìṣà to absorb their global environments and reinterpret or, even, reinvent those environments out of their own ethos underscores its cultural àṣẹ. Abiola Irele states,

> Ritual, in particular, although rooted in the deeply affected narrative of myth, is ultimately no more than a strategy of negotiation: between gods and humans and between social actors. Both myth and ritual involve a constant symbolic reshuffle of the cards, so to speak, according to the needs of the moment and of circumstance, and thus present themselves as forms of discourse that serve to position the motives and interest of the collectivities, as a function of the modes of insertion in the scheme of things. They are thus, we might say, relational by definition and function.[73]

Yorùbá culture, history, and myth, we may venture to say, are like a social glue. That glue holds diverse people, diverse ideas, diverse life experiences, diverse goals and values, and scattered interrelationships together in a web of commonality that constantly defines and refines who the Yorùbá are. One should recall, as well, that the orisa source is not only godhead, as discussed earlier, but is also a communal voice. A bicultural and systemic approach to Yorùbá oral tradition can maintain a tie between the artists and their respective societies, cultural caretakers and historical knowledge. Here, the distinction between verbal-visual and oral-written creative artists may be clearer than the bridge that joins them. Both conceive of themselves as functioning within a social milieu that praises a communal *I*. As such, these artists project a voice among voices either directly or improvisationally, in call and response, a capella, choral, or harmonic mode. Like the orisa who commune musically with their co-divinities, artistic reproduction within the context of an evolving orisa nexus formulates an ensemble of social, cultural, political, and historical voices.

Methodology in Yorùbá Historiography and Aesthetics: Some Considerations

Methodologically speaking, bicultural partnership analysis of Yorùbá oral traditions script the interplay between humanity and divinity by constructing and deconstructing, as needs arise, its unified parts as well as its fragmented whole. The seeming contradictions in narrative and locale are indicators of developments and cultural-historical shifts in Yorùbá historiography. The verbal-visual corroboration of this process often contributes to archeological discovery, as exemplified by the recent finds in Ijebu-Ode. A linguistic and gendered approach to the political system supports the possibility of a more fruitful reanalysis of the notion of patriarchy, matriarchy, and gender ideology in Yorùbá hierarchy. More importantly, the interplay between divinity and humanity requires that we investigate the role of communalism in Yorùbá thought and historical behavior, for it sustains and justifies the fragmented whole. Those fragmented or polythetic whole(s) inform a Yorùbá cultural and historical world view, its verbal and visual language, and its plethora of meanings. It validates and negates the historical relevancy and aesthetic quality of diverse oracular texts by validating its own communal voice. Its artists accordingly form the basis for a communal critique. This creative yardstick means both consistency and innovation, a measure of the aesthetically "cool,"[74] a place to depart from and return to, an anchor for Yorùbá history and a moving creative artistry.

To extend the boundaries of Yorùbá knowledge requires that scholars engage its cultural caretakers as partners and master teachers, not mere informants, in the research process. In the twenty-first century, an appreciation of its linguistic complexity and a working knowledge of the language itself, including an awareness of its tonal and lexical dialects is a prerequisite to any valid research design concerning the Yorùbá. Essentially, research in Yorùbá historiography specifically requires that researchers engage the topic at its own acknowledged point of entry, that is, through its oracular texts and ideological narratives. It requires the careful discernment between mythologized fact, cosmology, and historiographical analogy. Indeed, approaching such data is more than mere cataloguing of information, for it demands that the researcher step inside the epistemological core of Yorùbá thought and know as the Yorùbá themselves know the *amewa* or beauty of its discourse between its oral traditions, its oracular pantheon, and its caretakers. In exchange are the keys that can unlock the doors to a bicultural investigation of Yorùbá historical data and thought. In short, I speak of *retrofitting* Western approaches to historiography, art history, archeology, theology, linguistics, and the like, to the discursive contours of Yorùbá culture, and by extension, to other non-Western systems, as Linda Smith suggests, and as Rowland Abiodun recommends, by replacing the Yorùbá in the study of their historiography.

Notes

1. Linda Tuhiwai Smith. *Decolonizing Methodologies: Research and Indigenous Peoples*. London: Zed Books, 1999, 170.

2. *Imo* and *Igbeede* are Yorùbá words for knowing and understanding.

3. Robin C. C. Law. *The Horse in West African History: The Role of the Horse in the Societies of Pre-Colonial Africa*. Oxford: Oxford University Press, 1980.

4. Babatunde Agiri. "Yorùbá Oral Tradition with Special Reference to the Early History of the Oyo Kingdom." In Wande Abimbola (ed.), *Yorùbá Oral Traditions*, Nigeria Ibadan University Press, 1975, 157–89.

5. Ibid., 158.

6. Ibid., 160–61.

7. Kola Folayan. "Yorùbá Oral History: Some Problems and Suggestions." In Abimbola (ed.), *Yorùbá Oral Traditions*, 89–114.

8. D. T. Niane. *Sundiata: An Epic of Old Mali*. London: Longmans Group. 1965.

9. Folayan, "Yorùbá Oral History," 94–96.

10. Ibid., 94.

11. Ibid., 95.

12. Ibid., 101.

13. Jan Vansina. *De La Tradition Orale: Essai de Methode Historique.* Tervuren, Belgique: Musee Royal De L'Afrique Centrale, Serie in 8, *Science Humanines*, 36, 1961.

14. Ibid., 21.

15. Smith, *Decolonizing Methodologies.*

16. David Henige. *Oral Historiography.* London: Longman, 1982.

17. Vansina, *De La Tradition Orale*, 7.

18. Rowland Abiodun, "Understanding Yorùbá Art and Aesthetics: The Concept of Ase," *African Arts*, July 1994: 69.

19. Wande Abimbola. "Ifa Divination Poems as Sources for Historical Evidence." *Lagos Notes and Records* 1(1), 1967, 17–26.

20. Omotoso Eluyemi. "The Role of Oral Tradition in the Archeological Investigation of the History of Ife." In Abimbola, *Yorùbá Oral Traditions*, 115–45.

21. Sandra T. Barnes (ed.), *Africa's Ogun: Old World and New.* Bloomington: Indiana University Press, 1989.

22. Akin Euba. *Yorùbá Drumming: The Dundun Tradition.* Bayreuth, West Germany: Bayreuth African Studies Series, 1990.

23. See the works of Abiodun, Abimbola, Eluyemi, Euba, and others cited here.

24. Agiri, "Yorùbá Oral Tradition."

25. Wande Abimbola, *Ifá: An Exposition of Ifá Literary Corpus.* Ibadan: Oxford University Press, 1976, v–vi.

26. Smith, *Decolonizing Methodologies.*

27. Reverend Samuel Johnson. *The History of the Yorùbás from the Earlies Times to the Beginning of the British Protectorate.* London: Routledge and Sons, 1921.

28. E. Bolaji Idowu. *Olodumare: God in Yorùbá Belief,* Longmans, Green, and Co, 1962.

29. Ibid., 4–10.

30. Ibid., 30–56.

31. Ibid., 18–22, 57.

32. Rowland Abiodun. "Woman in Yorùbá Religious Images." *African Languages and Cultures*, 2 (1), 1989, 3–7.

33. Idowu, *Olodumare*, 18.

34. A. A. B. Aderibigbe. "Peoples of Southern Nigeria." In *A Thousand Years of West African History*, J. F. Ade. Ajayi and Ian Espie (eds.), New York: Humanities Press, 1972, 191–205. See also, I. A. Akinjogbin. "The expansion of Oyo and the rise of Dahomey, 1600–1800." In J. F. Ade. Ajayi and Michael Crowder (eds.), *The History of West Africa*, vol. 1. New York: Columbia University Press, 1972, 304–43.

35. J. K. Olupona. *Kingship, Religion, and Rituals in a Nigerian Community: A Phenomenological Study of Ondo Yorùbá Festivals.* Stockholm, Sweden: Almqvist & Wiksell International, 1991, 43.

36. Ibid., 25.

37. Idowu, *Olodumare*, 25.

38. Ibid.

39. Abiodun, "Woman in Yorùbá Religious Images," 1.

40. Abiodun, "Woman in Yorùbá Religious Images," 58–60.

41. Idowu, *Olodumare*, 60.

42. R. C. Abraham. *Dictionary of Modern Yorùbá*, London: University of London Press Ltd, 1958.

43. Ibid., 239.

44. Sandra T. Barnes (ed.), *Africa's Ogun: Old World and New.* Bloomington: Indiana University Press, 1989, 12.

45. S. A. Babalola. *The Content and Form of Yorùbá Ijala.* Oxford: Oxford University Press, 1966.

46. Ibid., 3–55.

47. Ibid., 38.

48. Judith Gleason. *Oya In Praise of an African Goddess.* San Francisco: HarperCollins, 1987. 208–27.

49. Barnes, *Africa's Ogun*, 13.

50. Diedre L. Badejo. "The Orisa Principle Divining African Literary Aesthetics." In *Orality, Literacy and the Fictive Imagination.* Detroit: Bedford Publishers, 1999.

51. Rowland Abiodun, "Verbal and visual metaphors mythical allusions in Yorùbá ritualistic art of Ori." *Word & Image: A Journal of Verbal Visual Inquiry* 3(3), 1987, 252–70.

52. John Pemberton and Funso S. Afolayan, *Yorùbá Sacred Kingship: A Power Like That of the Gods,* Washington and London: Smithsonian Institution Press, 1996, 23–46.

53. Jacob K. Olupona, "The Study of Yorùbá Religious Tradition in Historical Perspective." *NUMEN,* 40, 1993, 240–73.

54. Robert Farris Thompson. *Flash of the Spirit: African and African American Art and Philosophy.* New York: Random House, 1983, 9.

55. Ibid., 252.

56. Ibid., 5.

57. Ibid.

58. Linda James Myers, 1993.

59. Babalola, *The Content and Form of Yorùbá Ijala.*

60. Ibid., 8–18.

61. Abiola Irele, Introduction, in Femi Osofisan, *The Oriki of a Grasshopper and Other Plays.* Washington, DC: Howard University Press, 1995, xxxiv.

62. Euba, *Yorùbá Drumming,* 38.

63. Wale Ogunbiyi, *Drama and Theatre: A Critical Source Book.* Lagos: Nigeria Magazine, 1981.

64. Barnes, *Africa's Ogun*, 13.

65. Diedre L. Badejo. *Osun Seegesi: The Elegant Deity of Wealth, Power, and Femininity.* Trenton, NJ: Africa World Press, 1996.

66. Babalola, *The Content and Form of Yorùbá Ijala.*

67. Abimbola, *Ifá Divination Poetry.*

68. Euba, *Yorùbá Drumming,* 388.

69. Wole Soyinka. *Myth, Literature, and the African World.* Cambridge: Cambridge University Press, 1976.

70. Johnson, *History of the Yorùbás,* 149–52, 169.

71. Idowu, *Olodumare,* 80–85; Thompson, *Flash of the Spirit,* 18–33.

72. Abimbola, *Ifa Divination Poetry,* 1.

73. Irele, Introduction, *The Oriki of a Grasshopper and Other Plays,* xxxiv.

74. Thompson, *Flash of the Spirit.*

15

LOCAL HISTORY IN POST-INDEPENDENT AFRICA

Bala Achi

The growth of local history in post-independent Africa has been phenomenal, particularly among minorities long ignored as historically insignificant (as evidenced in the lack of attention paid to their past). For example, in Nigeria alone the Zuru of Kebbi, the Moroa, Kagoro, the Ham, the Kataf of southern Kaduna, the Itsekiri and Urhobo of the Niger Delta, and the Okin Yoruba of Northeastern Yorubaland have, in the twentieth century, attempted to write their local histories. In all these cases, the attempts have been fully sponsored by ethnic unions and actively supported by the elite. Today almost every ethnic group once neglected in Nigeria's historical documentation has attempted to write its own local history. In most cases, the only available recorded history of the people's past had been that left behind by Europeans who got their information from colonial informers (often from hostile ethnic groups) who actively collaborated with the British to achieve their own objectives. Such cases, especially when tribal prejudice was at play, led to distortion of a people's history.

This chapter will first look at how the Atyap, a minority group in Southern Kaduna, Nigeria, has used available resources in writing its history and will then widen the topic to the general growth of local histories in post-independent Africa, the significance of this, and the obstacles faced.

Background

The Atyap form part of the Nok Culture Complex in the upper Kaduna River valley. They speak a language in the Kwa group of the Benue-Congo language family. Since the 1970s they have wanted a local history text of their own. They made a bold attempt in 1981 when efforts by the Kataf Youth Christian Association resulted in the first Kataf History Conference, which brought together the academic world, local historians, and traditional leaders of the community. This mass participation, although hampered by a language barrier, was useful in eliciting relevant information.

The proceedings of that pioneering work, even though bound, could not be presented as an authentic and acceptable history of the people. Nonetheless, it laid a solid foundation for collection of the fairly reliable data that formed the background information that eventually led to the publication of *A History of the Atyap*. Also, identification of those within the community who had valuable facts about the people's past became possible. The Tyap Literacy Committee, formed later to translate the Bible into Tyap language and produce relevant literature for use in primary schools, was useful during the research into Atyap past and subsequent publication of the people's history. This progress culminated in the formation of the Atyap History Committee under my chairmanship. Its mandate was to document and publish relevant aspects of Kataf history. However, it was the duty of the Literacy Committee to raise the needed funds for the work. The eight members who constituted the History Committee worked to produce a standard text on the Atyap, and visiting Professor J. E. Philips contributed an appendix. By January 1992, a 320-page manuscript had been produced and sent to press. Though the project sensitized the Kataf community to a common cause, the committee was faced with problems of logistics and finance.

Methods and Growth

Why did the Atyap engage in such a task, considering the availability of works by British anthropologists and colonial administrations? The answer lies in the absence of historical research in most areas of Nigeria, a problem within Nigerian historiography. A sharp contrast exists between the immense amount of literature produced on some groups while little or nothing is produced on others. This creates the impression within

Nigerian historiography that the smaller ethnic groups were not themselves actors but mere tools in the power game of more organized and centralized kingdoms.[1] British colonial writers such as C. K. Meek, Harold D. Gunn, Charles Orr, B. Sharwood Smith, Major Tremearne, and C. L. Temple, who write on the Kataf, portray them as "pagans," "tailed head hunters," and excellent slave raiders who in turn constituted Zaria's slave zone.[2] Yet others portrayed the Kataf as an isolated people who never related with the outside world.

British writers relied on Hausa as interpreters, and in some cases as direct sources of information. These writers were therefore not only handicapped by lack of local participation but also tempted to accept the claims to suzerainty of the emirs of Zaria and Jama'a[3] because the British needed allies to implement their indirect rule system. Many Hausa of the ruling class not only quickly pledged their loyalty to the invaders, they also assisted the British in a propaganda campaign designed to make resisters more conciliatory. Also, the British Administration realized that many Hausa Muslims were in Zangon Kataf. According to Lugard, they pressured the government to include them in the Zaria emirate administration and not place them under any autonomous pagan chiefdom.[4] Thus, Kataf history had to be deliberately distorted and used to maintain and perpetuate inhumane inequalities in the area by subjecting the Kataf to emirate rule managed and dispensed from Zaria, in an attempt to protect a Muslim minority there. British force was used to extend and maintain the machinery of emirate rule among the Atyap.[5] This has intensified conflicts and irredentism, thereby affecting Nigeria's unity and stability. Sensitization and the growing self-assertion of the Atyap seemed to have frustrated the government even more. Armed groups began to make forays into Atyap land, increasing polarization of the society.

The negative and false presentation of the people's past had affected the general understanding of the dynamics of the Atyap polity and society. The *History of the Atyap* was therefore aimed at filling a gap in Nigerian history, namely, the history of a Kataf minority long regarded as an appendage of Zaria with no history worthy of study. The intention was to stimulate interest, discussion and more research on the Atyap past. The tapping of information from those in possession of various forms of primary sources of Atyap history was aimed at preserving the richness of society's past, as recounted by its elders so as to be a source of guidance.

To the Kataf, if the British did deliberately distort their history to achieve a colonial aim of divide and rule, such a malicious strategy has no justification in the twentieth century. Thus, they mobilized members of their society to work with professional historians, as well as practitioners of allied disciplines like geology, archaeology, ethnography, and sociology, toward the production of a local Kataf history text. Such a text would extend from the earliest times to the present, using modern techniques to recapture the history of a nonliterate and politically disparate group. This collaborative effort of varied experts helped in the production of a fairly standard text on the Atyap.

The historical methodology adopted is a shift from the orthodox approach to history writing, a shift from the narrative-descriptive approach to the causal and analytical, from political history to more of a social and economic history. The Kataf history study is designed to fit into this new methodological framework, seeking to solve the polemical methodological problem that assumes that "stateless" societies have no real resources for writing their history.

Significance

The writing of local history is the story of minority groups, in search of peace and relevance in independent and competitive African states, attempting to write their own history in a variety of different situations. It is thus a modest contribution by the people themselves, using mainly local sources, to enhance society's comprehension of their past, and particularly of their problems, their reactions, and the government's measures. Communities use history as a reservoir that satisfies their curiosity, pleases them, and inspires them toward a greater future in which they gain respectability within new nation-states. This relevance of history is seen in the way Muhammad Bello, a leading Islamic scholar, ordered the burning of Hausa literature during the Jihad of 1804 because these were "works of infidels."[6] Even the Kano Chronicle, one of the few surviving works on pre-jihad Hausa kingdoms, was probably reedited to suit the Fulani administration. Also, in the nineteenth century, Salame, an Islamic university town, was invaded and partly burnt down by the French, who absconded with many valuable books.[7] Yunfa, the Hausa king of Gobir, attacked the Muslims of Gimbana in 1804, killing many of the ulama and burning their books and slates.[8]

Those in authority have typically tried to suppress the history of their opponents, and thus it is an error to assume that smaller ethnic groups could not be actors because they "had no history." Truly, even the smaller ethnic groups were actors in the history of Nigeria. Another erroneous assumption is that the historicity of a group is based on its size and political relevance in society. The work done succeeds in showing that the Kataf have the resources for the reconstruction of their own history. By using these resources to reconstruct the past, the people can now come closer to realizing their yearnings, their aspirations for greater self-determination.

Writing local history poses challenges, for such writing is not the monopoly of universities, commissioned research councils, or international publishers. The major sources for reconstruction of local history include oral traditions, totemism, archaeological remains, settlement studies, and other such sources that enable the community to be actively involved in its own history. For these reasons, such work is often seen as subjective. From whatever viewpoint the writers approach their task, they are sure to be criticized because the work is not based solely on the written sources customarily used by historians.

Nonetheless, such history often engenders local patriotism and nationalism, as well as tangible advantages. For example, land and political positions were becoming relevant to the Kataf in the late twentieth century, leading often to court cases. A history of the Kataf from the Atyap viewpoint was quite helpful.

The community as the true custodian of its own past can write its own history by examining itself historically. This participatory approach in local history can help reduce the misrepresentation suffered from the hands of sponsored "foreign" writers. However, the work is also a mirror of correction, not done merely for self-glorification. It is not intended to paint an image of any other group as monstrous, but instead to show how the Atyap have related in times of both peace and war, especially after ca. 1650 C.E. when Zangon Kataf became an important trading camp for Hausa itinerant traders.

Obstacles

Writing local history is never easy and usually takes a lot of time as well. The writers must be intimately involved in the sociocultural life of those about whom they write, a necessity to produce a fairly authentic and readable record. The Atyap history, for example, has endured years of protracted setbacks.

One other limitation of a work based mainly on oral traditions has to do with the documentation and analysis of all versions. A pioneering work on local history can never attain perfection but only be an initial attempt to spur scholars into more research for a more extensive work on a community's past. In a work of this nature, one is often faced with different and conflicting claims by different clans. Each claims to be aboriginal or the first settlers, in a desperate attempt to establish legal ownership to a particular expanse of land and to political positions, and this often presents problems. For example, the Kataf region has become a hotbed of crises as both the Kataf and Hausa claim ownership of Zangon Kataf, the commercial and administrative headquarters of Kataf-land.

A History of the Atyap, edited by Bala Achi and published by Tamaza Publishers, Zaria, was initially planned for early 1992 but has been delayed. Even in early 2001, the book had yet to see the light of day. Major General Zamani Lekwot (retired), chairman of the Tyap Literacy Committee, sponsors of the project, was imprisoned on controversial charges for five years along with fourteen other Kataf after an ethnoreligious crisis in Zangon Kataf involving the Kataf and the Hausa. Attempts to bring the book out of press following his release in late 1995 have not been easy either. Groups clamoring for a rewriting to reflect the 1992 crisis, and those who insist on inclusion of a new chapter on Kataf political organization, have contributed to the delay. Also, since the release of funds to the history committee depends on its good working relationship with the literacy committee, the amount to be paid to the publisher and that claimed by the writers have often discouraged the sponsors. Finally, the vibrancy of viewpoints advanced in the book in the early 1990s could be weakened, for the contents could become outdated with new developments, more research, and the passage of time. This will involve a review and possible rewrite even before the book is out.

One other reason for delay has to do with the community's insistence on being part and parcel of the work at every stage. Drafts had to be read by the editorial committee and passed to the literacy committee, who in turn would make comments and pass them to community leaders for their own comments. Obtaining consensus on viewpoints was not easy.

Despite these and other obstacles, the book will eventually be published and will fill a gap in Nigerian history.

Notes

1. Ibrahim James, "The Ham: Its People, Their Political and Cultural History," University of Jos, 1997, xii.

2. Major A. J. N. Tremearne, "The tailed head-hunters of Nigeria," *Journal of the Royal African Society* 40 (1912): 136–99; C. L. Temple (ed.), *Notes on the Tribes, Provinces, Emirates and States of the Northern Provinces of Nigeria* (London, 1965): 22.

3. "Native" reporters were noted for lying in official reports and were incompetent. J. E. Philips, *Spurious Arabic: Hausa and Colonial Nigeria* (Madison, 2000). I am grateful to John Philips for allowing me access to this manuscript before its publication.

4. Charles Orr, *The Making of Northern Nigeria* (London, 1957), 57.

5. M. Perham, *Native Administration in Nigeria* (London, 1937), 134.

6. R. M. East, *Hausawa da Makwabtansu* II (Zaria, 1970), viii–ix.

7. O. Bello, *Islamic Education in 18th Century Nigeria* (Sokoto, 1994), 3–4.

8. Muhammad Bello, *Infaq al-Maisuri* (Hausa translation by S. S. Mohammed and J. Boyd) (Zaria, 1974), 16–19.

16

AFRICA AND WORLD-SYSTEMS ANALYSIS

A POST-NATIONALIST PROJECT?

William G. Martin

Africa and World-Systems Analysis: A Paradoxical Relationship

World-systems analysis, like the capitalist world-economy, has deep African roots. Most of the original formulators of the perspective, if not African, had considerable experience in Africa—and they openly acknowledged how this drove them towards a methodology suitable to understanding capitalism as a world-scale, historical system. And certainly no continent has been as integral to the development of capitalism, or suffered as much in the process, as Africa. Indeed, given five centuries of Africa's transcontinental role in capitalist development—from enslavement, through colonialism, to today's deadly embrace with free marketers—the study of Africa would seem a most fertile ground for world-systems work.

Yet despite this, world-systems analysis—or, more broadly, world-historical studies—has had only a small role in the study of continental Africa in the last twenty-five years. At the very moment when Africa appears increasingly vulnerable to world-economic forces, when "globalization" is on everyone's lips, substantive studies that place Africa within the capitalist world-economy are hard to find. Why this is so cannot be attributed solely to a general lack of world-historical studies of capitalism; here one need only look to Latin America, South Asia, or East Asia, where it is easy to point out a large world-historical literature that has developed over the last generation.

This presents a paradox to the writer confronted with evaluating work on Africa from a world-systems perspective: how does one account for the paucity of world-system studies of Africa, when Africa has been so important to the creation of the perspective and indeed of the capitalist world? Is a world-systemic understanding of Africa possible?

The answers lie only partly in examining the relevance and record of a world-systemic understanding of Africa's place in the modern world. Equally important, as we shall see, have been the shifting contours of how the study of Africa has been both understood and institutionalized in North America and on the continent. And this relates in turn to the critical impact, for African and world-systems studies alike, of epochal shifts in world power relations and, in particular, waves of African antisystemic movements.

These relationships among power in the interstate system, waves of African movements, and the conceptualization and institutionalization of studying Africa have rarely been addressed, particularly if one includes the relationship between North America and the continent. Certainly they are largely absent or at best marginalized—if one sets aside steady complaints of underfunding—in the discourse on how Africa is conceptualized or studied in U.S. academic circles. This chapter, with its focus on world-historical studies of Africa, is thus exploratory.

The thesis here is nevertheless stark: world-systems analysis became possible in the 1970s due to the direct impact of African nationalist movements and the world-wide revolts in and around 1968. At the same time, world-system scholars reached back to previous waves and conceptions of world-historical social change—including, most notably, Pan-African conceptions and scholarship. Like the movements that surrounded its birth, however, world-systems analysis confronted the dilemmas of the institutionalization of nationalist power. These inexorably led to a new, territorial definition of what constituted Africa, and where and how it should be studied. It is the collapse in the last fifteen years of this nationalist-territorial conception and method[1]—as variously revealed in critiques of universal European theories, the rise of the rhetoric of "globalization," the increasingly wobbly foundations of Africanist area studies, and the revival of transcontinental African scholarship—that signals the potentials of a new wave of world-historical, radical scholarship, including the rebirth of world-systems analysis. Thus the question: is world-systems analysis a post-nationalist project, only now coming into its own?

Africa and the Origins of a World-Historical Perspective

The world-systems perspective is distinguished by a radical commitment to a world unit of analysis and a global division of labor driven by more than four hundred years of capital accumulation. More narrowly focused, it presumes a systemic character to the capitalist world-economy, as indicated by the use of such conceptions as core-periphery relationships and an interstate system marked by relationally formed, strong and weak, states. More broadly cast, one might use the term "world-historical" studies to include those disdainful of the "systemic" or structural legacies of Western scholarship in the 1970s, yet equally committed to a radical, global, and historical analysis of the capitalist world.

The perspective's African roots are easily traced in the career of Immanuel Wallerstein, its acknowledged founder. As Wallerstein noted in the introduction to the first volume of *The Modern World-System* (1994), it was his original passage to colonized Africa that radically altered his work:

> I went to Africa first during the colonial era, and I witnessed the process of "decolonization". . . . It did not take long to realize that not only were these two groups [Europeans long resident in Africa and young militants of the African movements] at odds on political issues, but that they approached the situation with entirely different sets of conceptual frameworks.[2]

And these led directly to new theoretical and methodological insights, most notably the questioning of national societies as units of analysis, and, conversely, the inherently world-relational character of social change:

> The nationalists saw the reality in which they lived as a "colonial situation. . . ." I thereby became aware of the degree to which society as an abstraction was heavily limited to politico-juridical systems as an empirical reality. It was a false perspective to take a unit like a "tribe," and seek to analyze its operations without reference to the fact that, in a colonial situation, the governing institutions of a "tribe," far from being "sovereign," were closely circumscribed by the laws (and customs) of that larger entity of which they were an indissociable part, the colony.[3]

As for tribes, so too for newly independent African states and the promises of modernization: consideration of Africa led directly to an ever-larger unit and the modern world-system.[4] As Jewsiewicki has pointed out at length,[5] the origins of Wallerstein's work are inexplicable without taking into account the specificity of the African political conjuncture.

Several of Wallerstein's key allies, particularly those central to the programs established at Binghamton University, had similar African or related experience. Terence K. Hopkins, Wallerstein's closest intellectual collaborator and methodologist-in-chief of the world-systems school, founded the Binghamton graduate program in 1970 and recruited Wallerstein.[6] Hopkin's early work, including his dissertation, had been on small groups. Later research experience in Uganda, and between 1968 and 1970 at the University of the West Indies in Trinidad, subsequently gave him a lifelong commitment to linking local social change with world-scale processes. Similarly, Giovanni Arrighi's teaching stints in Zimbabwe (1963–66) and Tanzania (1967–69) led to well-known publications on Southern Rhodesia, African socialism, imperialism and, after his arrival in Binghamton in 1979, several coauthored articles, books, and research projects with Hopkins and Wallerstein at the Fernand Braudel Center.[7]

What distinguished such work was not simply that it was radical scholarship on Africa, or was allied with nationalist movements, much less that it engaged in big case comparisons. One could point to many such examples after 1968, from radical readers[8] to large works by such authors as Paige, Skocpol, or Tilly. Rather, what made such work world-systemic was its methodological insistence on the world-relational character and unit of social change, and a long-term historical perspective. These methodological principles set it apart most starkly from those using a comparative-historical methodology, for world-historical scholars argued from the very beginning against reifying nation-states, as colonial scholars had reified tribes, and then comparing states whose histories were inextricably linked. Although this was most clear for economic relations, it held for cultural and political relationships as well. Hence the importance of the experience of the colonial relationship, resistance against it (including impacts on European colonizers and their cultures), and the endurance of colonial-like, world-economic relations after nationalist parties obtained state power.

In many ways the emergence of the world-systems perspective arose to offer a mode of conceptualizing the historical reach of such world-relationships, in a period when formal colonial relationships had given way to a liberal celebration of sovereign, developing states. In so proceeding, early world-systems work drew directly on scholarship by black authors who had sought to chart how capitalism, slavery, and colonialism had been forged through the exploitation of Africans world-wide, whether one spoke of local social groups or the international economy. As already suggested, African scholars such as Mafeje and Magubane (Magubane would later teach at Binghamton) had set the stage for world-relational methodologies by challenging European scholars' descriptions of African communities as self-sufficient "tribes," insisting that so-called tribes were really embedded in, and shaped by, the historical relationships of colonialism.[9] Far from "tribes" being a unit of analysis, the studies revealed instead, in Mafeje's pungent formulation, a European "ideology of tribalism" in the service of colonialism. Fanon's analysis of the colonizer/colonized relationship and the pitfalls of nationalist consciousness also pointed in the same methodological direction.[10]

An even longer anticolonial and pan-African tradition had steadily insisted that capitalism rested upon the transatlantic exploitation of black labor and nations. Work published during the black nationalist wave in the 1930s and 1940s was particularly influential, including most notably Eric Williams's 1944 account of how the British industrial revolution rested firmly on the expansion of slavery in the Caribbean.[11] Equally significant were the efforts of such scholars as C. L. R. James, who linked proletarian slaves and revolutions in Haiti, France, and the Americas (1938); Oliver Cox, who constructed one of the first accounts of global capitalism and global racial stratification (1948); W. E. B. Du Bois, who insistently linked Africa and America (1947); and others.[12] Indeed, early world-systems scholars sought to formalize these notions, for the postcolonial epoch, by conceptualizing an international division of labor marked by core-peripheral relationships, and state power as fostered or limited by an interdependent, interstate system.

What these efforts did not develop was a body of work rooted in Africa, despite the singular efforts of the African master Samir Amin, who sought to conceptualize Africa's place in the process of accumulation on a world scale. As Amin recounts in his intellectual biography, his early work on capitalism as a world process rested upon an engagement and commitment to African national liberation movements and later work in independent African states.[13] Yet despite such steady and striking work, no larger indigenous school developed over the course of the last three decades. If such had occurred, we might have inherited a very different product: an African-centered interpretation and research agenda of the world-historical processes that both formed Africa as a distinct location in the world-economy and linked Africans at home and abroad. Walter Rodney's work, most notably *How Europe Underdeveloped Africa*,[14] suggests how such an agenda might have been carried forward. Still, this project remains very much before us, as is all too apparent in today's rediscovery and tentative conceptions of "Diasporas" and "Black Atlantics."

A conundrum presents itself: at the very moment when African movements achieved political power, why did world-historical work, and more concretely world-systems work, slip out of the African orbit? To understand this, we need to examine the world-economy of the production of knowledge regarding Africa. And this is not simply the story of Euro–North American scholars' domination of this process, much less a fevered, Orientalist invention of Africa, but rather an engagement with the direct choices of African scholars and Northern Africanists. For the paths they took would reflect a shared nationalist consensus, one that for almost two generations would work directly against a world-historical understanding of the Africans' place in the modern world.

After Anti/colonialism: The Nationalist Interlude

The thesis of this section may be simply stated: as formal colonialism fell and new states emerged in its wake, the dominant North American Africanists, as well as African scholars, became committed to a nationalist— in the specific sense of a territorial nation-state—unit of analysis. This seeming advance on the study of "tribes" nevertheless worked irrevocably to build, and then shore up, a common consensus among Africanists and Africans alike: the primacy of the study of states and autonomous national initiatives. This had direct methodological implications: it acted to seal off the study of transnational social, cultural, and economic processes, and removed racial and imperial relations from view. The exception to this pattern during the 1970s and 1980s confirms the trend: areas where national liberation movements were still struggling to overthrow colonial and white minority rule, and which would achieve a late, national independence.

This story has many parts. Easiest to grasp are trends in what became the dominant center of African studies, namely North America. As I have recounted elsewhere with Michael West,[15] the rise of African studies in the United States generated not only new institutions wedded to state funding but also new conceptualizations of Africa. Rejected at the very beginning was the long, anticolonial and pan-African heritage of Africa as a transnational community; in its place a continental (and in practice only sub-Saharan) Africa composed of nation states was put in place. In this respect the Africa of the postwar period was a methodological *retreat* from the more global, anti- and pro-colonial Africa of the first half of the twentieth century. As the study of Africa moved from historically black to historically white institutions and journals, and Africanists embraced state funding and foundation largesse, an Atlantic wall was constructed between the United States and Africa. Even when scholars protested Cold War logics, African area studies remained committed to dividing Africa and Africans from the United States. Africanists, now a predominantly white group of scholars, constructed an Africa that could not have been imagined prior to World War II—and then they became liberal interpreters of this sub-Saharan Africa to the United States and promoters of national development planning and aid for Africa.

On the other side of the Atlantic wall the urgent tasks of displacing colonial mentalities were underway. Here anticolonial resistance gave way to nation-building, both for those who inherited and would perpetuate the colonial bureaucracy, and those who sought to build a modern Africa—most notably by providing mass and higher education. The exciting creation and expansion of universities led, to be sure, to vibrant new centers of research, from Dakar to Dar es Salaam, from Makerere to Ibadan. As part of the global expansion of higher education in those decades, African universities often drew on European or North American models, and indeed were often initially staffed by expatriates from England or France. Advanced training, particularly at the Ph.D. level and certainly in terms of theoretical and methodological advances, was firmly held in metropolitan centers for a very long time. This drove African scholars to establish their own research networks, agendas, centers, and perspectives. As Mkandwire has noted, this first post-independence generation, "Finding themselves scattered all over the continent, cut off from the research networks dominated by expatriates and isolated in small departments or institutions . . . strove to set up continental and subregional organisations."[16] Moreover, "this generation was self-consciously anti-neo-colonial and considered decolonisation of national institutions and even the intellectual terrain as major tasks."[17]

One facet of these endeavors was to close off local work and centers from the exotica-collecting of overseas "academic tourists," as a common formulation put it. As a result, throughout the 1970s and 1980s African scholars and Euro–North American scholars often pursued their work quite separate from each other; many key African research centers rarely engaged in collaborative research with northerners, by choice. Yet, as current discussions among African scholars note, this did not necessarily displace the domination of western concepts, units of analysis, disciplines, and epistemologies. As Paulin Hountondji notes,

> It would be enlightening to place the present state of affairs in Africa into its historical context and view present-day shortcomings and weakness in the field of knowledge as a result of peripherization, that is, forced integration into the world market of concepts, a market managed and controlled by the North.[18]

Kwesi Prah would go even further: "From the early beginnings of 'African studies' to the present, Western scholarship has dominated knowledge production and reproduction about Africa,"[19] with the result that "most of us have simply tagged on to these [European] traditions or eclectic mixtures of these. No robust or homegrown schools have been historically discernible."[20]

Although others would contest such assertions—as in Ife Amadiune's attack on Prah, where she uses the work of Cheik Anta Diop to construct an African sociological and historical tradition,[21] or Ben Magubane's titling of his latest work as *African Sociology*,[22] a broad consensus by scholars on the continent clearly existed throughout the 1970s, 1980s, and into 1990s: the production of knowledge needed to take place in continental Africa, by Africans. Yet as Prah suggests, decolonization might lead to national universities and scholarship and yet permit the reproduction of northern conceptual and theoretical paradigms. Central to this story, of course, was the insistence of Northern agencies that European models of knowledge production take precedence over crossdisciplinary, crosscontinental initiatives. This had direct effects in many intellectual centers, as recounted for example in Samir Amin's comments on the constraints he encountered in attempting to conduct collaborative, independent research in Egypt, Mali and Senegal, among other locations.[23]

Particularly relevant here are the methodological and historical implications of the post-independence production of knowledge on two now separate continents. For African and other Africanists came to share related premises, even if driven by different impulses and aims: both pursued the study of African societies and states as separate, bounded, historical constructs. Thus liberals and Marxists alike preached stages of (national) growth, and Africans and Africanists alike analyzed national societies, histories, and conflicts. Furthermore, the use of a national unit of analysis permitted constraining continental Africa's relations with Europe and North American to external, "international," or market-mediated linkages. Thus the narrowing of dependency theory to calls for the enhanced power of national states vis-à-vis faceless and actor-less markets.

These assumptions served to reproduce in Africa the European disciplinary boundaries that dictated separating the society, state, and economy—and worked strongly against, if not ruling out altogether, the conceptualization of fundamental social relationships that cut across these boundaries and, especially, regional and continental boundaries. This was a double exclusionary movement: the disciplinary division of subject matter into state/market/society/culture was matched by yet a further division in each of these four realms, as Africa became isolated from Europe and North America and divided into states.

These developments facilitated in turn the mutual exclusion of race as an attribute relevant to the study of Africa. Considerations of racial oppression, that had so united black pan-African and anticolonialist scholars in the 1930s, 1940s, and 1950s, disappeared. Rarely in African or Africanist journals did considerations of race ever enter, with the notable exception of settler rule in southern Africa—the solution for which was, of course, majority rule and true national independence. The demise of formal colonialism, it seemed, had permitted the demise of the subject of race: no colonial difference, no racial difference.

For their part, African scholars, focused on local or national phenomena, could aptly argue that "race" was not a problem among Africans, but a problem of Europeans and Americans. This distinction only held, of course, as long as continental boundaries and subjects were not broached; as a matter internal to nation-states, race didn't apply to independent African societies and states. Excursions into the historical, necessarily international, place of African labor—either manual or mental—in the forging of modern capitalism were thus rarely attempted. Of course whenever continental boundaries were crossed, race immediately mattered—as African academics who traveled North, or sought research funds from those who funded African studies, found out very quickly indeed.

For Euro–North American Africanists, the severance of independent Africa from the Americas had the great benefit of sheltering them from black insurgents at home, particularly in the 1960s: was not this surely a problem of "race relations," a problem of civil rights internal to nation states and not of Africa or African studies? And, if so, best left to Americanists? What could be more natural than to leave local problems to local scholars? Eruptions in the late 1960s of black protest against the dominant white cast of African studies in the United States were, for example, weathered by continuing reliance on the paradigmatic and institutional separation of Africa and African-America.[24] Attempts to analyze race in both the United States and Africa, most notably South Africa, by use of the concept of "internal colonialism"—which at least permitted introducing race in colonial, if nationally circumscribed, terms— subsequently failed to gain a foothold. As long as state power in Africa, and civil rights in the United States, remained the goal of antisystemic movements, the dominance of national units of analysis prevailed among both scholars and the movements. In this sense the dilemmas of the movements were those of scholars as well: both groups were unable to heed the warnings of such prophets as Fanon or Malcolm X, and overcome the limits of national consciousness and the lure of territorially based promises of liberation.

Globalization: A New World-Historical Project?

If there is one certainty about the future of the study of Africa today, it is that such divisions can no longer be maintained: the foundations for these paradigms and methodologies have inexorably eroded in the last twenty years. On the one hand developmentalism and its promise of state-led nation and national-economy building is dead. If glimmers of the stages of development may still be seen in East Asia, promises of such progress have clearly bypassed Africa. Gone is the language of import substitution, export-oriented industrialization, and dependency-schooled delinking. Few if any observers in the 1980s included African states, not even Nigeria or South Africa, on the lists of "newly industrializing countries"; equally few African states qualified in the 1990s for the new category of an "emerging market" state. Developmentalist illusions, based on the models and histories of state-led, national capitalist development, have evaporated and been replaced by straightforward dictation from core states and international financial institutions. At the same time, new movements from below for more accountable, transparent, and democratic political participation have destabilized old nationalist regimes and colonial boundaries.

   This shattering of territorial and intellectual paradigms has stimulated new research and theoretical agendas in Africa and in the North. While exploratory and numerous, this work might easily be seen as moving along two quite opposed paths: in one direction, analysis has moved from national to continental boundaries; in another, a strong movement harkens back to very local, cultural studies. Thus, on the one hand, we have the emergence of a series of continental-scale works in the 1990s by such scholars as Mamdani, Mkandawire and Soludo, and Zeleza[25]—all authors who had previously worked on the local or national scale. On the other hand, new works stand rooted in cultural studies, which while often highlighting transnational cultural flows, center on the necessity of rejecting any narrative of modernity and focusing upon local cultural studies.[26]

Where the two strains meet, however, is telling: at the level of linking their chosen subjects to transnational and international flows. For anthropologists, this is a startling transformation: gone is the tribe, ascendant is global cultural theory. For social scientists the movement is less spectacular, yet no less singular, as national societies and states, and even continents, now find their place in transcontinental networks.

Seen in this light, it is only natural to ask: might this trajectory point towards a revival, in new forms, of world-historical studies of Africa? Certainly there are strong forces outside the world of scholarship pushing in this direction, from the impact of the dissolution of state boundaries and power, through the rising international significance of race and black cultural flows, to the undeniable new powers of international financial institutions, multinational corporations, and the global market. Indeed, it is frequently argued that we all face a new globalized epoch, a radical historical rupture. As Achille Mbembe recently enthused in a lead editorial in the *CODESRIA Bulletin*:

> The continent is experiencing rapid, multifaceted, complex and muddled changes with paradoxical results. Whether it concerns new forms of conflicts, the evolution of cultural and artistic creativity (style, music, cinema, dance, painting): everything is changing.[27]

Such statements are most often extended, however, in a tracing of new configurations of power and relationships forged through global financial, technological, and cultural flows. By contrast to Africanist or more recent postmodern perspectives, this is a notable shift—and opens the door to a revival of the world-scale, historical inquiries and perspectives—including world-systems work—that flourished in the 1970s.

Yet it would be far too facile to simply project this conclusion and predict a new wave of large-scale, historical work that cuts across national and continental boundaries.

Methodologically it is evident there can be no return to the numerous comparative-historical studies of the past generation, which placed states and even cultures in international context. The large swath of studies that Frederick Cooper reviewed at the beginning of the 1980s and

1990s in his survey of "Africa and the World Economy"[28] are no longer tenable: few, if any, in the face of "globalization," would now presume that national economies, societies, or cultures can be so isolated as to meet the most basic of standards for comparative analysis. Even Charles Tilly, the past proponent of such procedures, has openly admitted the death of the big case comparison.[29] This is a significant advance; it removes the possibility, so long adhered to, of conducting studies that assume national units of analysis exist and may be linked through international commodity and financial markets. Comparative, international, and area studies—each with their own territorial compartments—stand equally indicted.

Yet a move into very local studies and histories is not plausible either. For over two decades the indictment of meta-narratives, positivism, and structuralist theory has swept through the humanities and social sciences, buttressing an insistence on local agency, local narratives, and the primacy of localized epistemologies. This has, however, generated its own counter-flow: can one, in this age of "globalization," maintain an insistence on the autonomy and autochthonous character of the local? Within cultural studies, the answer is increasingly "no"; one needs only to witness the calls for tying local observations and cultures to transnational frameworks and flows, "strategic essentialism," the relational construction of culture across national and continental boundaries, and even the reappearance of historical narratives—not to mention the rise of new transnational journals and book series dedicated to the study of diasporas.

Oceanic Cross-Currents: A New Wave of World-Historical Studies?

Reflection on the difficulties faced by both comparativists and culturalists reveal a common dilemma: how does one construct theoretical and methodological approaches that allow us to understand global relationships without sacrificing the temporal and spatial specificity of local actors and processes? How do we understand social phenomena in a world-relational framework, without imposing partial and yet universalized models based on Euro–North American theory and history?

It is at this pivot point that the possibility of a new wave of world-historical research enters. Indeed, movements toward this end are quite apparent in work related to Africa, Asia, and Latin America—and less evident, it must be noted, in Europe and North America where high theory based on western modernity and postmodernity still holds sway. A prime example is the reemergence of colonialism as a conceptual framework for analyzing post-independence relationships and power. Indeed the emergence of this work in the last ten years, from three different continents, is itself a world-historical phenomenon that needs explanation. The impetus is, however, evident: the search for historical, relational conceptions that both reject the previous generation's strict focus on state boundaries and state power and, simultaneously, seek to move beyond postmodern impulses by constructing large-scale relations over the long-durée. Such a movement is strongest in Latin America,[30] exemplified by the work of such scholars as Quijano and Mignolo.[31] It is also quite apparent in South Asia in post-subaltern studies that seek to place local histories, nationalism, and agency within transnational movements, histories, and imperial domination.[32] As these studies illustrate, models of nationalism predicated on earlier European models are explicitly rejected, and steps towards a transcontinental, relational perspective are underway.[33]

Such movements are less evident, it must be admitted, in African studies. In part this is due to the continuing tradition of large-scale historical studies, the far weaker impact of postmodernism, and the continuing African reaction against cultural anthropology as a partner in the more recent experience of direct colonial rule. The revival of Fanon, for example, has remained very much a Northern affair focused on his earlier, more psychological works.[34] It is also true that the reactions against European-constructed narratives of Africa remain strong. In the early 1990s Steven Feierman could argue that the end of the universal narrative of the rise of the West dictated the fragmentation of historical narratives, making large-scale methodological projects, and certainly world-historical projects, impossible.[35] Yet less than ten years later, even dedicated local historians seek to cast their work with transnational, historical processes. Where Feierman's thesis still holds is in it insistence that a single world history, told from structuralist conceptions of European development, is no longer possible.

The question that thus emerges is not one of a return to singular world narratives, but how the search for new world-embracing narratives might be pursued. This is, indeed, a quite different path than that suggested and expected by Feierman, that is, the fading away of histories of Africa in world perspective in favor of local African histories. As in Latin American and South Asian studies, such work has irrevocably returned to the ways local African life is embedded in larger world processes. As this work proceeds, it not only reveals the use of world-historical methods and theoretical perspectives but also may overcome the limits of the world-systems perspective, particularly in relation to gender and race, as it crystallized in North America, and to a lesser extent Europe, in the 1970s and 1980s.[36]

How might this take place? Let me give two examples, one from each side of the Atlantic.

State Formation and Colonial Racism

One of the more difficult and underdeveloped assertions of world-systems work is that state formation is a relational process. This is most commonly grasped by locating state power and legitimacy in an interstate system of diplomacy and military networks; the most extensive study of such relations can be seen in the large body of work on rivalry and hegemony among core states.[37] What such work leaves undeveloped is the application, across the core-periphery relationship, of methodological insight provided by Terence Hopkins very early on, namely that state formation in one location might be seen as related to state deformation in another. To state this via an analogy: as with free wage labor formation moving historically with the creation of coerced and slave labor, so too with state sovereignty and strength; as intimated in earlier studies by such scholars as Eric Williams and C. L. R. James,[38] one might easily cast the emergence of rich democratic states in the core within the same narrative as the construction of plantation, settler, and colonial territories across the periphery of the capitalist world-economy. Just how necessary such work is today can be seen if one simply pauses to relate the "collapse" of state boundaries, resources, and power in Africa with the increasing power of supranational institutions such as the IMF and the World Bank, and the emergence of yet larger state formations in Europe (EU) and North America (NAFTA). What we lack of course is the conceptual and historical work that might develop these insights across core-peripheral boundaries—or even continental boundaries.[39]

Movement forward toward these ends can be seen in the work of African scholars who have sought to explain the fate of African states and economies during the 1980s and 1990s, a period marked by long-term economic decline and the collapse of state structures. Scholars, states, and financial organizations in the North in the 1980s and 1990s readily attributed economic and political collapse to a generation of policies pursued by states variously theorized as neopatrimonial, criminal, kleptocratic, or captured by corrupt interests. The simple but elegant summary by Mkandawire and Soludo of African economists' under-standing of this history shows a very different, if implicit, understanding of state formation.[40] For while they aim to buttress the claim for African state capacity, their narrative carefully links post-independence African state forms and power to relationships with states and political agencies in the North. This is not simply confrontation with *external* states or market forces, but a shared history and a world-historical process. What this careful description does not achieve, however, is a conceptualization of the world-relational formation of state power, which would break with the disciplinary boundaries of political science and the continental boundaries of African research. Here again, the work stands before us—and it could well continue to be explored with the continent constitut-ing a unit of observation if not analysis, and thus only slowly push towards world-scale analyses.

A clear movement towards this latter end can be seen in the more recent movement by other historians and social scientists to reintroduce, as in South Asian and Latin American studies, the centrality of colonial and racial relationships to political power and state formation. The most notable work is Mahmood Mamdani's *Citizen and Subject*, which charts how an exclusive, racialized citizenship instilled under colonialism is car-ried forward in time. This is not, one must notice, a study of "neocolo-nialism" as developed by Nkrumah and others in the 1960s and early 1970s, or even Mamdani's own earlier work on Uganda.[41] Indeed, if there is a revival of "neocolonial" studies in any sense, these formulations harken back to the discussions of Black Power and other radical circles of "inter-nal colonialism" in the United States and South Africa in the 1960s and 1970s. Thus far from states being subject to external control, Mamdani examines how relations between citizen and subject, institutionalized via indirect rule during the colonial period, were reshaped across the conti-nent in the post-independence period by maintaining colonial differences between citizen and subject, particularly through the accentuation of eth-nic and urban-rural differences. Thus if "the bifurcated state created with colonialism was deracialized after independence, it was not democra-tized."[42] The way forward today follows directly: "to create a democratic majority is to transcend two divisions that power spontaneously imposes on resistance: the rural-urban and the interethnic."[43] Here Mamdani holds out the hopeful examples of Uganda under Museveni, which has sought to "democratize Native Authority," and South Africa, which has been "the home of the strongest and the most imaginative civil-society-based resistance on the continent."[44]

One must note where this argument does not extend: to the imbrication of Ugandan or South African democracy in a world-relational network; here Mamdani is explicitly concerned to reject the overdetermination of international forces common in dependency and structuralist formulations. Yet this too leaves state power and formation as a local, nationalized affair: a serious underestimation of the continuing colonial—in the sense of crosscontinental—determinants of the African states' power. Indeed, even when dealing with the colonial creation of "decentralized despotism," the operation of colonialism as a global system—and as formative for Europe as for Africa and Asia—remains outside the scope of Mamdani's inquiry.

Where this powerful argument stops is thus where we need to go: beyond the borders of individual states to the world-historical processes that have shaped, to parallel Mamdani's formulation, citizenship and subjecthood via the differentiation of national rights and state power on a world scale. This is, of course, very much a world-systems question, and raises key questions of the racialization of state formation and civil rights. How, we might ask, have citizenship and human rights been racialized on a world scale, precisely because formal decolonization was predicated on the deracialization of national political and civil rights? In this sense one might stand Mamdani's world upside down: has not racialization as a transnational phenomenon—indeed, *always* as a transnational phenomenon from the epochs of Atlantic slavery and colonialism onward—increased precisely due to the purported deracialization of the state in the post–World War II and now post-apartheid period? In this sense one might well ask world-systems scholars to apply Mamdani's insights to their work: how have relations emblematic of indirect rule, with all their implications for citizenship and subjecthood, been a fundamental feature of global state formation and deformation? In short, for the post-independence period: was not decolonization dependent on the racialization, in new ways, of the interstate system?

From America, Towards a World-Historical Africa

A second example of the potential for new world-historical work is offered by developments from the other, American, side of the Atlantic. For here too national conceptions and frameworks are giving way to world-relational ones, rooted yet again in the long-durée and global processes. And as in Africa, this represents a drive to overturn a generation of Africanist area studies, and in so doing reach out to the study of Africans worldwide.[45]

The stimulus for such work is not, it should be noted, to be found emanating from the centers of African studies. Even work on Atlantic slavery, which has flourished with explicit debts to Braudel[46] and operates on a transcontinental scale, remains contained within the boundaries of its historical subject. It is rather from African-American movements and studies that the push to break the postwar intellectual heritage has arisen. As anyone familiar with the field knows well, over the last fifteen years the study of African-American life has become transformed to the study of black life in the Americas—and increasingly bridging to a worldwide Diaspora. Indeed the flourishing of Diaspora studies seems to know no bounds, as illustrated by the exploration of such concepts as the "Black Atlantic," or the emergence of new journals (e.g., *Transition, Diaspora, Contours*), or the establishment of new Ph.D. programs in Diaspora studies.

Just how sweeping this movement has been, and how it challenges a generation of Afro-American and African studies, is well illustrated in Tiffany Patterson's and Robin Kelley's sweeping survey of the burgeoning African-American Diaspora literature.[47] As Patterson and Kelley proclaim, the aim is to create a "theoretical framework and a conception of world history that treats the African Diaspora as a unit of analysis."[48] As with world-historical studies, and the more recent African work noted above, this requires the recognition that "nation-states as units of analysis obscure as much as they reveal."[49]

What might replace a narrow sense of Diasporas contained within national boundaries, as has been the case for a generation, remains however very much an open question. Echoing Braudel, the notion of a Black Atlantic anchors many of these works, to which one might add a Black Mediterranean, a Black Indian Ocean, and even, following Michael West's suggestion, a Black Pacific.[50] In different hands these units bound and periodize slave relationships, colonial systems, and transnational working class formations.

Current conceptions and units of analysis of a Diaspora, much less a Black Atlantic, seem unable however to capture or contain the world-relational processes that have produced blackness and whiteness as foundational features of modern capitalist life. Kelley and Patterson conclude their essay with a strong plea for a new, transcontinental framework for understanding African peoples, modernity, and capitalism:

> Just as Europe invented Africa and the New World, we cannot understand the invention of Europe and the New World without Africa and African people. But as expansive and overwhelming as diaspora and Atlantic are as

frameworks for understanding the modern world and/or black internationalism, they are still not enough. . . . Africa—real or imagined—is not the
only source of "black" internationalism, even for those movements that
embrace a nationalist or Pan-Africanist rhetoric. And these movements,
whether they hold the banner of international socialism, women's peace
and freedom, anti-colonialism and Third World solidarity, or Islam, have
never been contained with the holy trinity of Europe, Africa, and the
Americas.[51]

This suggests, in turn, the need to understand the production and imagination of "Africa" as part of broader, and deeper, world-wide processes and
histories. It is also, implicitly, a critique of "Diaspora" studies, arguing that
we need to unearth the processes that produce the phenomena contained
within the leaky conceptual and geographical compartments of the
"Diaspora," "Black Atlantic," or even continental Africa, America, and
Europe.

Reprise

Such conclusions point the way forward toward a world-historical understanding of the lived experiences of Africans as they have shaped and been
shaped by the modern capitalist world. To the extent this path is pursued,
it will mark the abandonment of conceptions of Africa and Africans by
nation-state boundaries, and the emergence of a new tradition, spanning
the continents, of black world-historical studies. Such a tradition might,
at last, develop the early world-systems assertion that the invention of
race, and global processes of racial stratification, have been essential to
the construction of the capitalist world-economy from the long sixteenth
century onward. For world-systems studies, this would mark a new age.

Finally, it is worth pausing to consider what has in the past propelled
such initiatives, and might now do so again. For in large part the emergence today of continental and transcontinental conceptions of Africa,
which seems so novel to us, is but a return to a long-standing vindica-
tionist and pan-African tradition. However we might chart this genealogy,
it is clear that successive waves of global black nationalism set the stage for
the flourishing of black world studies by such authors as Du Bois, James,
Cox, and Williams in the 1940s and early 1950s, and then again, briefly,
in the world-wide upsurge of Black Power in the late 1960s and early
1970s.[52] It is not too difficult to see how the reemergence of such work

in the 1990s reflects another wave of movements across the black world, whether we reference new movements in Africa or the Afrocentric and black nationalist marches and protests in the Americas.[53] And as I noted at the beginning of this chapter (and have argued at greater length elsewhere[54]), world-systems analysis is itself very much a product of the anti-systemic movements of the late 1960s and early 1970s.

Conditions in the early twenty-first century are, of course, much different. Yet the parallels across these waves of scholarship and resistance are too evident to ignore. Just as open colonial repression triggered anticolonial movements, so too has open, global capitalism—now set amidst rising racial difference and inequality, and the failure of liberalism as a legitimizing ideology—served to re-ignite popular as well as academic awareness of and resistance to world capitalist, world-racial, systems. The questions before us thus remain very much world-systemic ones. Can we understand this world, imagine different ones that might replace it, and act towards these ends?

Notes

1. As will become apparent below, we are using "nationalist" in this time and place to reference claims for nation-state independence and sovereignty—which must be distinguished from alternative notions of nationalism based on the pursuit of liberation for a "nation" or "people" that bridge across the boundaries of a state, or even a continental collection of states.

2. Immanuel Wallerstein, *The Modern World-System, 1: Capitalist Agriculture and the Origins of the European World-Economy in the Sixteenth Century* (New York: Academic Press, 1974), 4. See as well his earlier work on Africa, including *Africa: the Politics of Independence* (New York: Vintage, 1961), *The Road to Independence: Ghana and the Ivory Coast* (Paris & La Haye: Mouton, 1964), *Africa: The Politics of Unity* (New York: Random House, 1967), his later collection, *Africa and the Modern World* (Trenton, NJ: Africa World Press, 1986), as well as Immanuel Wallerstein, Sergio Vieira, William G. Martin, et al., *How Fast the Wind? Southern Africa 1975–2000* (Trenton, NJ: Africa World Press, 1991).

3. Wallerstein, *The Modern World-System, 1*, 4–5.

4. Ibid., 507.

5. Bogumil Jewsiewicki, "The African Prism of Immanuel Wallerstein," *Radical History Review*, 1987, 39:50–68.

6. See his resume on the web at: http://fbc.binghamton.edu/tkhcv.htm htm (accessed April 1, 2000), and a brief obituary at: http://fbc.binghamton.edu/tkhobit.htm (accessed April 1, 2000); see also Immanuel Wallerstein, ed., *Mentoring, Methods, and Movements: Colloquium in Honor of Terence K. Hopkins by his former students* (Binghamton: Fernand Braudel Center, 1998).

7. See his resume on the web at: http://fbc.binghamton.edu/gacv.htm htm (accessed April 1, 2000).

8. See, for example, Peter Gutkind and Peter Waterman, eds., *African Social Studies: A Radical Reader* (New York: Monthly Review Press, 1977).

9. Archie Mafeje, "The Ideology of Tribalism," *Journal of Modern African Studies*, 1971, 9, 2:253–61, and Bernard Magubane, "A Critical Look at Indices used in the Study of Social Change in Colonial Africa," *Current Anthropology*, 1971, 12:419–31.

10. Frantz Fanon, *The Wretched of the Earth* (New York: Grove Press, 1963).

11. Eric Williams, *Capitalism and Slavery* (Chapel Hill: University of North Carolina Press, 1944).

12. C. L. R. James, *Black Jacobins: Toussaint L'Ouverture and the San Domingo Revolution* (London: Secker and Warburg, 1938); Oliver Cox, *Caste, Class and Race: A Study in Social Dynamics* (Garden City, NY: Doubleday, 1948); W. E. B. Du Bois, *The World and Africa: An Inquiry into the Part which Africa has Played in World History* (New York: Viking, 1947).

13. As Amin recounts his days in Paris in the 1950s: "Because of the solidarity between our group of young Egyptians and black African students, I followed the embryonic sub-Saharan liberation struggles with great enthusiasm. . . . We were convinced that Asian and African liberation struggles were in the foreground of the world scene after 1945." *Re-Reading the Postwar Period: An Intellectual Itinerary* (New York: Monthly Review Press, 1994), 34–35.

14. Walter Rodney, *How Europe Underdeveloped Africa* (Dar es Salaam: Tanzania Publishing House, 1972).

15. William G. Martin and Michael West, eds., *Out of One, Many Africas: Reconstructing the Study and Meaning of Africa* (Champaign, Ill.: University of Illinois Press, 1999), and especially the chapter (pp. 85–122) by Martin and West, "The Ascent, Triumph, and Disintegration of the Africanist Enterprise, USA."

16. Thandika Mkandawire, "Three Generations of African Academics: A Note," *CODESRIA Bulletin*, 1995, 3:9–12; 9.

17. Ibid.

18. Paulin J. Hountondji, "Producing Knowledge in Africa Today: The Second Bashorun M. K. O Abiola Distinguished Lecture," *African Studies Review*, 38, 3 (December 1995): 1–10; 5.

19. Kwesi Prah, "African Scholars and Africanist Scholarship," *CODESRIA Bulletin*, 1998, 3/4:25–31; 25.

20. Ibid. 27.

21. Ifi Amadiume, *Re-inventing Africa: Matriarchy, Religion and Culture* (New York: Zed Press, 1997), 5–15.

22. Ben Magubane, *African Sociology* (Africa World Press, 2000).

23. Amin, *Re-Reading the Postwar Period*, 139–46.

24. See Martin and West, "The Ascent, Triumph, and Disintegration."

25. Mahmood Mamdani, *Citizen and Subject: Contemporary Africa and the Legacy of Late Colonialism* (Princeton, NJ: Princeton University Press, 1996); Thandika Mkandawire and Charles Chukwana Soludo, *Our Continent, Our Future* (Dakar: CODESRIA, 1999); and Tiyambe Zeleza, *A Modern Economic History of Africa* (Dakar: CODESRIA, 1993).

26. See for example Jean Comaroff and John Comaroff, *Ethnography and the Historical Imagination* (Boulder, Co.: Westview Press, 1992) and their "Introduction," in Jean Comaroff and John Comaroff, eds., *Modernity and its Malcontents: Ritual and Power*

in Postcolonial Africa (Chicago: University of Chicago Press, 1993), xi–xxxvii, or Amina Mama, "Shedding the Masks and Tearing the Veils: Cultural Studies for a Post-colonial Africa," in Ayesha Imam, Amina Mama and Fatou Sow, eds., *Engendering African Social Sciences* (Dakar: CODESRIA, 1997), 63–80.

27. Achille Mbembe, "Editorial," *CODESRIA Bulletin*, 1998, 3/4:3.

28. Frederick Cooper, "Africa and the World Economy," and "Postscript: Africa and the World-Economy," in Frederick Cooper et al., *Confronting Historical Paradigms: Peasants, Labor and the Capitalist World System in Africa and Latin America* (Madison: University of Wisconsin Press, 1993), 84–201, and 187–201.

29. Charles Tilly, "Macrosociology, Past and Future," *Newsletter of the Comparative and Historical Sociology Section of the American Sociological Association*, 1995, 8, 1/2, Winter:1,3,4.

30. See the overview by Steve J. Stern, "Feudalism, Capitalism, and the World-System in the Perspective of Latin America and the Caribbean," in Cooper et al., *Confronting Historical Paradigms*, 23–83.

31. Anibal Quijano, "Modernity, Identity, and Utopia in Latin America," *Boundary 2*, 1993, 20, 3:140; Anibal Quijano and Immanuel Wallerstein, "Americanity as a Concept, or the Americas in the Modern World-System," *International Social Science Journal*, 1992, 44, 4:549–58; and Walter Mignolo, *Local histories, Global Designs: Coloniality, Subaltern Knowledges, and Border Thinking* (Princeton: Princeton University Press, 2000).

32. See for example Partha Chatterjee, *The Nation and Its Fragments* (Princeton: Princeton University Press, 1996), and Gyan Prakash, "Colonialism, Capitalism and the Discourse of Freedom," *International Review of Social History*, 1996, 41:9–25.

33. Thus Chatterjee appropriately rejects Benedict Anderson's influential argument that Europe provided "modular" forms of nationalism for adoption later and elsewhere in the world (*The Nation and Its Fragments*, 3), and locates South Asian nationalism instead on its own, inside colonial India. From a world-systems perspective, what we need to inquire is how the European nationalism and Indian nationalism were formed in relation to each other—a methodological project quite different from that pursued by Anderson or Chatterjee.

34. See as a critique Cedric Robinson, "The Appropriation of Fanon," *Race and Class*, 1993, 35, 1:79–91.

35. Steven Feierman, "African Histories and the Dissolution of World History," in Robert Bates, V. Y. Mudimbe, Jean O'Barr, eds., *Africa and the Disciplines: the Contributions of Research in Africa to the Social Sciences and Humanities* (Chicago: University of Chicago Press, 1993, 167–205).

36. See William Martin, "The World-Systems Perspective in Perspective: Assessing the Attempt to Move Beyond Nineteenth Century Euro-North American Conceptions," *Review*, 1994, 17, 2 (Spring): 145–86.

37. See as a beginning Giovanni Arrighi, *The Long Twentieth Century* (London: Verso, 1994), and Giovanni Arrighi and Beverly Silver, eds., *Chaos and Governance in the Modern World System.* (Minneapolis: University of Minnesota Press, 1999).

38. Williams, *Capitalism and Slavery*, and James, *Black Jacobins.*

39. One small attempt is my own (see "Region Formation Under Crisis Conditions: South vs. Southern Africa in the Interwar Period," *Journal of Southern African Studies*, 1990, 16, 1:112–38, and "The Making of an Industrial South Africa: Trade and Tariffs in

the Interwar Period," *International Journal of African Historical Studies*, 1990, 23, 2: 59–85), where I tried to show that South Africa's industrial leap forward in the interwar period depended not only on changing relations with a weakened Great Britain, but also the creation of a new relational structure in the region—indeed giving coherence for the first time to southern Africa as unequal regional relationships accelerated under industrializing conditions in South Africa.

40. Mkandawire and Soludo, *Our Continent*, 21–30.

41. Mahmood Mamdani, *Politics and Class Formation in Uganda* (New York: Monthly Review Press, 1976), and *Imperialism and Fascism in Uganda* (Dar es Salaam: Tanzania Publishing House, 1983).

42. Mamdani, *Citizen*, 8.

43. Ibid., 296.

44. Ibid., 297.

45. This movement also has grave implications for the intellectual and institutional separation of Latin American from American and/or Latino studies—analogous to the tensions and transformations in the United States posed by the postwar division of African and African-American studies, and the current challenges signaled by the rise of Diaspora studies. This is, however, a theme we cannot pursue here.

46. E.g., John Thornton, *Africa and Africans in the Making of the Atlantic World, 1400–1680* (New York: Cambridge University Press, 1992).

47. Tiffany Patterson and Robin D. G. Kelley, "Unfinished Migrations: Reflections on the African Diaspora and the Making of the Modern World," *African Studies Review*, 43, 1 (2000): 11–45.

48. Ibid., 13.

49. Ibid., 29.

50. See Patterson and Kelley, "Unfinished Migrations," 29–30, and "Commentary" by Michael O. West, *African Studies Review*, 43, 1 (2000): 61–64, esp. 62.

51. Patterson and Kelley, "Unfinished Migrations," 32–33.

52. For an account of how this directly affected the institutionalization and racialization of the African studies establishment in the U.S., see Martin and West, "The Ascent, Triumph, and Disintegration," esp. 97–106.

53. See the four waves of black nationalism as charted in Michael West, "Like a River: The Million Man March and the Black Nationalist Tradition in the United States," *Journal of Historical Sociology*, 1999, 12, 1, March: 81–100.

54. See William G. Martin, "World Revolutions and World-Systems Analysis: Still Antisystemic Partners, Still Possible?," paper presented at the twenty-third annual conference of the Political Economy of the World-System Section of the American Sociological Association, March 26–27, 1999, the University of Maryland, College Park.

17

"WHAT AFRICA HAS GIVEN AMERICA"

AFRICAN CONTINUITIES IN THE NORTH AMERICAN DIASPORA[1]

Joseph E. Holloway

During my graduate years at UCLA, the great French cultural anthropologist Jacques Maquet once posed a theoretical question in class: How does one reconstruct the history of a symbolic object that long ago lost its meaning in a culture? No answer was satisfactory because current anthropological methods did not provide the methodology for answering this hypothetical question. Maquet knew the problem was of great complexity, but solvable. He used an example from mathematics: "To find a solution that will provide a method and give the outcome, correlational modeling might be useful." Maquet went further, saying, "Anthropological studies must go beyond current methods and map out new territories that have not yet been crossed."

The research problem I was trying to solve had to do with the similarities in masking tradition between the Ijaw of southern Nigeria and the Dan of Liberia. Here were two almost identical material objects, yet the content, structure, form, and meaning were understood only in one culture. I approached Maquet during his office hours for some direction, and his advice was that my approach should be multidisciplinary, using all available resources and methods at hand to reconstruct an anthropological past that had been lost in time. I got a map of West Africa and mapped similar masking traditions throughout the region, using what I called the

"Shot Gun" method. That is, I did a crosscultural comparison within a radius of five hundred miles analyzing similar cultural objects. After finding that the mask being studied exists in the above two cultures only, I used oral tradition to discover that a group had migrated from what is now Nigeria some five hundred years earlier and resettled in the Liberian region, and that they were most likely responsible for preservation of the masking tradition in the Dan region. In other words, by mirroring the symbolic object as it relates to their religion, ceremonies, aesthetic, folktales, dance, and so forth, the original meaning and purpose of the aesthetic object could be reconstructed from the anthropological and historical past. Years later these methods would be used to reconstruct African content in contemporary Gullah culture in North America.

This chapter focuses on various methodological approaches to the study of Africanisms in North America. At present the Diasporic approach has given the debates a new focus.[2] E. Franklin Frazier, in his deculturization hypothesis, had asserted that the institution of slavery destroyed any surviving African culture in North America. Melville J. Herskovits responded that, on the contrary, African cultural traits and carryovers were retained in the process of acculturation and adaptation; thus, an African continuity was present in African American culture. At present, the Diasporic approach uses a transnational framework to look at distinctive African cultural expressions, trying to see how African culture has changed over time and adapted itself to diasporic conditions while experiencing slavery, forced labor, and racial discrimination. This new focus includes methods such as linguistics, correlation modeling, crosscultural analysis, cultural mapping, cultural clustering, the immuno-chemical method, and finally the "Shot Gun" method of historical research.

Cultural Clustering and the Correlation Model

There have been numerous attempts to record the African cultural zones from which African Americans originated. Herskovits, in "A Preliminary Consideration of the Culture Areas of Africa,"[3] was the first scholar to identify broad cultural areas of Africa. His preliminary inquiry established eleven cultural areas, based on geographic regions, and his further inquiry into the ancestry of African Americans recognized the need for some kind of systematic collection of demographic data that would assist scholars in identifying the various ethnic groups. Although Herskovits saw the importance of multiplicity in the ethnicity of African American culture, he was not successful in identifying the precise African ethnic groups or cultural clusters and geographical areas of Africans who came to the North America, because he used an exclusively West African cultural baseline for assessing New World Africanisms. In sum, his methodology was valid in establishing a cultural baseline from which to assess the different Africans' traditions and customs found in the New World, but his model did not go far enough to include the Central Bantu groups. He looked for Africanisms in the wrong places, thus noticing only West African cultural survivals and ignoring most Bantu culture in the New World.

In 1944, the International African Institute in London began an Ethnographic Survey of Africa, in which the idea of cultural "clusters" was first developed: "Small groups of neighbouring peoples are taken as units within broad geographical regions."[4] These clusters were limited, however, in that they ignored the factor of language. Alan P. Merriam in 1959 further developed this concept, introducing the language variable and applying it to the then Belgian Congo in identifying Bantu music.[5] The concept has since become influential in anthropology.[6]

Philip Curtin's 1968 work[7] was one of the first studies that addressed African ethnicity in the New World by taking a census of Africans, tabulating the ethnic groups brought by the Atlantic slave trade. Instead of clearing up the confusion, his work added to it by failing to put related groups together into cultural clusters. To do this would have made the data more relevant by eliminating overlapping groups such as the Bambara, Mandingo, Malinke, and Temne, all Mande-related peoples sharing a common cultural identity.

Joseph H. Greenberg[8] was able to place the African languages into related categories by grouping Africans into related linguistic groups in his classic 1966 study on African languages. Greenberg used only the factor of linguistics. Other factors for cultural clustering are history, religion (cosmology), aesthetics (arts, music, musical instruments, dance, folklore), traditions, customs, food culture, and occupations.

In 1993 Vass and I used cultural clustering of related African linguistic groups to identify African linguistic survivals in American English.[9] In 1990, I had revised Herskovits's cultural zones into small cultural clusters: Mande, Mano River, Akan, Sudanic, Niger Cross River, Niger Delta, and Bantu. The Bantu cluster is further subdivided into Bakongo, Ovimbundu, and Luba Lunda.[10]

The revised Herskovits culture regions of Africa have an even wider application than the cultural mapping described above: they help identify and assess origins of African culture in certain southern United States communities with strong African cultural survivals, and they also have far-reaching implications for linguistics, genealogical research, biomedicine, and genetics, among other fields. For example, the biomedical community benefits tremendously from the potential to identify regional origins of genetic diseases found in both Africa and the United States, the cultural map can locate and help identify certain ethnic, genetic, or cultural traits, and the map is also useful for the genealogical research by which Americans of African descent trace their genetic ancestry back to specific regions of west and central Africa.

Using the cultural map, Patricia Fraser was able to identify African ethnic groups by using immuno-chemical methods.[11] By analyzing complotypes unique to individuals of African origin, she has identified four, FC (I, 90)O, FC63, SIC2, 17 and SC (3,2,90), that are found in Africa and the Americas.

For analyzing African cultural survivals in North America, the correlation model goes beyond Herskovits's regional model and allows for a more accurate assessment of the different African groups contributing to American culture. The correlation model can be used for identifying and categorizing each African "retention" traceable to a specific African origin. This approach entails an examination and listing of all Africanisms found in American culture in language, religion, aesthetics (arts, crafts, music, dance, instruments, occultism [voodoo], coiffure), family life, and food culture. A survey of demographic data on enslaved Africans, and a study of the African traits retained in their different settlements, can be used as a dating methodology for Africanisms found in North America and demonstrate how the demographic movement of African groups over time and space can transport elements of their culture from one geographical region to another.

For example, Puckett[12] observed in South Carolina among the Gullah in 1925 that the children of a dead parent were passed over the coffin. This practice is not as common as it was in past years but is still practiced from Georgetown to Savannah. All my informants recalled witnessing this custom recently.[13] None of the old people knew or remembered why they did this except for a local minister, who said that young children are passed over the coffin of the dead person to prevent the spirit of the parent or loved one from entering the body of the young child. "When a child is very young and don't understand what is happening because their souls is not fully developed, and their identity is not formed. Because of this a dead person's spirit can enter the body of the child causing it great harm. Children can hear the voices of the dead, especially if they were close to the individual which had died."[14]

One day the minister's daughter was found walking down a country road about the same time her grandfather died. She was found wandering in the wilderness by a niece and was questioned as to where she was going; she replied, "Granddaddy called me!" The elders of the community were consulted about how to deal with this problem. Their solution was based on what had worked in the past. They revealed that this was a very serious problem and asserted that the child would have to attend the funeral because she was in danger until it was over. In the minister's words, "Kids don't understand what death is all about, and because the child is young their spirit is not as strong as the dead. The child has to witness the funeral and be shown where the grandfather is going down into the ground." The child is therefore passed over the coffin to separate the spirits. The moment when the child is passed over the coffin signals the separation of the two spirits. Informants asserted that two other children who did not attend the funeral and were not passed over the coffin experienced serious psychological problems for about six months in adjusting to the death of the grandfather.[15]

Using the correlation method, we were able to identify the original African sources for this practice. The same custom is found today in Bonny and Opobo and has remained almost identical in form and meaning, as we shall now see. An informant from Opobo remembered this custom enacted when her grandfather died in the 1960s. She recalled that at the funeral the great-grandchildren and grandchildren were passed over the coffin. Her cousin performed this ceremony, passing the children from one end of the coffin to the other. One of the children, as she was being passed over the coffin, landed on top of the coffin and began to scream. The whole community was upset about this serious violation of custom.

According to my informant, the children were passed over the coffin so that the spirit of the dead would not be so attached to the children that it would keep visiting them. The visitation by the dead loved ones to the children is viewed as a serious matter because the children could become alarmed and because they are considered too young to understand they might become ill and die. The rite is performed to separate the bond between the dead person and the living children. This is done as an act of love and to keep the spirit from coming back into the house. The child passing over the coffin signals a break in the close bond between the dead loved one and the living relative, so that the spirit will go on its way and not come back to visit the children.[16]

Thus, this phenomenon of passing children over the coffin is still practiced identically by the Gullahs of South Carolina and by the Ibani of

Bonny and the Opobo in Nigeria. In the historical literature, Bonny was one of the major ports from which Africans were brought to North America. A close examination of slave importation records into South Carolina show that a total of 1,975 Africans arrived from Bonny in 1739.[17] These figures suggest that the core group of people from Opobo arriving from Bonny in 1739 formed a critical mass. The evidence suggests that the transportation and foundation for this passing-over custom first arrived in South Carolina in 1739 when the majority of Ibanis arrived from the African port kingdom of Bonny. No other substantial imports of Africans from Bonny occurred until 1800. Intense slave activities in the Bonny area began again between 1800 and 1807, just prior to the closing of the legal slave trade. Shipments identified by Elizabeth Donnan as arriving from Bonny ports include 530 Africans in 1805 and only 368 Africans at the close of the legal slave trade in 1807.[18] Thus, the correlation model has a potential for historical dating. Based on the above, one can assume that the "passing over" tradition was brought to the Sea Islands between 1739 and 1807.

Oral History and the Study of the African American Past

Oral history has been used for years as a valid historical methodology—in, for example, the Federal Writer's Project of the Works Progress Administration, which recorded the testimonies of ex-slaves. A scholar such as Lawrence Levine[19] reminds us that traditional historical methodology is inadequate for examining African American history because a preliterate people express their culture similarly to other preliterate African societies in their oral tradition, cooking folklore, folktales, music and religion. Several sources use oral interviews to good effect.[20]

Now, how does one use oral history as a methodological tool for reconstructing and analyzing the African American past? While in the field in St. Helena, South Carolina, I found a whole area of inquiry that had not been examined by previous scholarship. In conducting limited interviews, I found a direct parallel between the Gullah concept of time and history and that of their African ancestors. Time and history were remembered and recalled in relationship to major episodic events such as the earthquake of 1886, the tidal wave and hurricane of 1893, and the storm of 1911.

The Gullah also calculated their ages similarly to their African ancestors. Age was not numerically calculated but recorded instead in relationship to major episodic events such as the "de big Gun Shoot" ("de fust gun what shoot on Hilton Head [island] enduring de Civil War"). For example, when the census was being taken the Gullahs replied to the inquiry about how old they were in the following ways: "Well, Ma'am, I can't rightly tell, but I tell you dis, when gun shoot." This meant the speaker was born at the beginning of the Civil War. Another replied, "When gun shoot I bin so leetle I tink it bin tunder. I bin jest big nuf to tie de cow out." Another ex-slave remembered "birth de berry day gun shoot." Still another said, "I bin a grown [w]oman wid chillum," and another ex-slave admitted that "Dey did told me ma age, Ma'am, but when gun shoot I ben a leetle boy in shirt tail." They remember the "de big gun shoot" days and record their ages from that important event in their lives.[21]

Eva L. Ver dier, taking the census among the Gullah in 1930, noted that "the coastal Negro does not date time by *Anno Domini*, but from events of great excitement or danger. Instead of 'gun shoot' days, the younger ones reckon from the 1886 earthquake and still younger ones from the 1893 storm when over two thousand of them lost their lives in the storm and hurricane."[22]

The old people still recall the great devastation caused by the tidal wave and hurricane that hit St. Helena Island in 1893, destroying both crops and livestock. More than 2,000 people died.[23] Ben Mack, once the oldest man on the island, who died not long before I could do field research on his island, remembered the events as he recorded them in a song telling about all the things the storm had destroyed.[24]

Remembered in relationship to the storm of 1911 was an African turnip-like plant called *Tania* by the local people. The storm of 1911 was the historical reference point for recalling this particular root plant. One informant explained, "We had an old fashion thing that came from Africa called *Tania*." It had an elephant-ear-like leaf and below was something like a turnip. After the storm of 1911, "Everything vanished and it don't grow no more."[25] In the Georgia Sea Islands the people were also familiar with *Tania*. One informant interviewed in regard to an African-born ex-slave remembered that he (the African) "ate funny kine uh food. Roas wile locus an mushruhm and *tanyan* root. It lak elephant-eah and tase like Irish potatun."[26] In identifying this African root plant, we know that *tania* is a root plant that appears to be indigenous to West Africa. Of the two known varieties, one is called old coco-yam (Colocasia antiquorum), also called Eddo in the West Indies and Koko in Ghana and Nigeria. The other variety is called cocoyam Tania [Xanthosoma sagittifolium].[27]

The storm of 1893 was also used as the reference point for locating a group of Africans that lived at the Wallace plantation on St. Helena. One informant recalled that her mother said that she was Grebo,[28] and another informant recalled an African community or community of Africans that lived on the "de Wallace Plantation" about five miles from the present site of the Penn Center. On St. Helena some of the old people remembered what their parents and grandparents told them and in their turn handed down the experience of the race. "Oh, yes'm, he can remember hearing about the landing of those African people there at Lonesome Hill. Many died, and many ran away, and I spec dey ran back to Africa."[29] Whether this was a group of Africans who came to the islands after the 1850s or some isolated group of Africans that never acculturated into the general population is not known. One possible explanation is that they were smuggled into the areas by the *Wanderer* or some other illegal slave ship but not recorded.

Another possible connection with the *Wanderer* was Isaac Smith. Mrs. Bernice Brooks recalled the African stories and recollections of her great-grandfather,[30] Isaac Smith, who said he came over on a slave ship in his teens and did not remain a slave for long because freedom came soon after his arrival. He died in 1932 and was near ninety or in his early nineties. He recalled being in his teens, about sixteen seasons, at the time of his arrival in Georgia. He remembered being on deck with longhorn cattle (Africans were smuggled in by mixing them with the legitimate cargo), and that it was very hot when he arrived (probably during the summer). Based on these data he was probably born in Africa around 1842 and arrived in North America in 1858. He was captured in Africa with his father, but they were separated after they landed in Georgia. He never did learn how to speak good English and talked with a strong Gullah accent, meaning he probably arrived in Georgia in his mid-teens. In North America, he was employed as a "house boy" and never really worked the fields. He fished all the time and drank strong coffee.

The fact that enslaved Africans were being smuggled into the area on a regular basis contributed to a strong African presence. Slave traders continued to unload cargoes of slaves directly from Africa into the Sea Islands until the middle of the nineteenth century. The last recorded ship to land a cargo of Africans in the Sea Islands was the *Wanderer*, which came to Jekyll Island in Georgia with 420 Africans in 1858. They were unloaded on the Dubignon Plantation, and about half of them were taken to the Butler and Tillman Plantations near Hanburg in Edgefield Country, South Carolina. Although most of the Africans were later scattered throughout the South, many of them remained in South Carolina and

Georgia, living within a radius of from two to thirty miles from where they originally landed.[31]

Emory Campbell on Hilton Island recalled that his "great aunty" told him how these illegal Africans were smuggled in wagons that were covered to keep the authorities unaware.[32] As late as 1862, Miss Towne noticed that one woman from Gabriel Eddings Plantation on St. Helena had been brought from Africa. Her face was tattooed and she was of more "vigorous stock" than the others.[33] It is quite possible that the African community mentioned above had existed since slavery time and had helped preserve a continuing African presence, as reflected in Gullah burial practices, cosmology, basketry, handicrafts, and folklore. In 1893, the local population was very African in its own cultural heritage, yet the local residents identified the people on the Wallace Plantation as African. One informant explained, "Dem people dat can give you mo' history, dey all done gone now. Dem people on de Wallace Plantation dey were Africans and I know dis to be true. Dey was the people dat know all about Africa and African things. Dey all now gon'. Dey wuz wiped out when de storm uh 1893 came."[34] The fact that the Wallace Plantation was the only plantation on St. Helena with people identified as "Africans" by the local people suggests that Mr. Wallace was in the illegal smuggling business. On January 19, 1829, L. R. Wallace incurred penalties for slave trading.[35] The official slave trade had ended legally in 1808.

Critical Mass Theory and the Bantu

By tabulating the number of Africans coming into South Carolina, we were able to establish that they formed a critical mass by cultural group. The slave trade data suggests that the Bantus were the largest group of Africans in South Carolina, and possibly in other areas of the southeastern United States as well. Given the homogeneity of Bantu cultures and their strong similarities in language, this group doubtlessly dominated and influenced surrounding West African groups of larger size by becoming a critical mass. Also, as the Bantus were predominantly field hands or used in activities that required little or no contact with Euro-Americans, they did not confront the problem of acculturation as directly and intensely as did the West African domestic servants and artisans. Coexisting in relative isolation from other groups, the Bantus were able to maintain a strong sense of unity, and a cultural heritage, which they passed on to their American descendants.

Elizabeth Donnan's collection of the records of slave-importing companies[36] (1935) shows the number of Africans carried by each vessel and the ports from which they were received. These data indicate that planters in South Carolina and Virginia showed some preference for Africans from the Senegambian Coast and its hinterland. It is quite possible that South Carolina merchants sent their male Igbo cargo to North Carolina because of the refusal by local planters to purchase Igbo men and Africans from the Bight of Biafra. However, Igbo women were highly prized as concubines.

In the early years of the slave trade, Senegal was the most important region in the trade. In the late eighteenth century, however, slave ships turned their attention increasingly to Central Africa, a shift that accelerated with British suppression of the Atlantic slave trade in 1807. By the 1780s, Kongo-Angola traffic was already exceeding West African traffic. The Bantu regions of Africa (Angola, Congo, Benguela, and ·Cabinda) sent significant slave cargoes to South Carolina. These Africans brought a homogeneous culture identifiable as Bantu.[37]

Once the African Bantus reached the Sea Islands of South Carolina, they were able to retain much of their cultural identity because "New Africans" (many Bantus among them) were continually brought from Africa as field slaves to reinforce the labor supply. The strong African tradition of the Sea Islands of South Carolina is a result of this continued influx directly from Africa (not from the West Indies as was once commonly believed).

Curtin identified the African coastal region as the place of origin of slaves imported into Virginia and South Carolina. Senegambia, Windward Coast, and Gold Coast people represented 49 percent of the Africans brought into South Carolina. Collectively, West Africans from Senegambia through the Bight of Benin represented 60 percent of the Africans imported into South Carolina. Still, the Angolans clearly formed the largest single ethnic group (40 percent) imported into South Carolina, and they also formed a culturally homogeneous group on North American plantations.[38]

African cultural patterns predominating in Southern states clearly reflected the specific cultural groups imported into the United States. That is, the Upper South tended to be populated by Africans from West Africa, and the Lower South by Africans from Central Africa. The Upper South generally reached from Maryland and Virginia west into Kentucky. The Lower South, or Deep South, included South Carolina and Georgia as well as the fertile Delta region of Mississippi, central Alabama, and Louisiana. North Carolina and Tennessee were culturally intermediate areas. Southern Virginia and South Carolina were centers of dense African American populations that were derived from different regions of Africa and spread west with the western expansion of the United States following the Revolution.

The Bantu Versus the Mande on the Plantation[39]

Africans transported during the Colonial period were from the Guinea Coast, primarily Wolof, Fulani, Mandingo, and Bambara. Africans from the Senegambia were considered taller and of lighter complexions. "A preference for light-skinned slaves to work in the house existed in Charleston, New Orleans, and some other cities."[40] While the Mandes were often enslaved as craftsmen, artisans, and house servants, the field slaves were mainly Central Africans who, unlike the Senegambians, brought a homogeneous, identifiable culture. As field workers, the Bantus were kept away from the developing mainstream of white American culture, an isolation that enabled Bantu culture to escape acculturation and maintain homogeneity.

The Bantus also had metallurgical and woodworking skills, including a particular skill in ironworking that they used in making the wrought-iron balconies of New Orleans and Charleston. Certain ethnic groups from the Kongo-Angola region had a reputation for being adept at acquiring mechanical skills. Also, many were trained in, and even dominated, the barbering trade in South Carolina, performing the same tasks as free barbers: shaving, dressing hair, and setting wigs. They also worked as personal body servants and were employed in shops owned by their masters.

Bantu contributions to South Carolina and Louisiana include not only the popular wrought-iron balconies but also forms of wood carvings, basketry, woven cloth, and early aspects of ceramics such as clay-baked figurines and pottery. Cosmograms, grave designs and decorations, funeral practices, and the wake are also Bantu in origin. Distinctive Bantu musical contributions include Bantu instruments such as banjos, drums, diddley bows, mouthbows, quilts, washtub bass, jugs, gongs, bells, rattles, idiophones, and the lokoimni, a five-stringed harp.

The Bantus were the largest African group in South Carolina, and possibly in several other areas of the southeastern United States, including Alabama and Louisiana. Under the influence of his student Lorenzo Dow Turner Herskovits noted that there was a center of Bantu influence in

North America in the South Carolina Sea Islands off the coast of Carolina. He apparently saw this as an exception to the predominately West African nature of African American culture.[41]

Given the homogeneity of Bantu culture and the strong similarities among Bantu languages, this group no doubt influenced West African groups of larger size. Also, since the Bantus were predominantly field hands or did other work that required little or no contact with European-Americans, they did not suffer from the acculturation problems experienced by West African domestic servants and artisans. Coexisting in relative isolation from other groups, the Bantus were able to maintain a strong sense of unity and retain a cultural vitality that laid a foundation for African American culture. Thus, whereas the Mande had a greater influence on the developing white American culture, the Bantu had the greatest influence on the developing African American culture.

African Ethnicity on the American Plantations

The planters' preference in South Carolina was for Africans from the Gambia region, the Windward Coast, the Grain Coast, the Bight of Benin, and Angola. One possible reason why Africans from Dahomey were rare in Charleston might be their notoriously strong military tradition, which aroused fear of possible insurrections in the mind of Charleston's planters. South Carolinians liked Gold Coast Africans (Akan), but not as much as Virginia and Maryland did. Although Africans from the Upper Guinea Coast were highly prized, planters were more willing to invest in Angolans as prime field slaves.

Slave merchants took great care, throughout the entire history of the South Carolinian trade, to inform potential buyers of the African region and geographic point of origination of the slaves being sold. Many advertisements refer to the Southern planters' familiarity with African ethnic origins, and advertisements for slave cargo occasionally gave the source from which the Africans originated. A cargo from Angola was advertised in the 6 June 1771 *South Carolina Gazette* as "mostly of the Masse-Congo country and are esteemed equal to the Gold Coast and Gambia slaves."[42] Also, a notice in the *Virginia Gazette* during the eighteenth century gives clear evidence that planters distinguished escaped enslaved Africans by the various parts of Africa they came from, describing the escapees as "a young Angola Negro," "a very Black Mundigo [Mandingo] negro man," "a native

Madagascar," "a Congo Negro Slave, of the Suso Country," "New Negro Fellow . . . calls himself Bonna (Bonny) and says he came from a place of that name in Ibo country, in Africa," or "marked in the face as the Gold Coast slaves generally are."[43]

It was once believed that North American planters were unsophisticated about African ethnicity, but an examination of sources suggests they were familiar with the rice, cotton, and indigo production in Africa and were often able to relate the various African ethnic groups to the types of agricultural cultivation found in Africa. It seems clear that South Carolina planters did not purchase Africans blindly to work on their plantations. Instead, planters knew and understood cultural backgrounds and purchased with the expectation of using agricultural knowledge and skills on the North American plantations: for example, tending cattle, fishing, boating, house service, and blacksmithing.

The planters in North America were known to purchase Africans from West Africa to serve as house servants and artisans. Senegambians (Mandingo, Wolof, Serer, Fulani, and Bambara) were considered the most intelligent of Africans (because believed to be of mixed heritage, with Arabic ancestry) and were trained for domestic service and as handicraftworkers. Mandingoes were considered gentle in manner but prone to be thieves. Since they were thought to tire easily because of their delicate physiques, they served as watchmen against fires rather than as field slaves.[44]

Africans transported during the colonial period were from the Guinea Coast, largely Wolof, Fulani, Mande, Bambara, and a few Yoruba during the early period. Africans from the Senegambia were taller and lighter in complexion. "A preference for light-skinned Africans to work in the house existed in Charleston, New Orleans, and some other cities."[45] While the Senegambians (Mandes) were preferred as house servants, the Kongos, Angolans, and Igbos were preferred for the field, except for Igbo women, who were highly sought after as concubines. Having technological skills was also important, and planters explored ways to apply such skills to agricultural pursuits.

Most Angolans were used primarily as field slaves because they were large and robust. They were imported in large numbers, especially in the eighteenth century, and were the dominant group in South Carolina and Louisiana. Because they were primarily field slaves, they had little contact with the planter class; their acculturation during the colonial period was long and slow in contrast to house servants, who lived in close proximity to whites.

In short, South Carolina's planters wanted Gambians first, and next, "Healthy young Fantees, Coromantines, Negroes from Bassa on the Windward Coast, from Bance Island," and Angolans from Central Africa. Africans from the Bight, Igbos, and Calabar (Efik-Ibibio) were the least desired of all, and "captains were frequently urged not to bring them to the South Carolinian market."[46]

African Crops to the New World

Crops brought directly from Africa during the transatlantic slave trade include rice, okra, tania, black-eyed peas, and kidney and lima beans; Africans ate them on board the slave ships. Other crops brought from Africa included peanuts (originating from South America), millet, sorghum, guinea melon, watermelon, yams (Dioscorea cayanensis), and sesame (benne).[47] These crops found their way into American foodways and appeared among the ingredients in the earliest cookbooks written by Southern American whites.

As early as 1687, a young physician living in the West Indies, Sir Hans Sloane, found many of these crops growing on the island of Jamaica. These plants reached the mainland of North America either directly from Africa or with enslaved Africans destined for North America by way of trade with the West Indies. The crops may have found a home in North America even before Sloane's encounter. Eventually, however, these crops went from use exclusively by Africans in North America to being part of white southern cuisine.

Black-eyed peas first came to the New World as food for slaves during the transatlantic slave trade, arriving in Jamaica around 1675, spreading throughout the West Indies, and finally reaching Florida by 1700, North Carolina in 1738, and Virginia by 1775. Slave planter William Byrd mentions black-eyed peas in his writings in 1738. By the time of the American Revolution, black-eyed peas were firmly established in America as part of the general cuisine.

George Washington wrote in a letter in 1791 that "pease" (black-eyed peas) were rarely grown in Virginia. In 1792 he brought forty bushels of seeds for planting to his plantation. Black-eyed peas became one of the most popular food crops in the southern part of the United States. Washington later referred to them as "callicance" and "cornfield peas" because of the early custom of planting them between the rows of field corn.

Okra arrived in the New World during the transatlantic slave trade in the 1600s. Okra, or gumbo as it is called in the deep South, found exceptional popularity in New Orleans. In French Louisiana, Creole cuisine and African cooking came together to produce the unique cuisine of New Orleans. Gumbo is a popular stew or soup that mixes other vegetables with okra, the main ingredient, and is thickened with powder from sassafras leaves (gumbo file). One observer in 1748 noted that thickened soup was a delicacy liked by blacks. Even before the American Revolution, American whites already commonly used okra.

Enslaved Africans used the young okra, which contains the vegetable mucilage, to eat by boiling. The leaves were also used medicinally to soften a cataplasm, and seeds were used on the plantations of South Carolina to make a coffee substitute. Okra was popular among women to produce abortion by lubricating the uterine passage with the slimy pods. In West Africa today, women still use okra to produce abortion, using the same method.

The next important crop to arrive in the United States by way of Africa was the American peanut, which is also known by several other names, including groundnut, earth nut, and ground peas. Two other words of African origin are *pindar* and *goober*. Among other recorded sources of the use of these African names, both Thomas Jefferson and George Washington called peanuts *peendar* and *pindars* (1794, 1798). The word was in use before the American Revolution. The word *goober* was used principally in the nineteenth century. The period of greatest popularity was the 1860s, when the Civil War song, "Goober Peas," appeared. When it was published after the war, the words were attributed to "A. Pindar" and the music to "P. Nutt."

The American peanut has an interesting history. Although indigenous to South America as a crop, it was first brought to Africa by Portuguese sailors and then to Virginia from Africa by enslaved Africans. The peanut was used to feed Africans on the middle passage. One New World observer noted, "The first I ever saw of these [peanuts] growing was the Negro's plantation who affirmed, that they grew in great plenty in their country." In Africa, peanut stews, soups, and gravies serve as an important part of any meal. However, nut soups in the American South, although of African origin, are no longer enjoyed by the descendants of Africans but are associated with Euro-Americans instead.[48]

George Washington Carver researched the peanut as a crop, and from his experiments he found that they contained water, fats, oils, gums, resins, sugar, starches, pectins, pentosans, and proteins. From these compounds he identified more than three hundred possible peanut products, including Jersey milk that could produce butter and cheese. Other products were instant coffee, flour, face cream, bleach, synthetic rubber, and linoleum. Dr. Carver found that rubbing peanut oil on muscles helped rejuvenate them. Dr. Carver also created a peanut milk and a soy bean formula for Gandhi that Gandhi found to be a healthy part of his diet.

Sesame first arrived in South Carolina from Africa by 1730, and in the same year a Carolinian sent sesame and sesame oil to London. This was a matter of considerable importance in Colonial America and England because table oil was one of the products England hoped to obtain by colonizing the New World. To avoid importing olive oil for cooking, Britain encouraged production of table oils by offering bounties on edible oils. By 1733, a book on gardening published in London noted the cultivation of the sesame plant and its usefulness as a source of "salletoil." Enslaved Africans also grew sesame for other uses. Thomas Jefferson noted in the 1770s that benne (another name for sesame) was eaten raw, toasted, or boiled in soups by African slaves. Jefferson also noted that slaves baked sesame in breads, boiled it in greens, and used it to enrich broth. Today sesame is used primarily as bread topping.

The first successful cultivation of rice in the United States was accomplished in the South Carolina Sea Islands by an African woman who later taught her planter how to cultivate rice. The first rice seeds were imported directly from the island of Madagascar in 1685, with Africans supplying the labor and technical expertise.[49] African experts in rice cultivation were brought directly from the island of Goree to teach Europeans how to cultivate this cash crop.

House servants, while learning from the planters, also brought their own African culinary tastes into the plantation mansions. African cooks in the "Big House" introduced their African crops and foods, thus becoming intermediaries in the melding of African and European culinary cultures. African cooks introduced deep fat frying, a cooking technique that originated in Africa. Long before refrigeration, Africans understood how deep fat frying of chicken or beef could preserve these foods for a time.

Using their indigenous crops, enslaved Africans recreated traditional African cuisine. One example is fufu. In South Carolina this dish is called "turn meal and flour" and is prepared by boiling water and adding flour while stirring the ingredients, hence the name. Throughout Africa, fufu is a highly favored staple, a traditional West and Central African meal eaten from Senegambia to Angola. Africans prepare fufu by mixing palm oil and flour. From these fufu mixtures, slaves made hoecake in the fields that later evolved into pancakes and hot water cornbread. Cornbread, prepared by African slaves, was similar to African millet bread. In the reports of slavers found in the journal entry from the ship *Mary,* June 20, 1796, "Cornbread" is mentioned as one of the African foods provided for their cargo. The report also mentions a "woman cleaning rice and grinding corn for corn cakes." Corn fried into cakes is still prepared throughout Africa today.

As early as 1739, naturalist Mark Catesby noted that slaves made a mush from the corn meal called pone bread. He also noticed that slaves took hominy Indian corn and made grits, a food similar to the African dish called Eba. Catesby observed in 1747 that Guinea corn (*sorghum vulgare*) and Indian corn (*Zea mays*) were used interchangeably by blacks. He wrote that "little of this grain is propagated, and that chiefly by negroes, who make bread of it, and boil it in like manner of firmety. It[s] chief use is for feeding fowls. . . . It was first introduced from Africa by the negroes."[50] Lawson noted that Guinea corn was used mostly for hogs and poultry by whites, adding that enslaved Africans ate nothing but Indian corn.[51]

African food traditions contributed greatly to the culinary taste of America, and Southern cooking is therefore a cultural experience to which both blacks and whites contributed. Today's black American cuisine is strongly influenced by the African style of cooking, a carryover of this antebellum period. "Soul food" itself goes back to days when plantation owners gave slaves discarded animal parts, such as hog maw (stomach), hog jowl, pig's feet, ham hocks, and pig intestines. Blacks took this throwaway and added a touch of African culinary technique to create tasty dishes. Collard greens and dandelion greens were first recorded in 1887. Poke greens, turnip greens, and black-eyed peas were first brought to Jamaica from Africa in 1675 and arrived in North America in 1700. All of these African foods contributed to the great diversity of American cuisine.[52]

Mande and Wolof on the Plantation

Mande and Wolof were the two most widespread languages of the Senegambia. Bilingualism was important for trade and commerce in the region. During the 1700s, Wolof was by far the most dominant African culture found in the upper Guinea Coast and the coast of South Carolina.

The West African traders traded between Sierra Leone and Liberia, transmitting folklore, cuisine, and language.

Because of their Civil War between 1685 and 1700, many Wolof arrived in Colonial America as war captives, the only time that they came into North America in such numbers. Later, in 1772, Fenda Lawrence, a Gambian slave trader, visited the American South as a free tourist and to conduct business. The government of Georgia issued her a certificate stating that "a free black woman and heretofore a considerable trader in the River Gambia on the Coast of Africa, hath voluntarily come to be and remain for some time in this province," with permission to "pass and repass unmolested with the said province on her lawful and necessary occasion."[53] Fenda Lawrence probably spoke Wolof and some creole pidgin English, the trade language of the West African Coast. She apparently moved through the South without any problems and returned back to the Gambia to continue her trade in slaves and other commodities.

Another African from the Gambia, Job Ben Solomon, spent a brief time as a slave in Maryland. He attracted the attention of James Oglethorpe by means of a letter written in Arabic (which indicated the slave was literate in the Arabic language). Oglethorpe had Solomon purchased from his master and sent to England, where he was presented at Court, given gifts, and later, in 1734, sent home as a free man. He returned as a celebrity among his fellow Foulahs and neighboring Jolofs (Wolofs) and Mandingoes. Abd al-Rahman Ibrahim (known as Prince on the plantation), a West African prince from the kingdom of Tambo located in the Gambia, was as not fortunate as Fenda Lawrence. Instead of seeing the South as a tourist, he was sold into slavery in New Orleans in 1788 at the age of twenty-six. He was Fulbe (Fulani) and spoke fluent Arabic, Wolof, and Mande as well as several local dialects. Wolof was the lingua franca of the American South prior to the 1730s when Bantus were brought in. Following the intercession of President John Quincy Adams, Ibrahim was set free after forty years of bondage. Southern planters generally accorded Muslims a greater degree of respect than Africans from non-Muslim regions.[54]

Tales out of Africa

Br'er Rabbit, Sis' Nanny Goat, and others were characters in Wolof, Hausa, Fula (Fulani), and Mandinka (Mandingo) folklore transported to the New World. Other West African tales, such as those involving a Trickster Hare, were also introduced. The Hare (Rabbit) stories can also be found in parts of Nigeria, Angola, and East Africa. The Tortoise stories are found among the Yoruba, Igbo, and Edo-Bini people of Nigeria. Other examples of folklore from West Africa are tales such as the "Hare Tied in the Bean Farm," or the "Three Tasks of the Hare" (where he goes to ask God for more Wisdom). These tales are widespread among the Mandinka and Wolof of West Africa and also common in black American folklore.[55] Most of the Uncle Remus stories, as retold in the Sea Islands (cf. Walt Disney's "Song of the South"), are African in origin, especially Hausa and Mandinka. These Africans tales, especially such stories as "Chicken Little," laid the foundation for American nursery tales. More recently, the influence of Br'er Rabbit on contemporary America's most famous trickster rabbit, Bugs Bunny, has been noticed.[56]

The Anansi (Spider) stories, Akan in origin, remained intact in the New World. In Surinam, these stories are referred to as *Anansitori*. The West Indian black people of Curaçao call them *Cuenta de Nansi*. The Spider Trickster Anansi tales maintain a peripheral existence as the "Aunt Nancy" stories of the Georgia and South Carolina Sea Islands. The Anansi stories were told in nineteenth-century United States among a limited group of people, mainly Gullahs. After the twentieth-century influx of West Indians into America, the Anansi tales again became widespread.

The Hare and Hyena tales correspond to Br'er Rabbit and Br'er Fox tales as Trickster figures brought to North America by the Wolof. These tales from the Mandinka heartland spread south to countries such as Liberia, Sierra Leone, and Côte d'Ivoire. As the Mandinka Jula traders migrated, they brought these tales with them. The Africans who came from those areas during the transatlantic slave trade brought the folklore and tales as part of their oral tradition. African slaves who fled to the Creek Indians introduced these West African Trickster tales, and the Seminoles in Florida also adopted them.[57]

African Dances in North America

Dance is part of folk tradition. Enslaved Africans maintained continuity in their music, song, and dance cultures, as well as in the religions that influenced those cultures, as they adapted to life in North America.

Many African dances survived because they were reshaped and adopted by Euro-Americans, while others remained intact, or changed with the new circumstances. For example, the ring shout started as a sacred Kongolese dance but later found expression in nonsacred dance. In both Africa and the New World, the circle ritual meant different things in different cultures. In the Kongo, the ring shout-circle is identical to the Gullah counterclockwise dance, which is linked to the most important African ceremony, the rite of passage. Among the Mande, the circle dance is a part of the marriage and birth ceremonies, and in Wolof culture, the ring circle is central to most dancing. The Bamboula and the Calinda, variations of voodoo dance, became popular forms of dance expression in early New Orleans. The Cakewalk and the Charleston traveled from Africa to become integral to American dance forms on the American plantation.

The Calinda, also known as La Calinda, is one of the earliest forms of African dance seen in America. This Kongo/Angolan dance first became popular in Santo Domingo, then in Haiti and New Orleans. La Calinda is first reported by Dessalles in 1654, and later by a French monk, Jean Baptiste Labat, who went to Martinque as a missionary in 1694. The Calinda is a variation of a dance used in voodoo ceremonies and is always performed by male and female dancers in couples. The dancers move to the middle of the circle and start dancing. Each dancer chooses a partner and performs the dance, with few variations, by taking a step in which every leg is straightened and pulled back alternatively with a quick strike, sometimes on point, sometimes with a grounded heel. This dance is performed in a manner slightly similar to that of the Anglaise. The male dancer turns by himself or goes around his partner, who also makes a turn and changes her position while waving the·ends of a handkerchief. Her partner raises his hands in almost clenched fists up and down alternately, with his elbows close to his body. This dance is vivid and lively. In 1704, records show that a police ordinance was issued prohibiting night gatherings from performing the Calinda on plantations.[58]

The dance now known as the Charleston had the greatest influence on American dance culture of any imported African dance. It is a form of jitterbug dance, which is a general term applied to unconventional, often formless and violent, social dances performed to syncopated music. Enslaved Africans brought it from the Kongo to Charleston, South Carolina, as the Juba dance, which then slowly evolved into what is now the Charleston. This one-legged-sembuka-step, over-and-cross arrived in Charleston between 1735 and 1740. Similar in style to the "one-legged" sembuka style of dancing found in northern Kongo, the dance consists of "patting" (otherwise known as "patting Juba"), stamping, clapping, and slapping of arms, chest, and so forth.

The name "Charleston" was given to the Juba dance by Euro-Americans. In Africa, the word Juba (or Djouba) was used for many things, such as songs sung on the plantation, the food given to the field slaves, and the dance that later became known as the Charleston. The Juba dance itself was primarily a competitive dance of skill.

Later, the Charleston, which had evolved over the centuries, spread northward as African Americans migrated North. At first, the step was a simple twisting of the feet to rhythm in a lazy sort of way. When the dance hit Harlem, a new version surfaced. It became a fast kicking of the feet both forward and backward, later done with a tap.

The Charleston and other African dances started out as spectator dances, then became participant dances. Nevertheless, the Charleston became so popular that a premium was even placed on hiring of black domestics who could dance it well enough to teach the lady of the house. The dance can also be seen in other parts of the world: in Haiti, it is called La Martinique. Josephine Baker, a famous black entertainer, introduced this dance to European audiences in the 1920s. It became increasingly popular during the 1920s and today, when we hear of the Charleston dance, it is usually associated with those years known as the "Roaring Twenties."[59]

The Ombliguide was a dance performed by slaves in La Place du Congo, Kongo Square, in old New Orleans. An ordinance of the Municipal Council, adopted on October 15, 1817, made the name of this traditional place law. It was considered one of the unique attractions of old New Orleans, ranking second only to the Quadroon Ball. At the square, women wore dotted calico dresses, and brightly colored Madras headgear tied about their hair to form the popular headdress called the tignon. Children wore garments with bright feathers and bits of ribbon.

Slaves came regularly to Kongo Square to perform the Ombliguide and other Kongo dances, such as the Calinda, Bamboula, and Chica, all transplanted directed from Central Africa.[60] The Ombliguide was criticized in 1766 by the New Orleans City Council. Performed by four men and four women, it involves sensual movements with navel-to-navel contact, a common trait of Angolan traditional dancing.

Folk Medicine and the Root Doctor

African medical knowledge of diseases in both the Old and the New Worlds crossed the Atlantic Ocean and contributed to the medical well-being of Americans. Although African American practitioners as a group were considered folk and root doctors as compared to their European counterparts, African American medical practices were generally superior in that era.[61] For example, Africans are credited with introducing certain folk treatments for smallpox. Anthropologist R. S. Rattray reported that inoculation for smallpox was practiced "from time immemorial by the Akan of Ghana." Likewise, the Scottish explorer Mungo Park, during his travels to the windward coast at the end of the eighteenth century, was informed by a European doctor stationed there that the people of the Gambia practiced inoculation for smallpox as their traditional prevention.[62]

Lieutenant Governor William Gooch of Virginia in 1729 manumitted a slave named Panpan for his secret concoction of roots and herbs because it was a cure for yaws and for syphilis.[63] He was freed from slavery at a cost of sixty pounds. Bryan Edwards, listening to one of his Akan women, learned that vaccination was a medical technique used on the Gold Coast to inoculate children with infectious matter from yaws, thus giving them a mild case of the disease and providing resistance later in life. "Mothers inoculate their infants about the period of weaning, which they may be indulged in nursing them until their recovery; and many believe, from an African opinion and custom in that country, that children should undergo the disease at an early period of life."[64]

In another example, a slave by the name of Caesar was known to have cured several persons who had been poisoned. One, an overseer named Henry Middleton, found Caesar's antidote very effective. Caesar cured Middleton from intolerable pain in the "stomack and bowels" after he had found no cure or relief in the medicines of the "most skilful doctors of the country."[65] Caesar also cured a person bitten by a rattlesnake and a man afflicted with yaws with his body covered from "top to toe" with scabs. The cure for yaws required the use of flowers of sulphur and burnt niccars. He also cured those afflicted with the deadly symptoms of pleurisies.[66] For Caesar's antidote to poison and snake bite,[67] he was given his freedom and financial compensation for life.

Sampson, another slave, gained his freedom as a reward for discovering a cure for rattlesnake bites (see Appendix).[68] His cure was said to have been even more effective than Caesar's.[69] Colonial planters generally had more respect for their enslaved Africans' knowledge of herbs, medicines, and poison than did the so-called doctors of the era. Enslaved Africans brought indigenous skills and knowledge to North America directly from Africa. They contributed these cultural traditions concerning the uses of plants, as well as the new flora they encountered in South Carolina, in many ways similar to that of West and Central Africa.

Sampson walked into the Commons House of Assembly of South Carolina on May 9, 1754, and offered a cure for rattlesnake bites. To demonstrate the effectiveness of his medicines, he held in his hand poisonous snakes and then pressed them against his flesh and was bitten several times. He was bitten by so many venomous snakes that it was doubtful if he would recover. Sampson declared that he would return in three days alive and well. To everyone's surprise, he returned alive and offered the cure. "In proof of the efficacy of his medicines, Sampson on several occasion suffered himself to be bitten by the most venemous Snakes, and once let his Wounds come so near a Mortification, that it was doubted whether he could recover, yet he cured himself with them; he disarmed any Snake of its Venom with some one of the Herbs."[70] He was immediately given his freedom and a cash annuity for life.

Likewise, Africans knew that smallpox inoculation was done by simply taking some of the sap from the scalp and inoculating those who were not exposed. Smallpox was the most feared epidemic in Colonial America. Charleston, for example, had several smallpox epidemics during that period. However, an outbreak in the spring of 1760 was the most widespread. South Carolina had adopted the African practice of using individuals who had previously had smallpox to inoculate the population. In Charleston, townspeople had protested the government's activity: "negroes seized with that Distemper in the country are immediately brought to town and many others Persons are daily inoculated in order to go through the disease in Charles Town. . . ." In other words, "Persons are brought in from the Country, to take the Disease by Innoculation, which was Practice in their own country, it not speedily prevented. . . ."[71]

Through the root doctor, Africans brought holistic health practices to American plantations. African healers brought a knowledge of treatment for many diseases, and health practitioners such as midwives and nurses contributed to New World health care services. During antebellum plantation slavery in the early nineteenth century, midwives delivered more than 90 percent of the children born, as had been the custom in

Africa. Africans contributed to cures of numerous New World diseases based on their knowledge of similar diseases from the Old World. Their gift of medicine enriched the medical development of America, fusing the worlds of Africa and Europe, adopting practical use as well as a holistic approach to curing and treating diseases.

African Cultural Influences on Euro-Americans[72]

Most people are not aware that one in every five of the cowboys of the American West was black, contrary to the usual media portrayal of white cowboy historical figures. Also, cowboy culture has some African roots, only recently being recognized. The annual north-south migratory pattern followed by the cowboy is unlike the cattle-keeping patterns of Europe but analogous to the migratory patterns of the Fulani cattle herders, who live scattered from the Senegambia through Nigeria and Niger to the Sudan. Texas (African) longhorns were on the first slave ships to Mexico, followed by African cattle egrets that later migrated farther north. Many details of cowboy life, work, and even material culture, such as open grazing of cattle, can be traced to Fulani antecedents, but historians of the American West have rarely investigated this.

The literature on black cowboys, like that for African contributions to American culture in general, is meager. Major works about cowboys and the American West have ignored black Americans. Black cowboys have been left out of most movies and historical accounts of this period. Also omitted are the accounts of African cattle brought with enslaved Africans to the New World.

Even the search for surviving African culture among white Americans has largely ignored cowboy culture. Historian Peter Wood, however, found that the survival of African culture among white Americans was pervasive and specific, reaching almost every aspect of American culture. He has argued that the American cattle industry owes its origins to Africans.

For example, Fulanis from the Futa Jallon, accustomed to cattle raising, oversaw the rapid expansion of the British American cattle herds in the middle of the eighteenth century. They were responsible for introducing patterns of "open grazing," now practiced throughout the American cattle industry. Wood believes that the word *cowboy* originated from this early relationship between cattle, Africans, and Europeans in the colonial period when African labor and skills were still closely associated with cattle raising. As late as 1865, following the Civil War, Africans whose livestock responsibilities were with cattle were referred to as "cowboys" in plantation records. After 1865, whites associated with the cattle industry referred to themselves as "cattlemen" to distinguish themselves from black "cowboys."[73]

Many words associated with cowboy culture and originating from this relationship have found their way into American English. For example, *bronco* (probably of Efik/Ibibio and Spanish origins) was used centuries ago by the Spanish and by enslaved Africans working with cattle and horses. *Buckra*, also deriving from this relationship, comes from *mbakara*, the Efik/Ibibio word for "white man." *Buckaroo*, also coming from *mbakara*, was used to describe a class of whites who worked as broncobusters. *Dogies*, a word that even found its way into popular cowboy songs, as in "get along little dogies," originated from the Kimbundu *kidogo*, a little something, and (*ki*) *dodo*, small. After the Civil War, when large cattle roundups became necessary because of neglect during the war, black American cowboys introduced such Africanisms to cowboy language and songs.

Wolof Influences on American English

As noted above, the Wolof arrived in large numbers in the American South between 1670 and 1700 as a result of political disturbances in Senegambia with other Senegambians.[74] The Wolofs were the largest group of Africans to come to the American colonies in the seventeenth century and were predominantly house servants. Having extensive, close contact with Euro-Americans, they may have been the first Africans whose cultural elements and language were assimilated into and retained within the developing culture of America. They also had greater opportunity for admixture and interaction with whites than any other African group in the early years.

As a result of numerous Wolofs on American plantations in the early years, Wolof served as a lingua franca during the 1700s, and many words of Wolof origin found their way into American English. The Wolof had a greater impact on the language than their numbers would indicate. For example, one Wolof/Mande word now used throughout the world is "okay," or "O.K." Americans were mystified by its origins from the time of its popularization around 1839. Clues were found in the nineteenth-century black English of Jamaica and Surinam, and in the Gullah speech of South Carolina, all of which have numerous forms of the word. Two prime examples from Mande and Wolof are *o ke*, "that's it" or "all right," and Wolof, *waw kay*, "all correct." "O.K." is recorded in the speech of black Americans from 1776, but was probably used earlier in the 1700s.

Another Wolof word popular in black English is "dig," as in "dig this man." This word originates from Wolof *dega*, meaning either "look here" or "to understand," used to mark the beginning of a sentence and pronounced similarly to the English "digger." In black English of the 1960s, "dig" meant "to understand something." For example, in Wolof is *dega nga olof*, "Do you understand Wolof?"

David Dalby draws a direct parallel between the Wolof term *gay* and the American term guys, used informally to mean "persons" or "fellows." In Wolof it is always used as a plural. Other Africanisms found in American English include "uh-hum" (yes) and "unh-unh" (no), which occur in various parts of the world but nowhere as frequently and regularly as in Africa and the United States. The word "cush" was used in the American South during the slavery period to describe "cornmeal soaked in water." A similar word is used in Wolof for millet meal soaked in water.

Honkie, a term popular during the 1960s, was first used to describe white men who would drive to the African American community and honk automobile horns for their black dates. The word *hong* in Wolof means red or pink, and whites are described in most African languages as "Red." The word *sambo*, considered an abusive term by African Americans, is respectful in Wolof and a common family name throughout West Africa.

Several Wolof words were popularized during the jazz era. For example, "jive" in Ebonics means "misleading talk," which is code language originating from the Wolof word *jey*. The American words "hep," "hip" and "hippie" translate roughly into "to be aware or alive to what is going on," including drugs. In Wolof, the verb *hipi* means "to open one's eyes." The American slang "cat" means a person, as in hep-cat or cool cat, and is similar to the Wolof *kai* used as a suffix following the verb. The Wolof lexicon *jamboree* is now a standard part of American language. Originally, a jamboree was a noisy slave celebration. A jamsession in the old days of the plantation was slave musicians and slaves assembling for dance and entertainment. The origin is the Wolof word for slave, *jaam*.

The verb "sock" in the sense of "to strike" or the sexual connotation of "sock it to me, Baby" is found in Wolof and has a similar sound and meaning, "to beat with a pestle." The word "bug," as in jitterbug or Bugs Bunny, denotes an enthusiastic person. The word "fuzz" has been used by African Americans to mean "police." Historically, it meant a policeman, or those who patrolled the plantation at night and hunted down runaways on horseback. In Wolof the word *fas*, pronounced between fas and fuss, means a horse.

Enslaved Africans used the term "masa" for master, leading many planters to believe their slaves could not use the king's English properly. However, the word *mansa* was a title for many kings of West Africa; during the empire of ancient Mali, it meant chief or leader. (One such leader of note was Mansa Musa.) Enslaved Africans saw the masters as persons of authority and simply used their indigenous word for leader, *ma[n]sa*. On the American plantation, the "n" in *mansa* became silent.

A large number of Wolof words survived in American English because many Wolof interpreters were used during the early European voyages along the coast, and thus the Wolof names for African foodstuffs, such as yam and banana, became part of standard English.

African lexical items found their way into American English speech. The American Southern dialect in particular has been greatly influenced by Africa. Black servants, who raised the children of the Southern aristocracy, passed on their distinctive pronunciations, which then became uniquely southern. The musical quality of Southern speech is also believed to have derived from Africa. Generations of interaction with African speech patterns gave white Southerners their distinctive drawl. Charles Dickens, commenting on the speech of Southerners, noted that there was little difference between the speech of whites and slaves. Edward Kimber, a traveler in the South in 1746, wrote that "one thing they [whites] are very faulty in, with regard to their Children, which is, that when young, they suffer them too much to prowl amongst the young Negroes, which insensibly causes them to imbibe their Manners and broken Speech."[75] Black speech patterns are now found in the larger speech pattern of Americans, particularly among the youth.

White Southerners have adopted and assimilated African speech patterns and have retained expressions and words that were once Africanisms but are now Americanism, such as (aside from those already mentioned) bowdacious, bozo (stupid), cooter (turtle), goober, peanut, guy, hippie, hullabaloo, hully-gully, jazz, jamboree, juke(box), moola (money), pamper, Polly Wolly-Doodle, wow, daddy, buddy and tote, to name a few. Other English words first used by Africans include banana, banjo, Kola (as in Coca-Cola), elephant, gorilla, gumbo, okra, tater, tote and turnip.

White Southerners also borrowed the elaborate African social etiquette system, with its terms of endearment and kinship in speaking to neighbors, using such titles as "aunty" and "uncle" as signs of respect for elders. This tradition of respect for elders not only continued but also was reinforced by African social etiquette in the New World.

Other Cultural Influences

Finally, Herskovits noted similarities between black and white religious behavior, particularly in Pentecostal sects, such as ritual dancing, drumming, trances, and speaking in tongues. He traced many of these behaviors to the Sango cult. That trance form is characteristically African, but it is often found among whites who belonged to churches with large numbers of African Americans and those of certain Pentecostal sects.

Other Africanisms found among white Americans, according to Peter Wood, are such practices as leaving gourds on poles for birdhouses and using African techniques of alligator wrestling. As late as the 1930s, whites used funerary pottery in a manner identical to blacks. Both African and Europeans cultures contributed fairly evenly, given the circumstances, to what was to become American. Culturally, Americans shared many experiences—some born in Europe and some in Africa. For example, African house servants learned new domestic skills, including the art of quilting, from their mistresses. They took this European quilting technique and Africanized it by combining it with their applique style, reflecting a pattern and form still found in the Akan and Fon textile industries of West Africa, patterns and forms which then influenced white Americans.

Conclusion

A variety of African cultures has contributed to the richness and diversity of American and African American life. Many years ago, Melville Herskovits identified five areas in which African culture influenced the United States: music, speech, social etiquette, cuisine, and religion. Today, we know much more about how American life in those areas has been affected, and we are also discovering the location and nature of African origins for what has now become so fully "American."

For example, African culture has contributed substantially to American musical traditions, particularly through spirituals, jazz, blues, gospel, and bluegrass. All these musical forms have influenced popular American music, with spirituals remaining the most indigenous music to develop in America, coming close to bluegrass as the most authentically American music. Many Africanisms, such as the banjo, became Americanisms. Indeed, today the banjo is more characteristic of whites than blacks, and Appalachian banjo music is now considered as American as apple pie, without any distinguishing African characteristics.

Contrary to the popular belief that only West Africans contributed to North American culture, other African groups, especially the Bantu of Central Africa, also brought their own unique contributions. West Africans had more of an influence on white American culture because of their dominant presence in the plantation "Big House," and scholars had previously assumed the same West African dominance in black American culture. However, recent scholarship suggests a Bantu origin for much of the African American culture because, unlike the more numerous Senegambians (Mandes), the Central Africans brought with them a common culture and language that gave them greater focus despite their smaller number. Among others, Winifred Vass has documented survivals of Bantu vocabulary in American place names, folklore, lexicon, and literature, and Dena Esptein has shown that the banjo is of African origin.

The culture of the Mande had a profound effect on America by way of plantation "Big House" interactions. European culture was transmitted to the Africans, but African culture was just as certainly transmitted to the Euro-Americans. This acculturation process was mutual and reciprocal: Africans assimilated white culture, and meanwhile planters were adopting African customs and practices, including agricultural methods such as rice cultivation, African cuisine ("southern cooking"), open grazing of cattle, and use of herbal medicines and other procedures to cure and treat diseases such as smallpox. The African house servants learned new domestic skills from their mistresses, and in turn taught other skills to them.

In sum, a diversity of Africans, including the Bantu of Central Africa as well as the West Africans, signficantly changed North American culture.

APPENDIX

These cures were published in *South Carolina Committee for the Humanities Journal, South Carolina Department of Archives and History Commons House Journal* November 29, 1749, 304; *The London Magazine* 19 (1750): 367–68; and *The Gentleman's Magazine* 20 (1750): 342–43.

Caesar's Cure for Poison

Take the Roots of Plantane [Plantain] and wid Hoarse-bound fresh or dried, three Ounces; boil them together in two Quarts of Water to one Quart, and strain it: of this Decoction let the Patient take one their Part three Mornings, fasting successively, from which if he finds any Relief, it must be continued till he is perfectly recovered. On the Contrary, if he finds no Alteration after the third Dose, it is a sign that the Patient has either not been poisoned at all, or that it has been with Poison as Caesar's Antidotes will not remedy, so may leave off the Decoction. During the Cure the Patient must live on a spare Diet, and abstain from eating Mutton, Pork, Butter, or any other fat or oily Food.

N.B. the Plantan [Plantain] or Hoar Hound will, either of them, cure alone, but they are most efficacious together.

In Summer you may take one Handful of the Roots and Branches of each, in Place of three Ounces of the Roots of each.

For Drink during the Cure, let them take the following,

Take the Roots of the Golden Rod, six Ounces, or in Summer two large Handfuls of the Roots and Branches together, and boil them in two Quarts of Water to one Quart (to which also may be added a little Hoarse Hound and Sassafras); to this Decoction, after it is strained, add a Glass of Rum or Brandy, and sweeten it with Sugar for ordinary Drink.

Sometimes an inward Fever attends such as are poisoned for which he order the followings,

Take a Pint of Wood Ashes and three Pints of Water; stir and mix them well together; let them stand all Night, and strain or decant [the Lye of] in the Morning, of which ten Ounces may be taken six Mornings following, warmed or cold, according to the Weather. These Medicines have no sensible Operation, though sometimes they work in the Bowels, and give a gentle Stool.

The Symptoms attending such as are poisoned are as follows, A Pain of the Breast, Difficulty of breathing, a Load at the Pit of the Stomach, an irregular Pulse, burning and violent Pains of the Viscera above and below the Naval, very restless at Night, sometimes wandering Pains over the Body, a Reaching and Inclination to vomit, profuse Sweats (which prove always serviceable), slimy Stools both when costive and loose, the Face of a Pale and yellow Colour, sometimes a Pain and Inflammation of the Throat; the Appetite is generally weak, and some cannot eat any; those who have long been poisoned are generally very feeble and weak in their Limbs, sometimes spit a great Deal; the whole Skin peels, and likewise the Hair falls off.

Caesar's Cure for the Bite of a Rattle Snake

Take the Roots of Plantene or Hoarse Hound (in Summer Roots and Branches together) a sufficient Quantity; bruise them in a Mortar, and squeeze out the Juice, of which give as soon as possible, one large Spoonful; if he be swelled you must force it down his Throat. This generally will cure, but, if the Patient finds no Relief in an Hour after, you may give another Spoonful, which never fails.

If the Roots are dried, they must be moistened with a little Water.

To the Wound may be applied a Leaf of good Tobacco moistened with Rum.

Notes

1. This title was selected in honor of Melville J. Herskovits, who wrote a brief essay that mapped the field: "What Africa Has Given America," *New Republic* 84 (1935): 92–94; reprinted in *The New World Negro*, ed., Frances S. Herskovits (Bloomington: Indiana University Press, 1966), 168–74.

2. See Michael O. West and William G. Martin, "Future with a Past: Resurrecting the Study of Africa in the Post-Africanist Era," in *Africa Today* 44, 3 (1997): 309–26.

3. Melville J. Herskovits, "A Preliminary Consideration of the Culture Areas of Africa," *American Anthropologist* 26 (1924).

4. *Ethnographic Survey of Africa: Belgian Congo 2* (London: International African Institute, 1951).

5. Alan P. Merriam, "The Concept of Culture Cluster Applied to the Belgium Congo," *Southwestern Journal of Anthropology* 15, 4 (Winter 1959): 381–82.

6. Simon Ottenberg, and Phoebe Ottenberg, *Cultures and Societies of Africa* (New York: Random House, 1960).

7. Philip Curtin, *The Transatlantic Slave Trade: A Census* (Madison: University of Wisconsin Press, 1968).

8. Joseph H. Greenberg, *The Languages of Africa* (Bloomington: University of Indiana Press, 1966).

9. Joseph E. Holloway and Winifred K. Vass, *The African Heritage of American English* (Bloomington: Indiana University Press, 1993).

10. Joseph E. Holloway, ed., *Africanisms in American Culture* (Bloomington and Indianapolis: Indiana University Press, 1990), 3.

11. P. A. Fraser, E. J. Yunis, and C. A. Alper, "Excess admixture proportion of extended major histocompatability complex haplotypes of Causcasian origin among rheumatoid arthritis associated haplotypes in African Americans and Afro-Caribbeans," *Ethnic Health* 1, 2 (May 1996): 153–59.

12. N. N. Puckett, *Folk Beliefs of the Southern Negro* (Chapel Hill: University of North Carolina Press, 1926).

13. Personal interview with the Rev. Ervin L. Greene Jr., pastor of the historic Brick Baptist Church, on January 16, 1984, in Beaufort, South Carolina.

14. Ibid.

15. Ibid.

16. Interview with Ruby Iyman at the University of California at Los Angeles in 1975. Ruby Iyman was born in Opobo Nigeria (Rivers State) January 1, 1954.

17. Elizabeth Donnan, *Documents Illustrative of the History of the Slave Trade in America* (Washington, DC: Carnegie Institute, 1935), 4: 296.

18. Ibid.

19. Lawrence Levine, *Black Culture and Black Consciousness: Afro-American Folk Though from Slavery and Freedom* (New York: Oxford University Press, 1977).

20. One of the better uses of oral history to examine African survival is *Drum and Shadows: Survival Studies Among the Georgia Coastal Negroes*, by the Savannah Unit, Georgia Writers' Project, Work Project Administration, with foreword by Guy Johnson, and photographs by Muriel and Malcolm Bell Jr. (Athens: Univesity of Georgia Press, 1940). Other early works that include the use of oral interviews are Charles W. Joyner, "Slave Folklife on the Waccamaw Neck: Antebellum Black Culture in the South Carolina Low Country," Ph.D. diss.; John Blassingame, "Ex-Slaves: Approaches and Problems," *Journal of Southern History* 41 (1975): 473–92; C. Vann Woodward, "History from Slave Sources," *American Historical Review* 79 (1974); Gladys-Marie Fry, *Night Riders in Black Folk History* (1975); and Kathryn Lawson Morgan, "The Ex-Slave Narratives as a source for Folk History," Ph.D. diss. (1970). Also see the chapters (6 and 7) by David Henige and Barbara Cooper in this volume.

21. Eva L. Ver dier, "When Gun Shoot: Some Experiences While Taking the Census Among the Low Country Negroes of South Carolina," Beaufort Township Library, Beaufort, South Carolina (1931): 3–4.

22. Ibid.

23. Ibid.

24. Recording master tape of Mr. Ben Mack August 2, 1972. Penn Community Center Tape Archive. St. Helena Frogmore, South Carolina.

25. Doyle, personal interview.

26. *Drum and Shadows*, 71.

27. F. R. Irvine, *A Text-Book of West African Agriculture Soils and Crops* (London: Oxford University Press, 1934), 135–41.

28. Interview with Mrs. Magie Smalls on St. Helena, Frogmore, South Carolina, January 19, 1984; also found in J. Herman Blake, "'Doctor Can't Do Me No Good': Social Concomitants of Health Care Attitudes and Practices Among Elderly Black in Isolated Rural Populations," paper presented at the National Conference on the Black Aged, Washington, DC, May 27, 1977, p. 11.

28. Rossa B. Cooley, *Homes of the Freed* (New York: New Republic, 1926), 77.

30. Personal interview with Mrs. Bernice Brooks in Los Angeles on August 3, 1983.

31. J. Herman Blake, "New Perspectives on the Black Family Heritage," unpublished manuscript (Santa Cruz, 1977). I am grateful to President J. Herman Blake for giving me the opportunity to consult his unpublished manuscript and discuss with him his extensive Sea Island experience and contact. Also, I am thankful for the assistance of his brother once I arrived in Beaufort. The Rev. J. Henry Blake looked out for me and showed me the Islands. Without their assistance this research would had been much more difficult.

32. Personal interview with Emory Campbell on St. Helena at the Penn Center, January 1984.

33. Cooley, *Homes of the Freed*, 77.

34. Doyle interview.

35. W. E. B. DuBois, *The Suppression of the African Slave Trade to the United States of America 1638–1870* (New York: Schochen Books, 1969).

36. Donnan, *Documents*, 2: 36.

37. Holloway, ed., *Africanisms in American Culture*, 6–9; also, see William S. Pollitzer, "A Reconsideratrion of the Sources of the Slave Trade to Charleston, SC," unpublished essay used with permission; Donnan, *Documents*, 4: 310, passim.

38. Curtin, *The Transatlantic Slave Trade*, 157.

39. For a general study of Bantu influences in the U.S., see Winifred Kellersberger Vass, *The Bantu Speaking Heritage of the United States* (Los Angeles: Center for Afro-American Studies, UCLA, 1979), which is the source of much of the information in this section.

40. Eugene D. Genovese, *Roll Jordan Roll: The World the Slaves Made* (New York: Pantheon, 1974).

41. Melville J. Herskovits, "The Present Status and Needs of Afro-American Research," *Journal of Negro History* 36 (1951): 125–26; Donnan, *Documents*, 4:175–244, passim; Pollitzer, "Reconsideration of the Sources." See also Peter H. Wood, *Black Majority: Negroes in Colonial South Carolina from 1670 through the Stono Rebellion* (New York: Knopf 1974), 6., and Giberto Freyre, *The Master and the Slaves: A Study in the Development of Brazilian Civilizations* (New York: Knopf, 1946); Robert Farris Thompson and Joseph Cornet, *The Four Momets of the Sun: Kongo Art in Two Worlds* (Washington, DC: National Gallery of Art, 1981).

42. J. D. Duncan, "Servitude and Slavery in Colonial South Carolina 1670–1776," Ph.D. diss. (Emory University, 1971).

43. *Virginia Gazette*, November 5, 1736; April 21, 1738; August 17, 1739; December 8, 1768; January 15, 1767; August 13, 1772; Lorenzo Dow Turner, *Africanisms in the Gullah Dialect* (Chicago: University of Chicago Press, 1949), 34.

44. Ulrich Bonnell Phillips, *American Negro Slavery: A Survey of the Supply, Employment, and Control of Negro Labor as Determined by the Plantation Regime* (New York: D. Appleton, 1990), 42.

45. Genovese, *Roll Jordan Roll*, 324.

46. Donnan, *Documents*, 1: 817.

47. Victor Boswell, "Our Vegetable Travellers," *The National Geographic Magazine* 96, 2 (August 1949): 193–211.

48. Helen Mendes, *The African Heritage Cookbook* (New York: MacMillan, 1971) and Holloway and Vass, *The African Heritage of American English*, are the source of most information in this section.

49. Duncan Clinch Heyward, *Seed from Madagascar* (Chapel Hill: University of North Carolina Press, 1937), 4.

50. Mark Catesby, *The natural history of Carolina, Florida, and the Bahama Islands: containing two hundred and twenty figures of birds, beasts, fishes, serpents, insects, and plants; [rev. by Mr Edwards]; with an introduction by George Frick; and notes by Joseph Ewan* (Savannah: Beehives Press, 1974), Appendix, 81–82. I used the original version of 1743 located in UCLA Special Collection Library.

51. John Lawson, *A New Voyage to Carolina* (London, 1799).

52. For more information on African contributions to American cuisine see Mendes, *African Heritage Cookbook*.

53. Phillips, *American Negro Slavery*, 16.

54. In Donnan, *Documents*, 2: 420–27, and Terry Alford, *Prince Among Slaves: The True Story of an African Prince Sold into Slavery in the American South* (New York: Harcourt Brace Jovanovich, 1977).

55. Personal interview with David P. Gamble, December 5, 1985, and D. J. M. Moffett, "Was Uncle Remus A Hausaman?" *Southern Folklore Quarterly* 39 (1975): 151–66.

56. For examples, see David Roediger, "The Long Journey to the Hip Hop Nation," *St. Louis Post-Dispatch*, March 18, 1994, and Joe Adamson, *Bugs Bunny: Fifty Years and Only One Grey Hare* (New York: Henry Holt, 1990), both cited in Shelley Fisher Fishkin, "Reframing the Multiculturalism Debates and Remapping American Studies," *Journal of American Studies of Turkey* 1 (1995): 3–18.

57. Holloway and Vass, *The African Heritage of American English*, xxiii.

58. Moreau de Saint Mery, *Description topograpique, physique, evile, politique et historique de la partie Francaise de l'ile de Saint Domingue Tome 1* (New Orleans, 1704), 52–56.

59. Robert Farris Thompson, "Kongo Influences on African-American Culture," in Holloway, ed. *Africanisms in American Culture*, 151.

60. The partial Europeanization of some of these African movements eventually created the national dances of Latin American countries, such as the marcumbi, a dance learned by the Spanish and later brought to the New World through Spain. The fandango, the national dance of Spain, originated in Cuba from African dances. Other dances derived from the Ombliguide are the Chacharara, Cabomba, Melongo, Malamba, Gati, Semba, rhumba, Conga, and Tango. See Joseph Holloway Papers, #4511 Division of Rare and Manuscript Collections, Cornell University Library.

61. William D. Pierson, *Black Legacy: America's Hidden Heritage* (Amherst: The University of Massachusetts Press, 1993), 99.

62. Bryan Edwards, *The History, Civil and Commercial, of the British Colonies in the West Indies*, 3 vols. (London, 1794–1801) and R. S. Rattray, *The Tribes of the Ashanti Hinterland*, 2 vols. (Oxford: The Clarendon Press 1932).

63. J. H. Russell, *The Free Negro in Virginia* (New York: New York University Press, 1969). See *South Carolina Gazette*, May 9, 1740, also quoted in Ira E. Harrison, "Health Status and Healing Practices: Continuations from an African Past," *Journal of African Studies* 2, 4 (Winter 1975/6) and Wood, *Black Majority*, 289.

64. James Steward, *A View of the Past and Present State of the Island of Jamaica* (1808; reprint. Edinburgh, 1823), 303–4.

65. *South Carolina Archives [South Carolina Department of Archives and History] Upper House Journal*, March 16, 1750, 478.

66. Ibid., South Carolina Committee for the Humanities, November 28, 1749.

67. See Appendix above. These cures were published in *SCCHJ, SC-AR Commons House Journal* November 29, 1749, 304; *The London Magazine* 19(1750): 367–68; and *The Gentleman's Magazine* 20 (1750): 342–43.

68. Certificate No. 1876 mark by Negro Sampson, August 23, 1775, Treasury Receipts, 1774–1778, South Carolina Archives, 280.

69. Sampson's Cure was reported by the committee to the House on March 6, 1775 in the *SC-ARR Commons House Journal*, no. 30, part I, p. 295.

The Cure for the Bites of a Rattle Snake by Sampson a Negro. Take Heart Snake Root, both Root and Leaves, two Handfuls, Polyphony leaves one handful, bruise them in a MORTAR press out a Spoonful of the Juice and give as soon as possible after the bite, then scarify the wound, and take the Root of the Herb Avens, bruise it, poor [sic] a little Rum over it, and apply to the part, over which it is to be put the Heart Snake Root and Polyphony which remains after the Juice is squeezed out. These Medicines and Applications must be repeated according to the Violence of the Symptoms, so as in some dangerous Cases it must be given to the Quantity of eight spoonfuls in an Hour and the wound dressed two or three ties a day.

The above Herbs may also be bruised and beat up into a Paste with Clay, and when necessary may be scraped down to the Quantity of half a Common Spoonful and given amongst a little Rum and Water, and repeated as the doses of the Juice above mentioned. A little of this Paste may be wet with Rum and rubbed over the Wound.

N.B. He always uses this method when he cant find the Green Herbs.

Sometimes the Cure is entirely performed by the Patients chewing the Heart Snake Root and swallowing the Juice and applying some of the same Herb bruised to the Wound.

When the part is greatly inflamed and swelled, all the Herbs in the following List are taken to the quantity of some handfuls of each and boiled into a strong decoction with which it is to be fomented several times a day. The Herbs presented last by Sampson are:

1. Asarum cyclamini folio or Heart Snake root of this Province.
2. Polypodium Vulgare or common Polypody.
3. Caryophyllidae Virginiana radices inodora or Virginian Avens (Called here five Fingers).

4. Lonchitis Aspera or rough Spleenwort.
5. Hypnum julaceum or small erect Clubmoss.
6. Gnaphaliem huile or Creeping Gold Locks.

The public was informed of these additions to science in *The South Carolina Gazette* on April 8, 1756, and the House did provide Sampson with an annual annuity of £50.

70. Terry W. Lipscomb, ed., *The Colonial Records of South Carolina: The Journal of the Commons House of Assembly*, November 21, 1752– September 6, 1754, xxviii.

71. *South Carolina Gazette*, April 19, 1760.

72. For a groundbreaking study of African cultural survivals among whites in the United States that prepares the way for more research in this important but neglected area, see John Edward Philips's "The African Heritage of White America," in Holloway, ed., *Africanisms*, 225–39.

73. Peter H. Wood, "More Like a Negro Country: Demographic Patterns in Colonial South Carolina, 1700–1740," in Stanley L. Engerman and Eugene D. Genovese, eds., *Race and Slavery in the Western Hemisphere: Quantitative Studies* (Princeton, NJ: Princeton University Press, 1975). Also see Wood, *Black Majority*.

74. D. P. Gamble. *The Wolof of Senegambia* (London: International African Institute, 1957).

75. "The Speech of Negroes in Colonial America," *The Journal of Negro History* 24, 3 (July 1939).

18

HISTORY AND MEMORY

Donatien Dibwe dia Mwembu

I would like to discuss the relationship between history and memory in the Democractic Republic of the Congo. African history in general, and Congolese history in particular, are problematic as much in their reconstruction as in their interpretation. History and memory, in my opinion, each offers help to the other. History can be reconstructed thanks to memory, among other things, and memory in turn can be better interpreted thanks to history.

The connection between history and memory has already been the object of numerous scientific studies, unnecessary to mention here. The union of history-memory is significant in the reconstruction of what has gone before. Official history, faithful servant of current political institutions, omits certain facts, or falsifies past events, to legitimize power: the domination of one people by another, the occupation and exploitation of a territory by those who are strongest. In South Africa, for example, European settlers have created a history to legitimize the taking of almost all land, to the detriment of black Africans. Even more dependent on source materials than the craftsman is on the model, history is partial, relative, and fragile to the extent that its recovery is political.

Thus, I share the point of view of Pierre Salmon, according to whom, "la perception des faits n'est jamais parfaite; la transmission des faits est infidèle et la sélection des faits entraîne une déformation systématique de la vérité. Il s'ensuit que notre connaissance est inexacte, incomplète et superficielle" [the perception of facts is never perfect; the transmittal of facts is unreliable, and the selection of facts entails a systematic distortion of the truth. It follows that our understanding is inexact, incomplete, and superficial].[1]

A concern for historical truth leads the searcher beyond the written word to other sources, especially archeology, oral tradition, memory, and so on. As was emphasized so effectively by Bogumil Jewsiewicki and Valentin Yve Mudimbe, "There, as in other places on the planet, Africans tell, sing, produce (through dance, recitation, marionette puppets, and so forth), sculpt, and paint their history."[2] These various sources bring to history some pieces of information without which the historic past cannot be fully reconstructed.

Memory reveals a solution to the difficulties of the historian in the sense that it offers a raw material for the rewriting of history after achieving a better understanding of the experience of the participants themselves. In that specific framework, it enriches history and even makes it more alive and closer to reality. History, for its part, validates memory—or not—and also allows it to be understood in context whenever its account is considered accurate.

In what follows, I shall first summarize Congolese historiography. The second topic will be the question of memory and its contribution to the writing and rewriting of Congolese history. I will then address the methodology of investigation and the problems that arise from it. Finally, I will end with an attempt at interpretation of a Songye myth, one form of memory.

Congolese Historiography

For many years, history meant a history of "others." In Africa, the examples are legion. Colonial history is a history of whites in Africa insofar as it focuses on the deeds and activities of the colonizers and leaves in the shadows the contribution of those being colonized to the birth and development of the colonial enterprise. Most often, blacks pass by as mere supernumeraries on the stage of history.

In the Congo, at the beginning of the colonial period, the explorers, travelers, missionaries, and officers and agents of the State had been self-taught anthropologists, historians, or linguists. These amateur historians created the history of colonial achievement, of missionary achievement, in the Congo. And that situation has prevailed everywhere in colonial Africa where the European amateur historians produced a eulogy for the colonial pioneers as heroes and representatives of a civilization brought to the

African barbarians.[3] These views went well with those that King Leopold II affirmed for the Conférence géographique de Bruxelles on September 12, 1876, in that subsequently celebrated passage from his remarks, "To open to civilization the only part of the world where it has not yet penetrated, to pierce the darkness that envelops entire peoples, that is, I dare to say to you, a crusade worthy of this century of progress."[4]

Thus colonial history centered on colonial administration, colonial business enterprises, and the religious missions. All who were part of that trilogy sought, by means of the printed matter devoted to their work, to praise the purposes assigned to it and the results it achieved. It was within that framework that numerous works were published on the occasion of fiftieth anniversaries of colonial enterprises such as the *Comité Spécial du Katanga* in 1950, *l'Union Minière du Haut-Katanga, la Forminière et la Compagnie du chemin de fer du Bas-Congo au Katanga* in 1956 . . . biographies about important European political personalities who left a mark on colonial history, or monographs on the foundation of various religious missions, church-schools, etc.

Study of the African people in general and the Congolese in particular was limited to ethnologists and ethnographers. The unavowed purpose was to seek out ways and means of subduing the colonized subjects and thus serve the metropolitan interests, the ethnologists and ethnographists beginning to study the customs, clothing, and obscure beginnings of the colonized. Clearly, it was that context that brought forth the works of, among others, C. Van Overberg, E. Torday and T. Joyce, A. Hutereau, R. Beaucorts, J. Maes and O. Boone, C. Van Der Kerken, E. Verhulpen, and others.[5]

This behavior of the colonizers was dictated by the notion in vogue in that era that Africa had no history because it had no written documents before the Europeans arrived. (The positivist historians thought the oral traditions, which resided in the memory of individuals, could not be considered authentic given that they were at the mercy, over time, of continuous alterations and falsifications. The historians believed, thus, that the oral transmission of facts was not as faithful as that of written matter. One must wait until the 1960s to see J. Vansina do research on the true character of oral tradition and develop a method destined to examine the veracity of oral tradition. Since then, oral tradition has been considered a source of history.) It is the reason why the history of the Congo generally begins with the (European) explorations. When the Congolese are cited, it is not to show their contribution to the birth and development of the colonial society but to highlight the impact of the European presence on the colonized population, which could do nothing but submit.[6] "The history of the colonial era," Catherine Coquery-Vidrovitch observed, "was history made by Europeans, by conquerors of an Empire, and they wished, consciously or unconsciously, honestly or not, that that history should be noble. Historians always believe themselves good historians, therefore honest, but nevertheless reveal to some degree the full context of their work. And that context was such, during colonial history, that everything was printed to the benefit of the Europeans."[7]

The movement for professionalism of the discipline of history took place in two stages in the Congo. The first stage, a little after World War II, began with the arrival on the scene of the first Africanist professional historians with academic training. They carried with them, although hesitantly at the beginning, a different conception of history. They were beginning to be interested in the deeds and activities of the Congolese, caring about the recovery of objective history. However, each one wrote an African history colored by the ideology of his own school of origin. All the same, when Congolese history was written with a critical eye, it must be acknowledged that it was the eye of a foreigner.

Some other factors had worked in favor of that new orientation of Congolese historiography. Wartime, and the postwar period even more, had experienced many movements of protest and claims. It was also in the course of that period that one saw the emergence of the *évolués*. These latter, amateurs, began to interest themselves in the past of their tribe, ethnicity, or clan, whichever was appropriate. Thanks to a newspaper, *La Voix du Congolais*, the *évolués* could convey their opinions of colonial society. L'Université Lovanium (now the Université de Kinshasa) and l'Université du Congo belge et du Rwanda-Urundi (now the Université de Lubumbashi) were founded at that time, in 1954 and 1956 respectively. These events and many others did not leave the Africanist historians unaware of the study of social problems faced by the Congolese. Congolese historians had the duty, as Jewsiewicki emphasized to them, "de rendre aux peuples de ce continent leur propre histoire, élément nécessaire de la conscience nationale. En même temps, ses investigations doivent permettre l'intelligence des processus de formation de la société et de l'Etat actuels" [to restore to the peoples of that continent their own history, a necessary element of the national conscience. At the same time, their investigations ought to permit an understanding of the process of formation of a present-day society and State].[8]

Until the 1970s, Congolese historiography existed almost completely in the hands of Africanists mostly from Europe, both eastern and western, and North America. Those are the Africanists that in 1965 founded the first department of history at l'Université Lovanium, with the aim of responding to postcolonial needs by teaching and research in African history.[9] Historiography was called on to enlarge its field of action, to open itself to other domains until then kept in the shadows or simply neglected.

The first class of Congolese historians with academic training graduated in 1970. In the course of time, historiography divided into four options: social and economic history, political history, cultural history, and the history of the population.

Social and economic history looks at socioeconomic aspects to know about the economic activity of various administrative entities (provinces, districts, and territories); of the recruitment of African manpower, the rural exodus, the work parties and forced labor communally drafted at random and so on; of the works of an educational type; of the native peasants and the white settlers; of industrialization and the social problems it has entailed; of commerce, transportation, the supplying of worker populations with subsistence provisions, the land problems, and so on.

Political history has taken up the administrative and territorial problems relative to territorial organization, that is to say, the division of the national territory into provinces, districts, territories, sectors, and urban communes; to the connection between the colonial political authorities and the traditional African chiefs; to the banishment of the Africans; to the municipal elections; to the origin and multiplication of political parties; to rebellions; to labor unions, and so forth.

Cultural history includes many of the same themes: among others, teaching, African art, the style of dress, the messianic movements such as Kitawala (derived from the Watch Tower), Kimbanguisme, the cultural resistance of Africans confronted by the European penetration, the problems of acculturation and of cultures, and the like.

Study of the history of the African peoples was oriented toward the spatial evolution and distribution of population within provinces, districts, territories, and urban centers. It was necessary, on one hand, to show that not all towns in the Congo were colonial creations, but instead that most of them had only submitted to changes due to contact with the techniques and rhythm of the life introduced by the colonizers; and, on the other hand, to analyze the factors that have worked in favor of their spatial extension. That analysis emphasizes formation of the urban population and its ethnic distribution. Finally, the study of the evolution of the people from the heart of administrative entities (provinces, districts, and territories) aims, among other things, to show whether the uneven distribution of population observed in the Congo is an ancient phenomenon or a new one attributable to events of the end of the nineteenth century, and to supply the explanatory elements. Another theme that caught the attention of the historians is medical history. The object was to show the impact of the penetration of colonialism on the health of the indigenous peoples. The first works published made reference to the relationship between industrialization and health, to illnesses that were raging among the people. Numerous masters' theses were dedicated to analysis of the impact of the medical-social infrastructure on working people, causes of infant and child mortality, and qualitative analysis of death.

The second stage of Congolese historiography therefore began in the 1970s, a period after which the Congo had its own professional historians with academic training. Also from that period onward, those African historians began to research their cultural identity, to decolonize and to detoxify history—in short, as M. Achufusi has so well emphasized, "donner une image véridique de l'histoire, image nécessaire à la prise de conscience historique des masses dans leur lutte pour l'indépendance nationale, politique, économique, sociale et culturelle" [to give a truthful image of history, a necessary image for the holding of the historical consciousness of the masses in their struggle for national political, economic, social and cultural independence].[10]

Until that point, most studies dealt with the precolonial period (to rehabilitate African history) and more studies of the colonial period took into account, it is said, the availability of archival documents and the fact that it was necessary to understand the previous period before claiming to resolve current African problems. Interest in the postcolonial period is, however, one of the important gaps in Congolese historiography. The postcolonial period therefore still remains an almost virgin territory in which to work.

Nationalist history had scarcely begun in Africa in the 1960s with the accession of countries to political independence. One of the dangers to which such a history finds itself exposed is that of occasional instability and chauvinism. And it is to put the searchers on guard against that broken vision that Jewsiewicki noted:

Nous constatons, dans l'historiographie actuelle de l'Afrique, une assez regrettable tendance à simplifier singulièrement les problèmes sociaux et politiques de l'époque coloniale. Tout conflit est volontiers réduit à l'opposition fondamentale et schématique: colonisé-colonisateur, tandis que l'on oublie trop facilement l'existence de conflits sociaux entre les colonisés eux-mêmes aussi bien qu'entre les colonisateurs.[11]

[We confirm, in the actual historiography of Africa, a rather regrettable tendency to conspicuously simplify the social and political problems of the colonial era. Every conflict is readily reduced to a fundamental and schematic opposition: colonized-colonizer, so that the existence of social conflicts among the colonized themselves, or for that matter the colonizers, is very easily overlooked.]

In spite of the Africanization of academic and scientific personnel in 1976, research remains dominated by themes formerly used by the Annales school, the Anglo-Saxon approaches emphasizing the role of the State in national construction, and the neo-Marxist approach centered around the concept of underdevelopment.[12]

On the other hand, for a long time study of the past continued to be dominated by a masculine point of view, in the sense that women's share in the birth and development of the modern industrial world has been forgotten. Women always lived in the shadow of men, part of the private life of men. Victims of a patriarchal ideology dominant in the precolonial and colonial eras that drops them to second place, women are forgotten persons, objects rather than subjects.

Generally valued to the degree that they demonstrated their fecundity and therefore their ability to perpetuate the clan in the traditional societies, African women were, at the advent of colonization, at first considered instruments of pleasure required to make the workers' environment favorable after the hard hours of service. Later, they were required to become maids in Western households. In this framework they achieved the right to education. Some schools for girls were founded not only for the betterment of women but because the colonial society wanted to have at the side of the educated workers some women at their level. But everywhere women played the part of followers. History ignored them or spoke of them little. The statistics of the Union Minière du Haut-Katanga remain silent until 1967 as to the number of women employed at the heart of that enterprise. If the history of women begins to be interesting, it is due not only to the increasing number of women historians but even more because researchers became aware of the part women really played in the construction of history.

According to Jewsiewicki, "l'histoire est la reconstruction toujours problématique et incomplète de ce qui n'est plus" [history is always an incomplete and problematic reconstruction of that which is no more].[13] The Congolese historiographer who does not avoid that definition therefore reveals the gaps, the omissions, and the falsifications that characterize official history and are the cause of its fragility, its bias, its relativity. After all, it cannot be said that the discipline of African history is still young. History therefore needs to be rewritten, reworked, and enriched. In that context, as I have emphasized before, memory constitutes an important material for reconstruction.

Taking advantage of individual or collective memory makes possible the analysis of perception, behavior, attitudes, opinions, and judgments of the Congolese people at any given moment of their history and in a given milieu. In that context, the historian is not alone in attempting the reconstruction of the past but does it in combination with the participants, thus becoming the co-re-creator of the past.

Because the productions of history are many and varied, that based on memory is still in its beginnings, poor and covering only a few domains. The themes investigated are a function of social, political, economic, and cultural preoccupations. From the first day of independence in the Congo, the initiators of contemporary history have gleaned oral information at the side of political operators with the goal of weaving the political history of the Congo. It was thus that the CRISP dossiers were published from 1960 to 1965.[14] And, as Isidore Ndaywel è Nziem observed, those studies proved to be sound. As the 1970s opened, the harvest of life stories, that Jewsiewicki compares to the archival documents, began in the Congo. Indeed, the archival documents that the colonizers had developed and left had not covered all domains of life nor touched in a thorough manner all the socio-professional categories. This resulted in quite a few gaps that only oral investigation could enhance. In that context, the harvest of life stories from the national bourgeoisie supplemented the gaps found in the archival documents about the formation of the Congolese national bourgeoisie. Various publications of life stories, then autobiographies and religious testimonies, appeared during the 1980s. This happened when photocopied texts were new and therefore did not have wide distribution.

Finally, during the 1990s, studies and publications increased to a substantial distribution of memory in the Democratic Republic of the Congo. The domains covered by those studies are also varied: the first life stories harvested at the time of collection were brought together in a work published under the direction of Jewsiewicki. The studies were diversified and touched on some other domains such as religious testimonies, the life of the workers of l'Union Minière du Haut-Katanga, the political debates dealing with the exclusion of people of Kasai origin from Katanga

Province, the liberation of the Congo by the troops of l'AFDL, the biographies of personalities who had made a mark on the country's history, and so forth. All these studies contributed to an understanding of the history of the Congo. And these examples demonstrate that memory makes possible the reconstruction of the past.

The Contribution of Memory to History

An adage says that "an old person who dies is a library that disappears." And Joseph Ki-Zerbo agrees when he notes: "chaque vieillard qui meurt emporte dans sa tombe un trésor irremplaçable d'un enseignement particulier, à la fois matérielle, psychologique et spirituel fondé sur le sentiment de l'unité de la vie et dont la source se perd dans la nuit de temps" [each old person who dies carries into the grave an irreplaceable treasure of special teachings, at one and the same time material, psychological, and spiritual, based on a feeling of the unity of life, of which the source is lost in the night of time].[15] Those expressions stress the very important role that memory plays in the writing and rewriting of history. In fact, to seek to know the collective or individual mentality, the feelings, the judgments of a society at a given moment in its past—that is, in my opinion, to aspire to grasp the history of that society in all its universality.

So, for Jewsiewicki, memory is a library. But one must recognize that memory is subject to the whims of time insofar as forgetfulness intervenes and distorts certain historical facts, and sometimes mixes up their context. Memory also finds itself under the yoke of the current political situation. Under these conditions, it plays false because it does not reproduce the most faithful remembrance of the past. Memory will thus be subjective or objective depending on the individuals and the concerns of present-day interests. It is variable and therefore can be manipulated at will.

However, memory constitutes the raw material for history insofar as it enriches history thanks to the oral testimonies. Thus, history sets itself as a guardrail for memory in the sense that it justifies or rejects certain untrue memories. "La mémoire ainsi reconstruite," notes Jean-Pierre Chrétien,

> est la défense et illustration d'une communauté et c'est le travail de l'historien que de décrypter, sous la façade apparemment lisse de récits continus et intégrateurs, les failles, les aspérités, les contradictions qui révèlent des évolutions plus chaotiques et moins reluisantes. Ces mémoires sont aussi fondées sur l'oubli des autres références légitimantes.[16]

[Memory so reconstructed is the defense and illustration of a community, and it is the work of the historian to decipher, under the apparently
clear façade of continuous and uncorrupted narratives, the faults, the
roughness, the contradictions that reveal more chaotic and less shining
evolutions. These memories are also based on the neglect of other legiti-
mating references.]

In what follows, I am going to try to show, with a few examples, the
link between memory and history, that is to say, to show in what relates to
the Congolese population, the contribution of memory to historical
understanding and, on the other hand, the role that history plays in the
interpretation of memory.

Popular art is one illustration of the memory of a society. It provides
to history the feelings, perceptions, and representations of the population
at a given moment from its past and makes possible the analysis of those
variables. Two examples are going to illustrate the link that exists between
history and memory through popular art.

In 1985, inspired by a pictorial reproduction, I published an article
about the pain of the whip in the Belgian Congo.[17] That penalty has
marked the collective memory in the sense that it recalls one of the humiliating penalties of the colonial period, inflicted on the blacks against what
the colonizers called a lack of discipline at work (absence from work, lazi-
ness, desertion, etc.) and at the worker's camp. The punishment was established to avoid overloading the prisons. And the pain of the whip was a
humiliating practice, a symbol of alienation and domination. To be not
yet beaten but to let drop one's trousers or pants and submit to blows of
the whip on one's naked buttocks is degrading and humiliating. Nudity is
not an ordinary event in black Africa. To show one's nudity to another,
whether youth or adult, except for one's husband, wife, or lover, is considered a sign of sorcery or a curse and is punishable in the traditional
Congolese society. To publicly undress an adult person depersonalizes that
person. That is why the pain of the whip depersonalizes and was counted
among the penalties that humiliate. The number of blows of the whip to
be inflicted on delinquent blacks varied from one hundred to four before
being abolished on the eve of the accession of the Congo to independence
in 1960. According to colonial literature, the reduction in number of
blows of the whip paralleled the evolution of the Congolese people's mentality.

On June 30, 1960, the first Prime Minister, Patrice Lumumba,
repealed that humiliating penalty inflicted on the Congolese. In his short

speech, given June 30, 1960, Patrice Lumumba said, most notably, the following: "Nous avons connu les ironies, les insultes, les coups que nous devions subir matin, midi et soir, parce que nous étions des nègres. . . ." [We have known the humiliation, the insults, the blows that we experience morning, noon, and night, because we were black. . . .] The Congolese painters crystallized the collective memory concerning the pain of the whip, reproducing it on canvas. Those paintings about the pain of the whip were and are bought and hung on living room walls. That Congolese painters reproduced that sad scene on canvas for a long time after independence was not risky. In fact, it functioned as a message addressed to the dictatorship of Mobutu, which continued to apply the pain of the whip in the prisons of the special research squad and of the national services of intelligence and defense. The pain of the whip was here one of the tortures and a form of intimidation applied to persons considered by the regime to be subversives, anti-revolutionaries, etc. Those whipped with extreme cruelty are incapable of sitting on their buttocks. That penalty scars the memory of people who, for many reasons, have stayed for some time in the jails. To reproduce on canvas the pain of the whip during a clearly dictatorial regime is therefore a form of protest against that regime, one that also conducts itself as a colonizer with regard to the governed.

At the end of the 1990s, the memory of Congolese painters and intellectuals was once more scarred by the pain of the whip under the regime of President Kabila. The painters reproduced on canvas the kadogo soldiers as they applied that penalty to "liberated" Congolese people. The only difference from the paintings representing that scene during the colonial period is that the whites, the office of the territorial administrator, and the colonial flag are here replaced by kadogo soldiers, whipping their victims not only on their naked buttocks but on their naked stomachs at the navel. The kadogo, Rwandan soldiers, have replaced the Belgian colonizer.

During the scientific days organized by the faculty of letters of the University of Lubumbashi, participants likewise recalled that humiliating penalty, and noted especially that currently it was also applied to women. "Les Congolais qui ont toujours vécu au pays, note Lwamba Bilonda, ont été désagréablement surpris par la manière forte d'agir des troupes de libération qui ont amené avec eux le fouet au nombril, administré même aux femmes, chose que même les colonisateurs belges n'avaient jamais faite" [The Congolese who had always lived in the country had been disagreeably surprised by the severe manner of acting of the troops of liberation, who had brought with them the blow to the navel, administered even to women, a thing that even the Belgian colonizers had never done].[18] The admiration and friendship that the Congolese people felt toward the kadogo soldiers had given way to aversion. However, one can also understand the mentality of these Rwandan soldiers. "The Tutsi," it was said in Congolese country, "never weep for their dead parents, friends, and acquaintances. They weep instead for their cows." It is only one step from that to believing that in the eyes of the Tutsis the Congolese were worth nothing. And that explains this: He who strikes is great and more powerful; he has dominated the one struck. The interpretation of that memory is that the Tutsi want to show by that attitude, in the manner of the Belgian colonizers, that they dominate the Congolese and are recolonizing them. In this context, we permit ourselves to borrow this extract from Mathieu Kalele ka Bila:

> Avec l'avènement de l'AFDL, le pays a tragiquement cessé de nous appartenir! Il est devenu . . . une propriété privée exclusive des Erytréens, des Ougandais et des Rwandais! . . . Quant à nous-mêmes les natifs, nous sommes réduits au silence et nous avons été simplement transformés en leurs petits nègres esclaves, parias! . . . Ils nous confisquent à loisir nos véhicules, nos maisons, nos femmes! Ils nous arrêtent arbitrairement, nous chicotent impitoyablement au ventre pour un petit rien et nous gardent empilés dans les cachots infectés des mois durant sans jugement, sans nourriture et sans eau dans l'unique but de nous voir tomber malades et mourir![19]

> [With the arrival of the AFDL, the country tragically ceased to belong to us! It has become . . . the exclusive private property of the Eritreans, Ugandans, and Rwandans! As for us, the natives, we have been reduced to silence, and we have been simply transformed into their little black slaves, pariahs! They confiscate at will our vehicles, houses, and women! They arrest us arbitrarily, whip us mercilessly for a mere trifle, and keep us stacked in infected dungeons for months without trial, without food, and without water for the sole purpose of seeing us fall sick and die.]

The Tutsi therefore behaved like conquerors toward the "liberated" Congolese people. The behavior of the kadogo soldiers can be condemned. In black Africa, a child cannot under any circumstances hit his father, and even less a very old person. That the kadogo soldiers inflicted blows of the whip on aged persons, and on both sexes together, constitutes transgression of an African tradition based on the respect of young people toward adults.

As we have been able to demonstrate, that analysis clearly shows that the pain of the whip is a Congolese matter of multiple memories of domination.

Popular art is also an expression of urban Congolese memory. It reveals the important stages of Patrice Lumumba's political life from his speech of June 30, 1960, until his death. During the 1970s, the painter Tshibumba Kanda Matulu reproduced on canvas a large work about Lumumba, the national Congolese hero. That painting later evoked the curiosity of researchers and was the origin of many studies that permitted the enrichment and comprehension of Congolese history. In 1996, in a study dedicated to Lumumba as shown in popular painting, Jewsiewicki did not hesitate to speak in these terms:

> Le Lumumba de la peinture populaire semble être cette figure qui sur le plan esthétique comble l'espace entre l'homme élégant et le fils de Dieu devenu homme pour sauver les Congolais des chaînes de l'esclavage colonial. . . .Lumumba y est ce héros moderne qui rend aux Noirs non seulement l'espace de l'action politique mais aussi l'accès au sacré sécularisé. Il est un héros, une figure prométhéenne, qui rend à l'homme noir sa dignité, sa respectabilité, valeurs qui trouvent leur origine dans sa propre personne. . . . Comprendre cette métaphore a une valeur heuristique pour l'historiographie du Zaïre contemporain. La mise en image par Tshibumba, un peintre populaire de Lubumbashi dont s'inspirent au Shaba de nombreux tableaux représentant Lumumba, dit explicitement la métaphore narrative qui fait converger en sa figure christique l'histoire sainte et l'histoire politique. Elle engendre une mémoire de Lumumba comme martyr: son libre consentement à mourir pour son idéal en fait un héros. A l'instar de l'histoire sainte, il s'agit du récit apocalyptique d'une fin de l'histoire où celle-ci s'érige en tribunal.[20]

[The Lumumba of the popular painting seems to be this figure who, on the esthetic plane, takes up the space between the stylish man and the son of God-become-man to save the Congolese from the chains of colonial slavery. . . . Lumumba here is this modern hero who gives back to the blacks not only the space of political action but also access to the secularized sacred. He is a hero, a promethean figure, who returns to the black man his dignity and his respectability, values that find their origin in his own person.

Comprehending this metaphor has a heuristic value for the historiography of contemporary Zaire. The creation of an image by Tshibumba, a popular painter of Lubumbashi who has inspired in Shaba numerous tableaux representing Lumumba, presents explicitly the metaphoric narrative that brings together in this Christ figure the sacred and political stories. It produces a memory of Lumumba as a martyr: his willingness to die for his belief makes him a hero. Following the example of sacred history, it is an apocalyptic narrative of the end of a story where he set himself up in the judgment seat.]

In 1999, the catalogue of an exposition of Congolese pictorial memories of Lumumba, held at the Museum for African Art of New York, was published. The exposition brought together paintings by popular Congolese artists, of whom the most important was Tshibumba Kanda Matulu. In the manner of the pain of the whip, history and memory find themselves united in the understanding of that great and charismatic personage who left an impression on the history of the Democratic Republic of the Congo. The case of Lumumba shows that memory is one and many, objective and subjective, according to the individuals, the eras, the concerns, and the interests of the moment. In 1961 Lumumba was assassinated, as were his two companions, Mpolo and Okito, by the political authorities of Katanga, at that time a province in secession. Paradoxically, from the 1970s on, popular painters lived in Katanga province; the painter Tshibumba Kanda Matulu reproduced Lumumba on canvas to remind the Katangan people how important a role that man had played in the process of national emancipation of the Congo.

The memories of Lumumba have changed over time and place. Indeed, first considered as liberator of the Congo and of the Congolese people, Lumumba was diabolized at the same time by the Katangans, who saw him as a dictator and a Communist who had sold out to the USSR, and by the Kasaians, who considered him an assassin. The Mobutu regime, wanting Mobutu to appear as the political heir of Lumumba, rehabilitated him and made him a national hero. His effigy appeared on the twenty-makuta bank note, showing Lumumba breaking the chains of slavery. The memory of Lumumba as liberator revived the spirit of the Congolese people. A boulevard in the town of Lubumbashi carries the name Lumumba. From the 1970s on, attempts were made to analyze and understand the political method of Lumumba. In 1979, the Third Historical Conference of Zaire organized by the Historical Society of Zaire on the theme, "Elites and Understanding the Future of Zairois Society," among other activities, showed that Lumumba played an important role in the national emancipation of the country and was a model for the present-day political elite to emulate. Here, the painters and intellectuals threw a message to the political class, that of having Lumumba as a model to imitate in the management of *res publica*. In the world of painting, the painters reproduced Lumumba on canvas, reconstituting his political life and his martyrdom.

The most-used pictorial memories show Lumumba breaking the chains of colonization, signing the white book of independence, shaking the hand of King Baudouin I, haranguing the Congolese masses, and then arrested, tortured, and taken to Katanga where he was assassinated along with his two collaborators, Mpolo and Okito.

In the rising flash of Mobutuism, the memory of Lumumba was forgotten. The portrait of Lumumba on the twenty-makuta note was replaced by that of President Mobutu on the coin of the same face value. "Le Lumumba historique," notes Jewsiewicki, "a été renvoyé aux archives et progressivement banni de la vie politique et de l'espace public monopolisé par l'omniprésence de l'image du chef, maître des lieux, Mobutu lui-même" [The historic Lumumba has been sent to the archives and progressively banned from the political life and from the public space monopolized by the omnipresence of the image of the chief, master of everything, Mobutu himself].[21]

At present, after the downfall of the Mobutu regime, the painters are reproducing on canvas Lumumba passing his spirit on to Laurent Desire Kabila as in the Old Testament the spirit of the prophet Elias enters into the prophet Elijah. That means that Laurent Desire Kabila was chosen by God to replace Lumumba and bring the Congo out of the dictatorship of Mobutu. Indeed, the current regime presents itself as the continuation of Lumumba's politics and his thought.

Another representation of Lumumba is that comparing him to Christ.[22] Lumumba (killed by his own) dies with two companions in order to liberate the Congolese people from colonial slavery just as Jesus Christ died (killed by his own) in order to save the world from the slavery of Satan, in the company of two other people. A cult to Lumumba is dedicated to Lumumba in a church called Kabukulu in the East Kasai province.

Not only painting, but also the life story, is a genre of individual or collective oral history insofar as it comprises the history of a person, a family, a clan, etc. Here there is a dialogue between the narrator and the interviewer. The life stories also contain elements no less important to history. "Ils fournissent," according to Léon Verbeek, "l'explication de certains faits et comportements que l'histoire écrite ne donne pas" ["They provide," according to Léon Verbeck, "the explanation of certain facts and behaviors that written history does not give."][23] In the framework of current history, for example, life stories become an important source. We have been able to study, thanks to the life stories, the reintegration and reentry into Kasai Province of workers' families of Kasai origin expelled from Katanga Province. In addition, two publications on the liberation of the Congo by AFDL troops have been made possible thanks to the memory of the people. They constitute a considerable contribution to the history of the Democratic Republic of the Congo after the downfall of the Mobutu regime.[24]

Besides life stories, religious testimonies also bring a new element to cultural and religious history and to the history of the family. As we know, the churches, prayer groups, and religious sects provide moralization, mediation, and negotiation for many families. After the 1980s, Katanga Province in general, and the town of Lubumbashi in particular, have recorded the proliferation of charismatic prayer groups, as often Catholic as Protestant. Many people, especially women, reveal their family problems and wait for the priest, the pastor, or the shepherd of the prayer group to offer a prayer of intercession or deliverance, or to give lavish advice generally to couples to solve family problems and restore harmony within families. Here and there, some couples are invited to discuss and look for solutions to problems that could affect their relationships. The people healed or consoled then make public testimonies about their (re)conversion, that is to say, how from a lawless, worldly, and satanic life they have moved on, thanks to the action of the Holy Spirit, to a new life, pious, healthy, and harmonious, a necessary condition for being called children of God and meriting His mercy.[25] Religious testimonies complement the life stories. They, among others, set the tone for organization of social networks without which the survival of the population would be almost impossible in a country like the Democratic Republic of the Congo, which is openly in a many-faceted crisis. Religious testimonies therefore help history to understand how the Christians or members of other religions and non-Christian religious sects survived or found spiritual solutions to their material problems of existence.

Memory is also present in songs and popular drama. Musical and theatrical productions help the historian and history to better encompass the problems presented from political, economic, social, and cultural points of view. Music and the theater provide a snapshot of society at any given time during its history. They translate its political, social, economic, cultural, and mental circumstances. They have the mission of exploring the behavior of the people, of critiquing, of informing, of shaping, and of upbraiding the people. They allow the following, step by step, of the different vicissitudes of social life: the past, the present, and the profound aspirations of the people. They are therefore responsible for many representations, conceptions, and inspirations, for society's fears and hopes. They revive and glorify the past at the same time that they set up an imperturbable critique of the modern mind. They express the soul and mind of the people and play an important role in the reconstruction of the mentalities of the urban Congolese population. Private life is exposed to broad daylight and the whole world is found there, in the sense that daily life is presented in a satiric manner. The gathering and analysis of songs and oral theater productions can reveal to us the striking recollections that people preserve from their past.

At present, the biographies of important political, economic, social, cultural, and religious functionaries—those having marked the history of the country so well from the colonial period up to the postcolonial period, the history of the liberation of the Congo by the AFDL troops, of the formation, organization, and functioning of social researches in the urban centers, and of the reintegration and reentry into Kasai Province of Kasai workers' families expelled from Katanga Province—would not be possible except for the gathering of life stories and oral testimonies. Here, memory contributes greatly to the understanding of present-day history.

Research Methodology

I have collected some life stories and oral testimonies subsequent to September 1990, in the framework of our research on popular urban culture. We have collected life stories of workers of l'Union Minière du Haut-Katanga/Gécamines, then those of the petit bourgeoisie of the town of Lubumbashi, of painters, of abandoned children (commonly called "street children"), photographs, and so on. I myself am also interested in religious testimonies in which the relevance is not so obvious. Isidore Ndaywel è Nziem notes:

> Ce qui est davantage digne d'intérêt; c'est le récit des égarements, des méfaits et des erreurs confessées. La volonté de conversion constitue la meilleure garantie de la vivacité des faits énoncés dont la gravité cesse d'avoir de l'importance dans la psychologie collective, puisqu'elle fait précisément objet de dénonciation. A priori, on se trouve donc en présence des informations affectées d'un haut coefficient de véracité.[26]
>
> [What is more deserving of interest is the narrative of aberration, mistakes, and confessed errors. The will of conversion constitutes the best safeguard of the intensity of stated facts whose seriousness ceases to be important in the collective psychology, since it is precisely the object of denunciation. Theoretically, it is found in the presence of information marked by a high degree of truth.]

It goes without saying that the collection of data requires a team of people well-trained in the materials. The quality of the results of an inquiry depends on both the competence of those who lead it and on the equipment used (recording apparatus, cassettes, batteries, papers, pens, etc.) The gathering of memory is done by gathering life stories and oral testimonies from the people selected. However, the political conjuncture in the Congo is such that the people mistrust all inquiries and inquirers, and that situation at times affects the interviewers in selecting informants. Generally, they begin with people they know. At the end of the research, the informant is asked for a recommendation to friends, and so on and on. It is a matter of confidence. Those who receive the researcher are comfortable and can respond without ulterior motives to questions put to them. The presence of women researchers is indispensible. In fact, there are some questions that only the African women can put to other women and some things that women cannot reveal except to other women.

During the period of conflict between the Katangans originally from Katanga and the Kasaians, investigators were constrained to not put questions that would reveal their tribes or ethnic groups or respective provinces. Thus, for example, investigators of Kasai origin found the natives of Kasai Province while the investigators of Katangan origin put their questions to those of Katangan origin. The narrators then opened themselves up readily to their "brothers" of tribe or province.

The conversation is aimed at the object of the investigation. For example, a narrator tells the history of his life or that of his family. He usually touches on points such as his family origins, his childhood, a description of his migratory travels (recruitment and arrival at an urban milieu, his being taken in charge by members of his clan or ethnic group; work, lodging); life in the camp; composition of the family; the future of children; source(s) of income for the family, and so on. The investigators let the narrators talk but guide them, when that might prove necessary, towards the object of the study. Fortune does not always smile on the investigators. At times, they find themselves in the presence of very talkative people, also at times they endure people who suffer a certain verbal constipation. They must then push them to speak by some precise questions. The conversation is then translated and transcribed into literal French in order to be as close as possible to the sense of the testimony collected. Throughout the process, difficulties are not lacking in this gathering of oral data. However, the attitude of the historian should be the same for oral sources as for written sources.

The narrator's discourse can be true or false according to the identity of the investigator and the kind of relationship that binds the narrator to the investigator. The facts and interpretations that narrators furnish to investigators during reconstruction of the past depend also on the time and space context in which narrators find themselves. Thus, narrators can avoid talking about problems they consider intimate, that they wish to keep secret and therefore do not wish to share with the investigator. They will therefore talk of facts they find of interest and put to the side those that they themselves judge to be minor or not important. An African married woman, for example, will doubtless avoid talking about her sexual adventures before marriage. The personal history of the narrator is therefore incomplete. But, gathering the history of each member of the family permits the lifting of the veil on certain hidden aspects of one or another member.

We are at times confronted with a divergence of the narrators' versions on a given aspect. That situation is quite simply due to several reasons of a political, ideological, and tribal nature. Facing such situations, we resort to history, to written information on the period in the course of which the event has taken place,[27] or we choose a comparison of narrators, or, in the absence of these, the testimonies in person, the eyewitness testimony, can be trusted most often. We ourselves take our own position after due consideration, and we justify our choice.

As we have emphasized before, interpretation of memories assumes knowledge of the history of the region or the people. For example, at the beginning of the 1990s, Zaire entered a new era, the process of democratization. But that period of political transition saw the resurgence of regional collective identification. As for Katanga, the reconstruction and development of the province was considered the business only of native Katangans, who had a better understanding of the interests of their province. This required the exclusion of nonnatives, particularly the natives of Kasai province, from the development of provincial government.

That circumstance was also a way of exalting memories of the great Katangan political leader who fought against colonial occupation. Msiri was considered by the native Katangans of that province as a national hero and defender of the province's interests. According to the political discourse in vogue at that time and justifying the low proportion of Katangans among the effective workers in the big businesses developed in Katanga, the Katangans had refused to work for Belgians because of the assassination of Msiri, the defender of the interests of Katanga. In fact, it is known that the Garenganze empire created by Msiri had commercial power in the region that later (after 1910) became the province of Katanga. Msiri, who carried out commercial activities (ivory, slaves, copper, etc.), was assassinated in 1891 by Bodson, a Belgian officer, for being opposed to the establishment of another commercial power represented by the Belgian king, Leopold II. The memory of Msiri came back when the Katangans, in their struggle for control of political and economic power, wanted to (re)construct a regional collective identity against the strangers, who were not only numerous but especially too powerful and who had occupied, to the disadvantage of the natives, almost all the high positions in the different companies established in the province. Msiri's attitude was here considered a model to follow by every Katangan leader who struggled for liberation of Katanga and Katangans. In this context, the governor of the province, Kyungu wa Ku Mwanza, set up as a defender of Katangan interests, was also considered a liberator of the Katangan people from domination by the Kasaien people. For that he was given the name Mandela, in memory of Nelson Mandela, the president of South Africa, liberator of black South Africans from the yoke of apartheid.

But history teaches us that Msiri wasn't a native of Katanga. Coming from Tanzania, he set himself up in Katanga around 1850 and took power also over peoples southwest of Katanga, in particular the Basanga, the Balambe, the Baushi, the Balomotwa, etc. Besides, his assassination was sought by tribes southwest of Katanga, in particular the Basanga, to recover their freedom and their independence. Captain Stairs himself said it explicitly when he noted: "la mort de Msiri fortifie énormément notre situation dans le pays, et ce sera cause que les Basanga vont devenir nos amis très dévoués. Ce sont du reste les véritables propriétaires du pays" [The death of Msiri helped greatly to fortify our position in the country, because the Basangans will become our very devoted friends. They are moreover the real owners of the country].[28] However, as the Belgians had placed Mukanda Bantu, a son of Msiri, at the head of the kingdom, most of the natives had refused to work for the whites, whom they considered to be enemies for being friends with their Yeke enemies.[29]

Another example appears in the embellishment or demonization of the past by the speaker. That attitude is a function of the present social or political position of the speaker. After the liberation of the Congo by the AFDL troops, certain women, formerly called "100 kilo musiki" and fanatical supporters of Mobutu, started to demonize the regime. Yet, from the time of Mobutu, they continued to use the slogan, "*Otumoli ba mama, otumoli Mobutu; otumoli Mobutu, otumoli ba mama*" [if you arouse the mothers, you arouse Mobutu; if you arouse Mobutu, you arouse the mothers] in order to suggest the existence of a certain relationship between them and the deposed president, formerly their source of happiness. "The flatterers' meaning depends on who is listening," it is said.

A third example is that of persons who glorify the colonial past yet demonize the next day the achievement of independence. One comes to believe that this nostalgic attitude for the colonial period would be a sort of preference for slavery over liberty, just as the children of Israel, after their exodus from Egypt, faced difficulties in the desert.[30] We think that such nostalgic attitudes must simply be considered a form of protest by a population concerned about the poor conditions of their present life. However, that takes nothing away from the meaning that makes up the testimony.

A Songye Myth

We will finish this study with an attempt to analyze a myth on the origin of the power achieved by the Bena Totwe group, which belongs to the ethnic group the Songye. The Songye live in a region made up of the Lomami and Sankuru areas, between the fifth and sixth parallels south. Today they are divided among four provinces: West Kasai, East Kasai, Maniema, and Katanga. The Bena Totwe belong to the Songye of East Kasai. They live in the territory of Kabinda, in the district of the same name. The most important groupings in Kabinda are the Bena Milembwe, the Belands, the Basanga, the Bakankala, the Bena Majiba, the Bena Mpaze, and the Ben'Eki. The Bena Totwe belong to the Ben 'Eki tribe in the Ludimbi-Lukula collectivity. They are found in four villages: Totwe Ngiefu, Nguba Totwe, Kabangu ka Totwe, and Bakile ba Totwe.

That which the Bena Totwe say of themselves and which all the Ben 'Eki know is summed up in an enigmatic phrase: "*Totwe emenene te Mpaze te Milembwe t'Eki dia Kalanda.*" Literally, this means: "The Totwe people have come forth, they are not of the Mpaze tribe, nor of the Miembwe, nor of the Eki of Kalanda." In other words, the Bena Totwe have come forth like mushrooms and don't count as brothers to the Bena Mpaze, nor the Bena Milembwe, nor the other clans of the Ben 'Eki tribe.

To that is added another fact much more important to the political setup. None of the *mwin'eki* Nkole can go through the Totwe villages carried in a typoï; none of them can stay the night in the Totwe villages. In addition, the Bena Totwe don't pay tribute to them. The result is that the Bena Totwe behave like a state within a state in the sense that they seem

politically autonomous. Nevertheless, the Bena Totwe are not demo-
graphically nor economically more important than the other Songye villages of the Eki tribe.

The first impression to come out of all this is that the Bena Totwe
are the natives, that is to say, the descendants of the original local population, found in place. This will justify, then, the term *emeneme*, which
comes from the verb *kumena*, meaning to germinate, to sprout, or to
spring. That version can be shown to be true to the degree that the Bena
Totwe natives didn't have brothers among the neighboring "stranger" populations (Bena Mpaze and Bena Milembwe) newly settled in the region,
who later on with the others came to make up the Ben 'Eki group.
However, that interpretaion proves to be totally false when one knows that
in the manner of the Ben 'Eki, the Bena Mpaze, and the Bena Milembwe,
the Bena Totwe are not the source of an indigenous population.

When one investigates the oral tradition, the Bena Totwe will be
descendants of Luba hunters from Katanga who were introduced into the
current area of Ben'Eki in pursuit of a sacred animal. These hunters were
under the control of a powerful Luba chief. They prepared to return to
their own country when the chief fell sick and died. They decided to bury
the corpse of the deceased chief and to remain in the place to guard his
tomb. In contrast to the first, the second version holds that the Luba
hunters were installed in the region and their chief had already established
commercial relations with the neighboring populations, which sold produce of the hunt and taught them the use of fire. All this gives us the
image of human migrations that operate in successive waves at different
epochs. On the other hand, all the Ben'Eki are unanimous that the directions of migrations were from a point of departure at the Sanga-Lubanga
site. And, one of the proofs of the coexistence in time of the Songye and
the Luba of Katanga in Sanga-Lubanga would be the *lubuku*. As Kabamba
Mabuija notes,

> Le *lubuku* est une institution qui, tout en défiant le naturel empirique que
> l'homme expérimente, se pose en intermédiaire entre les ancêtres défunts
> et les vivants. Les vivants se réfugient derrière les prêtres du *lubuku* pour
> demander aux défunts les raisons des malheurs ou des calamités qui s'a-
> battent sur un individu ou un groupe d'individus. Le langage utilisé par
> ces prêtres songye dans le *lubuku* est le kiluba.[31]
> [The lubuku is an institution which, completely in defiance of empirical
> nature which man experiences, poses itself as an intermediary between the
> dead ancestors and the living. The living take refuge behind the priests of
> lubuku to demand from the dead the reasons for their unhappiness or

the calamities that affect individuals or a group of individuals. The language used by the Songye priests in the lubuku is Kiluba.]

In the belief of Kankieza Kantu, the present Songye territory in East Kasai had known an invasion of hunters coming from Sanga-Lubanga. It is a question of *Pibwe* (hunters) Kitengie, Lubamba, and Kabongo.[32] Munono sha Nsenga places Pibwe Lubamba at the head of Bena Totwe, Bena Mpaze, and Bena Milembwe. In any case, under the leadership of a powerful chief hunter, the Bena Totwe had constituted one of the waves of migrants and installed themselves in the Eki region. As they were newcomers, the Bena Totwe did not have brothers among the populations found in the place. It appears that, as we have demonstrated, the term *emenene* is not justified.

When one digs out more oral tradition, it seems that a mysterious lake had surged up at the place where the Bena Totwe had buried the corpse of their late first chief. This lake, called *Mbebe*, still exists today. This was a miracle as much to the eyes of the Bena Totwe as to the neighboring populations. Very quickly this lake acquired a great reputation.

Before the arrival of the Bena Totwe in the Eki territory, the title of *Nkole* existed. The Nkole was, and is considered even today, a supreme chief. He represents the founding ancestors of the Eki community. The Nkole exists on three levels: the Nkole of the village, the Nkole of a group of villages, and the Nkole of all the Ben'Eki. Before becoming Nkole, the candidate ought to have reached the grade of *Mfubana*. And, this last grade is found only in certain families among the Bakwa Lubo, the Bena Mulemba, the Bena Eyongo, the Batshimbwe, and the Bena Kasongo. To become Nkole among all the Ben'Eki, it was necessary to belong to the families of the Bena Kasongo Ntundu, of Kabongo or of Kibambi.[33] At the time of his investiture, the Nkole, whatever might be his degree, ought to drink the water of the river Edikulyi. As the chief of the Bena Totwe might be Nkole, the emergence of a mysterious lake where his corpse was buried gives cause for reflection. The lake became the "lake of Nkole." This is why all the aspirants to the grade of Nkole ought to drink the water of lake Mbebe. This water carried strength and power to the new chief, overwhelmed all evil power, and purified the impure. According to oral tradition, a wizard could not cross the river. Likewise, it would be difficult if not impossible for a canoe carrying the relics of human remains to cross a body of water or a lake if the carrier (of these relics) had not thrown something in (a piece of money, for instance). Beginning at that moment, Lake Mbebe replaced the Edikuluyi River and became the lake of confirmation of the power of the Nkole in all the territories of the Ben'Eki. And every time this occasion of investiture occurred, it was this Nkole of the Bena Totwe who made the candidate drink the water of Mbebe and invested him with the leopard skin.

The investiture at Lake Mbebe was always accompanied by the redistribution, by the future Nkole, of material goods including human offerings. Young boys and girls were thrown alive into the lake and thus offered to the mânes. After Munono sha Nsenga, chief Mwana Kankieza had been the last Nkole of the Ben'Eki confirmed at Lake Mbebe. Since the arrival of the Europeans and their occupation of the Eki territory, the investiture of the Nkole at Lake Mbebe has not taken place. The confirmation was extremely expensive in both material goods and human lives. Colonization and evangelization could not permit the Ben'Eki to continue in such practices.

Lake Mbebe was without parallel in the whole Eki territory, among the Bena Mpaze and the Bena Milembwe. The Bena Totwe could correspond their tradition with that of Lake Mbebe. In fact, it was not the Bena Totwe who had power, but rather Lake Mbebe. In other words, if the Eki chiefs did not spend the night in a Totwe village or cross it seated in their typoï, this is due to the respect that they owed to Lake Mbebe, of which the Bena Totwe were the owners. The Totwe villages were thus considered a "no man's land," and this is why the Bena Totwe did not pay tribute to the cheif of the Ben'Eki. The origin of Lake Mbebe comes therefore at the origin of the time of the political role the Bena Totwe played among the Ben'Eki, and this enigma was known by all who understood *"Totwe emenene te Mpaze te Milembwe t'Eki dia Kalanda."*

Notes

1. P. Salmon, *Histoire et critique*, Bruxelles, Editions de l'Université de Bruxelles, 1987, p. 43.

2. B. Jewsiewicki and V. Y. Mudimbe, "Africans' Memories and Contemporary History of Africa," in *History Making in Africa*, Wesleyan University, 1993, p. 3.

3. P. Salmon, *Introduction à l'histoire de l'Afrique*, Bruxelles, Hayez, 1986, p. 33.

4. G. Martelli, *De Léopold II à Lumumba*, Paris, Editions France-Empire, 1964, p. 33.

5. C. Van Overberg, *Collection des monographies ethnographiques*, Bruxelles, 1907–13. This work consists of eleven volumes that deal with Bangala, Bayombe, Basongye, Mangbetu, Warega, Kusu, Ababwa, Mandja, Baholoholo, and Baluba-Hemba; E. Torday, and T. Ajoyce, *Notes ethnographiques sur le peuple communément appelé Bakuba ainsi que sur les peuples apparentés les Bushongo*, Bruxelles, 1910; A. Hutereau, *Histoire des*

peuples de l'Uele et de l'Ubangi, Bruxelles, 1922; R. Beaucorts, *Les Bayanzi du Bas-Kwilu*, Louvain, 1933; J. Maes, and O. Boone, *Les peuplades du Congo belge*, Bruxelles, 1935; E. Verhulpen, *Baluba et Balubaïsés*, Antwerpen, 1936; G. Van der Kerken, *L'Ethnie Mongo*, Bruxelles, 1944, etc.

6. Salmon, *Introduction à l'histoire de l'Afrique*, p. 18.

7. Cited by M. Amengual, *Une histoire de l'Afrique est-elle possible?*, Dakar-Abidjan, Les Nouvelles Editions Africaines, 1975, p. 25. "L'histoire à l'époque coloniale c'était l'histoire faite par les Européens, par les conquérants d'un Empire; et ils voulaient, consciemment ou inconsciemment, honnêtement ou pas, que cette histoire soit belle. . . . Et un historien se croit toujours un bon historien, donc honnête, mais il révèle, en partie, tout son contexte. Et le contexte était tel, pendant l'histoire coloniale, que tout était tiré du côté des Européens."

8. B. Jewsiewicki, "Notes sur l'histoire socio-économique du Congo (1880–1960)," in *Etudes d'Histoire africaine* 3(1972), p. 209.

9. Mumbanza Mwa Bawele and Sabakinu Kivilu, "Historical Research in Zaïre. Present Status and Future Perspectives," in B. Jewsiewicki, and D. Newbury (eds.), *African Historiographies: What History for which Africa?*, London-New Delhi, Sage Publications, 1986, pp. 224–34.

10. M. Achufusi, cited by Salmon, *Introduction à l'histoire de l'Afrique*, p. 19.

11. It is to show that social conflicts also existed among the colonizers themselves that B. Jewsiewicki published "Contestation sociale au Zaïre (ex-Congo belge). Grève administrative de 1920," in *Africa-Tervuren* 22 (1976) 2/3/4, p. 57.

12. Bawele and Kivilu, "Historical Research in Zaïre," p. 230.

13. B. Jewsiewicki, "Aide-mémoire," document polycopié, Québec, 30 août 1998.

14. See the publications of CRISP: Congo 1960–65, etc.

15. J. Ki-Zerbo, "Tradition vivante," in *Jeune Afrique*, Stock, II (1980), p. 199.

16. J. P. Chrétien, and J. L. Triaud, p. 30.

17. Donatien Dibwe dia Mwembu, "Sur la peine du fouet au Congo Belge."

18. M. Lwamba Bilonda, "Le vécu de la libération de la ville de Lubumbashi du 7 avril au 17 mai 1997," in D. Dibwe dia Mwembu, J. J. Hoover, and (sous la direction de) B. Jewsiewicki, *Récits de libération d'une ville. Lubumbashi*, Paris, L'Harmattan, Collection Mémoires, lieux de savoir, Archive congolaise II, 1999, p. 87.

19. G. De Villers, and J. C. Willame, "République Démocratique du Congo. Chronique politique d'un entre-deux-guerre. Octobre 1996–Juillet 1998," in *Cahiers Africains*, nn. 35–36, Paris, L'Harmattan, 1998, p. 108.

20. B. Jewsiewicki, "Corps interdits. La représentation christique de Lumumba comme rédempteur du peuple zaïrois," in *Cahiers d'Etudes africaines*, 141–42, XXXVI-1-2, 1996, pp. 128–29.

21. Ibid., p. 134.

22. Ibid., pp. 113–42.

23. L. Verbeek, "Histoire et littérature orale," in *Cahiers de littérature orale*, n. 45, 1999, p. 167.

24. Crispin Bakatuseka Kolamoyo intitulée, "La 'Libération' de Lubumbashi," and "Récits de Libération d'une Ville. Lubumbashi" (1997).

25. I. Ndaywel è Nziem, "Un nouveau champ heuristique à Kinshasa au Zaïre: le groupe de prière," in G. Thoveron and H. Legros (eds.), *Mélanges Pierre Salmon* (I). *Méthodologie et politiques africaines*, Bruxelles, E. Guyot, Civilisations, vol. 40, n. 2, 1992, p. 57.

26. Ibid.

27. J. Vansina, "Comment l'histoire se construit: la conquête du royaume Kuba (1899–1900)," in Thoveron and Legros (eds.), *Mélanges Pierre Salmon*, pp. 41–49.

28. A. Verbeken, *Msiri, Roi de Garenganze. L'homme rouge du Katanga*, Bruxelles, 1956, p. 246.

29. A. Delcommune, *Vingt années de vie africaine*, Bruxelles, 1892, p. 140; see also Kalukula Asani bin Katompa, "L'opposition sanga à Msiri et à l'administration coloniale belge, 1891–1911," travail de fin de cycle, Lubumbashi, Université Nationale du Zaïre, campus de Lubumbashi, 1977.

30. G. De Villers, "A propos d'un recueil de témoignages zaïrois sur la période coloniale. Témoignages et réalités," in J. Omasombo Tshonda (sous la direction), *Le Zaïre à l'épreuve de l'histoire immédiate*, Paris, Karthala, 1993, p. 195.

31. Kabamba Mabuija, "Essai d'histoire des Songye. Cas des Eki. Des origines à 1900," mémoire de licence en histoire (in press), Lubumbashi: Université de Lubumbashi.

32. Kankieza Kantu, "Introduction à l'organisation socio-politique des Ben'Eki," travail de fin de cycle, Lubumbashi, CIDEP, 1973, p. 15.

33. Kampa Kamikudi Lubo, "Contribution à l'histoire socio-politique traditionnelle des Ben'Eki de Ludimbi-Lukula," travail de fin de cycle, Lubumbashi, CIDEP, 1982, pp. 71–72.

19

WRITING ABOUT WOMEN

APPROACHES TO A GENDERED
PERSPECTIVE IN AFRICAN HISTORY

Kathleen Sheldon

The inclusion of women and gender in African history has been flourish-ing in recent decades.[1] Initially the focus of research was on women as his-torical actors, and historians showed that women were present and active despite their omission from much historical writing about Africa. Later more nuanced approaches discussed gender as the social construction of male and female roles, though frequently "gender" was a stand-in for women.[2] Eventually studies of masculinity surfaced, demonstrating fur-ther that male behavior and experience should not be the norm against which women were measured, but that all history was gendered—that is, events were affected by the maleness or femaleness of the people involved.

Before the 1970s there was little published research on African women's history. Information on women in Africa was more often found in anthropological and ethnographic studies.[3] This focus continues to be evident in the preponderance of research on African women in develop-ment rather than history *per se*. The first publications in the 1970s in the new wave of research dealt with women and economic change and with women as political activists.[4] By the early 1980s the history of African women had emerged as a vibrant and steadily expanding area of research and study. Scholars were motivated, as with women's history in other world areas, by the development of the international feminist movement, and from the beginning there was a political component to much of the research and writing in African women's history. African women's history

465

also paralleled the expansion of African history following World War II, as scholars inside and outside of Africa began to focus on historical transformations on the African continent. By the mid-1980s there were a number of important extended studies as well, still primarily focusing on women's public lives,[5] though studies of family and sexuality were also beginning to appear.[6] Only in the 1990s did a substantial number of monographs on specific topics begin to appear, although most new research is still found in journal and anthology articles.

Despite these advances in the historiography, many standard histories of Africa still omit women and ignore the implications of gender.[7] Helen Bradford refers to "androcentric sins," observing that often when women are neglected the author (usually male) will note their absence and offer an apology, but continue to write a historical analysis that ignores gender and women. For instance, in his preface to the revised edition of *The Rise and Fall of the South African Peasantry*, Colin Bundy comments that his analysis "would have been enhanced had it included a discussion of *women*," yet he excludes women despite his recognition of their importance. Bradford also decries the practice of using a general term such as "people" as if referring to both men and women when in fact the reference is only to men, thus effacing and negating women's experiences.[8]

This essay will consider sub-Saharan Africa only, following the practice of African studies in general, which treats North Africa as a separate entity culturally and historically. I will be focusing on methodological issues—what kinds of evidence can we employ to write African women's history—rather than attempting an overview of historical studies of African women.[9]

Early History and Elite Women

Scholars have been able to retrieve some information about African women in the distant past by utilizing historical linguistics to examine changing patterns in women's roles as wives and mothers within pastoralist and agricultural communities.[10] As David Schoenbrun demonstrates for the Lakes Region in present-day Uganda, linguistic evidence can help explain the gendered development of banana farming and cattle pastoralism at the end of the first millennium (ca. 1000 C.E.).[11] Other researchers have begun to look at archaeological evidence as a way to understand the division of labor in early societies, though they caution that scientific evidence collected through archaeological research does not prove that women or men did particular work, but only provides a basis for explication and analysis.[12]

Nonetheless, archaeologists have helped retrieve some of that earlier history. Debates about the development and decay of Great Zimbabwe rely heavily on interpretations of archaeological evidence concerning royal wives, their housing, female initiation rites, and male and female images. Some have suggested that a major factor in the decline of this urban settlement after the sixteenth century was the scarcity of nearby firewood for cooking. When women refused to walk great distances to gather wood the people dispersed into smaller, less urban settlements.[13] Heidi Nast has developed an approach she calls "spatial archaeology" to investigate the history of the palace at Kano, Nigeria. The physical information, gleaned in part from archival documents, provides information about the growing influence of Islam in the fifteenth century. The results allow Nast to assess the roles of male and female slaves as well as to examine the seclusion of royal wives when male rulers became concerned about controlling their wives' sexual behavior in order to prove their paternity.[14]

Items such as pots, jewelry, and other material goods can provide some evidence about women's activities in earlier historical periods. Marla Berns opened up the discussion of who made the ancient pottery statues in West Africa, noting that it is often assumed that these items were made by men because the statues were put into the category of "art" rather than "craft" and because they were believed to have a spiritual component, both categories generally associated with men. The conventional interpretation actually runs counter to the fact that women are mainly responsible for pottery-making in the twentieth century, including items used in ritual events as well as pots for everyday use. Thus researchers should consider the role that women may have had in making the widely known two-thousand-year-old Nok ceramic heads from what is now Nigeria, as well as other figures from Chad. Berns suggests that patterns used in working with clay are repeated in tattoo designs on women's bodies, and that those designs reflect social ideas about womanhood and femininity. She further proposes that if we recognize that women may have made some of these items and designed the emblems decorating the pottery we should accept that "women, through what they make, contribute to the construction of symbolic systems," and thus to the development of culture.[15]

Finding information concerning earlier historical eras can be difficult. Because many African communities were decentralized and nonliterate, written materials from before the nineteenth century, especially from an African woman's perspective, were scarce. In a few cases historians have been able to use unusual archival sources to retrieve the stories of elite women. Thus researchers have found material for Queen Nzinga, a sixteenth-century ruler in what became Angola,[16] for Dona Beatriz, a religious leader in seventeenth-century Kingdom of Kongo,[17] for and wealthy traders along the West African coast.[18] A more recent group that garnered recognition was the Asante queen mothers who exerted substantial political influence in nineteenth-century central Ghana.[19]

The available sources have allowed historians to describe aspects of these women's lives in some detail, but interpreting their place in history remains open to discussion. For example, Nzinga was adopted as a symbol of anticolonial and anti-Portuguese struggle during the Angolan war for independence in the 1960s and 1970s. Yet a closer examination of choices she made suggest that she was quite willing to cooperate with the Portuguese when it suited her need for political survival or advancement, leading others to characterize her as a collaborator. There is a similar variety of opinion concerning the women who traded with Europeans along the west coast of Africa, with some seeing their willingness to improve their life situations through trade and sometimes marriage with Europeans as an early form of treachery. Others view them as strong and independent women who chose their own path and even played an important role in keeping control of African trade by not allowing Europeans access to all parts of the coastal societies.[20]

In South Africa, "the most written about African woman" is arguably the Khoena girl who became known as Eva. Though not of elite background, she was in contact with the first European settlers, who recorded information about her. From a young age she worked for the household of the Dutch commander, Jan Van Riebeeck, and she later married a Dutch surgeon. Her proximity to the European community resulted in an unusual amount of documentation as compared to most African women of the seventeenth century. Her story has been told many times, and has recently been reassessed by Julia Wells, who laments the "unfortunate loss of her Khoena identity in the historical accounts."[21] This comment could apply to all of those mentioned above, since the reason there is any documentation about these women is that they were removed from their African society and integrated to some degree into the developing European coastal settlements. As with the elite women mentioned above, historians have displayed a variety of opinions about the meaning of Eva's life. She has been described as a "woman in between," sometimes being presented as emblematic of the harsh treatment of African women by

European conquerors, while at other times as the "mother of the Afrikaner nation," or an example of Africans as "irredeemable savages."[22]

In all of these cases our understanding of the options these women faced and their motives for making the choices they did are obscured because the available sources are almost entirely written by European men. For Dona Beatriz, for example, nearly every source was written by Italian priests who were not only observers and recorders but, as John Thornton notes, instigators of events that involved her.[23] Surviving sources written by Kongolese are rare, and those by women nonexistent. Though there are useful insights in the available sources, historians must acknowledge the sexist and ethnocentric assumptions that are evident as well.

In another instance, Nakanyike Musisi has shown how close study of a variety of materials including colonial publications and documents, local histories, and archival sources, can illuminate the changes in the lives of elite women in Buganda (part of the modern nation of Uganda). Musisi comments that she was initially resistant to using sources written by men (both European and Bugandan), but those sources did have useful information if she read and analyzed them with an awareness of their inherent biases.[24] Rather than discuss one woman, she introduces information about a range of women in the royal family. Although noble Bugandan women in earlier periods had some privileges, by the nineteenth century the kingdom became more centralized with the result that female members of the royal family lost power relative to men. As land was increasingly privatized in the hands of the king and his top advisors, women had access to land only through men. The sexual behavior of royal princesses also came under increasing scrutiny as control of ascension to the throne became a political issue.[25]

R. A. Sargent investigated royal women among the Bunyoro-Kitara, another example from what is today Uganda, to analyze why knowledge about women's power in the past has been lost. Sargent suggests that men's oral histories tended to omit the stories about women who ruled in the past, and that the obscurity where such women remain is directly a result of their being female, as they were considered "an aberration rather than a real political force." He argues that one such woman, Daca (active in the sixteenth century), "should be clearly regarded as a Lwo heroine, and must be considered an influential figure in the political transformation of the northern interlacustrine region."[26] Oyeronke Oyewumi has demonstrated how gender-neutral histories about Oyo royalty in Nigeria have been rendered male as those stories were written down. She enumerates cases of female rulers who were not specifically named as women in Oyo tradition, because Yoruba language does not designate gender. Several of these women have been erroneously transformed into male rulers by modern historians.[27] Information on them is present in archival sources as well as oral traditions, but is often ignored or downgraded.

Both the production of art and the representation of women in artistic images can add to our knowledge of women's roles in history. Suzanne Blier discusses royal women in particular in her recent book, including illustrations of carvings of queen mothers from several African kingdoms. The figures suggest the exalted position royal women held in their societies as well as some of their ritual and actual responsibilities. Details regarding hairstyle, dress, and adornment in particular set royal women apart from ordinary women. In one example, the Mangbetu Queen Nenzima is depicted with unusually long fingernails, clearly a possibility only for someone who did not do any manual labor.[28] A similar source of information on the royal women in Benin is found in court photographs taken over many decades that document the royal family. Flora Kaplan discusses how the Bini royalty prized owning photographs of family members and important events, as well as how useful these were as source materials in improving her understanding of kinship and family in the court. Many of the available photographs were of royal women posed in their best clothing and involved in ritual activities.[29]

The approaches used by researchers has shifted since the 1970s, as exemplified by Edna Bay in her work on the women of the royal court at Dahomey, who included the women soldiers who have often been called Amazons. When Bay first began to study African history, she chose to focus on these women because they were known and there was extant information. As Bay comments in her later work, however, though this initial research satisfied her "search for women of historical importance, [she] was troubled by a nagging sense that not all of [her] evidence fit."[30] As she investigated further she learned that the important role of the royal women in the eighteenth century and early nineteenth century was lost over time. She discovered that part of the evidence was in the history of spirit cults and local religions and that shifts in those arenas could be linked to the end of the slave trade and the rise of trade in palm oil. Her work portrays a transformation in the reasoning of feminist historians away from simply writing about women as women to analyzing changes in social configurations that are illuminated by understanding women's situation. She also demonstrates how gendered histories can help us comprehend not only women's experiences but the history of society more generally.

The study of elite women such as those in the Dahomey palace has continued to attract many researchers, as these women were both more visible in the historic record and demonstrate one kind of power wielded by women. As Flora Kaplan notes in her introduction to a recent collection of essays on queen mothers and other powerful African women, there was an earlier ethnographic literature on elite women.[31] As scholars have begun to examine those women in a historical context, they are beginning to comprehend the complex development and decline of the elite position of royal women.

Oral Testimony

While some historians have turned to women's life histories and the use of oral testimony to fill lacunae in published sources, this has limitations in researching earlier periods.[32] Oral testimony has been used with much success in collecting information about women's lives today or in the recent past, with one result being the development of life stories about ordinary (rather than elite) women.[33]

Claire Robertson has written about her experience collecting life histories of Ga women in Ghana, some of which were incorporated into her book.[34] Her article addresses such methodological issues as maintaining the informant's privacy, sharing the researcher's own comparable information so that it is not so intensely an exploitative situation, the good and bad aspects of hiring an interpreter from the local area, problems of language and translation more generally, choosing women to interview, balancing the process by asking questions and eliciting more free-form stories, being concerned about the factual or fanciful nature of the stories told, and payment for those who were interviewed (she paid informants if she spent more than one hour talking with them). She also addresses the issue of gender, including both the researcher and the interviewees. She found that the woman-centered housing arrangements in central Accra, where women usually lived in compounds with female relations rather than with their husbands, favored interviews. This contrasted with interviews conducted with women in suburban housing where co-resident husbands intervened on more than one occasion, either forbidding the continuation of the interview or sitting in and overriding any comments his wife made with his own opinions.

Christine Obbo provides some interesting anecdotes in her discussion of research in a variety of East African communities. On the one hand men assumed that they knew about women's history while women did not have that knowledge. On the other hand, women would often allow men who interrupted to have their say, and then continue with their own stories by stating, "As I was saying . . ." Obbo suggests that researchers need to create a space in their interviews and conversations so that women can talk, especially when they need to recover from male intrusions.[35]

Francesca Declich's discussion of history in Tanzania and Somalia reveals how oral histories vary between men and women. She demonstrates how women and men have distinct histories to tell because their own experiences varied by gender, and this was compounded because in retelling their stories male and female audiences heard and remembered the information differently. This became essential when looking at the historical development of ethnicity and identity, as women from a matrilineal background focused on female ancestors as founders of their group, which later gained an ethnic cohesion centered on the female progenitors. Male narrators completely elided this important source of identity. The broader understanding of this history was damaged because researchers often only wrote down the male versions, entirely omitting the female interpretation of historical experiences.[36]

Oral testimony can also be useful in learning about modern elite women. Nakanyike Musisi discusses the process of collecting information for a biography of the last Bugandan queen mother who had died in 1957. It was a predicament because the ex-queen mother had been involved in a scandal in the 1940s, and had retreated to live a secluded life after that event. Musisi was concerned with how she approached the gatekeeper to those who had information about this woman. She surprised herself when she spontaneously adopted a more religious attitude than she normally exhibited when she felt that would ease the relationship and perhaps allow access. The biography has implications far beyond the story of one elite woman's life, as it "demonstrates the intimate relationship between royal women's sexuality, power, and state machinery."[37] Those implications also made this a delicate topic in terms of collecting information, and indicate that a certain amount of flexibility is a virtue when doing historical research.

Onaiwu Ogbomo describes how Owan men in Nigeria were uncomfortable when he interviewed women about precolonial history. He realized the local men were not only concerned with interactions in general between an outsider man and "their" women, but that the men were disturbed about the process of women telling their version of that history, as that was seen as possibly "empowering the oppressed gender."[38] Ogbomo suggests that though there are obstacles to men pursuing research in women's history, they can be overcome, and in fact must be in order for history to be as honest as possible. He hired a female research assistant to conduct some of the interviews, in order to avoid antagonizing husbands who were unwilling to allow Ogbomo to spend time with their wives. In addition to interviewing women, Ogbomo also collected songs and poems and observed marriage ceremonies for clues to the past. This attention to process brought out new information on the history of that region, as men began the story with the establishment of male control, but women's version began earlier, when women had power. Ogbomo emphasizes that it is not enough to collect political narratives to reconstruct precolonial history, but researchers must also examine other forms of oral tradition and ritual to discover what women's roles were in the past.

Leroy Vail and Landeg White also turned to songs as a source for history from the point of view of women. They analyzed Tumbuka women's songs from Malawi, and were able to suggest a new periodization of history as a result.[39] For Tumbuka women the late nineteenth century was marked by a loss of power resulting from a shift away from matrilineal descent patterns, an issue ignored in the conventional regional histories of Ngoni raids and population migration. Heidi Gengenbach also reveals that women's ideas about their own history in southern Africa are not congruent with the political changes most often used to organize written history. Through elderly women's life stories, she reconstructs a world centered on the agricultural calendar, family obligations and responsibilities, and the occasional ecological disaster (such as floods and drought).[40]

Other forms of oral information can be found in stories and sayings, rather than from direct questioning. Researchers can retrieve information on marriage, kinship, and social expectations regarding women's behavior from folktales, where such issues are presented in allegorical forms. Mary Bill suggests that Tsonga stories about eating and drinking are really cautionary tales about who is a legitimate potential sexual partner, and who is outside of social boundaries regarding relationships. These stories also indicate the centrality of relationships between sisters in southern African societies.[41] The danger is that folktales may appear to be timeless, yet they reflect the era in which they are told and retold. The stories undoubtedly change over time as different people tell them. But they can echo ideas about marriage and sex as well as political power, and often include gendered notions of those subjects.

Proverbs are a similar source of folk wisdom about important issues. An unusual source of sayings is the *kanga* or cloth wrap used by women all along the east coast of Africa. Such cloths are often printed with aphorisms, and as Sharifa Zawawi demonstrated, "the kanga represents . . . a Swahili woman's cultural and literary heritage [as] they encapsulate in a particularly pithy and epigrammatic way the social parameters of their wearers' existence."[42] Women will purchase kangas that have sayings they appreciate, and by wearing the kangas the words are seen and enjoyed by their community. Many of the mottoes apply to family and marriage, and suggest proper female behavior.

Oral testimony is not always a remedy for gaps in the literature, however, as I learned when doing research on women and work in Beira, Mozambique. I interviewed nurses, garment workers, and women who worked in cashew factories.[43] In general, the best-documented group was the nurses, who were also the best educated, and the most articulate about their own histories. Their own experience of education gave them some insight into my goals as a researcher and their identity as professional women contributed to their level of comfort when being interviewed. The garment workers were also educated, and there was also some information in the factory archives. There was much less information for the cashew factory in Beira, where I was told that files and reports from the colonial era had been destroyed after independence. Women who worked in the cashew factory were more likely to have had no formal educational experience, and were often hesitant and anxious when being interviewed. Thus the women who were least present in written and published material were also the most attenuated sources of oral information. In the end, though the women's accounts did provide information not available from any other source, the level of detail in the interviews tended to replicate the hierarchy of data that already existed.

Researchers have used oral information to good effect in women's history, finding information that was not in archival or other written sources, and bringing women's perspective to the study of social change. The words that become documents of women's history have many potential sources, from formal and informal interviews and the collection of complete life histories, to songs, folktales, and sayings.

Marriage and History

The use of marriage patterns as a guide to historical periodization has been suggested by several researchers, as a way of developing history from women's point of view. Marcia Wright shows how changes in marriage were related to larger political and economic changes in her article on Tonga women and maize production in Zambia in the twentieth century.[44] In this case the arrival of plows altered the dynamic of marriage, which had previously relied on bridegrooms providing service to their in-laws as part of the marriage agreement. As agriculture developed, settlements became denser, and women lost rights to land and to the proceeds of their labor in the fields. Colonial agents emphasized male control of income, which combined with the advent of plow agriculture to shift the system of marriage from matrilineal brideservice patterns through a period when men paid bridewealth (rather than do the work required in brideservice), and finally evolved to a system of paternal control over polygynous families. The changing patterns of marriage allow an insight into social changes more broadly.

Another source that uses marriage as a way of studying social change is found in Barbara Cooper's study of marriage and social history in Niger. Her introduction provides a model of the ways in which a research project can be changed in the field when confronted with the realities of those arranging interviews and those being interviewed. Cooper comments that she planned to write a "gendered history more broadly understood rather than women's history in the recuperative sense."[45] Yet in the field she found that her personal research interests were forced aside in light of what people in Niger believed she wanted to research, as the gendered nature of doing research came to the forefront. That is, if she wanted to interview women, then topics such as political history were off limits (at least for some people), and marriage was generally seen as a more appropriate subject for queries. As it turned out, she was able to use marriage as a lens to view the colonial experience in this Hausa society. But she was not able to interview men, as the women clearly felt that would be a violation of the trust they gave her when relating confidential aspects of their lives. She has written a detailed study of colonial law, access to land and housing, urbanization, education, religion, and politics (especially regarding women's organizations), based to a great extent on female informants. In one chapter she elucidates economic transformation through a study of changes both in the process of exchanging of marriage gifts and in the goods involved in the transaction. The twist of looking at broader issues through the intimate experience of marriage rather than such familiar lenses as labor or politics suggests what is possible when historical study centers the experience of women and uses a gender analysis.

Marital relations were also at the base of Kenda Mutongi's research on Kenyan widows. Most literature dealing with widows in Africa has discussed the levirate, the system where widows were inherited by their husband's brother or sometimes other male kin. Rather than assume that the levirate was the main concern for widows, Mutongi interviewed widows to learn about their priorities. She discovered that widows in the 1940s and 1950s were more concerned with how to survive with male help without resorting to remarriage. One of the key issues beyond their personal survival was contracting good marriages for their daughters. Women would invoke their position as "poor widows" in order to solicit aid from men in the community. The gender construction of masculinity meant that men could position themselves as good men in the community by assisting widows who publicly acknowledged their need for help. The widows' efforts also played a role in defining proper male behavior during a time of social and political upheaval.[46]

Approaches to Finding Women's Stories

Oral testimony has been long used, and its limitations noted, in retrieving women's history. In addition to the innovative methods already mentioned, historians have turned to a variety of other sources in their search for information on women. Colleen Kriger analyzed weaving techniques found in nineteenth-century fabrics from Sokoto in West Africa. Her close study of textiles suggests that women's weaving was more varied, had a higher value, was more organized, and was better known than earlier studies indicated.[47] Among the many topics covered by Jean and John Comaroff in their studies of the interaction between the Tswana and missionaries in South Africa is the ideology of domesticity and proper housing among the Tswana. They combined the traditional research method of a close reading of mission documents with the study of the architecture of Tswana homes and communities. The round homes and the circular arrangement of housing was an obstacle to European missionaries, who saw the lack of "squareness" as resonant with a lack of civilization. The attempts by the Europeans to develop houses with four walls involved a shift from women to men building those homes.[48]

Heidi Gengenbach investigated the tattoo designs with which women in southern Mozambique decorated their bodies, and showed how the practice of tattooing was characterized by female bonding, women's selection of what gave pleasure and was considered beautiful, and the persistence of African preferences regarding their bodies in the face of colonial and missionary disapproval. The changing practice of fashioning tattoos as seen in alterations in the designs and their placement on women's bodies can be correlated to larger social changes, providing a way to develop a periodization of history from the perspective of nonliterate women.[49] Thus women's bodies as well as the physical space they inhabited have been used as historical "documents."

Centering Women in Familiar Narratives

Reexamining familiar issues from a woman's perspective has altered African history. In her study of nineteenth-century Lesotho, Elizabeth Eldredge describes in detail the daily round of work for which women were responsible. With the development of plow-based agriculture, women became more dependent on men, but they also were able to take some economic initiative. She demonstrates that technology such as harrows for weeding, which was usually women's work, were not adopted.[50] Research on Swahili women's spirit possession cults suggested the changes in religious and spiritual beliefs that occurred as the East coast of Africa was incorporated into the global economy.[51] Other religious women in West Africa played an important role in the spread of Islam, and left a written record of their beliefs and teachings.[52] Studies of women and religion have also included the role of women in developing local churches that were off-shoots of larger denominations,[53] and the sources of female spiritual power in local religions.[54] In all of these cases earlier research on agricultural work, the spread of Islam, and other religious activities, had not incorporated the presence and contributions of women.

As we have seen, the availability of sources influenced what kind of research could be done. This is a partial explanation for the prominence of studies of slavery, as this was a topic with unusual depth in documentation. Yet earlier studies of slavery did not discuss women except as victims of the slave trade. Marcia Wright's study of women's vulnerability in Central Africa also brought the issue of gender differences in pawning to the forefront.[55] And in their important collection, Robertson and Klein demonstrated that slaves within Africa were more likely to be women, a reflection of their productive and reproductive contributions to their communities. This has included attention to women as slave owners, and to women's experiences as slavery ended.[56]

By focusing on women during the colonial era, we are gaining a new understanding of the gendered differences of the impact of colonialism. For example, studies of women's work during the colonial period often showed how they had lost power and economic autonomy with the arrival of cash crops and their exclusion from the global marketplace, in contrast to men who were more likely to benefit from these economic changes.[57] Analysis of the development of legal systems under colonialism has shown that women were at a disadvantage as "customary" laws were established based on male testimony that gave men, especially elite men, advantages over women in issues of marriage and divorce.[58] Further inquiry on women's lives during the colonial period can be found in a special issue of the *Canadian Journal of African Studies*, where changes in marital practices and expectations provide a common theme.[59]

Research on this era also exhibits a tension between women as victims and women as powerful agents within their communities, as female agricultural innovations were described as essential to community survival,[60] and women became politically active because of their experiences.[61] In Cheryl Johnson's study, the development of three different market women's associations in Lagos suggests the ethnic and class divisions present in the city.[62] Others have investigated women's changing position in arenas formerly seen as only male, such as mining compounds.[63] Another essay took a new look at patterns of women's urban migration, based in part on court records in a smaller city.[64] Shula Marks exploited an unusual set of letters to discuss the relationship between South African women of various backgrounds. Her book not only describes the complexity of such connections, but discusses the problems and advantages of using such an unusual documentary source.[65]

Catherine Coles used three linked life histories to give vibrancy to the urban development of Kaduna, Nigeria. Her informants' own stories portrayed what it meant to women to live in the city as society changed, from the grandmother who lived the secluded life of a proper Muslim Hausa wife, to her daughter's greater freedom in her work, and her granddaughter's access to education. In this case what might have been a dry retelling of economic and political change was infused with the story of this family, which was intertwined with twentieth-century urbanization.[66]

Studies of European and American women travelers, government agents, researchers, and missionaries assess their position within their own societies as well as their interaction with African communities.[67] In some cases female travelers and agents wrote documents that focused on women, in a historical period when women were more commonly ignored. The editors of a collection of French documents concerned with women and colonization observe that "sources from European women are very different from male sources." They suggest that European women were able to get closer to local women, especially in Islamic societies where men were often separated socially from women, and they were interested in more "feminine" topics including children, girls' education, cooking, women's work, and marriage.[68] Ghislaine Lydon discusses one such woman and the thousand-page report she wrote for the colonial government in French West Africa in the 1930s. The unpublished account contains a great deal of useful detail concerning women's lives, labor, marriage, health issues, and the law throughout the region, yet it has languished in the national archives in Senegal.[69] Certainly its existence suggests the material yet to be discovered in archives across the continent.

Another potentially large source of documents that has yet to be exploited lies in the private papers of African women. In writing a biography of a woman leader from Ibadan, Nigeria, LaRay Denzer has demonstrated that such papers include detailed information on the development of women's organizations as well as on political activity more generally.[70] The introduction of western education, European ideas about domesticity, and the changing role of women in urban centers have all been studied, drawing on a variety of published and archival sources, colonial documents, and interviews with women about their experiences.[71] In all of these cases researchers made use of extant documents that had been overlooked or unknown to earlier historians.

In an exemplary illustration of feminist historical analysis, Helen Bradford reexamined documents related to the Xhosa cattle-killing of 1856–57, one of the most noted incidents in nineteenth-century South Africa.[72] In the customary retelling of that millenarian event, Nongqawuse was a young girl who was seen as a prophet. She called for the Xhosa people to stop cultivating and to kill their cattle, actions that resulted in forty thousand deaths and weakened the Xhosa so they were unable to withstand British colonial advances. Bradford begins with the idea that women's labor as agricultural workers must be centered in this narrative; it was the lack of crops that led to mass starvation, rather than the more dramatic cattle-killing, which was recorded by European observers. By showing how marriage, sexuality, adolescent girls, and cattle are interconnected, Bradford makes clear how social expectations of male and female behavior led to the disaster. But further, Bradford rereads documents where she discovers the actual words of Nongqawuse and other women that have been systematically omitted from existing studies. Those African women voiced oblique referrals to witchcraft, defilement, adultery, and incest; their references to incest in particular were simply removed from many published versions of the testimony. Bradford argues that Nongqawuse, an orphan living in her uncle's homestead with numerous male and female relations, exhibited behavior that indicated possible abuse by her uncle or other men in that homestead. This negative experience could not be talked about directly, and Nongqawuse began having visions in which her father and other powerful men denounced unacceptable male behavior in Xhosa society. Of course there were larger social changes that made the Xhosa susceptible to her imprecations, but previously the personal sexual history of those involved has not been included among the factors that led to such wide-spread misery. By centering African women in this well-known event, Bradford demonstrates how women and gender are essential components to writing a complete and honest history.

Studies of political activism reversed previously accepted ideas of women's passivity in the face of such changes. In an influential article Judith Van Allen demonstrated that women drew on precolonial practices to make clear their displeasure with the colonial powers.[73] By using a judicious combination of archival sources and interviews with participants, researchers have reassessed the Mau Mau resistance movement in Kenya to include the significant role played by women.[74] The story of Charwe, a woman possessed by the female spirit of Nehanda who was a pivotal actor during an anticolonial struggle among the Shona (now in Zimbabwe) in the 1890s, has been told and retold.[75] Susan Geiger's study of the leadership activities of illiterate Muslim women in Dar es Salaam fundamentally changed the view that the Tanzanian anticolonial movement was led solely by men who were products of Christian mission education.[76] This was a complete switch from arguments that the colonial powers had brought about their own end by educating the men who formed the anticolonial organizations and then came to power after independence. If women who were outside the colonial educational system were involved in the struggle to end colonialism, there were obviously other factors involved in developing an anticolonial consciousness. Geiger's book presents this information in an unusual format as an extended plural biography of the women who were involved in the nationalist movement in Tanzania (then Tanganyika), switching between a narrative history of that era, the particular stories of individual women, and the extended account by Bibi Titi Mohammed of her life. As Geiger comments, she uses these life histories "to confront the biases, silences, and resulting distortions found in existing histories of the period of Tanzania's nationalist movement."[77]

As African women were primarily responsible for agricultural labor, studies of the formal sector of the economy eclipsed women's actual economic activity. In Africa, studying women's economic contributions meant paying attention to rural agricultural work as well the urban efforts of market vendors, both sectors previously neglected in African labor history. As Jane Guyer has shown, a social history of the Beti in Cameroon can be derived from a close study of women's agricultural work. She points out that female agricultural work "can seem stagnant" as women continue to grow crops for family consumption using short-handled hoes, while changes apparently go on around them. She pursued her research by participating in the daily and seasonal round of labor, and came to focus on the field itself, "with its deep associations with female life and labor," and which led outward to the surrounding economy. The introduction of cocoa as a cash crop had a profound impact on the economy, though less so on women's work. By taking women's fields as the starting point she learned about changes in women's lives that were not obvious when beginning with the larger issues of cash crop production and the incorporation of the Beti into the global economy.[78]

In an attempt to learn about women's perspectives on their own local agricultural and ecological history, Louise Fortmann describes a map-drawing project. In this study women were asked to draw with sticks on the ground, and to indicate where they gathered firewood, where certain fruits were found, and related topics. When men intervened in the community map-drawing, the result was often a distortion of what the women perceived. As part of the process women were asked what had changed in the past ten or twenty years, and they most often answered that there had once been more trees.[79] This unusually "grounded" project made it possible to learn from women about their own agricultural history.

In another approach to centering women in the study of agricultural history, Claire Robertson investigated the cultivation and marketing of varieties of beans in Kenya. She found that despite the centrality of beans to good nutrition and to women's budgets, they were "often as invisible and taken for granted as the woman farmer and her labor . . . a fate commensurate with their status as a women's crop among the Kikuyu and other peoples."[80] Beans also had symbolic importance, and Robertson suggests that the displacement of beans by maize as a primary food crop was related to the degradation of local religions. Attention to women's fields and women's crops has the potential to transform African agricultural history, just as regard for women's organizations has changed African political history.

Gender and Masculinity

Although most of the work cited here assumes a gender distinction based on the biological differences between male and female humans, this approach has also been critiqued. Oyeronke Oyewumi compared Yoruba (Nigeria) ideas about gender with Western constructs, and concluded that Yoruba culture does not view the world through the lens of biology that groups all people into "female" and "male" categories. Instead people are classified by age and by their relationship to those around them—there are parents, children, and siblings, but not mothers, daughters, and sisters.[81] Although it appears that people in most African societies do recognize distinction in social roles as being derived from biological differences, her findings caution all researchers to be wary of assumptions about social and biological identities.

Recently work has expanded on gender and masculinity, as in Burke's recent examination of ideas about consumption and cleanliness in Zimbabwe and Luise White's reexamination of Mau Mau and gender.[82] Dorothy Hodgson's publications on Maasai gender issues have expanded the field as well, in particular as she has investigated changes in relations between men and women under colonialism. One major shift she discusses is how women came to be seen as "possessions" who were "owned" by men. Earlier evidence indicated that women and men had held complementary responsibilities that came to be spatially separated under British colonialism, resulting in the development of a particular form of patriarchy. This gender formation was not inherent in the pastoral social economy as is sometimes suggested, but was specifically related to historical changes under colonialism.[83]

One of the issues continuing to be debated is that of representation. Discussion about who is writing this history and for what audience can be quite contentious, despite the growing numbers of African women historians and the developing self-awareness of non-African men and women who are writing histories of African women.[84] All of these developments and controversies can only contribute to the expansion and improvement of our knowledge about African women's history. The use of the varied methodologies discussed in this chapter has helped retrieve previously obscured aspects of African history, especially related to women and gender, by reexamining territory already covered and opening new topics. The infusion of history with the voices of African women as scholars and subjects indicates the direction African women's history will take in the near future.

Notes

1. A small part of this chapter previously appeared in Kathleen Sheldon, "Women's History: Africa," *Encyclopedia of Historians and Historical Writing*, Kelly Boyd, ed. (London: Fitzroy Dearborn Publishers, 1999), 1308–11.

2. For a detailed discussion of these issues in South African historiography, see Linzi Manicom, "Ruling Relations: Rethinking State and Gender in South African History," *Journal of African History* 33 (1992): 441–65.

3. For example, see the contributions to Denise Paulme, ed., *Women in Tropical Africa* (Berkeley: University of California Press, 1963; originally published as *Femmes d'Afrique noir* [Paris: Mouton, 1960]); E. Dora Earthy, *Valenge Women: The Social and Economic Life of the Valenge Women of Portuguese East Africa* (1933; reprinted, London: Frank Cass, 1968); Sylvia Leith-Ross, *African Women: A Study of the Ibo of Nigeria* (London: Faber and Faber, 1939); and M. F. Smith, *Baba of Karo: A Woman of the Muslim Hausa* (New York: Philosophical Library, 1955). For an interesting set of essays analyzing the work of that generation of women researchers, see Shirley Ardener, ed., *Persons and Powers of Women in Diverse Cultures: Essays in Commemoration of Audrey I. Richards, Phyllis Kaberry and Barbara E. Ward* (Providence, RI: Berg, 1992).

4. *Canadian Journal of African Studies* 6, 2 (1972); *African Studies Review* 28, 3 (1975); Nancy J. Hafkin and Edna G. Bay, eds., *Women in Africa: Studies in Social and Economic Change* (Stanford, Stanford University Press, 1976).

5. Nina Mba, *Nigerian Women Mobilized: Women's Political Activity in Southern Nigeria, 1900–1965* (Berkeley: Institute of International Studies, University of California, 1982); Claire C. Robertson, *Sharing the Same Bowl: A Socioeconomic History of Women and Class in Accra, Ghana* (Bloomington: Indiana University Press, 1984); Margaret Strobel, *Muslim Women in Mombasa: 1890–1975* (New Haven, Conn.: Yale University Press, 1976).

6. Kristin Mann, *Marrying Well: Marriage, Status, and Social Change Among the Educated Elite in Colonial Lagos* (New York, 1985); Luise White, *The Comforts of Home: Prostitution in Colonial Nairobi* (Chicago: University of Chicago Press, 1990).

7. Tiyambe Zeleza has provided a very helpful discussion of how women have been omitted from traditional African histories (or included in the most perfunctory ways): "Gender Biases in African Historiography," in *Engendering African Social Sciences*, ed. Ayesha M. Imam, Amina Mama, and Fatou Sow, 81–116 (Dakar: CODESRIA, 1997).

8. Helen Bradford, "Women, Gender and Colonialism: Rethinking the History of the British Cape Colony and Its Frontier Zones, c. 1806–70," *Journal of African History* 37 (1996): 351–70, Bundy reference on 351; Colin Bundy, *The Rise and Fall of the South African Peasantry* (London, 1988). This is not to single out Bundy as being especially neglectful; he is simply one example among dozens of possibilities.

9. Such a history can be found in Iris Berger and E. Frances White, *Women in Sub-Saharan Africa: Restoring Women to History* (Bloomington: Indiana University Press, 1999). There are several essays that assess the direction of African women's history: Margaret Jean Hay, "Queens, Prostitutes, and Peasants: Historical Perspectives on African Women," *Canadian Journal of African Studies* 22, 3 (1988): 431–47; Nancy Rose Hunt, "Placing African Women's History and Locating Gender," *Social History* 14 (1989): 359–79; Ayesha Mei-Tie Imam, "The Presentation of African Women in Historical Writing," in *Retrieving Women's History: Changing Perceptions of the Role of Women in Politics and Society*, ed. S. Jay Kleinberg, 30–40 (Providence, RI: Berg/UNESCO, 1988); Claire Robertson,

"Developing Economic Awareness: Changing Perspectives in Studies of African Women, 1976–1985," *Feminist Studies* 13, 1 (Spring 1987): 97–135; Claire Robertson, "Never Underestimate the Power of Women: The Transforming Vision of African Women's History," *Women's Studies International Forum* 11, 5 (1988): 439–53; Margaret Strobel, "African Women," *Signs* 8, 1 (Fall 1982): 109–31; and Zenebeworke Tadesse, "Breaking the Silence and Broadening the Frontiers of History: Recent Studies on African Women," in Kleinberg, ed., *Retrieving Women's History*, 356–64. There are also sources focused on specific countries, such as Iris Berger, "'Beasts of Burden' Revisited: Interpretations of Women and Gender in Southern African Societies," in *Paths Toward the Past: African Historical Essays in Honor of Jan Vansina*, ed. Robert W. Harms, Joseph C. Miller, David S. Newbury, and Michele D. Wagner (Atlanta: African Studies Association Press, 1994), 123–41; and Penelope Hetherington, "Women in South Africa: The Historiography in English," *International Journal of African Historical Studies* 26, 2 (1993): 242–69. I will not be discussing guides to research that are directed at anthropologists or other nonhistorians, though they have much useful advice regarding fieldwork. Nor will I be addressing philosophical problems in feminist research in Africa; among many provocative sources, see Marjorie Mbilinyi, "Research Methodologies in Gender Issues," and other essays in *Gender in Southern Africa: Conceptual and Theoretical Issues*, ed. Ruth Meena (Harare: SAPES Books, 1992).

10. Christine Ahmed, "Before Eve was Eve: 2200 Years of Gendered History in East-Central Africa," Ph.D. diss., University of California, Los Angeles, 1996.

11. David L. Schoenbrun, "Gendered Histories Between the Great Lakes: Varieties and Limits," *International Journal of African Historical Studies* 29, 3 (1996): 461–92.

12. The best overview is Susan Kent, ed., *Gender in African Prehistory* (Walnut Creek, Calif.: Alta Mira Press, 1998).

13. For a useful discussion of some of these debates, see David Beach, "Cognitive Archaeology and Imaginary History at Great Zimbabwe," followed by comments by others, *Current Anthropology* 39, 1 (1998): 47–72.

14. Heidi J. Nast, "Islam, Gender, and Slavery in West Africa Circa 1500: A Spatial Archaeology of the Kano Palace, Northern Nigeria," *Annals of the Association of American Geographers* 86, 1 (March 1996): 44–77. She also addresses these issues and uses this methodology in "Engendering 'Space': State Formation and the Restructuring of the Kano Palace Following the Islamic Holy War in Northern Nigeria," *Historical Geography* 23 (1993): 62–75; and in "The Impact of British Imperialism on the Landscape of Female Slavery in the Palace of Kano, Northern Nigeria, 1903–1990," *Africa* 64 (1994): 34–73.

15. Marla C. Berns, "Art, History, and Gender: Women and Clay in West Africa," *African Archaeological Review* 11 (1993): 129–48.

16. Joseph Miller, "Nzinga of Matamba in a New Perspective," *Journal of African History* 16, 2 (1975): 201–16; John Thornton, "Legitimacy and Political Power: Queen Njinga, 1624–1663," *Journal of African History* 32 (1991): 25–40.

17. John K. Thornton, *The Kongolese Saint Anthony: Dona Beatriz Kimpa Vita and the Antonian Movement, 1684–1706* (Cambridge: Cambridge University Press, 1998).

18. George Brooks, Jr., "The *Signares* of Saint-Louis and Gorée: Women Entrepreneurs of Eighteenth-Century Senegal," in Hafkin and Bay, eds., *Women in Africa*, 19–44.

19. Agnes Aidoo, "Asante Queen Mothers in Government and Politics in the Nineteenth Century," in *The Black Woman Cross-Culturally*, ed. Filomina Chioma Steady

(Cambridge, Mass.: Shenkman, 1981); Ivor Wilks, "She Who Blazed a Trail: Akyaawa Yikwan of Asante," in *Life Histories of African Women*, ed. Patricia W. Romero, 113–39 (Atlantic Highlands, NJ: Ashfield Press, 1988).

20. E. Frances White, *Sierra Leone's Settler Women Traders: Women on the Afro-European Frontier* (Ann Arbor: University of Michigan Press, 1987).

21. Julia Wells, "Eva's Men: Gender and Power in the Establishment of the Cape of Good Hope, 1652–74," *Journal of African History* 39 (1999): 417–37.

22. All quotes from sources cited in Wells, "Eva's Men," 417.

23. Thornton, *The Kongolese Saint Anthony*, 3.

24. Nakanyike B. Musisi, "Women, 'Elite Polygyny,' and Buganda State Formation," *Signs* 16, 4 (1991): 757–86, comment on sources, p. 761–62.

25. Musisi, "Women, 'Elite Polygyny.'"

26. R. A. Sargent, "Found in the Fog of the Male Myth: Analysing Female Political Roles in Pre-Colonial Africa," *Canadian Oral History Society Journal* 11 (1991): 39–44, quotes on 42.

27. Oyeronke Oyewumi, "Making History, Creating Gender: Some Methodological and Interpretive Questions in the Writing of Oyo Oral Traditions," *History in Africa* 25 (1998): 263–305.

28. Suzanne Preston Blier, *The Royal Arts of Africa: The Majesty of Form* (New York: Harry R. Abrams, 1998): 22; other images and discussion on 14, 35, 48, 85, 137, 185, 188, 220–21, and 246.

29. Flora S. Kaplan, "Fragile Legacy: Photographs as Documents in Recovering Political and Cultural History at the Royal Court of Benin," *History in Africa* 18 (1991): 205–37.

30. Edna G. Bay, *Wives of the Leopard: Gender, Politics, and Culture in the Kingdom of Dahomey* (Charlottesville: University of Virginia Press, 1998), xi; see also her earlier "Servitude and Worldly Success in the Palace of Dahomey," in *Women and Slavery in Africa*, ed. Claire C. Robertson and Martin Klein, 340–67 (Madison: University of Wisconsin Press, 1983).

31. Flora Edouwaye S. Kaplan, ed., *Queens, Queen Mothers, Priestesses, and Power: Case Studies in African Gender*, Annals of the New York Academy of Sciences Vol. 810 (New York: New York Academy of Sciences, 1997), xxxi. Most of the earlier sources were written by anthropologists, for example, E. J. Krige and J. D. Krige, *The Realm of the Rain-Queen: A Study of the Pattern of Lovedu Society* (London: Oxford University Press, 1943).

32. Susan Geiger, "Women's Life Histories: Method and Content," *Signs* 11, 2 (1986): 334–51; and essays in the Personal Narratives Group, *Interpreting Women's Lives: Feminist Theory and Personal Narratives* (Bloomington: Indiana University Press, 1989).

33. Among those examples that also discuss the methodology used, see Marjorie Mbilinyi, "'I'd Have Been A Man': Politics and the Labor Process in Producing Personal Narratives," in Personal Narratives Group, *Interpreting Women's Lives*, 204–27; and Sarah Mirza and Margaret Strobel, eds., *Three Swahili Women: Life Histories from Mombasa, Kenya* (Bloomington: Indiana University Press, 1989).

34. Claire Robertson, "In Pursuit of Life Histories: The Problem of Bias," *Frontiers* 7, 2 (1983): 63–69; and Robertson, *Sharing the Same Bowl*.

35. Christine Obbo, "What Do Women Know? . . . As I Was Saying!" in *Oral Narrative Research with Black Women*, ed., Kim Marie Vaz, 41–63 (Thousand Oaks, Calif.: Sage, 1997).

36. Francesca Declich, "'Gendered Narratives,' History, and Identity: Two Centuries along the Juba River among the Zigula and Shanbara," *History in Africa* 22 (1995): 93–122.

37. Nakanyike B. Musisi, "A Personal Journey into Custom, Identity, Power, and Politics: Researching and Writing the Life and Times of Buganda's Queen Mother Irene Drusilla Namaganda (1896–1957)," *History in Africa* 23 (1996): 369–85. See also Sondra Hale, "Feminist Method, Process, and Self-Criticism: Interviewing Sudanese Women," in *Women's Words: The Feminist Practice of Oral History*, ed., Sherna Berger Gluck and Daphne Patai, 121–36 (New York: Routledge, 1991); and Jane Turrittin, "Aoua Kéita and the Nascent Women's Movement in the French Soudan," *African Studies Review* 36, 1 (1993): 59–89. Kéita wrote an autobiography, *Femme d'Afrique* (Paris: Présence Africaine, 1975), available only in French, which provides a great deal of detail about women, politics, and the family during the colonial period in French West Africa.

38. Onaiwu W. Ogbomo, "Oral Field Techniques and Women's History: The Case of Owan, Nigeria," *Ufahamu* 22, 3 (Fall 1994): 7–25, quote on page 11.

39. Leroy Vail and Landeg White, "The Possession of the Dispossessed: Songs as History among Tumbuka Women," in Vail and White, eds., *Power and the Praise Poem: Southern African Voices in History*, 231–77 (Charlottesville: University Press of Virginia, 1991).

40. Heidi Gengenbach, "Where Women Make History: Pots, Stories, Tattoos, and other Gendered Accounts of Community and Change in Magude District, Mozambique, c. 1800 to the Present," Ph.D. dissertation, University of Minnesota, 1999.

41. Mary C. Bill, "Refusal to Eat and Drink: A Metaphor for 'Safe Sex' in Tsonga Folktales," *African Languages and Cultures* 7, 1 (1994): 49–77.

42. Sharifa M. Zawawi, "Cloth and the Message among the Waswahili," paper presented at the Annual Meeting of the African Studies Association, Denver, Col., November 1987, p. 4.

43. Kathleen Sheldon, "Working Women in Beira, Mozambique," Ph.D. dissertation, University of California, Los Angeles, 1988.

44. Marcia Wright, "Technology, Marriage and Women's Work in the History of Maize-Growers in Mazabuka, Zambia: A Reconnaissance," *Journal of Southern African Studies* 10, 1 (October 1983): 71–85.

45. Barbara M. Cooper, *Marriage in Maradi: Gender and Culture in a Hausa Society in Niger, 1900–1989* (Portsmouth, NH: Heinemann, 1997), xvii. And see Cooper's contribution (chapter 7) to this volume.

46. Kenda Mutongi, "'Worries of the Heart': Widowed Mothers, Daughters and Masculinities in Maragoli, Western Kenya, 1940–60," *Journal of African History* 40 (1999): 67–86.

47. Colleen Kriger, "Textile Production and Gender in the Sokoto Caliphate," *Journal of African History* 34 (1993): 361–401.

48. Jean and John L. Comaroff, "Home-Made Hegemony: Modernity, Domesticity, and Colonialism in South Africa," in Karen Tranberg Hansen, ed., *African Encounters with Domesticity* (New Brunswick, NJ: Rutgers University Press, 1992), 37–74.

49. Heidi Gengenbach, "Boundaries of Beauty: Tattooed Secrets of Women's History in Southern Mozambique," paper presented at the African Studies Association Annual Meeting, Chicago, Illinois, October 1998.

50. Elizabeth A. Eldredge, "Women in Production: The Economic Role of Women in Nineteenth-Century Lesotho," *Signs* 16, 4 (1991): 707–31.

51. Edward A. Alpers, "'Ordinary Household Chores': Ritual and Power in a Nineteenth-Century Swahili Women's Spirit Possession Cult," *International Journal of African Historical Studies* 17, 4 (1984): 677–702.

52. Jean Boyd and Murray Last, "The Role of Women as 'Agents Religieux' in Sokoto," *Canadian Journal of African Studies* 19, 2 (1985): 283–300.

53. Bennetta Jules-Rosette, ed., *The New Religions of Africa* (Norwood, NJ: 1979).

54. Iris Berger, "Fertility as Power: Spirit Mediums, Priestesses and the Pre-colonial State in Interlacustrine East Africa," in *Revealing Prophets: Prophecy in Eastern African History*, ed. David M. Johnson and Douglas H. Anderson (London: James Currey, 1995), 65–82.

55. Marcia Wright, "Women in Peril: A Commentary on the Life Stories of Captives in Nineteenth-Century East Central Africa," *African Social Research* 20 (1975): 800–819.

56. Claire Robertson and Martin Klein, eds., *Women and Slavery in Africa* (Madison: University of Wisconsin Press, 1983, reissued, Portsmouth, NH: Heinemann, 1997).

57. For example, see Achola Pala Okeyo, "Daughters of the Lakes and Rivers: Colonization and the Land Rights of Luo Women," 186–213, and Mona Etienne, "Women and Men, Cloth and Colonization: The Transformation of Production-Distribution Relations among the Baule (Ivory Coast)," 214–38, both in *Women and Colonization: Anthropological Perspectives*, ed. Mona Etienne and Eleanor Leacock (New York: Praeger, 1980).

58. Martin Chanock, "Making Customary Law: Men, Women, and Courts in Colonial Northern Rhodesia," in *African Women and the Law: Historical Perspectives*, ed. Margaret Jean Hay and Marcia Wright (Boston: African Studies Center, Boston University, 1983).

59. This special issue includes an introductory essay by Dorothy L. Hodgson and Sheryl McCurdy, "Wayward Wives, Misfit Mothers, and Disobedient Daughters: 'Wicked' Women and the Reconfiguration of Gender in Africa," *Canadian Journal of African Studies* 30, 1 (1996): 1–9; see also Jean Allman, "Rounding Up Spinsters: Gender Chaos and Unmarried Women in Colonial Asante," *Journal of African History* 37 (1996): 195–214.

60. Margaret Jean Hay, "Luo Women and Economic Change During the Colonial Period," in Hafkin and Bay, eds., *Women in Africa*, 87–109; Maud Shimwaayi Muntemba, "Women and Agricultural Change in the Railway Region of Zambia: Dispossession and Counterstrategies, 1930–1970, in *Women and Work in Africa*, ed. Edna Bay (Boulder, Col.: Westview, 1982); and Sherilynn Young, "Fertility and Famine: Women's Agricultural History in Southern Mozambique," in *The Roots of Rural Poverty in Central and Southern Africa*, ed. Robin Palmer and Neil Parsons, 66–81 (Berkeley: University of California Press, 1977).

61. Cora Ann Presley, "Labor Unrest among Kikuyu Women in Colonial Kenya," in *Women and Class in Africa*, ed. Claire Robertson and Iris Berger, 255–73 (New York: Holmes and Meier, 1986).

62. Cheryl Johnson, "Class and Gender: A Consideration of Yoruba Women during the Colonial Period," in Robertson and Berger, eds., *Women and Class in Africa*, 237–54.

63. Jane L. Parpart, "Sexuality and Power on the Zambian Copperbelt: 1926–1964," in *Patriarchy and Class: African Women in the Home and the Workforce*, ed. Sharon B. Stichter and Jane L. Parpart (Boulder, Col.: Westview, 1988).

64. Sean Redding, "South African Women and Migration in Umtata, Transkei, 1880–1935," in *Courtyards, Markets, City Streets: Urban Women in Africa*, ed. Kathleen Sheldon (Boulder, Col.: Westview, 1996*)*, 31–46.

65. Shula Marks, ed., *Not Either an Experimental Doll: The Separate Worlds of Three South African Women* (Bloomington: Indiana University Press, 1987); also see her essay on the process of writing the book, "The Context of Personal Narrative: Reflections on '*Not Either an Experimental Doll'—The Separate Worlds of Three South African Women*, in Personal Narratives Group, *Interpreting Women's Lives*, 39–58.

66. Catherine M. Coles, "Three Generations of Hausa Women in Kaduna, Nigeria, 1925–1985," in Sheldon, ed., *Courtyards, Markets, City Streets*, 73–102.

67. Margaret Strobel, *European Women and the Second British Empire* (Bloomington: Indiana University Press, 1991).

68. Yvonne Knibiehler and Régine Goutalier, *"Femmes et Colonisation": Rapport terminal au Ministère des Relations Extérieures et de la Coopération* (Aix-en-Provence: Université de Provence, 1986), 8–11.

69. Ghislaine Lydon, "The Unraveling of a Neglected Source: A Report on Women in Francophone West Africa in the 1930s," *Cahiers d'Études Africaines* 37, 3 (1997): 555–84. The document she discusses is Denise Moran Savineau's "La famille en AOF: condition le la femme." Barbara Cooper brought this article to my attention.

70. LaRay Denzer, *Folayegbe Akintunde-Ighodalo: A Public Life* (Ibadan: Sam Bookman, 2001).

71. For example, see the articles in Hansen, ed., *African Encounters with Domesticity*; and in Sheldon, ed., *Courtyards, Markets, City Streets*.

72. Helen Bradford, "Women, Gender and Colonialism," especially 360–68.

73. Judith Van Allen, " 'Aba Riots' or Igbo 'Women's War'? Ideology, Stratification, and the Invisibility of Women," in Hafkin and Bay, eds., *Women in Africa*, 59–85.

74. Tabitha Kanogo, "Kikuyu Women and the Politics of Protest: Mau Mau," in *Images of Women in Peace and War: Cross-Cultural and Historical Perspectives*, ed. Sharon Macdonald, Pat Holden, and Shirley Ardener (Cambridge, UK: Macmillan Education, 1987); and Cora Ann Presley, *Kikuyu Women, the 'Mau Mau' Rebellion, and Social Change in Kenya* (Boulder, Col.: Westview, 1991).

75. D. N. Beach, "An Innocent Woman, Unjustly Accused? Charwe, Medium of the Nehanda Mhondoro Spirit, and the 1896–97 Central Shona Rising in Zimbabwe," *History in Africa* 25 (1998): 27–54, discusses the events as well as the variety of interpretations that scholars and activists have attached to this woman's actions.

76. Susan Geiger, "Women in Nationalist Struggle: TANU Activists in Dar es Salaam," *International Journal of African Historical Studies* 20, 1 (1987): 1–26.

77. Susan Geiger, *TANU Women: Gender and Culture in the Making of Tanganyikan Nationalism, 1955–1965* (Portsmouth, NH: Heinemann, 1997), 6; see also Susan Geiger, "Tanganyikan Nationalism as 'Women's Work': Life Histories, Collective Biography and Changing Historiography," *Journal of African History* 37 (1996): 465–78.

78. Jane I. Guyer, "Female Farming in Anthropology and African History," in *Gender at the Crossroads of Knowledge: Feminist Anthropology in the Postmodern Era*, ed., Micaela di Leonardo (Berkeley: University of California Press, 1991), 257–77, quote on 267. The lack of attention to female farming in Africa has often been lamented, and existing statistics are woefully incomplete. A few of the many sources (mostly not by historians) include Ruth Dixon, "Seeing the Invisible Women Farmers in Africa: Improving

Research and Data Collection Methods," in *Women as Food Producers in Developing Countries*, ed. Jamie Monson and Marion Kalb (Los Angeles: UCLA African Studies Center, 1985), 19–36; Anita Spring, "Women Farmers and Food in Africa: Some Considerations and Suggested Solutions," in *Food in Sub-Saharan Africa*, ed. Art Hansen and Della E. McMillan (Boulder, Col.: Lynne Rienner, 1986), 332–48; and Kathleen Staudt, "Uncaptured or Unmotivated? Women and the Food Crisis in Africa," *Rural Sociology* 52, 1 (1987): 37–55.

79. Louise Fortmann, "Gendered Knowledge: Rights and Space in Two Zimbabwe Villages; Reflections on Methods and Findings," in *Feminist Political Ecology: Global Issues and Local Experiences*, ed. Dianne Rocheleau, Barbara Thomas-Slayter, and Esther Wangari, 211–23 (New York: Routledge, 1996).

80. Claire C. Robertson, "Black, White, and Red All Over: Beans, Women, and Agricultural Imperialism in Twentieth-Century Kenya," *Agricultural History* 71, 3 (1997): 259–99, quote on 259. She also presents this material in *Trouble Showed the Way: Women, Men, and Trade in the Nairobi Area, 1890–1990* (Bloomington: Indiana University Press, 1997).

81. Oyeronke Oyewumi, *The Invention of Women: Making an African Sense of Western Gender Discourses* (Minneapolis: University of Minnesota Press, 1997).

82. Timothy Burke, *Lifebuoy Men, Lux Women: Commodification, Consumption, and Cleanliness in Modern Zimbabwe* (Durham, NC: Duke University Press, 1996); Luise White, "Separating the Men from the Boys: Constructions of Gender, Sexuality, and Terrorism in Central Kenya, 1939–1959," *International Journal of African Historical Studies* 23, 1 (1990): 1–25; and Mutongi, " 'Worries of the Heart.' "

83. Dorothy L. Hodgson, "Pastoralism, Patriarchy and History: Changing Gender Relations among Maasai in Tanganyika, 1890–1940," *Journal of African History* 40 (1999): 41–65. For an overview of gender studies in Africa, see Nancy Rose Hunt, "Introduction," *Gender & History* 8, 3 (1996): 323–37, special issue on "Gendered Colonialisms in African History."

84. Shireen Hassim and Cherryl Walker discuss this in "Women's Studies and the Women's Movement in South Africa: Defining a Relationship," *Women's Studies International Forum* 16, 5 (1993): 523–34; see also Sondra Hale, "Some Thoughts on Women and Gender in Africa: Listening to the Whispers of African Women," *Journal of African Studies* 16, 1 (1998): 21–30; and Tiyambe Zeleza's comments in his extended book review, "Gendering African History," *Africa Development* 18, 1 (1993): 99–117.

PART IV

Conclusion

20

WRITING AFRICAN HISTORY

John Edward Philips

Academic writing should be organized logically, as this chapter is. Academic research, on the other hand, is part of life, and therefore is not logically organized by nature, however much researchers might wish it were. Although we try to organize our research logically, we have to gather data whenever, wherever, and however we can. Thus we must be ready to modify our research and writing plans according to contingency, and always be ready to improvise.

Researchers put order into the confusion of information we have gathered from various sources at various times, in order to tell a story from, or answer a question with, that information in ways that make sense to readers and listeners. This chapter is organized logically, to explain the stages of data collection and presentation in a logical order, but in fact the logic of real life research is rarely so neat and tidy.[1] Instead, each stage blends into another, overlapping, with unexpected gaps and breaks throughout the process. At any moment the researcher must be ready and willing to jump into any other stage of research and writing, whether in logical sequence or not.

Scholarly research in any field involves collection of data, analysis of those data according to an algorithm or method, and derivation of conclusions based on methodical analysis of the data. This is true whether the field is English literature or astrophysics. The data are not necessarily facts, of course. If one works in literature, one's data are fiction, not the facts that are the obsession of the historian. Nonetheless, even when the methods, data, and purposes of research are different in different fields, the basic process is the same.

The logical order of research is also the same: decide on a topic, gather data, evaluate the data, organize the data and, finally, write up the results. But of course the actual process of producing history is more complicated and messy, and the chronological order of the stages is almost always very mixed, rarely following this logical order exactly.

Because natural scientists use generally accepted methods, they can expect re-analysis or reproduction of the same data to produce the same conclusions, a process referred to as *replication* and an important means of testing scientific findings. On the other hand, although certain historical methods, such as source criticism, are generally accepted, different historians using the same data may come to radically different conclusions. Much, though by no means all, historical research involves testing hypotheses to see if they can be falsified through the gathering of factual data, yet the production of historical literature remains as much art as science. To speak of historical "methods" rather than of "method" may be more accurate, for different historians will evaluate evidence differently, even if a core of shared assumptions still unites historians in a common discourse, whatever their disagreements about the events of the past and the effects of those events on subsequent events.

It is important to keep in mind what the term *data* means, and how it differs from *knowledge* and *information*.[2] Data is a Latin plural word, although English-speakers often forget its plural nature and use it in a collective sense. Its singular form is "datum" and its literal meaning is "given." Thus in French it is translated literally from Latin as *les donées*, or "the givens." In history data are any existing sources about the past. Data exist out there—to be discovered, interpreted and given meaning by human historians. Information is processed data, organized and put into a useful form by human action: the interface between data and knowledge. Knowledge exists in human brains, since manuscripts, databases, and even computers cannot think.

All three terms are relative, of course. Oral historical data are other people's knowledge that we access as data to create information. Secondary sources are knowledge that a historian has turned into information, thus making it also data for further research. Most useful data are also information, so that the terms "data" and "information" are often used interchangeably, even by specialists in information science. But the distinction between data and information can be important. All the written data collected in the ancient Meroitic script will never be information until someone develops the ability to read the Meroitic language.

As Susan Macintosh has pointed out in chapter 2, data are perhaps better thought of as "capta" since they are not "given" so much as "taken." We can't make them up of course, since that would amount to fraud. We do have to find them, though, and the search for data, the work of accessing and "taking" data, is often the most difficult and time-consuming aspect of writing history.

Data are "capta" in another sense. The Latin word "captus" or "capta" (the masculine and feminine singular form of the words, respectively) could mean "slave." Data are tools we use to construct historical literature about the past. We cannot use them to do anything beyond their natural limits, any more than a Roman slave owner could have ordered his human property to fly like a bird. Neither are they our property alone, since, as David Henige pointed out in chapter 6, they should be available to all researchers, so that our conclusions can be tested for plausibility and probability. Nevertheless, we take data from sources so that we can use them to construct historical narratives. We must put them to work. Without them we could construct history from nothing but our own memory.

Accessing data about the past to create information with which to create historical literature in order to spread knowledge about the past is what historical research is all about. Let us examine that process in more detail.

Choosing a Topic

The logical first step of any research is to decide the topic. What is it we want to find out? We may want to solve some historical problem, we may have a question to answer, or perhaps we just want to know what the real story was. The question or problem or story may already be on our minds, or on the minds of others, whether the general public or a funding agency. The topic may have been suggested to us by a curious student, or by previous research we have done. A teacher or colleague who no longer had time to carry out all the necessary research may have suggested it to us. In a reverse pattern, many historians have researched a particular topic simply because they found material in the available sources that told a good story or answered an important question. However we have come to history, our curiosity about the past has brought us to it.

Whether originating in a problem to be solved, a question to be answered or a story to be told (and most history is a little bit of all three) research about the past, like any research, boils down to questions we want answered. We want to find information and pass it on to others, in whatever form we find most appropriate. Some form of the journalist's questions—Who? What? When? Where? Why? and How?—should always be at the back of our minds as we gather data from sources.[3]

History is always about people, and therefore "Who?" is an important question for research, and biography is a major genre in popular historical writing. Even when the topic is primarily a particular individual it can help us to keep a list of the most important characters in their life story, so that we can track what they were doing through time. This technique is especially useful with a complicated story involving a number of characters over a number of years, but no matter how many characters there are in the story, "Who?" is always a vital question.

What happened is almost as important as to whom it happened (or who did it), but we must answer more than merely "What happened?" or even "What details are important?" even though we do have to decide what to leave in and what to take out. To decide what is important we first must decide the meaning of the story, which sometimes cannot be identified until we have finished our research and begun to write it up. Therefore, gathering more data than we will finally need is safer than risking the possibility of having gathered too little. Recognizing the meaning of the story can also help locate the climax, so it can go at the appropriate place in our narrative.

Different sources will contradict each other, so to answer the question "What happened?" we must decide which sources are most likely to be accurate. Also, if we want our readers to trust us, we must give them access to information that may contradict our conclusions. We must keep in mind alternative plausible explanations, even as we seek for the most likely explanation. Knowing the difficulty of proving anything about the past, which no one can revisit, should help us respect the reconstructions others make of the past, no matter how much theirs differs from ours.

"When?" is another critical question. Chronology is one task of the historian not because it is the basic task of historians to fix dates to events and persons but because chronology is critical to arguing (if not necessarily proving) causation, as explained in the first chapter. Furthermore, although not all history books and articles are organized on strict chronological lines, many of them are, and most of them have major parts that are chronological. Events also unfold in chronological order, even if no one learns about them in exactly that way, because human beings exist in space as well as in time. Thus constructing a timeline can also help us in doing research, but it is also good to remember that events unfold in space as well as time. Distance and geography have their own influences. "Where?" can be as critical a question as "When?"—or perhaps they are the same question, time being simply another dimension in the space-time continuum. We can't travel in time to experience the past, but we can travel in space to see where it happened. Sometimes pacing out an old battlefield, or walking around an old palace, can help us understand the past as the people of the past experienced it themselves in those very same places at some other time. Fieldwork is considered an important part of African history, but African history it is not the only field of history where fieldwork can be an important part of research.[4]

"Why?" is one of the hardest questions, and one of the most critical. Causation is what makes history different from mere chronology. But causation is not a simple matter. The characters in our story had their own ideas of causation, and even when they left written memoirs they may not have been honest (even to themselves) about their personal motivations, which are only one aspect of causation. Social science has given us more and more information about causation, and the relationship between the social sciences and history is mutually beneficial. We historians must do our best to keep up with the latest social science research to know what theories might be relevant to our own research and interpretations.

The "How?" question is related to the "Why?" question, and may help to answer it. If we can understand the processes by which events unfolded in real time in the past, that understanding may help us to explain them. This involves unraveling the interlocking and interacting threads of events that are taking place in different places all the time everywhere. Finding their connections, the effects they had on each other, can help us to understand causation more easily than simply asking "Why?"

All of these questions interlock and overlap, influencing each other. *What* is important in our story helps tell us *who* is important in it. After all, each person is the center of his or her own life, but some are more important in the story we are writing. Figuring out causation can help us decide what is important, and both these questions can help us limit our study in time and space, helping to answer the "When?" and "Where?" questions for us. Reality, including past, present and future in all places, is actually a seamless, interacting web, the complete understanding of which is beyond human intelligence. But eventually we should be able to find enough information to generate a coherent, plausible answer to a particular question or group of related questions about the past that have been on our mind, or just to be able to tell an interesting story that is worth reading. At that point all the relevant data should be organized and used in a book, article, film, lecture, CD-ROM or other work of history to answer questions and/or tell a story about a given topic.

Data Collection

Once we have decided the topic of research and limited it to a workable size, we have to assemble all the evidence, from whatever sources we can find. "Pas de documents, pas d'histoire" is true if translated as "no sources, no history." We do not need "documents" in the sense of written records to write history, of course, but we do need some remains of the past, without which the past would be forever unknowable.

The sources we discover may suggest new questions to us. They may constrain our answers not only because they rule out certain possibilities and confirm others, but also because they do not provide answers to all the questions we can pose. Historians today are adept at asking new questions and teasing new information out of old sources to come up with new answers. Africanist historians in particular are famous for their use of new sources. All historians, Africanist or not, have a responsibility to avoid limiting their sources in any way. Instead historians must use as many sources as they can find as carefully as possible. A good detective tracks down every lead, even if the best detective cannot always find all the evidence he or she would like. Sometimes our sources determine our questions, instead of the other way around, or perhaps it would be better to say that there is a mutual dependence between our questions, the sources we find, our conclusions, and the histories we write. As we gather more data we are influenced by the data we have already found, and by the stories and hypotheses that we are forming about them in our mind.

No individual historian can gather and evaluate all the various types of evidence that have been discussed in this book. (That is one reason this book has been written by several specialists, rather than by a single individual.) But as historians we all need to use sources that we have not ourselves gathered, if only because we must be familiar with the relevant secondary sources in order to add our own contributions to the literature of history. African history, because it uses a greater range of sources than most other areas of history, requires a greater range of expertise from those who write it. A good historian, in any field, must be able to critically evaluate not only the raw source materials gathered with a variety of techniques by a variety of disciplines, but he or she must also be able to evaluate the use made of those materials by various other historians.

The first sources from which to gather information are usually secondary sources. We have to know what has already been written about our own and related topics. We have to know what questions have already been answered satisfactorily, what unanswered questions have been raised, what stories have already been well told, and what stories seem to be most promising for telling in the future. We have to get a sense of where our own research and writing will fit into the overall existing historiography. Much information can come from books and articles already written. There is little point in spending a lot of time doing research, only to find out that the information we collected was already common knowledge to other researchers. Reference works, such as encyclopedias, are therefore often the best places to start research.

We need to read secondary sources at least as critically as we read primary sources. We need to ask how and from where the information in them was obtained, and how reliable it is. We need to know what the authors' biases were, and how they might have affected their research and their interpretation of the information they and others discovered. Thus a historian will usually look at a history book differently from the way most of the reading public does. Most readers perhaps glance at the title page, then go straight to the narrative, maybe stopping to read the introduction or preface on the way. They are so averse to footnotes that popular histories often do not contain academic footnotes, and popular historians are forced to compromise the form of their citations between academic standards and the demand of the book market.

Trained historians, on the other hand, will often look at the back of the title page, to find the publication data. Who supported the publication of a work is often as important a question as what data were found in researching the book. In many cases, unfortunately, it can even determine not only what was said in the book but even what data were found and considered. The date of publication provides not only the historical context of the work, but gives a clue to what sources were available, and what perspectives were common. After finding out who wrote and published the book and when, a good historian will read the footnotes and the bibliography, to find out what sources this historian consulted, and how they know what they claim to be the facts of history. Unless history is based on the most reliable information from the broadest possible range of sources, it cannot represent the best possible reconstruction and explanation of the past.

Reading the notes is the first way a historian evaluates a fellow historian's work, but it is also how research is usually begun. By finding what sources other authors have consulted we can begin to build a research bibliography of both primary and secondary sources. Copying the bibliographies of available secondary sources onto notecards is the beginning of further research. Such a new bibliography will help us to identify the primary and secondary sources related to our topic. Online, searchable databases can now be used to supplement such bibliographies, and there are various published bibliographies that we should consult as well,[5] but there is no substitute for copying the bibliographies found in the secondary literature.

Consulting the notes of previous authors allows us to trace the supporting evidence they used in drawing their conclusions. While the secondary sources they use may help us identify the place their work occupies in the ongoing debates about the past, it is the primary sources they use which are ultimately the most important, not only for their arguments, but especially for our own research. Since secondary sources themselves are based on primary sources, it is usually best for us to find the primary sources, not only to evaluate the conclusions others have drawn from them, but to be able to come to original conclusions of our own.

Without consulting primary sources it is difficult to do original history. Of course important historical works have been written using nothing but secondary works, but such works are usually either popularizations or critiques of existing historical literature. To add information to the sum of historical knowledge in the world today usually requires research into primary sources. In the case of African history, this means finding data in public and private archives and libraries, in archaeological field reports and artifacts (the sites no longer exist as primary sources, having been destroyed by the process of excavation), in oral traditions and other oral historical accounts preserved in the minds of Africans, in African languages themselves, and anywhere else we can find data about the African past. We do not necessarily need to find new primary sources, because sometimes new information can be teased out of old ones by careful analysis. There is almost always something that some previous researcher missed in analyzing the data, or declined to use in writing up.

Data Evaluation—Turning Data into Facts

To test the data we have collected from such primary sources is the logical next step. Raw data must be evaluated and checked for reliability before they can be used as information in the historical reconstruction of the past. Since the past is unknowable even in the limited sense that we know the present, much less in an absolute sense, we can realistically apply to each datum only a relative probability, a likelihood that it actually verifies a fact about the past. In addition, we are likely to be confronted with contradictory evidence, even from the same source. In such cases we must try to decide which evidence, if any, is more reliable. Then we can usually generate a series of fairly reliable and more or less trustworthy facts with which we can begin to build a hypothesis about the past. This evaluation of the raw data enables us to use those data and thus learn facts about the past.

Archaeology and historical linguistics provide most of the primary evidence for history's earliest periods. Even in ancient Egypt, written documentation is only a few thousand years old, and in most of the rest of the continent it is far more recent. In more recent periods oral traditions survive, and for the very recent past first-person oral history is available. In addition, scientific methods can be used for specialized purposes, and at various time depths. Such methods can test the validity of archaeological and written documentation in particular.

Archaeological data are important, and have an air of objectivity about them that convinces many historians to accept the writings of archaeologists at face value. But archaeological data are still spotty for much of Africa, and what survives in the soil is only a small sample of what once existed. In recent years looting has often destroyed archaeological data before it was gathered and analyzed to produce information, and the information that could have been gained was thus lost forever. Even where excavations have been carried out, archaeologists are as likely as others to make mistakes. Knowing the air temperature and other weather conditions when a site was excavated is often helpful. Such variables can affect the quality of the notes taken about the artifacts found. And of course some artifacts survive better in the soil than others, and soils differ in their ability to preserve artifacts.

Historians who are not themselves archaeologists must learn to critically evaluate archaeological data, lest they jump to unsubstantiated conclusions. For example, some researchers into the history of cannabis use claimed that the earliest known use occurred in water pipes from fourteenth-century Ethiopia, since a water pipe with cannabis resin had been found in a cave in the Ethiopian highlands associated with a date of 1320 ± 80. This would have meant that smoking pipes were used for the consumption of cannabis centuries before the introduction of tobacco and pipes from the new world, and that the probable site of the origin of such smoking would have been in Ethiopia. This might have called into question the assumption of archaeologists working in West Africa that smoking pipes were evidence of a post-Columbian date. But by looking at the excavation report, I learned that the pipe was not directly associated with the date, but that both the pipe and the date were from a very disturbed layer, and were perhaps not related at all.[6] This called into question the conclusions that had been drawn from the date attributed to the pipe. Subsequent testing of the pipe, however, was able to provide a more reliable date directly from the residue in the pipe bowl, which did turn out to be consistent with an early date for cannabis smoking in Ethiopia. However, cannabis pipe bowls from eastern and southern Africa turned out to be water-pipe bowls of a different shape from the tobacco pipes introduced to West Africa during the slave trade. The water pipe bowls of eastern and southern Africa were not found in West Africa, where only tobacco pipe bowls, bent at an angle, were found. So the assumptions of archaeologists working in West Africa were confirmed, even though they could not be uncritically extended to other regions of Africa.[7]

Historical linguistic data analysis is a very recent and controversial method, although Greenberg's historical classification of African languages is now generally accepted. The correlation of linguistic and archaeological evidence is still very speculative, and can be upset by new findings in either field. There is no guarantee that people who used a common set of artifacts (and the only artifacts we can know about are those artifacts that may leave some trace in the archaeological record) necessarily spoke the same language, or that all the people who spoke the same language would have left similar collections of artifacts in the archaeological record. Languages and cultures are continuously evolving and interacting, and trade has been important in Africa for many centuries.

Language is an especially important source of data in and of itself, even without being correlated with other data from other sources. This is so because language is an important medium of thought and communication that expresses the way humans view and think about our world. It thus reflects not only the particular physical environment in which humans live and which they describe to each other in the course of their daily lives, but also the mental and social environment of those who use the language in question. It thus becomes a way to get inside the minds of the people of the past even more readily than can be done by using archaeological finds.[8]

Both archaeological and linguistic data share an important trait that is not always shared by oral traditions and written documents: they are evidence "in spite of themselves."[9] Archaeologists love to find rubbish pits, piles of garbage on the edges of settlements. These show what was used, and then thrown away, by people in the past. Because these people were not throwing away their garbage deliberately in order to leave a record for archaeologists in the future, we can be fairly certain that, if we analyze the finds properly, we have an objective record of what they were using in their daily lives. They were not placing articles on the pile just to fool us.

Alas, the same cannot always be said of written records. Although they can bring to life the words and thoughts of the individuals who wrote them (unlike historical linguistics, which can help to reconstruct only the collective physical, mental and social environments of the speakers of particular languages), written records are always created for specific purposes, even if they are often preserved by accident. Their purposes make their testimony less objective than that of the archaeological and linguistic evidence discussed above. The training of historians usually emphasizes the evaluation of written documents largely because it is often more difficult than the evaluation of some other types of evidence, requiring more skill on the part of the historian.

The great breakthrough of Ranke in the nineteenth century, which made history into the modern academic discipline it now is, was to emphasize those documents written for purposes other than to create historical literature. Instead of using memoirs and existing narrative histories, as previous historians had tended to do, Ranke as much as possible used primary sources that had not been created with an eye towards history, and were therefore created with less of a bias towards a particular interpretation. Such records allowed Ranke to reconstruct the past far more accurately than previous historians had done, and constituted a revolution in historical method.[10]

This is not to suggest that Ranke and his followers made all advances in the analysis of written documents. The evaluation of written documents by historians had already seen a number of advances since the Middle Ages. For example, documents that exist in multiple copies must be analyzed according to the relationship that each copy has to the others, in order to account for possible corruptions and additions in each. Furthermore, in 1681 Jean Mabillon published *De Re Diplomatica* [On Diplomatics],[11] a volume laying out methods for detecting forgeries of documents, especially charters and treaties. From then on historians could begin to separate out the more reliable documents from the forgeries, first on the basis of internal evidence such as vocabulary and style, and more recently on the basis of their physical material. For example, if an alleged eighteenth-century Islamic charter from Bornu or a medieval Ethiopian chronicle were found to have used ink or paper manufactured in the twentieth century, they could be dismissed as forgeries, although it is possible that they might be recent copies of old documents. The documents could not have been written before the ink and paper used to write them had been manufactured.

Evaluation of written documents involves more than the mere verification of authenticity. Biases are usually at least as important. Of course, written documents reflect the viewpoints of the literate members of society, but bias has more to it than that. What kinds of information did they record? Why was that particular information recorded and preserved? How did the author(s) of the document gain access to the information recorded? How would they know about it? How do we know they weren't making it up? People can be mistaken, or lie, as easily in authentic, contemporaneous documents as they can orally in person, sometimes more easily, because the written document might never have been read by anyone else who knew about the events being described. These and similar questions suggest plenty of opportunities for the creative use of the historian's intelligence, and a skeptical imagination. This part of source criticism is not yet an exact science, and probably never will be. It requires historians to think like detectives, which is what we often are, detectives who work on a case after the statute of limitations has run out.

What do we do if written sources contradict each other, as they often do? When linguistic or archaeological findings contradict each other the contradiction is often only apparent, not real. The archaeologists or linguists may be using different methods, such as different classification schemes, to organize and interpret their data. Thus an apparent contradiction between data sets may be only a contradiction of interpretation by specialists, which can be resolved by an informed scholar evaluating the data systematically or by collecting more information. Sooner or later a consensus will usually emerge among specialists. However, written records and oral traditions, because they record the observations of fallible and interested human beings, are much more likely to directly contradict each other. In such cases the historian should always recognize and record the existence and nature of their disagreement, but must also try to decide which source is more reliable, or perhaps just less unreliable. It may be the one recorded nearer in time, or space, to the events in question. It may be the one written by a disinterested outsider. It may be the one written by someone intimately involved in the events portrayed. It may be the one written by a direct eyewitness, or by someone who later interviewed a more reliable witness. A historian may have to combine the testimonies of several sources, and written and oral sources should always be interrogated by use of data from other sources, including physical as well as oral and linguistic evidence.

One famous example of contradictory written sources in African history is the alleged Songhay conquest of several of the Hausa states. It was described in detail by Leo Africanus, who wrote shortly after the time, and who had traveled in the Songhay empire, though not in the Hausa kingdoms themselves. Yet this purported conquest is mentioned in none of the chronicles written in the Hausa states, including the famous *Kano Chronicle*, an annotated king-list of unknown date, which is a major source for the history of Kano before the Sokoto Jihad of 1804. The *Kano Chronicle* had no hesitation about mentioning, even describing in detail, the many defeats Kano faced in its history, and the many times it was sacked. Reluctance to mention such a defeat is therefore not an adequate explanation for its failure to mention the Songhay conquest recorded by Leo Africanus.[12]

Some historians would trust Leo Africanus, since his account was written closer to the time. The *Kano Chronicle* was probably written centuries later when the Songhay conquest may not have been considered as important or traumatic as others.[13] Other historians would trust the *Kano Chronicle*, which was written closer in space. Surely historians from Kano would be expected to know their own city's history better than an outsider like Leo, who never visited the town at all. Even the famous Timbuktu chronicles mention only a brief Songhay campaign against Katsina. But comparing documents still requires a judgment call on the part of historians. By using data from other sources we can test these contradictory written documents for reliability.

The Hausa language contains many words for government and administration that were borrowed from Kanuri, the language of the Bornu Empire to the east of Hausaland. It contains few loanwords of any sort from Songhay, and almost none whatsoever for words related to government or administration.[14] Since no Hausa state has titles that it might have borrowed from Songhay, there is no linguistic evidence that anyone from the Songhay empire played a role in the government or administration of any Hausa state. Therefore we may confidently conclude that Leo Africanus was at best mistaken about Songhay rule in Hausaland. Probably, like Marco Polo more famously before him, he was credulously repeating stories he had heard, without bothering to verify them. Certainly his apparent mistake about the relations between Hausaland

and the Songhay Empire may call into question the reliability of his other information.

Oral traditions, like memoirs and narrative histories, were created to present particular interpretations of the past, and are thus much like secondary sources. They contain a bias; in fact they contain not only the biases of their original authors but the accumulated biases of their transmitters as well. As a form of folklore they have multiple authors, being continually recreated as they are transmitted from brain to mouth to ear, and on to another brain in the cycle known as the folk process. Historians who combine the methods of folklore with the methods of history can still use them. In fact, the application of modern historical methods to oral traditions, to interrogate them and to make them, as Marc Bloch famously said of written documents not created with one eye on history, "witnesses in spite of themselves"[15] is one of the main innovations that marked the rise of African history in the second half of the twentieth century. Much of Jan Vansina's revolution in oral tradition consisted of treating oral traditional materials with the same skeptical approach that historians had used for written documents since the time of Ranke. It is what the reciters of oral tradition recall inadvertently, what the oral traditions say "in spite of themselves," that is often most valuable, and the most interesting stories are the least likely to be true.[16]

Data Organization

One cannot simply jump straight from collecting data into writing up conclusions. Data must first be organized. The structure we give our data is as important as their contents in determining the effectiveness of our writing in conveying information to our readers, and in convincing them of the accuracy and relevance of our reconstruction of the past. Whether we are intent on proving a hypothesis about the past or simply telling a story, the structure of our prose is of the utmost importance. The facts must be put together in a coherent sequence that leads inevitably to a conclusion.

The organization of data is also the first step in actual writing, the creation of an outline. At this point a historian has to decide how to answer the question or tell the story. If information has been collected on notecards, now is the time to shuffle those notecards according to an outline. In the twenty-first century more and more historians are collecting their information in electronic databases, which can be organized and reorganized with a few key strokes on a computer keyboard. Either way, but especially with electronic databases, a field on each item by which the data can be sorted is imperative. Dates are one important field by which data can be sorted, especially if one is going to write one's story chronologically, but other tags can be even more important. For writing a book, with an outline of chapters in mind, a field for chapter or perhaps a separate file for each chapter may be necessary.

All writing is either narration, exposition, description, or a combination. Historical writing always involves an aspect of narration, although exposition became increasingly important in the twentieth century as social science became more important in history. Description has also always been necessary in history, but has generally been subordinate to exposition and narration. Which of these three is to be emphasized in any particular historical work is critical to deciding the organization of that work. Social science history is generally problem-oriented, and thus often expository, with a thematic organization. Humanistic history is more often narrative, although the narrative structure doesn't always follow strict chronological lines. Most history is neither pure social science nor pure humanistic literature, but a mixture of the two styles.

Many forms of organization work satisfactorily for narrative writing. While a strictly chronological organization is easier for many readers to follow, and thus is common in popular forms of history such as biography, to begin in the middle, perhaps at the most exciting point in the narrative, is often more effective. This technique, called *in media res*, or "in the middle of things," can be especially effective in history, where the outlines of a story may already be well known to many readers. Narratives can also proceed in reverse chronology, with the narrator seeking to show the causes of each event. Sometimes parallel narratives can come together at the end as various characters meet in the climax, but perhaps with multiple, interacting endings to match the multiple beginnings.

In all narrative the author must keep the plot line in mind. Whether the story is a tragedy or has a happy ending, it will have characters, setting, and action. It will have a beginning, a middle, and an end, with dramatic tension rising to a climax, and a denouement. It must be paced fast enough to maintain the readers' interest without losing essential detail. It must keep track of connections between events and characters, and it must be attentive to questions of causation and explanation, both immediate and long term. Finally, it should in some way return to the beginning at the end. This return to the origins provides a satisfying feeling of closure to the reader of any narrative.

Carefully reading recently written history that one admires, and/or which is popular, can alert one to how other historians tackle these questions of organization. For example, in his recent best-selling book *King Leopold's Ghost*,[17] Adam Hochschild made transitions between different sections of his narrative by telling how and where the main character of the preceding section probably, unwittingly, crossed paths with the main character of the following section. This technique suggests cinematography, where a camera can move from one character to another and start following the second character, having finished telling the story of the first. In the future more and more literary techniques will be borrowed from other media as other media become more familiar to readers and writers alike. Hypertext opens up possibilities for nonlinear narratives whose structures are defined more by individual readers' curiosity than by the author. This should have a profound impact on the production and consumption of historical literature in the future.

The Write-Up

Once one has constructed an outline and organized one's data with it, the writing is half over. In the old days of physical note cards one could simply go through the note cards as one wrote one's article or book, turning each card over in turn as the information it contained was entered into the draft. Today, with software databases, it is not uncommon to press a few keys and have a properly configured database turned directly into a draft, without having to tediously retype all the information. This draft must be read carefully and rewritten, over and over, to ensure that it becomes the best possible article or book. Here we must not trust our own judgment alone. Such drafts should be shown to trusted colleagues, and/or read at conferences, for feedback about their strengths and weaknesses. An editor who is not a specialist in our own field can also be helpful. We ourselves, and our colleagues, often do not realize the necessity of explaining what is common knowledge among specialists; we have been in the discipline for so long that we have ceased to think about such things. If we want to reach a wider audience we will have to consider them.

Our purpose in creating historical literature is to turn dull facts into good writing that will convey something important about the past to people in the present and future. Since the purpose is to reach our audience, to interest and influence them, like all writers we must keep our audiences in mind. Whom are we writing for? The vocabulary, style, and even grammar of an undergraduate textbook will be different from those of a specialized monograph. Popular history and articles for newspapers are very different from dissertations and presentations at scholarly conferences. As scholars we should never water down the complexities of our subject matter, but if we are interested in reaching an audience larger than that of history professors and other historians we must pay attention to the needs, interests, and especially the knowledge and preconceptions of that audience. All people interpret new information in the context of knowledge they already have. We should never overestimate the knowledge they already may possess, although we must try to guess it, but we should never underestimate their intelligence, either.

While a good story is often not likely to be true, we must turn a true story into a good one. This may involve the use of flashbacks and flashforwards, foreshadowing, and other literary techniques, especially in narrative history. Even the most technical social scientific history can benefit from good writing style and regular consultation of a manual such as Strunk and White's *The Elements of Style*. Much good advice can also be gleaned from various author's handbooks, especially those written for academic authors. No one enjoys reading poorly written prose.

If we have prepared our data and outline well, the actual writing can be the simplest task of all in writing history. All that remains is to polish one's prose until it shines, and then to set it loose so that others can appreciate its luster.

Notes

1. E. H. Carr spoke of the assumption that historians did all their research first and then wrote it up. His own experience was that, after a brief initial period of research, the tasks of research and writing were combined, further research being guided by the thinking caused by writing. *What is History* (New York, 1961), 32–33.

2. I am grateful to my colleague Tomoyuki Nagase of Hirosaki University, Faculty of Science and Technology, Department of Electronic and Information System Engineering, for helping me understand the nuances of "data," "information" and "knowledge." He is, of course, in no way responsible for any of my mistakes or misunderstandings here.

3. A good summary of the "wh" questions as relevant to historical research is contained in William Kelleher Storey, *Writing History* (New York, 1996), 19–21.

4. An African example of how unfamiliarity with geography can lead historians astray is the Bantu expansion. Some of the linguistically derived schema have proposed movements through impossible terrain. For details see John H. Robertson and Rebecca Bradley, "A New Paradigm: the African Early Iron Age without Bantu Migrations," *History in Africa* 27 (2000): 287–323.

5. One of the most famous is Joseph C. Miller's *Slavery and Slaving in World History: A Bibliography 1900–1991* (Millwood, NY, 1993).

6. J. E. Philips, "African Smoking and Pipes," *Journal of African History* 24, 3 (1983): 303–19.

7. R. E. M. Hedges, et al., "Radiocarbon Dates from the Oxford AMS System," *Archaeometry* 29, 2 (1987): 289–306.

8. Jan Vansina's *Paths in the Rain Forest* (Madison, 1990) is a good example a work produced by means of such methods.

9. Marc Bloch, *The Historian's Craft* (New York, 1953), 61.

10. "The introduction of a critical approach to the sources into mainstream history-writing was Ranke's most important achievement." John Tosh, *The Pursuit of History*, 2nd ed. (New York, 1991), 56.

11. Cited in Mark T. Gilderhus, *History and Historians*, 4th ed. (Upper Saddle River, NJ, 2000), 33, and Bloch, *Historian's Craft*, 81.

12. Mahdi Adamu, "The Hausa and their Neighbors in the Central Sudan," in *UNESCO General History of Africa*, vol. 4, ed. D. T. Niane (Berkeley, 1984), 280–81.

13. John Hunwick, in "Not yet the Kano Chronicle: Kinglists with and without Narrative Elaboration from Nineteenth Century Kano," *Sudanic Africa* 4 (1993): 95–130, argued that the Kano Chronicle was written at the end of the nineteenth century. Murray Last, on the other hand, argued in his "Historical Metaphors in the History of Kano before 1800," *History in Africa* 7 (1980): 161–78, that it was begun in the seventeenth century and periodically updated. See also John Hunwick's "A Historical Whodunit: the So-called 'Kano Chronicle' and its Place in the Historiography of Kano," *History in Africa* 21 (1994): 127–46.

14. For the early development of the Hausa language and its loanwords, see J. E. Philips, *Spurious Arabic: Hausa and Colonial Nigeria* (Madison, 2000).

15. Bloch, *Historian's Craft*, 61.

16. "The more perfect the structure of a text, the more likely it is that it has been altered for artistic reasons." Jan Vansina, *Oral Tradition* (Harmondsworth, 1965), 64. The same author's more recent *Oral Tradition as History* (Madison, 1985) has since superceded this work as a guide to the use of oral traditions in reconstructing history.

17. Adam Hochschild, *King Leopold's Ghost* (New York, 1998).

CONTRIBUTORS

The late **Bala Achi** was a lecturer at the Federal College of Education, Ahmadu Bello University, Zaria, as well as Director of Research at the National Museum, Abuja, Nigeria. He was the author of a number of articles on Nigerian history published in Nigeria, Japan and elsewhere. It is not known if his book on the history of the Atyap will ever be published.

Isaac Olawale Albert is currently Senior Research Fellow, Sub-Dean of Postgraduate Studies and Co-ordinator of the Peace and Conflict Studies Programme at the Institute of African Studies, University of Ibadan, Nigeria. He has won many honors for his research into such fields as the social history of Africa, security studies, conflict resolution, gender studies, and African oral traditions and folklore. His publications include *Women and Urban Violence in Kano, Nigeria* (1996) and *Introduction to Third Party Intervention in Community Conflicts* (2001).

Diedre L. Bádéjo is Professor of African World Literatures and Cultural Histories and Chair of the Department of Pan-African Studies, Kent State University, Ohio. She received a Ph.D. in Comparative Literature from the University of California, Los Angeles. Her areas of emphasis are African and African American literary criticism, oral historiography, gender, and cultural studies, especially Yoruba and Akan oratures. Among her publications is *Òsun Sèègèsí: The Elegant Deity of Wealth, Power, and Femininity* (1996). She is currently working on a collection of her essays.

Dorothea Bedigian investigates indigenous sesame varieties and the natural history of wild species of Sesamum, as well as peoples who use them, in Africa and Asia, with an interdisciplinary approach employing agronomy, anthropology, archaeology, chemistry, genetics, geography, history and linguistic analysis.

Barbara M. Cooper, Associate Professor of History at Rutgers University, is the author of *Marriage in Maradi: Gender and Culture in a Hausa Society in Niger, 1900–1989*. Her publications have addressed female labor and slavery, gift exchange as social discourse, oral genres and the oral re-performance of pilgrimage, movement and the construction of gender, and the negotiation of a shifting political economy through the re-definition of marriage. She is currently writing a history of a minority evangelical Christian community in Niger.

Donatien Dibwe dia Mwembu has a Ph.D. in History from the Université Laval, where he worked under the direction of Bogumil Jewsiewicki on popular urban culture in Lubumbashi since 1990. He is currently Professor in the Department of History at the University of Lubumbashi (République Démocratique du Congo) and also Président of the *comité scientifique* for the project: "Mémoires de Lubumbashi."

Henry J. Drewal, Evjue-Bascom Professor of Art History and Afro-American Studies at the University of Wisconsin-Madison, has lived, worked, and researched visual cultures and histories primarily in West Africa for forty years. He is the author of several books, catalogues, and numerous articles, including *Gelede: Art and Female Power among the Yoruba, Yoruba: Nine Centuries of African Art* and *Thought, and Beads, Body, and Soul: Art and Light in the Yoruba Universe*. He is currently preparing two publications and a major exhibition on arts for Mami Wata and other African and Afro-Atlantic water spirits.

Christopher Ehret is a historian and historical linguist, with particular interests in early African and human history, the linguistic methods of historical reconstruction, and the comparative historical study of African language families. He has published eight books and more than sixty articles on these topics. His most recent book is *The Civilizations of Africa: A History to 1900* (2002).

Toyin Falola is the Frances Higginbothom Nalle Centennial Professor in History at the University of Texas at Austin. He is the author of numerous books, the coeditor of the *Journal of African Economic History*, Series Editor of *Rochester Studies in African History and the Diaspora*, Series Editor of the *Culture and Customs of Africa* by Greenwood Press, and Series Editor of *Classic Authors and Texts on Africa* by Africa World Press. He has received various awards and honors for both research and teaching. His students and colleagues have presented him with a set of Festschriften. His memoir is to appear in 2004.

David Henige founded *History in Africa* in 1974 and has been editor since. He is particularly interested in comparative historiography, source criticism, and oral tradition. He has published several books, including ones on the sources for Columbus's first voyage and the role of numbers and quantification in history, and has a forthcoming work on historical evidence and argument. He has also published numerous articles on a range of historiographical and editorial topics.

Joseph E. Holloway was a Fulbright Scholar at the University of Botswana, 1994–95, a Visiting Scholar at Cornell University, 1988–89, and a Ford Foundation Postdoctoral Fellowship for Minorities Program participant in 1983. He is Professor of Pan African Studies at California State University, Northridge, where he has taught for more than nineteen years, and is the author or editor of six books, including *Neither Black Nor White: The Saga of An American Family* (2003) and *Africanisms in American Culture* (1990).

John Hunwick is Professor of History and of Religion at Northwestern University, and director of its Institute for the Study of Islamic Thought in Africa. His publications include *Timbuktu and the Songhay Empire* (1999), and two volumes (1995 and 2003) of the *Arabic Literature of Africa* series that he jointly edits.

S. O. Y. Keita is biological anthropologist and physician with a long-standing interest in African history and historiography, as well as the way human biological diversity has been conceptualized in Africa. He has done research on the skeletal biology of early Nile Valley people, and northwest Africans. Dr. Keita was trained in skeletal biology at the Smithsonian Institution. He holds an M.D. from Howard University and a doctorate in biological anthropology from Oxford University. He is currently Senior Research Associate at the National Human Genome Center at Howard University, and Research Associate, Department of Anthropology, Smithsonian Institution.

William G. Martin is a Professor of Sociology and Africana studies at Binghamton University, and coordinates research on world movements at the Fernand Braudel Center. Among his publications are articles on the world-system, southern Africa, and the volumes *Out of One, Many Africas: Reconstructing the Study and Meaning of Africa* (with Michael West); *Semiperipheral States in the World-Economy,* and *How Fast the Wind? Southern Africa 1975–2000* (with Sergio Vieira and Immanuel Wallerstein).

Daniel McCall earned a B.A. (History) at Boston University; and a Ph.D. (Anthropology) at Columbia University. He was Professor of Anthropology and Adjunct Professor of History at the African Studies Center of Boston University, from its founding in 1954 to his retirement in 1983. He has taught courses on Peoples and Culture of Africa; Art and Society in Africa; African Prehistory from Archaeology and Linguistics; African History to 1800; West African History 1800 to Present; and other topics. Among his many publications are *Africa in Time Perspective,* and numerous articles. He has edited three volumes of *Boston University Papers on Africa.*

Susan Keech McIntosh has been a Professor of Anthropology at Rice University since 1989. She is the coauthor or editor of five books, three of which are major monographs on her archaeological research in West Africa. In addition, she has authored or coauthored over forty articles on West African archaeological fieldwork or issues relating to complex societies in Africa. She has also authored a series of overviews of West African archaeology and is currently writing a book on the Holocene archaeology of West Africa. Her main fieldwork has concentrated on the development of iron-using societies in the two great floodplains of the Middle Niger and the Middle Senegal Valleys. She has codirected field research in Mali and Senegal for nine seasons since 1980, funded by grants from the National Science Foundation, the National Geographic Society, and private foundations. In 1989–90, she was a Fellow at the Center for Advanced Study in the Behavioral Sciences at Stanford. She has served as a member of the Archaeology Panel at NSF and has served or is currently serving on the editorial boards of numerous journals, including *Current Anthropology,* the *Journal of African History, Journal of World Prehistory, Antiquity,* the *African Archaeological Review,* and the recently inaugurated journal, *Public Archaeology.* Currently, she is president of the Society of Africanist Archaeologists.

John Edward Philips is a professor in the Department of International Society, Faculty of Humanities, Hirosaki University, Japan. A former

Fulbright graduate student to the University of Sokoto (now Usmanu Danfodiyo University) Nigeria, he is the author of *Spurious Arabic: Hausa and Colonial Nigeria* (2000) and several articles. His current research interests include historical methodology, ethnic cooperation, and conflict in the Nigerian middle belt, and slavery.

Kathleen Sheldon is an independent historian affiliated as a Research Scholar with the Center for the Study of Women at the University of California, Los Angeles (UCLA). Her articles on African women's history have been published in edited collections and in *History in Africa, International Journal of African Historical Studies, Lusotopie, Signs,* and *Canadian Journal of African Studies.* Her books include *Courtyards, Markets, City Streets: Urban Women in Africa* (Westview, 1996); *Pounders of Grain: A History of Women, Work, and Politics in Mozambique* (Heinemann, 2002); and *A Historical Dictionary of Women in Sub-Saharan Africa* (Scarecrow Press, forthcoming).

John Thornton earned his Ph.D. in African History at UCLA in 1979. He has taught at the University of Zambia, Allegheny College, the University of Virginia, and Millersville University before joining the faculty at Boston University. A specialist in central Africa, he is the author of *The Kingdom of Kongo* (1983) and *The Kongolese Saint Anthony* (1998) among other books and articles.

Masao Yoshida was educated at Hobart College (B.A.), University of Tokyo Graduate School of Social Sciences (M.A.) and University of East Africa at Makerere, Uganda (Ph.D.). His main interest is rural development, especially the history of agricultural marketing. While working for the Institute of Developing Economies in Tokyo, and Chubu University, he has written many books and articles in English and Japanese, including *Agricultural Marketing Intervention in East Africa: A Study of the Colonial Origins of Marketing Policies 1900–65* and *A Contemporary History of Eastern Africa.* He was recently a visiting professor at the Department of History, Makerere University.

INDEX

Abbott, L. A., 150n102

Abimbola, Wande, 354, 372n19, 372n25, 373n67, 373n72

Abiodun, Rowland, 346n13, 352, 357, 371, 372n18, 372n32, 373n50

Abiola, J. D., 270

Abitbol, M., 248n56, 249n67

Abraham, R. C., 372n42

Abu-Lughod, Lila, 213n12

Achi, Bala, 15, ch. 15

Achufusi, M., 463n10

Adamu, Mahdi, 510n12

Adenaike, C. K., 189n7

Aderibigbe, A. A. B., 372n34

AFDL (Alliance des forces démocratiques pour la libération du Congo), 18, 447, 450, 454, 455

Afigbo, A. E., 277, 307n37

Afolayan, Funso S., 373n52

Africa in Time Perspective, 1, 51, 80n1, 82n35

Africanizing history, 35, 43–45, ch. 14

Africanus, Leo, 275

Afro-Asiatic languages, 7, 94, 103–4, 107, 136, 140–44, 151n114

Afrocentrism, 399

Agiri, Babatunde, 349, 371n4, 371n5, 371n6, 372n24

Agorsah, E. K., 347n28

agriculture, 3, 10, 14, 19, 58, 82n24, 94, 99–104, 108, 118–24, 143, 152, 156, 308, 310–13

Ahmed, Christine Choi, 111n17, 484n10

aid, 14, 291

Aidoo, Agness, 484n19

Ajayi, J. F. A., 289, 293

Ajisafe, 270

Ajoyce, T., 462n5

Ake, 306n13

Akinjogbin, I. A., 372n34

Akinyele, I. B., 270

Alawiye, Imran Hamza, 244n1

Albert, Isaac, 13–14

Alford, Terry, 436n54

Ali, Mohamed Nuuh, 110n5

Allman, Jean, 487n59

Alper, C. A., 434n11

Alpers, Edward A., 487n51

Amadiune, Ife, 388, 400n21

Ambrose, Stanley, 111n17, 148n55

Amengual, M., 463n7

Amin, Samir, 385, 388, 400n23

Aminu, Muhammad, 46n4

Amselle, J.-L., 146n29

Anderson, Benedict, 401n33

Angel, J. L., 145n5, 146n14, 147n39, 148n53

Annales school, 17, 445

anthropology, 5, 9, 162, 331, 336–38, 343, 353, 465 (*see also* ethnography); physical, 9, ch. 4, 169–70, 174, 182, 196, 198, 201, 202, 205, 210, 268, 375, 393, 403–5

Appleby, Joyce, 45n3, 213n19

Arabic, 12–13, ch. 8, 275, 277

Araujo, Emanoel, 347n29

archaeology, 5–6, 14, 40, ch. 2, 94, 99, 104, 107–8, 111n17, 111n18, 111n19, 119, 169, 172, 188, 191, 317, 331, 338–39, 353, 377, 378, 466–67, 500, 501–2; New Archaeology, 53; Post-processual, 56

architecture, 337

archives, 12, 170, 173–74, 267, 296, 318–19, 478–79

Ardener, Shirley, 483n3

Armelagos, G. J., 146–47, 147n50, 148n54

Arnett, E. J., 275

Arnoldi, M. J., 345n11

Arrighi, Giovanni, 384, 401n37

art, 9, ch. 13, 448

arthritis, 120–21

Arua, O. A., 270

Asante, 18

Asare, Kofi Opoku, 368

Ashlock, P. D., 148n60

Asia, 16, 381, 393

Atkinson, P., 307n28

Atlantic, 13

Atyap (also Katab or Kataf), 15, ch. 15

Aufderhide, A. C., 148n55

Austen, R., 326n21

Ayandele, E. A., 306n2

Baba, Ahmad, 226

Babalola, S. A., 373n45, 373n46, 373n47, 373n59, 373n60, 373n66

Badejo, Dierdre, 15–16, 373n50, 373n65, ch. 14

Bahn, Paul, 80n2

banana, 10

Bantu, 6, 10, 31–33, 55, 83n37, 92, 93–94, 411, 412, 413–14

Barber, Karin, 200, 214n26

Barnes, Harry Elmer, 2, 20n5

Barnes, Sandra, 359, 361–62, 364–66, 372n21, 373n44, 373n49, 373n64

Barnett, Sylvan, 345n7

Barth, Heinrich, 164, 167n39

Bar-Yosef, O., 151n119

Bassani, Ezio, 346n18

Bassett, Thomas J., 246n31

Bates, R. H., 316

Bauer, P. T., 310

Bawele, Mumbanza Mwa, 463n9

Bay, Edna, 18, 470, 483n4, 485n30

Beach, David, 484n13, 488n75

Beaucorts, R., 463n5

Beckingham, C. F., 244n2, 265n24, 265n25

Bedigian, Dorothea, 10

Beidelman, T. O., 212n8

Bello, O., 380n7

Bello, Sultan Muhammad, 246n27, 377, 380n8

Ben-Amos, Paula, 331, 333, 345n3, 345n4

Bender, M. L., 110n2, 151n114

Benin City, 331

Berger, Iris, 483n9, 484n9, 487n54

Bergslund, Knut, 110n15

Berkhofer, Robert J., 45n3, 47n31

Berlin Conference, 41

Berns, Marla, 347n35, 467, 484n15

bias, 11, 29, 40, 53, 56, 58, 61–62, 266–68, 270–71, 276, 279, 302, 304, 469, 480, 504

Bible, 34, 170, 279. *See also* Jesus of
    Nazareth
Big Bang, 41
Bill, Mary C., 486n41
Bilonda, M. Lwamba, 463n18
Binford, Lewis, 60, 82n27
Blackmun, Barbara, 345n3
Blake, J. Herman, 435n28, 435n31
Blakey, M. L., 147n46
Blassingame, John, 434n20
Blench, R., 151n114
Blier, Suzanne, 470, 485n28
Bloch, Marc, 45n3, 307n27, 510n9,
    510n11, 510n15
Bobboyi, Hamidu, 237, 252n124
Bocoum, H., 84n51, 84n56
Bohannon, Laura, 194, 212n7
Boodle, Leonard, 153
Boone, O., 463n5
Bosch, E., 148n58
Bosman, Willem, 264n15
Boswell, Victor, 436n47
botanical gardens, 153, 158–60, 164
Bowcock, A., 148n68, 150n100
Boyarin, Jonathan, 214n22
Boyce, A. J., 150n102
Boyd, Jean, 248n58, 487n52
Bozzoli, Belinda, 202, 205, 214n31
Bradford, Helen, 466, 479, 483n8,
    488n72
Bradley, Rebecca, 509n4
Braudel, Fernand, 81n5, 114, 116,
    145n2, 145n8, 397
Brazil, 16–17, 257, 260
Brenner, Louis, 248n57
Br'er Rabbit, 16–17
Briggs, L. C., 146n30
Brooks, A. S., 149n88
Brooks, George, 484n18
Brown, W. A., 253n134, 253n138

Brues, A., 148n61
Bugs Bunny, 17
Buikstra, J. E., 147n44
Bundy, Colin, 466, 483n8
Bunyoro-Kitara, 18
Burke, Peter, 47n34, 489n82
Busson, F., 167n34

Campbell, Robert, 273
Canada, 16
capta, 62, 64
Caribbean, 16–17
Carlson, D., 145n3, 147n34
Carnes, Mark C., 46n8
Carney, Judith, 347n28
Carr, E. H., 45n3, 307n16, 509n1
Carver, George Washington, 418
Casirer, Ernst, 9
Catesby, Mark, 436n50
causation, 41–42, 53, 64, 81n4, 117,
    135, 333, 353, 507
Cavalli-Sforza, L. L., 145n6, 148n58,
    148n68, 149n72
Cerulli, E., 251n107
change, 3, 4, 6, 12, 18, 19, 25, 31, 40,
    53, 58, 86, 169, 185, 293
Chanock, Martin, 197, 487n58
Chatterjee, Partha, 401n32
Cherbonneau, M. A., 249n68
Chhabra, S. C., 167n36
Chippendale, Chris, 62, 82n34, 83n36,
    83n40, 84n49
Chrétien, Jean-Pierre, 447–48,
    463n16
Christelow, Alan, 248n58, 253n128
chronology, 5–6, 35, 42, 59, 64, 66–67,
    68, 78–79, 83n45, 172, 185,
    496–97. *See also* dating;
    glottochronology; radio-carbon
Cigar, N., 248n56

Clarke, David, 53, 60–61, 81n7, 81n8, 82n30, 82n31
Cliffe, L., 326n12
Clio, 35
Close, A. E., 111n19
cognate, 92
Cohen, David, 213n16
Coles, Catherine, 478, 488n66
Collingwood, R. G., 145n7, 146n15
Collins, R. O., 306n1
colonialism, 14, 26, 39, 81n17, 124, 184–86, 197, ch. 10, 290–92, 305, 309–13, 315, 318–19, 328n41, 375–76, 381, 383–86, 389, 393, 395–96, 440–42, 462, 478
Comaroff, John and Jean, 400n26, 476, 486n48
computers, 334
Congo, Democratic Republic of, 17–18, ch. 18
Constandse-Westermann, T. S., 150n101
Cooley, Rosa B., 435n28, 435n33
Coon, C., 126, 127, 148n58, 148n63
Cooper, Barbara M., 8, 214n33, ch. 7, 475, 486n45, 488n69
Cooper, Frederick, 391, 401n28
Coplan, David, 200, 214n25, 214n32
Coquery-Vidrovitch, Catherine, 309
Cornet, Joseph, 435n41
Cornia, G. A., 327n36
correspondence, regular sound, 92–93, 99
Cosentino, Donald, 347n29
cowboys, 426–27
Cox, Oliver, 385, 398, 400n12
Cresswell, R., 85n65
Crowder, Michael, 342, 347n32
Crowther, Samuel, 271–72
Cuoq, Joseph, 244n7

Curtin, P. D., 327n39, 405, 434n7, 435n38
Cushitic languages, 6, 90, 98

Dahalo, 6
Dahomey, 19, 469–71
D'Andrade, R., 149n71
Danfodiyo, Usuman, 41
Danish, 11, 255–63
Dapper, Olfert, 277
Darnton, Robert, 214n22
Dar Tichitt, 53
Darwin, Charles, 82n23
data, 30, 32–33, 36–38, 43, 52–54, 58, 60, 62–64, 86–87, 97, 99, 104, 114, 119, 122, 134–35, 141, 144, 188, 191, 298, 301, 305, ch. 20. *See also* capta
dating, 41, 66–67, 68, 71, 78, 84n47, 186. *See also* chronology
Davidson, Basil, 46n7
Davison, Jean, 213n12
Dawson, M. H, 289
Declich, Francesca, 472, 486n36
Deines, H., 167n30
Delafosse, M., 246n36
Delcommune, A., 464n29
Denett, R. E., 268
DeNiro, M. J., 148n55
Deny, J., 252n119
Denzer, LaRay, 479, 488n70
Derrida, Jacques, 47n31, 347n33
detectives, 37–39, 295, 504
De Villers, G., 463n19, 464n30
Diakonoff, I. M., 150n99, 151n114
Diamond, Jarred, 2, 20n4, 57, 82n24
diaspora, 44, 309, 386, 392, 397, 402n45, ch. 17
Dibwe dia Mwembu, Donatien, 17, ch. 18, 463n17

dilogicality, 353
Dingwall, E. J., 147n32
Diop, Cheikh Anta, 388
Dixon, Ruth, 488n78
DNA, 9, 113, 116, 129, 131, 135, 138, 144. *See also* genetics
documents (written), 1, 7–12, 15, 38–40, 52, 58, 62, 169, 171, 175, 180, 184–85, 191, ch. 8, ch. 9, ch. 10, 289, 292, 318, 378, 441, 494, 498, 503, 505
Donnan, Elizabeth, 412, 434n17, 434n18, 435n36, 435n41, 436n46, 436n54
Drewal, Henry, 9, 346n13, 347n29, ch. 13
Drewal, Margaret T., 346n26
DuBois, W. E. B., 385, 398, 400n12, 435n35
Duncan, J. D., 435n42
Dunn, Ross E., 245n20
Dupuis, Joseph, 253n130

Earthy, E. Dora, 483n3
East, Rupert, 250n90, 380n6
eclipses, 186
economic history, 14, 288, ch. 12
Edwards, Bryan, 437n62
Egharevba, Jacob, 269, 270, 275
Egypt, 44, 108, 113, 115–16, 119, 123, 124, 133, 141–43, 146n13, 146n21, 157, 170, 216, 222–23, 279
Ehret, Christopher, 6–7, 10, 20n2, 110n2, 110n3, 110n4, 110n6, 110n7, 110n8, 110n9, 110n10, 110n11, 110n12, 110n13, 111n16, 111n17, 149n71, 151n114, 346n25
Ekegha, O. O., 270
Eldredge, Elizabeth A., 486n50

Elkins, 345n2
Ellison, J. R., 346n21
Eluyemi, Omotoso, 372n20
Embleton, Sheila, 110n14, 111n18
Enwezor, Okui, 347n27
Equiano, Olaudah, 318
Ethiopia, 11, 106, 110n3, 143, 140–41, 216, 235, 237, 259
ethnicity, 9, 115–16, 119, 131–32, 135–36, 197, 247n38, 302, 336, 404–5, 414–16
ethnography, 14, 273–74, 278, 294, 296–98, 377, 441, 465. *See also* anthropology
Etienne, Mona, 487n57
Euba, Akin, 363, 367, 372n22, 373n62, 373n68
Eurocentrism, 38
Evans, Richard, 45n3
evidence, 38, 353
évolués, 17, 442
Excoffier, L., 145n6, 150n95

Fabian, Johaannes, 347n36
Fagan, Brian, 80n2
Fage, J. D., 265n30, 270
Fagg, William, 331
Falola, Toyin, 12
Fanon, Frantz, 400n10
feedback, 184
Feierman, Steven, 213n18, 393, 401n35
feminism, 196, 203, 205, 208, 213n12, 294, 302, 465
Fieldhouse, D. K., 310
film, 27
Finley, M. I., 48n37
Fischer, David Hackett, 45n2
Fishkin, Shelley Fisher, 436n56
Fix, A. G., 148n67
Flight, Colin, 46n16

Folayan, Kola, 349, 371n7, 371n9
Foley, R., 149n82
folklore, 9, 34–55, 47n24, 152, 183, 202
Ford, John, 28–29
Forde, Daryll, 270
Fortmann, Louise, 481, 489n79
Foucault, Michel, 347n33
Foundation for African Archaeology, 346n23
Fraser, P. A., 434n11
Frazier, E. Franklin, 404
Freedberg, David, 345n9
Freeman, Derek, 174, 182, 189n6
Freund, B., 327n29
Freyre, Gilberto, 435n41
Friday, Sergeant Joe, 37
Friedlander, Peter, 207
Fry, Gladys-Marie, 434n20

Gaballah, M. F., 146n13
Gabel, C., 145n6
Gambia, 420
Gamble, D. P., 438n74
Garlake, Peter, 339, 346n22
Geiger, Susan, 213n13, 480, 485n32, 488n76, 488n77
gender, 273, 293, 314, 356–57, 370, ch. 19. *See also* feminism; women
genetic relations (languages), 33, 87–89
genetics, 2–3, 6, 9, 10, 14, 20, 112–17, 121–25, 129–32, 134, 137–40, 142–44, 155, 406. *See also* DNA
Gengenbach, Heidi, 473, 476, 486n40, 486n49
Genovese, Eugene D., 435n40, 436n45
Ghali, Noureddine, 248n57
Ghana, 339
Gibb, H. A. R., 275
Gilderhus, Mark, 3, 20n6, 510n11
Gleason, Judith, 373n48

glottochronology, 105–7, 110n15
Gluck, S. B., 213n13
Gnawa, 114
God, 41, 98
Gold Coast, 11
Gomez, Michael, 250n92
Goodman, A., 147n48, 147n50
Goody, Jack, 199, 213n20
Gordon, April A., 326n26
Goutalier, Régine, 488n68
Grant, T., 147n33
Gray, Richard, 190n14
Greenberg, J. H., 6, 32, 46n13, 405, 434n8
Greek, 12
Guez, Nicole, 346n27
Guglielmino, C. R., 148n58
Gunn, Harold D., 376
Guthrie, Malcolm, 32, 46n14
Gutkind, Peter, 400n8
Guyer, J., 326n24, 481, 488n78
Gwarzo, H. I., 247n49

Habraszewski, T., 247n46
Haerdi, F., 167n25
Hafkin, Nancy, 483n4
Hale, Sondra, 486n37, 489n84
Hall, J. R., 145n2
Hall, Martin 55, 80n2, 81n11, 81n14, 81n15
Hallet, R., 306n5
Hamet, Ismael, 249n74
Hamilton, Carolyn, 214n34
Hamitic hypothesis, 112, 277
Hamlet, 39
Hammersley, M., 307n28
Hanson, John, 248n58
Harlan, J. R., 10, 153–55, 165n2, 166n3, 166n4, 166n5, 166n6, 166n7, 166n8, 166n9, 166n10,

166n11, 166n12, 166n13, 166n14, 167n35

Harmann, Ulruch, 247n50

Harney, Elizabeth, 346n27

Harpending, H., 146n12

Harrak, Fatima, 227, 248n52, 248n54

Hassan, F., 151n118

Hassan, Salah, M., 347n27

Hassan, Yusuf Fadl, 252n111

Hassim, Shireen, 489n84

Hausa, 8, 12, 15, 203–5, 216, 224, 227, 229, 233, 251n95, 269, 272, 274–75, 280, 376, 378, 379, 475, 505

Hausman, A. J., 145n6

Havelock, Eric, 213n20

Hay, M. J., 213n14, 483n9, 487n60

Hayashi, K., 327n27

Hayden, B., 82n34

Hayes, W. C., 146n22

Hedges, R. E. M., 510n7

Heine, B., 109n1

Heintze, Beatrix, 263n1

Henige, David, 7, 189n4, 192, 265n29, 351, 372n16

Hermon-Hodge, H. P., 274, 282n38

Herodotus, 34, 42, 157, 170, 349

Herskovits, Frances, 433n1

Herskovits, Melville, 16, 404, 430, 433n1, 433n3, 435n41

Hetherington, Penelope, 484n9

Heusch, Luc de, 195, 212n8

Heyward, Duncan Clinch, 436n49

Heywood, Linda, 347n28

Hiernaux, J., 145n6, 148n57, 148n59, 149n78, 149n81, 150n96

Hill, Polly, 326n11, 326n13

Hill, Richard, 252n120, 274

Hilliard, Constance, 251n102

Hilton, Anne, 263n2

Hinderer, Anna, 272

Hinton, R. J., 146n25

Hobsbawn, Eric, 213n15, 288–89

Hochschild, Adam, 508, 510n17

Hodder, Ian, 81n18, 83n43, 145n2, 146n17

Hodgkin, Elizabeth, 244n1

Hodgkin, Thomas, 274

Hodgson, Dorothy, 482, 487n59, 489n83

Hoffman, M., 146n21

Hofmeyr, Isabel, 201, 214n30

Holloway, Joseph, 16–17, ch. 17, 434n9, 434n10, 435n37, 436n57

Honigmann, E. A. J., 47n32

Hooker, J. D., 164, 167n38

Hopkins, A. G., 310

Hopkins, H. C. F., 166n21, 244n8, 248n56

Hopkins, Terence K., 384, 394

Horton, Robin, 13, 84n46

Houdas, Octave, 247n41, 249n65, 249n69, 250n86

Hountondji, Paulin, 388, 400n18

Howells, W., 150n103

Hudson, G., 150n89

Huffman, Tom, 55, 81n11, 81n12

Huizinga, A., 150n101

Hunt, Lynn, 45n3

Hunt, Nancy Rose, 483n9, 489n83

Hunter, Thomas, 250n92

Hunwick, John, 12, 13, 248n56, 249n65, 250n78, 250n90, 251n106, 253n127, 510n13

Huss-Ashmore, R., 147n50

Hyden, Goran, 326n12

Ibn Battuta, 220, 222, 245n15, 245n16, 245n17, 245n18, 245n19, 245n20, 246n37, 275

Ibn al-Hakam, 12
Ibn Khaldun, 12–13, 35–36, 47n26, 220, 246n29, 275
Idigo, M. C. N., 270
Idowu, E. Bolaji, 355, 357, 372n28, 372n29, 372n30, 372n31, 372n33, 373n71
al-Idrisi, 222–24, 246n28
Ifa divination, 354
Igbo, 18, 60, 211, 272, 412, 415
Ilahiane, Hsain, 145n11
Iliffe, J., 313–14
Imam, Abubakar, 269
Imam, Ayesha Mei-Tie, 483n9
Indian Ocean, 13, 16
Indirect Rule, 15
Indo-European languages, 3
Inikori, J. E., 327n39
interviews, 299–301
Irele, Abiola, 363, 373n61, 373n73
iron smelting, 64, 73–80
Irvine, F. R., 435n27
Irwin, Paul, 181–83
Isaac, Glynn, 82n32
Italian, 13
Iwekawune, I. E., 270

Jacob, Margaret, 45n3
James, C. L. R., 385, 394, 398, 400n12, 401n38
James, Ibrahim, 379n1
Japan, 11
jargon, 27
Jenkins, T., 146n12
Jenne jeno, 53
Jesuits, 11
Jesus of Nazareth, 30
Jewsiewicki, Bogumil 145n2, 399n5, 440–47, 451–52, 462n2, 463n8, 463n11, 463n13, 463n20, 463n21, 463n22
Johnson, Cheryl, 478, 487n62
Johnson, Guy, 434n20
Johnson, Matthew, 81n5, 81n9, 81n10, 81n16
Johnson, Samuel, 269, 270, 275, 355, 368, 372n27, 373n70
Joyner, Charles, 347n28
Jones, Adam, 263n1, 263n3, 265n30
Jones, G. I., 267–68
Jones, H. H., 146n22
Jos, 45n1, 46n4
Joyner, Charles W., 430n20
Judd, M., 147n42
Jules-Rosette, Bennetta, 487n53
Junaidu, Al-Hajj, 269

Kaduna, 15
Kamil, 'Abd-al-'Aziz' Abd-al-Qadir, 146n13
Kano, 26, 314, 467
Kano Chronicle, 20, 34, 377, 505
Kanogo, Tabitha, 488n74
Kantu, Kankieza, 464n32
Kaplan, Flora, 470, 471, 485n29, 485n31
Kasai, 17, 446
Kasfir, N., 326n12
Kasfir, Sydney, 346n27
Katab or Kataf. *See* Atyap
Katanga, 18
Kati, Mahmud, 249n62, 249n63, 249n64
Katompa, Kalukula Asani bin, 464n29
Keddie, Nikki, 47n38
Keita, Shomarka, 9, 145n3, 148n62, 149n72
Kelley, Robin D. G., 397, 402n47, 402n48, 402n49, 402n50, 402n51

Kennedy, Jean, 346n27
Kennedy, P., 314
Kent, S., 147n44, 484n12
Kenya, 6, 90, 141, 164, 312–13, 315
Keynes, J. M., 26
al-Khathlan, Saud H., 244n1
Khoisan, 6, 90
Khury, Fuad, 310
Killick, David, 84n48, 84n51, 84n54, 85n62
Kimambo, I. N., 324
Kirk-Greene, Anthony, 47n33
Kitagawa, Katsuhiko, 323
Kittles, S. A., 148n62, 149n72
Kivilu, Sabakilu, 463n9
Ki-Zerbo, Joseph, 447, 463n15
Klein, Martin, 487n56
Knibiehler, Yvonne, 488n68
Kobusiewicz, M., 151n118
Kojiki, 34
Kolamoyo, Crispin Bakatuseka, 463n24
Kongo, 11
Koponen, J., 326n15
Kosso, Peter, 58, 82n26, 82n28
Krige, E. J. and J. D., 485n31
Kriger, Colleen, 476, 486n47
Kroeber, A. L., 9–10
Kuper, Adam, 55, 81n11
Kurawa, Ado, 250n88
Kurosawa, Akira, 28–29
Kyekshus, H., 326n15

Labor, U.S. Department of, 30
LaDuke, Betty, 346n27
Lahr, M., 149n83
Lang, Dierk, 245n14
Lang, P. D., 150n98
Langaney, A., 145n6
Lange, D., 249n61

language, 6, ch. 3, 114, 172, 260–61, 466, 501, 502
Larsen, 146n23, 146n26, 147n35, 147n45, 148n55, 148n56
Last, D. M., 250n84, 487n52, 510n13
Latter, B. D., 148n70
Law, Robin, 263n6, 264n18, 371n3
Lawson, John, 436n51
Leenhouts, P. W., 166n17
Legassick, M., 327n27
Lekwot, Zamani, 379
Leo Africanus, 20
Lerner, Gerda, 18
Levine, Lawrence, 434n19
Levi-Strauss, Claude, 8, 42, 47n35, 47n36, 195
Levtzion, N., 244n8, 248n56, 250n91, 253n130
Lewicki, Tadeusz, 12, 245n23
Leys, Colin, 326n21
Lhote, H., 151n116
Leith-Ross, Silvia, 18, 483n3
Linares, R., 149n71
Lindsay, Arturo, 347n29
Linnaeus, Karl, 158
Lipscomb, Terry W., 438n70
literature, 25, 27, 35, 201
Little, M., 164, 167n42
loanwords, 95–98
local history, 12, 15, 269–71, 289, ch. 15
Loret, V., 166n15
Louvanium University, 17
Lovejoy, Paul, 47n27, 327n39
Lubo, Kampa Kamikudi, 464n33
Lucas, A., 166n16
Lugard, J. F. D., 274, 376
Lydon, Ghislaine, 479, 488n69

Mabillon, Jean, 503
Mabuija, Kabamba, 460, 464n31

Macbeth, 34
MacGaffey, Wyatt, 212n8
Mack, Beverly, 248n58
Macmichael, Harold, 252n111
Maes, J., 463n5
Mafeje, Archie, 400n8
Magaji, Habou, 203
al-Maghili, 217
Maghreb, 13
Magnin, Andre, 347n27
Magubane, Ben, 388, 400n8, 400n22
Maini, Amar, 323
Maire, R., 167n40
maize, 158
Malinowski, B., 307n26
Malson, Micheline, 213n13
Mama, Amina, 401n26
Mamdani, M., 326n20, 400n25,
    402n41, 402n42, 402n43, 402n44
Man Who Shot Liberty Valance, The,
    28–29
Mangat, J. S., 325n9
Manicom, Linzi, 483n2
Mann, Kristin, 483n6
Manning, P. E., 327n39
al-Maqrizi, 244n2
Maquet, Jacques, 16, 403
Marks, Shula, 47n27, 478, 488n65
Marquart, Jos., 245n21
Martelli, G., 462n4
Martin, B. G., 247n47, 247n49,
    250n89, 250n94
Martin, D. R., 148n54
Martin, G. J., 167n31
Martin, R., 146n19
Martin, William, 19, ch. 16, 399n2,
    400n15, 400n24, 401n36,
    401n39, 402n52, 402n53,
    402n54, 433n2
Marty, Paul, 249n66

Marxism, 55–56, 208, 302
Mason, John, 347n29
Masri, F. H. El, 248n56
Matamba, 18
Mayr, E., 148n60
Mba, Nina, 212n11, 483n5
M'baye, Alhadji Ravane, 245n10
Mbembe, Achille, 391, 401n27
Mbilinyi, Marjorie, 208, 484n9, 485n33
McCall, Daniel, 51, 63, 80, 80n1, 82n35
McCann, M., 147n33
McCurdy, Sheryl, 487n59
McEvilley, Thomas, 346n27
McHugh, Neil, 252n111
McIntosh, Roderick J., 81n6, 83n44,
    84n51, 346n15, 346n24
McIntosh, Susan K., 5, 81n6, 82n22,
    83n44, 84n51, 246n35, 346n15
McKie, R., 149n82
McLuhan, Marshall, 198, 213n20
McNeill, William H., 82n24
Mead, Margaret, 174, 182
Meek, C. K., 268, 376
Meglen, R. R., 147n51
Mehta, N. K., 310
Meillassoux, Claude, 245n13
Mendes, Helen, 436n48, 436n52
Menozzi, P., 145n6
Merbs, C. F., 147n40
Merriam, Alan P., 405, 434n5
Mesopotamia, 3
Mico, Ted, 46n8
Middle Range Theory, 60
Mignolo, Walter, 401n31
Miller, Joseph, 192, 195, 200, 212n2,
    484n16, 510n5
Miller-Monzon, John, 46n8
millet, 164
Miquel, Andre, 246n30, 247n39
Mirza, Sarah, 485n33

Mirzoeff, Nicholas, 345n10
Mischlich, 251n95
missionaries, 11, 12, 255, 258–59,
  ch. 10, 441, 478
Mkandawire, Thandika, 400n16,
  400n17, 400n25, 402n40
Moffat, Robert, 272
Moffett, D. J. M., 436n55
Molnar, S., 143n24
Monteil, Vincent, 245n12, 245n15
Moore, Henrietta, 214n34
Moorehead, Alan, 44, 48n39
Moraes Farais, Paolo F. de, 245n9
Morgan, Kathryn Lawson, 434n20
Morikawa, J., 328n42
Morris, B., 167n28
Morrissey, Charles, 212n3
MTV, 334
Mudimbe, V. Y., 145n2, 440, 462n2
Muhammad, Akbar, 244n1
Muhammad, Baba Yunus, 253n139
Muhly, J. D., 84n55
Munson, Patrick, 81n6
Muntemba, Maud Shimwaaji, 487n60
Murdock, G. P., 10
Musisi, Nakanyike, 469, 472, 485n24,
  485n25, 486n37
Musonda, Francis, 82n25
Mutongi, Kenda, 475–76, 486n46,
  489n82
Myers, Linda James, 373n58
myth, 34–35, 195

Nadel, S. F., 167n33
Nafziger, E. W., 327n37
Nagase, Tomoyuki, 509n2
Nagel, D. A., 146n22
narration, 34–35, 52, 114, 180, 182,
  187, 195–96, 293, 301, 392, 507
Nast, Heidi, 467, 484n14

National Endowment for the
  Humanities, 2, 47n25
national history, 12, 276, 304, 387–89
nationalism, 12, 39, 382, 384, 386,
  399n1
National Science Foundation, 56
Neuwinger, H. D., 167n29
Newman, J. L., 148n58, 150n95
newspapers, 12
Niane, D. T., 349, 371n8
Niditch, Susan, 189n2
Niger, 13, ch. 7, 475
Niger-Congo languages, 6, 92, 93–94
Nigeria, 15, 211, 222, 228–29, 232–35,
  238, 240, 243–44, 268–69, 296,
  chs. 14–15, 403, 407–8, 469, 472,
  482
Nile, 13
Nilo-Saharan languages, 7, 87–89, 90,
  91, 95, 98–108, 109n2, 140, 143
Nkotsoe, Mmantho, 205, 214n31
Nkrumah, Kwame, 41
Nok, 15
North Africa, 3, 224
Novick, Peter 38, 46n5, 47n28
Nubia, 102, 105, 119, 123, 140, 142,
  147n51, 216–17
Nurse, D., 109n1
Nurse, G. T., 146n12
Nyerere, J. K., 326n15
Nyong'o, P. Anyang', 326n13
Nzegwu, Nkiru, 346n27
Nziem, I. Ndaywel è, 463n25
Nzinga, Queen, 18, 468

Obbo, Christine, 471–72, 485n35
objectivity, 27, 28–30, 36–37, 62, 177,
  198, 378
Ocholla-Ayago, 168n44
Odhiambo, E. S. A., 213n16

Oduduwa, 16
O'Fahey, R. S., 248n55, 248n56,
    249n60, 252n110, 252n123
Ogbomo, Onaiwu, 472–73, 486n38
Oguibe, Olu, 347n27
Ogunbiyi, Isaac A., 253n129, 373n63
Ojo, Chief, 270
Okediji, Moyosore, 346n13, 347n27
Okeyo, Achola Pala, 487n57
okra, 417
Okwui, Enwezor, 346n27
Oliver, Roland, 32, 46n15, 83n41
Olupona, J. K., 356
Olusola, J. A., 270
Ong, Walter, 213n20
oral history, 8, 19, 38, 187, ch. 7, 289,
    299, 324, 408–11, 434n20,
    455–56, 471–74, 494, 500
oral traditions, 7–8, 10, 14, 15, 38, 40,
    ch. 6, 191–92, 199, 254, 268,
    270–71, 299, 317–18, 349–50,
    378, 441, 461, 500, 501, 506
Orans, Martin, 189n6
Orr, Charles, 273, 376, 380n4
Ortner, D., 146n23, 147n45
Osofisan, Femi, 373n61
Othello, 39
Ottenberg, Phoebe, 434n6
Ottenberg, Simon, 347n27, 434n6
Owsley, D. W., 146n17
Oyarinde, 270
Oyewumi, Oyeronke, 469, 482,
    485n27, 489n81
Oyo, 18, 41

Pacific, 4
Palmer, H. R., 249n61, 250n90,
    252n124, 274–77, 279
Park, Mungo, 424
Parpart, Jane L., 487n63

Passerini, Luisa, 212n10
Patai, D., 213n13
Patterson, Thomas, 81n17
Patterson, Tiffany, 397, 402n47,
    402n48, 402n49, 402n50, 402n51
Paulme, Denise, 483n3
p'Bitek, O., 165, 168n45
Pellegrini, B., 145n6
Pemberton, John, 346n13, 373n52
Penny, D., 148n71
performance studies, 340
Perham, Margery, 380n5
Perinbam, B. Marie, 246n34
Perks, R., 8
Person, A., 84n53
Pierson, William D., 436n61
Philips, J. E., 1, 4–5, 19–20, 345n1, 375,
    380n3, 438n72, 510n6, 510n14
Phillips, Ulrich Bonnell, 436n44, 436n53
Phillipson, D. W., 32, 46n19, 46n20,
    46n21, 149n83
Phiri, K. M., 306n7
Piazza, A., 145n6
Pilaszewicz, S., 251n97
plantain, 10, 160–61
Plato, 43, 126
Pollitzer, William S., 435n37
population genetics, 14
Portelli, Alessandro, 212n10
Porter, Philip W., 246n31
Portugal, 11, 257–58, 260–62, 277, 279
Posnansky, Merrick, 346n25
postmodernism, 29, 56–57, 74, 78,
    182, 198, 201, 205, 294, 302,
    333, 343, 393
Prah, Kwesi, 388, 400n19, 400n20
Prakash, Gyan, 401n32
prehistory, 1, 52, 64, 78
Presley, Cora Ann, 487n61, 488n74
Priest, J. D., 146n22

Ptolemy, 12, 219–21
Puckett, Newbell Niles, 434n12
Putschar, W. G. J., 146n23, 147n45

Quechon, Gerard, 84n52, 84n53, 84n58, 85n63, 85n64
Quijano, Anibal, 401n31
Qur'an, 43

Rabb, Theodore, K., 345n5
race, 9, 112–13, 117, 124–31, 134–37
Radin, P., 8
radio-carbon, 6, 64, 66, 71–79, 84n47, 85n65, 501–2
Ramchandani, R. R., 325n9
Ranger, Terence, 197, 213n15
Rannala, R., 150n89
Rashomon, 28–29
Rattray, R. S., 424
Redding, Sean, 488n64
Rehder, J. E., 84n55
Reichmuth, Stefan, 253n129
religion, 98, 268, 293, 454
Renfrew, Colin, 80n2
rhetoric, 333
rice, 10, 158, 418
Robertshaw, Peter, 81n3, 82n23, 83n41, 85n67
Robertson, Claire, 212n11, 471, 481, 483n5, 483n9, 484n9, 485n34, 487n56, 489n80
Robertson, John H., 509n4
Robinson, David, 248n58
Robinson, Frederick, 401n34
Robinson, James Harvey, 20n1
Rodney, Walter, 385, 400n14
Rohr, A., 145n3
Rolands, Michael, 81n17, 82n19
Roosevelt, A. C., 84n60
Rosa, P., 145n4

Rose, J. C., 147n48, 147n50
Rossel, G., 10, 166n22
Rotberg, Robert I., 345n5
Rubin, Arnold, 344
Rudney, J., 145n3
Russell, J. H., 437n63
Russian, 13

Saad, E. N., 150n97
Sa'd, Mustafa Muhammad, 244n3
Saeki, M., 323
Sahara, 13, 39, 59, 81n4, 81n6, 105–6, 108, 111n19, 309
Sai, Akia, 270
Saint Mery, Moreau de, 436n58
Salmon, P., 462n1, 462n3, 463n6, 463n10
Sanchez-Mazas, A., 145n6
Sandford, M. K., 147n51
Sankofa bird, 40
Sanneh, Lamin O., 250n92
Sansonnet-Hayden, H., 82n34
Sargent, R. A., 469, 485n26
Sarnat, B. G., 147n49
Saul, J. M. and S. P., 145n4
Scheub, Harold, 214n24
Scheven, A., 168n43
Schiffer, Michael, 61, 82n33
Schild R., 110n13, 111n19
Schlippe, Pierre, de, 162, 167n37
Schmidt, Peter, 55, 81n13, 81n17, 346n24
Schmitt, B. E., 293
Schmucker, B. J., 146n28
Schön, J. F., 271–72
Schoenbrun, David, 108–9, 111n21, 466, 484n11
School of Oriental and African Studies (SOAS), 3, 32
Schour, I., 147n49

Schwartz, M. S., 307n29
Scott, James, 208
seeds, 153
Seligman, C. G., 145n1, 147n31, 148n58
semiotics, 332
Senegal, 18, 217–18, 221–25, 234
sesame, 152, 163–65, 418
Shakespeare, William, 39, 40, 47n23
Sharkey, Heather, 252n116
Shaw, Thurstan, 60, 82n29
Sheldon, Kathleen, 18, 196, ch. 19, 483n1, 486n43, 488n71
Schmidt, Peter, 212n1
Sethuraman, S. V., 327n33
Shivji, I. G., 327n30
Shostak, Marjorie, 196, 213n12
Silver, Beverly, 401n37
Simon, C., 145n6
Slatkin, M., 150n89
slave trade, 26, 256–58, 309, 318, 377, 381, 396, 397, 408, 410–11, 416
Smith, B. H., 146n27
Smith, C. D., 326n12
Smith, Charles, 274
Smith, Linda Tuhiwai, 351, 371, 371n1
Smith, M. F., 8, 196, 213n12, 483n3
Smith, M. G., 47n27
Smith, Sharwood, 376
social science, 5, 36, 42, 47n25, ch. 11, 377
Social Science Research Council, 47n25
Soforowa, A., 167n27
Soludo, Charles Chukwana, 400n25, 402n40
Songhay Empire, 20
sorghum, 10, 158, 164
Soulillou, Jacques, 347n27
sources, primary and secondary, 46n6, 500

Sow, Alfa Ibrahim, 251n98
Soyinka, Wole, 367, 373n69
Spear, Thomas, 345n1, 346n16
Spring, Anita, 489n78
Stace, C. A., 166n19
Stacey, M., 307n30
Stahl, Ann, 56, 81n19, 82n20, 85n67
Stahl, Kathleen, 310
Staudt, Kathleen, 489n78
Steinbock, T., 147n45
Stern, Steve J., 401n30
Steward, James, 437n64
Storey, William Kelleher, 509n3
stratigraphy, 6, 67, 86–87
Stringer, C., 149n82
Strobel, Margaret, 212n11, 483n5, 484n9, 485n33, 488n67
structuralism, 55, 196, 393. *See also* Levi-Strauss, Claude
Stuart-MacAdam, P. L., 147–48n51, 148n52
Stuessy, T. F., 166n20
style, 330
Swahili, 12, 216, 230, 278

Tadesse, Zenebeworke, 484n9
Talbot, P. A., 268, 274
Tanzania, 55, 313, 320–22, 324, 480
tax, 316
teeth, 118–19, 122
Temimi, A., 247n52
Temple, C. L., 268, 273–74, 376, 379n2
Templeton, A., 148n69, 150n93
Tepowa, Adebiyi, 275
Terrell, J., 149n80
Theal, George M., 264n19
theory, 4, 14, 19, 26, 52, 55–57, 61, 292–94, 302, 383–84, 390
Thomas, H., 327n39
Thomas, Rosalind, 189n2

Thompson, A., 8
Thompson, Robert F., 347n29, 373n54, 373n55, 373n56, 373n57, 373n71, 373n74, 435n41, 436n59
Thorne, A. G., 149n72
Thornton, John, 10, ch. 9, 402n46, 468, 484n16, 484n17, 485n23
Tichenor, C. C., 146n22
Tilly, Charles, 392, 401n29
Tishkoff, S. A., 150n94
Tolmacheva, M., 248n58
Tominaga, C., 325n9
Tonkin, Elizabeth, 201, 214n28
Topolski, J., 145n10
Torday, E., 462n5
Torney, D., 147n33
Tosh, John, 510n10
toss zone, 60
Townsend, Henry, 272–73
trade, 14, 26, 39, 44, 59, 79, 84n45, 153, 157, 160, 224, 227, 242, 246n32, 246n34, 247n50, 256–58, 278–79, 308–10, 314
translation, 175–76
Tremearne, A. J. N., 268, 279, 376, 379n2
Trevor-Roper, Hugh, 3, 193, 290, 304
Triaud, J.-L., 245n13, 248n56, 253n125, 463n16
Trigger, Bruce, 82n21
Trinkhaus, E., 147n36
Tuchman, G., 307n21
Tunis, Irwin, 345n3
Turkish, 13
Turner, Lorenzo Dow, 435n43
Turrittin, Jane, 486n37

al-Umari, ibn Fadl Allah, 12–13, 244n2
UNESCO, 7, 166n18
Union Miniere du Haut-Katanga, 18

Urvoy, Y., 275
Uya, O. E., 306n10

Vail, Leroy, 213n21, 473, 486n39
Van Allen, Judith, 480, 488n73
van Beek, W. E. A., 189n9
Van der Kerken, G., 463n5
van der Merwe, N., 85n65
Van Gerven, D., 145n3, 147n34, 147n51, 148n54
van Onselen, 327n27
Van Overberg, C., 462n5
Vansina, Jan, 7, 11, 17, 32, 46n11, 46n12, 46n17, 46n18, 48n37, 84n61, 85n66, 85n68, 108–9, 111n20, 146n29, 170–71, 189n3, 189n7, 193–94, 199–200, 212n4, 338, 346n17, 350–51, 372n13, 372n14, 372n17, 441, 464n27, 506, 510n8, 510n16
Vantini, G., 244n3
Vartevan, Christian de, 153, 165n1
Vass, Winifred Kellersberger, 435n39, 436n57
Vaughn, Megan, 214n34
Vavilov, N. I., 10, 154, 156
Venzlaff, H., 167n26
Verbeek, Léon, 453, 463n23
Verbeken, A., 464n28
Ver dier, Eva L., 409, 434n21, 434n22, 434n23
Verhulpen, E., 463n5
Vermeersch, P. M., 149n86, 149n87
Vernet, J., 246n24
Vieira, Sergio, 399n2
Vigilant, L., 148n71
visual culture, 333–35, 345n11
Vlach, John, 347n28
Vogel, E. F. De, 166n18
Vogt, Hans, 110n15

Waldron, T., 146n20
Walker, Cherryl, 489n84
Walker, Roslyn, 346n13
Wallerstein, Immanuel, 382–84, 399n2,
    399n6, 401n31
Waterman, Peter, 400n8
Watt, J. M., 166n24
Webster, J. B., 189n4
Weiner, J. S., 150n101
Weiss, K., 146n15
Wells, Julia, 468, 485n21, 485n22
Wendorf, F., 110n13, 111n19
Wertime, T., 84n55
Wesseling, Henk, 47n34
West Africa, 13, 221, 224
West, Michael, 386, 397, 400n15,
    400n24, 402n50, 402n52,
    402n53, 433n2
Westermarck, E., 167n32
Wet, J. M. J. de, 155, 166n6
wheat, 153, 156–58
whip, 448–51
White, E. Frances, 483n9, 485n20
White, Hayden, 347n34
White, Landeg, 213n21, 473, 483n6,
    486n39
White, Luise, 212n11, 482, 489n82
Wilks, Ivor, 233–34, 248n56, 250n91,
    485n19
Willame, J. C., 463n19
Williams, Eric, 394, 398, 400n11,
    401n38

Willis, John Ralph, 244n1
Wilson, E. O., 2, 20n3
Wilson, F., 327n27
Wolf, Diane, 213n13
women's history, 18–19, 314, 445,
    ch. 19. *See also* feminism; gender
Wood, Peter, 426, 430, 435n41, 438n73
Woodward, C. Vann, 434n20
Woolley, Sir Leonard, 3, 20n7
World systems theory, ch. 16
Wright, Marcia, 197, 213n14, 474–75,
    477, 486n44, 487n55
Wrigley, C. C., 326n20
Wylie, A., 84n57

X, Malcolm, 390

Yang, Daqing, 46n9
Yankah, Kwesi, 201, 214n29
al-Ya'qubi, 12
Yellen, J. E., 149n88
Yoruba, 15–16, 200, 238, 270–72, 275,
    277, 289, 329–30, 336, 345,
    346n13, ch. 14, 374, 482
Yoshida, Masao, 14, 326n17
Yoshikuni, T., 323
Young, Sherilynn, 487n60
Yunis, E. Y., 434n11

Zaria, 15
Zawawi, Sharifa M., 486n42
Zeleza, Tiyambe, 325n1, 400n25,
    483n7, 489n84

Writing African History is an essential work for anyone who wants to write, or even seriously read, African history. It will replace Daniel McCall's classic *Africa in Time Perspective* as the introduction to African history for the next generation and as a reference for professional historians, interested readers, and anyone who wants to understand how African history is written.

Africa in Time Perspective was written in the 1960s, when African history was a new field of research. This new book reflects the development of African history since then. It opens with a comprehensive introduction by Daniel McCall, followed by a chapter by the editor explaining what African history is (and is not) in the context of historical theory and the development of historical narrative, the humanities, and social sciences. The first half of the book includes chapters on sources of historical data, including oral tradition (David Henige) and oral history (Barbara Cooper), indigenous written documents (John Hunwick), precolonial European documents (John Thornton), and colonial and mission documents (Toyin Falola), as well as chapters on archaeology (Susan Keech McIntosh), biology (Dorothea Bedigian), physical anthropology (S.O.Y. Keita), and historical linguistics (Christopher Ehret). The second half of the book includes chapters about different perspectives on history. Covered in this section are social science (Isaac Olawale Albert), art history (Henry John Drewal), Africanizing history (Diedre L. Badejo), economic history (Masao Yoshida), local history (Bala Achi), memory and history (Donatien DIBWE dia Mwembu), world systems theory (William G. Martin), African links to the African diaspora (Joseph E. Holloway), and gender perspectives (Kathleen Sheldon). The editor's final chapter explains how to combine various sorts of evidence into a coherent account of African history. *Writing African History* will become the most important guide to African history for the 21st century.

Praise for *Writing African History*:

"African history has taken wing and spread into different questions and newer ways to answer those questions since Daniel McCall's *Africa in Time Perspective* came out in 1964. To bring us up-to-date, John Philips has brought together an outstanding group of scholars to introduce the questions that attract Africanists and the methods used to answer those questions. The result will stimulate students and teachers and should be the standard work on African history methodologies for years to come."
— Martin Klein, Professor Emeritus, University of Toronto

"Philips presents the first comprehensive update to foundational methodological works from the 1960s on writing African history. His scope is imaginative and wide, covering source methodologies and issues of perspective and interpretation. Contributors include recognized masters and thoughtful newcomers, with important statements from Africa-based scholars. The result is a serious, balanced, and useful work."
— Joseph C. Miller, T. Cary Johnson, Jr. Professor of History, University of Virginia

"African history has clearly come of age with this monumental, comprehensive guide. The volume demonstrates the wealth of sources available for African historians, from the archaeological and botanical to newly appreciated Arabic documents and extensive African oral traditions. Philips is to be congratulated on his eminently readable epilogue and background chapters that provide a unity all too often lacking in similar anthologies."
— Merrick Posnansky, Cotsen Institute of Archaeology at UCLA

"This is essential reading for anyone interested in African history. The essays, written by many of the leading experts in the field, brilliantly assess the current state of knowledge of the African past and discuss how we have come to know what we think we know."
— Paul E. Lovejoy FRSC, Distinguished Research Professor, Canada Research Chair in African Diaspora History

CPSIA information can be obtained
at www.ICGtesting.com
Printed in the USA
FFOW03n1339060516
23858FF

9 781580 462563